D0990346

COMPETITION AND MONOPOLY

# COMPETITION *and* MONOPOLY

## *Legal and Economic Issues*

By MARK S. MASSEL

THE BROOKINGS INSTITUTION · WASHINGTON, D.C.

Published June 1962

Library of Congress Catalog Card Number 62-17634

THE BROOKINGS INSTITUTION is an independent organization devoted to nonpartisan research, education, and publication in economics, government, foreign policy, and the social sciences generally. Its principal purposes are to aid in the development of sound public policies and to promote public understanding of issues of national importance.

The Institution was founded December 8, 1927, to merge the activities of the Institute for Government Research, founded in 1916, the Institute of Economics, founded in 1922, and the Robert Brookings Graduate School of Economics and Government, founded in 1924.

The general administration of the Institution is the responsibility of a self-perpetuating Board of Trustees. The Trustees are also charged with maintaining the independence of the staff and fostering the most favorable conditions for creative research and education. The immediate direction of the policies, program, and staff of the Institution is vested in the President, assisted by the division directors and an advisory council, chosen from the professional staff of the Institution.

In publishing a study, the Institution presents it as a competent treatment of a subject worthy of public consideration. The interpretations and conclusions in such publications are those of the author or authors and do not necessarily reflect the views of other members of the Brookings staff or of the administrative officers of the Institution.

# *Foreword*

The law of competition and monopoly has never been successfully reconciled with the economics of competition and monopoly. Lawyers and economists have recently made some progress in mutual understanding, but much research remains to be done before the needs of public policy are met.

The present study is an attempt to explore further the interrelations of economics and law and to clarify them both for the layman and for the professional specialist. As one part of a broader program of relating economic and legal analysis in the treatment of competitive issues, the study was conceived in response to a number of requests for an expansion of the author's lecture on the subject, delivered during the Brookings Lectures 1958-1959 on *Economics and the Policy Maker.* It continues Brookings' interest in studies of competition carried out over the years by such economists as Edwin G. Nourse, John Maurice Clark, A. D. H. Kaplan, and Corwin D. Edwards.

The book has been written in such a manner that the text can be read without reference to the footnotes. The voluminous notes, appearing at the end of the text, are for those who may want to explore some of the suggestions and ideas more fully.

The study was a project of the Economic Studies Division, directed by Ralph J. Watkins. An advisory committee consisting of John Maurice Clark, Corwin D. Edwards, Loyle A. Morrison, Sigmund Timberg, and John Stedman made helpful comments on the manuscript. To them and to others who reviewed the manuscript and made suggestions, the author and the Institution are especially grateful.

The Institution appreciates the support of the Ford Foundation, which financed this study.

The views expressed in the study are those of the author and do not necessarily reflect the views of the Ford Foundation, those serving on the advisory committee, or the staff of the Brookings Institution.

Robert D. Calkins
*President*

April 1962

# *Author's Acknowledgments*

Many acknowledgments are in order here. The members of the advisory committee have been most helpful in their comments and suggestions. Robert D. Calkins has made many personal contributions to understanding and clarity. Ralph J. Watkins has been generous with his support and patience during the progress of the study. A. Evelyn Breck has improved the book through her skilled editorial work, with the able assistance of Medora Richardson. Virginia Angel indexed the volume. Jean Birch Christopher and Carole E. Chase have supplied the secretarial and checking assistance that helped to make the work of drafting more enjoyable. Finally, Jean Magnus Massel has combined the qualities of severe criticism and wifely forbearance.

The merits of the book are due in large part to the support of all of these and several others. Its deficiencies fall, of course, within the province of the author.

Mark S. Massel

# Contents

# 1 / *Perspective and Plan**

PROBLEMS OF COMPETITION have no national boundaries. Under the private enterprise system there is competition among firms. Under totalitarian regimes competition appears in the rivalries among bureaucratic units and among industrial trusts. Under some mixed systems competition develops among public and private entrepreneurial units. Currently, an international "competitive" struggle derives from the conflict between totalitarian and free-market systems.

While competition exists in various forms in other countries, the United States of America has given more sustained attention to issues of competition and monopoly than any other nation. Problems of the free market have influenced public policies since the founding of the republic. Issues of monopoly, government regulation, government economic activity, and free trade have attracted attention ever since the thirteen states decided to confederate. In many different guises, competitive issues permeate most of the affairs of the body politic. They affect many facets of living patterns—economic, political, and social. They are intimately related to basic questions concerning the role of government, business, agriculture, and labor.

We, the American people, however, have not appreciated the broad influences of these issues on public policy and on our everyday lives. The narrow word association of competition is with "antitrust." Hence, the pervasive influences of these broader issues are not recognized even though they are implicit in such diverse features in the recent news as: the Buy-American plans for the Development Loan Fund, the congressional investigations of inflation and of administered prices, the President's appeal to the steel industry to hold the price line, the spec-

* Because the footnotes are voluminous, they are presented at the end of the text. Footnotes for Chapter 1 begin on page 341.

tacular attack on price-fixing in the electrical equipment industry, and the establishment of a European Common Market.

## *Confusion of Goals*

National concern about antitrust problems was manifested about seventy years ago in the passage of the Sherman Act.[1] That statute prohibited monopolization, attempts and conspiracies to monopolize, and restraints of trade. Its enactment let loose a continuing flood of debates, legislative considerations, investigations, and prosecutions. The debates have taken hold in every corner of the land. Political campaigns have regularly called forth oratory against sin and monopoly. Various business groups have jousted with each other and with farm and labor organizations on the legislative battleground. Government agencies, congressional committees, bar associations, and individual academicians have had a continuing interest in the field.

Throughout these debates two features stand out: first, public statements portray almost universal support of the competitive or free enterprise system as an ideal; and second, a body of clear policies to achieve that goal has not been formulated. Why do we experience such difficulty in clarifying the means to the alleged ends? Is this state of affairs caused by confusion about the relationship between the ultimate goal and the means for achieving it? Does it mean that while we maintain a theological belief in competition, we have no substantive basis for such teaching? Or, is the difficulty inevitable because there are too many diverse objectives involved in "competition" to permit us to settle on any organized set of principles?

One possible explanation of the disparity between the agreement on goals and the differences concerning the means to achieve them is the difficulty of maintaining competition. Some students of the subject feel that although competition may be highly desirable, it is practically impossible to keep the economy competitive.[2] They argue that governmental intervention cannot activate competition.[3] As a matter of fact, even Adam Smith, the exponent of competition, had doubts. These appear immediately after his often cited passage: "People in the same trade seldom meet . . . but the conversation ends in a conspiracy against the public. . . ." For, he went on to say, "It is impossible indeed to prevent such meetings, by any law which either could be executed or would be consistent with liberty and justice."[4]

Smith's attitude was echoed when the Sherman Act was passed in 1890.[5] Many prominent economists of the day scoffed at the notion that it would be possible to restore "lost" competitive pressures through government intervention. As some saw it, social trends pointed to increased direct regulation, rather than revitalized market competition.[6]

Another factor which may affect the disparity between goal and means is the lack of agreement about what competition is. There are serious differences among economists, lawyers, and businessmen about the general meanings of competition and monopoly and about evaluations of conditions in specific markets. Unfortunately, the underlying facts do not make for simple concepts. Possibly one of the reasons for the dissension is a general desire to simplify a complex concept that has more attributes than many are willing to recognize.

In the early days of neoclassical economic thought, a clear-cut distinction was made between competition and monopoly. Competition implied many buyers and sellers in the market. No individual could influence price, demand, or supply.[7] Competitors dealt with one uniform commodity and enjoyed no trademark or patent protection. Nor did any seller enjoy customer good will because of differences in product quality, reliability, service, or location. Anyone could easily become a buyer or a seller. Against the pure white of competition, the black of monopoly was clear. A monopolist was the only seller of a commodity in a market. He brooked no interference because no one could compete with him. His was the power to command.

While this clear distinction between competition and monopoly may be easy to grasp, it does not describe actual market situations. Market rivalry takes many forms. Though price competition has occupied the center role in economic analysis, there are many other forms of rivalry:[8] quality of product, style, brands, delivery service, warranties and repairs, advertising and other forms of sales promotion, discounts and allowances to distributors, cost reduction, investment in capacity, developing "market segments" in order to sell to one group at lower prices without disturbing the higher prices charged to others, and achieving favored positions with suppliers or distributors.

Given these diverse forms, analysis of market rivalry calls for the consideration of more factors than price alone.[9] Some types of rivalry tend to give the consumer a better price-quality deal; some tend to raise costs and prices; some give the customer a wider range of choices in quality, style, and service. Indeed, some rivalry serves to restrain competition in the long run.[10] Whatever its influence, each of these forms of competition must be taken into account.

It is clear that pure competition and pure monopoly do not exist in any market. Each market situation is a complex of varied competitive and monopolistic forces.[11] Therefore, any market analysis calls for inquiry into which forces dominate and what might or should be done to change the balance, or to change the nature of the competitive forces.

Contributing to the disparity between goals and means is the uncertainty about what results can be achieved through competition. On the surface, the national interest in maintaining competition seems to be economic. We want to raise living standards, to hold high the banner of efficiency, to encourage the growth of the economy, to provide "full" employment, and to avoid serious inflation.

A closer examination reveals many other public policy aims that are tied up with competition: some political; some social; and quite a few ethical. We dislike great concentration of economic power because it may lead to political domination.[12] We desire to be assured of fair play and of freedom from undue interference by other individuals.

There are many differences among these goals. On the one hand, competition is regarded as a means of lessening the need for direct government regulation; on the other, government is frequently looked to for means of stimulating the economy. There is a desire to encourage numerous small enterprises in industry, commerce, and agriculture because such dispersal of power will help to nurture our democratic framework.[13] At the same time, large corporations frequently appear to be necessary for the application of modern, low-cost methods of production and distribution.

A policy to encourage international trade is offset by fears of unemployment in certain industries if the doors to imports are opened wide. In order to improve our cold-war position, there is a strong interest in encouraging economic development in other countries, including such steps toward economic-political integration as the Common Market. At the same time, there is a concern about future international competition and the construction of differential barriers which will harm American industries.

## *Policy Dilemmas*

This complex of goals has created many dilemmas for public policy. For example, in some industrial sectors, aggressive competition may promote greater efficiency; yet it may tend to eliminate many small businesses and to concentrate the manufacture of some lines of product in a few hands. Building codes can prevent slums and fire hazards; yet, if they are too stringent, they may inflate costs unduly and curtail construction, or they may keep new companies and products out of the construction and materials industries. Increased imports of low-price goods may raise standards of living and stimulate domestic competition; however, they may reduce employment in some industries or eliminate some domestic enterprises.

Perhaps the broadest of these dilemmas reflects a major social problem today: the conflict between the desire for personal security and the maintenance of the incentive system.[14] There is considerable pride in the accomplishments of the free enterprise system, which depends on personal incentives. At the same time, there exists a strong drive for personal security[15]—against such diverse uncertainties as loss of jobs, declines in income, losses of markets, and price wars. Driven by these desires and by the feeling that an affluent society[16] need not tolerate substandard living conditions for anyone, the body politic may have become preoccupied with these protections without re-thinking the relationship between incentives and personal security.[17]

The incentive system provides rewards for greater efficiency and penalties for inefficiency. This system of carrots and sticks presumably finds expression, in a free market, through competition.[18] Yet this drive may be at odds with a full-blown personal security program since a sharply competitive system may entail ruthless consequences.[19] Individual companies may be driven out of business.[20] Employees of those firms may suffer along with the owners. Entire communities may be hurt by ensuing cuts in purchasing power.

Given the possibilities of such ruthless results, there have been many attempts to temper the system.[21] These protections have taken many forms in both the government and private sectors. Government has been given some responsibility for full employment.[22] Such developments as old-age benefits, corporate pensions, medical coverage, and minimum wages have also contributed to a broad pattern of personal security protection. The government-sponsored growth of labor unions has promoted a number of measures for the job security of the individual.

This drive has extended into the business domain. On many occasions, industries appeal to the government to promote their economic security. Substantial sectors of industry and of labor press for protection against foreign competition, through such mechanisms as tariffs, quotas, and Buy American programs. Many campaigns are waged for protection, public and private, against internal competition. The protective mechanisms cover a wide area: tacit price agreements, the regulation of price differentials, agricultural price supports, the development of marketing cooperatives, resale price control, long-term agreements to buy and sell, an increasing fixity of manufacturer-distributor relations, the widespread growth of many forms of insurance, the development of strong brand positions, and corporate mergers that will provide a broader, diversified base of operations in order to avoid the incidence of risk.

Concurrently, new theories are developing about business statesmanship.[23] Large corporations are being "endowed" with souls[24] and justice —attributes which imply that they are concerned about the public weal because of enlightened, long-run self-interest rather than because they are driven by competitive forces.[25] Accompanying the new theories of corporate responsibility are implications that the community need not be too concerned about competition and concentrations of economic power. The extreme form of this viewpoint seems to imply that by allowing giant companies the comforts of life,[26] the public will, in turn, be assured of comfort and protection.[27]

We are witnessing an interesting ethical shift. Economic teachings since Adam Smith[28] have been based on the theory that the organization of capitalistic markets compels entrepreneurs to contribute to the public weal through their search for private gain.[29] In contrast, the recently developing theme is that large corporations will benefit society because of their new-found public responsibility.[30] A new *Wealth of Nations* is yet to be written—one which produces a theoretical formulation for the shift in somewhat the same fashion that the original book justified a move from state regulation to free markets.

This ethical shift is not without danger.[31] There is no doubt that corporate responsibility and the level of business morality has improved. However, if the thesis of corporate trusteeship should be oversold and gain public acceptance, large companies will be expected to promote the public weal rather than their own gain.[32] Such standards could ultimately lead to increased pressures for government supervision of industrial operations. A quasi-public-utility status could be decreed for entire sectors of industry. The occasional public scandal, such as the successful criminal prosecution of General Electric, Westinghouse, and several of their executives, could drive such companies over the brink into direct government controls precisely because of their self-advertised public responsibility.[33]

These developments may herald a weakening of the entrepreneurial drive. Increasingly, promising young men desire to work for large companies. Occasional spectacular successes, such as those of a handful of scientists who have developed electronic and other engineering businesses, have not affected this widespread desire. University students look for greater employment security and the expectation of comfortable pensions in retirement, rather than the rewards of entrepreneurial risk. Similar aims are manifested by many small businessmen who seek greater security by selling out to larger corporations.

At the same time, there are substantial forces in the economy that interfere with the security quest of many. Successive waves of technological development in manufacturing, in design, and in distribution make the business situation less certain for large numbers of enterprises. Many companies are concerned about the unknown competition "around the corner" from the firms in other industries, employing different materials and production methods. Diversification is a notable feature of corporate development. Goods flow through a number of different types of channels. Supermarkets, drug, variety, and hardware stores seem intent on invading each other's domains. These changes produce new rivalries with innovating competitors.

In addition, the geographical attributes of competitive markets are changing. Markets for manufactured products are spreading wider and wider. Competition in many markets is shifting from a regional to a national basis. Indeed, some markets have been pushed into international shapes. Improvements over several decades in communication and transportation are exerting profound influences on market size. The progress of national retail chains and wide-ranging regional chains is destroying the stability of local markets, many of which had maintained strong monopolistic elements.

The push to national markets is tied up with the erosion of regional differences in tastes, customs, and attitudes. Variety in "Main Streets" is gradually disappearing. Differences in local accents are less marked —due in part to radio, television, and the cinema, and in part to great cross-migrations of people. There is more nationwide uniformity in clothing, housing, and other styles. In the process, many aspects of competition are changing. Some make for more, some for less market rivalry. All point to changes in competitive patterns.

There seems to be a public feeling that reasonable personal security should be provided without unduly limiting—or destroying—the effectiveness of the enterprise-incentive system. This public desire creates one of the basic problems of modern society. In a free-market economy the problem is entwined in the issues of competition. Efforts to avoid competitive forces or to achieve the comforts of monopoly are elements in the quest for personal security. As Judge Wyzanski has said: "Some truth lurks in the cynical remark that not high profits but a quiet life is the chief reward of monopoly power."[34]

Because of these dilemmas about policy, our attitudes toward government regulation are distinctly ambivalent.[35] In general discussions about a wide range of economic problems, many prefer a more substantial role for government. Such a role would place heavy emphasis on business regulation and direct government participation in economic activity. At the same time, however, our halls are rife with criticism of the regulatory agencies.[36] There are frequent castigations of their inefficiency, their tedious legal procedures, their inability to face up to policy issues, and their general ineptitude.

An interesting intellectual quirk has entered public considerations of competition and government regulation: comparing the actual of one process with the theoretical ideal of another.[37] Those who underscore the shortcomings of competition contemplate an idealized picture of the efficiency of government and of its ability to promote the public interest. In contrast, critics of government regulation are inclined to compare it with an idealized version of the benefits of free competition. Many accept the view that the forces of competition are weakening but scoff at the shortcomings of government regulation, citing the National Recovery Administration as an example.

## *Policies and Administration*

This pattern of diverse national goals and ambivalent attitudes toward government is the root cause of many difficulties in formulating and administering clear and consistent policies which bear on competition. Antitrust laws, both national and state, are avowedly dedicated to competition. Yet many aspects of the supervision of regulated industries, of barriers to imports, of government research and development programs, and of state and local regulations blunt the edge of competition. We have not followed any coordinated plan in setting up the agencies that administer antitrust and related laws. There is no mechanism or organizing device for coordinating policies regarding competition or indicating their relationships with the ultimate public policy goals.

The diversity of goals makes it impossible to construct a precise set of policies and administrative mechanisms.[38] Some goals are complementary. Some are in conflict: for example, policies favoring small business must give way to the exigencies that influence public health and safety; thus, it would appear that the development of the new biological drugs and of atomic energy must be assigned to a manageable number of large companies.

Many of the relationships among the goals vary with the times. The cold war created conflicts between policies concerning national security and international market competition. The great depression changed many policies regarding business and agricultural competition. World War II called for the effective employment of the capacities of large companies even at the risk of disadvantaging smaller enterprises. Clearly, changes in conditions, internal and external, require changes in policies.

Nevertheless, we can develop greater consistency in policies. We can avoid the spectacle of agencies working at cross-purposes. For example, after the Department of Justice had successfully prosecuted a railroad under the antitrust laws and prevented it from seizing control of another, the Interstate Commerce Commission approved a merger which negated the antitrust decree.[39] In 1961 there was talk of an antitrust proceeding to compel the American Telephone and Telegraph Company to divest itself of its international communication system;[40] meanwhile, the same company is being encouraged to take the lead in setting up a communications satellite,[41] which would probably be applied mainly in international operations.

The issue has two aspects: first, most policies should be patently consistent; second, any apparent inconsistencies should be generally understood by the interested public. Thus, if the two A.T.&T. moves are compatible, a public explanation would be in order. On the surface, the satellite development would strengthen the company's market position particularly in the field of international communications. Further, the satellite would permit it to improve such communication, possibly with cost reductions. Hence, the two moves are hard to rationalize.

Accompanying the lack of consistency in regulatory functions has been a failure to develop a compatible set of government policies. Regulatory and commercial activities of the government have not been used to support each other in attaining public goals. For example, pertinent tariffs on individual items have not been reduced in order to inject foreign competition into a specific monopolistic market, and the buying power of the government has not been widely employed to induce substantial companies to become competitors in a given market.

There has been only desultory progress in administering the antitrust laws and in testing their efficacy. This task has been treated in large part, as if it were solely a legal problem, with inadequate attention to the essential economic nature of this type of regulation. There has been too little economic analysis in choosing companies to prosecute—analysis which would enable the government agencies to concentrate on the more strategic influences on competition. Economic inquiry has not been used widely in settling antitrust proceedings, either by negotiation or litigation. Above all, antitrust authorities have been preoccupied with pinning "guilty" tags on defendants and have paid insufficient attention to the task of formulating realistic remedies which will inject new competitive forces into the market place.

## *Relations Between Lawyers and Economists*

The formulation and administration of competitive policies require, in large part, the application of law to the solution of economic and related problems. It is true that the antitrust and other regulatory laws are administered through legal procedures. Yet, they deal with problems that involve a number of other social sciences: economics, statistics, political science, psychology, accounting, and sociology.

Because of the nature of problems of competition, economics is the major discipline, other than law, which is involved. It serves, on many occasions, as a coordinator bringing together the statistical-accounting inquiries, the psychological testing methods (through market surveys), and the political science analyses. At times, economists "cross lines" and provide parallel skills in other fields, notably statistics. Therefore, this volume concentrates on the uses of economic analysis, bringing into focus the various other disciplines where they seem most pertinent. Similarly, it discusses the economics profession as illustrative of the other professional groups in the social sciences.

A principal thread in this volume is that the treatment of problems of competition necessitates further coordination of the economic and legal disciplines and more effective cooperation between the two professions. While recent decades have witnessed progress in the use of economic analysis to solve antitrust and related questions, this application has been far from adequate. The need for improved coordination will not be met unless and until there is a clearer understanding of the difficulties inherent in utilizing economic analysis in the administration of the laws affecting competition. These difficulties stem from differences in the legal and economic disciplines, differences which have been glossed over by both professions.

To promote the progress that society requires, the two disciplines must be brought closer together. This requirement is broader than antitrust. It is germane to the development of practical solutions to many other fundamental problems of government regulation.

It would be tempting, indeed, to assess the blame for the poor coordination on either the lawyers or the economists. A favorite indoor sport among some antitrust lawyers is to reminisce about the shortcomings of economists. In turn, some economists can entertain themselves with the naiveté of the legal profession. However amusing such parlor games may be, impartial consideration will demonstrate that the situation stems mainly from differences in the methodologies of the two disciplines rather than from the intellectual provincialism of either profession.

Adequate use of economic analysis in the treatment of competitive issues will require a wider appreciation of the substantial differences between the two disciplines and their practitioners. Both professions deal with many of the same problems. However, the divergence in their methods of tackling these problems is both strategic and subtle. The intellectual curtain between the professions will not be torn away until each appreciates these differences.

On the legal side, an obstacle to coordination is the lawyer's disposition to work with other lawyers. By and large, lawyers seem to prefer to work out their problems on a free-wheeling basis within their own professional boundaries. The legal profession, generally, thinks of other disciplines largely in the use of expert witnesses.[42] Whether they are engaged in litigation, negotiation, or policy formulation, lawyers are not enthusiastic about working on a professional par with experts from the other disciplines, be they economists, doctors, chemists, engineers, or accountants.

On the other hand, economists have their own problems in applying economic analysis in these legal areas. First, they have frequently overlooked the distinctions between the application of economic analysis in formulating legislative policy and its uses in administering existing policies. Second, economists have not always appreciated the differences between the functions of analysis in the competitive area and in other areas of public policy. Occasion for litigation is rare in such fields as economic stabilization, monetary and fiscal policy, international trade, and economic growth. In contrast, government regulation of business, including antitrust, proceeds within the context of litigation. Even the policy issues in such fields as antitrust are involved in the conceptual framework of lawsuits. The courts and the pertinent administrative agencies, such as the Federal Trade Commission, function through legal adversary procedures. Hence, competitive issues reflect an emphasis on litigation-oriented administration and policy-making, in contrast to most other areas of economic policy.

Because of this legal focus, lawyers have naturally dominated the administration of antitrust as well as other types of business regulation. Lawyers represent the government, private plaintiffs, defendants, and respondents, in litigation and negotiation. Judges adjudicate the controversies. Lawyers generally run the antitrust agencies and the pertinent congressional committees.

Therefore, a prerequisite for the successful application of economic inquiry in the administration of antitrust is the development of analytical tools that are effectively adapted to the needs of the lawyer. In effect, if economists are to make an important contribution in this area, they must forge economic tools of analysis which meet the operational requirements of the professional groups that administer policy.

For more effective administration of those policies which are dedicated to maintaining competition two aims must be pursued: first, to advance the use of economic analysis in policy-making and administration; second, to improve the methods of economic inquiry which are applied to the solution of competitive problems. These two aims are closely related. Progress in the application of economic studies in litigation will compel economists to develop more pointed empirical methods. Additionally, increased use of economic inquiry in the solution of competitive problems will attract more able economists to the field.

To make an effective contribution, the economist must take into consideration the complexity of public aims that affect the regulation and stimulation of competition. As indicated above, these aims encompass much more than economic goals. Hence the task of indicating desirable policies regarding competition cannot rest exclusively on economic analysis.[43] However, it can help us to understand our objectives and to develop effective balances among them. To this end, economic inquiry can throw light on the economic costs of various policy alternatives. Together with such other learned disciplines as law and the other social sciences, it can promote a clearer understanding of relationships among the ultimate goals in the consideration of specific policy questions.

## *Plan of Study*

This volume deals with the problems of formulating and administering public policies which bear on competition. It describes the complex structure of ultimate goals which form the basis for these policies and reviews the confused skein of rules and administration. Finally, it discusses the current use of economic analysis in helping to solve these problems and what might be done to improve its application.

Several sets of relationships figure importantly in this exploration. First is the wide range of public aims which affect these issues—political, social, and ethical as well as economic. Second are the connections between antitrust and other forms of regulation, as well as the government's commercial and developmental activities. Third is the association of activities on the several levels of government—federal, state, and local. Fourth is the interplay of policy formulation, litigation, and other features of administration, an interplay which sets practical limits on what can be accomplished. Fifth is the interplay of the legal and economic disciplines, a relationship that has a substantial bearing on both policy and administration.

The book discusses: the nature and complexity of the policy goals and of the government activities affecting competition; the process of policy formulation and the needs for economic studies; litigation procedures and opportunities for using economic inquiry; and a survey of the use of economic analysis in three specific problem areas—indicators of competition, the problems of defining a competitive market, and the uses of statistical evidence. Finally, it suggests several methods for improving the use of economic analysis in working out the problems of competition.

# 2 / *Basic Public Goals**

THE USES OF ECONOMIC ANALYSIS in the formulation and administration of policies that bear on competition are strongly influenced by the background of national goals—goals which are political and social as well as economic[1]—and of current government activity. Accordingly, this and the next chapter review this background. This chapter deals with a wide range of objectives which affect these policies. Chapter 3 covers the involved patterns of pertinent government operations, federal, state, and local.

There are several types of pertinent public goals. Political and social objectives involve issues of political power,[2] freedom, equality of opportunity, health, safety, fair play, and ethics.[3] Economic aims cover such features as economic growth, inflation, and stability. Another group of goals relates to specific sectors of the economy: labor, agriculture, and small business. Finally, the goals of national security reflect international, military, atomic, and space implications.

Each of these public objectives has a substantial bearing on policy issues affecting competition. For example, even though some believe that industrial concentration might lead to higher efficiency, national concern about political power may stimulate policies against concentration of economic power.[4] The protection of public health may require safeguards that limit competition. Control of inflation may influence policies regarding union power. Improvement in international relations may call for increasing imports, a move which may create concern about the effects of foreign competition. Military exigencies may make it desirable to award research and development contracts to a handful of companies, though such a policy may limit future competition.

* Footnotes for Chapter 2 begin on page 344.

## *Political and Social Objectives*

A range of political and social objectives have had a profound influence on the attitudes of the United States toward competition.[5] Prominent among these aims are: avoidance of concentrated economic power,[6] free political parties, personal freedom,[7] equality of opportunity, and limited direct controls of government.

Policies favorable to competition have always been regarded as basic features of a free enterprise system and individual liberties.[8] Since the early days of our nation, there has been much concern about the relationship between liberty and concentrations of economic power.[9] Many have feared that large aggregates of economic power will strengthen antidemocratic forces.[10] Accordingly, with Jefferson,[11] they feel that the maintenance of a competitive free enterprise system is a basic requirement for continuing a democratic government.

The same attitudes were reflected in the early days of antitrust,[12] even in the debates regarding the Sherman Act. In his illuminating study of those debates, Thorelli concluded: "Active competition was [regarded as] the mainspring of what we have labeled economic egalitarianism. It was the dispenser of justice to consumer and producer alike."[13]

More recently, Justice Douglas emphasized political and social objectives. In his disssent in the *Columbia Steel* case he argued:

> Industrial power should be decentralized. It should be scattered into many hands so that the fortunes of the people will not be dependent on the whim or caprice, the political prejudices, the emotional stability of a few self-appointed men. The fact that they are not vicious men but respectable and social minded is irrelevant. That is the philosophy and the command of the Sherman Act. It is founded on a theory of hostility to the concentration in private hands of power so great that only a government of the people should have it.[14]

The theory of a private enterprise system places competition in a strategic role.[15] The essence of a free enterprise system is that numerous independent decisions—regarding price, for example—are tested when they meet in the market place.[16] Individual enterprises win or lose by these decisions. Mistakes affect only a fragment of the economy and are offset by the successes of others. Contrariwise, in a controlled system one decision is made—by a commission, by a monopolist, or by the joint agreement of a group of "independent" enterprises. In such an economy, the consequences of errors are large; private independence is lost; political and social pressures flow from the activities of the single decision makers. In brief, the free enterprise system depends on practical dispersion of power.

There are, however, differing attitudes regarding concentration of power in the hands of "big business"[17] and "big labor." On the one hand, some maintain that big business and labor have developed a capacity for substantial public responsibility.[18] They believe that far-sighted self-interest combined with the good will of the big organizations will provide a healthy state of economic affairs. On the other hand, some argue that they do not want to rely exclusively on business or labor statesmanship.[19] They prefer to rely on market pressures with lesser dependence on business or labor responsibility. They are unwilling to risk the "power" system which may emerge from substantial reliance on such statesmanship.[20] Accordingly, they urge that society should strive for competitive markets instead of relying on the sense of responsibilities of the big-business managers, or for that matter, of the leaders of big unions.[21] A few feel so strongly that they advocate setting some limits on company size[22] in terms of assets or employees or as percentages of the output of an industry.

The relationship between competition and personal freedom has changed with the times. At one time personal freedom meant absence of government interference.[23] Currently, it has a much broader connotation. It has taken on elements of economic and political freedom. It relates to immunity from private as well as governmental interference.[24] It is recognized that the various freedoms do require some government restrictions which lay down the general rules of the game.[25] Therefore, there is little support today for the contention that government should not interfere with the liberty of individual businessmen to enter into contracts which will restrict competition.[26] Instead, there is a feeling that such restrictions may affect the freedom of others who want to enter a market and of consumers who would like to make their own choices.[27]

Further, the license to make restrictive agreements may be self-defeating in the long run. Such private restrictions, if they entail drastic consequences, may lead to direct government regulation. One of the most powerful arguments for competition has, of course, been that it will minimize the need for positive government controls.[28] Supporters of a militant competitive policy have been impressed with competition as a self-regulator in the market, whereas they fear that monopoly will breed extended government controls.[29] On the other hand, some believe that there are practical limits to the effectiveness of competition[30] and that in many fields public policy will call for direct government intervention even in the presence of active competition.[31]

Many feel that concentration of economic power is not compatible with a democratic political system.[32] Thus, it has been argued that competition is an important factor in the maintenance of a political system of more than one party.[33] E. V. Rostow, in *Planning for Freedom,* makes the point that competitive capitalism is a necessary element of a democratic society.

> Unless the members of an opposition can make a living without the permission of the government; unless they can function as a political party, obtain newsprint and presses, hire meeting halls, publish freely; unless they can have access to television without complete dependence on the good will and sporting instincts of the government in power, their opposition is bound to be a feeble, meaningless force, existing only by sufferance. Capitalism is a vital part of the price of liberty.[34]

Another social goal that affects public policy regarding competition is the maintenance of the individual's opportunity to improve his economic and social position, free of interference.[35] This basic democratic tradition permits every individual to choose his own calling and to move out of his "class" within the limits of his personal resources, unhindered by either governmental or private control.[36]

Related to this desire for free opportunity is that of fair play.[37] Ethical considerations have had an important influence on much of our thinking about competition.[38] For example, there is a distinct moral overtone to the feeling that it is unfair for a large company to cut prices in one town, driving local competitors out of business, while maintaining its prices elsewhere.[39] The expression, "predatory practices," reflects such an overtone as do "boycott," "conspiracy," and "unfair" methods of competition.

Because of this drive for fair play many people tend to equate the protection of individual competitors with the maintenance of competition. While there is a substantial relation between the two, as Wilcox observed, "The preservation of competitors may have some value in itself. But it is not the preservation of competition and should not be defended as such."[40]

The semantic attributes of morality are employed in interesting ways to defend opposing points of view. Proponents of antitrust exemptions, which permit a manufacturer to set the prices of retailers, call their program "Fair Trade." State regulations which set minimum mark-ups for retailers are dubbed "Unfair Trade" laws.[41] Some of the appeals against competitors who cut prices refer to the practice as "unethical." The great national experiment in recovery-through-restriction, the National Recovery Administration, set up "Codes of Fair Competition."

These semantic gambits are not merely disingenuous forensic maneuvers. They reflect ambivalent attitudes in our society. We do want fair play in a clean competitive struggle. Wanting lower prices and better quality, we respect the companies which provide them. Yet, we sympathize with the underdog, especially if he is smaller. We rush to protect the less able competitors who might be hurt and tend to disparage some of the ruthless upstarts who upset the carts of comfortable vested interests, but we favor the results.

The relationship between freedom and economic efficiency has assumed world-wide significance.[42] Important questions have been raised here and abroad about which combinations are preferable. Many people assume that a totalitarian system can provide superior economic progress. Most of those in the well-developed economies of the West choose freedom with a willingness to sacrifice some economic efficiency if it should be necessary, though they do not believe that freedom and efficiency are inconsistent. However, some in underdeveloped areas seem convinced that the problems of subsistence come first.

These assumptions are of considerable national and international import. They raise many basic analytical questions. Are freedom and economic progress incompatible or mutually dependent? Will central authority produce better results in a modern economy? Will it produce better armaments and public works because it can depress living standards, or can a determined free nation demonstrate superior performance if it chooses to "gird its loins"? Can a modified free-market economy turn in a better performance because it utilizes the drives of private initiative and imagination and has greater flexibility?

The course in the United States seems clear: we want freedom even at economic cost.[43] Yet, we need a clearer understanding of the relationships between the two elements. It seems likely that freedom and economic progress go hand-in-hand. Indeed, it seems probable that rounded analysis would indicate that civil liberties constitute the underpinning of our high productivity—rather than a luxury that we can afford. Thus, such objective inquiry might have a telling influence on the intellectuals in the undecided nations.

There are several indications that personal freedom—an important basis for decentralized operations—may add to over-all efficiency rather than detract from it. To test such an hypothesis a clearer inquiry into the Soviet experience is needed. Comparisons of productive progress in the United States with Russian developments should be reviewed in the light of differences in phases of development. As W. W. Rostow has suggested, greater relative progress seems possible—even likely—in earlier phases.[44] We need to know whether the Soviet economic achievements have been balanced, have occurred only in the public works and big projects sector, or if comparable progress has been made or can be made in consumer goods and services.

Yugoslavian experience seems to indicate that a decentralized, competitive framework does improve the output of consumer goods and services. Starting with deficient production around 1950, Yugoslavia effected a decentralized operation about 1956 when all enterprises were turned over to the workers. Much reliance was placed on competition among the enterprises.[45] Some economic reports indicate that the country is pleased with its progress since this move.[46] There are other signs that the government would like to find out how to make the system more competitive.[47]

## *Regulating Levels of Competition*

A set of social policy goals concerns the protection of health, safety, and honesty.[48] These aims have a profound influence on the competitive tone of the economy. Some of the pertinent regulations merely set the ethical levels on which competition operates, such as regulations against fraudulent representation. Certain controls set standards of fairness and safety to guide competitive operations. However, others go further and blunt the edge of competition or serve as the basis for a system of control.[49]

Minimum standards for the protection of health and safety set the plane of competition by limiting its form. Building codes, milk inspection, and food and drug regulations compel all competitors to meet certain minimum standards. While these requirements may eliminate some substandard firms, public policy may make this result unavoidable.

On the other hand, such controls may be used as instruments to limit competition.[50] For example, building codes and inspections may exclude potential contractors and craftsmen from an industry; may make it impossible for new products to be used; may keep new material suppliers out of a city; or may compel the use of more costly materials and production methods than safety requires.[51] Similarly, health measures may be used to confine a city's milkshed unreasonably.[52] They can be employed to keep potential milk distributors out of an area. Again, licensing of trades and professions—such as barbers, plumbers, doctors, lawyers, and opticians—may be perverted into a mechanism to reduce the number of competitors or to eliminate price cutters.

Standards of nomenclature and of representation,[53] applying to advertising and product labels, also influence the plane of competition.[54] For example: a requirement that textile labels show fiber content in accordance with standard rules prevents representations of high quality for shoddy materials. Such standards ensure that the old-style medicine man's colored water cannot be sold as a newly discovered antibiotic. Such regulations do not constitute outright prohibitions of sales or production. Rather, they are developed in order to promote honesty on the part of the seller and knowledge on the part of the buyer.

These standards have two purposes: the social objective of raising levels of morality and fair play;[55] and the economic objective of improving the efficiency of competition.[56] The underlying premise supporting competition is that the consumer should be the final arbiter in the market. Since it is assumed that he makes his selection on the basis of price and quality, the rewards go to the more able producers and distributors. Unless he can make effective quality comparisons,[57] the system cannot operate efficiently since some gains would depend on ability to mislead rather than on productive performance.

A continuing problem is how to facilitate competition by maintaining standards of nomenclature which keep pace with technological developments. An illustration of the use of standards to retard technological improvement was introduced at a congressional hearing.[58] Rigid trade association standards for rating the capacity of certain types of household furnaces were used to hold down the rating of a new type of furnace. Though the heat output of the new product was substantially higher than that of a conventional furnace with the same outside dimensions, the rating system showed that their capacities were equal. The implication of the testimony was that the old rating system was continued in order to minimize the competitive advantages of the new item.

On occasion, there are delicate balances between the goals of health and safety and competition.[59] Some public protection may reduce competitive influences. However, most standards serve to lift the plane of competition. Given the proper perspective, such regulations may serve to improve the efficiency of the competitive mechanism by improving consumer choices.

## *Economic Growth and Standards of Living*

The outstanding economic goal which bears on competitive policy is the desire to promote the growth of the economy and to raise standards of living.[60] Since this aim depends on improvements in the efficiency of production and distribution, it has an intimate relationship with the dynamics of market rivalry.[61]

The relationship between competition and efficiency has always been an important element in economic thought.[62] From its inception modern economic theory has been concerned mainly with efficiency in the allocation of resources—land, labor, and capital. In its early days the operating advantages of competition were stressed. Adam Smith argued that the competitive mechanism and the "invisible hand"[63] of the market stimulated the use of resources to produce the largest volume of goods and services possible. The greater efficiency led to larger production at lower prices. Hence, a competitive economy produced higher standards of living than one which was dominated by monopolistic forces[64]—whether they were created by business or by the state.

Some attention was devoted to the shortcomings of monopoly profits. Since the competitive system would keep prices at the lowest levels, larger shares of total production would be turned over to worker-consumers than they would receive from monopolies. On the other hand, the monopolist could collect large tolls from the flow of economic activity, tolls which depressed standards of living for everyone except himself.[65]

Some thoughtful economists doubt that competition is associated with the greatest increases of efficiency[66] and living standards.[67] One prominent contention is that because of the dynamics of technology, gains in efficiency depend mainly on innovations.[68] Larger aggregations of capital have funds for research and find it profitable to develop new improved products and equipment if they are protected from strong competitive influences. As the argument goes, the resultant innovations create higher productivity with lower costs and greater increases in standards of living than would be generated by competition. Another position, suggested by two British economists, is that "technical progress is encouraged by a favorable balance between safety and competition. . . ."[69]

Discussion of this contention has moved from the consideration of competitive forces to the issue of size.[70] Thus, it is argued that large companies do not promote efficiency[71] and innovation;[72] that smaller companies can and do innovate;[73] that they can develop greater efficiency because they avoid bureaucratic drags; and that they sell at lower prices because they are more competitive.[74] The one side argues that large companies create innovations more frequently and efficiently because of superior organization, better equipment, and higher volume;[75] the other side argues that smaller companies accomplish more because they have less overhead and more flexibility, and because they are more strongly influenced by competitive pressures.[76]

Public support of invention and innovation has a long history in the United States as well as in other developed countries.[77] Our patent system was designed to grant a legal monopoly to inventors, who disclosed the nature of their inventions, in an effort to encourage invention and to protect risk investment in its application. However, in recent years important questions have been raised about patent rights and their influences on innovation and competition.[78] Possibly, because of these doubts, the United States courts seem to have become less and less protective of patent rights.[79] The more immediate policy problems under consideration are whether to reinforce or weaken the rights of patentees, whether to hold them to strict conformity with the antitrust laws in the application of their patent monopoly,[80] and how to treat government-financed patent developments.

It has been suggested that under certain conditions a reduction of competition will spur substantial increases in efficiency together with lower costs and prices.[81] For example, one producer in a small industry could use large-scale automatic machinery and manufacture at much lower costs than a number of companies that operate on an inadequate scale. The same contention has been applied to distribution. For example, it has been reported that an industry arrangement in one European city effected substantial decreases in the costs and prices of home-delivered milk by reducing the number of milk trucks making daily deliveries on each block from 30 to 3.[82]

Another phase of the discussion about competition and company size involves union relations. Some contend that only large companies can cope with the power developed by large labor unions.[83] This discussion of size factors has given rise to the concept of countervailing power,[84] a theory that power on one side of the market begets power on the other. If either a buyer or a seller has monopoly power, a large number of small independent units on the other side of the market would create an imbalance that will not endure and should not be encouraged. The prerequisites of a healthy economy include a rough equality in the economic power on the buying and selling sides of the market.[85] Therefore, as the theory goes, when large aggregations exist on one side, society's interests are best protected by similar power groups on the other side.

Serious question has been raised about the validity of countervailing power as the protector of the public interest.[86] It has been suggested that these large industrial units frequently "gang up" on the consumer.[87] The employer may be a selling monopolist as well as an employing monopolist.[88] In that event, he can accept increases in labor costs because he can raise prices. Similarly, a powerful union's position may be used by a small group of competitors—through industry-wide collective bargaining and union cooperation—to effectuate restrictive business practices which dull the edge of competition.

Even if countervailing power should be discounted as a practicable basis for the protection of the public interest, its proponents have thrown an important point into sharp relief. The effects of competition may depend on the balance between the two sides of a market.[89] Aggressive seller competition will be influenced by the rivalry among the buyers. For example, a monopolistic buyer (a monopsonist) can play one supplier off against another. In extreme cases, such a tactic may induce the sellers to cooperate with each other in self-defense.[90] Similarly, a monopolist's position will be seriously influenced by the nature of the competition among his customers. If his customers should be engaged in aggressive rivalry, he can extract more from them. If they are not in direct competition with each other, he can use a series of differential prices and charge what the "traffic will bear." If they should work out a concerted program in opposition to him, his position might be weakened substantially.

Consideration of the government's role in fostering economic growth is closely related to many competitive issues. As suggested above, a basic argument for competition is that it reduces the need for governmental activity. On the other hand, many public programs seem to render competition more effective in stimulating economic growth. For example, the construction and maintenance of roads, water supplies, and sanitary facilities permit more companies to push for growth and greater efficiency. Additionally, governmental measures to reduce economic fluctuations may increase the efficiency of the competitive system by providing enough stability of demand to encourage individual competitors to assume risks in innovation and production.

Unfortunately, most of the debates about the relations between competition, efficiency, and the standards of living have been on theoretical grounds.[91] On this theoretical level, the arguments in favor of competition are supported by the majority of economists.[92] However, the theory has not been subjected to close empirical tests. There is no organized body of field analysis to establish that, on the whole, efficiency is increased under competitive conditions.[93] Nor is there clear evidence that monopolistic elements increase profits significantly. Similarly, the evidence regarding the relationship between innovation and competitive conditions is incomplete, though there is enough information to raise substantial doubts about the assumption that large, monopolistic companies are the principal innovators.

There are a number of interesting findings that a competitive system develops operating superiorities.[94] For example, several teams of engineers, production executives, and accountants who were sent to the United States by the Anglo-American Council on Productivity were impressed by the influence of competition on efficiency and costs.[95] Said the industrial engineers, "It is our opinion that, more than any other factor, competition provides the drive for the more frequent analysis of costs and the application of industrial engineering techniques in the U. S., and the constant effort to achieve the most economic usage of men, materials, machines and money."[96] Similarly, the accountants concluded: "The freedom of competition which exists in the United States undoubtedly is a most important reason for the drive for lower unit costs."[97]

However, there is a clear need for careful field studies of the operational advantages of competition. Such research might indicate that there is no adequate generalization which applies to all industries and to all societies. It might show there are substantial differences in the potential contributions of competition, depending on industrial, marketing, and even cultural conditions. Conversely, it might indicate that the underlying theory in support of competition applies to all economic activity.

Such empirical analysis of the influence of competition on efficiency and on standards of living would be useful, among other reasons, because it would serve to clarify many concepts, such as the meaning of competition in its various forms[98] and the basic definitions of productivity and efficiency. Thus, the several elements in the competitive process would be analyzed; quality and investment rivalry may be as important as that of price; even competition in selling effort may have played a substantial role in our economic progress. There is evidence that certain types of rivalry drive certain costs down directly,[99] while other types increase some costs, such as those for advertising and design. However, the broader effects of these forces on the standard of living need fresh analysis.[100]

In these efforts there is a serious need for study of the structure and behavior of cost itself. Most analytic economics is premised on assumptions about costs which seem to fit a more elementary technology and market organization than we now enjoy.[101] There is considerable evidence of changes in the nature of costs,[102] changes which are so substantial that a clear understanding of the nature of competition requires a re-examination of cost factors. Such a reappraisal should help to illuminate the effects of competition on growth and inflation.

There is a clear need for better understanding about the behavior of costs and their relationship to competition.[103] Thus, sharp market rivalry may be the spur that compels industrial management to effectuate reductions of costs in manufacturing and distribution.[104] Most economic theory does not take account of many important factors affecting costs but tends to consider only the effect of a given schedule of costs on price.[105] Such an analysis logically leads to the concept of monopoly profits. If monopoly leads to higher prices without affecting costs, the resulting margins must be greater than under competitive conditions. However, these assumptions have no empirical basis. They overlook the influence of low prices on the drive to lower costs and greater efficiency.[106]

Further, the nature of market rivalry can have a profound influence on the composition of costs. Manufacturers set their market strategy with an eye on several factors—price, design of product and package, methods of distributing, service, warranties, and sales promotion. Should the product and package be improved so that the market will "accept" a price increase? Is it possible to make the product improvements without increasing unit costs? Can a new machine reduce costs substantially? With lower manufacturing costs will it be more profitable to reduce prices or to use the cost savings to pay for a sales promotion campaign? Will an advertising campaign produce such great increases in volume that it will more than pay for itself? Will the use of "trading stamps" increase sales in a supermarket to such an extent that profits will be increased without raising prices?

These cost factors influence market strategy because of a range of influences relating unit costs to volume and profits.[107] There are signs that the total costs of a firm are becoming less responsive to changes in volume.[108] Larger and larger proportions of total expenditures are not influenced directly by changes in the volume of sales in any one year. Increased mechanization, more elaborate factory office systems, research and development programs, and various methods of insurance tend to develop a central core of costs which does not shrink or expand with changes in volume. Therefore, volume factors have become more important, together with long-run decisions about cost commitments and other investments.[109]

This range of influences on costs makes the analysis of competition more complex.[110] It reflects the variety of components which make up modern competition. It impinges on the differences in the cost consequences of the various types of competition, those that increase and those that decrease costs. It sheds light on the consequences and possibilities of price competition and its effect on problems of inflation.

## *Controlling Inflation and Ensuring Stability*

The goals of controlling inflation and ensuring economic stability have an important influence on policies affecting competition.[111] These issues seem to occupy a more prominent place in current public concern than does competition itself.[112] There have been general claims that competitive pricing puts limits on price and wage increases.[113] However, these claims have not been backed up either by a full theoretical treatment or by substantial analytical research.[114]

The recent discussions of "administered prices" is a case in point. Briefly defined, "administered prices" are set by managerial decision as opposed to those set by the automatic operation of the market. In its original form, the concept has little significance since almost every price is "administered" whether it is influenced predominantly by monopolistic or competitive forces. Because of government administration, such "free-market" prices as those of many agricultural products have become "administered." Recent discussions have content only if one reads into the phrase "administered prices" a lack of price flexibility[115]—especially a resistance to price reductions—because the market is dominated by monopolistic forces.[116]

The initial attack on "administered prices" came during the depression of the 1930's.[117] Gardiner Means, the originator of the term, contended that administered prices were relatively inflexible,[118] and that they had been held fairly steady in the face of reduced demand while sales, production, and employment declined.[119] Meanwhile, in the free-market sectors, prices had fallen and physical sales volume had been relatively steady. The implication of this thesis was that administered prices contribute to depression while free, competitive prices do not.[120]

More recently, the Kefauver Committee hearings have revived the "administered price" attack. A new thesis has been advanced: that such pricing has contributed to the inflationary spiral.[121] Briefly, this argument is that noncompetitive industries do not offer substantial resistance to wage increases and that high profits stimulate union pressures for such increases. The resulting hikes in prices, together with the wage increments, stimulate demands for higher wages in other parts of the economy. The full pattern of the attack would then appear to be that such administered prices accentuate depressions and magnify inflation.

A number of studies have challenged these conclusions.[122] Serious questions have been raised about their assumptions and the proof offered.[123] It has been contended that increases in many administered prices have been moderate during the postwar inflationary boom and that this moderation has helped to restrain inflation. On the other hand, E. V. Rostow argues that these price policies have delayed the process of adjustment to inflation and have prolonged "the agony."[124]

Related contentions have been advanced regarding the administered wage rates of labor unions.[125] As this argument goes, their monopoly power has enabled unions to resist wage decreases effectively and to press constantly for increases. Because wage increments sometimes run ahead of changes in productivity, runs the argument, they produce a "cost push" upward on prices.[126] On the other side of the coin, the higher wages create additional purchasing power without a proportionate increase in the supply of goods and services. This juxtaposition of the "cost push" and the "demand pull' spells inflation.[127] Thus, it is maintained, monopolistic industries and monopolistic unions contribute jointly to strong inflationary movements.[128]

The influences of administered prices and wage rates on inflation have received considerable national attention in recent years.[129] Presidents Eisenhower and Kennedy have appealed to both labor and industry to hold off wage and price increases voluntarily.[130] In mid-1961 President Kennedy "warned" the steel industry not to increase prices.[131] All of these appeals were premised on the theory that prices and wages in many industries and unions are not controlled by competition; hence, voluntary choices could either spur or restrict inflationary forces.

These appeals have stirred up considerable economic debate.[132] One side argues that monetary and fiscal measures constitute the only means to control inflation. Some urge that current government policies are breeding inflation and that exhortation for private restraints avoids the basic problem. The other side argues that voluntary restraints are an important supplement to monetary and fiscal steps.

Current monetary theory seems to assume that the monopoly problem has little to do with inflation.[133] Basically, the teaching of monetary theory is that an imbalance between the quantity of goods and total purchasing power, or the quantity of money, creates inflationary pressure.[134] "Too many dollars chasing too few goods" is a fairly accurate, popular cliché about inflation. This imbalance relates to total quantities of goods and money, not to individual items. Hence, following the theory, if the price of one item is higher, there is less purchasing power left over to buy other goods. Conversely, a lower price simply releases more purchasing power for other products and services. Thus, the tenets of monetary theory do not seem to include any specific factors to reflect the competitive situation.

There is a need to clarify the relationship between competition and the inflationary process.[135] A key factor might be the influence of competition on efficiency and prices. Conceivably, if competitive drives should accelerate improvements in productivity to keep pace with wage increases in substantial industrial sectors, total production might keep pace with purchasing power,[136] or at least narrow the gap. At the same time, the higher productivity would tend to cancel the effect of wage hikes on unit costs. In that case, both the cost-push and demand-pull would be tempered. For such inflation depends, in good part, on the relative movements of average wage rates and productivity.

Further, if prices in a substantial competitive sector were stable, increases in purchasing power might be sopped up by larger purchases of these lower-priced goods. Such a result would depend, of course, on the influence of price on the volume purchases in the pertinent markets. If lower prices in the highly competitive industries should not induce consumers to step up their use of the goods and services, the low prices would only release purchasing power for the products of the monopolistic industries.

Such lower competitive prices might also have a profound influence on wage rates. If these lower prices held down the costs of living, they could relieve pressures for higher wage rates, pressures which are significant in both organized and nonunion industries, under both escalation contracts and flat-rate agreements. While there are differences in the timing of wage increases, depending on organization and contract provisions, extended pressures for wage adjustments will in time affect most industries.

Similarly, active competition might compel employers to resist wage demands more strongly when they exceed productivity improvements.[137] Individual competitors are concerned about their ability to recover the increased labor costs since their market rivals may not increase their wage rates unless there should be industry-wide wage bargaining.

Another factor in the analysis of the competition-inflation complex is the influence of profit margins.[138] If profits were substantially higher in monopolistic markets, the high gains might encourage additional investment in plant and equipment in that and in other industries during an inflationary period. The new investment would not be limited to the increased dollar profits, since the high profit rate would induce other financing. Because the purchasing power generated by the new investment would not be offset by a greater flow of consumer goods, it would add more power to the inflationary forces. Conversely, if competition keeps profits in check, such inflation-generating forces would be controlled.

The increased capacity created by the additional investment may ultimately lead to greater production and higher productivity. Such forces would, of course, be anti-inflationary. However, if the influences of the new plant are too long in the making, the profit inflation would not be offset in time.

Even if competitive forces do not restrict inflation directly, an important issue remains for fiscal and monetary theory: Will the effectiveness of the counterinflationary moves be influenced by the competitive state of affairs?[139] Much monetary theory seems to assume a competitive market situation.[140] Conceivably, the effectiveness of fiscal and monetary moves can be offset by monopolistic pressures for higher wages and prices.[141] Thus, restraint in the money supply might be met by increased velocity in the circulation of money—with resulting additions to purchasing power.

Public concern about inflation enters into policy considerations about competition in two ways: first is the influence of competition on inflation; second is the influence of inflation on the competitive drive for efficiency. A strong inflationary trend may help the inefficient to continue because of the margins inherent in an upward price movement except, of course, in those markets in which prices are based on historic costs. If final prices should reflect substantial increases in material prices and wage rates, a producer who bought materials and employed labor at the lower levels will automatically add a factor for the price inflation to his margin. Thus, the competitive tests of efficiency would be tempered.[142] Hence, government measures to reduce inflationary forces can improve the performance of the competitive system by helping to eliminate the inefficient or compelling them to improve their operations.

## *Protecting Labor, Agriculture, and Small Business*

National efforts to protect the interests of labor,[143] agriculture, and small business[144] affect public policy regarding competition in several ways. On the one hand, there are signs that untrammeled competition may injure certain vital elements of society, and affect the tone of the entire economy. On the other hand, some of the protections provided for these groups may dull the edges of competition and injure other sectors.[145]

The basic concept of the labor union is anticompetitive.[146] The union is organized to avoid competition among its members.[147] It prevents the employer from playing one worker off against another in order to control wages and working conditions. In effect, the power of the employer, as a buying monopolist—in technical jargon, a monopsonist—is offset by the union.[148] At the same time, the power of the union may, following the theory of countervailing power, beget similar power on the other side of the bargaining table.

Because countervailing influences are needed, the formulation of public policy regarding union monopoly power is particularly difficult. Some economists feel that there exists a public need to restrain this power.[149] For example, Chamberlin argues that "the objection from a public point of view to labor monopoly is no whit different from the familiar objection to industrial monopoly."[150] Yet, even he feels that there are differences between the business and union issues. Hence, he urges that "comprehensive study of this whole range of problems by economists from a public point of view is desperately needed."[151]

The advent of powerful national unions gives rise to a troublesome set of public questions. In one respect, the weakening of a union may upset an important balance of power. In another, a national union can wield monopoly power, or it can cooperate with employers in raising prices to levels that are out of balance with the rest of the economy.[152] In McKie's words, "The view that unions counteract the monopsony power of employers is no doubt partly true, but when the employer has monopoly power in product markets the monopoly power of the union is not merely countervailing but concurrent or even additive."[153] Indeed, union power has been used on occasion to enforce industrial restrictions on competition.[154] Unions have helped industries to police minimum price agreements, to set limits on who may enter an industry, to keep certain goods off the market, and to foreclose innovations of productive equipment and processes.

The union issues present another competitive dilemma: what to do about competition among union leaders.[155] The president of a powerful national union, anxious to keep his job and maintain his organization's strength, may drive for better working conditions and larger wage increases than other unions obtain. In this competitive drive, he may assist his industry in the promotion of restraints on competition or push effectively for increases in wages and fringe benefits which far exceed changes in productivity.

One suggested solution for this problem is the development of a national wage and price policy.[156] Some employers and union officials in the United States, as well as in England,[157] have proposed that conferences of employer and union organizations be held to formulate general principles to guide wage increases.[158] Some countries, such as the Netherlands, have employed such a practice.[159]

An argument for establishing such national policies[160] is that they would avoid the inflation-breeding interunion competition. On the other hand, such conferences entail substantial questions of administration,[161] of applicable principles, and of conflict with some political and social objectives. In essence, the union problem poses a serious need for objective analysis.[162]

Agricultural goals have, in the main, led to restriction on competition.[163] During the great depression, *laissez faire* produced agricultural conditions which were regarded as seriously injurious to public welfare. Overproduction, in the face of low purchasing power, led to prices that depressed the agricultural segment of the economy and injured the agricultural-supporting industries. The crisis threatened to affect the peaceful order of society in many communities. Waves of mortgage foreclosures took place and guns were used to prevent more of them. Farming practices in many sections deteriorated so badly that land and equipment were run-down and the productive capacity of the nation was reduced. These conditions, together with the associated human misery, forced a public policy of direct government support and control programs. At the same time, farmers were encouraged to improve their financial welfare through buying and marketing cooperatives.

The temporary cures turned into permanent problems. Today's policy makers have inherited the task of reconciling substantial differences between agricultural policies and those favoring competition.[164] How long and how extensively should the farm control and subsidy programs be supported? Since agriculture does not always adjust to market conditions, what competitive elements should be maintained in the pricing and distribution of farm products?[165] What limits should be set on the efforts of agricultural marketing cooperatives to limit production and control primary marketing?[166] In brief, how can a balance be established between competitive and control policies so that we can have an efficient farm economy without penalizing the consumer?[167]

Public efforts to preserve small business[168] and small farmers provide another series of intricate policy problems with competitive overtones.[169] There is strong support for these efforts based, in part, on the belief that such programs will avoid undue concentrations of power[170] and, in part, on the voting strength of small entrepreneurs. Programs have been instituted to maintain high agricultural prices, to weaken chain and discount stores, to encourage cooperatives, and to prevent retail price-cutting.[171]

Against a general desire for efficiency and growth, are set off the fears inherited from the depression with its spectre of ruin for the small business.[172] In this respect, our feelings about competitive efficiency are ambivalent. We expect the more efficient companies to compete vigorously. Yet, when they are conspicuously successful, we entertain moves to restrain them. Judge Hand was troubled by this problem in the *Alcoa* case, saying, "The successful competitor, having been urged to compete, must not be turned upon when he wins."[173] This simple maxim provides no guide for a complex policy issue. There are signs that many large companies hold their competitive power in leash lest they drive their rivals to the proverbial wall and are faced with antitrust attack.[174]

A related dilemma is the effect of some antitrust laws on industrial concentration. The clearest antitrust rules attack collusion among competitors and the control of customers or suppliers.[175] At the same time, an individual company can maintain programs that two or more firms are forbidden to establish by agreement. If two competing companies agree on prices, there would be a clear antitrust violation. On the other hand, if the two plants are owned by one company, common prices can be fixed. Therefore some companies solved their pricing difficulties by merging.[176] So, for example, after losing an antitrust case involving a price conspiracy in 1899, the defendants merged and avoided the effect of the decree.[177] Similar instances are reported in the United Kingdom.[178] We have, of course, tried to counteract such tendencies by the Celler-Kefauver Antimerger Act. However, this regulation has only limited effect.

A similar problem affects relations with distributors, both wholesale and retail. A manufacturer invites antitrust prosecution if he sets resale prices for independent distributors (unless permitted by state law), or enters into agreements which compel distributors to use his products exclusively. However, if he sets up his own distribution outlets, those facilities will sell his products exclusively, at the prices he sets. Hence, this vertical integration permits the manufacturer to pursue policies which are illegal when they affect the practices of independent distributors.[179]

In effect, except for the Antimerger Act and the monopolization provision of the Sherman Act, the antitrust laws appear to encourage the extension of one's own operations.[180] This pattern seems to counter efforts to maintain small business.

Unfortunately, problems affecting labor unions, farmers, small entrepreneurs, and big businesses have developed such emotional sensitivity that the application of impartial analysis is very difficult. Objective analysis of the power of labor unions subjects one to the accusation of being antilabor. Impartial analysis of the powers of agricultural and small-business trade associations is attacked in similar vein. Critical comments about big companies are labeled as "antibusiness" or "anticapitalist." However, in the face of these significant policy problems affecting competition, growth, and inflation objective study is required to achieve a sensible balance which will accommodate our broad policy objectives.[181]

## *International Problems*

A wide range of international problems further complicates national goals. With the growth of interest in international relations, new forces have intruded into the complex of antitrust and related policies. And the signs point to further intrusions. These international problems involve exports and imports, foreign trade agreements, international raw material arrangements,[182] participation in international cartels,[183] and foreign investment. They directly affect antitrust policies, raising questions about the application of our own laws to the activities of United States nationals in other countries[184] and the operations of foreign nationals in the United States.[185] They have substantial bearing on many international political and economic relationships. The various moves toward international integration, such as the European Common Market, will intensify these problems.

Intricate political factors of international relations and the problems of international trade have a growing influence on public goals. At the same time, specific legal problems stem from basic differences in the domestic law of other jurisdictions which reflect a wide spectrum of attitudes concerning competition and monopoly.[186] Many industrial establishments in other countries are state-owned monopolies.[187] Some monopolies are state-sponsored.[188] Some cartels are not only tolerated but are encouraged by the state.[189] On the other hand, there is a growing interest, abroad, in eliminating restrictive business practices and encouraging competition.

The United States has adopted several positions in this spectrum. It has maintained a general competitive policy for domestic trade, while limiting foreign competition through protective tariffs, quotas, and "Buy American" preference.[190] Meanwhile, in interesting contrast, Switzerland has encouraged domestic cartels[191] and promoted free trade in its international policy. Similarly, Americans who pride themselves on maintaining the most aggressive domestic antitrust policy in the world, permit some resale price maintenance, while several countries—such as Sweden, Canada, France, and Denmark—have virtually eliminated it.[192]

It has been difficult to set clear and consistent policies regarding competition in international relations. On the one hand, we have tried to persuade other countries that there are great advantages in promoting competition.[193] On the other hand, we present the face of a protective tariff to many foreign industries. Similarly, we have enacted the Webb-Pomerene Act which appears to permit American competitors to cooperate, in cartel fashion, in foreign operations.[149] Such inconsistencies have led some foreign observers to wonder whether Americans feel that the benefits of competition should accrue to the United States economy but should not be transferred to others.[195]

Nor have we presented a consistent appearance in our positions regarding international raw material agreements.[196] An example is our attitude toward the international coffee agreement which was set up to protect farmers, and even entire economies, from the extremes of *laissez faire*. For a long time we refused to cooperate with some of these international efforts to protect farmers, even though we applied similar policies in solving our own domestic farm problems. Recently, of course, we reversed our stand and are currently cooperating in such international plans.[197]

Some American antitrust prosecutions have affected business operations in other countries.[198] These interferences were based on findings that specific international agreements violated United States antitrust laws because they set restraints on American imports or exports. In the course of some prosecutions, we have influenced or attempted to influence business operations abroad. For example, an antitrust decree was issued covering various operations of du Pont and Imperial Chemicals[199] in the United Kingdom; another decree affects Timken's[200] operations in the United Kingdom and France; the United Fruit decree covers its operations in several Latin American countries. Other governments have objected, some vociferously, to American interference with their domestic affairs.[201] However, it is hard to see how the antitrust laws can be administered without such effect.[202] In each such case, competition in our domestic markets was affected by the business practices through their influence on exports from or imports into the United States. Thus, if United Fruit had cornered the supply of bananas in the producing countries, it would automatically enjoy a domestic monopoly because of its foreign controls.

We require a sensible balance between domestic and international policies affecting competition. If there were a general conviction that antitrust enforcement has a substantial effect on the economy, national efforts to promote competitive policies through international agreements might be increased. We might even find that the economic problem is so serious that we are willing to take some chances with international good will. Conversely, inquiry might indicate that the total impact of such antitrust cases is not substantial. Or, it might show that the economic effects of such prosecutions are not significant because our control is not complete. In either event, we might decide that because of the current sensitivity in international relationships we would not continue such prosecutions. Domestic companies might be permitted to participate in international cartels. Or, we might set one policy for some industries and another policy for others. At any rate, appreciation of the economic effects of various alternative policies would help us to formulate clearer policy positions in this area.

## *Military, Atomic, and Space Issues*

Closely related to our international objectives are a series of military, atomic,[203] and space goals.[204] The combination of highly accelerated technological development and the enormous sizes of individual projects in these areas creates a new set of competitive problems.

Effective prosecution of military, atomic, and space projects may make it desirable to follow practices that nurture monopolistic forces.[205] There are arguments for concentrating certain technological developments in few hands. Such a program offers great advantages to the favored few. It gives them superior positions for further government awards. It presents them with exclusive knowledge of technological products and processes, developments which may provide substantial applications to a host of civilian products. It aids them in the construction of productive capacity that can be transferred to other uses.

This pattern creates a serious dilemma. Military preparation and space development constitute basic national objectives. Must they be so planned that they conflict with competitive policy or can the two objectives be reconciled in whole or in part? Must technological development be confined to the few or can it be broadened? Would it be practicable to spread the newly emerging knowledge in these fields by publishing technical information, making patents available and awarding small, pilot contracts to a number of companies or do security problems prevent it? How do these issues influence policies regarding government patents? If the government made patents and know-how freely available to all applicants, would the favored companies refuse contracts? Would such a policy stimulate more companies to compete for the government research and development work?

The issues were raised clearly during World War II. There were congressional investigations of the concentration of war contracts. Relatively unsuccessful efforts were made to spread work among smaller companies through several programs. However, no objective analyses were made of the reasons for the concentration. We do not know whether such concentration is inevitable, whether it is the product of procurement methods, or whether it results from competitive maneuvering. More important, we do not have practical methods to avoid it.

## *The Over-All Problem*

The problem of relating this variety of ultimate public goals to policies bearing on competition is a complex and never-ending one. It cannot be solved by simple maxims. It clearly will not be met by an extreme *laissez faire* position.[206] Nor can it be settled once and for all time. It requires broad general understanding of the various goals and their relative importance in meeting changing conditions.

Entwined in all policies affecting competition are threads of political, social, economic, and international goals. We are interested, primarily, in the maintenance of a democratic society. We desire to provide maximum personal freedom, and to maintain personal economic security at the same time that we nurture incentives for greater efficiency and high standards of living.

With all of these currents—now comingling, now opposing[207]—policy formulation assumes great importance. In this process, economic analysis should help to clarify many issues.[208] It should help to attain sensible balances in the promotion of the various objectives—balances which are prerequisite to satisfactory policy formulation and administration in many areas.

Policy formulation in this area can be improved. First, we can develop a clearer understanding of the complex of objectives—an appreciation of the fact that most public policy issues in this area cannot be guided by a single national goal but must take several into consideration. Second, we can clarify the role of competition in meeting some of the goals. We can establish basic premises through field research regarding the influence of competition on efficiency, growth, stability, and international trade. While such premises may not have the same application in all industries, we might for policy purposes rely on the effects that obtain from competition in the bulk of markets.

Most important, we can single out those areas which can be analyzed systematically in order to reduce our great dependence on personal hunches and emotional value judgments. In the end, the political process provides a composite value judgment. The thesis here is that we provide a firmer analytical basis, where and when we can, for these public policy decisions. Further, since economic inquiry can make a substantial contribution to this end, ways and means should be found to stimulate such studies.

# 3 / *Government Activities**

THE POSSIBILITIES of applying economic analysis in the formulation and execution of public policies regarding competition are influenced by the existing structure of government activities. Such consideration calls for a review of the present legislative and administrative framework.

The complex of public policy goals affecting competition is reflected in a hodge-podge of legislation and administrative agencies. The statute books contain a confusing array of legislation which, in part, promotes competition and, in part, supports monopoly.[1] Since this array is the result of a long process of accretion without the benefit of periodical over-all review, it does not reflect a clear consistent body of policy. Many statutes that were passed to meet temporary exigencies remain on the books even when conditions change. No effort has been made to review all of the pertinent statutes as a whole to see if they meet currently accepted policy objectives. Indeed, legislative attention is directed to new enactments rather than the repeal of old ones.

The wide spectrum of legislative policy is reflected in an inconsistent structure of administrative agencies and methods of enforcement. A cursory review indicates that about twenty federal agencies are charged with the administration of antitrust and related statutes. There is considerable direct overlapping in the functions of many agencies, an overlapping that is serious because of a lack of uniformity in administrative policies.

The statute books contain a potpourri of procedures for enforcing the substantive laws. Many procedures depend on judicial enforcement. Others depend on administrative action. Some provide for injunctions; some for criminal action; others for the cancellation or with-

* Footnotes for Chapter 3 begin on page 359.

holding of franchises. Among them are many curios: the power to forbid use of the Panama Canal; the seizure of imported goods or of goods in interstate commerce; and the suspension of federal enforcement of interstate compacts.

Thorough analysis of the broad spectrum of government activities affecting competition—both regulatory and nonregulatory—would be practically impossible. The nooks and crannies are so deep that the eye of the general viewer quite frequently misses important elements. Many regulations harbor serious subsurface influences that indirectly but profoundly affect the shape and nature of competition in a market. Indeed, it is difficult to visualize many types of government regulation that do not have some influence on competition.

Examples of such indirect influences on competition are within the ken of everyone who has participated in government activity, either regulatory or commercial. To illustrate: When the Interstate Commerce Commission allows a reduction in railroad rates for coal, it gives coal an advantage over petroleum products; when it permits lower railroad rates, it affects the trucking industry. When the Federal Power Commission approves a natural gas pipeline, it may aid natural gas companies and injure producers of other fuels. A substantial government contract for electronic research and development may give the contractor a significant edge over his competitors. The Wool Products Labeling Act[2] helped producers who had lived up to its standards of consumer information in their rivalry with those who had not.

The complete picture of government activities bearing on the state of competition covers a wide area. In addition to federal regulatory functions, a number of other factors must be taken into account. Some are industrial activities, such as purchasing, research and development programs, and the generation of electric energy. A few deal with taxes. Others are found on the levels of state and local governments.

The following treatment covers a generalized picture of: antitrust laws; the regulation of the plane of competition through the protection of health, safety, and honesty; import and export control; the patent system; state regulation; and the pertinent federal nonregulatory functions. It is not an exhaustive compilation. It is intended only to demonstrate the need for broad policy review and to establish the setting for the process of policy formulation and the role of economic analysis.

## *Federal Regulatory Activities*

Federal regulations cover a broad, confusing spectrum. It is generally assumed that governmental policies of the United States favor competition, in contrast to those of most other countries. Yet, in the face of a widespread public objective of maintaining competition, those policies are not clear. In fact, a significant sector of the regulatory activity of the federal government is substantially anticompetitive.[3] Further, there are indications that the balance of recent legislative proposals would weigh against, rather than for, competition.

While most policies are directed to fostering competition in the bulk of industry, many elements in the supervision of the so-called regulated industries[4] have been designed to curtail competition.[5] For example, the Interstate Commerce Commission has set truckers' rates high enough to protect the railroads' rate structure.[6] Indeed, the efforts of the I.C.C. to limit exemptions from the trucking regulations, for farmers and for contract carriers, are designed to hold rates high rather than low. Similarly, the Civil Aeronautics Board has granted no certificates for new scheduled carriers since it started operation. As Walter Adams points out, "After twenty years of regulation, and despite a 4,000 per cent increase in traffic, there are four fewer trunk lines than when the Civil Aeronautics Act was passed."[7] For some time the C.A.B. was slow in awarding additional routes to the existing certificated carriers so that new competition among the chosen few would not be generated. Recently, however, it has been more liberal in granting additional routes.[8]

Substantial doubt has been expressed regarding the competitive effects of certain laws which bear antitrust labels. For example, some suggest that the Robinson-Patman Act has promoted "soft" competition, sacrificing the "hard" competition of the Sherman Act.[9] They charge that it has eliminated important elements of price competition, and that it has provided special protection for brokers.[10]

A number of recent congressional proposals raise serious questions regarding the general trend of public policy. Revisions have been proposed for the Robinson-Patman Act to promote a one-price system.[11] There is considerable congressional support for a national fair trade act that would authorize resale price control in every state, without depending on state enabling legislation.[12] Similarly, bills have been introduced to compel manufacturers to extend conventional functional discounts to all wholesalers and retailers.[13] Such a requirement might block experimentation with new distribution methods and eliminate the pricing flexibility of individual firms—damaging many smaller manufacturers who can outmaneuver their large competitors by cutting prices "on the spot" in order to obtain an order.

## *Federal Antitrust Laws*

There is an extensive but disorganized body of antitrust regulation on the federal statute books. A number of acts promote competition, while many oppose it. They are so diverse that it is impossible to trace a consistent policy thread running through them.

Three major acts cover the main features of the antitrust laws: the Sherman Act, the Clayton Act, and the Federal Trade Commission Act. Each has been subject to some modification and extension by amendments.

The Sherman Act[14] (1890) contains two important provisions. Section 1 outlaws *restraints of trade* by agreements, combinations, and conspiracies in interstate and foreign commerce. Section 2 outlaws *monopolization* of such commerce; and covers attempts or conspiracies to monopolize. The Wilson Tariff Act[15] (1894) applies the basic provisions of the Sherman Act to the importation of goods. The McGuire[16] and Miller-Tydings[17] amendments permit resale price control contracts in those states which allow them.[18] The Norris-LaGuardia Act[19] (1932) provides a specific exemption for labor unions.

The Clayton Act[20] (1914) was premised on the assumption that the broad provisions of the Sherman Act were not adequate and that more specific rules against incipient monopoly and restraints of trade were required. Accordingly, this act contains a number of provisions outlawing specific practices. Section 2, frequently referred to as the Robinson-Patman Act[21] (1936), which amended it, forbids *price discrimination* that may lessen competition substantially, injure competition, or tend to create a monopoly; additionally, it forbids the payment of brokerage fees to buyers as well as furnishing services to customers or making payments to them except on "proportionally equal terms." Section 3 contains a provision against *exclusive dealing contracts* or *tying arrangements,* whereby a customer agrees not to purchase the goods of the seller's competitors, if such arrangement may lessen competition substantially or tend to create a monopoly. Section 7, also known as the Celler-Kefauver Act[22] (1950) or the Antimerger Act, which amended it, forbids the *acquisition of shares or assets* of other corporations if such acquisition may substantially lessen competition or tend to create a monopoly. Section 8 makes it unlawful for anyone to be a director in two or more competing corporations, any one of which has the net worth of one million dollars or more.

The Federal Trade Commission Act[23] (1914) was enacted during the same year as the Clayton Act. This act establishes the Federal Trade Commission and describes its functions. Section 5, as amended by the Wheeler-Lea Act,[24] declares that "*unfair methods of competition*" and "*unfair or deceptive acts*" are unlawful.[25]

In addition to these three broad statutes, a substantial number of federal regulations relate to the problems of competition. Some laws give specific support to the basic statutes; some merely provide for separate administration of the laws; many provide exemptions—for certain types of practices, for specified "regulated" industries, and for specified unregulated activities; while others apply to imports, disposition of government property, advertising, and the use of trade-marks.

A number of related statutes apply antitrust policy to specific industries. For example, there are laws that apply to: meat-packers and stockyard operators;[26] producers, importers, and distributors of alcoholic beverages;[27] bank holding companies[28] and banks;[29] the electric power and natural gas industries;[30] and users of nuclear materials;[31] importers and exporters in other countries.[32]

### *Exemptions*

A number of statutes provide exemptions from the application of the antitrust laws.[33] Some cover specified unregulated activities; some relate to "regulated industries"; and some permit the individual states to make the ultimate determination regarding the scope of the exemption.

General exemptions are provided for labor unions,[34] export associations[35] that do not restrain domestic commerce, voluntary arrangements which contribute to national defense,[36] and certain types of organizations of small businesses.[37] Provisions are made for administrative exemptions from antitrust for farm marketing cooperatives,[38] agricultural marketing agreements,[39] cooperatives of fishermen,[40] associations of marine insurance companies,[41] and lessees of federal oil and coal lands.[42]

Another series of exemptions from federal antitrust laws clothe state governments with supervisory power. Among these exemptions are insurance companies[43] and tobacco growers.[44] Interstate compacts that limit the production of petroleum are exempt under one act,[45] while another prohibits interstate shipment of products that do not comply with these compacts.[46] However, the latter exemption can be suspended when the President feels that the state programs levy an undue burden on interstate commerce.[47]

### *Regulated Industries*

Regulated industries are given separate antitrust treatment. These exemptions from the general application of the antitrust laws have been confirmed by judicial interpretations. A doctrine of "primary jurisdiction"[48] has evolved to rationalize the judicial holding that the pertinent regulatory agency may exempt approved transactions from the antitrust rules. This doctrine has precluded a number of prosecutions by the Department of Justice.

These exemptions have been quite effective. In one outstanding proceeding, the Department of Justice sued to prevent one railroad from controlling another. After his victory in the Supreme Court, the Attorney General stood helplessly by while the Interstate Commerce Commission approved the merger of the two railroads.[49] The House Antitrust Subcommittee has contended that the I.C.C. helped the oil pipeline industry to circumvent a consent decree.[50]

Regulatory agencies are authorized to grant exemptions from the antitrust laws in a number of industries. Important among these are joint rate agreements between railroads,[51] truckers,[52] water carriers,[53] telephone and telegraph carriers,[54] and airlines.[55]

Entry into business is controlled in a number of industries: railroads[56] and trucklines; hydroelectric power generation; natural gas and other pipeline operations;[57] radio, telegraph, and telephone communications;[58] radio and television broadcasting;[59] food packing and certain types of food distribution;[60] applications of atomic energy for electrical power generation and other industrial and medical purposes;[61] the use of public lands for grazing and the extraction of mineral resources;[62] the operation of airlines and helicopter service;[63] the distilling, wholesaling, and importation of alcoholic beverages,[64] and the importation of agricultural products and biologicals.[65] Licenses for specific locations or routes are used for controlling operations in transportation,[66] communications,[67] power generating facilities,[68] and gas transmission lines.[69]

Many features of competitive operations in regulated industries are controlled in addition to entry.[70] Rates are regulated in the transportation,[71] communications,[72] and power industries.[73] Most rate controls set ceilings on charges. However, some provide floors as well, notably in railroad and truck transportation.[74] Uniform prices are set for hog cholera serum and virus.[75] Federal milk marketing orders set minimum prices for dairy farmers.[76] Quality of service is regulated especially in the transportation fields. Passenger service of both railroads and airlines is controlled quite closely.

The government's role in the production of electrical energy presents an interesting set of competitive problems.[77] There has been a running fight between one group which favors government regulation of private companies and another which favors public power. The Tennessee Valley Authority interposed a strong competitive public facility in its region—strong enough to become a virtual monopoly. Besides federal projects, publicly owned properties include those of state and municipal governments and public power districts. Some support for the public production of power is based on the theory that such production will provide a yardstick for rates—partly to inject competitive pressures and partly to strengthen rate regulation. As Caulfield points out, "Few, if any, areas of Federal domestic economic policy involve so much political tension and so sharp and deep a schism in political thought, interest, and action as Federal electric power policy."[78]

The use of competition as a means of control in the regulated industries has been a subject of some concern.[79] Some have favored it strongly and feel that the regulatory agencies have not relied on competition when they can.[80] The problem has received some prominence recently in discussions about mergers in the rail and air transport industries.

The issue of competition as a method of regulation is not new.[81] In 1874 the Windom Committee of the Senate recommended that there be no direct regulation of the railroads. Instead, it favored government-owned railroad lines for freight and an improved public waterway system.[82] In 1886 the Cullom Committee recommended to the Senate that direct regulation of the railroads be undertaken through the passage of the Interstate Commerce Commission Act. The committee also endorsed public improvements of navigation in order to develop more active competition with the railroads.[83]

*Raising Levels of Competition*

Regulation to protect public health and to raise the ethical levels of competition center on setting minimum standards, on curtailing misrepresentation, and on requiring informative labeling.[84] This activity is intended not only to raise standards of safety and ethics but also to improve the consumer's effectiveness as the final arbiter in free markets.[85] Through assurance of reasonable quality or informative labels, they help the consumer to place less reliance on well-advertised brands. In this respect, they may enhance price competition.[86]

The regulation of the distribution of food and drug items[87] together with the control of the production of biologicals[88] provide minimum standards to protect public health. They prevent dilution of the products covered and curtail competition based on quality deterioration.[89] Minimum standards of quality are set for canned fruits which are imported, while standards of identity and purity are set for other imported foodstuffs.[90]

Another set of minimum standards is administered under the Poultry

Products Inspection Act,[91] the Federal Meat Inspection Act,[92] and the Imported Meat Act.[93] Through federal inspection, meat which is diseased or which fails to meet sanitation requirements is condemned; labeling is supervised and grades are established. Similar rules are applied under the Process and Renovated Butter Act[94] and the Virus-Serum-Toxin Act.[95] The Flammable Fabrics Act[96] prohibits the manufacture, importation, or sale of fabrics and wearing apparel that are dangerously flammable.

One type of regulation helps to provide the consumer with quality information. The Wool Products Labeling Act of 1939,[97] the Fur Products Labeling Act of 1951,[98] the Textile Fiber Products Identification Act of 1958,[99] and the Hazardous Substances Labeling Act of 1960[100] cover appropriate consumer information for furs, textiles, and hazardous household products, especially chemicals. The Insecticide Act[101] contains specific labeling requirements, as does the Naval Stores Act[102] (covering turpentine and resin). The Federal Alcohol Administration Act[103] requires labels on alcoholic beverages to indicate product identification, size, and fill of containers.

The Department of Commerce promulgates commercial standards which are standards of nomenclature.[104] The use of these standards is voluntary. However, misuse opens the path for a charge of unfair methods of competition. The department also administers a voluntary labeling plan for consumer items and a program of simplified practice recommendations set up to reduce the number of sizes and varieties of manufactured products.

A number of grading regulations are set up for the protection of farmers, while several operate at the wholesalers' level. Under the United States Grain Standards Act of 1916[105] inspection service is provided for grading and certification of grain. Under the Federal Seed Act of 1939[106] false labels and advertising of agricultural and vegetable seed are prohibited; the dissemination of noxious weed in agricultural seed is restricted; germination standards are set for vegetable seed; and minimum standards are set for imported seed. Under the Tobacco Inspection Act[107] tobacco is graded on an auction market after the program is approved by two thirds of the growers who sell on the market. Under the Cotton Acts[108] a cotton classification service is furnished to certain groups. Under the Perishable Agricultural Commodities Act[109] inspection service and standards of nomenclature are provided for the benefit of farmers and dealers. Standard specifications of size and capacity are developed and enforced for baskets and hampers used in marketing fresh fruits and vegetables.[110]

Planes of competition are raised and manipulative activities are prevented on commodity and stock exchanges. Under the Commodity Exchange Act[111] activities on commodity futures exchanges for agricultural products, mainly wheat, corn, and cotton, are regulated. The Securities and Exchange Commission administers regulations regarding securities issues, securities exchanges, brokers, dealers, investment advisers, and investment companies.[112]

A somewhat curious requirement for giving the consumer information is contained in the Automobile Information Disclosure Act of 1958.[113] It requires that labels showing the manufacturers' suggested retail prices should be attached to every car.

Under Section 5 of the Federal Trade Commission Act as amended —which outlaws unfair competition and deceptive practices—the F.T.C. prosecutes companies for misrepresentation and for deceptive advertising of foods, drugs, and cosmetics. Its campaigns against misleading practices have accounted for more proceedings than its antimonopoly work.[114] Hence, it has appeared to be more interested in raising the plane of competition than in rooting out anticompetitive market forces.[115] Several organizational changes in mid-1961 may imply that the antimonopoly activity of the F.T.C. will become more important.

## *Functions of Federal Agencies*

The administration of competitive policies has been entrusted to a surprising number of agencies with considerable overlapping in functions and little coordination.[116] The functions of some are dedicated primarily to the prosecution of a competitive policy; others are concerned mainly with direct regulation;[117] a few are given regulatory functions as an incident to operating responsibility; some regulate broad sectors of economic activity; others confine their attention to specific industries.

*Two Principal Agencies*

The two principal antitrust agencies are the Federal Trade Commission and the Antitrust Division of the Department of Justice. The F.T.C. is an independent commission empowered to issue cease and desist orders, which are enforced by the courts. The Commission combines investigative, prosecuting, judicial, and advisory functions. Its Enforcement Bureaus check protests sent in by private individuals or companies to see if a formal complaint should be issued. Some minor legal trespass has been handled by an agreement or stipulation that a company will discontinue the complained of practice.[118]

The Enforcement Bureaus prosecute the complaints. The Commission's hearing examiners conduct trials along judicial lines. These are adversary proceedings between the F.T.C. counsel supporting the complaint and the counsel for the respondent. After the examiner issues an initial decision, including his discussion of law and facts, either counsel may petition for an appeal before the F.T.C. in order to persuade it to reverse the examiner.

However, most of the orders issued by the Commission are negotiated with the respondents without a hearing. For many years F.T.C. procedure called for such negotiations after a formal complaint had been issued and before formal hearings were started.[119] Some orders were negotiated after hearings were instituted but before the hearing examiner issued his decision. On a few occasions there were some negotiations before the complaint was filed. In 1961, the procedure was changed.[120] The new practice is to negotiate a consent order before a complaint is filed. After such filing the proceeding must go to formal hearings and decisions.

The Commission also attempts to promote voluntary compliance by holding Trade Practice Conferences with individual industries and issuing rules after such conferences.[121] These rules have no legal status[122] and add little substance to the administration of the laws. Occasionally, the F.T.C. issues explanations of its policies in the form of guides[123] or staff memoranda. It offers advice to businessmen and lawyers regarding its interpretation of the propriety of specific business practices and mergers.[124] While this advice is informal and not binding, the Commission recognizes the good faith of companies that have requested and followed such advice.[125]

In its enforcement of the acts relating to misrepresentation of textiles, furs, drugs and cosmetics, the F.T.C. issues rules under its statutory authority.[126] Further, it examines advertising, in both printed and electronically broadcast forms.

The Office of Export Trade administers the Webb-Pomerene Act, which covers export associations. It maintains a register of such associations and is charged with observing their operations.[127]

The Department of Justice prosecutes criminal cases and civil proceedings ending in equity decrees that cover future actions.[128] While it litigates many civil cases ending in judicially formulated equity orders, most of its equity decrees are formulated through negotiations with the defendants. These consent decrees are then presented to the courts.[129] The department has recently announced a change in practice whereby the proposed decree will be published before filing, in order to permit interested parties to suggest changes.[130] On occasion, a judge will review a consent decree before accepting it; usually these decrees are regarded in the nature of agreements between the parties and are not subjected to substantial judicial review.

The two agencies have overlapping jurisdictions. The major substantive provisions of the Clayton Act are enforced mainly by the F.T.C. and the Department of Justice, although other agencies have certain limited duties. The Department of Justice enforces the Sherman Act, which covers monopolizing and restraints of trade. The F.T.C. enforces Section 5 of the Federal Trade Commission Act, which covers unfair methods of competition,[131] as well as deceptive practices. Since violations of the Sherman Act may also be considered violations of the Federal Trade Commission Act,[132] either agency may prosecute. However, some practices that violate the F.T.C. Act do not come under the Sherman Act.

The relationships between the functions of the two agencies have not been clearly resolved either by the Congress or by the agencies, themselves. The overlap has been criticized[133] and defended—though rarely on substantive grounds. Its defenders point to the virtue of competition, even between government agencies. Further, they claim that there is significant cooperation between the two agencies. Such cooperation appears to be confined to a procedure to establish "squatters' rights." Each agency notifies the other when it starts a proceeding[134] so that both organizations will not prosecute at the same time. Nevertheless, on occasion both agencies have prosecuted the same companies for the same offenses.[135] Apparently, there is some agreement that certain industries will be covered by only one of the agencies in the administration of Section 7 of the Clayton Act, the antimerger statute.

Yet, many questions about the overlapping and the lack of affirmative coordination remain unanswered. Are some types of problems best handled by a commission and others by the courts? What types fit into each category? Does the regulation of some industries require the supervision of a "quasi-judicial" agency while others call for an executive agency? Since most proceedings are settled through negotiation, is there a basic difference in the agencies' policies so that one requires a procedural safeguard—the Administrative Procedure Act,[136] which applies to the F.T.C.—and not the other?

While the two agencies try not to interfere with each other to any appreciable extent, neither has availed itself of the services it can obtain from the other. For example, Section 6 of the Federal Trade Commission Act[137] authorizes the Attorney General to request the F.T.C. to use its broad subpoena powers to investigate suspected antitrust violations and compliance with outstanding antitrust decrees. Yet, according to the public record, before 1961 the Attorney General requested the F.T.C. to review compliance with a decree on only three occasions[138] and has never asked it to investigate a suspected antitrust violation.[139] Instead, the Department of Justice has made repeated requests to be given a power of civil process, which is akin to a subpoena, in order to strengthen its own investigations.[140] Recently, the department seems to have instituted a new policy when it requested that the F.T.C. investigate compliance with 56 decrees, and supported the Commission's budget request to conduct the inquiries.[141]

Similarly, the F.T.C. can, when it wants to enjoin a merger that might violate Section 7, ask the Department of Justice to exercise its authority to sue for an injunction. Yet, it apparently has not made such requests. Instead, it has asked Congress for the power to sue for an injunction on its own.

Despite the claims of cooperation[142] there are signs of strong differences between the two organizations. W. C. Kern, a member of the Federal Trade Commission, complained publicly about the attitude of the Department of Justice. He referred to occasions when the department "refused to enforce our orders by way of penalty proceedings—even when it admits that there exists no price competition in the industry and among the respondents involved, but concludes the situation might not convince a court and therefore proceedings would be impolitic."[143] Further, "All too often Justice made application for writs of certiorari ostensibly undertaken in our behalf [but] more like the kiss of death."[144]

In its antimonopoly work the F.T.C. has placed considerable emphasis on the Robinson-Patman amendment to Section 2 of the Clayton Act. Though the Antitrust Division shares jurisdiction over Section 2, until recently it showed no sympathy with the Robinson-Patman amendment.[145] A large proportion of the F.T.C.'s proceedings under the Robinson-Patman Act seem to have little connection with competitive problems. Rather, they deal with the enforcement of the provision which forbids the payment of brokerage fees to buyers, Section 2 (c)[146]—a species of class legislation which, at best, has not affected competition and merely prevents reductions in the costs of distribution.

The Federal Trade Commission was empowered to conduct studies that would keep the Congress and the President informed about competitive conditions. However, it has not demonstrated an outstanding interest in such studies. Nor, in due justice, has either the President or the Congress seen fit to encourage such investigations by providing the Commission with budgetary means therefor. The F.T.C. has made a number of studies.[147] The chain store investigation,[148] its study of public utility holding companies, its recent antibiotics and coffee studies are conspicuous examples. On several occasions, its studies have served as underpinnings for legislation.

The Department of Justice has several functions relevant to competition in addition to its responsibilities under the Sherman and Clayton Acts.[149] The Attorney General is required to notify the Atomic Energy Commission whether a proposed license would tend to create an antitrust violation.[150] He supervises antitrust exemptions which may be given by the Small Business Administration.[151] The department is further charged with advising the appropriate agencies on the competitive effects of sales of government-owned plants to private buyers[152] and of contemplated bank mergers.[153] It has the authority to attack bank mergers even if they are approved by one of the appropriate agencies. Additionally, as the chief law enforcement unit of the federal government, it represents the other agencies in enforcement litigation.

### *Other Agencies*

A wide range of other agencies also participate in antitrust administration. Some have direct enforcement roles; some are empowered to exempt certain practices; a few are authorized to suspend statutory exemptions; others are charged with suspending or refusing licenses if they are involved in an antitrust violation. Several agencies have sole antitrust jurisdiction over specified segments of industry. Some share functions with others—mainly with the Department of Justice. All agencies are required to inform the Attorney General whenever there is a suspicion that the bids they receive involve an antitrust violation.[154]

The agency roster is long. The President is charged with overseeing the operations of the Interstate Oil Compact[155] (which are exempt from antitrust). He is authorized to declare import embargoes on any products in order to avoid certain unfair methods of competition.[156] The Atomic Energy Commission has reporting duties and may suspend licenses for antitrust reasons.[157] Banks, bank holding companies, and bank mergers come under the antitrust jurisdiction of the Board of Governors of the Federal Reserve System,[158] the Comptroller of the Currency, the Federal Deposit Insurance Corporation, and the Attorney General.[159] Pertinent regulated carriers are subject to the antitrust jurisdiction of the Interstate Commerce Commission,[160] Federal Communications Commission,[161] Civil Aeronautics Board,[162] Federal Power Commission,[163] and Federal Maritime Board.[164]

The Department of Agriculture[165] exercises antitrust supervision over farm cooperatives and agricultural marketing agreements. It shares jurisdiction over meat packers and stockyards with the F.T.C.[166]

The Department of the Interior is the antitrust watchdog over cooperatives of fishermen;[167] it can give antitrust exemptions to certain combinations of lessees of federal mineral rights.[168] The Securities and Exchange Commission can grant antitrust exemptions for certain public utility mergers.[169] The Treasury Department exercises partial antitrust jurisdiction over production, importation, and wholesaling of alcoholic beverages,[170] and enforces import embargoes that are laid down by the President because of unfair methods of competition.[171] The Secretary of the Treasury administers provisions against tied sales by exporters from other countries.[172] The Tariff Commission is directed to investigate unfair methods of competition in importation (including dumping) which may restrain or monopolize trade.[173] The Secretary of Commerce is directed to make special investigations regarding trusts.[174] The Small Business Administration can exempt certain joint ventures with the approval of the Attorney General.[175] The Administrator of General Services is charged with notifying the Attorney General when large government plants are to be sold so that antitrust features may be reviewed. He is required, also, to notify the Attorney General when he receives identical bids that he believes evidence antitrust violations.[176]

There exists no mechanism for coordinating the activities of these agencies. On many occasions the conflicts in their policies are evident and the need for coordination is obvious. For example, the Department of Justice has filed several suits to block bank mergers only a few days after the transactions were approved by the banking authorities.[177] The Federal Reserve Board approved a merger after serious objections were interposed by the Department of Justice.[178]

Similar problems have affected the regulation of the railroads. In a Sherman Act case in 1922 the Supreme Court ordered the separation of the Southern Pacific Railroad and the Central Pacific.[179] Soon after that decision the Interstate Commerce Commission, acting within its jurisdiction, approved the merger.[180] Again, there were sharp differences of opinion between the I.C.C. and the Department of Justice in the consideration of rate agreements. The department felt that some agreements did not allow the parties to take independent action, in accordance with the enabling statute. Nevertheless, the I.C.C. approved the agreement.[181]

More recently conflicts have developed in the public press regarding a communication satellite. The Federal Communications Commission, and others, have considered awarding a joint license to the American Telephone and Telegraph Company and other companies to construct, orbit, and operate such a satellite.[182] Meanwhile, the Assistant Attorney General, Antitrust Division, has discussed the possibility of a proceeding to compel A.T.&T. to divest itself of its international communications operations.[183] The satellite would, of course, be used mainly in international communications.

## *Federal Sanctions*

The methods for enforcing the laws and the pertinent sanctions are about as confused as the structure of laws and agencies. Some means are used so frequently that they are well known. Some are curios that merely fill space in the statute books. Comparatively little attention has been given to how effective the full set of methods may be or to the extent of their use.

The most prominent methods of enforcement are court decrees and administrative orders. Under the Sherman Act[184] and certain provisions under the Clayton Act,[185] the Department of Justice may obtain equity injunctions ordering companies to follow certain practices and to desist from others. If these injunctions are not obeyed, fines and imprisonment may be ordered by a court.[186]

Under the Clayton and Federal Trade Commission Acts, the F.T.C. is empowered to issue cease and desist orders.[187] Violations of such orders after they are final are punished by civil penalties of not more than $5,000.[188] The Commission's subpoenas are enforced by court orders; fines can be levied for noncompliance and imprisonment can be ordered.[189] Fines and imprisonment can be ordered for furnishing a false statement of fact to the F.T.C.[190]

Criminal punishments are provided for several types of violation.[191] A violation of Section 1 or 2 of the Sherman Act can be prosecuted as a misdemeanor subject to a fine not exceeding $50,000 and imprisonment of not over one year.[192] Violation of the provisions of the Federal Trade Commission Act against false advertising of foods, drugs, devices, or cosmetics, under the Wheeler-Lea amendment, provides similar penalties. If the use of the commodity is injurious, or if the advertising was intended to defraud or mislead, the violation is a misdemeanor that calls for a fine of not over $5,000 and imprisonment of not over six months; a second conviction calls for a double fine and imprisonment.[193] The Packers and Stockyards Act provides for a fine from $500 to $10,000 and imprisonment of from six months to five years for a violation.[194] The Shipping Act of 1916 provides a fine of not more than $25,000.[195]

Forfeitures of rights are provided in some acts. The Lanham Trade-Mark Act provides for the cancellation of trade-mark registrations when they are misleading or when they are used to effectuate an antitrust violation.[196]

Some rights may be curtailed or lost through judicial determination. Patent rights may be subject to compulsory licensing under the equity power of a court. A contract which violates an antitrust law may be declared unenforceable.

Under the Atomic Energy Act of 1954, licenses may be revoked or suspended if they are involved in an antitrust violation.[197] The Communications Act of 1934 provides that a court which has found that the licensee of a broadcasting station has violated the antitrust laws may revoke the license. No license may be granted to the licensee thereafter.[198]

Several embargoes are set up as sanctions. The Panama Canal Act provides that ships belonging to violators of the Sherman Act will be excluded from the use of the Canal.[199] Ships that are owned or operated by persons who have violated the antitrust provisions of the Shipping Act of 1916 are to be refused right of entry to United States ports until the Federal Maritime Board certifies that the violation has ceased.[200] The Tariff Act of 1930 authorizes the President to embargo import items that are involved in unfair competition.[201]

Several acts provide for forfeitures of property to the federal government as penalties. Section 6 of the Sherman Act provides that property in interstate or foreign commerce can be seized and condemned if it is owned under a contract or combination that is proscribed by the act.[202] Under another statute, coal lands or deposits that were purchased or leased from the federal government shall be forfeited if they are employed in a conspiracy in restraint of trade.[203] Goods that are imported following a practice which would violate the Sherman Act are subject to forfeit under the Wilson Tariff Act.[204]

Damages for violations can be collected under Section 4 of the Clayton Act.[205] Persons who are injured can sue for treble the damages they prove.[206] Under Section 4A the federal government can sue for single damages. Under the Automobile Dealer Franchise Act, a dealer may institute a damage suit for a violation.[207]

## *Patents, Copyrights, and Trade-marks*

Competition is influenced also by the system of patents, copyrights, and trade-marks.[208] To encourage invention and innovation, the Founding Fathers established a patent system.[209] Under it the inventors of novel features of products and processes can obtain letters patent which provide limited-term monopolies. A patent is a seventeen-year grant of the exclusive right to make, use, and sell the invention.

In recent years the relations between patent monopoly and antitrust policy have attracted substantial attention.[210] The use of patents to promote market restrictions has been prominent in a number of antitrust cases.[211] In many proceedings, the monopoly hold of patents has been weakened through decrees requiring that the patents be licensed to applicants.[212] Discussions of industrial concentration have included references to the concentration of patent ownership. Questions have been raised about the practice of "sitting on patents" in order to forestall innovations which might weaken established positions for old products.[213] Indeed, the usefulness of the present patent system has been questioned.[214]

The patent system gives rise to many questions regarding competitive policy. Should a patent owner be permitted to order a licensee to confine his sales to a limited geographical area, to a specified product, or to certain industries? Should he be permitted to set the prices charged by licensees for a patented product or for a product that includes a patented feature? For an extreme illustration, may a license agreement covering a patented pen-point set the price for the finished fountain pen? Should courts outlaw every contract that compels the buyer of a patented article to buy other nonpatented articles? For example, should a sale or lease contract for a patented salt-dispensing machine provide that the purchaser will buy all of his salt from the machine-manufacturer?[215]

Patents have been considered an important feature in several antitrust cases which involved issues of economic power.[216] A company that has cornered the important patents covering a product can prevent others from entering the market.[217] In certain circumstances, the owner of a patent can achieve substantial power if he can compel every licensee to give him a cross-license covering every improvement patented by the licensee. A patent-pool to which all the members of an industry contribute their patents can allocate markets, limit volume, and set prices.

The nonuse problem poses interesting competitive issues.[218] Under United States law a manufacturer can prevent the introduction of new products by patenting a new development and failing to use the invention. Many other countries—even some which are not noted for their competitive policies—provide sanctions against such a custom.[219] The practice has been under attack in many quarters. One of the clearest criticisms has been made by a leading patent attorney, William H. Davis, who said that "Since one great object of the patent privilege is to bring inventions into actual use . . . it would seem not unreasonable to declare . . . that prolonged and unjustified failure to use or license is an abuse of the patent right. . . ."[220]

Because of the great increase in the federal government's expenditures for research and development, its control over patents covering inventions developed at its expense has become an important public issue.[221] The government's use of these inventions has been protected since 1910 when Congress provided for compulsory free licensing to the government of all patents which are derived through work for the government.[222] Recently, the practice of permitting government contractors to apply for patents in their own names has been questioned widely because of the monopoly they are granted on nongovernment uses.[223]

This issue has been tied up with the charge that the government curtailed competition by awarding the bulk of research and development contracts to a handful of large companies. Daniel Hamberg supported such a charge in his testimony before the Senate Small Business Committee. "For the five years ending June 30, 1956, of 6,788 pending patent applications that resulted from government-sponsored R and D work, 52 per cent belonged to 15 large companies."[224]

Copyrights involve a number of similar competitive problems: monopoly grants, barriers to imports, and compulsory licensing. A copyright is a monopoly grant to the owner of such things as an original writing, drawing, or musical composition.[225] As in the case of patents, the copyright owner may issue limited licenses subject to restriction.

Copyright law provides an interesting illustration of early antitrust attitudes. The Copyright Act of 1909[226] provides that if one company is licensed to record copyrighted music, a similar license must be given to any applicant at royalty fees which are set by statute. The 1909 committee report indicates a concern that one member of the infant recording industry was well on the way to a monopoly of reproducing rights.[227] However, in a study for the Senate Patent Subcommittee, W. M. Blaisdell reported that "Since that time, the author and music publisher groups have sought to eliminate the compulsory license provision, while the recording companies have exerted every effort to maintain it."[228] Further, he concluded that today no producer could monopolize the industry, raising a basic question about the desirability of continuing the regulation.[229]

Trade-mark law provides for protection of brands—one which developed in the common law. The use of another's mark has been held to be illegal because it constitutes unfair competition and is misleading to the consumer. The federal government provides for registration of trade-marks in the Lanham Act,[230] as do most states. If trade-marks are used to implement an antitrust violation, the F.T.C. can take action to have the federal registration canceled. Trade-marks have been used to allocate markets.[231] They are, of course, the basis for a number of types of distributive controls, such as fair trade. A few antitrust cases have involved the use of trade-marks in restraint of trade.

## *Import and Export Barriers*

Competition in many United States markets is influenced by tariffs[232] and other barriers. Some regulations embargo all imports of specified types of articles.[233] Others set limits to the volume of imports through quotas.[234] Many influence price competition with domestic industries through protective tariffs. Some are intended to protect domestic industry against "dumping" of foreign goods[235]—a practice of selling goods here at prices that are substantially below those charged in the originating country plus transportation costs and tariffs. This regulation serves to promote what is regarded as fair competition. On the other hand, there have been several export subsidies in effect: cotton, wheat, and flour.[236] Recently, embargoes have been placed on certain exports, notably to Cuba and Russian-dominated countries.[237]

Import restrictions can have a number of influences on domestic competition, both intended and unintended.[238] They can be used to establish price floors to protect domestic industries.[239] As an incidental effect, this protection may encourage domestic newcomers to enter an industry.[240] Since they increase the prices of imported goods at the ports-of-entry, they may permit domestic manufacturers who are located inland to sell their goods at points that are closer to the seaboard. Therefore, a by-product effect is the promotion of national markets for some goods.[241]

Import embargoes have been established largely as health measures. Some exceed the limits required for health and serve as a means of protecting domestic producers.[242] For example, a cattle disease in one section of Argentina has served as the basis for an embargo on all cattle coming from that country.[243]

Quotas have had a considerable influence on competition in certain markets. For example, the sugar quota[244] has provided such protection for the domestic beet and cane sugar industry that United States prices have usually been considerably higher than free world sugar prices plus import duties and delivery costs.[245] Such procedures have the same effects as protective tariffs, except that they raise the prices paid to foreign producers. Quotas have been established as a phase of United States policy to allocate its sugar imports among various producing nations. They figured prominently in recent news when they were revised as an economic measure against Cuba. Another current news item has concerned the international coffee agreement that will set quotas for producing and importing countries.[246]

"Voluntary" import quotas have been set up through international agreement. For example, Japan has limited its textile exports to the United States on a voluntary basis.[247] Recently, discussions have been held between Japan and Hong Kong, as textile producers, and the

United States and other countries, as textile importers, regarding import quotas that are clearly calculated to affect domestic competition.

A direct limitation on imports is administered through the "Buy American" programs.[248] Starting with the Buy American Act of 1933,[249] a number of controls were instituted to favor United States produced products in federal procurement. All of these policies[250] call for such preferences, with some exceptions when price differences are too large.[251] Along with other import restrictions, they set direct limits on competition.

## *State Regulations*

Public consideration of policies bearing on competition has emphasized federal regulation and neglected state activities. State authorities, with few exceptions,[252] have not been active in enforcing their antitrust statutes.[253] State and local governments seem to display more interest in restricting competition than in maintaining it.

A substantial case can be made for devoting more attention to the state regulations and their influences on competition. Only sparse information is available regarding the effects of a host of state activities.[254] Yet, the total of these may have significant nationwide effects. A number of similarities found in state regulations suggest that some types of legislation may have wide geographical impact. For example, there was a rash of "fair trade" legislation patterned on the California law. In fact, seven states literally copied the California statute, including typographical errors.[255]

### *Regulating Competition*

State antitrust legislation provides even more variety than the federal provisions. There are general statutes against trusts, combinations in restraint of trade, and monopolies. Some laws outlaw agreements between two or more persons not to compete. There are rules against tying contracts and exclusive dealing arrangements, against pools to regulate the quantities sold or the prices charged, and against business restraints in specific industries.

On the other hand, a substantial amount of state legislation sets limits on price competition,[256] entry into business, and free movement of goods. For example, a number of state statutes permit resale price maintenance,[257] limit entry into certain trades,[258] and make it difficult to sell goods produced in others states.

Using their police power, many state and local governments[259] have instituted regulations that limit or avoid competition.[260] For example, as a health measure, many prohibit the sale of fresh milk[261] that has not been produced in inspected dairies. Since the inspectors travel within a circumscribed area, a milk-shed is established limiting competition to the dairies within the area. Further, requirements covering the construction of barns and the methods of operation serve to restrict production within the milk-shed area and to raise costs.[262]

An amusing illustration of the extremes to which these milk regulations may go is contained in a statement made at a 1942 conference on state trade barriers. "Milk, no matter how pure or cheap, cannot come into Washington, D.C. markets unless it has come from cows that have been wiped clean, teat by teat, with a hemstitched linen towel of certain dimensions used by a man sitting on a three-legged stool in a barn that has a smooth ceiling. This would seem to put the dairyman right into the laundry business."[263] We were recently informed that these regulations have been changed to permit paper towels, to compel the use of a metal stool which may have four legs, and to require smooth walls as well as ceilings.

Seemingly simple rules against loss leaders,[264] or provisions against selling below cost, have presented interesting complications. As a practical matter, selling "costs" are sometimes set by statutes which establish prima facie costs,[265] such as 6 per cent of the price paid by the retailer.[266] In some jurisdictions, "costs" may be based on local surveys of the average costs of retailing. Such "costs" may be rebutted by proving the retailer's own costs, following a uniform definition—an expensive procedure for the average store. However, as the Marketing Laws Survey pointed out, "Attention has been so concentrated upon issues concerning the constitutionality of statutes prohibiting sales below costs that there has been little, if any, actual enforcement."[267]

There are many provisions for administrative supervision over prices of agricultural commodities and foodstuffs, milk, fuels, and gasoline. Several states require that the prices paid to farmers for cream should be publicly posted;[268] one requires the posting of milk prices;[269] two require the posting of prices for bread and bakery products;[270] one prohibits rebates and discounts on the sale of bread and bakery products.[271] Some statutes provide that all gasoline prices must be posted publicly, and that there can be no variation from posted prices—a mechanism that prevents gasoline stations from cutting a price to any customer unless they cut prices to all.[272]

Alcoholic beverages are given special treatment.[273] In the liquor "monopoly" states,[274] liquor prices are fixed in the state-operated stores, the only retail sources permitted. A number of other states require that distillers and importers set the wholesale and retail prices of alcoholic beverages.[275]

Another type of regulation provides for the control of various professions and trades through licenses.[276] Many license boards are composed entirely of members of the pertinent profession or trade. While such licensing arrangements may be set up to control the quality of the professional services rendered, they serve as an effective way to limit the number of competitors. There are occupational regulations covering: abstractors, accountants, architects, attorneys, barbers, beauticians, chiropodists, chiropractors, contractors, dentists, embalmers, engineers, massage operators, medical technicians, midwives, naturopaths, nurses, optometrists, osteopaths, pharmacists, photographers, physicians, surveyors, and veterinarians.[277]

Local building codes[278] have provided somewhat notorious forms of competitive restrictions. The primary purpose of these codes is the protection of the community against fire and health hazards. Additionally, they may be dedicated to protect the unknowing consumer who cannot see what lies behind the opaque walls of the finished house. Starting with the twin aims of community and consumer protection, it was no long step to compel the use of high-cost materials, the employment of licensed building tradesmen[279] (whose numbers are limited), and the discouragement of prefabricated components, labor-saving equipment, new materials, and new distribution methods.[280]

Other regulations have permitted groups of competitors to set prices with government approval. For example, state laws permit rate-setting in the insurance field,[281] as well as price-setting and marketing cooperation by agricultural producers.[282]

A number of states have regulated competition by controlling production. This has been a notable feature in the oil-producing states which have set allowable production quotas through state regulatory agencies.[283]

Some state and local governments attempt to control methods of distribution.[284] Chain-store taxes are intended to protect local independents.[285] Regulations of door-to-door salesmen have combined consumer protection with efforts to prevent outsiders from selling in a community.[286]

### *Interstate Trade Barriers*

A relatively ignored pattern[287] of state regulation has been directed to limiting interstate commerce for the protection of local industry.[288] Writing in 1939, Henry A. Wallace, then Secretary of Agriculture, expressed alarm about this development. "Today, we cannot say that we have free trade between the States. It develops that public health and sanitation measures may be so designed as to restrict trade across state lines. The same may be said of certain tax laws, of motor-truck regulation, of quarantines, of grading, labelling, and packaging laws, and of state-financed advertising of farm products."[289]

A comprehensive description of these barriers would require an extended inquiry, state by state, into the formal regulations,[290] their enforcement, and their effectiveness—a task which far exceeds the boundaries of this review. Several types of hurdles are listed here to illustrate the range of activity that has been undertaken.

Michigan levied a tax of 4 cents a gallon on wine made from home-grown grapes and 50 cents on the product made from California grapes.[291] Alabama levied an annual tax of $1,000 on each winery. However, if 75 per cent of the materials used were home-grown, the tax was only $25.00.[292]

At one time California declared an embargo on strawberries grown in Louisiana, which state retaliated with an embargo on California citrus.[293]

One state prohibited the importation of eggs unless they have *non-tremulous* air cells—a regulation which is quite effective in keeping out-of-state eggs off the market[294] since it is difficult to maintain such an air cell in an egg which is subject to the normal jouncing of transportation.

A host of labeling statutes and labeling requirements greatly complicate the marketing of certain goods throughout the country.[295] Many types of drugs and other products require tags which are specified by the individual states. Since these label specifications are not uniform, a manufacturer must affix a special label for each of a number of jurisdictions. An interesting variety in the requirements for margarine labels[296] is listed in the Marketing Laws Survey. Some states required that containers be labeled on top, side, and bottom; others, top only; some, top and side; and some on two sides. The printing types used on the containers are specified in sizes from ¼ inch to 1 inch and in a variety of letter styles such as plain, bold, Roman, and gothic.[297]

In 1932, one state established a Bang's disease quarantine[298] which kept out all dairy cattle unless they came from herds that had been fully inspected three times within the year before their arrival. At the time only 1,500 herds in the country could qualify. None of these were located in the state that maintained the requirement.[299]

Another state empowered its commissioner of agriculture to declare an embargo on any fruit or vegetable whenever the domestic products were sufficient for the state's market.[300]

Motor vehicle regulations covering equipment, weight, and size, as well as license fees, have affected truck movements from state to state.[301] For example, a truck going from Louisiana to Arkansas is limited to a height of 12′6″ in Louisiana and 13′6″ in Arkansas; yet it can have a gross weight of 64,000 pounds in the former state and is limited to 56,000 pounds in the latter.[302]

The extent and effect of state trade barriers has not been evaluated.[303] Presumably, many are ineffective enough to warrant neglecting them. Others may engender some serious competitive consequences. However, without detailed analysis of their operations, their importance cannot be appraised, nor can the combined effects of the federal, state, and local business regulation.

*State Taxes*

State tax systems seem to influence the nature and extent of interstate competition. Under the federal Constitution, states may not levy duties on interstate or foreign shipments. However, their internal tax regulations do exercise substantial indirect influence.

A number of states have established programs to forestall evasion of their sales or excise taxes and to protect their merchants located in areas bordering on low-tax states. Some states levy use taxes[304] on products which are brought into the state by consumers or sent directly to them.[305] To the same end, there are limits to the amounts of specified products that consumers may bring into some states. For example, limits have been set on the consumer importation of alcoholic beverages,[306] which are subject to special taxes. To enforce these regulations, some states have informal "border patrols" which watch cars bearing the state's license plates when they are parked at retail liquor stores located in adjacent low-tax jurisdictions. The patrols seize the liquor as soon as it is brought over the state line and arrest the buyer.[307]

State income taxes also affect interstate commerce. In order to subject "foreign" companies to their jurisdiction, most states impose registration requirements on out-of-state firms which are "doing business" within their borders. Such registration provides the basis for subjecting the companies to the states' judicial and tax jurisdictions.[308] It applies only to companies who engage in sufficient activity within the state to satisfy the technical legal requirements of "doing business."

Recently, a number of states, in quest of revenue, have inaugurated campaigns to collect income taxes from all companies which sell in their territories even if no registration is required.[309] A Supreme Court decision has upheld the states' rights to levy such taxes.[310] A new federal statute provides for an investigation of the problem.[311] There is no accepted basis for an equitable allocation of a corporation's income among the states in which it produces and sells. As a result, a company with an interstate business may be compelled to pay higher taxes than a firm which carries on the same volume of business within one state.[312]

These tax features raise complex policy issues.[313] On the one hand, it seems only reasonable to subject all competitors to the same tax burdens and only fair to domestic companies to levy equal taxes on everyone who sells in the state. On the other hand, out-of-state competitors may be subjected to two sets of taxes on the same income, one in the state of their residence and the other in states into which they ship goods. Further, as Justice Frankfurter pointed out, such tax procedures will subject many companies to a multitude of regulations requiring keeping separate records, making returns, and engaging counsel in a number of states.[314] This, he suggested, could create cost burdens which "may well exceed the burden of the taxes themselves, especially in the case of small companies. . . ."[315]

## *Federal-State Relations*

Federal and state regulations complement each other in many respects. There is considerable cooperation in regard to some health and deceptive practice regulations.[316] Several federal statutes enable states to follow policies that may burden interstate competition.[317] At the same time, the federal government has protected state and local procurement programs from market restrictions.[318]

Various federal acts, mentioned above, support local restrictions of competition. The Miller-Tydings and McGuire Acts permit states to authorize resale price control. The Interstate Oil Compact and State Tobacco Compact Acts permit interstate agreement controlling production. The Connally Act prohibits interstate shipments of petroleum and its products if they do not comply with state regulations. The McCarran Act exempts insurance companies from the federal regulations to the extent that state laws control such operations.[319] The act has been interpreted to mean that federal antitrust laws apply only to boycotts and to rate-making in those states that do not themselves provide antitrust protection.[320] However, there appear to be reasonable bases for the contention that the federal antitrust laws can be applied when they do not conflict with direct state controls of insurance.[321]

Some federal studies have pointed out the danger of state barriers. The Marketing Committee of the National Association of Commissioners, Secretaries, and Directors of Agriculture expressed the fear that the federal government would be forced to intervene if the states went too far.[322] Yet, no federal action has been taken.

Some of the state regulations, such as those covering labels, may result from federal inactivity in important areas. In such instances, the sensible method for avoiding the variety of state requirements appears to be to institute federal controls.[323] For example, the new federal Hazardous Substances Labeling Act[324] may well induce individual states to follow uniform rules or even to cancel their own label controls, relying on federal regulation.

In antitrust enforcement, the federal authorities have cooperated regularly with procurement authorities of state and local governments. Complaints from purchasing officials about collusive pricing have received careful antitrust attention.[325] Recently, Robert A. Bicks, then Assistant Attorney General in charge of the Antitrust Division, suggested a stepped-up cooperation of this type in an address before the Association of State Purchasing Officials.[326]

Such cooperation is maintained, also, in the federal regulation of price differentials. The Robinson-Patman Act, which is opposed to price discrimination, was amended in 1938 to exempt purchases by schools, public libraries, and charitable institutions.[327] Several judicial decisions hold that state and local government agencies enjoy the same exemption.[328] The federal agencies have never attacked any price cutting that redounded to the advantage of such local governments.

## *Governmental Nonregulatory Activities*

A broad array of nonregulatory activities of government exert profound influences on the state of competition.[329] Most prominent in this group are taxation and government purchases, including research and development contracts. Some of these functions appear to encourage concentration and the growth of large companies. Conversely, some activity may be employed to encourage competition directly, to discourage excessive company growth, and to promote the effective functioning of small companies.

*Federal Taxes*

Many general statements have been made about the effect of taxes on industrial concentration.[330] However, there has not been enough empirical work to test these hypotheses. The major tax issues concern the effect of taxes on spin-offs of parts of a large company,[331] the incentives that the tax system offers to owners of small companies to sell their holdings,[332] the tax pressures forcing them to sell, the tax advantages obtained by the purchasers, and the tax bite that keeps young, small companies from expanding through earnings.[333]

Tax rules can penalize a large company or its shareholders when the corporation sells a division or divests itself of stock in another company. Such sales involve heavy tax payments for the capital gain, while a dividend distribution composed of shares in another company builds up an immediate income tax liability for the shareholders. In either event, the bill for taxes discourages the divestiture.[334]

This tax feature appears to have been the major reason for du Pont's resistance to the government's efforts to force it to distribute its holdings of General Motors stock to its own shareholders.[335] Before recent changes in the tax laws, du Pont individual shareholders would have had to pay regular income taxes on the market value of the General Motors shares they received. Additionally, these taxes would have compelled many to sell the GM stock soon after receipt. Such selling might have depressed the price of GM stock with, some argued, unfortunate effects on the stock market.

Another aspect of the same problem influenced the Hilton Hotels' consent decree, which provided that the company sell some of its hotels.[336] For, in that instance, the corporation would be required to pay a heavy capital gains tax.

This problem was given much consideration by the Congress. Hearings were held[337] regarding bills to solve the du Pont type of situation. Some follow the pattern of the tax exemption which was granted to those companies that were compelled to sell properties under the Public Utility Act of 1935.[338] A bill was finally passed, approved February 2, 1962, to avoid this heavy tax incidence.[339]

There has been some concern about the tax pressures on the owners of small companies, encouraging them to sell.[340] Such a sale produces a substantial tax saving because the owner pays a capital gains tax of 25 per cent on his gain instead of paying much higher income taxes on the dividend distribution of the profits. Further, it has been suggested that the tax penalties for undue withholding of corporate dividends has increased the desire to sell.[341]

Another pressure on the owner of a small, successful business is generated by the heavy estate and inheritance taxes which must be paid on his death. These may be so large that his estate may have to sell the entire business in order to raise funds for the payment of taxes. Such a sale may not only lose family control of the business, but might well depress the sales price because of the pressure to sell. Some efforts have been made to alleviate this situation by change in the tax laws. However, no data are available on the effects of the changes.[342]

Provisions for the carry-over of losses have added attractions for the purchase and sale of small companies. Under these regulations, a company which suffered losses may subtract them from current profits before figuring its tax bill. Therefore, a company which suffered heavy losses can offer a potential purchaser substantial tax savings. The owner-sellers can reap some benefit from these losses, while the purchasers can buy substantial tax savings for moderate prices.[343] Though new regulations have set some limits on such tax inducements to acquire small companies, the benefits still exist.

One study of these tax influences casts doubt on their seriousness.[344] However, the repeated presentations of the arguments, as well as indications that they have affected some sell-outs, seem to warrant further inquiry. A broad analysis would require consideration of many factors in addition to the tax elements. For example, many owners of small, successful companies have not built up a stable, well-balanced management to run their companies. With one-man management, the prospects for the company when that man dies or retires may be dim.

The unusual number of sellouts may be a temporary condition due to a long period of high incomes and to industrial changes that are still in process. These conditions may not be sustained over the long run. For example, a low-cost supermarket operation which was started during the depression may have expanded with the rapid growth in the economy, combined with the slow progress of the national chains in shifting to supermarket merchandising. The owner may now have a profitable, attractive business. However, the firm may lack a managerial team to carry on successfully without him. Conceivably, his only recourse, or that of his family, would be to sell the business rather than to continue it independently. That condition may obtain regardless of what changes are made in the tax structure.

It has been contended that corporate tax rates do not permit new small firms to expand as easily as older companies did when tax rates were much lower.[345] Therefore, it is urged that the rates be made more progressive, lowering the rates on small incomes and raising them on large. Currently, the first $25,000 of a corporation's income is taxed at a rate of 40 per cent while a 52 per cent rate applies to all additional profits, regardless of how large the income is. Hence, the advantage to the small firm is not very substantial.

This argument is based on several premises. Large companies grew when low income taxes permitted them to retain the bulk of their profits for expansion. At present, large depreciation charges reduce tax payments, and these businesses can "throw off" large amounts of cash which are available for expansion.[346] Further, large corporations have easy access to new equity and borrowed capital, in contrast to small firms.

Additional advantages were offered to large companies during the wars. Special provisions were made for accelerating depreciation charges for new plant and equipment that were tied in with the war effort.[347] For example, instead of taking 5 per cent of the cost of a building as an expense during a high-tax year, a company could take 20 per cent. Large companies, especially those with war contracts, were enabled to obtain new productive facilities with quick return of their investments because they enjoyed such heavy write-offs when they could save substantial excess profits taxes.

Here, too, is a need for clarification of objectives. Public policy goals may push for the encouragement of new small business, in order to diffuse economic and political power and to encourage innovation. In that event, we may want to lighten the tax burden on these enterprises even if such a step calls for higher taxes for larger corporations. Or, we may want to give priority in tax relief to the new enterprise without changing the rest of the structure. Conversely, if the push of our objectives does not favor new or small companies, we may be satisfied with the present tax structure.

*Government Purchasing and Research and Development*

Government purchases have had important influences on the working of competition in recent years. As indicated above, they have been used as a phase of import control through the "Buy American" programs. Their current programs may influence the basic structures of many new industries, such as atomic energy, space satellites,[348] and new electronic applications.[349] The total amounts spent on government purchases of goods and services loom large in the economy. In 1961 federal expenditures of this type were estimated at $45 billion, while expenditures of state and local governments accounted for over $40 billion. Hence, out of a total gross private product of $413 billion, government spent $85 billion on goods and services or over 20 per cent.[350]

The proportions of gross national product accounted for by government purchases may understate their effects on competition. Their impact is substantially greater than the 20 per cent average on such activities as the production of defense items, atomic energy equipment and applications, hydroelectric power equipment, electrical power generation and distribution, space equipment,[351] computing and other mathematical-accounting machinery, and certain types of transportation and construction equipment.[352]

There is a two-way relationship between government purchases and competition. The purchasing authorities are anxious to maintain competition in order to buy at low prices.[353] The purchase programs, in turn, affect the nature and extent of market competition.

The federal government makes a special effort to maintain competition among its suppliers.[354] The Armed Services Procurement Act of 1947[355] and the Federal Property and Administrative Services Act[356] provide that agency heads refer identical bids to the Attorney General when they believe that there may be an antitrust violation.[357] The Antitrust Division of the Department of Justice has cooperated with state procurement officials in a program for checking state bids. As Robert A. Bicks, then Assistant Attorney General pointed out, the reporting of identical bids helps the division to locate violations.[358]

On the one hand, if governments favor purchases from large companies, those suppliers can strengthen their positions vis-à-vis smaller companies. On the other hand, government purchasing can be used to encourage small companies and to induce new entrants into important industries in order to weaken monopoly positions.

The use of government purchases to eliminate monopoly was illustrated during World War II. The federal government induced the entry of two major aluminum producers, as part of its campaign to break the Alcoa monopoly.[359] In a less spectacular way, it helped many companies to diversify their activities through the awards of contracts that were large enough to serve as a basis for excursions into new products and processes. In fact, this war development was one of the strategic factors leading to the remarkable diversification in the activities of many companies in the past decade.

In contrast, there have been many criticisms of purchasing procedures that favor the large companies.[360] During World War II, the large proportions of war contracts going to the largest corporations were a source of public concern.[361] The balance between the need for quick development of products and production and the encouragement of small companies was a bothersome, unsolved problem.[362]

Many of these problems have remained, though they have taken other forms. The same issue seems to be shaping up in the research and development programs,[363] in atomic energy,[364] and in the exploration of space, with their far-flung technological by-products. Some argue that, in the absence of war pressures, the military purchasing departments[365] could step up their purchases from smaller companies. It has been suggested that large companies are favored on open bid procedures for two reasons: representatives of large companies help procurement agencies to formulate specifications that make it difficult, if not impossible, for smaller manufacturers to bid; and some of the invitations to bid call for such large quantities that only larger manufacturers can fill the order.[366]

Some efforts have been made to alleviate this situation through the activity of the Small Business Administration, which certifies companies as "small business." The armed services then attempt to award specified amounts of work to such "small companies."[367] A similar program calls for organizing a pool of small companies to cooperate in taking on a large order.

However, these programs have not been outstandingly successful.[368] Procurement officers have not been eager to cooperate because they feel that prices paid to "small business" are too high, and they find it easier to let substantial contracts to individual large companies. Some efforts have given smaller companies direct contracts in place of subcontracts—for the same work that they would have obtained from prime contractors.[369]

Some procedural aspects of government procurement for research and development favor large companies. During World War II a company with large, profitable, production orders could afford to take substantial risks on research and development contracts because of the procedures for the renegotiation of profits on war contracts. If a large company suffered a loss on any contract because of errors in cost estimates, the loss merely reduced the substantial profits earned on its production orders. Since its profits were renegotiated on its total military sales, the losses on research and development contracts merely reduced the renegotiation refunds to the government. In fact, since such contracts increased its total military sales, a contractor might be permitted to retain higher dollar profits because allowable profits were measured as a percentage of total sales to the government. In contrast, a small company which had no production orders would have no way of recovering any losses on such a research and development contract. Hence, renegotiation permitted the large contractor to outbid smaller companies for such work.[370]

The advantages of such development orders are substantial. Improvements in civilian items, from accounting machines to shoes, from hearing aids to insecticides, have been developed through military research and development contracts.[371] Many such improvements benefit the commercial operations of the contractor. A company that completes development work has a first chance at future production orders. Its development work gives it production skills as well as the know-how to estimate costs more accurately and to start production more quickly. Additionally, it has been claimed that some government agencies have given contractors who develop new items an unfair patent advantage.[372] Instead of dedicating patented improvements that were researched with government funds to public use, it has permitted contractors to obtain valuable patent rights.[373] The requirements that a royalty-free license be given to the government has not interfered with patentees use of the franchise in private commerce.[374]

The use of government purchases to influence competition has not been fully appreciated.[375] Because of their importance in many industries, such purchases may be used to raise the plane of competition; low wages paid by some producers may be forced upward; humane methods of production may be instituted; minimum standards of health and safety for consumer goods may be effectuated. The Walsh-Healy[376] and Davis-Bacon[377] Acts require that "prevailing wages" be paid in the production of goods or in construction for the federal government.[378] These provisions have raised wage rates in many areas. In some industries, such as coal-mining, they have confined government purchases to large, unionized producers.[379]

Federal purchases are being used to implement the Humane Animal Slaughter Act[380] of 1958. The only sanction under that act is the requirement that all meat sold to the government should be produced in accordance with its provisions.[381]

Government specifications can have a profound influence on health and safety. For example, when automotive equipment was developed to eliminate noxious gas fumes, federal purchase specifications for automobiles were changed to require such equipment. Some state and local governments used the same specification. This development has simplified the problem of getting a voluntary agreement from the industry that all new cars will carry such equipment.[382] There are signs that such a program had an influence on the industry policy of installing equipment for safety belts on all cars.

Government sales of plants, inventions, and goods can have a profound influence on competition. These disposals were quite large at the end of World War II. The Federal Property and Administrative Services Act[383] was passed in 1949. It provides that when the federal government plans to sell plants that cost over $1,000,000, personal property costing over $3,000,000, or any patents or inventions, the Attorney General is to advise the Administrator of General Services if the disposition would be inconsistent with the antitrust laws. A similar provision was enacted with specific reference to rubber producing plants.[384]

*Aid to Small Business*

On the positive side, there remain questions regarding the function of the government in promoting research and in furnishing advisory aids to small business.[385] What should be the government's task in developing research work for the benefit of all business, including small? Should such research cover new technological improvements in products and processes? Should statistical work in analyzing markets, marketing methods, and management problems be increased? Should the government attempt to supply small business with free research to improve their operations?[386] Should the government affirmatively aid the formation of small research firms, in order to make such services generally available to other small companies? Would such encouragement enable more smaller companies to enter into new industries?

Some have urged that the government give small business the same type of advisory service it provides farmers through the county-agency system and related research activities.[387] The Small Business Administration has undertaken a series of programs. It publishes educational material advising small businessmen on the problems of starting and running their firms, makes arrangements for classes and discussions for small businessmen at local educational institutions, and offers advice to small businesses.[388]

The Automobile Dealer Franchise Act of 1956[389] is an unusual statute passed in order to aid small business. It permits an automobile dealer to sue a manufacturer who has terminated or not renewed his franchise if the manufacturer did not "act in good faith." While the act is intended to offset the power of the manufacturers, it is not at all clear that it is directed toward strong competition.

On various occasions the federal government has undertaken financial aid programs for small business.[390] It has made direct loans[391] and given commercial banks loan guarantees. Special programs have been instituted for small business in devastated areas. Inducements have been developed to encourage the formation of private organizations to help small business in its financial arrangements. While there have been signs of substantial activity, it is difficult to evaluate the effectiveness of these programs.

## *The Problem*

Government activities, federal, state, and local, which influence competition are in a serious snarl.[392] It is clear that some inconsistency must be tolerated in policies regarding competition because of the diverse public goals which bear on the subject. However, the diversity of public goals cannot explain many elements in the current confusion.

The existing hodge-podge pattern of uncoordinated regulations and activities lacks an organized body of principles because there has never been a general review of the statutory framework. This body of law has developed through haphazard accretion over the past seventy years. Some legislative enactments were responsive to the problems of their day, considering then current economic conditions and political beliefs about the role of government. Some acts were depression-born. Some reflected strong public feelings about the powerful robber barons of the day. Some were responsive to the needs of an economy domiated by agricultural activity. But these differ from the requirements of 1962, and these will not endure indefinitely.

The diverse state and local activities have contributed to the tangle. In the environment of local interests, pressure groups have found less resistance to their desires for self-protection than exist on the national level. Therefore, a substantial number of state and local regulations tends to counteract federal efforts to maintain a free national market.

Little attention has been paid to the difficult problems of reconciling policies favoring competition and those which are founded on other important objectives. For example, direct regulation was undertaken to provide positive promotion of the services of transportation and communication as well as supervision of operations that could not be left entirely to a free market.[393] In this process, few efforts were made to secure the advantages of those forms of market rivalry which could be permitted within the scope of regulation,[394] for example, competition between trucks and railroads and between established and new air carriers. Similar problems of reconciliation affect procurement and tax policies.

The confused pattern of administration parallels the uncoordinated structure of policy. Overlapping functions, as well as unexplained differences in methods of operation and in available remedies, characterize the administration of the antitrust laws. This situation is made more serious by conflicts in the administrative policies of the many agencies charged with this administration.[395]

The overlap of the two principal agencies has escaped the scrutiny of both the executive and legislative branches. It is mainly by chance that an alleged violation is treated by one or the other of these agencies. On several occasions, the Antitrust Division has instituted antitrust suits taking little or no account of previous action by the Federal Trade Commission for the same practices. Lawyers for potential defendants try to have their problems handled by one agency or the other, depending on their feelings about which will give their clients easier treatment. In the same way, lawyers who seek informal clearance of prospective mergers or other business ventures select the agency that pleases them most.

There are strategic differences in the remedies available to the two agencies. A defendant in a Department of Justice action may be faced with a broad, sweeping equity decree. If he is prosecuted by the F.T.C., the most he will have to face is a limited cease and desist order, unless the proceeding falls under the Celler-Kefauver antimerger statute. Because of these differences, the Antitrust Division can negotiate consent orders which are much broader than those of the F.T.C. The F.T.C. may consider economic defenses under such statutes as the Clayton Act, Section 3, while most courts do not allow such defenses when the Antitrust Division prosecutes.

There are marked differences in the policies of the two agencies regarding the same statute. The F.T.C. assiduously enforces the Robinson-Patman amendment of the Clayton Act. The Department of Justice has successfully ignored the statute.

Similar divergences exist between the Department of Justice and some of the regulatory agencies. The department has supported antitrust policy in regulatory matters while the agencies hold that the "public interest" is broader than competition.[396] Hence, they believe that their charters require them to consider competition as only one of the factors to weigh in their decisions. Meanwhile, no effective mechanism exists for coordinating their policies and for settling their differences.

It is possible that our belief in competition is so broad that it extends to the activities of government agencies. It might be argued that overlapping jurisdictions will keep the agencies on their toes. However, no one has seriously advanced lack of coordination as a technique for improving the regulatory process. Nor has anyone shown that these conflicts have served to implement public objectives.

These are pressing problems of public policy. They require substantial review of the present structure of laws and agencies. They call for a definition of the general direction of the roads we want to follow, in the light of the various public goals which relate to competition.

We must recognize that government cannot play a completely neutral role in a highly industrialized society. Its diverse activities inevitably exert substantial influences on competition. It is unrealistic to picture government as a hovering policeman, settling disputes and ensuring fair play, without affecting the competitive struggle. It is doubtful that such an idealized theory of government ever fitted the factual situation. Nor does it serve today as a realistic frame of reference for formulating public policy.

An understanding of these policy problems and of methods for treating them calls for an appreciation of the nature of the process of policy formulation. How are the policy issues expressed? What are the major types of issues? How is policy formulated through our legal-administrative institutions? With this background, we can turn to the problem of effectively employing economic analysis in the solution of these problems.

# 4 / *Policy Formulation**

THE FORMULATION of public policies bearing on competition is strongly influenced by public goals and current government activities. Therefore, the use of economic analysis in the consideration of these policy problems is influenced by this setting. At the same time, the opportunities for applying economic inquiry are guided by the general process of formulating government regulatory policy.

As Chapter 2 indicates, there is such a diversity of public aims regarding competition that economic analysis alone cannot resolve these policy issues. As that discussion showed, our attitudes toward competition are tinged with ambivalence.[1] We want competition, but we also want to protect certain industries and their employees from foreign rivalry. We want the impersonal market place to determine success and failure, but we want to protect small business. We look to government for the solution of many economic problems, but we nurture an antipathy toward the regulatory agencies. We desire the highest standards of living, but we also choose to avoid concentration of economic power in the hands of the few even if such concentration were to improve industrial efficiency.[2]

This mixture of attitudes is reflected in current activities of government. As noted in Chapter 3, many regulations are dedicated to maintaining competition, some are intended to raise the level of market rivalry, and others are constructed to take the sting out of competition. Inconsistencies have developed because of the gradual accretion of policies that were adopted at various times under differing conditions and public attitudes.[3]

In these circumstances, there is a pressing need for a continuing review of policies, a review that would engender greater consistency.[4]

* Footnotes for Chapter 4 begin on page 384.

Such inquiry would call for a substantial contribution from economic analysis. While our policies must reflect the variety of public goals, economic analysis can help to set a perspective for the reconciliation of these aims. Such analysis can suggest alternative ways to satisfy some aims and indicate their economic consequences.[5] It can assist the policy makers in reviewing the current state of affairs, in defining the issues which must be resolved, and in understanding the relationships between contemplated changes and the remaining policies.

There are four fairly distinct phases of policy formulation which present opportunities for useful economic inquiry: evaluating competitive conditions, establishing the nature and extent of the economic analysis that is required in applying the rules, determining the nature of the remedies for noncompetitive situations, and setting up effective administrative operations to carry out the rules. The evaluation of current conditions calls for a review of the present state of competition and the factors that influence it.[6] The formulation of the competitive rules requires analysis of how flexible and how specific they should be. The development of effective remedies for noncompetitive markets requires organized study to set up guides for the development of antitrust decrees and other steps which would help to improve conditions in specific markets. The analysis of the agencies that administer the programs calls for a combination of economics, political science, and organization theory.

The specific application of economic analysis in working out the solutions of these policy issues is influenced by the mechanisms of policy-making. The process of formulating regulatory policies—through legislation, litigation, and administration—provides the setting for injecting economic analysis. The procedures for enunciating rules and for reviewing current policies are important elements in the total policy process.

It is only against this background that the role of the economist, as a technician, can be appreciated. The policy-making process sets strategic boundaries for the role of the technical expert and the opportunities to apply his discipline. Public policy must accommodate a variety of goals, along with an ever-changing pattern of political pressures and administrative requirements. These influences profoundly affect the methods for applying the contributions of economics and related disciplines in the process of policy formulation.

This chapter, therefore, has two phases. First, is an outline of the nature of the policy problems—evaluation, nature of rules, remedies, and administration. Second, is a discussion of the policy-making process as the setting for economic analysis.

## *Evaluation of Competitive Conditions*

The obvious first step in formulating policies is to evaluate current conditions to see what may be the needs for change. Such evaluation involves several bench marks. What is tolerably satisfactory competitive performance in a market? How much reliance do we want to place on competition as an industrial regulator? In what areas do we want direct control? What signposts can be developed to indicate whether the economy is getting more competitive or less?

Setting standards for satisfactory competitive performance requires adaptation to current conditions. An extreme example of such a need is the onset of a war. Concern about competitive influences may be submerged under the press of war production. In order to increase some productive efficiencies, competitors may be encouraged to cooperate by concentrating the production of specific items in individual plants and by assisting the government in parceling out limited supplies of material. A lesser illustration would be the tendency to limit competition during severe depressions in order to protect small business.

Evaluation of competitive conditions includes inquiry into those government activities that bear on market rivalry.[7] Barriers to international trade, public procurement methods, federal research and development programs, direct industry regulation, and tax rules can have strategic influences on the state of competition. State-administered limitations of price, distribution, and production can exert market influences which may be even more effective than private agreements in restricting competition. Government development programs can serve to mold the structure of an industry in a monopolistic shape.

The direct controls of industry raise a number of specific questions regarding the extent to which we want to rely on competition. Should we attempt to promote competition among the members of a regulated industry or to limit it?[8] Should parallel railroad lines be combined?[9] When competing forms of transportation developed, such as trucks, should railroads have been given freer rein to change their rate structure instead of instituting truck regulation to support the established freight rates? Would our transportation system have been more efficient if we had depended more on methods of stimulating competition, improving waterways, building roads, and affirmatively encouraging the development of buses and trucks? Are we injuring the railroad system by giving preferential benefits to other forms of transportation?

Such evaluations must include analyses of alternatives. What is the present state of competition? How much competition can be injected? What would be accomplished by more competition? Or, by less?

An example is the Federal Communications Act, which is intended to improve the programs of television stations. Given the technological limitations on the number of stations that can operate within a locality, could the cultural and educational levels of programs be raised by discouraging competition? Suppose that three independent stations believe that 75 per cent of the viewers at a given hour want to see "Westerns" and that the next largest group, say 10 per cent, want to hear a symphony. Is it reasonable to expect any of these stations to satisfy the 10 per cent symphony audience instead of trying to attract one third of the much larger "Western" audience, with the chance of capturing 25 per cent? Would one station program a symphony if all three were owned by one company? Conversely, should we attempt to break through the technological limitation and increase the number of stations in order to cater to minority tastes, following the lead of radio with its "good music" stations?[10] For if seven stations were in "viewing distance," one of them might find its largest viewing audience by broadcasting a symphony.

A basic feature of any broad evaluation of general policies is the analysis of the state of competition within the economy. Any judgment about the over-all effect of government activity—about what we want from competition and about whether we want to adopt new policies to stimulate competition—will depend on how the present competitive conditions are evaluated.

We need to develop satisfactory analyses of the general state of competition.[11] For the most part, competition has been treated as an issue of microeconomics, dealing with the problems of the individual firm or market. Scant attention has been given to objective methods of evaluating the degree of competition in the economy, a problem in macroeconomics.[12]

There have been a number of conflicting evaluations.[13] Some have said that there is more market rivalry today than there has been for a long time.[14] Others feel that competition has been lessening steadily.[15] Some argue that, as a practical matter, there is not enough competition to be a substantial economic force; others contend that there is adequate competition in the economy.[16]

None of these conflicting evaluations rest on substantial empirical foundations. We have few field studies which deal with the state of competition either today or in the past.[17] We have yet to develop a theory or a body of data that can supply a firm conceptual and analytical base for examining such trends.

There are no data covering the state of competition in bygone days to support any evaluation of trends.[18] The economic literature of the times can be misleading. Economic theorists of the neoclassical school developed a conceptual description of pure competition. In a spirited opposition to the governmental interferences of his day, Adam Smith contended that competition *would* provide the most efficient allocation of resources.[19] However, he made no pretense of portraying the existing state of affairs in his theoretical treatment.

In mid-nineteenth century, John Stuart Mill, a leader of the neoclassical school, was concerned about the positions taken by some of his contemporaries. Of them he said, "They are apt to express themselves as if they thought that competition actually does, in all cases, whatever it can be shown to be the tendency of competition to do. . . . But it would be a great misconception of the actual course of human affairs to suppose that competition exercises in fact this unlimited sway."[20]

General evaluations of the competitive state of affairs require an organization of the types of economic analyses that are germane to the problem. To begin with, broader concepts than price competition are needed. Competition takes many forms.[21] Some drive toward lower costs and prices; others may engender higher costs and prices. For example, it has been suggested that market rivalry in the automotive industry concentrates on design and model changes, rather than prices.[22] Such changes have required heavy investments and substantial increases in unit costs. As a result, prices may be appreciably higher than those that would have obtained had there been relatively few model changes. However, this pattern does not indicate the absence of competition. Rather, it calls for more precise analysis of types of competition and their relation to national objectives.

The analysis of competitive trends calls for inquiry into the effects of the various forms of competition on prices, production, and quality. Such analysis requires long-range studies. Industry studies provide interesting clues and analytical methods, but they are not enough. The analysis must comprehend general price trends and related changes in cost factors. Measurements of industrial concentration may show up important trends, though meaningful data is not available at the moment.

Another analytical area that might be considered would be an organized review of changes in market forces—due to technological developments, to innovations in distribution, and to governmental operations. New competitive forces have supplanted former factors in many industries due to several dynamic influences:[23] technological innovation has produced new competition in materials, products, and manufacturing methods; the drive to diversify has brought established companies into new markets;[24] new methods of distribution have cut across old channels; and changes in economic conditions have introduced new competitive factors affecting both imported and exported goods.

Such an examination should encompass the influences of the fear of unknown competition around the corner.[25] If a manufacturer develops the impression that new entrants may be attracted into his market,[26] employing either the same materials and processes or new ones, his attitudes may change substantially. Recent technological development has been so pervasive and so rapid that the conventional definitions of industries and markets tend to become out-of-date.[27] Hence, the industry study is hard to fit into long-run trend analysis. Even the use of such a stable industry category as "steel" may become obsolete as a market classification in the foreseeable future.

## *Nature of the Rules*

The nature of the statutes and other rules governing competition and monopoly constitutes an important policy issue. A mechanical rule[28] may be easy to administer but have undesirable economic consequences. A rule that calls for involved economic analysis may prove to be impractical for current methods of administration.[29] Hence, there is a need for an appropriate balance between the desire for certainty and the requirements of economic inquiry.[30]

The problem can be illustrated by a rule regarding contracts which require the buyer to purchase exclusively from the seller. Certainty can be achieved by a fiat against all such contracts. Or the rule might outlaw only those exclusive arrangements which lessen competition substantially.[31] It might be modified by permitting small manufacturers to use such contracts or by allowing these agreements for limited periods when the buyer is a large company that purchases the commodity for its own use in a market where it needs assurance of supply.

The quest for certainty[32] affects antitrust along with other types of government regulation. Since most of the antitrust statutes turn on the effects of given practices on competition, however, the area for simple legal rules must be limited.[33] If we are willing to forego consideration of the economic effects of the practices, we can establish clear, rigid rules for all. If we maintain that only those practices which restrain competition shall be prevented, we cannot provide complete certainty because of the need to consider market effects.

There remain, however, issues of degree. Can *more* definiteness be provided?[34] Is it true that confusion permeates antitrust?[35] Can the businessman get competent legal advice which will, in the great bulk of cases, serve as reasonable predictions? Is this "confusion" a manifestation of dissatisfaction with laws which compel people to forego profitable industrial practices? How much of the uncertainty can be cured by improving the applications of economic analysis in administration and litigation?

The issue of certainty in antitrust law has found expression in an interesting dichotomy between "per se" and "rule of reason" violations. Briefly, per se rules[36] cover certain practices which are held to be illegal in and of themselves; while a rule of reason[37] violation requires a showing of probable competitive effects.[38] To prove a per se violation, the prosecution need show only that certain practices exist without any evidence regarding their competitive effect. The prominent per se rules concern price-fixing arrangements, boycotts, and agreements among competitors to divide markets.[39] The rules are founded on the judgment that these practices are inherently anticompetitive.

Evidence concerning the economic effects of a per se violation is not considered by the courts.[40] In a price-fixing case there is no consideration of the reasonableness of the prices which were fixed.[41] If two competitors agreed on prices, they would violate the antitrust laws even if the agreement were ineffective. Even if they accounted for only 5 per cent of the market and competed with one hundred other manfacturers, no defense would prevail.[42]

At the other extreme, under the rule of reason principles, the prosecution must show that the pertinent practice will probably lessen competition substantially or tend to create a monopoly. For example, to attack a merger successfully, the prosecutor must establish a likelihood that the combination will lessen market competition substantially.

In the pure forms of the two types, economic consequences are all important in a rule of reason case and are ignored in a per se case. When the rule of reason applies, the prosecution must prove harm to competition, and the defense can use economic evidence to prove that competition is not affected substantially. In theory, the prosecution need not introduce economic evidence in a per se proceeding, and the defense cannot.

The usefulness of this black-and-white distinction is limited.[43] Conceptually, it describes the extremes. However, most procedures fall between the two. Many rules are more flexible than one extreme or less rigid than the other. Many per se violations must be proved by circumstantial evidence which includes economic analysis of the market. Many violations that bear a rule of reason tag can be established by simple evidence that the business of the defendant is "substantial."

Consider, for example, the application of Section 3 of the Clayton Act, a provision that outlaws exclusive selling agreements which may "substantially lessen competition or tend to create a monopoly in any line of commerce." This section has not been regarded as providing a per se rule. Yet, in the *Standard Stations*[44] and the *International Salt*[45] cases, the courts held that such exclusive agreements were outlawed because a "substantial" amount of business was involved.[46] No further economic evidence was considered.[47]

Another illustration of the limitation of these categories is provided by Section 2 (a) of the Robinson-Patman Act. This section forbids a price discrimination which may substantially lessen competition. The F.T.C. and the courts have presumed rather consistently that any price discrimination has the required effects without inquiring into market consequences.[48] However, this presumption has not placed the section into a clear per se category[49] because there have been some successful defences based on an affirmative showing that the price discrimination would not have the required effect, or that competition was actually flourishing.[50]

The value of the simple dichotomy is further reduced by practical evidentiary problems. Substantial economic evidence must be introduced in many cases that involve per se rules.[51] Consider a common garden variety price-fixing complaint—a classic illustration of a per se violation. While the government can prove a violation without proving market consequences, "conspiracies are seldom capable of proof by direct testimony and may be inferred from the things actually done."[52] A prosecutor rarely has the good fortune to uncover an express price agreement, either written or oral. Therefore, he tries to establish the existence of price-fixing by circumstantial evidence or inference. His evidence is calculated to prove that market prices did not behave as they presumably would in the absence of collusion.[53] Hence, instead of proving that the agreement lessened competition, the government "proves" first that prices in the market are not competitive and then argues that this condition would not have obtained in the absence of an agreement.

The essential policy problems seem to be obfuscated when they are stated in terms of the dichotomy. The issues are further confused by other positions which are taken by some critics of the per se rules. While they argue that evidence of economic effect should be considered in antitrust proceedings, they also contend that there are too many uncertainties in the antitrust laws. Yet, a persuasive support for the per se form is found in its quality of certainty.

It seems fair to say that the policy issues will not be furthered by this war of words. The classification is useful to indicate the two extremes for purposes of exposition. However, the basic problems revolve about the degree of flexibility that should be applied under the various rules and the respective evidentiary burdens that should be borne by the prosecution and the defense. The technicalities of the dichotomy would have been avoided if Congress had considered a statute declaring that price-fixing, market-division, and exclusive sales agreements are illegal without any reference to competitive effect. In that event, the issues would have been faced squarely. Consideration would be given to a contention that such arrangements always hinder competition and to the argument that it would be impractical and unnecessary to require the courts to consider substantial economic evidence in such cases.

The basic issues are broader and deeper than the choices offered by this dichotomy. They bear on fundamental problems regarding substantive law and procedure. To illustrate some of these issues, consider the following problems:

Should certain practices be forbidden without regard for economic effect? Example: Should all price discrimination be proscribed or should the prosecution have to offer affirmative proof that a reasonable probability exists that a price discrimination will injure market competition, or that it will harm certain types of competitors?

Are there types of practices whose monopolistic market consequences should be presumed[54] unless the defendant proves affirmatively that competition will not be affected?[55] Example: Should the government be required to prove that each merger it attacks will tend to lessen competition substantially, or should the defendants have to carry the burden of proving that mergers of specified types will strengthen competition?[56]

Should every law be applied equally to all businesses or should stricter rules apply to companies which enjoy substantial market power?[57] Example: Should minor suppliers in a market be exempt from the Clayton Act provisions against exclusive arrangements?[58] Should the prosecution have to prove effects on competition when it attacks a relatively small company for such a violation and rest on a presumption of such consequences when it prosecutes a large company?

Such issues relate to how strong a case will be required for a successful prosecution, who will bear the affirmative burden of proving economic consequences, and what limits will be placed on such proof. Conceivably, a thorough study would indicate: (a) that certain practices almost always tend to lessen competition;[59] (b) that certain others usually do so; and (c) that there are some that will in particular circumstances. If such categories were developed, clearer rules could be established. For example, such rules might provide that: no economic proof would be required to establish a violation in the group (a) cases; the burden of justifying its actions would rest primarily on the defendant in group (b); the burden of proving economic effect would have to be carried by the government in class (c); while the government would have the burden of proof in any proceeding which involves a novel point.

In such analysis, consideration must also be given to the costs of these cases, in administrative time, in dollar expenditures, in court time, and in business uncertainty. What would be the budgetary costs of full economic considerations in more cases? How would they affect the cost of litigation? What is the economic effect of business uncertainty about the status of changes in market practices or investments? In brief, such analysis would balance the costs against the advantages.[60]

At the same time, analysis and experimentation is needed to develop improvements in our system of adjudication. How can the economic issues be tried more clearly and efficiently? What help can be given to judges? How can the agencies' procedures be improved for more effective consideration of economic factors? What would be the effect of the clearer rules on the practice of negotiating decrees and orders? Should these consent procedures be improved and encouraged?

## *Remedial Policies*

Prognosis is a major gap in the enforcement of policies regarding competition. Substantial consideration has been accorded to the definitions of violations under the antitrust laws. However, scant attention has been given to how to cure a violation: What decree or order shall be issued and what affirmative steps can be taken to stimulate competition in the market involved? As Justice Brennan has said, an antitrust "suit has been a futile exercise if the Government proves a violation but fails to secure a remedy adequate to redress it."[61] This deficiency is traditional in antitrust legislation. Thorelli points out that in 1890 "Congress placed considerable faith in the capacity for self-enforcement of the Sherman Act."[62]

The main thrust of antitrust policy has been to inject competitive forces into markets which need them.[63] This objective cannot be advanced in most markets by penalties, criminal or civil.[64] Nor is it affirmatively promoted by broad orders to discontinue a violation. It requires decrees that provide positive guides for future operations.[65] In some instances it requires other forms of government action.

The arsenal of available remedies requires major policy consideration.[66] Current remedies are confined to several forms: the cease and desist order of a commission and the injunction of a court to discontinue a practice; the compulsory patent license; the break-up of a company; the compulsory sale of specified assets; compulsory trusteeship over certain assets; and the order to follow specific business practices. They are accompanied by several penalty provisions: fines, imprisonment, and treble-damage actions. Meanwhile, practically no attention is paid to several other means for stimulating competition: the elimination[67] of a protective barrier against foreign competition;[68] the withdrawal of anticompetitive devices maintained by federal, state, and local government regulation; the affirmative use of government purchases and research programs to induce new competition; and the enactment of tailored legislative programs to change the structure of the market.

There is a striking lack of policy guides for the current judicial remedies. Neither the courts nor the administrative agencies have satisfactory bench marks for the formulation of the decrees and orders they are empowered to issue or negotiate. As a result, many decrees deal with the symptoms of monopoly without considering the underlying factors that create the condition.[69] The courts have no practical guide lines for the supervision they must exercise over some decrees. There is a striking absence of consideration of the use of governmental powers other than those that fit the judicial mold.

These policy issues are found on several levels: the lack of legislative directions for the courts and agencies; the lack of operating guides for judges and administrative bodies; and the need for the development of nonjudicial programs to reduce monopolistic forces.

*Legislative Guides for Remedies*

Legislation covering antitrust remedies is confined to rough procedural rules. There is little consistency between the remedies that are available to the courts and those that lie within the powers of the Federal Trade Commission. Further, while the various acts contemplate substantial differences in the gravity of their violations, there are no parallel directions concerning the appropriate remedies.

As Chapter 3 indicates, the legislation covering antitrust remedies is surprisingly sparse. The general language offers little indication of the nature of the decrees which may be written, whether formulated by judges or negotiated by the Department of Justice.[70] In contrast, the Federal Trade Commission's authority is sharply limited.

The Sherman, Federal Trade Commission, and Clayton Acts provide vague legislative guides. Section 4 of the Sherman Act and the Clayton Act authorize the Attorney General "to institute proceedings in equity to prevent and restrain such violations" and gives the federal courts appropriate jurisdiction. Section 5 of the Federal Trade Commission Act and Section 11 of the Clayton Act authorize the F.T.C. to order a violator "to cease and desist from using such (unfair) method of competition." Similar authority is given to the other regulatory agencies under the Clayton Act.

There is an interesting paradox in the powers wielded by the F.T.C. and the courts. The Commission was set up because the courts did not possess the expert knowledge and investigative ability which was needed to maintain competition.[71] Nevertheless, the Commission's authority was confined to issuing orders instructing respondents to discontinue a practice,[72] with one exception: under the Celler-Kefauver Act it can order a company to divest itself of assets obtained through an illegal merger. Meanwhile, the courts have been permitted wide latitudes for constructing remedies.

Having visualized a commission endowed with the *expertise* to tailor mandates which would meet the requirements of specific markets, Congress confined its remedies to simple "stop" orders, while it expected the courts to produce equity decrees which are tailored to the needs of individual markets. Its powers of investigation, its staff of economists and accountants, and its specialized experience should, in theory, equip the F.T.C. to construct affirmative plans to stimulate competition. Congress relied on this ability when it passed Section 7 of the Federal Trade Commission Act. That provision enables a judge to call on the Commission to advise him about an "appropriate form of decree." Yet, the broad powers were given to the judges who, incidentally, have not taken advantage of Section 7. The same wide latitude is given to the Department of Justice in its negotiations of consent decrees.

Another policy problem, long neglected in legislation and administration, is what should be the relationship between the statute which is violated and the choice of remedies. While a violation under the Sherman Act is considered more serious than one under the Clayton Act,[73] there appears to be no difference in the available equity remedies.[74] As Chapter 3 indicates, the Sherman Act applies to accomplished restraints and monopolization, while the Clayton Act is dedicated to the prevention of such restraints.[75] Because of this difference, the prosecution bears a heavier burden in proving a violation in a Sherman Act case than in a Clayton Act proceeding[76] except for such a clear per se violation as a written price-fixing agreement. Yet, there are no differences in the legislative guides for the judicial remedies. Both acts provide the Attorney General with the same authority and establish the same general jurisdiction in equity for the federal courts.

Nor have the courts spelled out any fundamental distinctions between Sherman and Clayton remedies. This lack was clearly indicated in the recent *du Pont-General Motors* case.[77] The Sherman Act charge in the Attorney General's complaint was disregarded by the Supreme Court. Instead, it found that the Clayton Act had been violated. Nevertheless, the remedies which are under consideration by the Supreme Court and the District Court are the same as would have been obtained had the Supreme Court found a Sherman Act violation.

The influence of this quirk raises questions about the logic of the structure of antitrust law. A practice which probably will restrict future competition may call for the same remedy as one which has restricted competition already. An Attorney General who has a choice of prosecution under either the Clayton Act or the Sherman Act can secure the same decree under either statute although he has a lighter burden of proof in a Clayton Act proceeding.

This factor does not mean that the nature of the defendant's practice has no effect on the decree. A more serious anticompetitive practice and a clearer intent to restrict competition will persuade a judge to issue a more drastic decree.[78] Therefore, a Sherman Act proof may provide firmer support for a far-reaching decree than evidence of a Clayton Act violation. The Antitrust Division could play it safe by bringing Clayton Act charges, when applicable, and providing as strong a proof as would be required by the Sherman Act.

However, given the judicial hesitation about radical antitrust orders, this distinction may be of limited importance. As Walton Hamilton said, "an attempt to amend or revise the structure and practices of an industry by resort to judicial process is a task fraught with uncertainty. The legal process . . . was never shaped for so stupendous and alien a task as causing the channels of commerce to run straight, or fitting an industry out with a new and different set of practices."[79]

The net result of these patterns is that the nature of the remedy for an antitrust violation may be strongly influenced by chance. If the Federal Trade Commission takes jurisdiction, the available remedies are limited, except under the Celler-Kefauver Act. If the Department of Justice institutes an action under one act, it may fail; under another act, it may succeed; under either act, it may obtain the same remedy. The decree can reach further than an order issued by the Federal Trade Commission. Similarly, the consent decree of the Department of Justice can have a more affirmative cast than the Commission's consent order.[80] Hence, the defendant faces greater risks when the department attacks him than when the F.T.C. starts proceedings.

## *Judicial and Administrative Guides*

Procedural problems aside, there is a dearth of principles of substance to guide judges and agencies in the formulation of antitrust decrees and orders. Little is known of the influences of previous decrees on market competition or industrial performance.[81] Therefore, those who write decrees have no basis in experience for predicting the effect of their orders. Indeed, the few bits of information[82] available concerning the effects of decrees and orders leave little basis for confidence that the "common sense" approach of judges and lawyers has injected competition into many markets which are dominated by monopolistic forces.[83]

The deficiency cannot be ascribed to the individual judges or lawyers. They must do with what they have. They cannot carry on research into the effects of past decrees in order to tell what type of order was successful, and what was unsuccessful, in market situations that were similar to the one under consideration. They have precedent and analogy in determining whether the antitrust laws were violated. However, they have no bench marks or criteria for determining what alternative prognosis will be most effective in encouraging new competitive drives, or in awakening old ones.

There are few guides for or limits on the shaping of equity decrees in antitrust. Only on rare occasions has the Supreme Court upset a decree formulated by a District Court after it has accepted a decision that a violation has occurred.[84] Judicial discretion has not been hemmed in by precedent. Indeed, the Supreme Court has held that antitrust decrees "will be upheld in the absence of a showing of abuse of discretion."[85] Nor has the Antitrust Division been restricted by precedent in negotiating consent decrees, though it tends to follow the general rules. Perhaps, the judicial decrees have been less drastic than they might have been with clearer guidance, especially since many of the prosecution's proposals for decrees are not supported by substantial evidence and analysis.[86] Perhaps, also, the deficiencies in such prosecution requests are due to the same lack of analytical bench marks.

In the main, there has been a tendency to narrow the purview of the decrees.[87] For the most part, the courts and the agencies have tied the order to the specific practices covered in the complaint. In the *National Lead* case the Supreme Court held that the authority of the Federal Trade Commission to fashion orders was limited by the test: "Does the remedy selected have a 'reasonable relation to the unlawful practice found to exist'?"[88] If unjustified price discrimination is found, a cease and desist order is issued. If a forbidden merger takes place, the marriage is annulled. Yet, the violation may be a manifestation of an underlying situation that calls for a more basic cure.[89] The price discrimination may be symptomatic of monopolistic forces in the industry structure; conversely, the discrimination may be a significant outlet for market rivalry. The merger may signify a reaction of weaker competitors against a dominant firm with monopoly power.

The strange fact is that no attempt has been made to analyze the substantial history of antitrust in order to establish guideposts for decrees and orders.[90] Since 1890 the Department of Justice has instituted more than 1,500 antitrust proceedings and approximately 600 decrees have been written.[91] In the first forty-five years of its existence the F.T.C. issued more than 5,600 orders,[92] including over 1,000 orders dealing with antimonopoly charges.[93] Yet, with all this experience, only a modicum of information is available concerning the economic effects of these decrees and orders on competition and industrial efficiency.

The cryptic generality of the laws has allowed wide judicial latitude for developing the law through experimentation case by case.[94] Such experimentation calls for a regular review of the effects of past experiments—a basic requirement of the trial-and-error method. However, the experiments are made without observation. Decrees are written following hunches, some of which are dressed in the intellectual cloth of theory. After a decree is written, some attention may be paid to its enforcement, but there is no mechanism for a systematic analysis of the effects of such decrees, either individually or collectively.[95]

Some analysis has been undertaken. A few congressional investigations and economic studies[96] on particular subjects or industries have shed some light on the subject.[97] They have not been broad enough, however, to relate the effects of various types of decrees to any classification of market conditions. Some industry studies have produced interesting insights,[98] but these have not compared the results of various types of decrees. There exists no body of knowledge that would provide clues regarding the potential effects of alternative remedies. No field analysis has been made of experience with the type of order which may be proposed in a proceeding: whether the decree will effectively stimulate competition; whether it will merely change the forms of business transactions without influencing competition; or whether it may entail side effects that will actually lessen competitive forces.

To illustrate the need for such empirical inquiry, consider what order should be issued after a finding of a price conspiracy. The usual decree merely instructs the defendants to stop conspiring. Yet, there has been no study of the effects of such orders. Active enforcement of the order might force a discontinuance of the overt agreement, yet each company may maintain the agreed prices; market influences may create only minor or gradual price changes; and prices three or four years later may be quite close to those which would have obtained had the agreement continued in force.

Several recent decrees have proceeded beyond the maxim, "Do not conspire." These decrees require that companies establish new prices which are based on their costs, plus the profits they desire, and "other lawful business considerations."[99]

Economic theory tells us that such decrees reflect a lack of understanding of the competitive process. Setting a price by adding a desired profit to total unit costs has been associated, in some current economic teaching, with the behavior of a monopolist, who need have no concern about competitors. When he increases his price, unit sales volume may be reduced because some consumers stop buying. Yet, within limits his total dollar sales may increase while total costs decrease, providing a higher profit. In contrast, in a perfectly competitive market, when a seller increases his prices and his competitors do not follow, his sales will fall to a mere trickle or to zero. Hence, the cost-plus formula of the decree would appear incompatible with competition.

It is conceivable, however, that such an order, calling as it does for "monopolistic" pricing by each individual company, might be the most effective way to eliminate the influence of a price conspiracy. The order might compel each conspirator to wipe the slate clean and to price like a monopolist, unconcerned about competitive factors in the market. Each seller would offer his goods at prices that differed from his competitors' because of variations in costs and in profit goals. Head-on clashes among the competitors would ensue: one producer might find that he had priced one product out of the market; another might face this problem on another product; and so on. In self-defense each might have to cut some prices to meet competition. This is, in effect, the general pattern of price rivalry.

Accordingly, it is possible, under certain market conditions, a decree which appears to foster monopoly pricing might be the most effective way of establishing active and continuing price competition. But data and the mechanism for testing such a hypothesis are lacking.

Another illustration of the need for reviewing the effects of decrees may be found in Justice Douglas' dissent in the *Standard Stations* case.[100] Standard Oil of California had sold its products under agreements which provided that independent operators of gasoline stations would purchase all their supplies from Standard. The majority of the Supreme Court held that the agreements violated Section 3 of the Clayton Act because they foreclosed a substantial amount of trade from other refiners and wholesalers. Justice Douglas was concerned about the effect of such a holding. In dissenting, he argued that if such contracts are forbidden, Standard might be encouraged to sell at retail through its own stations instead of selling to independent retailers.[101] He believed that American social and political objectives would best be served by maintaining these independent operators, even if they were confined by exclusive supply contracts, instead of encouraging Standard and its competitors to substitute employees for the independents.[102]

Here, then, is a basic conflict regarding the effects of the decree. Did it increase competition? Did it eliminate independent station operators? Did Standard start to operate its own stations? When the contracts were canceled, did the retailers voluntarily buy from Standard exclusively because they felt that the practice was more profitable for them? There has been no effort to test any of these questions.

Recently the Senate Subcommittee on Patents, Trademarks, and Copyrights demonstrated the need to review the consequences of decrees. The findings of its staff report on *Compulsory Patent Licensing Under Antitrust Judgments*[103] cover a survey of the effects of 81 decrees requiring that licenses be granted for reasonable royalties. The report indicates that no licenses were issued under 31 decrees, almost 40 per cent of those studied.[104] Inquiries about acquiring licenses were received in only 7 out of the 31 cases; 4 companies reported receiving 1 inquiry each; 2 companies received 2 inquiries each; and 1 company received 7 inquiries.[105] Further, 69 of the 81 decrees were negotiated; licenses were issued under only 39 of these negotiated decrees or 55 per cent; no inquiries were received by companies subject to 23 of these consent decrees.[106] Based on this and other evidence, the report suggested that in a consent decree negotiation "a defendant may offer for compulsory licensing, a substantial group of patents with no competitive significance. . . ."[107] Further, the report visualized the possibility that, "if misapplied, compulsory licensing relief may harm rather than advance the objectives of both the patent laws and the antitrust laws."[108]

The report does not cover the differences in the aftermaths of decrees which require: patent licenses with reasonable royalties; royalty-free licenses; divestiture of patent rights; nonenforcement of patents; and programs to make know-how available. Further, the review did not go into the market significance of the patents in question to see what influence their importance had on licensing activity. However, it illustrates the basic needs for continuing review.

The Celler Antitrust Subcommittee made similar findings in its investigation of the A.T.&T. consent decree. It found that "the patent licensing and technical information provisions of the decree neither materially aid independent manufacturers of telephone equipment to compete with Western (the A.T.&T. manufacturing subsidiary) nor materially hamper Western in the enjoyment of its predecree patent monopoly."[109]

Robinson-Patman orders provide another example of the need for such continuing review. Stripped of their verbiage, many orders provide merely that the respondent should stop violating a specified section of the act.[110] Some orders relate to specific practices—for example, offering discriminatory prices to one purchaser or to a class of purchasers, such as chain stores.[111] It is difficult to determine what orders the Federal Trade Commission should use in given situations. A general order to comply with the Robinson-Patman Act may have little effect on another violation by the same respondent if it is unrelated to the first proceeding.[112] For example, the first proceeding might cover a price concession to one customer while the second violation concerns an advertising allowance. An order which is confined to a specific violation might be evaded by a simple subterfuge. Thus, if a manufacturer is compelled to discontinue advertising allowances to one class of customers, he might comply with the order but reduce his prices to the same buyers. A mere change in the form of the allowance—calling it a price discount rather than an advertising allowance—would constitute compliance with the order, but the change would have no significant effect on the market situation. Hence, careful analysis is required to devise orders that will ensure the desired market effects without, on the other hand, curtailing competitive forces. For, if an order forces the respondent to sell "at his peril" whenever he competes actively, the ultimate antitrust purpose is lost.

Inquiry into the effects of orders requires the investigative powers of a government agency which can institute the study soon after a decree is issued.[113] This need was highlighted by Corwin D. Edwards' excellent study for The Brookings Institution covering the economic effects of the Robinson-Patman Act.[114] During the investigation he found that it was impossible to secure reliable information on the market effects of most orders which had been issued years before. In many instances, company executives who were in office during the F.T.C. proceeding had retired or died. Further, it was too late for an outside study of market conditions before and after the orders were issued.

### *Continuing Judicial Supervision Over Decrees*

Another important study of decrees would cover continuing judicial supervision over the application of the orders.[115] The *Hartford-Empire* decree[116] provided for such supervision over the royalties paid and the terms of the contracts entered into by Hartford-Empire and its licensees.[117] The Antitrust Division had to participate extensively in the negotiations of these contracts. Because of the time and effort required of its personnel, the division has not proposed any other decree requiring such extensive judicial supervision, except in the proceeding against the American Society of Composers, Authors and Publishers (ASCAP).[118] The division has advocated decrees that require patent licenses at reasonable royalties and provide that potential licensees may petition the court to set such fees when they cannot be fixed through negotiations.[119] Up to 1960 there were only six occasions when a court was asked to set the royalty rate. The Justice Department participated in only three of these.[120]

It may well be that the policy for the division is desirable. Close judicial supervision may go so far down the road of direct regulation that the flavor of competition is lost.[121] Analysis might demonstrate that the task of gauging adequate rates requires too much economic analysis for practical application. Possibly, the additional effort required by such supervision would best be spent elsewhere. The fact remains, however, that there is no satisfactory basis for evaluating the division's policy.[122] It appears to have been dictated by administrative convenience and general antitrust philosophy rather than consideration of its competitive effect.

The basic question remains: How much judicial supervision over the application of decrees is desirable? On the one hand, there is the pitfall of edging into direct governmental regulation through close judicial and administrative supervision over market practices. On the other hand, the lack of continuing supervision may lead to stentorian decrees with little substance. Obviously, public policy requires some clues regarding the effectiveness of these procedures.

It should be noted that this discussion has not touched on the enforcement of decrees or on the problems of revising decrees after they are promulgated. These problems are considered in the chapter on litigation and negotiation.

*Nonjudicial Remedies*

Policy issues regarding the means for stimulating competition are broader than those which involve antitrust decrees. A strong procompetitive program would call for a reconsideration of the limited administrative basis for antitrust and would cover a wide range of other remedies. Currently, the channels for administering competitive policies lie mainly with the Federal Trade Commission, the Department of Justice, and the courts. They have no authority over anticompetitive factors in other functions of the government nor over its nonregulatory activities.

As suggested above, a market may be made more competitive by governmental action which lies outside of the antitrust field. The removal of a protective tariff or of another trade barrier may bring foreign competition into a market.[123] A defense contract for research or for supplies may induce a substantial company to enter a market or even aid in the development of a new competing firm. The modification of state and local restrictions, as in the case of milk-sheds, by providing federal inspection, may open up protected markets. A rigorous program of informative labeling may assist the consumer in placing less dependence on entrenched brands and stimulate price competition or strengthen smaller competitors.

The most effective remedies in some important markets might be developed through the legislative enactment of programs that are tailored to the requirements of specific industrial situations.[124] The Congress has passed such legislation, for example, the Public Utility Act of 1935,[125] the Copyright Act of 1909[126] (which provided for compulsory recording licenses of musical compositions), and the Automobile Dealer Franchise Act.[127] But it has not considered such action as an integral phase of antitrust policy. It is conceivable that a full-blown program would call for congressional action regarding international trade barriers, patents, government purchasing, and taxes confined to specific markets and industries in order to cure serious monopolistic conditions.[128] Such action might in extreme cases go as far as the Public Utility Act of 1935 in changing the structure of the market.

Such programs would, of course, call for affirmative recommendations to the Congress from the existing agencies or from a new agency charged with a continuing watch over competitive trends and the effects of current antitrust activity. The agencies have not been encouraged to make affirmative recommendations regarding measures for specific markets. The ones that are made fall within the purview of the conventional antitrust remedies.

While some public attention has been given to remedies in recent years, it has been confined to procedural issues.[129] Should fines be increased? Should F.T.C. orders be final or subject to judicial review? Should the Federal Trade Commission be authorized to issue temporary orders? Should consent decrees be published before they are entered in order to permit third parties to make suggestions? The basic problems of remedies have been overlooked.[130] Little progress has been made in tailoring orders to meet the needs of specific markets. There has been almost no use of government action outside of antitrust decrees and orders to stimulate competition. There has been practically no consideration of the possibilities of congressional action to take care of serious situations that require special treatment.

## *Policies Regarding Administration*

The administrative framework for effectuating these public policies presents a substantial policy problem, in itself. An excellent body of substantive law can help to set the tone for the economy. Furthermore, the law can be applied through private suits. In the final analysis, however, much if not most of its effect will depend on the work of government agencies.

The administrative structure is highly significant. The relationships among the functions of the many agencies can affect their accomplishments profoundly. The organization of the individual agency is important. Should it be an "independent" commission[131] or a single-headed executive department? Is an "administrative court" needed, or is the problem best handled by a regulatory agency with its *expertise?* Should a specialized court be instituted to try regulatory cases or antitrust proceedings? Should economists be appointed as members of the commissions or of a specialized court, as a matter of practice, or should the agencies depend on a staff of economic advisers?

The relationships among the twenty-odd agencies that participate in antitrust enforcement is confusing. Some are dedicated to competition. Others must take account of direct regulatory assignments, the use of public lands and other property, the promotion of specific economic activity, or tax-collection and related functions. Few guide lines are set for the relationships between their primary functions and their antitrust work. Hence, there is a great lack of coordination among the agencies. There are severe clashes between agencies. For example, the Interstate Commerce Commission approved a merger that had been successfully prosecuted, in another form, by the Department of Justice. Several bank mergers which had been approved by the Comptroller of the Currency and the Board of Governors of the Federal Reserve System were attacked by the Department of Justice.

Even the two principal antitrust agencies are not coordinated. As shown in Chapter 3, both the Federal Trade Commission and the Antitrust Division fail to take advantage of the cooperation which is permitted by statute. They have exhibited substantial policy differences in such areas as the enforcement of the Robinson-Patman Act. Their apparent agreement regarding specialization in certain industries seems to be based on squatters' rights rather than a well-organized plan.

No single agency carries basic responsibility for the development, review, or formulation of policy.[132] None bears over-all administrative responsibility. Even the President lacks general authority and responsibility over all such activities because of the "independence" of the regulatory commissions.[133]

Few efforts have been made to analyze the budgetary requirements of administration. The antitrust agencies do not have the advantage of a "constituency" to support them in the Congress. They have no strong political basis for demanding the funds or personnel they require.[134] Hence, it is especially important that objective inquiry be employed to analyze the size of their burdens and the related budget needs. Is a budget of around $8 million for the F.T.C. and $5 million for the Antitrust Division enough? Do they have sufficient staffs of competent economists? Are these positions likely to attract able economists or are salary changes required?

Such budget evaluations must, of course, be related to the nature of the substantive rules and the procedural burdens. A rule of law which requires the evaluation of the competitive effects of a practice is more costly in application than one which does not. An agency that participates in the development of policy, by trying test cases and making recommendations to Congress, needs a larger budget than one that merely administers well-established rules.

## *The Economist's Role in Policy-Making*

There appears to be universal acceptance of the need for economic analysis in the development of public policy regarding competition. Some believe that more economic analysis is needed, some think less;

a few feel that the current situation is tolerably good. But no one would deny the usefulness of economic inquiry in the formulation of policy.

Little consideration has been given to the methods of applying economic analysis in this policy development. Should economists confine their advice to the Congress? Should policy issues be settled by economic analysis? Where and when should economic inquiry fit into the policy-making process?

The confluence of several forces bears on the usefulness of economic analysis in policy formulation as it affects competition. Government enforcement of competition essentially is a regulatory process in the broad sense. It may reflect many differences in objectives and mechanics from such other activities as railroad and power regulation. Yet, like the others, it is a political process. Its problems cannot be solved within the four corners of an analytical exercise. Its programs cannot be written on a clean slate. It must accommodate a wide range of established objectives, customs, and legal structures, as well as the institutional patterns of regulation.

In the development of such regulatory policy, there are several factors that influence the role of economic analysis: the methods for developing policy—who makes policy and how the rules are developed; the process of policy review; and the role of the technician in policy formulation. It is only against this background that the opportunities for employing economic analysis, and its limitations, can be developed.

### *The Policy-Making Process*

The policy-making process has a direct bearing on the problems of using economic analysis in the formulation of competitive policies. The institutional mechanisms for developing policy can be classified on a number of levels. Broad policies are developed through legislation and treaties. In turn, some of these general charters are expanded through the rules and practices of the regulatory agencies.[135] Such rules may be formal or informal, publicly announced or privately developed. At the same time, significant policy developments are evolved through the decisions of the courts and the orders of administrative agencies.

Congress enacts broad policies. It is influenced by the President's legislative recommendations,[136] as well as by those of the regulatory agencies and by judicial decisions. Congressional investigations[137] and debates have substantial influences both on drafting legislation and on subsequent interpretations.[138] In these proceedings, Congress is a focal point in the political process, reflecting and articulating the pertinent political pressures.

Congressional discussions, debates, and committee reports have been particularly important in interpreting statutory meanings in antitrust because of the general "constitutional types"[139] of phraseology employed in the statutes. The statutes employ such vague phrases as "substantially to lessen competition," "unfair methods of competition," "tendency to create a monopoly," and "discrimination."[140] Issues debated in the Congress and reviewed in its committee investigations[141] necessarily have a profound bearing on the work of the administrative agencies. At the same time, congressional appropriations for the agencies influence antitrust enforcement and administrative policy by setting the size of staffs and by offering administrators budgetary rewards for favorable responses to congressional wishes.

The President's role in policy-making in this area is complex.[142] When he exercises his powers of political leadership, he can have a profound influence on congressional action. In his executive capacity he can, if he chooses, dictate the policies of those regulatory agencies that are located in the executive departments, such as the Antitrust Division of the Department of Justice. However, his position vis-a-vis the independent commissions, such as the F.T.C., is not clear.[143]

The independent commissions, clothed in the phrase "arms of the Congress," constitute a focal point in the rivalry between the legislative and the executive branches.[144] Congress set them up to be independent of the Executive.[145] Yet, the President appoints the members of each commission and the chairman, except the chairman of the Interstate Commerce Commission who is selected by the members on a rotating basis. Their budgets and legislative recommendations clear through the Bureau of the Budget, though they can appeal directly to the Congress.[146] The President has severely restricted powers to remove members of a commission. Hence, the ultimate controls over the commissions are in such a confused state that "independent" may mean neither free nor responsible to anyone.

The regulatory agencies—both executive departments and commissions[147]—play important roles in policy development.[148] A highly significant process—one which needs more attention—is the selection of cases to prosecute. In such selection the administrative agency makes basic determinations concerning the types of activity that pass muster and those that are considered violations of the antitrust laws. It must then decide which cases rate high priorities since it lacks the means to prosecute all. Neither courts nor private individuals can raise policy issues unless and until an agency decides to file a complaint, except for those rare private suits that raise novel points. A judge has little opportunity to make policy interpretations unless a government agency or a private party brings a case and argues a pertinent legal theory.

Policy is also made by the agencies through their own quasi-judicial decisions. Federal Trade Commission decisions regarding antitrust violations figure directly in policy development. The decisions constitute precedents for the agency and its staff. Some of these policies depend on judicial interpretations, but many do not. For example, the Supreme Court held, in the *Standard Stations* case,[149] that the courts do not have to consider the economic effects of exclusive purchase contracts which affect a "substantial" volume of commerce in order to find a Clayton Act violation. Nevertheless, the F.T.C. decided that it should consider such evidence in its *Maico*[150] decision. Its later decisions,[151] which did not follow *Maico,* were made on its own without any judicial influence.[152]

Related to the influence of formal agency decisions in the development of policy are their determinations regarding consent orders and decrees. The negotiation of such orders is an important element in such policy formulation. The use of certain provisions in consent decrees negotiated by the Antitrust Division will not necessarily persuade a judge to incorporate them in a decree of his own making. But such provisions do affect subsequent consent orders and probably have an indirect influence on congressional and judicial policy-thinking.[153]

Policy-making functions of regulatory agencies include the issuance of interpretations of the law. This method of developing policy has not been used under antitrust laws as widely as under other regulatory statutes which contain specific provisions for such interpretative rule-making.

The Federal Trade Commission has issued some rules. It has followed this practice in administering the various textile and fur labeling acts, which do provide for the promulgation of rules.[154] It has had some success with guides regarding advertising and the use of demonstrators for cosmetics.[155] It has not, however, always followed its own guides.[156] During a spirited public controversy regarding basing-points and delivered prices, it issued an important policy statement in the form of a staff memorandum.[157] It set up a Trade Practice Conference procedure to issue rules of fair practice for individual industries; This endeavor has not been an outstanding success; the rules are not binding on either industry or the F.T.C. None of the other agencies that administer the antitrust laws have promulgated any rules under those statutes.

The generality of the language employed in antitrust legislation has kept policy formulation dependent to a major extent on the determination of particular issues in litigation.[158] This process is influenced by the somewhat passive role of the judiciary. By and large, judges are not expected to strike out on their own and formulate legal theories which have not been advanced by one of the litigants.

The bar plays a strategic part in this process of policy evolution. Theories presented by counsel are vital elements in the judicial process. The plaintiff's selection of a case and the defendant's decision to fight present an occasion for judicial determination. Thereafter, the lawyers' development of issues and data, their formulation of legal theories, and their persuasiveness in presenting evidence and argument are key factors in the court's contribution to the development of the law.

Judicial precedent is as important in antitrust as in other fields of law, but there are unique difficulties in the application of legal precedent in the consideration of competitive problems. Because many decisions in this field depend on economic interpretation, the application of its rules of law differs from that followed in such areas as the laws of real estate, corporations, and commercial transactions.

The principle of precedent depends on analogy. Its application calls for finding a settled dispute that has decisive features which are like those affecting the case under consideration and reviewing the judicial determination laid down in that situation. When factual findings can be separated from legal rules, the use of precedent is not particularly complicated. Thus, the interpretation of the effect of a deed on an easement permits a clear separation between the facts that the deed was signed and contained the provision, and a problem of interpreting their legal effects. When the legal rule depends on economic interpretation, however, the application of precedent requires the determination of analogous market situations. This is primarily a task for economic, rather than technical legal analysis.

Consider, for example, the question of what is the pertinent market within which competition takes place, an issue which is discussed at length in Chapter 8. The strategic conclusion of the outstanding *Cellophane* case[159] was that the pertinent market included cellophane and a wide variety of other flexible wrapping materials. As a result, it was held that the defendant did not occupy a monopoly position, and it won the case. In the *du Pont-General Motors* decision,[160] the pertinent market was confined to paints which are used on automobiles, excluding paints and finishes applied on other products. Hence, the defendant lost the case because of its influence in the small market. In *Alcoa*[161] the market was interpreted to cover virgin aluminum ingots, excluding aluminum scrap and other competing materials, such as copper. Again, the smaller market led to a finding that the defendant had monopolized it.

Rationalizing these cases in order to establish their consistency calls for economic analysis. Why were substitute materials included in the market in one case and excluded in another? Why was one market construed so widely that it included many flexible wrapping materials, while another market was defined so narrowly that it did not include all paints and even excluded the use of the paint in question on products other than automobiles? Were the three situations analogous, or are there significant factors that distinguish them?

The application of consistent legal precedents for determining what is a pertinent market is clearly a problem of economic analysis. Nevertheless, it frequently has to be undertaken by the courts without, it must be acknowledged, effective help from the litigants. The resulting relationships between the decisions are so unclear that their usefulness as precedents is limited. The use of precedent requires analytical principles that produce consistent interpretations. Hence, the development of various aspects of rules regarding competition will be improved if better methods can be fostered for applying economic analysis in the litigation process.

Consistency aside, there is a great need to demonstrate the rationale for decisions about important subjects. Otherwise, the fine art of opinion writing would not have been developed. Judges would merely hand down their final decisions without discussing principles.

However, legal tradition may have placed too much dependence on the judiciary. Burdened as they are with the need to make reasonably quick decisions on a wide range of subjects, the judges cannot be expected to formulate well-organized principles in every important case. Nor can they begin to carry out such responsibilities without substantial help from the lawyers before them and from scholarly studies. This need is accentuated, of course, when the underlying principles fall into the spheres of other organized disciplines, such as economics, sociology, statistics, psychology, or accounting.

Furthermore, in the quest for principles we must consider how they should be developed in the light of their uses. Society would be greatly convenienced if the first court which considered a new area could lay down a broadly conceived set of principles to guide us; if, for example, a full code of behavior under the Sherman Act had been laid down in the early 1890's. A judge who could decide the next case as well as the one at bar would perform a great service for his fellow man. However, all of our experience—particularly the development of the common law, which underlies so much of our legal traditions—indicates that such attempts would be doomed to failure.

Judicial principles develop through accretion. After some experience with an issue, as it arises in a number of cases, a body of principles can be drawn. Hence, the timing of the synthesis is important. Premature formulation in a new area can produce a body of a priori analysis which is ill-suited for the policy needs. On the other hand, untoward delay may produce a body of inconsistent decisions and make it doubly difficult to rationalize the field.

Since the problems of society tend toward increasing complexity, the formulation of principles calls for carefully considered analysis. Since few judges have the opportunity for such reflection, there is a great need for scholarly commentary which encompasses legal studies and other analyses. This requirement indicates a great need for substantial analytical collaboration between legal scholars and their associates in the other disciplines. In the formulation of principles dealing with competition such cooperation entails considerable analytical contribution from the economists.

### *The Promulgation of Rules*

A universal debate in regulatory administration concerns the issuance of rules.[162] Many legal discussions of regulation are founded on the assumption that it consists of two separate phases: rule-making and adjudication.[163] The one sets policy, the other applies it.[164] This contention implies that Congress should pass more specific legislation and that the agencies should be charged with the task of spelling out detailed rules rather than developing them case by case.

The debate has taken several forms in the antitrust field. Many complaints have been registered, mostly from the business community, that the antitrust laws are so indefinite that the businessman does not know how to comply with them. Some would have Congress pass more precise statutes so that the agencies and the courts are not given the power to legislate.[165] Others would have the agencies, notably the Federal Trade Commission, issue clear-cut rules.[166] A corollary point has been the suggestion that the agencies should issue binding rulings about new ventures or practices before business undertakes them—a preclearance procedure.

The neat dichotomy of rule-making and adjudication fits the black-and-white of hornbook learning. But it fails to portray the complex grays of regulation as it exists. To describe policy formulation as a simple process of rule-making, entirely separate from any case-by-case development, is to disregard substantial elements of the legal system.[167] Indeed, it overlooks the policy process in any organization whether it be business, charity, education, or government.

In modern society regulatory policies have always been made through a combination of rule promulgations and the case-by-case decisions of courts and administrative agencies.[168] Under our legal system, legislation is only the start of policy development, regardless of who legislates. Courts, government agencies, and prosecutors participate in further development extending the statutory rules. This situation maintains in all legal fields: divorce, crimes, corporations, real estate, public utility regulation, or antitrust. Even when an administrative agency issues formal rules, no matter how definite, the application of those rules to the specific situation is rarely a mechanical operation. Interpretations are always required—interpretations which necessarily add to policy development.

Policy-making in a business corporation parallels the governmental process. A board of directors has a unique position in that it is wholly occupied with policy—not that it is the sole policy maker. Policy-making is a two-way function with communication both up and down the lines of authority. Many policy questions are raised by people on the operating levels. They supply the data which are considered in setting policy. When the decision is made, whether by the board, the president, a department, division, or unit head, it may be modified in its application in successive steps down the line. In this way, anyone who does more than a completely mechanical task may participate.

Within the dynamism of administration, whether by an independent commission or an executive department, any literal application of the dichotomy of rule-making and adjudication would probably block action. No one in the agencies could negotiate a consent order, agree to a stipulation, or agree that a proposed practice complies with the antitrust law unless the specific type of situation was covered by a specific rule. Under such a system department heads and judges would have to beat a regular path to Congress or to pertinent commissions for policy rulings.

The place of formal rule-making in the policy process depends on the nature of the problem. In some fields, we have sufficient knowledge to construct rules and to make tolerable forecasts of their effects. In others, we must proceed by steps, following a trial-and-error method of building up a structure of policy. At times, a body of law which has emerged from the case-by-case process can be effectively codified and supplemented through the promulgation of rules, but such codification requires a development through a succession of cases.

The antitrust field has its share of legislation founded on inadequate consideration. An outstanding example is the cost provision of the Robinson-Patman Act, the provision which is intended to eliminate that price discrimination which may lessen competition. When the act was considered, there was some concern that the provisions against price discrimination might penalize efficiency and prevent the development of new methods of distribution. Therefore, it was provided that a seller could justify a price discrimination by proving that the price difference was no greater than his cost savings in dealing with the favored customer, even though the discrimination might lessen competition.[169] No consideration was given, however, to the state of the art of cost-accounting.[170] No inquiries were made regarding the practicability of the provision.

Unit costs for each product were, and are, accounted for generally as average costs of an establishment, rather than as specific costs of dealing with each customer or class of customers.[171] Costs of production are taken as the average for a specific product.[172] Administrative and selling costs, the principal areas in which cost differences may be found, are usually measured as average percentages of sales.[173] Only slight progress has been made in measuring differences in the costs of selling to various types of customers. While economic analysis deals with the concepts of cost differentials, cost accountants were not accustomed to using such methods for this purpose when the Robinson-Patman Act was written. Nor were there any recognized accounting principles to cover such differentials. Indeed, after twenty-five years of administering the act, no principles have emerged.[174] Therefore, such justification has been offered and accepted by the F.T.C. or the courts only on rare occasions, and the provision has not had the effect that Congress apparently intended,[175] despite the reasonable attitude of the F.T.C.[176] It seems possible that some members of Congress might have had second thoughts about the act in its present form if they had realized that this "safeguard" was illusory.

*Policy Review*

Effective policy formulation requires an overview of the effects of existing policies. An understanding of future problems and alternative solutions must rest heavily on a full appreciation of experience, past and current. Thorough review is needed for realistic evaluation of the needs for policy changes affecting either violations or remedial measures.

The application of economic analysis in such policy consideration faces two hurdles: we do not have an organized mechanism for thorough policy surveys; and we lack practicable methods for giving the reviewers the advantages of economic advice.

Established patterns for studying regulatory policies are inadequate. We depend too much on the judicial case-by-case review. Judicial consideration cannot, by itself, fill all the needs of a rounded policy examination.[177] A judge's scope is confined to the case before him. Regardless of his capacities, he has no base for reviewing the operations of a regulatory agency and the laws it administers. He has no means for changing other government activities which are not involved in the litigation but which may have a profound effect on the market under consideration. He cannot investigate the agency's policies in uncovering situations which require attention, in selecting cases to try, or in settling problems through informal negotiations. He cannot review the consent orders of the Federal Trade Commission nor can he check its contested orders unless the respondent appeals. Above all, he has no power to investigate the economic effects of his own decrees, let alone other proceedings. Other means of review are inadequate. While congressional committees have conducted many excellent investigations of specific phases of policy, they are subjected to so many immediate pressures that they cannot maintain a continuous analytical review. The Executive and the agencies themselves have demonstrated little interest in such policy review. No President has commissioned a continuing analysis. No agency has the function of reviewing the competitive effects of all government activity.[178] The Bureau of the Budget and the Council of Economic Advisers are not burdened with this task. One experiment in joint review by the Executive and Legislative branches, the Temporary National Economic Committee, was temporary in fact.

It would not seem desirable to charge the antitrust agencies with the responsibility for such a review.[179] The two major agencies, the Federal Trade Commission and the Antitrust Division of the Department of Justice, are essentially enforcement organizations. As such, they cannot be expected to review policies on the broad basis which is needed.[180] Their divided responsibility would prevent either one from maintaining an objective review. Equally important would be the restraining influence of their limited jurisdiction. Both agencies operate within the circumscribed area of antitrust and have little contact with other governmental activities—some of which limit competition and some of which can be employed to stimulate market rivalry. It should be made clear that this lack of a broad review mechanism for regulatory processes is not peculiar to antitrust. It affects all regulatory programs. However, the problem is more complex in the area of competition than in some other fields.

### *The Technician and Policy Formulation*

The role of economic analysis in the formulation of public policies regarding competition is affected by a general problem: the role of the technician in formulating public policy.[181] How central a part should be assigned to the expert? Should he make policy? Should his advice be accepted without question? What responsibilities should he bear?

Since regulation of industry is essentially a political[182] process, the accommodation of its objectives cannot be confined to an organized intellectual exercise.[183] The pressures within our society make themselves felt so effectively that policy development cannot rest exclusively on a technical basis.

This pattern is not only inevitable but desirable.[184] As long as we maintain our stand against a fully planned economy, it will be impossible to draft public policies on the technician's drawing board.[185] As long as our knowledge and analytical methods are not capable of balancing all public objectives and the market forces in the economy through the operation of one gigantic computer, we must rely on the voices of the various pressure groups.[186] The influences of the farmer, of labor, of industry, of small business, and even on rare occasions of the consumer, can be read into many elements of current regulation. These are the hallmarks of a free society. The pressures and counterpressures, the conflicts of objectives, and the resolution of those conflicts constitute the warp and the woof of the democratic fabric.

In this environment disciplined analysis has a substantial function.[187] Economists, together with lawyers and political scientists, play important roles in the regulatory process. Theirs is the task of pointing out the available policy alternatives and their relation to existing policies, of making predictions about the effects of the alternatives, and of analyzing the results of past decisions.[188]

At first blush, this process may seem inefficient. Given special competence in his field, the technician may appear best equipped to formulate policy. He enjoys a sophisticated understanding of the problems in his area. Applying his analysis directly to a policy problem should be more effective than employing him in an advisory capacity. As a technician, rather than a competing participant, he can better understand and defend the "public interest."

Yet there is much to be said for the political process.[189] It can help to bolster the professional standing and competence of the adviser. It may well produce results which are superior to the technical conclusions. The technician who makes the political decision can all too easily give up his integrity to meet the practical requirements of the situation.[190] If he should disregard the pressures or overlook objectives which fall outside his field of competence, his decision will not endure. If he should "bend with the wind," he would fail to make the intellectual contribution that public policy requires. Above all, if the policy decision is based entirely on his predictions—a most uncertain procedure in any process which must accommodate human reactions—any ensuing error could "swing the pendulum" and reduce the effectiveness of other technical analysis in future policy consideration.

The practice of the professional turned policy maker lends support to this thesis. Lawyers who become administrators of government departments or businesses retain legal counsel. Experts in the study of public administration are apt to depend heavily on advisers when they take on administrative functions. The economist turned senator consults economists even more than do his lay colleagues.

To make his contribution, the professional adviser must appreciate the policy-making process, its idiosyncrasies and its irritations.[191] In turn, the decision framers must appreciate the role and the integrity of the technical adviser in order to employ his services to best advantage.

### *The Role of Economic Analysis*

Several disciplines, notably law, economics, and political science, participate in the formulation of policies regarding competition.[192] Since the lawyers control the regulatory processes, they play a leading role. At the same time, theirs are the strongest voices in policy development because of their positions in the Congress and in the administrative agencies.

However, effective solutions for these policy issues call for economic inquiry. Analyses of competitive and monopolistic forces are economic problems. Any exploration of the pertinent policy problems calls for predictions about the economic effects of the various alternative policies under consideration.[193]

The skills of the political scientist are required in this area because many aspects of these policies are tied up with general problems of government. Any regulatory policy requires governmental administration, whether it is oriented toward competition or against it. The pertinent administrative elements are seen clearly in their application to the independent commissions.[194] Yet, when the rules are administered by the Executive departments, the regulatory problems are essentially the same. The review of policy alternatives frequently calls for consideration of their administrative practicability.

The posture of the economist in policy-making differs from his function in the administration of the policies. In advising on new legislation the economist is not fettered by existing regulations. While current regulations and their administration must be covered in his studies, they constitute operating data and do not set limits on his analysis. In contrast, the economist must accept the limits of the established regulations and procedures when he is employed in their administration, a role which is reviewed in Chapter 6.[195]

The economist's function in policy formulation calls for broad-gauged analyses of the alternative policies under consideration.[196] He is not only free of the bonds of current antitrust regulation, but he may consider many other features of public policy. He may seek the lawyer's advice about the current situation and about the legal side effects of the policies he has to analyze. But, he is not bound by the lawyer's point of view. He is free to raise questions about such related policies as government purchasing, research and development, tariffs and quotas, and taxes.

The tools of economic analysis must be operational in policy formulation just as in administration.[197] Policy decisions are formulated by legislators, administrators, and judges. Administration is supervised by lawyers. Therefore, there is a clear need for tools of economic analysis which can be utilized by people who lack backgrounds in economic theory.[198]

To be effective, the economist must differentiate between the analytical tools he employs in formulating his own conclusions and those which will be utilized by others, especially lawyers.[199] An economist is free to consider long, involved chains of reasoning, technical statistical measures, and mathematical formulas in developing his own evaluations of a condition and its remedy, but, he must overcome almost impassable hurdles if he wants to stay with his original analysis in advising others.[200] Hence he must translate his conclusions and the reasons therefor into linguistic concepts and paths which are within the ken of the layman.[201] The legislator, the administrator, or the lawyer who accepts the basic premises of technical economic theory and analysis is rare, indeed. These individuals exhibit neither familiarity with nor interest in the technical vocabulary and the abstract concepts of economic theory.

This problem is not unique. Other professions have to cope with similar tasks. In advising a business client, the lawyer cannot stop with a technical analysis of the juridical problem. On most occasions, he must translate his conclusions and supporting reasons into terms that are understood by his client. The medical professions, the natural and physical scientists, and the engineering professions must translate in the same way.

Above all, to be effective in the formulation of competition policy, economic analysis must be empirical. The great contribution of economic theory rests on its methodology. It helps to identify the pertinent questions which should be raised, to formulate problems precisely, to indicate the types of data which should be employed, and to apply methods of formulating and testing hypotheses.

While a broad framework of theory may be helpful to the economist in his policy activities, he cannot be effective if he simply produces the final answers of theory. Crises aside, policies cannot be writ on a clean slate. Policy formulation rests upon policies in being and calls for modification and alteration. Though the form of a policy enunciation may be a fiat, policy is developed through accretion. Hence, a policy recommendation which calls for a radical switch to a novel theoretical concept falls short of the mark except for those unusual crises which produce inexorable pressures for substantial change.

The ready answers provided by economic theory will not do.[202] Their philosophical bases contribute to methodology. But, their untested conclusions, taken out of a conceptual framework of static equilibrium, hardly fit the economy in being. Their generality, lacking the pointedness of an empirical approach to specific problems, is wide of the mark.

Progress in economic research and in its application is in the making. Industry studies are contributing to the development of meaningful research methods. Policy makers are employing economic analysis more widely than ever before. Congressional committees, lawyers, and judges show ever-increasing realization that antitrust policies are economic in nature. On their side, economists are developing greater facility in communicating with the policy makers.

The essential problem is how to accelerate these developments. A wider scope for policy consideration in this area must be sought. The framework for continuing policy review on a wide front must be forged, a review that takes cognizance of the whole spectrum of government activities that affect competition. The legal-judicial limits of antitrust contain no room for consideration of the host of government activities, federal, state, and local, which influence competitive forces —trade barriers, taxes, government purchasing and research, consumer information, direct controls, aids to small business, and special rules for various economic groups. Nor do they allow for economy-wide consideration of industry structure and specialized legislative enactment. It is precisely in this quest for a broad-gauged approach that economic analysis can make its greatest contribution to the formulation of public policy.

The importance of the policy role of economic analysis does not deprecate its potential contribution to the administration of existing policies. We turn now to a review of the uses of economic inquiry in antitrust litigation and negotiation.

# 5 / *Litigation and Negotiation**

TO APPRECIATE THE PROBLEMS of applying economic analysis in the administration of the antitrust laws, one must consider the nature of litigation. These procedures provide the setting for introducing economic evidence and argument.[1] They limit the application of economic inquiry in the consideration of competitive and regulatory problems.[2] The litigation process influences the relationships between the lawyers and the economists in antitrust administration. Because of this it sets the framework within which the economist must operate in order to make an effective contribution to antitrust enforcement.

Litigation has not been an ideal process for the trial of economic issues.[3] Early court procedures were not tailored to ferret out economic issues or to deal efficiently with economic evidence and analysis.[4] Recent decades have witnessed forward strides in the treatment of economic issues in the courts. However, it is apparent that effective administration of policies regarding competition requires further progress in this direction.

The processes of litigation have not been conducive to efficient settlement of competitive issues. On the average, it has taken some five and a half years to complete a litigated antitrust case.[5] The proceeding against the Aluminum Company of America was extended for twenty years.[6]

Under the pressure of increasingly complex economic problems, there has been a growing trend toward the enforcement of antitrust and other regulatory laws through the administrative process, rather than the courts. In antitrust this movement has taken the form of administration through the Federal Trade Commission and other regu-

* Footnotes for Chapter 5 begin on page 399.

latory agencies, as well as the negotiation of consent decrees by the Antitrust Division of the Department of Justice.

While the administrative procedures have lightened the physical burden of the courts, they have not eliminated the influences of litigation. The formal procedures of the Commission are based on the judicial model.[7] In the place of a federal district judge, it substitutes a hearing examiner.[8] The members of the Federal Trade Commission, sitting as a body, adopt a posture similar to an appellate court. After the Commission has approved the filing of a complaint, it maintains a judicial aloofness. Counsel supporting a complaint is supervised by the Enforcement Bureaus and maintains a litigant's arm's-length relationship with the hearing examiner and the commissioners, treating them as judges.[9] The Commission in its appellate role consults no one who has had any organizational connection with the case in point—no hearing examiner, member of the Enforcement Bureaus, economist from the Bureau of Economics or accountants from the Bureau of Restraint of Trade.[10]

## *Litigation*

Litigation is directly important in several areas. The Department of Justice is principally occupied as a prosecuting agency. The Federal Trade Commission acts as a plaintiff or defendant in court proceedings to enforce or defend its actions. On such occasions, it changes its quasi-judicial robe for that of the barrister. Private suits, whether for treble damages or for injunctions, follow the conventional course of judicial proceedings. Such trials are carried on in the same manner as government suits.

Accordingly, any evaluation of the uses of economic analysis in the administration of the policies regarding competition must be set against the background of litigation. Any suggestions for improvement in the application of economic inquiry must take account of the process of antitrust litigation and its companion consent procedures. The relative strengths and weaknesses of these procedures must be considered in any review of the current uses of economic analysis or of potential improvements. Similarly, the limitations of the scope of a judge's powers—his inability to consider the problems of an entire market at one time and his lack of authority over other government functions which may influence competition—set clear boundaries for the uses of economic analysis in dealing with competitive issues.

A full description of all applicable forms of litigation and negotiation would be too involved for the present purpose. There are many distinguishable types of antitrust litigation: a civil proceeding in equity before a judge; a criminal prosecution before a judge and jury, or before a judge sitting alone; an appeal from an order of the F.T.C. before a panel of judges; a treble-damage action before a judge and jury or a judge sitting alone; a hearing on an appeal from the decision of a lower court before a circuit court of appeals or the Supreme court, composed of several judges; a hearing before a master-in-chancery, appointed by a judge to make findings of fact; a hearing before a trial examiner of the Federal Trade Commission; or a hearing before the Commission, itself. Each of these forms has its own technical intricacies.

The applications of economic analysis can be demonstrated most clearly by concentrating on one procedure, the government's civil prosecution, which is the most prominent. This process provides a fair guide to the others and offers a clearer picture of the problems of utilizing economic evidence.

### *The Judge's Function*

The conceptual framework of the judicial process colors the basic pattern of litigation, its strength, and its weaknesses. The judicial task is essentially one of selection.[11] The primary function of the judge is to make a choice of alternatives based on the evidence and legal arguments presented to him in open court.[12] As Judge Clark sees it, "only rarely and perhaps fortuitously may an opinion be expected to rise above its source in the presentations of counsel."[13] It is presumed that each adversary will put his best foot forward, presenting the strongest evidence and arguments on his side.[14] Accordingly, the judge is not expected to conduct factual investigations or to develop legal theories of his own.[15] He sifts through the evidence and arguments that have been presented to him in the presence of both parties. He does not engage in side discussions with either the adversaries or with others who may be interested. On infrequent occasions, he may hear from *amici curiae,* "friends of the court," who are not directly involved in the litigation. He may even appoint such "friends" to investigate and report. He may order a master-in-chancery to hold hearings on the facts and to report back conclusions. But these statements and advice are rendered in open court and are limited by criteria of relevance.

This procedure comports with our ideas of justice and contributes to the efficiency of the process. As Lon Fuller observed, the "moral force of a judgment is at maximum if a judge decides solely on the basis of arguments presented to him. Because if he goes beyond these, he will lack guidance and may not understand interests that are affected by a decision outside the framework."[16]

The open trial gives each adversary full notice of the evidence and legal arguments that enter into the judge's consideration. Hence, each adversary can confine his presentation to the evidence and arguments he believes will be necessary to win his case. He does not have to speculate about secret evidence, advice, or influence. Therefore, he need not attempt to present all of the information and arguments which could possibly be useful to his side in order to counteract any evidence or argument that the judge might learn without his knowledge.

Within narrow limits, a judge may take "judicial notice" of certain facts. The doctrine of judicial notice, however, is narrowly circumscribed. It covers data which are available to everyone in standard publications and "general knowledge." Usually, the information is referred to in open court,[17] giving the parties an opportunity to controvert it.

In addition to his function of selection and conclusion, the judge supervises the conduct of the litigation.[18] He is concerned with the pleadings before the trial proper, the presentation of the evidence and arguments. He may hold pretrial conferences to clarify the issues and to arrange for sensible handling of extended evidence.[19]

Finally, he must decide whether the antitrust laws have been violated, and he must issue a decree if he finds that a violation has taken place. Occasionally, a judge's functions continue after he issues his judgment. Some decrees provide that the court will supervise their execution. For example, if the judge orders that certain patents must be licensed to any applicant on the payment of reasonable royalties, the decree may provide that the court will fix the royalties if the licensor and applicant cannot agree.

### *Defining the Issues*

The stages of an antitrust trial consist of the following: (1) the definition of the issues of the litigation; (2) the collection of evidence; (3) the presentation of the data, in accordance with the technical rules of evidence; (4) the presentation of arguments by the lawyers analyzing the evidence and the law; (5) the judicial sifting and determination of whether a violation has taken place; and (6) the formulation of a decree, if a violation has been found. In some instances, step (6) calls for separate evidence and arguments regarding the decree.

The definition of issues is the keystone of litigation.[20] It is particularly important in antitrust.[21] In the absence of clear issues, neither party could tell what information and arguments to develop.[22] Similarly, the judge would have a difficult time understanding the purpose of a tremendous amount of intricate evidence which may be presented. Nor could he control the trial and exclude extraneous information without ignoring pertinent data.

To begin with, the adversaries must state issues that have secure legal bases. Thus, if the plaintiff should allege merely that the defendant had a monopoly position, he would not have stated an antitrust issue. The Sherman Act challenges the process of "monopolizing" not "monopoly." Therefore, an important element in such a proceeding is that the monopoly was achieved with "intent" or that the defendant engaged in various "abuses" on his way to the summit.

The definition of issues provides an organizing mechanism for both sides. A complaint that the defendant violated Section 2 of the Sherman Act will require broad evidence of actions, practices, and policies over a period of time, tracing out the path to "monopoly" with pertinent intent and "abuse" evidence. In contrast, a charge that Section 7 of the Clayton Act was violated when the defendant acquired the assets of a major competitor narrows the scope of the trial. Here the issue centers on specific acts of acquisition.

The issues in a case are defined generally through the pleadings which are presented before the trial proper[23] and in the pretrial conferences.[24] On occasion, the parties outline the evidence that will be presented in trial briefs in order to permit all concerned to place the information in perspective. More and more frequently, judges hold pretrial conferences with counsel for both sides. These conferences are designed to clarify the issues involved and to review problems of evidence. During this preparatory phase the judge may order each party to furnish specific information to its opponent so that the latter can help to clarify the issues before the trial is started instead of discovering new issues during the course of the courtroom proceedings.[25]

However, this process is not always effective in defining the pertinent issues. It frequently permits legal maneuvers[26] which are calculated to obfuscate, to confuse the other side and the judge, and to ward off clear definitions so that the opposition is not prepared to counter the evidence and arguments that finally emerge. At times, the economic issues are so poorly conceived and defined that what may be a strong case for either side is lost.

Until the issues are defined, it is difficult to tell what economic analysis is needed. If the case should turn on the existence of a conspiracy which can be proved with direct evidence, economic data and analysis may not be applicable. A criminal proceeding under Section 1 of the Sherman Act will illustrate the point. It will be recalled that the section outlaws conspiracies to restrain trade. The *General Motors Acceptance Corporation*[27] (GMAC) case turned on the question whether General Motors and GMAC conspired[28] to compel GM's dealers to finance their car sales with GMAC. Several dealers testified that they had been forced into such exclusive financing agreements. The defense offered testimony from other dealers that they had not been subjected to such coercion. However, the court refused to hear the defendants' dealer witnesses, holding that: the issue in the case was whether GM and GMAC had conspired to violate the Sherman Act; all the prosecution had to prove was the existence of a conspiracy even if it had affected a limited number of dealers; for if a conspiracy existed, neither its extent nor its economic effects were relevant. Similarly, the court would have denied the pertinence of any evidence to show that competition was flourishing.

However, if the case involved separate agreements between General Motors and each of a handful of dealers to finance all his sales with GM, there would have been no basis for a conspiracy charge because the manufacturer made each agreement alone without the cooperation of a third party. That case would come under Section 3 of the Clayton Act,[29] against tying contracts and evidence regarding probable economic effects might have been pertinent. The *GMAC* case turned on the treatment of GMAC as a third party which conspired with GM even though the latter was its parent corporation.

The type and amount of evidence required is affected by the legal rules regarding the nature of proof and who has to bear the principal burden. Such rules are subject to change, as in the case of the provision against exclusive purchase agreements contained in Section 3 of the Clayton Act. Before the *Standard Stations*[30] and *International Salt*[31] cases, the rule seemed to be that the plaintiff should introduce economic evidence to show that the agreements would tend to lessen competition and that the defense could employ economic evidence to counter this hypothesis. After those cases it was believed that the prosecution in a judicial proceeding need prove only that a "substantial" volume of commerce was affected by such exclusive agreements without going into evidence about competitive effects. A more recent case, *Tampa Electric*,[32] indicates that evidence about economic effect will be considered in reviewing a single exclusive contract with a large buyer-user.

At times the issues of a case turn exclusively on questions of legal interpretation based on economic argument without any presentation of evidence. In such instances the economic argument is based on presumptions about the business background of the case. Some of these presumptions are assumed by one side and not challenged by the other. Some presumptions are accepted by the judge as general knowledge, available to everyone, evidence of which he can take "judicial notice" without requiring testimony or documents.

An instance in point is the *Automatic Canteen* case,[33] an attack on a buyer who benefited from a discriminatory price. The pertinent statute, Section 2 (f) of the Robinson-Patman Act, imposes liability on the buyer who "knowingly" benefits from a lower discriminatory price. Defense counsel argued that the F.T.C. had not shown that Automatic

Canteen "knowingly" obtained the advantage of an illegally low price since the F.T.C. had not proved that the company had known that it had the benefit of a discrimination which could not be justified under the act. He stated that since the company did not know the manufacturer's costs it could not possibly know that the price discrimination was not justified. Canteen would have been hard put to prove that differences in the sellers' costs would justify the discounts—a problem of economic proof. Hence, its counsel did not attempt to show that the price was justified but instead argued the legal point and gained a victory. His argument that buyers generally do not know their sellers' costs is, of course, an economic one.[34]

The importance of clarifying the issues in antitrust litigation cannot be overemphasized. Such clarity is a strategic factor influencing the significance of both economic evidence and argument.

### *Collecting Data*

After the issues have been visualized, a start can be made to collect evidence. The parties, especially the plaintiff, would need to develop some evidence before filing a complaint. The defendant might also make some investigation before filing an answer. Frequently, however, the detailed inquiries are started in earnest only after the pleadings are filed and pretrial conferences are held, or after preliminary skirmishes to determine what will be the strategic elements of the trial.

This stage may call for interviews with potential witnesses, field studies, reviews of file materials, and industry or market studies in order to establish the economic setting of the problem. At this point many skills come into play.

Collecting and organizing evidence is a practical problem. Basic plans must be developed regarding what types of evidence best support the arguments. The opposition's probable evidence must be visualized. Technical decisions must be made about what evidence would be admitted by the court, what data can be made clear to the judge, and what will be most persuasive. At the same time, substantial consideration must be given to the costs of collecting the data and presenting it.

The costs of data collection can be so expensive that it can dictate what points will be made or stressed. For example, in the *Investment Bankers* case,[35] the government and the defendants agreed on a compilation of all significant issues of securities over a stated period of time. It was reported that the defendants spent not less than $350,000 on this compilation.[36] Obviously, many defendants could not afford such a defense.

The use of such published information as reports of the Bureau of the Census, the Bureau of Labor Statistics, and the Department of Agriculture can affect the costs and time of preparation. At times, trade association data, industry studies, and the internal reports of a company can be used.

Field studies can be developed in various ways. Frequently, as in the *Investment Bankers* case, both parties will agree on the survey, enabling the one to undertake it without chancing the possible refusal to admit the expensive survey into evidence.

The use of statistical samples of such evidence as prices, costs, or shipments into a regional market can determine whether a field study is practical or not. As Judge Wyzanski observed in the *United Shoe Machinery* case,[37] "If antitrust trials are to be kept manageable, samples must be used. . . ." A sample study can have several advantages: it can reduce cost substantially; it can be completed quickly; it permits more detailed information at each point; it has more flexibility, permitting more changes if the original questions are inadequate. The problems of sampling and of the use of samples and of statistical tabulations are reviewed in Chapter 9, below.

*Presenting Evidence*

The problems of presenting evidence are interrelated with the collection of data. Some issues relate to technical evidentiary problems, others affect methods of compilation and presentation. Consider, for example, evidence that a company's sales increased sharply after a specified event. If a judge were shown the original sales invoices, he would find it almost impossible to interpret the operations of any company which made more than a handful of sales. Accordingly, such evidence calls for a compilation of the basic data and proof of its reasonable accuracy. A tabulation of daily sales might not show the trend clearly, while annual or monthly figures would. A chart might drive the point home. On the other hand, if the opposition wanted to show that the specified event did not contribute to a firm's growth, it might present a chart comparing the company's sales with those of its competitors in an effort to prove that the industry's sales increased more rapidly than those of the firm.

The presentation of evidence can call for a combination of legal and economic skills. The lawyer must be able to show that the data are admissible as proper evidence under the technical legal rules. He must consider how to make the evidence persuasive and how to relate it to his argument. The economist can provide means for summarizing, presenting, and interpreting the data and for relating them to the issues and the argument.

The method of presenting results of a survey can have a profound influence on its persuasiveness. Calling up several hundred dealers or consumers would be impractical and expensive. A judge would probably resent the intrusion on his time. Accordingly, such a survey may be presented through statistical compilations of the results. However, as shown in Chapter 9, many judges retain an innate suspicion of statistics. Hence, a combination of a handful of live witnesses and a compilation may be preferable.

In such presentations, expert witnesses may be used.[38] In certain circumstances, an expert may be called on to interpret the data developed by other witnesses. Or the expert may be called on to testify regarding his conclusions based on his own studies. In this way, the judge is given the benefit of an expert's interpretation of the data though he may also be confused by a radically different interpretation offered by an expert for the other side.

During such presentations, the opposition can utilize several means to disprove the evidence or to cast doubt on it. Cross-examination of experts can be used effectively, especially if the examiner has a substantial grasp of the technical problems. Cross-examination may raise doubts regarding the accuracy or significance of the data and the competence or integrity of the witness. A favorite gambit is to read from an expert's previous writings if a section can be found to controvert his testimony. In many instances, of course, the opposition's method for breaking down the persuasiveness of data is to present counterevidence.

Considerable importance attaches to the technical legal rules concerning admissibility of evidence. Over a period of time, the courts have developed a set of rules regarding what types of evidence can be admitted. The most significant rule affecting the admissibility of economic evidence has been the "hearsay" rule. This regulation has had substantial influence on the types of economic evidence that can be considered during a trial. Strict application of the rule, as originally formulated, would deny consideration of many, if not most, types of statistical evidence.[39] However, as Chapter 9 demonstrates, the rules have been liberalized substantially in recent years.[40]

Despite this recent liberalization, the rules of evidence currently affect the types of data which can be introduced and the methods of introducing them. Consideration must be given to the demonstration that the data have a substantial bearing on the issues of the case and that they are reliable. This process calls for substantial consideration of how to define the issues, what evidence can be developed and used. and how the data can be presented persuasively.

The rules of evidence have had a strong limiting effect in many instances. In the *Alcoa* case, the Department of Justice submitted two pages of import statistics in evidence. Before it was accepted, about one week had to be taken to review evidence in support of these tabulations. The review included all statutes covering the government's collection of such statistics since 1890, all supporting administrative regulations, and the original books of record.[41]

However, many judges do not share the same attitudes about the technical proof that should be required before such tabulations are accepted in evidence. The pretrial order in the *Borden* case[42] provided that any records or publications of the United States Department of Agriculture or of any federal milk administrator would be accepted in evidence. An order in the *Imperial Chemical* case[43] allowed any report, document or publication of any agency of the United States Government or any foreign government to be introduced in evidence. A similar order, covering United States agencies was issued in the *Cellophane* case.[44]

With the increased importance of economic evidence, there is a strong movement in legal-judicial circles to allow the introduction of tabulations, providing that opposing counsel is given a reasonable opportunity to examine both the tabulations and the underlying data before the trial proper. This procedure offers an opportunity to object to the introduction of evidence on substantive grounds regarding the specific data, rather than because of general rules of evidence.

Some of these technical problems can be solved by using alternative methods for introducing the data. Thus, after reviewing the problem of introducing import statistics in the *Alcoa* case, Corwin Edwards suggested that a qualified expert witness could have testified as to his opinion based on his study of the material "even though it was derived from sources which the court might have rejected as improper."[45]

### *The Lawyer's Arguments*

The lawyer's arguments regarding the interpretation of the facts, their relation to the issues, and the state of the law are frequently crucial. In many cases all of the preceding phases of the trial emerge only as preliminary steps leading up to the "clincher," developed in the free-wheeling atmosphere of the final debate.

In these arguments in antitrust cases, issues of law and fact blend together. Given the generality of the statutory phraseology and the need for economic interpretation of precedent, the legal arguments themselves provide substantial opportunity for economic interpretation,[46] as in the *Automatic Canteen* case,[47] discussed above.

At this stage of the trial the lawyer has the greatest leeway. He can infer economic conclusions from his own evidence and that of the opposition. He can utilize some economic inference to build up his side or to demolish the opposition. In short, he runs in an open field. The judge has no legal basis, comparable to his power to exclude evidence, for challenging an argument because of the lack of logic in the inferences that are drawn. Though he may not be impressed by the argument, he cannot refuse to listen to it.[48]

The full import of this stage of the trial and of the opportunities it offers for employing economic analysis can be appreciated when the techniques of circumstantial evidence are considered.

*Circumstantial Evidence*

The general outline of the steps leading up to the stage when the judge must take over, is thrown into bold relief by the problems of circumstantial evidence. The typical antitrust proceeding turns on circumstantial rather than direct evidence. Most antitrust issues turn on analytical conclusions—that competition may be lessened substantially, that a company is trying to monopolize, that trade is being restrained unduly. There can be no direct observations of these phenomena.[49] Therefore, circumstantial evidence is required.[50] True, an occasional antitrust case may be tried on such direct evidence as a written agreement fixing prices, but such clear-cut situations rarely go to trial.

Direct evidence can be sufficient when a proceeding turns on simple, uncomplicated issues of fact. For example, the direct testimony of an eye-witness who saw a hold-up proves that the act took place.

As the Supreme Court pointed out in the *Eastern States Lumber Association* case, in 1914, however, even "conspiracies are seldom capable of proof in direct testimony and may be inferred from the things actually done. . . ."[51] As a matter of fact, if a written price-fixing agreement were available, the equity case would probably be settled by a consent decree. (Of course, the formalities of a trial cannot be avoided in a criminal case, although there may be negotiation beforehand. For example, the parties may agree to a plea of *nolo contendere* whereby the defendant does not contest the position of the prosecution. But we are dealing here with civil proceedings only.)[52] Usually, circumstantial evidence that supports an inference that there is a price agreement is the only proof available.

The treatment of circumstantial evidence rests on the methodology of testing a hypothesis.[53] In stating the issues of the case, the plaintiff presents a working hypothesis, for example, that the defendant's distribution practices have lessened competition substantially. Then he offers evidence in support of this thesis. He may or may not produce expert witnesses to testify that there is a strong relationship between his hypothesis and his evidence.[54] Counsel for the plaintiff usually carries the argumentative burden himself. On completing his evidence, he argues: (a) that the evidence is clearly compatible with his hypothesis;

and (b) that it is not consistent with any other inference; or (c) that, while it might be compatible with another hypothesis, the possibilities are so remote that his is the only reasonable one. In opposition, the defendant's counsel seeks to destroy the plaintiff's hypothesis. He may try to persuade the court that the plaintiff's evidence and inference are not compatible, without presenting any further evidence. But this procedure is rare. More frequently, the defense undertakes to upset the force of the plaintiff's evidence in several ways: by cross-examining the latter's witnesses in order to cast doubt on their testimony; by introducing new evidence to controvert the plaintiff's witnesses; or by presenting new information which does not controvert the plaintiff's evidence but is employed to defeat his hypothesis. Then, the defense argument is that the reliable elements in the plaintiff's evidence do not support his hypothesis; that the total evidence,[55] including the defendant's, is not compatible with such an inference; or, affirmatively, that the evidence is more compatible with a new hypothesis which would destroy the plaintiff's claim.

The methodology of testing a hypothesis is the core of most antitrust cases.[56] Take a price conspiracy case, for example. Suppose that the government proves that when the General Services Administration invited bids for plastic rulers, it received several bids—each for $17.84345 per gross, delivered in Washington, D.C. It shows further, that for several years all producers changed their list prices and discounts during the same week. It argues that such events could not have transpired unless there had been a price agreement because such price behavior is not compatible with competition.

The defendants counter with evidence that the precise bid prices are simply arithmetic results which were obtained by applying a series of percentage discounts to list prices, in accordance with an industry custom of long standing.[57] They prove that these discounts are customarily allowed to wholesalers who buy in largest volume brackets; further, that the industry has allowed these wholesale discounts to the federal government[58] since 1935 when some departments threatened to switch to wooden rulers because the plastic prices were too high. They prove that each manufacturer has always charged uniform delivered prices at all points in the country. They establish that, although all companies changed list prices at approximately the same time, everyone made a number of sales at off-list prices. Further, on several occasions a company which raised its list prices had to cancel the increases because other competitors did not follow suit. Therefore, they argue that the evidence presented, taken as a whole, is not compatible with a price conspiracy, but supports the hypothesis that prices are set by lively competitive forces.[59]

In this setting, the judge must weigh the two hypotheses—the one, that there was a price conspiracy and the other, that prices were competitive.[60] He must consider which evidence is more plausible. He must decide which inference is more compatible with this evidence.

This process of formulating hypotheses and testing them through observation constitutes the essential methodology of modern empirical economic analysis. For that matter, it is the methodological foundation for the physical, natural, and social sciences. As Cohen and Nagle point out in discussing scientific method, "all inquiry which deals with matters of fact employs probable inference. The task of such investigations is to select that hypothesis which is the most probable on the factual evidence. . . ."[61]

While a trial calls for an adversary proceeding—which is not common to research—it does throw empirical methodology into bold relief precisely because it involves adversaries.

## *Decisions and Decrees*

When all the evidence and arguments are before him, the first task of the judge is to decide whether there was an antitrust violation. Frequently, he will combine this decision with a decree regarding the defendants' future actions.[62] Ordinarily, a judge will hold separate hearings on the decree after he decides that a violation exists.[63] At such hearings, evidence, arguments, and suggestions may be offered by the parties in conflict. For a clearer view of these determinations, the finding of a violation and the formulation of a decree are treated as separate stages here.

### *Finding Violations*

There is a considerable variety in the judicial practice of writing opinions and findings of fact.[64] Some judges issue one memorandum which combines the findings of fact, the opinion regarding the law, and the decision. Some add the decree, when appropriate. Others write separate findings of fact before or after[65] writing their opinion and decision.

Some judges regard the drafting of findings of fact as one of their most important functions.[66] They may ask one or both parties to submit suggested findings and hear arguments about them before writing their own findings. A judge may submit his proposed findings to both counsels and listen to their arguments before issuing the statement in final form. Other judges prepare such findings merely to satisfy the formal requirements rather than as a step in arriving at their conclusions. The formal requirement enables higher courts, on appeal, to review the application of the law to the facts. This feature is obviously of special importance in antitrust litigation because the legal conclusion is so often woven into the economic interpretation.

In this stage of a trial, the judge must sift the evidence and arguments and make his choice among the hypotheses that were presented. At this point, he works alone: reviewing and interpreting the data, analyzing the proposed hypotheses, applying his interpretation of the law, and writing his opinion and findings for the benefit of the parties before him, for appellate courts, and for the guidance of others.

### *Formulation of Decrees*

The prime purpose of an antitrust suit in equity is to obtain a decree covering future action[67] by the defendants. In a criminal suit, the objective is to set a punishment, usually in the form of a fine. Imprisonment may be ordered. Except for the recent electric equipment case, this punishment has been applied sparingly in antitrust.

The ultimate purpose of a decree is to make a market more competitive.[68] The order may prohibit a repetition of past violations. Or, it may be drawn to inject new competitive elements into the pertinent market. The formulation of a decree is a difficult and serious problem.

There are surprisingly few legal or practical[69] guides laid down for the judge in his task of drafting a decree.[70] Major guides relate mainly to what he may not do. As a point of law, the judge is told by the Supreme Court that:

> [He] may not impose penalties in the guise of preventing future violations. . . . The court may not . . . place the defendants, for the future, "in a different class from other people." . . . The decree must not be "so vague as to put the whole conduct of the defendants' business at the peril of summons for contempt"; enjoin "all possible breaches under the law"; or cause the defendants hereafter not "to be under the protection of the law of the land."[71]

There is a wide range of discretion available to the judge. A decree may contain a general edict, a narrow order covering specific violations, or a plan for substantial change. It may merely order the defendants to obey the law, for example, to discontinue a conspiracy. It may be quite narrow in its application—ordering the cancellation of a special discount to one company. At the other extreme, it may call for such drastic action as the division of a company into several parts.

An equity decree may forbid a past practice and proceed to prevent another practice which would achieve the same results. For example, in the *International Salt* case,[72] the court found that the defendant violated the Clayton Act by its practice of leasing salt dispensing machines on the condition that the lessees buy all the salt used in those machines from the lessor. The court felt that the defendant might circumvent the mere prohibition of this practice by charging substantially lower rentals to those lessees who did buy its salt. Therefore, in addition to forbidding the practice, the decree required the company to lease its machinery to all applicants at rates which are not discriminatory.

The most difficult type of decree to formulate is one that changes the structure of a company. To write such a decree, a judge must visualize the structure which will effectively inject competition into a market without being unnecessarily punitive. Should a company be broken up into three independent firms, four, or seven? Is there ground to believe that four companies will be more competitive than the two who are in the market? Should all the companies in an industry be of similar size? Should any company have more than one plant? How should the products and functions (manufacturing, wholesaling, and retailing, for example) be split up among the companies? How will the resultant companies fare in their competition with the rest of the industry?

Divorce and divestiture have always posed such massive problems for judges that they have been used infrequently.[73] The court felt that the *Hartford-Empire* decree, with all of its problems of administration, was preferable to the break-up which the government had requested.[74] Judge LaBuy's recent task of determining how to eliminate du Pont's influence in the General Motors Corporation[75] is an excellent illustration of the intricate workings of divorcement. In that case, the nub of the difficulty rested not on the competitive issues, settled as they were by the Supreme Court, but on how to develop a practical program whereby du Pont would give up its GM stock. The court was concerned about avoiding a heavy tax burden on du Pont's shareholders if they were given the GM shares, and the effect on the market prices of this stock if large blocks were sold, with potential repercussions on other parts of the market. In fact, the problem was so serious that Congress in January 1962 put through a form of tax relief to alleviate it.[76]

The ultimate aim in drafting a decree is to tailor an order which will reduce the monopolistic forces in a market. If separate proceedings are held to consider the decree,[77] after finding a violation, the judge can consider a number of significant factors which bear on the order. What was the underlying cause of the violation? Did it stem from specific features in the structure of the industry? Was the specific violation merely a symptom of underlying monopolistic forces or an independent anticompetitive practice?

After considering the underlying causes of the violation, the next step would be to view the alternatives to see how these causes can be eliminated. At this stage, information about the effects of various types of decrees in analogous market situations would provide practical guidance. Since many decrees and orders have been handed down over the seventy years of antitrust administration, it should be possible to review the effects of the types that have been imposed. However, as indicated in Chapter 4, no analytical guides of this type are available.

Nor do judges obtain practical, objective help in decree formulation. As stated above, in 1914, an effort was made to assist courts in the task of writing decrees. Section 7 of the Federal Trade Commission Act[78] empowers a judge to ask the F.T.C. for aid in drafting antitrust orders after he has determined that a violation has taken place. The F.T.C. is authorized to conduct hearings under such rules as the judge may prescribe, and to file a report with him. The court may adopt or reject the report, in whole or in part, and "enter such decree as the nature of the case may in its judgment require." However, the courts have not availed themselves of this assistance.

Judges continue to formulate decrees on their own. If separate hearings on the decree are held,[79] they are frequently confined to arguments about the plaintiffs' suggestions. But this procedure does not provide an analysis of the problems to be solved by the decree. The Antitrust Division has a Judgment Section, staffed by lawyers with experience in drafting decrees, who probably are of considerable aid to the courts in formulating decrees after litigation, and to the division in drafting consent decrees.[80] The Federal Trade Commission recently established an Office of Consent Orders under the General Counsel.[81] There are no signs that either section has undertaken analysis of the economic effects of past decrees although there have been investigations of compliance with such orders.

### *Judicial Modification and Supervision of Decrees*

After entry of a decree there may arise a need for judicial modification of the order or supervision over its operations. Courts have the inherent power to modify, enforce, and terminate their decrees.[82] Some decrees make specific provision for modification, though that is an inherent power of the court. A few decrees provide for supervision of their application.

While the general power of the courts to reconsider decrees seems to be well established, consent decrees have provided specifically for this power.[83] The Federal Trade Commission Act empowers the Federal Trade Commission to modify any of its orders, subject to specified procedural requirements.

There has been an interesting development in judicial supervision—the use of a "wait-and-see" approach.[84] After finding an antitrust violation in the *Alcoa* case,[85] the court postponed the writing of a decree until it could review the government's progress in inducing new entrants into the industry. After ordering the United Shoe Machinery Corporation[86] to discontinue certain practices and to follow others, the decree provided that either party could petition for a change in ten years, since the judge was not willing to accept the government's more drastic proposal to break up the company.

A similar trend may be found in consent decrees. The recent orders in the *United Fruit*[87] and *International Business Machines*[88] cases provide for a reopening if specified conditions are not met within a given time. The *United Fruit* decree called for the formation of a new independent company to which United would transfer enough assets to handle 900,000 stems of bananas annually. The *IBM* decree provides that seven years after entry of the judgment "IBM shall divest itself, upon terms and conditions approved by this Court, of such part of its then existing capacity for the manufacture of tabulating cards as may then be in excess of 50% of the total capacity" in the United States, unless it can satisfy the court that competitive conditions do not warrant such divestiture.

Decree revision has been infrequent.[89] Courts are not overly anxious to consider applications for such revision,[90] nor is the Antitrust Division. There is no regular procedure for reviewing existing decrees to see whether changes in market conditions require a rewriting. In fact such market changes[91] can be so substantial that an old decree may affirmatively discourage competition. Consider, for example, the decree against the meat packers.

The big four meat packers are restrained from the wholesale distribution of nonrelated grocery items and from any retail distribution. Strategic changes have taken place in the meat packing industry and in the distribution of grocery products since the decree was written in 1920.[92] Hence, it is possible that currently the decree may serve to reduce competition in the distribution of groceries by excluding the four companies.[93] Recent efforts by the meat packers to revise the decree have been unsuccessful. A word of caution: this discussion is not premised on the conclusion that this decree should be changed. It is intended solely to demonstrate the need for later analyses of market situations to consider whether decrees of long standing should be revised.

Judicial supervision over the operations of a decree has assumed increased importance in recent years. Two striking examples call for such supervision that they border on rate regulation. These are the decrees in the *Hartford-Empire*[94] and *ASCAP* (American Society of Composers, Authors and Publishers[95]) cases. The *Hartford-Empire* decree provided for compulsory licensing of patents and compulsory leasing and sale of machines at reasonable rates and prices. Forms of leases, sales, and licenses, as well as rates and prices had to be judicially approved; existing agreements had to be rewritten and credit arrangements reformulated—all under court supervision. The Hartford licensees formed a committee to represent them in the procedure. The Antitrust Division had to participate in the entire process.

The *ASCAP* decree provided for supervision of the rates charged to users for royalties on the works of members of ASCAP and of the formulas for distributing these royalties to the members.[96] The decree was based on the premise that ASCAP is a necessary restraint of trade. On the one hand, the individual member has no practical way to police the users of his works and to collect royalties. On the other hand, without some supervision ASCAP could extract unreasonable royalties from users since it covers the bulk of the artistic works which might be employed.

ASCAP and the Department of Justice have had a number of trips back to the courts to readjust royalties, the organization of ASCAP, and the distribution of its proceeds. Perhaps because of the great administrative burden of these decrees, perhaps because it feels that the decrees call for regulation rather than the restoration of competition, the Antitrust Division has avoided such supervisory decrees since these two were formulated.[97]

There is an extensive area of judicial supervision on a less detailed basis than in the *Hartford-Empire* and *ASCAP* cases. A substantial number of decrees call for compulsory patent licenses at reasonable royalties. Similarly, the *United Shoe Machinery*[98] decree calls for the sale of machines at reasonable prices. All of these decrees provide that if the negotiation of a sale or a licensing agreement is not successful, either party may petition the court to set the reasonable price or rate.

With the growing complexity of industrial operations and of the antitrust remedies, it seems likely that the trend toward increased judicial supervision over the operation of decrees will continue. The burden imposed by such supervision seems so substantial that the courts will require appropriate aids. The place of the administrative agencies in the process seems to require a re-evaluation.[99]

## The Judge's Burden

The federal district judge's task in antitrust and related fields is singularly difficult.[100] He must try cases of considerable economic complexity within the framework of judicial processes which were developed for much simpler trials.[101] He has to cope with involved economic problems[102] and is expected to exercise unusual power which may have profound far-reaching effects. He must do all this at the lonely summit, with no help from staff or colleagues.

In the typical antitrust case, the judge must contend simultaneously with complex issues of fact and of law. He must weigh the evidence and relate it to the hypotheses urged on him by the adversaries. He must follow economic analysis even in his interpretations of the antitrust law.

These imposing legal-economic tasks are made doubly difficult by the clumsy methods for ferreting out the germane issues and facts. As Judge E. Barrett Prettyman stated so forcefully,[103] our trial procedures are not adapted to complicated cases. They were constructed to cope with legal problems which can be solved by oral testimony and quick decisions. The technical rules and procedural requirements compel the judge to engage in a type of intellectual juggling—moving between technical questions regarding the admissibility of evidence and the consideration, step by step, of what the evidence means. Technical information and interpretations are offered by experts and others with conflicting views. "The tribunal does the best it can to decipher the truth from the resultant welter. Nothing could be sillier."[104]

The guidance for running such trials is obscure since the procedures are fitted for simpler, nontechnical issues. Judge Gregory F. Noonan once complained, "there appear to be no accepted standards or practices for gathering or presenting evidence of an economic nature."[105] Further, "efforts to prove complex economic facts by conventional rules governing the admissibility of evidence have proved tedious and burdensome, resulting in long drawn-out trials."[106]

After the trial itself, the physical burden of wading through the massive amounts of material in the record of a Big Case is formidable. Analyzing, assembling, and reviewing the disorganized mass, discarding extraneous detail and organizing the bits and pieces into a coherent factual review call for herculean efforts.

The size of the trials, in many cases, merits the appellation "Big Case."[107] The *Sugar Institute*[108] trial took one year. Following the trial, the judge spent fourteen months writing a 178 page opinion and 50 pages of findings of fact.[109] The trial against the Aluminum Company of America took two years and two months. The judge had to consider 58,000 pages of testimony coming from 153 witnesses. Additionally, he had to review 15,000 pages of documentary evidence.

The trial in *Ferguson* v. *Ford*[110] produced 70,000 pages of records and 45,000 exhibits. There were more than 700,000 pages of documents.[111] The *A & P* record covered 45,000 pages of testimony and 7,000 exhibits. The *National Lead* case[112] involved 1,400 exhibits.[113]

In the *United Shoe Machinery* case,[114] the government submitted an imposing trial brief before the trial: this covered 634 pages for the summary of facts; 87 pages for the law of the case; and 6,224 pages of excerpts from documentary evidence.[115] In the *Investment Bankers* case,[116] the government itself introduced 10,640 documents. Judge Harold Medina was moved to say that, "unless some way be found to confine within reasonable bounds the material to be read and studied by the Court, the determination of the issues by the ordinary process of absorption and ratiocination will be a physical impossibility."[117]

The size of the judge's task is so great that in some Big Cases he must review as much economic data as would be covered in a respectable economic study of an industry. He must review this material and develop his conclusions on his own. He does not enjoy the advantage afforded to the economist in discussing his ideas with colleagues, as well as businessmen, during the course of his study. Further, it is the rare jurist who has had any experience with economic analysis before he faces the problems of such a case.[118]

In the course of his review, the judge must weigh the complicated evidence and test the proffered hypotheses in order to decide whether the violation has occurred. If he should find a violation, he must undertake the heavy task of formulating a decree. If he should hold separate hearings concerning the order, he must consider further evidence and arguments regarding the various alternatives. In some instances, as in the *Hartford-Empire* case,[119] he may later be faced with a number of new problems in his supervision of the application of his decree.

The import of this tremendous burden which is piled on a judge's back in the trial of these cases has been largely ignored.[120] It induces many judges to avoid Big Cases whenever possible.[121] The issue involves much more than the personal comfort of the federal judiciary. It concerns the efficacy of antitrust policies.

As both industry and economic analysis take on additional complexity, the task of determining economic conditions and trends becomes increasingly difficult. Some recent developments have made antitrust law more intricate. While there have been some moves toward simplification,[122] some statutory and judicial development has made interpretation more involved. For example, the doctrine of "quantitative substantiality" seemed to ease the burden of judging the effects of exclusive dealing contracts with a large number of customers since economic interpretation was no longer needed if the arrangement affects a substantial amount of trade. However, the recent *Tampa Electric* case[123] seems to open the door to economic analysis when a large buyer enters into an exclusive arrangement to purchase material which he uses rather than resells. Similarly, the new anti-merger statute and recent interpretations of what is the relevant market (covered in Chapter 8) have introduced more complicated types of analysis.

As the law grows more complex—a trend which seems inevitable—the judicial task grows heavier.[124] As more and more economic interpretation is injected into antitrust consideration, the judge's analytical burdens become more burdensome.[125] On the one hand, progress in the application of economic analysis—such as the definition of the relevant market, reviewed in Chapter 8; the more refined indicators of competition, discussed in Chapter 7; and statistical evidence, covered in Chapter 9—will place greater strains on judicial capacity. On the other hand, if no means are developed for practical assistance to the courts, there will be substantial limits on the possibilities of practical applications of economic analysis in antitrust enforcement.[126]

Another element in the judicial burden raises profound implications for public policy. Because of the dependence on litigation for antitrust administration, affirmative remedies for monopolistic situations depend on individual judges. Their decisions can serve to reorganize the structure of companies or change basic industrial practices with serious effects on markets, competitors, owners, and employees. Yet a judge is required to make these significant decisions unaided.

The unusual power given to judges in this field has a marked effect on their attitudes. Because of their sense of responsibility, they hesitate to provide drastic remedies.[127] This tendency was clearly stated by Judge Wyzanski in discussing his decision to refuse a government request that he break up a company. He stated that:

> In the antitrust field the courts have been accorded, by common consent, an authority they have in no other branch of enacted law. . . . They would not have been given, or allowed to keep, such authority in the antitrust field, and they would not so freely have altered from time to time the interpretation of the substantive provisions, if courts were in the habit of proceeding with the surgical ruthlessness that might commend itself to those seeking absolute assurance that there will be workable competition, and to those aiming at immediate realization of the social, political, and economic advantages of dispersal of power.[128]

The existence of this power has not raised many questions because judges hesitate to exercise[129] it unless they can be convinced beyond any doubts.[130] As a result, we may not have given our antitrust policies an affirmative chance to be fully effective.[131]

A basic policy issue, therefore, is: How serious are we about our competitive policies? If we satisfy our national goals by broad statements, the restraining influence of the judicial responsibility is appropriate. On the other hand, if we do want to carry out our enunciated policies effectively, we must seriously explore methods to lighten the judge's load.

The judicial problem has a serious influence on administrative decisions. Court decisions and decrees guide the Antitrust Division in its selection of cases. If the division feels that no judge will consider an order which would inject competition, it will not, and it should not, file a complaint. Furthermore, judicial action provides the setting for the negotiation of consent decrees. A defendant will not agree to a strong consent decree if he believes that a litigated order will be much easier. He may accept a negotiated decree which may be somewhat tougher than he believes a court would prescribe, but there are limits to how far he will go. Hence, the burdens on the judiciary have far-flung effects.

## *Consent Decrees and Orders*

The consent procedures[132] constitute a major element in the administration of the antitrust laws. Like other regulatory functions, antitrust depends heavily on negotiation. Such procedures take the form of consent decrees in the Antitrust Division and of consent orders and stipulations in the Federal Trade Commission. On occasion, the division has secured voluntary compliance through informal discussion.[133]

Until recently the F.T.C. followed a stipulation procedure which was less formal and not as binding as an order. In this program, a Commission counsel would review the practice which it found objectionable with the potential respondent. If an agreement was reached, a stipulation was executed whereby the respondent agreed to discontinue specified practices.[134] While the stipulation lacked the legal force of a formal order, the F.T.C. seemed to believe it to be fairly effective within the limited area in which it was used. This practice was abandoned recently. The more formal consent procedure is required currently.[135]

It is difficult to evaluate these procedures. They represent the bulk of antitrust activity. While they are strongly influenced by the litigation process, they are not strictly bound by judicial precedent. Because of their nature, they do not provide the same public opportunity for evaluation as the open hearings of litigation.

Consent decrees and orders are used in the majority of antitrust proceedings. There are indications that they have been used somewhat more frequently in recent years.[136] From 1954 to 1958 inclusive, 88 per cent of the successful equity proceedings of the Antitrust Division ended in consent decrees.[137] During the same period, 71 per cent of the orders issued by the Federal Trade Commission were negotiated; to this might be added another 4 per cent to cover orders that were entered without an active defense.[138]

The consent procedure calls for private negotiations without a public record of the evidence and arguments of either the prosecution or the defense and without the supervision of a judge or trial examiner.[139] In the past, some consent decrees were worked out after a public complaint had been filed with the court or the Federal Trade Commission. Other negotiations preceded the filing of a complaint.

After negotiations, a public record is made. Until recently, the Department of Justice and the defendant would file the consent decree with the appropriate court with a short explanatory statement after they had concluded their negotiations; similarly, the Counsel Supporting the Complaint and the respondent would file it with the F.T.C. hearing examiner. In theory, either the judge or the examiner could reject the decree. On occasion the judge or examiner would raise some questions with the adversaries before accepting the decree. However, the usual procedure was to accept the filing simply because both sides had agreed to it.[140]

There has been a substantial difference between the practices of the Department of Justice and the Federal Trade Commission in the treatment of consent orders. There are persuasive indications that a high proportion of the consent decrees were negotiated by the department before the complaint was filed. Between 1935 and 1945 approximately 75 per cent of the consent decrees were entered by the court within three days after the complaint was filed.[141] Considering the time required for the negotiation of such decrees, it seems fair to presume that they were agreed on before the complaint was finally drafted.[142] In contrast, the evidence concerning past procedures of the Federal Trade Commission indicates that complaints were usually filed with the Commission before negotiations for a consent order were instituted.[143]

Recently, both organizations announced rather drastic changes in their consent procedures. The Department of Justice will file a prospective consent decree with the court thirty days before it is finally submitted,[144] or make it available to interested persons in order to permit other parties to offer suggestions. The Attorney General may permit exceptions to this policy.[145] In contrast, the new procedure of the Federal Trade Commission calls for the filing of consent orders before any publicity is given to the proceeding. The order must be filed with the F.T.C. within thirty days after the party in question is informed of the opportunity to negotiate, unless the time is extended. If no agreement is consummated in time, a public complaint is filed. There can be no negotiation after a complaint is issued.[146]

The two agencies apparently have "reversed their fields." The Department of Justice, which apparently negotiated many final consent orders even before there was any public notice of a proceeding, will now give the proposed order some publicity before finally agreeing to it. The Federal Trade Commission, which had negotiated orders after a complaint was made public, will now negotiate only before there is any public notice of a proceeding. No reasons for these shifts have been made public.

When a decree is negotiated before a complaint is filed, it seems only reasonable to infer that the complaint will be confined to practices that are covered in the decree.[147] No open record exists to indicate the setting for the negotiation. There is no public basis for evaluating the nature of the competitive problem that concerned the government before starting the proceeding.

The consent proceedings raise some interesting questions regarding administrative policy. On balance, it is difficult to evaluate their place in antitrust enforcement. On the one hand, the practical administrative problem indicates a substantial need for them. On the other hand, the procedures make it extremely difficult to evaluate the effectiveness and the fairness of the antitrust program.

Administratively, the consent procedures seem to be highly desirable.[148] Without them, the range of activity of both the Federal Trade Commission and the Antitrust Division of the Department of Justice would be reduced substantially. Judge Hansen, the former Assistant Attorney General in charge of the Antitrust Division, said that during one period the average litigated case took 66.2 months while the average consent settlements took only 29.7 months. As he pointed out, the substantial differences in elapsed time would be accompanied by at least a comparable savings in man power and effort.[149] While no studies have been published, it would seem possible that the financial savings would be proportionately large.

In theory, consent procedures should enable the antitrust agencies to develop more meaningful orders than those produced through contests.[150] Serious shirt-sleeve discussions permit a better organized, more affirmative approach to sensible solutions than the cumbersome courtroom procedures with their formalities and technical maneuvers.[151]

A shortcoming of these informal negotiations is that they do not always provide opportunities to consider the effects of a decree on third parties.[152] This would appear to be the reason for the recent change in the procedure of the Antitrust Division. While litigation does not always uncover the effects of an order on third parties, public proceedings do offer more opportunities for obtaining such information than private discussions.[153] With adequate information regarding the effects of a contemplated decree from competitors, distributors, users, and suppliers, it should be possible to formulate more significant orders.

The consent procedures increase the difficulty of evaluating the effectiveness of the antitrust program.[154] Because of the ease in writing consent orders and decrees, they could encourage a type of numbers game.[155] Over the years, the most important factors used to judge the work of the Antitrust Division or the Federal Trade Commission have been the number of cases they have instituted and the number of their wins.[156] Obviously, the consent procedure enables an administrator to exhibit a highly successful statistical record, even if the program has little effect on competition. Consent procedures invite an administrator to build a good record by filing cases against small companies in unimportant industries.[157] Such an opportunity is available also to the individual lawyers working for an agency.

There is no firm basis for an objective evaluation of either the consent procedures or their results. Little progress appears to have been made by either the Congress or the Executive in reviewing the effectiveness of antitrust operations, including the consent orders.[158] In this, as in other areas of government regulation, full reliance seems to have been placed on judicial case review rather than on broad policy review. Hence, the consent procedures seem to be subject to no general scrutiny outside of the agencies.

Negotiated decrees have been sharply criticized on two counts. On the one hand, it has been suggested that the consent procedures are not always fair because the government uses undue leverage in pressuring the defendant.[159] Therefore, many defendants are forced to agree to a number of conditions which may be overly harsh. Conversely, some consent orders have been criticized because they have not been strong enough,[160] or because they have not been effective. Some congressional committees have contended that litigated decrees would have provided more drastic solutions than certain negotiated orders.

A general or a case-by-case evaluation of the relative merits of consent and contested orders would be difficult. Such an evaluation would have to cover the advantages to the defendant in avoiding litigation. These gains, moreover, must be subjected to a two-pronged analysis: first, they give the defendant some advantages; second, these same advantages strengthen the government's strong bargaining position.

A defendant obtains a number of benefits from a consent decree or order.[161] First—and this applies mainly to small companies—negotiation avoids the high cost of a defense.[162] Any antitrust litigation entails substantial legal fees. The cost of gathering information and developing the case runs high even before the hearing or the trial. Costs are substantial, also, because much of the data must be produced by the company's own staff or by outside consultants. In addition, company officers, as well as customers and suppliers, may have to spend days at hearings.[163]

Another disadvantage in litigation may be the effect of the publicity in the general or trade press. Many businessmen are concerned lest certain customers or suppliers should resent the practices under review. Many fear the use which competitors will make of the publicity.

Finally, a most important pressure to accept consent decrees is created by the Clayton Act provision that enables injured parties to sue for three times the amount of damages they suffered because of the violation.[164] A litigated court decree is treated as prima facie evidence of the antitrust violation in subsequent damage suits. A consent decree does not constitute such evidence.[165] While the contested orders of the Federal Trade Commission cannot be used to the same advantage, public hearings can supply potential plaintiffs with substantial leads to useful evidence.[166]

Here then is the dilemma: on the one hand, consent procedures seem desirable for effective and efficient enforcement of the antitrust laws; on the other, they can lead to injustice and can induce an agency to overlook important problems while it builds a paper record of accomplishment.[167] Though such a record can be built through litigation, the consent process permits an even better showing with a limited budget. Further, the negotiation method can provide remedies which are too harsh or too lenient, and make it quite difficult for outsiders to evaluate the proceedings.

To pose this problem is not to deny that there are many capable, fair-minded prosecutors in the agencies. Rather, the issue is what can be done to assist these men and to provide more significant policy evaluations of the operations of our antitrust agencies. It should be observed, in all fairness, that the problem of evaluating negotiated proceedings extends throughout the entire range of regulation.[168] Antitrust is only one of the areas which seems to require broader policy review than can be provided by a judiciary, whose review is limited to the individual case.

## *The Issues*

Given a completely free choice, litigation would hardly be deemed an efficient tool for the enforcement of competitive policies. Aside from its limited purview, it is not a procedure which is tailored to an objective analysis of regulatory problems.[169]

Because litigation must rest on the narrow basis of antitrust law, it cannot provide a coordinated approach to other government activities. It must, by definition, be narrowly limited to the confines of the court's jurisdiction. It cannot, for example, encompass programs to change the government's purchasing methods or a protective tariff in order to induce more competition.

Since a judge is usually concerned with one competitor at one time, his scope is limited. He must temper the decree lest the defendant be placed at an unfair disadvantage in its competition with its rivals. This deficiency could be reduced by joining all the competitors in one suit.[170] However, such a practice would interfere with the agencies' incentive to file many suits in order to impress Congress. It would, in many instances, make the proceedings even more cumbersome than they are today.

Litigation procedures involve many features which interfere with impartial analysis.[171] They depend greatly on the "gamesmanship" of the counsel for each side. They are hemmed in by the four corners of the courtroom. Although they are regulated by the canons of relevance and judicial impartiality, they do not allow for independent inquiry.

Much antitrust litigation places an unfair and unrealistic burden on the judge's shoulders. He is asked to take on responsibilities for which he has no adequate preparation—either by way of his own background or by way of impartial analytical aids. His powers in antitrust actions are so extensive that it is unreasonable to expect him to use all of them. He has little chance to become deeply convinced that a far-reaching structural change in a company is needed in order to cure a monopolistic situation. Even if he should have such a conviction, he can affect only one competitor, and he may question the fairness or desirability of such a step.

In brief, the basic administrative patterns of enforcement set substantial limits on the effectiveness of antitrust. Litigation fails to meet the needs for either flexibility, analysis, or realistic cures. The participants in litigation are necessarily hemmed in by institutional pitfalls.

What, then, can be done? Two courses suggest themselves: first, to seek administrative-legislative procedures which avoid the confines of litigation; and second, to improve litigation procedures in order to better the application of economic analysis.

Improvements in administrative procedures affect the broader issues of the regulatory process as well as specific problems in antitrust. They pose such questions as how to relate the work of the two major agencies to each other and to the many others; how to relate executive and independent commission functions; how to relate antitrust enforcement to other government activities.

Improvements in litigation—a more immediate task—call for developing methods for utilizing economic analysis more effectively. They require several steps: aiding the judges with their heavy burdens; improving the application of economic inquiry through the stages of litigation and in administration generally; and improving economic analysis so that it can make a more satisfactory contribution. They call for objective consideration of the advantages of specialized panels of judges, or even specialized courts.[172]

Such effort would be worth while. Litigation is of such importance under our system that it will continue to be a key element in the administration of national policies regarding competition. Future improvement will depend on the development of more effective applications of economic analysis, making use of the advantages that can be derived from the trial process and retaining the attributes that have engendered public respect for the courts and the law. To this end we turn to the uses of economic analysis in legal antitrust proceedings.

# 6 / *Economic Analysis in Legal Proceedings**

THERE IS A TREMENDOUS NEED to improve the uses of economics and related disciplines in antitrust proceedings.[1] Though our competitive policies stem from a blend of economic, social, and political objectives, a major element in their administration is the solution of economic problems. Economic inquiry is a key factor in both litigation and negotiation.[2]

In this activity, economic inquiry uses a number of research techniques. They include such procedures as: analysis of markets, statistics, surveys of consumer attitudes, accounting, cost accounting, and industry studies. They require the skills of economists, statisticians, accountants, cost accountants, and occasionally sociologists and psychologists.[3] In antitrust work the economist serves as the general coordinator of the research methods applied by the others, though some economists do apply the other disciplines, notably statistics, themselves. Therefore, the functions of economic analysis cover the applications of the other techniques.

Progress is needed on three fronts. First, more effective means must be developed for applying current methods of economic analysis. Second, tools of economic analysis which are more appropriate to antitrust administration must be forged. Third, there is a need for a substantial number of economists who can apply these tools. These requirements are intimately linked. If economists are employed widely in antitrust administration, they will help to improve the administrative mechanism and to develop analytical tools which the lawyers can employ. At the same time, the improved opportunities will attract able young economists into the field.

A review of the problems of applying economic analysis in legal proceedings calls for consideration of two functions: prelitigation pro-

* Footnotes for Chapter 6 begin on page 409.

cedures; and the process of litigation and negotiation. Finally, such a review must deal with the touchstone for improvement: the relations between the legal and economic disciplines. The many opportunities for fruitful application of economic inquiry are limited by the mutual lack of understanding of the two disciplines.

It must be emphasized that there is a need for evolutionary improvement, not revolutionary change. Economists are currently employed by the agencies, the Executive Offices, and the congressional committees concerned. Advances have been made in applying economic inquiry in antitrust. However, there has not been sufficient progress to meet the needs. Nor will there be unless the task is taken seriously.

## *Prelitigation Procedures*

The administrative agencies carry out some of their most important functions before they decide to prosecute. They must investigate complaints[4] sent in by the public. They must consider whether a situation warrants prosecution; what can be accomplished by a proceeding; whether an informal disposition will take care of the problem; and whether the problem can be cured through consent procedures.

### *Investigation and Evaluation*

Currently, the agencies are not financed or organized to carry on these functions properly.[5] They are not equipped to carry on their own independent investigations of competitive conditions in important markets.[6] They do attempt such analysis regarding mergers. However, they depend on complaints from interested parties for the bulk of their work.[7] While such complaints are useful, they are not apt to uncover all of the important areas that require attention.[8]

Even the investigation of complaints calls for economic analysis.[9] Many protests merely reflect a competitive pinch which is felt by the complainant; some may cover damage to a group of competitors; others reflect injury to market competition. Field inquiry is needed to determine the economic import of these complaints.

An even more important use of economic inquiry would be a continuing review of important markets.[10] Such a review would spot problem areas and indicate which markets deserve close attention.[11] Without knowledge of sensitive points in the economy, a great deal of serious effort can be devoted to unimportant tasks while substantial monopolistic forces are overlooked.[12] This pinpointing would permit more effective use of the limited budgets, man power, and talent of the agencies. If prosecution could be focused on the strategic areas in the industrial structure, the antitrust program would be much more effective.[13] At the same time, such a program would enable the agencies to show Congress that their campaigns have greater meaning even though they might engage in fewer prosecutions.

Such pinpointing could improve the cumulative effect of enforcement and avoid the current discrimination in antitrust prosecution. Without adequate analysis of a market, an agency can make the mistake of prosecuting a troublesome seller who has injected strong competitive influences in a market. It can place one company in an unfortunate position vis-à-vis its rivals, and give the others an unfair competitive advantage.[14] In extreme cases, an ill-advised prosecution can reduce market competition. On the other hand, a market evaluation could uncover the key to more active market rivalry. It might call for prosecution of several companies at one time.[15] It might require a campaign against powerful suppliers of parts or customers rather than against the producers of the finished article.

Such market analysis could indicate what are the strategic factors in the competitive picture, as opposed to the surface manifestations of monopolistic forces. For example, it might be found that price discrimination is a symptom of an underlying monopolistic position of a seller or a buyer. Then, instead of striking blindly at the price discrimination, the prosecution might be leveled at such elements as a patent position, the power of one or two dominant enterprises, or a tacit price agreement. On the other hand, market study might indicate that it would be desirable to ignore the price discrimination because it is an effective competitive force.[16]

### *Decision to Prosecute*

The decision to prosecute is a basic function of legal administration. Such decisions turn on several practical factors: How clear is the evidence of a violation? What would be the theory of the case? Can a meaningful remedy be devised? How much time and effort would the proceeding require if it goes to trial? What are the chances of a consent decree? How important is the problem when compared with others on the docket—does it involve an important economic influence or a significant legal issue?

The bulk of these evaluations calls for some economic inquiry together with legal analysis.[17] Considerations of the importance of the problem, of the possibilities of developing effective remedies,[18] of the evidentiary burdens, and of the theory of the case call for economic inquiry. On occasion, these preparatory studies require extended work in both economics and law. For example, before drafting the complaint against the Imperial Chemicals Industry,[19] the government secured 20,000 documents from the company's files.[20] In its review, the government checked over 12,000 patents.[21] In proceeding against the United Shoe Machinery Corporation,[22] the Department of Justice had to conduct a legal-economic study of several hundred thousand papers in the files of the company.[23]

The selection of cases and the development of the theory of the prosecution are strategic elements in the development of antitrust law. If an agency believes that a statute has no application to a specific type of situation, the courts have no opportunity to rule on the question.[24]

The decision to prosecute calls for a judicial attitude.[25] It requires judgments about fairness, significance, and policy. At that stage of a proceeding the prosecutor can use the same type of analytical help that a judge requires later in making a decision and formulating a decree.

## *Litigation*

Economic inquiry can be useful at every stage of the trial procedures described in the previous chapter: defining the issues,[26] collecting the data, presenting the evidence, developing the arguments,[27] and assisting in the judicial decisions.[28] Since most antitrust litigation depends on circumstantial evidence, it turns on the formulation and testing of economic hypotheses, as demonstrated in Chapter 5. Hence, the skills of the economist can be usefully employed by the trial attorneys and the judge throughout all the phases of a case—from complaint to decree.

*Trial Procedures*

The definitions of the issues in most antitrust cases are both economic and legal in content.[29] The prosecution and the defense must contend with economic questions when they are engaged in clarifying the issues before the trial. The same types of problems must be handled when an adversary strives to confuse the issues.

The collection and presentation of evidence frequently call for extended economic inquiry. The economist can suggest the types of data that would be useful to prove the points which will be stressed. Similarly, he can spot those points that provide inadequate support for an argument as well as those which cannot be supported by persuasive evidence. Together with statisticians and other technicians, he can define and administer field surveys and other tabulations. Frequently, he can locate useful data in governmental and other studies or in a company's operating records.

The skilled economist should provide valuable guides to more effective administration in litigation. With a well-defined set of issues and clearly delineated evidence, the trial of complex problems can be shortened and simplified.[30] Many trial records reflect general excursions through masses of evidence that treat with tangential information.[31] In the process, essential elements are lost, and the trial is unnecessarily long.[32]

Many issues in antitrust litigation are primarily economic. For example, if an issue concerns the defendant's share of a market, the definition of the relevant market can be a strategic point. How then, can one side prove that the market is small; how can the other prove it is large? As Chapter 8 indicates, many characteristics affect these definitions. The determination of what are the important features and how they can be established calls for the skills of the economist. No single factor can describe a market adequately. On the other hand, it would be impractical to apply all of the criteria which have been used. Hence, the task for economic inquiry is to select the market dimensions that are pertinent to the case at bar and to determine which can best be covered by available data.

A principal issue in many cases is whether competition has been lessened or whether it is threatened. Again, the economist can help in the selection of the pertinent indicators of competition, which are reviewed in Chapter 7, and in the development of data and analysis that will help the argument.

Some of the most difficult problems in developing evidence in antitrust are statistical. What data are readily available? How should they be presented? Should a statistical sample be used or a complete census? For example, should a cost study cover all operations in all the warehouses of a company for a twelve-month period, or will it be sufficient to study one "typical" warehouse for one month? As Chapter 9, "Statistical Evidence," shows, the treatment of such evidence can determine whether a case is won or lost.

### *Formulation of Decrees*

Although economic inquiry can help to frame effective remedies in antitrust,[33] it has not been widely employed in this task.[34] By and large, the economists' participation in antitrust litigation has been confined to questions of violation. Decrees have been drafted by lawyers and judges without the assistance of the economist. However, the formulation of a decree is a significant exercise in economic analysis.[35] If the order fails to inject competition into a market, the essential purpose of the proceeding is lost.[36] In fact, unless it fits the needs of a market situation, a decree can hinder rather than encourage competition.

The formulation of effective remedies requires a substantial body of empirical data concerning the influence of various types of decrees. Meaningful predictions about the probable effects of the alternative orders under consideration must take cognizance of the influences of similar orders in analogous situations. General economic theory may be better than nothing as a help in drafting a decree. By itself, however, theory cannot meet the needs. Field analysis of the economic effects of previous decrees is a prerequisite for the formulation of significant antitrust orders.

Economic theory may explain how a market operates, but it does not provide a firm basis for determining how to make a market more competitive.[37] Theory, and common sense, tell us that a price agreement will reduce competition and that a market will probably be more competitive if the influence of the agreement is eliminated, but neither theory nor common sense tells us how to produce this result. Theory can supply the questions which should be researched, rather than the answers. It teaches that markets tend to be less competitive with fewer competitors. But, it cannot tell how many competitors are required for effective competition in a given market. That question calls for empirical investigation—comparisons with markets with similar structural characteristics in buying, manufacturing, selling, and distributing.

There is no operational theory for judging the effects of a merger. Nevertheless, theory can guide field analysis which will develop clues regarding the effects of mergers under various types of market situations as well as effective remedies for acquisitions which lessen competition. In this respect economic analysis is comparable to any other discipline. It helps to formulate the issues and to determine the data needed for solution. It does not provide simple, out-of-pocket answers.

A firm analytical basis for decrees is needed in the consent procedures as well as in litigation. Both sides require reasonable predictions of the effects of proposed orders. Without such evaluations their bargaining must be in the dark. The defendant might accept a decree which injures his competitive position by unnecessary restrictions. On the other hand, the government might settle for decree provisions that have little substantive content. For example, there is compelling evidence that a number of consent decrees containing provisions for compulsory patent licenses have been ineffective because the defendants have received no requests for such licenses.[38] In the final analysis, each side must decide whether to accept the most favorable order it can negotiate or to go to trial.

### *Enforcement and Supervision of Decrees*

After a decree has been issued, economic inquiry can be a powerful tool in enforcement. Clues to possible violations can be obtained through studies of market conditions. Searching questions can give substantial meaning to compliance reports. For example, reports covering price movements, sales volume, innovations, investment, new entrants to the market, and changes in distributive channels might produce more meaningful clues than general statements that a contract was canceled or that salesmen were instructed to discontinue a practice.

Similarly, when an order calls for judicial supervision—as in the *Hartford-Empire*[39] and *ASCAP*[40] cases and in reasonable royalty decrees—judges, administrative agencies, and defendants need analytical aids. Economic studies can provide some guides for judging the reasonableness of royalties and prices under such decrees. Without such analysis, judges are no better equipped for supervising the operation of a decree than in formulating it.

Another opportunity to apply economic analysis would be in the consideration of possible changes in existing decrees. Petitions to change a decree involve the same types of problems that are encountered in formulating the original order.

### *Treble-Damage Suits*

The measurement of damages in private antitrust suits creates another need for economic inquiry.[41] It will be remembered that the Clayton Act enables anyone who is injured by an antitrust violation to recover three times the amount of damages he suffered.[42] Treble-damage suits are similar to equity prosecutions except that a previous antitrust decree serves as prima facie evidence of the violation[43] and that the plaintiff must prove the amount of his damages.[44]

Establishing damages in such a case can be quite difficult.[45] In essence, the plaintiff must provide a reasonable[46] measurement of the effects of the violation on his business, comparing his operations with what his performance would have been in the absence of the violation. Such reconstruction calls for an "as if" inquiry.[47] Account must be taken of what would have occurred if "normal" market factors had been at work. The reconstruction[48] may cover such factors as market demand and supply, the influence of the specific interference on costs, the plaintiff's profit experience before the violation occurred, changes in profits which could reasonably have been expected because of subsequent capital and other improvements, profits of similar companies which were not affected by the violation, and changes in property values. The reconstruction might take account of such factors as changes in the economic conditions of the affected industry, changes in wages and prices, fluctuations in consumer demand, financial conditions affecting the availability of capital and credit, and analyses of cost. All of these elements are imbedded in the fabric of economic analysis. They can be researched and woven into the inquiry. They affect both the reconstruction of profits and the tests of its reasonableness.

An interesting problem arises when the plaintiff measures his damages by the excessive prices charged by the defendant. A common defense has been that the plaintiff recouped the overcharge by passing it on to his customers. This defense has been successful in all cases brought by each plaintiff who purchased for resale. There was one exception: in a recent proceeding against the United Shoe Machinery Corporation by a shoe manufacturer, the defense of "passing on" was rejected.[49] However, the cases have not dealt with the theory that the higher resale prices affected his volume adversely, with a reduction in profits.[50]

As more experience is developed in such cases, it seems likely that measurements of damages will become more refined. With such refinements, the need for such economic analysis will probably increase. In view of the recent increase[51] in the number of treble-damage suits this problem will acquire increased importance.

## *The Judge's Economist*

Means must be found to lighten the heavy burden borne by the individual judge in antitrust trials.[52] His duties call for exacting economic analysis—guiding the clarification of issues, sifting involved circumstantial evidence, relating it to the hypotheses advanced by each party, interpreting antitrust precedent, and formulating remedies. He requires help on many fronts.[53]

It will not be easy to develop practical means of assistance within the bounds of the judicial process.[54] Unfortunately, the most obvious solution for the problem is unsatisfactory. At first glance, a direct cure would be the employment of an economist to assist the judge.[55] Judge Wyzanski followed this procedure in the *United Shoe Machinery* case when he appointed Professor Carl Kaysen of the Harvard Economics Department as his "law clerk."[56]

While this step alleviates the judge's burden, it conflicts with the judicial tradition discussed above.[57] It provides neither adversary with an opportunity to present evidence and arguments to counter the advice which is given to the judge in private. Therefore, such a procedure might reduce respect for the judicial process and extend the proceedings beyond practical limits. For if each side knows that a judge will hear such ex parte advice, lawyers will feel compelled to present every facet of a market situation instead of covering only as much as they feel is needed to counter the presentation of their opponents.

Indeed, Judge Wyzanski himself seemed to be quite concerned about this point. About the time he had the *United Shoe Machinery* case under consideration, he took occasion in a lecture[58] to raise basic questions regarding the judicial use of the results of independent legal and economic research which are not available to the parties in open court.

The need for judicial assistance has become so pressing that the Judicial Conference of the United States has made several studies concerning it.[59] Several committees have proposed the appointment of an impartial, expert witness[60] who would be acceptable to each side as well as to the judge. It was suggested that such a witness would review the material supplied by both sides and conduct some studies himself.[61] He would testify on his findings in open court, being subject to cross-examination by each of the adversaries. Additionally, each of the adversaries would have a full opportunity to introduce evidence and arguments in opposition to or in support of the findings of the expert witness.

Another suggestion was the appointment of one or more experts to serve as masters-in-chancery.[62] Under this plan the master would hold hearings, following ordinary rules of procedure, in order to investigate specific issues of fact.[63] He would provide the court with reports, findings of facts, and recommendations.[64] These would be subject to examination and testing by both parties. In this way the judge would be relieved of a substantial part of the task of conducting long trial proceedings, and would have the benefit of the opinion of the "impartial experts."[65] None of these proposals has been put to test to determine its practicability.[66]

As Chapter 3 indicated, this problem was considered by the Congress as long ago as 1914, when it passed the Federal Trade Commission Act.[67] Section 7 of the act provides "that in any suit in equity brought by or under the direction of the Attorney General, as provided in the antitrust acts, the court may, upon the conclusion of the testimony therein, if it shall be then of the opinion that the complainant is entitled to relief, refer said suit to the Commission, as the master-in-chancery, to ascertain and report an appropriate form of the decree therein." After reviewing the report, the judge would make up his own mind and write the decree. The courts, however, have not seen fit to take advantage of this provision.[68] In fact, the committee of the Judicial Conference which considered the use of masters-in-chancery made no mention of this statute in its report.

The employment of economic experts to assist judges in antitrust proceedings has not met with universal approval.[69] The Attorney General's National Committee to Study the Antitrust Laws recommended against "an independent staff of economic experts" to assist courts in such trials.[70] Judge Yankwich in a commentary on the report of the Judicial Conference, discussed above, did not appear too sanguine about the use of economic experts because he feared that "economic theories" would be brought into the proceedings and that an economist might speculate about the "beneficial effect" of certain practices instead of confining his attention to the "restraint."[71]

The judicial burden in antitrust is a pressing problem. Until effective means are developed to improve the process of litigation, the practical implementation of these policies will be limited. The suggestions emanating from the judiciary are interesting. They reflect a problem which is as broad as the regulatory process itself. The antitrust question is a manifestation of an underlying issue affecting all government regulation—albeit a more dramatic one.

The current situation seems too serious to dismiss these suggested cures out of hand. They require concentrated consideration. They may or may not be sufficient.

A full solution to the problem calls for more than a program for supplying assistants to the judges. Effective consideration of these economic issues requires that all the parties involved in the litigation handle them with skill. A master-in-chancery may be of considerable help to a court. However, his analysis will be greatly influenced by the definition of the issues and the quality of the evidence presented to him. His contribution, as well as that of the judge and the impartial expert witness, will depend importantly on the understanding and preparation of the parties.

On the other hand, it seems reasonable to assume that superior understanding on the judicial level has a profound effect on the litigants. A judiciary which brings great legal skills to the courtroom will lift the level of legal craftsmanship of the lawyers who appear before it. Similarly a higher degree of economic sophistication on the bench would have an important bearing on the work of the bar—in the selection of cases, in defining the issues, in gathering and presenting evidence and arguments, and, finally, in dealing with the decree.

## *Relations Between Economists and Lawyers*

Further progress in the utilization of economic analysis will depend on an improvement in the mutual understanding of the legal and economics professions[72]—an understanding which requires that both groups recognize the hurdles that lie between them.[73] Recent years have witnessed significant progress in the application of economic analysis in the antitrust field,[74] but the requirements of public policy call for more substantial improvement.

Public policy will not be advanced by one-sided criticism of either profession.[75] Economists must accept the supremacy of the lawyers in antitrust enforcement.[76] They also have to understand the lawyers' predilection for working with familiar concepts,[77] some of which may not fit easily into the framework of economic inquiry. Above all, economists must realize that in order to be employed in antitrust, their tools of analysis must be operational—tools that fit the requirements of the legal system.[78] Economic inquiry will assume a substantial role in the regulatory process only through evolutionary steps since neither legal nor economic methods of analysis will be changed overnight.

On the other hand, lawyers must recognize the essential economic nature[79] of antitrust problems and appreciate the need to modify trial procedures in order to deal with economic problems effectively.[80] They must appreciate the economic aspects of both the evidentiary problems and the analysis of precedent in antitrust law—features that make it desirable to work with the economist as a professional equal[81] instead of considering him only as an expert witness[82] or a "handmaiden."[83]

There can be no doubt that a growing number of lawyers and economists are cooperating with each other effectively. Some economists have acquired a keen appreciation of antitrust law and of its processes. Some lawyers not only are accustomed to working with economists but display competence in economic analysis. They follow Justice Holmes' "The Path of the Law" in which "the man of the future is a man of statistics and the master of economics."[84] The issue here is not one of persons or personalities. Rather, it relates to the two disciplines. The number of "coordinators" is small. Progress in this professional cooperation is limited by the institutional structures of the courts and agencies and by the lack of interdisciplinary understanding.

The task of coordinating the work of economists and lawyers will not be easy. The problems will not be solved by lawyers' complaints that economists are too theoretical.[85] Lawyers must realize that many of the economic "facts" which they utilize in litigation and negotiation are founded on theoretical grounds.[86] For example, differences in costs are not "objective facts" but depend on theories about the behavior of costs. Cross-elasticity of demand, the market within which competition operates,[87] profits, and vertical integration are other facts that depend on theoretical premises.

Further, economists will not be stimulated to develop analytical methods which are useful to lawyers until they are called on for affirmative help. Nor will able young economists be attracted by this field until lawyers start to work with them as colleagues rather than as superiors.[88]

The employment of economists as expert witnesses[89] will not, in itself, produce the operational tools that are needed. Indeed, there are signs that some courts are not at all impressed by experts. To make progress, the lawyer will have to work with the economist in planning the general strategy of the case, in defining the issues, in collecting and presenting the data, and in formulating the arguments.[90] Many, possibly most, lawyers have yet to learn that some economists can make a greater contribution by analyzing evidence and helping with argument and strategy than by serving as expert witnesses.[91]

*Differences in the Disciplines*

To break through the barriers, both groups will have to appreciate the fundamental differences in their disciplines. Such understanding will require patience as well as the capacity to overcome the egocentric confidence that each profession has in its own methods. Progress will not be easy. The lawyer must realize that the conventional legal analysis may not be satisfactory for the solution of these current problems and that the "language of the market-place" must be employed in trying economic cases. On the other hand, the economist must accept the fact that antitrust problems are handled in a practical legal process which must encompass a variety of principles—social, political, ethical, and equitable, as well as economic.[92] Further, each profession must realize that the other has no simple clear rules to follow.[93]

There are several types of barriers to the mutual understanding of lawyers and economists. Differences in their activities have led to some disparity in the value judgments of many members of the two professions. Many terms which are used by both groups have different meanings. The frames of reference of the two disciplines are not similar, nor are their methods of settling disputes and testing predictions. The two professions do share one quality in common: both prefer to work within the boundaries of their own disciplines free of interference from others.

*Differences in Values*

The differences between the two disciplines have been accentuated by the disparity in the activities of many members of the two professions. Most economists who are concerned with antitrust are engaged in academic pursuits, while most lawyers interested in the field are engaged in administration—representing private defendants, private plaintiffs, and government agencies, or acting in judicial capacities. Academic economists tend to consider antitrust and related problems in terms of policy-making in the public interest, whereas practicing lawyers approach these regulatory issues as practical problems in the implementation of the law.[94]

This divergence in activities has led to apparent differences in the value judgments of some economists and some lawyers. Some academic economists tend to feel that many lawyers are not interested in the public welfare because of their professional work. They do not always recognize the lawyer's responsibility to plead his client's case in the gamesmanship of litigation and negotiation as forcefully as possible, regardless of what his own beliefs may be.[95] It is true that some practicing lawyers have attuned their beliefs to the narrow interests of their clients.[96] However, it must be remembered that their value judgments are shared by many business economists and consultants. Moreover, there is room for differences of opinion about what paths do lead to maximum public welfare.

This diversity, it should be noted, is not due entirely to characteristics of the disciplines. Many law teachers, and, indeed, many practicing lawyers share the attitudes of the academic economists. However, the disparities in the value judgments of many practitioners have helped to keep the two professions somewhat apart.

A more serious cleavage between the two disciplines rests on their basic premises.[97] Lawyers are largely preoccupied with issues of procedure in both practice and public policy. How should the laws be administered? What are the problems of litigation and interpretation, of drafting legislation, agreements, corporate charters, and debentures? Economists are concerned with the workings of the economic system, with the allocation of resources, with fiscal and monetary issues, and with the operations of the market.

Stemming from these diverse orientations are variations in the approach to public issues.[98] Lawyers tend to consider issues of government regulation as problems in the application of the current law. Many of them are concerned about the public policy aspects of legal procedures. Economists tend to analyze such regulatory issues in terms of economic effect. Lawyers, preferring to work with familiar concepts, are more comfortable with problems of ethics and fairness.[99] Economists, on the whole, are less concerned about intent and more interested in market results.[100]

### *Importance of Intent in Antitrust*

These differences find clearest expression in the consideration of intent in antitrust.[101] The legal problems concern the application of the antitrust laws. Currently, these laws involve issues of intent and abuse,[102] especially in such areas as unfair competition, monopolization, and conspiracies to monopolize.[103] In contrast, economists, who are not involved in the application of the law, are more concerned about public policy issues and the state of competition than about the application of the current legal rules.[104] Therefore, intent is not a key element in their analysis,[105] though some economists are concerned about intent and disagree with their colleagues.[106]

It should be noted that these differences about the importance of intent and abuse are not inevitable.[107] Lawyers regularly apply antitrust rules which call for no consideration of intent, for example, issues of price-fixing, allocation of markets, and boycotts. Similarly, in public utility regulation and in the application of such statutes as the Public Utility Act of 1935[108] few problems of intent or abuse appear.

As long as important antitrust laws contain elements of intent,[109] it will accentuate the differences between economic analysis in administration and in policy formulation. As the courts have interpreted the monopolization[110] provision of the Sherman Act, it covers the process of developing a monopoly position, not being a monopolist.[111] The courts have looked for evidence of abuse in the monopolization process, probably because policy makers have been influenced by social as well as economic objectives.[112] If the law should be changed to cover monopoly, it seems likely that part of the conflict between some members of the two professions would dissipate.[113]

*The Language Barrier*

A barrier exists in the differences in the meanings attributed to the language used by the two professions.[114] A striking example is to be found in the concept of price discrimination.[115] In economic theory, "price discrimination" covers undue similarities as well as undue differences in price.[116] A manufacturer who sells to two customers at the same price would discriminate if there were differences in his cost of selling to each of them.[117] In contrast, the lawyer employs the term "price discrimination" as it is defined in the Robinson-Patman Act and public utility regulations. In that context, discrimination occurs only when there is a difference in the prices charged to two customers; if the same price is charged, there is no price discrimination regardless of cost differences. Price differences can constitute a Robinson-Patman discrimination,[118] even if they are not illegal because they are justified by a difference in costs. However, in such a case, the price difference would not fit the economic definition of discrimination. Hence, some price discrimination as the economist defines it, will not fit the legal definition; some legal price discrimination will not satisfy the economic concept; while some price differences classify as price discrimination under either definition.

The language barrier is related to differences in the organization of the two disciplines. Lawyers must operate within a fairly well-organized linguistic system. Their terminology in any given legal field is substantially uniform. Their language is specialized, following definitions which are set by statutes and litigation in the specific field, or even in individual contracts. Because of the pressure of adversary proceedings, the law tends to a fairly high degree of precision in its terminology. The application or meaning of a term may be changed through legislation or court decision—but there is an organized mechanism to deal with such changes. The system works tolerably well except when it applies to such economic terms as "competition," "restraint of trade," and "monopoly."

Economists have no organizational framework that compares with the law. They have no authority which establishes terms and meanings that must be accepted by all. No statutory definitions can change economic terminology. Indeed, much of the discussion in respectable economic theory is tautological and deals with the meanings of terms. Further, the discussion is directed to universal definitions rather than specialized meanings for particular fields.[119]

For the most part economic terminology seems to be less specific than legal terms. Until recently few economists had to deal with the pointed problems of administration and adversary proceedings. Therefore there has been no organized pressure for the development of and application of more specific terms. As a matter of fact, the indefiniteness of economic terminology can be illustrated by the same term "price discrimination." Whereas economic theory contributes a clear concept of price discrimination, economists have been prone to follow the legal definitions in analyzing industrial situations.

These differences in language precision are differences of degree. Legal terminology reflects neither the precision of mathematics nor the stability of Gibraltar. On the other hand, economic terminology has some stability and considerable uniformity in use.

### *Frames of Reference: Disputes and Predictions*

There are substantial differences in the general framework for the exercise of the two disciplines.[120] Legal problems are treated within fairly well-defined frames of reference. Such frames are established by statutes and court interpretations. The application of precedent is of major importance—since both sides can usually find some precedent to use. Practicing lawyers do not have to visualize a broad theoretical background covering the general body of law in order to solve the problem at hand.[121] Their interests are immediate—to advantage their side in the litigation or negotiation rather than to seek universal academic truth.[122]

On the other hand, because of the nature of their work most economists do have to visualize a broad background since the problems they deal with are not methodically limited by a tight frame of reference. Whereas a lawyer can break a problem down into limited components, an economist usually has no such limits. A lawyer can parse a problem so that it involves issues in contracts and agency, for example. An economist dealing with the same contract might range over such wide fields as the structure of the market, international trade, channels of distribution, cost influences on price, and risks of cost increases.

The greatest contrast in the two disciplines centers on their methods for settling disputes. In the final analysis, serious legal controversy is settled by litigation. The highest court decides whether or not an adversary is right.[123] Other differences are settled through statutes. In either event, the legal profession enjoys organized means for settling controversies, and final conclusions are accepted by everyone, albeit with varying degrees of satisfaction. In contrast, the economists have no institution for settling differences. There is no economic supreme court. Nor is there a jury to hand down an enforceable verdict. No economist has to accept another's opinion. There is no end to differences in general economic analysis, and there cannot be.

Because of the lack of a unifying device, there is no formal consensus among economists.[124] As Chapter 2 indicated, economists harbor substantial disagreement about the influence and importance of competition.[125] There are wide variations in their uses of value judgments as well as individual differences in the process of analyzing and researching a problem. Economists cannot outclass lawyers in the quality of individualism, but their lack of an organized system permits differences of opinion to continue without end, in contrast to the mechanism for settlement that the legal profession employs.

Differences in the professions' treatment of predictions are related to their handling of disputes. Both lawyers and economists must make forecasts. Lawyers guess the outcome of specific cases and the legal consequences of business practices.[126] Ultimately, these predictions are put to a final test, the decision of the highest court involved.[127]

In contrast, the economist's forecasts are not subject to such an unequivocal test.[128] Nor, given the nature of economic problems, can they be. No institution is chartered to approve or disapprove. Even if an economist's peers were to accept his prediction, the ultimate test depends on what takes place in the economy or the market. Yet, even these do not provide conclusive proof. Even when the outcome matches the prediction, there always remains the uncomfortable possibility that some unconsidered factors will be regarded as the strategic ones in some future analysis.[129]

*Intellectual Provincialisms*

Related to these differences are the provincialisms of modern professions. Perhaps Alfred North Whitehead hit the target when he said, "Modern professionalism is the training of minds to conform to the methodology."[130] Both lawyers and economists want to follow their own methods free from outside interference.

Many economists seem to ignore the legal or other disciplines.[131] Others may uncritically accept legal conclusions without question. For example, public utility economics is based on the legal definition of a public utility, rather than on an economic classification of industry types. On the whole, economists assume that the economic problems are the most important ones. Hence, many overlook the ethical, political, and social objectives that must be fitted into the legal treatment of competition.

Many, if not most, lawyers prefer their own free-wheeling ways which they follow with great confidence. David Riesman's description of this feeling is somewhat exaggerated. "The lawyer's feeling that he could master anything in a pre-trial two weeks, that there is no expertise but his own, is often arrogant and Philistine, and I used frequently to have to argue with my brethren of the bar that neither economics nor anthropology could be so easily encompassed."[132]

Some lawyers have no need to work with other professions because they prefer such conventional legal fields as real property law and wills. Many are unenthusiastic about the development of administrative law which requires consideration of economic and sociological problems. In fact, many possess what Julius Cohen has called, "the ingrained habit of regarding law as genuine only if it is labelled 'judge-made.' "[133]

One of the protective devices for maintaining the lawyers' superior independence[134] is to stress the dichotomy between "fact" and "law," and to assume that questions of law lie entirely within their province. Yet, in such fields as antitrust many "legal" issues are essentially economic in nature. The application of precedent as a guide to decision is in point. Analysis by precedent is based on analogy: the "fact situation" in the immediate case is compared with that of earlier proceedings to determine which is most analogous;[135] then the rules of the earlier case are applied. Justice Cardozo described the finding of precedent as a process of matching "the colors of the case at hand against the colors of many sample cases. . . ."[136] Some economic analysis is implicit in applying precedents concerning such legal conclusions as what is the relevant market (demonstrated in Chapter 8) and what is an unreasonable "restraint of trade."

This blending of legal and economic analysis is inescapable. Yet, many lawyers and judges strive to avoid it. For example, the *Handbook of Recommended Procedures for the Trial of Protracted Cases* reflects a basic concern about "a tendency, particularly in antitrust litigation, for the parties to proffer expert opinions on issues which in essence are legal rather than factual. . . ."[137] Therefore, it is recommended that such practices be discouraged. No attention is paid to the difficulty of sorting out "fact" and "law," nor are any guide lines suggested for such classification.

### *Operational Differences*

Basic differences between the two disciplines stem from their historical applications. The law is centered on decision-making and the solution of circumscribed problems, usually through adversary proceedings.[138] Economics has tended in a more academic direction, concentrating more on analysis of how the economy operates. It has not been centered on problem-solving, decision-making, or adversary proceedings. Economic analysis has been occupied with appraising and guiding policy. With this focus, economists tend toward an interest in how decisions are made rather than in making them.

Only in recent times has the economist entered the arena of problem-solving.[139] For example, there were only sporadic efforts to apply economic analysis in antitrust before the great depression. Lacking a traditional emphasis on the solution of specific, pointed problems, economics has usually dealt with issues of general theory and description. During most of its development, economic price theory was not subjected to empirical tests. It has been concerned with broad-brush analysis rather than the more pointed determinations which are the bases for action. An economist who writes an industry study need not be as precise and careful as one who might advise a government agency that it should attempt to break up a corporation.

Probably because traditional economic theory was long confined to academic halls, it developed theories of markets which were not intended for practical application in the administration of antitrust and related laws.[140] These theories do not fit the needs of litigation or negotiation.[141] They require long chains of deductive reasoning about concepts which have no observational counterpart.[142] They tend to oversimplify analysis by using a restricted number of variables[143] which leave little room for important differences in degree.

### *Traditional Economic Theory*

A full discussion of the limited application of traditional economic theory would require more space than is available here. Several illustrations should suffice.

Much of price theory centers on comparisons of demand and supply under conditions of pure competition. Prices are determined where two geometric curves meet; one represents the quantities people will buy at various prices, and the other portrays manufacturing costs at each level of production. In a market which is perfectly competitive, the point where the two curves cross on a chart will indicate the market price and the quantity sold. At that same point the cost of the last unit sold will equal the price which is required to induce the last buyer to enter the market. This geometry turns on the use of the technical terms "marginal" cost and "marginal" revenue.[144]

In the hands of a skilled neoclassical theorist this exercise serves as a basis for a closed system analysis, which explains how markets would work under certain, fixed conditions. It serves only as a conceptual model and a pedagogical device. It is not conceived as an operational tool of analysis[145] for the review of actual market problems.

There is no pretense in traditional theory that the marginal concepts applied in this model have observational counterparts. Its use in empirical analysis would require a schedule that reflected the potential purchases of the item by all consumers at each price-point and a composite tabulation of the total costs of all of the sellers for each additional increment of production at one moment of time. But no one has ever been able to construct such tabulations for an individual company, much less a market. Nor can data be collected to establish what prices and volume would be in a given market under conditions of pure competition as a means of gauging the results. Some models have been constructed to show price behavior under a pure monopoly. These follow the same geometric plan and require the same types of unobserved data.

Models omit too many variables for practical application.[146] They were not intended for this purpose. They cover the effect of prices and costs on volume. However, they take no account of the many other factors which influence volume and competition.[147] They employ several basic assumptions: that there will be no variation in the quality or appearance of the products offered by each seller; that service, as well as credit and delivery terms, will be uniform; that no seller will enjoy any advantage of good will from distributors or consumers. Therefore, the models leave out some of the most significant factors that influence rivalry in the markets which produce antitrust problems:[148] trademarks; differences in product and packaging; differences in the various quality factors in the product; variations in service, guarantees, repair facilities, and credit;[149] differences in methods of distribution and distributive discounts; locations of retail distributors; variations in volume of advertising and sales promotion;[150] and the many differences in productive facilities which influence costs such as location, degree of vertical integration, degree of mechanization, plant size, and the firm's purchasing power.

Efforts to vary these models in order to fit the conditions of markets which lie between perfect competition and perfect monopoly have not been too successful. Economists have produced a substantial theoretical literature about markets with few sellers (called "oligopoly") or few buyers (called "oligopsony"). But these efforts have not yet produced tools of analysis which can be applied in policy formulation or administration.

There have been a number of efforts to design specific gauges of monopoly power.[151] Several indexes are based on measures of cross elasticity of the demand for the products of each individual seller.[152] These are based on the theory that in a purely competitive market the product of any seller is a perfect substitute for the product of every other seller. Therefore, any variation from perfect substitution will indicate variation from pure competition. But no method has been devised to measure demand or cross elasticity. Hence, no scales are available to set bench marks in the range from pure competition to pure monopoly.

Another group of indexes of competition turn on profits.[153] Differences between the current rate of interest and an industry's profit rates, based on investment, would indicate degree of competition. This gauge is premised on several assumptions: that monopoly always breeds higher profits; that accounting figures of individual companies are always comparable; and that all the sellers are one product companies. Again, there are no observations to support these assumptions and no practical methods for applying them.

The most widely discussed indicator of monopoly power in economic theory is the Lerner index.[154] This is derived from an arithmetic equation which is based on the long chain of deductive reasoning contained in traditional theory that prices equal marginal costs in a purely competitive market. Taking off from this theory, Professor Lerner assumed that the extent of monopoly could be measured by the difference between price and marginal cost—the greater the difference the stronger the monopoly. To develop a scale which would be comparable among many industries, this difference was divided by the price. The index is calculated from a simple formula, $\frac{\text{price minus marginal cost}}{\text{price}}$, or $\frac{p - mc}{p}$. When price equals marginal cost, the formula would produce an index of 0. For example, if both price and marginal cost are \$5, the formula would be $\frac{5 - 5}{5}$ or 0. If the price were raised to \$10, the formula would produce $\frac{10 - 5}{10}$ or .50. The value for a complete monopoly would never go as high as 1.00 since that index would require a marginal cost of 0.

This formula is based on many untested assumptions about the nature of costs and competition. If a company's marginal costs are less than average costs[155]—a fairly common case because of overhead—

basing the price on the out-of-pocket cost of the last unit would produce a loss. Therefore, as the formula goes, competition could take place only at a loss.[156] On the other hand, as Professor Lerner, himself, points out, a company may take less than "monopoly" profits because they might attract other entrants into the industry. Hence, at best, this formula could gauge only the sellers' use of his monopoly position, rather than the extent of his power.

Most important, the formula has no observational counterpart;[157] data are not available for its application; and its justification is too complex for litigation. Because it is more abstruse than some other formulas which have been suggested, it highlights the wide gap between traditional economic theory and the operational needs of policy makers and administrators.

Such patterns in traditional economic theory have led many lawyers to the mistaken belief that economics is concerned mainly with esoteric theory.[158] This belief overlooks the force of some empirical studies of competition and the sensible applications of economic analysis in a number of antitrust proceedings. In effect, judging economists by these theories would be comparable to judging the practical applications of law on the basis of the theoretical classifications of some legal philosophers.[159] Their explorations in jurisprudence are useful in general conceptual work. However, they, too, remain untried.

## *Application of Economic Analysis*

The methodology of economics provides many advantages, current and potential, for the treatment of market problems.[160] It furnishes a framework for such analysis: the definition of the problem; the important questions to be resolved; the nature of the evidence that bears on those questions; the methods of collecting and analyzing data; the comparisons of situations; and the methods of making predictions.

Illustrations of the specific applications of economic inquiry in the consideration of competitive problems are presented in some detail in the three following chapters. They deal with three central problems: data and criteria which can be employed in analyzing competitive and monopolistic forces in a market; definitions of a pertinent market under the various statutes; and the collection and use of statistical evidence in litigation.

None of these problems can be solved on the level of mathematical certainty either with or without market studies.[161] Economic analysis can provide basic aids for their solutions. It does not present a substitute for judgment.[162] It does furnish a basis for improvement in the understanding of operative problems and of the alternative solutions.

There is, today, no organized body of principles for economic analysis which will provide guide lines[163] for solving the pointed decisional problems affecting competition. Nor is there a large group of economists equipped for the tasks and available for ready employment.

Increased use of economic inquiry in antitrust, however, will stimulate the development of an improved methodology, one which can be applied in a practical way in litigation and negotiation. While such economic analysis has been developed largely in academic halls, substantial forward strides will depend on experience in solving practical problems in the enforcement process.

Two developments point to the practicable possibilities of such progress. First, an increasing number of judges have been asking for economic analysis to help them in deciding cases.[164] Second, a number of economists have demonstrated the utility of economic analysis in legal procedures.

Most of the judicial comments about the paucity of economic analysis have taken the form of criticism of the prosecution's case. For example, in the recent *Columbia Pictures* case, Judge Herlands was moved to state: "In other words, the Government's case on this issue ignores the types of information useful in determining whether the vigor of competition has been or will be impaired as a result of the Distribution Agreement."[165]

In the *Besser*[166] case, discussed in Chapter 8, the government introduced data on the entire industry manufacturing concrete blockmaking machinery. However, it could not, in response to the court's request, produce separate data about the high-production machinery that Besser and some others manufactured. Therefore, the court had to treat all the machinery—low as well as high production—as one market.

The judge's desire for more economic analysis is shown clearly in a study which Professor Kaysen and Dean Grether undertook in and for the Antitrust Division.[167] After a detailed review of several cases in which market definition was important, they concluded that judges are interested in economic evidence, but, they implied, the government has not supplied it properly.[168] A number of cases provide examples. Their report referred to the Supreme Court's criticism of the government's evidence in the *Columbia Steel* case:[169] that the sales data were inadequate proof that the eleven Western states constituted a market; that little evidence was produced to show that the two companies did sell the same types of structural steel products; that no data were produced comparing the production of large pipe by each of the two companies and competitors; that no proof was advanced to support the contention that Consolidated Steel might broaden its market by technological advances and internal expansion.[170]

Kaysen and Grether felt that the government's thesis in the *Paramount* case[171] was based on the assumption that the market for exhibiting movies is local and that there is no national market. The District Court defined the market to be national so that the defendants controlled only one sixth of the theaters. The government's appeal was based on the contention that the lower court's relief, based on its findings, was inadequate. The Supreme Court set aside the findings and defined the market as the "first-run field" in large cities. They concluded that, "The Supreme Court supplied the analysis necessarily implied in the Government's case. Perhaps, had the issue been dealt with more directly before the lower court, the decision in that case might have been different."[172]

The defense presented substantial economic data in the *Cellophane* case,[173] while the government merely repeated generalizations regarding the rule of law. In the *du Pont-General Motors* case[174] the court based its interpretation of the market on the defendant's argument that it had to supply highly technical service to the automobile producers. The point was not made by the prosecution. The defense presented this information, not as evidence of the market dimensions, but to show that it obtained the General Motors business because of excellent service rather than through stockholdings.

The progress made by economists when confronted with specific problems of antitrust litigation has been demonstrated on several occasions. There is no way to develop an organized roster of economists who have served ably in advising lawyers regarding analysis of the legal status of specific business practices and transactions and the economic problems entailed in the litigation of cases. Since economists do not appear "of record" unless they are members of the bar, there are no public records to indicate such advisory work. On the basis of personal knowledge, several can be mentioned: M. A. Adelman, L. S. Kellogg, J. W. Boatwright, Jules Backman, C. D. Edwards, J. J. Corson, T. J. Kreps, A. D. H. Kaplan, B. W. Lewis, P. W. Cook, Jr., J. P. Miller, and Joel Dean.

The writings of several illustrate this progress: Corwin D. Edwards' *The Price Discrimination Law,* Carl Kaysen's *United States Versus United Shoe Machinery Corporation,* Walton Hamilton's *Antitrust in Action.* A number of industry studies reflect a growing capacity to analyze antitrust and related problems. To mention a few: Joe S. Bain, *The Economics of the Pacific Coast Petroleum Industry* (1945-1947); Melvin G. de Chazeau and Alfred E. Kahn, *Integration and Competition in the Petroleum Industry* (1959); Robert F. Lanzillotti, *The Hard-Surface Floor-Covering Industry* (1955); Jesse W. Markham, *Competition in the Rayon Industry* (1952); James W. McKie, *Tin Cans and Tin Plate* (1959); Donald Wallace, *Market Control in the Aluminum Industry* (1937).

Further progress is demonstrated by the many articles by economists in leading law journals. Such names as E. S. Mason, M. A. Adelman, C. D. Edwards, J. W. Markham, G. W. Stocking, R. C. Brooks, Jr., A. E. Kahn, Carl Kaysen, and E. T. Grether are attached to a substantial number of articles dealing with various phases of antitrust. Yet, each of these is a member of an academic department of economics or business.

In this connection, the differences between general research, policy analysis, and administration are quite important. If all economic inquiry were confined by administrative limitations, the analysis of policy problems would be unduly limited. The broad-brush speculation and the formulation of theoretical hypotheses are essential to progress in public policy.[175] Just as both basic and applied research are needed in the physical and natural sciences, so are their equivalents required in such social sciences as economics.

Both professions will have to recognize these differences in the applications of economic analysis. The lawyers must understand the values of general economic studies and the development of economic theory. They must realize that such analysis can be applied by economists in devising the theory of a case and in developing proof. But this accomplishment requires that the economist be given a clear understanding of the lawyers' needs.

## *Economic Analysis in Policy and Administration*

There is a strong public need for broad-gauged economic analysis and commentary on the state of business regulation, especially antitrust. To be useful these commentaries must raise questions about legal procedures and administration. They should not be confined by current law. In fact the economist may reduce his contribution to public policy if he is preoccupied with demonstrating a capacity to handle legal categories. For in that preoccupation he may be drawn into the conventional legal framework, losing the valuable outlook of a broader vantage point.

Economists must recognize the distinction between their activities in administration and policy formulation. The solution of a practical administrative problem requires acceptance of the bounds of the current state of the law and legal procedures.[176] The review of the work of the administrators must take into account the limits of their functions. There is an important distinction between analysis of the effects of administration in carrying out existing law and discussions of the law itself. Economic commentaries about antitrust cases that overlook the limitations—statutory and decisional—within which the lawyers and the courts must operate frequently miss the strategic points. The lawyer does not regard economic commentary about a case seriously unless the writer shows a grasp of the nature of the legal problems and processes which were involved.[177] However, there are occasions when economic analysis of the effects of a proceeding or a program should look to final results and disregard the legal limitations, providing that the commentator clearly enunciates the nature of his analysis.

Similarly, lawyers must appreciate the distinction between policy issues and the application of current law. They have not always recognized the focus of economic analysis which deals with what the law should be. Nor have they clearly distinguished discussions of the economic and social effects of the law and those of the procedural and substantive aspects. Many have not accepted Lee Loevinger's pertinent comment, "There are established techniques and sources for answering the ordinary legal questions—although they do not always yield completely lucid answers—but there are no established techniques or sources for seeking answers to these [social and economic] questions."[178]

Opportunities for applying economic analysis in the administration of our antitrust laws seem to exist in every nook and cranny. Substantial progress has been made. However, it seems fair to say that this progress has not met the public need. While the antitrust laws are largely economic in concept, they are frequently enforced with a disregard for economic inquiry. Yet, we must realize that improved use of economic analysis presents difficult problems, problems that have their counterparts in other phases of business regulation.[179] Accordingly, both of the professions have a substantial task ahead if they are to meet their public responsibilities. One of the requisites of this progress is a clear recognition of the hurdles that lie between them. Such understanding may serve to remove some of the friction. Above all, it may weaken some of the professional provincialism and strengthen the possibilities of working cooperation.

# 7 / *Indicators of Competition**

WE TURN NOW to several illustrative applications of economic analysis in the solution of competitive problems: indicators of competition; defining the market; and statistical evidence. These are presented in this and the two succeeding chapters.

Since there are no direct measures of competition, consideration of the balance between competitive and monopolistic forces must depend on circumstantial evidence. This evidence centers on some recognized indicators, or criteria, of competition. For example, a large number of competitors of equal size is taken as a sign of active competition. On the other hand, the fact that one company accounts for 90 per cent of the sales in a market would be taken as evidence of lack of competition.

Indicators of competition are used in the formulation and application of policies bearing on competition. They are employed in gauging the extent of competition in a market and in the economy generally. Their specific applications in antitrust depend on the nature of the law. Some statutes call for the use of certain indicators, as in price-fixing cases; others call for the use of a number of other indicators, as in merger cases.

## *Concepts of Competition*

There are no precise definitions of competition and monopoly.[1] Neither economics nor law has produced a uniform classification of competitive and monopolistic situations.[2] True, there are well-ac-

* Footnotes for Chapter 7 begin on page 422.

cepted concepts of the two conditions in their pure forms. However, neither of these fits the world in being.

Unfortunately, there appears to be no way to set up definitive all-encompassing classifications of competition and monopoly.[3] This lack reflects the intricacies of modern economic activity. Practically every industrial situation reflects an amalgam of these two opposing forces. Pure competition and pure monopoly are useful as conceptual bench marks, but they do not, by themselves, describe any actual market. Their pristine purity does not provide a firm, feasible basis for policy. Hence, the practical analytical problem is to take account of all of the influences in a market in order to reach a balanced judgment and to prescribe what can be done to change an unsatisfactory situation.

The purely theoretical concepts can be summarized quickly.[4] Pure competition describes a market with several major characteristics which create an orderly balance between supply and demand. Individual businessmen in it have so little discretion in their decisions that their competitive moves border on reflex responses.[5] The market is composed of large numbers of buyers and sellers, no one of whom can influence a selling price. They buy and sell a standard commodity. All transactions are as impersonal as a purchase or sale on the New York Stock Exchange. Any individual can easily enter the market as a seller or a buyer, and he can leave the market just as easily without any untoward sacrifice. All buyers and sellers have equal knowledge of current market conditions—prices paid, volume, and cost. No buyer-seller loyalties exist. No supplier has any trade advantage through reputation, patents, or financial and family connections.[6]

Such a frictionless market, if it would work, would accord no advantage to any individual.[7] It would be self-policing with full freedom for all.[8] The only state interference needed would be the protection of the health and safety of the community. *Laissez faire* would be the order of the day, for in this, "the best of all possible worlds," everyone would work for the public good by pursuing his own gain. Efficiency has free play and limited resources—land, labor, and capital—are so allocated that the largest number of consumer wants which can be met are satisfied.

The opposite pole is just as clear. The perfect monopolist is the only seller in the market, and the monopsonist is the sole buyer. Competing with no one, the monopolist has full freedom of choice.[9] Each buyer has no alternative but to pay his price.[10] After estimating his volume of sales at various prices and his total costs for such volume, the seller sets the price which will give him the largest profit attainable.[11] His is the "nirvana" of free choice, free of outside interference or concern.

These concepts were developed in traditional economic theory. They were not conceived as literal descriptions of the economy.[12] Rather, they were used to support the thesis that a competitive economy would allocate the use of resources most efficiently. They were employed to show that such an economy would be most sensitive to consumer demands and would attain the greatest consumer satisfaction.

This thesis had a substantial influence. It convinced many that government should stop interfering with market operations because Adam Smith's "invisible hand,"[13] the free market, was the most effective regulator. It was dedicated to the removal of many governmental interferences with free trade. Tariffs and embargoes depressed international trade—a situation that was particularly serious for countries, such as England, the birthplace of the theory, which were engaged in trading and maritime activities. State monopolies and state-franchised monopolies dominated many markets. Restrictive guild-controls were prevalent.[14] The moral of free competition was the base for a campaign to remove these public influences. Some of the early writers went further and felt that the state should remove private barriers. Most important, the polar concepts of competition and monopoly were employed to support a general thesis; not to describe the actual state of affairs.[15]

After this conceptual dichotomy had been employed for a time, many saw the need for analyses which reflected the actual operations of markets and firms. Such writers as Alfred Marshall, who brought a background of wide observation to his work, became interested in the frictions that interfered with the articulated workings of the competitive process. The rise and fall of individual firms, along with scarcity elements which gave substantial advantages to some firms, were brought into the analysis.[16]

Later came empirical studies of industrial practices, which revealed the shortcomings of these uncomplicated theories and pointed up the need for changes in theoretical analysis.[17] Modifications were developed, still within the framework of a general, rounded theoretical pattern. "Imperfect competition"[18] was offered by Joan Robinson as a variation of the original theories.[19] Professor Edward H. Chamberlin developed the theory of "monopolistic competition"[20] to accommodate such forces as the market advantage of brands in a competitive framework. These and other works produced broad market theories in the tradition of previous economic theory.[21] However, they suggested the desirability and possibility of bringing economic analysis closer to the market place.[22]

In recent years, the concept of "workable competition" was suggested in an article by Professor J. M. Clark who called for a more realistic conceptual framework for the analysis of competition.[23] The thesis of the article is elaborated in Professor Clark's excellent new book *Competition as a Dynamic Process.* "Workable competition" is based on the principle that competitive and monopolistic forces are not mutually exclusive but interrelated.[24] In this, the theory gave expression to an existing state of economic inquiry. Industry studies[25] and work in antitrust enforcement had long since left the polar concepts of pure competition and monopoly and had proceeded to a more sophisticated and complex view of industrial markets.[26]

The shift to workable competition may be one of kind rather than merely degree.[27] Previous economic theory called for fully rounded, closed-system explanations of the market. The theoretical solutions told how the system *should* operate logically and what it should produce.[28] Many economists would like to see "workable competition" rounded out as a complete universal theory. Currently, the concept does not have such content.[29] In fact, its strongest contribution may be to discard the traditional counsel of perfection.[30] Unfortunately, it is somewhat difficult to develop a clear picture of what the theory represents.[31]

The most definite feature ascribed to workable competition is that it considers actual markets to see if they are reasonably competitive in the light of the limits set by inherent conditions. The theory sums up possibilities of improvement.[32] If competition in an industry cannot be improved, it is workably competitive.[33] In most situations this single criterion seems practicable. Moreover, it is only reasonable to suppose that anyone who applies the theory would be alert to markets in which substantial competition cannot be established, such as telephonic communication, which seems to require more direct regulation.

A further stage in theoretical development is implicit in recent empirical work and in this book. Briefly stated, its premise is that theory should constitute a framework for empirical methodology.[34] Price theory[35] will not be of much use for the solution of policy problems if it continues to be a philosophical exercise which purports to contain, within itself, the answers to all problems of the day. It must follow the current paths of theory in such other fields as the biological and physical sciences. Like medical theory, its major contributions will come when it shifts from the "Book of Answers" to the "Book of Questions."[36]

As a frame of reference for empirical analysis, economic theory can offer substantial guidance for the researcher, the policy maker, and the administrator. It can provide guides to the strategic questions involved in considering policy issues, to the types of evidence which are pertinent, and to the methods of relating the questions to the evidence. It includes the technique of formulating hypotheses and subjecting them to rigorous tests. Like legal methodology, it offers a method for applying precedent through the analysis of analogy, using previous experience and research.

If economic theory of the market is to serve in this way, it must encompass an organized framework for analyzing the indicators of competition. It cannot stop with a theological belief for or against competition. It must consider the content of competition as it exists and compare it with various alternatives.

Prevailing competition is far too complex to be captured in mechanistic or nominalistic terms.[37] Its diverse manifestations, its intricacies, and its limitations must be reconsidered seriously. It lacks that philosophical purity which characterizes a guiding faith. It calls, above all, for an open-minded, empirical approach, one which uses postulates as research aids, but which later challenges these assumptions. It requires serious reconsideration of the assumptions and the postulates at various stages of analysis by comparing them with empirical observation.[38]

In the development of a pragmatic approach to competition three major types of competitive indicators have been employed.[39] They relate to: (1) the structure of the market; (2) the behavior or conduct of the participants in a market; and (3) the performance of the industry or of the market.

Attributes of structure include such indicators as the numbers of buyers and sellers in a market, the geographical distribution of supply and demand, the difficulties of entry into the market, and the type and degree of vertical integration which exist. Attributes of behavior cover such factors as: collusion among the competitors regarding price or volume of output; exclusive contracts; and price discrimination. Attributes of performance relate to the results of the operations of an industry or market, measured by such indicators as: profit levels, the rate of growth of the industry, innovation and progressiveness, and the utilization of capacity.

These classifications are not watertight. There is considerable overlapping of the types of indicators,[40] and frequently it is difficult to classify a particular attribute as one of structure, behavior, or performance. For example, various types of marketing methods, such as exclusive agreements, are generally regarded as aspects of behavior. However, long-range exclusive agreements which have been employed regularly may be as important in analyzing the structure of a market as any corporate forms.

## *Uses of Indicators of Competition*

Indicators of competition are employed for several major purposes. The most prominent is to determine whether an antitrust law has been violated. Second, is the application of the criteria to determine the cure after a finding of a violation. Third, is the diagnosis of general competitive conditions in the economy.[41] Last, is the consideration of legislation and other aspects of public policy which may bear on competitive conditions.

The most prominent use of the indicators involves the determination of whether an antitrust violation has taken place. They may also show the need for employing methods outside of antitrust to stimulate competition. Initially, such indicators are applied in deciding whether to prosecute. Subsequently, they are employed in the trial of the issues or in the negotiations of consent orders. In some proceedings, the indicators may point to a clear violation; in others they may be used as circumstantial evidence in support of an economic conclusion. An express agreement to limit production is a direct indication that the Sherman Act was violated. On the other hand, evidence about concentration of production and high profits would be used to show that a merger may tend to lessen competition substantially—a prerequisite to a finding that there was a violation of Section 7 of the Clayton Act, the antimerger provision.

Indicators that are employed to judge the existence of a violation may differ from the criteria that are employed in constructing a remedy to cure the violation.[42] In this respect, the uses of criteria are similar to those applied in medicine. Indicators used in diagnosis usually differ from those used for prognosis. Medical procedure calls for the employment of separate criteria for the diagnosis and the treatment. Thus, temperature, location of pain, and other symptoms may indicate influenza; but the cure is medication and rest, not changing the temperature chart.

In antitrust, the differences between detecting a violation and formulating the remedy should be of great import. For example, if the finding of a violation is based partly on such indications as high profits and price leadership, an order to eliminate such conditions would be meaningless. Significant programs might include such steps as: making patents freely available to all comers; requiring the disclosure of know-how; splitting one division of a corporation from another; compelling the divestiture of stock in another company; canceling long-run requirements contracts; eliminating a protective tariff; and encouraging companies in other industries to supply government requirements of the pertinent product. A finding of a price conspiracy may call for more than a decree to, "stop conspiring."[43] It might call for an order setting up pricing formulas for the individual companies, for reducing some tariff barriers, or for making it easier for new competitors to enter the market.

The indicators used for evaluation of the state of competition in the economy as a whole differ from those used for individual industries. True, data on individual industry conditions are helpful, but broader indicators are required. For the most part, general evaluation rests on such criteria as measures of changes in concentration in large industrial sectors,[44] changes in the business population, failure and acquisition rates, changes in profit rates, responsiveness of prices to changes in market conditions, increases in price leadership, changes in the use of industry-wide wage agreements, and trends in prices paid and charged.[45]

At another level, competitive criteria are applied in analyzing issues of public policy. Do we want a national "fair trade" law? Should railroads be encouraged to merge? Should spin-offs of corporate divisions be encouraged? Should compulsory quality labels be instituted for various products? Should manufacturers be compelled to allow functional discounts to wholesalers? Should the brokerage provision of the Robinson-Patman Act be repealed? Such public policy questions require analytical criteria that may be quite different from those used to examine individual industries.

The need for different sets of indicators for policy making and for administration does not imply that we require completely separate sets of criteria for each purpose. Obviously, there is considerable overlapping. However, even when the same indicator is used for several purposes the methods of analysis and the degree of accuracy required may differ. A prosecution may entail measurements of industrial concentration which accurately gauge a specific market situation. On the other hand, an examination of the concentration of economic power in the hands of the largest corporations calls for a review of broad trends which do not require as fine a measure as the prosecution. Hence, an indicator that is inadequate for an inquiry into a specific market may fill the requirements of broad policy analysis.

## *Pressure for Simple Standards*

Because of the influence of antitrust on business operations, many lawyers, businessmen, and students have urged that more specific standards of competitiveness should be constructed. There have been frequent complaints about the indeterminate nature of the laws.[46] It has been argued that a more definite set of guides would make our antitrust policy more effective because it would stimulate voluntary compliance.[47]

Such certainty would have substantial advantages. It would help to satisfy the desire to see the laws applied consistently and fairly. Enforcement would become less dependent on the individual judgments of the participants in the administration of antitrust. Chance would play a smaller role in the uncovering and prosecution of violations. Litigation would be less costly for the government, private plaintiffs, defendants, and the courts. Voluntary compliance would be promoted.

On the other hand, the issue of certainty in antitrust produces an interesting variety of reactions. While some groups appeal for greater certainty, they also complain about the per se rules.[48] Others would like increased certainty through a substantial extension of per se principles. For example, it has been suggested that all mergers,[49] requirement contracts, and exclusive dealing arrangements be declared illegal, per se, if the amount of commerce involved is substantial.

As Chapter 6 indicates, some efforts have been made to formulate mathematical rules. Suggested yardsticks related to such factors as industrial concentration, profits, and measures of "degree of monopoly."[50] None of these seem to meet the needs.[51] At least for the foreseeable future, no meaningful formula seems likely.[52]

Measures of industrial concentration as a yardstick for monopoly have attracted the most attention. However, as demonstrated in Chapter 8 on definition of the market, such a formula is not very helpful. A concentration percentage is only one indicator of a market situation.[53] Competition among a small number of competitors can be very strong, while competitive forces can be weak in an industry with many competitors. As Professor Wilcox has pointed out:

> . . . The indexes of concentration are not indexes of monopoly. They may reveal the consequences of monopolistic restriction and exclusion or those of competitive innovation, market development, and reductions in cost and price. They may conceal the influence of potential competition, and the presence—on the other side of the market—of countervailing power. The studies of concentration are suggestive, but they fall far short of proving the monopoly that they are often said to prove.[54]

Profit rates have been suggested as a guide though not as the sole criterion.[55] For example, Professors Kaysen and Turner have suggested using profits—especially for single-product firms—as a "fairly good measure of long-run price-cost relations" which they feel is an important indicator of competitiveness in a market. "If normal profits are of the magnitude of say six to eight per cent on invested capital, an average profit rate of nine per cent over ten years could not be identified as supernormal with any confidence, but one of twelve per cent could."[56] Moreover, they felt that this measure need not be confined to single-product firms, "In most industrial multi-product firms . . . price-cost margins for the separate products can be defined."[57] This suggestion assumes that high profits go hand in hand with monopoly and that low profits accompany competition. Yet the empirical evidence on this point is scanty and desultory.

It seems likely that the principal influences of competition are on cost and on efficiency rather than on profits.[58] For example, the supermarket industry, which has been regarded as highly competitive, has shown a potential for high profit rates based on original capital investment, while competition has driven costs to low levels. It is reported that the industry's gross mark-ups average approximately 17 per cent[59] of manufacturers' prices while average profit rates run in the neighborhood of 1 to 1½ per cent of sales. However, there have been many spectacular financial successes in this industry. Entrepreneurs who started with one small store only twenty-five years ago now have enterprises valued in the range of 7 to 10 million dollars—despite the fact that no outside capital additions were made after the initial investment.[60]

This desire for a single yardstick to gauge the degree of competition stems partly from a feeling that only such a measure will prevent antitrust proceedings from becoming too complex for practical administration.[61] The wearisome court procedures and the apparent judicial inability to keep litigation within manageable limits have given rise to efforts to simplify the tests of competitiveness. While some advocate the extension of per se rules, and others seek a single economic gauge, many would like to limit the number of indicators used.

To succeed in the effort to solve the practical administrative problems of the Big Case, it seems likely that we need more, rather than less, economic analysis.[62] A single indicator for all cases might be desirable if the task must be handled by lawyers without economic advice. However, if the skills of the economist are utilized effectively, the total number of indicators employed in the single case should not interfere with efficient litigation.[63]

While, as this chapter indicates, there is a long array of competitive criteria, no proceeding need involve all of them. Economic analysis can contribute to efficient litigation by winnowing out those indicators which are not germane to the specific issues of the case. Through this process much of the chaff that fills the many pages of evidence would be eliminated.

Unfortunately, there is no easy road to efficient antitrust litigation. A single test of competitiveness might well disregard such important factors[64] that an antitrust prosecution would destroy competitive forces in some markets and overlook monopolistic forces in others. For example, low profits might conceal an inefficient monopoly, while high returns might reflect an active, innovating firm which has energized competition in several markets. Further, in the application of any such single criterion, allowances would have to be made for exceptions[65]—a process that might well bring any of the other indicators into play.

While analysis of competition may seem complex, it does not differ from other fields of economic inquiry or, for that matter, other disciplines. No single yardstick will do in the analysis of inflation, aerodynamics, corporate reorganizations, international relations, or medical ills. While we seek simplicity, scientific advances seem to head into complexity except for those fortunate phases when several factors can be so correlated that some can be eliminated.

Every discipline seems to require the application of skilled judgment to determine which criteria are important for a specific problem. No methodology seems to provide automatic flags to signal the significant aspects of a problem. In this respect, the selection of indicators of competition is no exception.

Progress is in the making in the analysis of competition. Economic market studies show greater sophistication. At the same time, the legal profession demonstrates more skillful dealings with the indicators. One has only to review the pleadings and evidence in several recent cases to see this progress. Such cases as *Bethlehem,*[66] *General Motors,*[67] *Brillo,*[68] and *Cellophane*[69] reflect forward movement in the pleadings, opinions, and subsequent commentaries.

The current problem is how to improve these analyses so that they will meet the various needs of policy formulation and administration. The never-ending search for simplification is desirable—not because the single indicator will be found, but because the exploration and experimentation adds to knowledge of the subject. For the immediate future we must use a full kit of tools, rather than rely on an all-purpose one.[70]

## *Structure of the Market*

The structure of a market encompasses characteristics of market relationships which are fairly stable.[71] Structural criteria are generally more permanent than those of behavior.

While all three types of indicators—structure, behavior, and performance—are influenced by the definition of the market, structural characteristics are affected most importantly. For example, without a definition of the market, analysis of industrial concentration would not be possible.

Several features of market definition, which are covered in the next chapter, bear on its structural characteristics. Cross-elasticity of demand affects not only the definition of the market but also the nature of competition within the market. For example, cross-elasticity between automobile finishes and other types of paint may be so low that there is a separate market for automobile finishes. However, within the market for automobile finishes, the cross-elasticities of demand for the products of the individual manufacturers influence the market structure. Further, automobile finishes may be substitutable for other types of finishes. Hence competitive alternatives in the other paint markets may influence competition in automobile finishes. Similarly, product differentiation and price relationships among products affect not only the dimensions of the market, but also its structural characteristics.

Though a review of structural aspects of a market usually concentrates on sellers, it also covers the buyers from and the suppliers to the sellers. For example, the structural aspects of the retail automobile market would not be understood without considering the structure and practices of the automobile manufacturers' market. A study of the structure of the canning industry would cover the framework of competition among vegetable and fruit farmers, among manufacturers of containers and container closing machines, and among wholesale and retail outlets. Thus, the position of the A & P and other national chains in grocery distribution might be important.

Analysis of the "other side of the market" would be essential in a review of the competitive forces among a group of sellers who buy from one manufacturer or who sell to one customer. A dominating supplier or customer can be strategic in such a review. For example, it has been suggested that in the early rate-fixing cases against the railroads insufficient account was taken of the practices of such large shippers as the original Standard Oil Company which played one road off against another and forced loss-breeding rebates.[72] The motion picture cases included several actions against powerful exhibitors.[73]

The most prominent features of market structure have been: number and concentration of competitors, barriers to entry, geographical distribution of buyers and sellers, differences in the degree of integration of competitors, product differentiation, and countervailing power. The list of indicators that follows is not intended to be complete nor does the order of presentation reflect relative importance.

### *Concentration*[74]

One of the most prominent aspects of structure is the relative concentration of sellers, buyers,[75] and suppliers within a market.[76] This criterion covers the number of firms[77] and their relative sizes. It is frequently assumed that a large number of firms, none of which are of predominant size, is an indication of active competition.[78] Concentration is usually measured by the percentage of the industry or market accounted for by the "Big Four" or "Big Eight" of the industry.

Measurements of concentration are frequently applied in public policy considerations and in such cases as *Alcoa,*[79] *Brillo,*[80] *Crown,* and

*American Tobacco*.[81] This aspect of structure is particularly important in connection with issues of monopolization[82] and mergers under the antitrust laws.

A measurement of concentration is strongly dependent on the definition of the market.[83] It is only one indicator of the competitive picture,[84] though a very useful one. It does not provide a direct gauge of the degree of competition.[85] While more active competition is generally associated with a large number of competitors, this assumption is subject to considerable qualification, as the court pointed out in the *Brown Shoe* case.[86] As a practical matter, one market with a small number of competitors may contain more active competition than another with a larger number.[87]

### *Entry*[88]

The relative ease of entry into a market by new companies[89] or by existing companies in other industries[90] is regarded as a prime factor in analyzing structure. High barriers to entry figured importantly in the *American Crystal*[91] and *Spalding*[92] cases. Because other companies could not enter the pertinent markets easily, the courts were inclined against those mergers.

If there are no substantial barriers to entering a market, strong monopoly elements will probably not endure.[93] High profits or opportunities to enter the market with lower costs will attract newcomers. Similarly, if the members of an industry felt that it was easy for others to enter the market, they would be less inclined to fix prices since more profitable prices would make the market more inviting to outsiders.

On the other hand, if entry is very difficult or impossible, monopoly power will be protected. In some industries problems of entry might limit the power of existing firms to increase capacity and place a premium on the acquisition of competitors.

There are no overt guides for gauging ease of entry into a market.[94] Therefore, analysis of this factor depends on several subsidiary issues: patents, trade barriers, costs, discounts, product differentiation, and previous history of entries and exits.

*Patent position*[95] affects potential entrants directly. Since patents are granted as legal monopolies, they may keep competing goods out of the market altogether.[96] The use of patents has been featured in many recent cases—but mainly because of abuse of the monopoly right, as in *Hartford-Empire*[97] and *General Electric.*[98]

*Trade barriers* at national, state, or local levels can influence entry into various markets. Protective tariffs, quotas, and embargoes for health or economic reasons, licensing provisions and labeling requirements can all contribute to barriers which shut potential competitors out of a market or increase their costs substantially.

*Long-run cost curves* of new entrants have been held by some to be a most important element affecting entry.[99] High fixed costs increase the capital requirements and add to the risks of potential entrants.[100] The Bethlehem Steel Company tried to use this argument to justify its acquisition of Youngstown.[101] Such factors may make it impossible for small companies to enter into a market. They may discourage entry in some markets because of the great risks involved.

Many of these high fixed costs are required by distribution rather than manufacturing.[102] For example, if all of the sellers in a market undertake tremendous expenditures on national advertising, small companies may have great difficulties in entering into the market. Such elements seem to have influenced the *Tobacco* case.[103] A company which is strongly entrenched in one market may acquire an unrelated company to take advantage of the latter's established position in its own industry. Such conglomerate mergers are frequently based on an effort to avoid high costs in breaking into a new market.

*Discounts* and other forms of price discrimination can be used as a barrier to entry into a market and can serve to prevent smaller competitors from making sales to substantial customers.[104] In the *American Optical* case,[105] the F.T.C. found that the cumulative discounts, based on total volume purchased from the respondent, restricted sales by competitors. American sold a wide line of products—stock merchandise, optical machinery and equipment, frames and prescription items. Its competitors, with one exception, sold a limited line, for example, frames only or prescription glasses only. Therefore, the smaller companies could not sell enough to any customer to institute a volume discount which would be comparable with that of American Optical.

*History of entries and exits* is a key element in the review of entry barriers. Many new entries into a market are a practical indication that entry is not too difficult. In contrast, if an industry's mortality rate is high, a feature of the *Spalding*[106] proceeding, and there are few new competitors, the problem of entry is a serious factor in analysis of the market.

*Alternative sources of supply*[107] influence ease of entry into a market as well as the definition of the relevant market. Thus, if lake sand has the same attributes as pit sand, the availability of this other type would affect the relevant market as well as competition within it. If the prices of lake sand are too high in the lakeside market, the other sand will be used even though transportation costs are high.[108]

### *Geographical Distribution*[109]

The geographical distribution of sellers, buyers, and suppliers to the sellers is an element of structure. Because of heavy transportation costs, the national market for certain products, such as steel, is affected by the location of both the mills and customers. This factor figured importantly in the *Bethlehem Steel*[110] and *Cement Institute* cases.[111] Many competitors may have limited advantages within certain geographical areas. However, if a competitor with a locational advantage presses his luck too far, other competitors may be enabled to undercut him.

### *The Regional Nature of the Market*[112]

This attribute refers not to the locations of the sellers and buyers but to the geographical dimension of a market—whether it is on a national, local, or regional basis. Milk markets are usually local with little intershipment between markets, a significant factor in the *Maryland-Virginia Milk Producers* proceeding. On the other hand, markets for men's readymade clothing are more or less national in scope. On the whole, retailing is more influenced by local conditions than is manufacturing. Similarly, consumer services are sold in local markets.

The geographical nature of the market can have a radical influence on the shape of competition and its interpretation. A number of proceedings such as *A & P,*[113] *Anheuser-Busch,*[114] and the movie cases, have involved local market competition between firms operating entirely within the market and those who sell in many regions throughout the country.

### *Independence of Rivals*[115]

Independence of rivals has been a prominent element in some cases and in two statutes. In the *Hamilton Watch* case[116] it was held that the purchase of the shares of one watch seller by another would have an illegal influence on the competition between the two of them. The joint ownership of the stock of several companies in the hands of one firm can influence both legal antitrust interpretations and the nature of competition. In *Kiefer-Stewart*[117] it was held that two wholly owned subsidiaries of one parent conspired with each other.

Interdependence of competitors is a direct objective of two sections of the Clayton Act.[118] Section 7 covers intercorporate stock acquisitions.[119] Section 8 stops one man from serving as director of two substantial companies which are in competition with each other.[120]

Protecting independence of rivals has been the basis for policy discussions about the influences of investment trusts and insurance companies on the competitive policies of firms in which they have substantial holdings.

### *Integration*[121]

In many considerations of competition, the problems of integration are key issues.[122] Such problems arise when some competitors supply their own products or services while other firms must sell or purchase those same products or services. If all fabricators of aluminum products mined bauxite and smelted virgin aluminum, there would be no competitive problems caused by the integration of the operations of some fabricators. At one time, however, the Aluminum Company was the sole producer of virgin ingot, part of which it sold to other fabricators while it used the remainder in its own fabrication. Integration was a key issue in the Antitrust Division's case against Alcoa.[123] It was argued that this integration permitted Alcoa to increase the raw material price and depress its charges for the final products, squeezing its unintegrated competitors between high costs and low selling prices. Similar questions regarding integration have arisen in connection with the production of lumber, pulp, paper, aluminum foil,[124] and steel products.[125]

The importance of integration is not confined to differences in mark-ups and "squeezes."[126] It also can affect differences in competitors' costs. For example, a mill which produces both pulp and paper has substantial cost advantages over a nonintegrated plant. In the nonintegrated operation pulp must be dehydrated for shipment and rehydrated to make paper. Since the integrated plant simply transfers the wet product from pulping equipment to paper machines, it is more efficient and enjoys a substantial cost advantage. (Some efforts have been made to overcome this advantage by shipping wet pulp in tanks.)

*Product Differentiation*[127]

In many markets, especially those for consumer goods, product differentiation is an important element in market rivalry.[128] With substantial product differentiation, through the use of trade-marks and design features, consumer attraction can become a meaningful element of market structure.[129] Product differentiation is related to issues of brands, patents, cross-elasticities of demand, and price relationships. A company may have several trade-marks for the same item, selling it at various prices.

The use of private brands can have a significant effect on market structure. Manufacturers of nationally advertised brands frequently sell the same product, or a specially designed one with private brand labels, to national distributors at lower prices. During the framing of the Robinson-Patman Act a suggestion that price reductions for private brands should be allowed was turned down by the House Judiciary Committee.[130] Several proceedings have involved price discrimination on private-brand commodities. For example, the Hansen Inoculator Company sold a product for 24 cents under its own brand and 15 cents under one buyer's private brand.[131]

The significance of product differentiation depends, of course, on consumer information regarding product qualities. Trade-marks may have a substantial effect on entry into the market and on the nature of competition among sellers of various sizes. For example, individual grocery or drug stores are rarely able to market goods with their own brands because they are not organized to design products and packages, manufacture the products, or control their quality when made by others, and promote the trade-marks. On the other hand, supermarket and drug chains do have the capacity to promote their own private labels.[132] As a result, the smaller retailer is more dependent on the manufacturer of national brands. Meanwhile, the larger distributor can counter the power of the national-brand manufacturer by promoting a private label item, or he may use this power to wring special price concessions from the seller. As Joe S. Bain analyzes this problem, grade labeling and adequate consumer information can have a substantial bearing on the breakdown of barriers to entry in many markets.[133]

### *Market Information*

Competition can be influenced by the mechanisms for disseminating information regarding prices, costs, and qualities, as well as data concerning supply and demand. With such information customers have full freedom of choice among the offerings of various sellers. The same data permit sellers to size up the competitive situation more effectively. Without such information pockets of monopoly or monopsony can develop. Availability of such data to consumers has been discussed in several important cases, notably *Sugar Institute*.[134] This aspect of structure deals with the market mechanism for promulgating such information.

While ready availability of such data can sharpen competition, it can also be tied in with collusive arrangements. Trade associations' information services regarding prices and volume of sales may serve as a competitive mechanism especially if they are available to buyers as well as sellers. However, it was held in several cases that open-price trade associations have been used to support prices—either by enforcing a specific agreement or reinforcing tacit understanding.[135] Some associations have kept sellers from cutting prices secretly in order to obtain additional volume. They required that the seller give his competitors preliminary notice before he changed a price, as in the *American Linseed Oil* case.[136] This elimination has curtailed some price competition.

### *Government Services*

A number of government activities, which do not come under the scope of antitrust, can affect the structure of a market. Such government supervision as compulsory grading, food and drug regulation and inspection, the control of warehouse receipts, and of weights and measures enables buyers to deal with sellers at long distance. These activities, together with the impartial administration of commercial law (covering sales contracts, negotiable instruments, and agency), permit sellers to extend their selling activities over wide areas. In many markets—for example, fresh, frozen, and canned fruits and vegetables—such governmental activities expand trading areas and aid entry into a market because they decrease the importance of established reputations and trade-marks.

On the other hand, certain types of regulation can and have dulled competitive forces. As pointed out in Chapter 2, some state regulations have made it difficult for outside manufacturers or distributors to send goods into a state in competition with domestic manufacturers or distributors. Protective tariffs, quotas, embargoes, and customs regulations have had the same effects on the national level.

### *Countervailing Power*

Even if countervailing power[137] is not considered as a substitute for competition, it does constitute an element in the study of a market structure. Its use as an indicator calls for somewhat complex inquiry. On the one hand, its mere existence reflects substantial anticompetitive elements in the market. On the other, it can denote factors that limit monopolistic forces. Thus, the fact that a large industrial purchaser or distributor has the ability to manufacture a commodity may limit the monopoly power of the established manufacturers of the item.

Many examples of such a situation can be found in modern industry: the ability of Ford and Chrysler to manufacture spark plugs themselves appears to influence the prices of those items;[138] A & P's demonstrated ability to manufacture has, it has been alleged, helped it to gain discriminatory concessions;[139] Sears Roebuck has designed and produced a range of consumer items when it felt that suppliers' prices were unreasonably high. At another level, the growth of buying cooperatives to purchase private label merchandise from small food packers and manufacturers (as well as from large producers with excess capacity) has limited the market power of large national-brand producers.

The existence of countervailing power has varying implications for market competition. At times, the power of a large buyer can upset an anticompetitive framework. At other times, it can increase the disparity between large and small competitors.[140] Similarly, the countervailing power between large employers and labor unions can offset each other. It can produce sufficient similarity in labor costs to influence competition. A number of cases have demonstrated that unions and employer organizations have conspired in very effective programs to limit production, increase costs and prices, and enforce other restrictive practices in a market, as in *Bradley Co.* v. *Local Union No. 3*.[141] The anticompetitive plans were enforced by the unions, which refused to supply labor to any employer who did not cooperate.

### *Potential Competition*

The fear of potential competition appears to be a prime motivating factor in some markets.[142] It is, of course, influenced by ease of entry. The force of this competitive factor is dependent on structural conditions in a specific market and on general conditions in the economy. Because of the dynamic trends in technology, coupled with a growing industrial interest in diversification, many companies do not know when and how new competitors may enter their markets. Wood items have faced new competition from products made from steel, aluminum, and plastics; manufacturers of metal castings have to contend with replacement by metal stampings and plastic extrusions; cotton competes with chemical fibers, plastics, and pulp products.

Diversification has become an important factor affecting competition in many markets.[143] Manufacturers are looking for new product markets. Distributors are branching into other areas: supermarkets sell drugs and clothing; department stores sell food; drug stores carry clothing and electric appliances. Distributors integrate backwards by going into manufacturing, while manufacturers integrate forward—producing more advanced products, taking on wholesale and even retail distribution.

The existence of such potential competition may have profound effects on the competitive framework in many markets. It may point up the impracticality of collusive arrangements or the desirability of maintaining low prices in order to avoid attracting newcomers.[144] In some markets, the danger of this unknown competition "around the corner" may constitute a major competitive spur.

## *Behavior of Participants in a Market*

Patterns of behavior[145] or conduct of sellers are the most frequent competitive indicators employed in the administration of antitrust. These indicators are utilized more frequently than criteria of structure and performance because they fit into the process of litigation more readily. Some behavior indicators deal primarily with intent; some reflect intent indirectly; while others are covered by specific legal rules, such as the Robinson-Patman Act.

Behavior indicators are, of course, not clearly distinct from all criteria of structure or performance. Interrelations are many and varied.[146] For example, the vertical integration of one company (an aspect of structure) may permit it to squeeze nonintegrated competitors (an aspect of behavior) as contended in the *Alcoa*[147] case. Product differentiation is an element of structure; at the same time it may be used to limit competition, or it may be the basis for the control of resale prices.

Similarly, some aspects of performance may be so dependent on behavior that the lines of demarcation between the two types must be arbitrary. Freedom of consumer choice, an aspect of performance, may be tied up with behavior. When a dominant company prevents distributors from selling other manufacturers' products (behavior), it may effectively limit consumer choice (performance). When sellers agree to apportion sections of the market among themselves, they limit consumer choice.

Rounded analysis of behavior frequently calls for consideration of the conduct of buyers as well as of sellers. It may, on occasion, require examination of the conduct of suppliers to the sellers. Marked differences in the size and power of buyers may be the force which sparks discrimination in the prices and services of sellers. If retailers must deal with powerful manufacturers who have strong trade-marks, many retailers may band together in order to make their purchases cooperatively or to force the manufacturers to control resale prices. A manufacturer's policy of selling only to exclusive distributors may curtail price competition among retailers, while a system of multiple distribution may push competing retailers into stiff price competition.

The patterns of behavor have so many interrelations that any system of classification cannot avoid overlapping. Some practices may fit under more than one classification; in some industries a given practice may automatically bring another into play. Hence, the following exercise in taxonomy does not and cannot develop watertight classifications.

### *Collusion*[148]

Elements of collusion or conspiracy thread through many antitrust cases. Many of these fit the category of per se violations. Hence they are taken not only as indicators of competition but also as antitrust violations, in and of themselves. Price agreements among competitors, frequently referred to as horizontal price agreements, have been set up as per se violations ever since the *Socony-Vacuum* case.[149] Agreements to divide territories, to limit production, and to allocate customers have been outlawed in such cases as *Johnson* v. *Schlitz*[150] and *Hartford-Empire.*[151]

A price agreement between two subsidiaries of one company has been held to be collusive.[152] While the economic effects of the arrangement do not differ from the operations of two divisions of the same company, the existence of separate corporate persons made possible a finding of conspiracy.[153]

### *Boycotts*

Boycotts constitute a specific aspect of collusive behavior. Agreements among suppliers, or among suppliers and their customers, to boycott a type of distributor or a specific retailer have been held to indicate a lack of competition. In the recent *Klor's*[154] case, boycotts were held to be violations per se. Various elements of fair play influence attitudes regarding such practices—elements which may have even more weight than competitive effect.

### *Character of Market Incentives to Competitive Moves*

This is a summary element suggested by some writers.[155] It presents a special problem in the case of oligopoly—a market with a limited number of competitors. In such a market, the individual company must visualize the quick reactions of its competitors when it makes a price cut, increases prices, or develops a new product or package. If a producer feels that a price cut will be quickly counteracted, he will be less likely to make the move. Hence, the time he expects to elapse before there would be a countermove will have an important bearing on his enthusiasm for a competitive maneuver. This element is, of course, a behavioral aspect of industrial concentration. It is related to a number of other indicators: conscious parallelism, price leadership, basing point prices, and matching competitors' prices.

### *Conscious Parallelism*[156]

There has been some interest in recent years in a doctrine of conscious parallelism.[157] Under this theory, the antitrust laws would be violated if each competitor copied the price moves of other sellers when he knows, with or without agreement, that everyone else would follow suit. There would be no need to prove collusion if conscious parallelism had developed as an independent basis for a finding of violation.[158]

Conscious parallelism has never been held to be an antitrust violation, in and of itself.[159] However, evidence of such practices have, as a practical matter, been used as support for a finding of conspiracy.[160] In *Interstate Circuit, Inc.*,[161] the Supreme Court held that "an unlawful conspiracy may be . . . formed without simultaneous action or agreement on the part of the conspirators. . . . Acceptance . . . of an invitation to participate in a plan, the necessary consequences of which, if carried out, is restraint of interstate commerce, is sufficient to establish an unlawful conspiracy. . . ."

### *Price Leadership*[162]

Price leadership obtains when one or more companies in a market lead price movements—both increases and decreases—that are matched by others firms.[163] This institution has been widely discussed as an indicator of absence of competition in economic writings. It has been found as an indicator of collusion or as an element in the pattern of competition in such cases as the 1915 *U. S. Steel*[164] proceeding. It was held to be evidence of an antitrust violation in *International Harvester*.[165] It affected the F.T.C. decision in the *Crown* case.[166]

The full significance of price leadership is not easy to detect. It may emerge as the result of a specific or tacit agreement. It may develop because the members of an industry follow the lead of one company when they believe that it has superior understanding of cost and demand conditions.[167] It may be forced by a powerful competitor who has a reputation for punishing recalcitrant smaller competitors by deliberate predatory practices.[168]

### *Basing Point Pricing*[169]

Basing point pricing is an important feature in some industries whose transportation costs are substantial in relation to price, for example, steel and cement. It has been involved in price discrimination cases, such as *Staley*.[170] It may be related to price leadership or agreement, and to the issue of meeting competitors' prices. Under a basing point system, delivered prices are set by adding transportation costs between a fixed base—which may not be the seller's plant—and the buyer's plant to a list price. Since the delivered price includes transportation costs from the basing point, there would be no differences in the price charged regardless of which plant shipped the item. An extreme illustration of this practice was the Pittsburgh-plus system, under which all steel producers used one city as their basing point for delivered prices for certain products. These prices included freight costs from Pittsburgh, even those of a plant which was located next door to the buyer.[171] A further development is to set up several basing points with prices stated for each point; or to set up each mill as a basing point in which case delivered prices are usually the lowest sum of mill price plus transport cost available from any mill.

This practice has attracted substantial attention in economic analysis. It has been interpreted by some as a clear indicator of price collusion, or at the minimum, as a drag on competitive pricing.[172] Under the system, a buyer would pay the same price to every plant which chose to sell to him, regardless of its location; therefore, the plan does make it possible to enforce a price-agreement even when transportation costs are high, as in the steel industry. Some economists disagree with the conclusion that basing-point systems of themselves indicate the failure of competition and feel that this pricing system must be analyzed as one element in a complex of factors.[173]

In industries with heavy transportation costs, a basing point system can be employed to implement price collusion. Such a system permits equalization of prices quoted by each seller at each customer's receiving point. The practice was hit strongly in the Supreme Court's *Cement Institute*[174] decision. Because the system produces discriminatory prices, that case involved the Robinson-Patman Act. However, the basic problem in the *Cement Institute* proceeding appears to have been price collusion rather than price discrimination because of other evidence developed in that case.

### *Freight Absorption*

Absorbing freight is another aspect of delivered pricing. It takes many forms. One is to add to a base price the freight from the competitor nearest to the customer regardless of where the shipping point may be—a form of basing point pricing practiced by an individual competitor. Another is to quote delivered prices with no separate element for freight. Delivered prices may be uniform throughout the country, or they may be regional prices. For example, some companies charge one uniform price east of the Rockies and another price west. In some markets, all sellers use the same delivered pricing system. In others, there are a number of systems—a practice which may give considerable importance to cutting prices to meet a competitor's charges.

### *Meeting and Matching Rivals' Prices*[175]

This practice has important implications in the administration of the Robinson-Patman Act. It was the central issue in *Standard Oil of Indiana,*[176] in which case it was held that meeting an equally low price of a competitor is a complete justification for a discriminatory price.[177] Legislative efforts have been made to curtail this defense. Questions have been raised about systematic plans for meeting competition, as in a basing point system, rather than meeting competition in individual transactions. Some cases have touched on the border of predatory practices. In *Anheuser-Busch,*[178] the F.T.C. objected to lowering the price of a nationally advertised product to meet the price of a local brand which customarily sells at lower prices. However, the commission lost the case on appeal. Analysis of this factor includes a review of general industry practices regarding meeting prices and of customary differentials for competing products in the industry.

### *Price Flexibility*[179]

Flexibility of prices has been advanced as an important aspect of the competitive picture.[180] Analysis of price flexibility includes a review of the frequency of price changes and their amplitude. This problem achieved substantial public interest recently under the heading "administered prices." Much of the discussion rests on the theory that in a competitive market, prices will change frequently because they are sensitive to changes in demand. The "inflexibility of industrial prices," relative to agricultural prices, has been interpreted by such writers as Gardiner Means as a sign of reduced competition in the economy.[181] Others, such as Alfred Neal, have challenged this interpretation.[182] Neal points to the need to consider the flexibility of the margins between the prices paid for the elements going into costs and the prices charged for final products, instead of considering the final prices only. It has been suggested that many prices which are not changed frequently have been relatively stable during inflationary periods.

The concept of flexibility of prices has been important in policy deliberations. In litigation, coincidences in the timing of price changes have been employed as circumstantial evidence of collusion; however, patterns of price flexibility have not figured prominently.

### *Frequency of Price Changes*[183]

This feature is closely related to problems of price flexibility[184] and of meeting competitors' prices. It covers such questions as: Are prices changed daily or do they continue for a year or two? Are all prices of all competitors changed at the same time? Gauging the frequency of price changes calls for clear definitions. For example, if a manufacturer's published prices are kept constant while his discounts to retailers are changed frequently or if he makes special price concessions,[185] a review of the changes of his prices can entail complex statistical problems, particularly because most price series are not very accurate for individual products.[186]

Another complicating factor is found in industries which follow price lines.[187] Many industries employ fixed prices over long periods, for example, a $19.95 dress or a 10 cent bar of candy. While the dollars-and-cents prices are maintained, the "effective" prices are changed by variations in style, quality, or quantity.

Other industries must continue the same prices over a fixed period of time. Because of catalog selling, mail-order houses must set prices which they observe for many months. Others, such as the automobile and farm implement manufacturers, set prices for annual models. However, season-end discounts and changes in trade-in allowances produce much more flexible prices than those in the published lists.

### *Methods of Determining Prices*

Methods of determining prices have been considered broadly in examining market situations. The use of standard formulas—as in basing point systems—has been treated as an element in competitive analysis. If an industry produces tailor-made items, such as the job printing trade, its only method for setting up a collusive scheme would be to establish a uniform price formula.[188] The formula might contain set hourly rates for the work and mark-ups over the cost of material; for example, it might be contained in a "cost book" for such special items as automobile repair services.

Another method which has been involved in several cases[189] is the use of bid depositories—a system under which each competitor notifies a central agency of bids before it submits them to customers. This information is made available to all competitors,[190] but not to customers. Some cases have featured the use of books of uniform prices, standard freight rates, and formulas for extra charges for modifications of standard items.[191]

### *Price Discrimination*[192]

The subject of price discrimination[193] has stirred up considerable debate in economic circles. It has been described both as an indicator of anticompetitive forces[194] and as the manifestation of active competition.[195] The anticompetitive argument has rested on the premise that price discrimination does not take place when sellers are engaged in active competition or when there are substantial differences in the buying power of customers. On the other hand, it has been argued that price discrimination is a competitive practice in many markets; that individual sellers who would not cut all of their prices in order to get an order are willing to reduce some prices;[196] therefore, price discrimination is the mechanism for instituting competitive price reductions. It can, of course, indicate dominant market positions of buyers.[197]

As suggested in Chapter 6, analysis of price discrimination has been somewhat confused by differences in the legal and economic definitions.[198] The practice is covered specifically by the Robinson-Patman Act. While the act outlaws only that price discrimination which may lessen competition substantially, the F.T.C. and the courts have in most proceedings presumed that any discrimination does so.[199] This presumption has been rebutted in only a few cases. While Section 2(f) of the law covers buyers who benefit[200] as well as sellers, it has been ineffective[201] until the recent *American Motor Specialties*[202] case. In a few proceedings, such as *A & P*,[203] there have been attacks on favored buyers under other antitrust laws.

### *Discrimination in Service*

A related aspect of market behavior is discrimination in service. Separate sections of the Robinson-Patman Act cover these practices. One section prohibits a seller from supplying service to favored buyers unless it is offered to others "on proportionally equal terms." A parallel section covers payments to buyers for services supplied by them, for example, advertising or special displays. Supplying free demonstrators to some distributors and paying them advertising allowances without making comparable contributions to other customers have been held to violate these sections. In a few cases, it has been held that the act is violated if a manufacturer does not make all of his goods available to all of his customers. For example, a soap manufacturer who would not sell his ten-cent size of soap to druggists, but required that they buy the larger size, was held to be a violator in the *Luxor* case.[204] The Robinson-Patman Act does not cover the buyers who are favored under the service sections. However, the F.T.C. has proceeded against favored buyers under Section 5 of the Federal Trade Commission Act, as in the *Food Fair* case.[205] Differential advantages in services were involved also in the *A & P*[206] antitrust case.

### *Predatory Practices*[207]

Predatory practices[208] have been regarded in some cases as indications of a lack of competition or the existence of monopoly-breeding power. The practices have been attacked not only because they are anticompetitive but also because of their ethical overtones.[209] Predatory behavior includes such practices as cutting prices in local markets in order to harm individual competitors,[210] spreading disparaging rumors about competitors or about their products, bribing personnel of competitors to harm their employers, threatening present and potential customers of competitors with possible patent or other suits, and sabotaging competitors' machines which are being used by potential customers.[211]

### *Marketing Methods*

Analysis of marketing methods covers a wide range that affects both structure and behavior. Products are sold by manufacturers direct to consumers, and through wholesalers, superwholesalers, retailers, chains, and agents. Many manufacturers use some or all of these channels. There are differences in the field representation of manufacturers: through factory-owned branches, through salesmen, through agents, or through franchise distributors. Distributors use a variety of similar methods.

Many patterns are so firmly established that they can be treated as elements in the market structure. For example, if each manufacturer sells to distributors who handle his produce exclusively over a period of years, a form of vertical integration develops.[212] In these circumstances entry of new manufacturers may be quite difficult. This issue was the determining factor in the *Standard Stations*[213] and the recent *Mytinger*[214] proceedings.

In some markets, differences in the marketing methods of individual manufacturers can complicate the analysis.[215] Some producers may extend their power through such practices as setting up exclusive dealerships and requirement contracts, while others do not. These differences in pattern can produce many problems similar to vertical integration of manufacturing.

Differences in the legal forms of marketing can have an important bearing on the effect of various antitrust laws on individual competitors. One manufacturer may be permitted to follow a practice which is forbidden to others because of differences in his contractual arrangements with distributors. For example, a manfacturer who sells through retailer "agents," as in the case of General Electric's distribution of light bulbs, can set retail prices without the benefit of fair trade, can establish territories, and can require exclusive contracts.[216] In contrast, a competitor who sells to "independent" retailers is stopped from these practices.

### *Exclusive Territories*[217]

Some producers designate one distributor—wholesaler or retailer—who can sell their products exclusively in a specified territory.[218] This issue is prominent in two recent F.T.C. complaints: *Container Stapling*[219] and *International Staple*.[220] Under some arrangements, no other distributors can sell in the franchised territory; under others, if another distributor makes a sale in the territory, the discounts are shared by the two resellers involved. Such systems can influence price competition at the wholesaler's or retailer's level. They may induce the distributor to handle the products of the manufacturer exclusively.[221] In some industries this practice is so firmly established that it has become a form of vertical integration in the structure of the market.[222]

### *Requirement Contracts*

Some sales agreements provide that the purchaser will buy all his requirements of the goods covered by the contract from the seller. Some provide that he will make no purchases from others. The practice is covered specifically by Section 3 of the Clayton Act. There has been some disagreement regarding the effects of such contracts on competition. In the *Standard Stations* case,[223] the Supreme Court seemed to feel that all such contracts reduce competition; in the *American Can* proceeding,[224] the Court felt that such a contract could be permitted for a limited period of time, one year, because of the business requirements of the buyer. In *Tampa Electric*[225] it upheld an electric power company's twenty-year contract to purchase its coal requirements.

It has been suggested there is a likelihood that such contracts constitute a form of competition in some markets and that they constitute a valuable service because they provide the buyer with an assured source of supply. In a study of the brewing industry in the United Kingdom, it was concluded that the use of a requirement contract had maintained smaller sellers in business.[226]

### *Tying Contracts*[227]

Tying contracts are sales agreements or policies providing that the purchaser must buy Product A in order to obtain Product B. If a company has a strong market position for one of its products, it can "force" the sale of other items through such an arrangement.[228] The practice is similar to a requirement contract for Product A and has raised problems under Section 3 of the Clayton Act.[229] Such arrangements have been held to violate the antitrust laws in a number of cases, ranging from the block-booking of motion pictures[230] to the compulsory purchase of salt for use in patented dispensing machines. The use of a patented item to force the purchase of an unpatented product has been especially important in the cases.[231]

### *Patent Pooling*

Pooling the patents of a number of competitors is a phase of patent control. It may serve to block others from the market. It may make competition among the members of the pool more effective. Conversely, it may be the keystone for a pattern of cooperation among the members, a conclusion reflected in the 1895 *National Harrow*[232] case and the later *Hartford-Empire*[233] proceeding. Obviously, a patent pool can become a significant attribute of market structure. However, it does not always constitute an antitrust violation. Thus, in the *Cutter Laboratories* case,[234] a pool covering a freezing process and related equipment was held to be satisfactory because the two companies involved were not competitors.

### *Cross-Licensing and Grant-Backs*

Cross-licensing is closely related to patent pooling except that it affects individual licensors. In a grant-back, a licensee agrees that he will give the licensor of a basic patent a license to use any patents which he, himself, might obtain relating to the same product or process. The procedure has enabled owners of basic patents to extend and retain control over manufacturing and marketing operations beyond the bounds of the original patent, as in the *Rail Joint Co.* case.[235]

### *Other Patent Controls*

A number of other patent practices may influence a competitive situation.[236] A company may obtain patents for a number of inventions and prevent innovation by "sitting" on the patents—not using them and not licensing anyone else to use them. A patentee might control the prices, volume of production, and sales of his licensees. The members of an industry may "voluntarily" recognize one or more weak patents held by one owner and accept licenses which contain such restrictive provisions as price and production limitations. A powerful company may use threats of expensive patent suits to whip others into line on pricing, methods of distribution, and product design.

### *Intent to Monopolize*

Intent to monopolize has been classed as an important indicator by some economists.[237] The intent looms importantly in legal aspects of antitrust.[238] This feature is, of course, a summary evaluation. On occasion, such an intent may be proven by specific evidence of conversations or writings. Usually, it is inferred from circumstantial evidence. At any rate, it can be a significant litigating factor in evaluating the behavior of a competitor who is powerful enough to influence the flavor of the market.

### *Merger History*

Clues to the background of competitive behavior may be drawn from the merger history of some of the leading companies in a market. Such a history has been used to analyze intent to monopolize or to evaluate the milder forms of controlling competition. Such evidence has been regarded as directly in point in many proceedings instituted under the new antimerger statute.[239]

Merger history can be an important element in an economic study of a market and of the economy generally. Of course, the competitive effects of mergers do not point in one direction. While some mergers may increase market concentration or eliminate bothersome competitors, others may enable smaller companies to survive and to attain more significant competitive influence. Some conglomerate mergers may stimulate competition because they bring a powerful new company into the market.

### *Seizure of Opportunities*

Intent has been related to a company's aggressiveness in seizing opportunities to expand, thereby preventing other companies from entering the market or from growing. This factor is most important in the natural resource industries. Much was made of this point in the *Alcoa* proceeding.[240] In his study of the aluminum industry, Donald Wallace concluded that the company had ignored opportunities to expand. However, the two points of view may be reconciled. Alcoa may have seized every occasion to keep others from obtaining a foothold in the industry at the same time that it overlooked affirmative opportunities to expand the market for aluminum.

### *Product Standardization*

Competitive behavior may be influenced by industry-wide standardization programs. Standards of dimensions can be undertaken to reduce costs and to permit the interchangeability of competing products, as in the standard electric light bulbs or phonograph records. This procedure can promote price competition or it can be used to reinforce price collusion and price leadership.

Standardization of descriptive nomenclature can help the consumer to make more rational choices, leading to more effective competition. On the other hand, such standardization may be employed for the opposite effect. For example, the Federal Trade Commission felt that although there are significant differences in the specifications of the cement produced by various companies, the industry pretended that its products were of uniform quality in order to support its price agreement.[241]

## *Performance of the Market*

Performance is a tricky indicator of competition.[242] At best, criteria of performance are instruments of diagnosis, not prognosis. They may indicate that a competitive situation should be improved, but they do not tell what steps are needed to effectuate the change. They are difficult to apply because there are no satisfactory yardsticks to gauge the adequacy of performance.[243] Analysis of performance provides many temptations to evaluate the total social contribution of an industry rather than to evaluate its competitiveness.[244] Yet judgment whether a market is tolerably competitive frequently requires some sensing of its performance.[245]

Conceptually, the ultimate judgment about the effectiveness of competition in a market should be its performance.[246] How competitive are the prices, the production, the innovations, and the consumer choices? The principal significance of indicators of structure and behavior is the light they throw on expectations of performance. In this respect, the indicators of competition are similar to those used in many other types of evaluation, for example, the appraisal of a new airplane. Engineering studies may be made of the physical structure of the airframe; the operations of individual features—such as engines, fuel, electrical and control systems—may be reviewed and tested carefully; but in the final analysis these studies are only indicators of what can be expected. Ultimately, the plane's performance is the important test.

While criteria of performance are useful for evaluation,[247] they do not, by themselves, provide the basis for determining the remedies.[248] When an airplane's performance is rated "unsatisfactory," improvement depends on changing the factors which cause the inadequacy. A decision to increase the plane's stability merely sets the goal. The improvement may require redesigning the airframe or the engine. Similarly, if high profits are regarded as an indication of monopolistic forces, an order to reduce a company's profits would not touch the heart of the problem. The indicator may show that some elements in the market need tinkering. However, if those elements are not spotted, the performance diagnosis has little practical value.

The indicators of performance require the construction of standards of adequacy.[249] What gauges can be used to tell when performance reflects a competitive situation? How can a final evaluation be made of the adequacy of an industry's growth, of changes in the design of its products and in its production methods, or of its profit levels?[250] Such evaluations must take account of many factors in addition to competition. Progressiveness, for example, may depend on developments in other markets in response to consumer tastes. Such shifts affected the markets for the horse-drawn buggy and the whalebone corset. Growth and innovation in the automobile industry were stimulated by strong consumer desires and a major public roads program in addition to competition, or the lack thereof.

Tied in with these difficulties is a serious analytical problem. How can performance evaluations be confined to the judgment of competitiveness?[251] Broad consideration of an industry's performance offers irresistible urges to make evaluations of social performance.[252] Consider, for example, one performance indicator that has been suggested: labor conditions. An industry that is dominated by monopolistic forces may agree to increase wages and fringe benefits freely because it can raise prices easily.[253] A competitive industry might resist union demands with greater vigor. Some social evaluation would rate the monopolistic industry high, the competitive one low. Yet, there is no suggestion that poor working conditions should be taken as an indication of competitive performance.

The difficulty of analyzing performance is compounded by questions regarding the place of competition in the implementation of our economic, political, and social goals. An industry might provide substantial stability of employment and considerable innovation because of a combination of monopolistic forces and a consumer demand that remains tolerably stable in the face of price increases. Such stability and innovation may indicate that the industry is in excellent working order and give it a high rating for social performance. But such an evaluation does not meet the issue of competitiveness. As we shall see, many of the tests of performance tend toward broad evaluations of social performance rather than the more specific analyses of competition.

The most prominent indicators of competitive performance which have been suggested are: profit levels, passing cost savings on to the consumer, innovation and progressiveness, rate of growth, capacity-output relations, freedom of consumer choice, wasted resources in selling activities, contribution to national defense, and labor conditions.

### *Profit Levels*

One of the most widely used indicators of performance is the level of profits.[254] This criterion has not been employed widely in litigation,[255] although it seems to have been involved in several cases, such as *American Tobacco*,[256] *Sugar Institute*,[257] and *Eli Lilly*.[258]

As suggested previously, the use of profit showings as an indicator of competition is founded on the assumption that monopoly breeds high profits. However, this assumption has neither firm theoretical foundation nor substantial empirical support.[259] The major influence of competition may well be to force competitors to seek ways to reduce costs.[260] With a profit margin of 5 per cent, a company will work hard to cut its cost, which represents 95 per cent of its price, whenever it has to pay more for materials or labor. Similarly, it must scramble for cost savings whenever competition forces its prices down or prevents its prices from rising after an increase in wages or in material prices.[261] However, if a firm can easily raise its prices because of its monopoly position, it may not be too concerned about reducing costs.

Studies have not indicated a clear pattern of monopoly profits.[262] Research has produced only desultory results.[263] There are wide ranges of profit showings for competitors in the same market. Hence, differences in costs or in accounting may account for a more substantial part of variations in profit showings than does monopoly position.

Comparisons of profit showings are uncertain at best.[264] One company may have purchased equipment at very low prices, another at very high prices. One may pay high salaries to officer-owners, another low salaries. One may engage in a costly long-run research program, another may spend little on research. The profit figures published for substantial companies are influenced by managerial decisions about what profits should be shown. This does not imply dishonesty in accounting. Honest accounting results are, and must be, influenced by corporate policies. To take a simple example, a corporation which wants to avoid high profit showings can expend substantial amounts on repairs, research, product development, building up a sales force, and developing other activities that will be charged as current expenses. These reduce published profits. In reverse, it can reduce these expenses and increase profit showings.

The use of profit levels as an indicator of competition is complicated by the widespread existence of multiproduct companies.[265] When a diversified company sells a number of items in several separate markets, its profit showings reflect the over-all operation of the company. Therefore, even if the company's published profits are low, it might have made tremendous profits in one market. Unless and until companies develop divisional profit and loss statements, it will be impossible to analyze profits for this purpose.[266] Further, even should divisional statements be made available, companies could exercise substantial discretion in allocating expenses—and in some cases, allocating income—to the various divisions. Hence, divisional profit showings might not reflect the operations of multiproduct companies in any particular market.

Nevertheless, showings of extraordinary profits by all firms selling in a market—compared with companies that follow similar production and distribution methods, but which sell in other markets—does affect analysis of competitive forces. Extraordinary profit showings over a long period of time may have substantial significance if it is one of a series of indicators. On the other hand, low profit showings do not indicate forceful competition.[267]

### *Passing Cost Savings to the Consumer*[268]

Passing cost savings on to the consumer has been suggested as another indicator.[269] It assumes that active competition will force such consumer benefits. Although this criterion is closely related to profit showings, it is not quite the same. Cost savings—especially those resulting from increases in productivity—do not necessarily bring about lower prices or higher profits. Instead, they may be drained off in many other ways: increases in wage rates and other labor costs;[270] higher executive salaries; greater expenditures for distribution and sales promotion; or expenditures for innovation and product development.

Practical application of this indicator is difficult. It requires an analysis that is even more complex than gauging profits because of the difficulties of pinning down unit costs. Obtaining such cost data is especially complicated because most substantial companies manufacture a number of products with a high proportion of joint costs, including overhead. Additionally, this indicator is founded on the assumption that when costs are reduced, competition will drive only in the direction of lower prices. In this, it overlooks other consumer benefits from competition which are not so easily measured: improvements in quality; innovation; new equipment or other improvements that may lower future costs substantially; and better consumer service.

### *Innovation*[271] *and Progressiveness*[272]

Many hold that competition will stimulate innovation and progressiveness. An industry with heavy investments in the manufacture of current products may want to avoid innovations that require changes in productive equipment in order to take full advantage of its investment in present capacity. Dynamic competitive pressures may make it impossible to maintain this protection.

On the other hand, it has been suggested that competition may not permit the accumulation of profits which are needed for changes and that it will make innovation less attractive because it offers no protection for the innovators' investment; hence, some monopolistic forces may accelerate innovation.[273] Conceivably, innovation will be generated most forcefully in a market which has an appropriate blend of competitive and monopolistic forces.[274] The premise of our patent system is that monopoly protection will encourage people to take the risks of innovation. Similarly, it has been suggested that innovation is a key factor which will upset monopoly positions, and that it acts as a self-generating substitute for competition.[275]

The judgment of satisfactory progressiveness is difficult.[276] We have not achieved practical yardsticks except, possibly, for extreme cases of backwardness. The range of technical engineering and production analysis required for final evaluation casts some doubt on the potential usefulness of this indicator.

### *Rate of Growth*[277]

Another proposed indicator concerns the rate of growth of an industry. Conceptually, a competitive market forces down costs and prices, with a concomitant increase of sales. Further, if competition forces innovation, an industry will grow; on the contrary, a comfortable monopoly position will tend to retard growth.

This indicator has a close relationship with the behavior indicator listed above, seizing opportunities for increasing capacity. As stated above, the *Alcoa*[278] decision referred to the company's practice of keeping potential competitors out of the market by using every opportunity to expand, while an able industry study indicated that opportunities for expansion were neglected. Here, too, is a complex index of competitiveness that poses substantial problems of evaluation.

### *Capacity-Output Relations*[279]

This indicator focuses on excess capacity.[280] In abstract theory, under pure competition prices are so low that sales volume equals practical capacity. If demand falls, prices are lowered until capacity is in full use.

Large excess capacity may mean that an industry is holding prices too high. However, it can be caused by a number of other factors as well: the general level of economic activity may be low; sales may have fallen off because the industry's products are going out of style; excess capacity may be due to past investment errors in the industry, or to anticipated increases in demand.[281] Since investment decisions constitute an element of competitiveness, current excess capacity may be due to the influence of past competitive forces. Indeed, cartels have purposely kept plant size in check in order to avoid the pressures of excess capacity on price. Further, in a tolerably competitive market, excess capacity may stimulate competitive maneuvers either through price reductions across the board or by discriminatory price concessions to selected customers.

### *Freedom of Consumer Choice*[282]

One of the advantages claimed for competition is that it gives the consumer[283] a range of choices from a variety of products and sources of supply;[284] in contrast, a monopolistic market may confine his choices. Similarly, a competitive market offers a range of alternatives to sellers.[285] Interestingly, this claim is at odds with the postulate of a standard commodity which is required for pure competition.

### *Wasted Resources in Selling Activities*[286]

This measure of performance requires an evaluation of the usefulness of selling activities in the relevant market.[287] It has received considerable public attention recently in the Senate hearings on the drug industry. The issue is related to issues of consumer information and truth in advertising. There are implications in the wording of this criterion, which seems to be founded on the assumption that price competition is the only desirable form of market rivalry, and that other methods of competing should be restrained. It may reflect a strong tendency to introduce evaluations of social performance into the analysis.

This indicator introduces the need for determining what are selling activities and how much selling is desirable. Would the repackaging of a line of products be classified as a selling activity? Would annual redesigns of automobiles be so classed?[288] Can any allowance be made for the contention that selling effort can increase total economic activity or that increases in a company's volume can generate savings in other costs which outweigh the selling expenses?

### *Contribution to National Defense*[289]

Some have suggested that the evaluation of competitive performance should take account of the industry's contribution to national defense.[290] This criterion illustrates again the difficulty of keeping the focus on competition when performance indicators are employed. While such contributions may raise some questions about a broad competitive policy, they hardly qualify as yardsticks of competitiveness. Indeed, some campaigns for protection against foreign competition have been based on the argument that an industry must be protected because of its potential contribution to national defense, as in the tariff campaign of the domestic watch industry. Further, during general defense preparations, antitrust prosecutions are commonly postponed in order to avoid interference with an industry's production.

### *Labor Conditions*[291]

It has been suggested that labor conditions should be taken as an indicator of performance.[292] The consideration of labor conditions in an industry may be significant in the evaluation of its social performance. Yet, it is difficult to visualize its practical use as an indicator of competition. Public policy has called for setting minimum labor conditions, partly to prevent individual competitors from gaining advantages by paying submarginal wages. However, as suggested above, unusually favorable labor conditions may reflect monopoly more frequently than competition.[293]

## *Antitrust Applications*

The uses of the various indicators of competition are not clearly defined in most of the antitrust statutes. A few acts are concerned with specific indicators, others are indefinite. In administration, some statutes involve only one criterion of competition while others require the application of several indicators.

The statutory language does not always define those aspects of competition that are covered. The Sherman Act[294] does not mention competition: Section 1 relates to contracts and conspiracies "in restraint of trade"; Section 2 covers anyone "who shall monopolize or attempt . . . or conspire . . . to monopolize."

The Clayton Act[295] uses the phrase "lessen competition or tend to create a monopoly" in Section 2, as amended by the Robinson-Patman Act (price discrimination), Section 3 (exclusive purchase contracts and tying arrangements), and Section 7 (mergers and acquisitions). Section 8 (interlocking directorates) of the Clayton Act relates to competing corporations.

Section 3 of the Robinson-Patman Act[296] refers to "destroying competition or eliminating a competitor." Section 5 of the Federal Trade Commission Act[297] covers "unfair methods of competition" and "unfair or deceptive acts or practices."

Even when the same statutory language regarding competition is employed, the indicators that are employed in enforcement may differ. Sections 2, 3, and 7 of the Clayton Act use the same phrase,[298] "lessen competition or tend to create a monopoly." Yet, Section 2 is guided by criteria of behavior—price discrimination and meeting competitive prices; Section 3 is influenced by other criteria of behavior—exclusive contracts and tying arrangements; and Section 7, the antimerger provision, involves indicators of structure and behavior. Further, there is a substantial difference in the way in which the indicators are applied.

In the main, the cases which have been decided under Section 2 and Section 3[299] have not taken account of economic effects,[300] while the Section 7 merger cases have involved substantial analysis of effect. Under the interpretation of Section 3 of the Clayton Act which was enunciated in the *International Salt*[301] and *Standard Stations* cases,[302] that section is guided only by considerations of behavior: exclusive dealing arrangements and tying contracts are illegal when they affect a substantial volume of business. In contrast, the recent *Tampa Electric*[303] interpretation of the same section makes allowance for the structure of the buying and selling industries in evaluating an exclusive contract. Hence, exclusive contracts were held to be illegal without considering the economic background for the arrangement in *Standard Stations,* and were upheld in *Tampa Electric* on the basis of an analysis of the market.

The cases under Section 7 have entailed considerable exploration of market factors. The effects of mergers are judged by reviewing a number of elements of structure—concentration, difficulties of entry, geographical distribution, and alternative sources of supply—as well as such indicators of behavior as merger history. These features have been considered, in detail, in such cases as *Bethlehem Steel,*[304] *Crown Zellerbach*[305] and *Pillsbury Mills.*[306]

A few laws are guided by single indicators, others tend to accentuate several criteria, while some do not involve a clear pattern. Cases under the Robinson-Patman and the Federal Trade Commission Acts, together with Section 1 of the Sherman Act, turn largely on issues of behavior. At the other extreme, Section 8 of the Clayton Act is confined to one issue of structure since it covers only interference with the independence of rivals through interlocking directorates.

Combinations of criteria, relating to structure and behavior, are taken up in cases under Section 2 of the Sherman Act (monopolization) and Section 7 of the Clayton Act (mergers). Cases of monopolization call, first, for a finding of a high degree of concentration among the sellers in a market, and second, for behavior that indicates intent to monopolize. On the other hand, attempts of conspiracies to monopolize may be proved by behavior alone. Merger cases turn largely on issues of market structure;[307] however, many proceedings involve elements of behavior.

Indicators of performance have not been used widely. Profits were considered in some restraint of trade cases, such as *Sugar Institute;*[308] in monopolization cases, as *Alcoa,*[309] *Cellophane,*[310] and *General Electric.*[311] In *Banana Distributors, Inc.* v. *United Fruit Co.*[312] the court held that, "Defendants' profit margin is another factor which may properly be considered by a jury in determining whether the defendants had monopoly power."

Several indicators of behavior have been employed in cases under Section 1 of the Sherman Act. Price agreements, patent pools, and other forms of collusion were considered in the *Socony-Vacuum,*[313] *Sugar Institute,*[314] *Hartford-Empire,*[315] *Klor's,*[316] and *U.S. Steel* cases.[317] Problems of entry were considered in the *American Tobacco* proceeding.[318]

Sherman Act Section 2 cases have followed two lines: monopolization and conspiracies or attempts to monopolize. The first step in a monopolization case is to analyze the concentration of production or purchasing in a market. Unless a high degree of monopoly is found, there can be no violation. Thus, in the *Cellophane* case[319] the successful defense turned on a finding that the defendant accounted for only a small part of the flexible wrapping material market. After finding a "monopoly" situation, the courts consider indicators of behavior to determine whether there was an intent to monopolize. For example, in *Alcoa*[320] intent was found because the defendant seized every opportunity to expand and prevented other companies from entering the market; in *United Shoe Machinery,*[321] intent was found on the basis of the use of tying contracts.

Findings of conspiracies or attempts to monopolize are based on the defendant's behavior. In *GMAC,*[332] the arrangement between General Motors and General Motors Acceptance Corporation, whereby some dealers in General Motors cars were forced to finance their sales through GMAC, was declared to be conspiracy to monopolize. In *Lorain Journal*[323] a boycott based on a tying arrangement was the basis of a finding of attempt to monopolize.

Section 5 of the Federal Trade Commission Act depends entirely on indicators of behavior. The proceeding against *Food Fair*[324] turned on inducing manufacturers to grant discriminatory advantages to the respondent; the *National Silver*[325] case involved misrepresentation. The *Cement Institute*[326] case involved price agreements. *Fashion Originators' Guild*[327] was a boycott case.

Robinson-Patman cases, technically under Section 2 of the Clayton Act, are concerned only with indicators of behavior. Discriminations in prices, payments for services, and furnishing services on discriminatory terms are the sole foundations for such cases, except for the payment of brokerage. Meeting or matching equally low prices of a rival was held to be a valid defense in the *Standard Oil of Indiana* case.[328] On occasion, elements of structure were introduced into the proceedings; however, they did not affect the final results. In the *Hansen Inoculator* case[329] a violation was found although the lower prices were charged for private-label items and the higher prices for an advertised brand. In *Anheuser-Busch*[330] the respondent defeated the attempt of the F.T.C. to consider the geographical nature of the market and the differences in the geographical distribution of the activities of the market rivals.

Section 3 of the Clayton Act covers agreements to buy exclusively from one seller and tying arrangements. Such cases as *Standard Stations*[331] and *International Salt*[332] centered on behavior without considering competitive effects. The F.T.C. decided that such effects should be reviewed in the *Maico* case,[333] but it decided to follow the Supreme Court's lead in the *Mytinger* proceedings[334] when it refused to consider the influence of the arrangement on competition. Since then the Supreme Court considered competitive effects in *Tampa Electric*[335] when it took account of such structural elements as the geographical distribution of coal and oil in the Florida area, barriers to the entry of coal in that area, and the relatively unconcentrated production of coal.[336]

Section 7 of the Clayton Act, governing acquisitions and mergers, has involved many competitive indicators, mainly of structure. Issues of concentration were prominent in the *Bethlehem Steel*[337] and *Brillo* cases.[338] Problems of entry were considered in *American Crystal*,[339] *Spalding*,[340] and *Bethlehem Steel*.[341] The history of exits from the industry affected the *Spalding*[342] decision. Vertical integration was a factor in the *Brown Shoe* case.[343] *Lake Erie Sand* case[344] contained questions of alternative sources of supply and of geographical distribution of production—which came up in the *Bethlehem* case.[345] The issue of the *Hamilton Watch* proceeding[346] was clearly the question of independence of rivals. In *American Crystal*[347] an issue of behavior, price competition among leading companies, was mentioned; however, it did not seem to be of substantial significance.

## *Improvements in the Uses of the Indicators*

The application of the indicators of competition poses squarely the need for improving the use of economic analysis in the consideration of problems bearing on competition. There is no simple do-it-yourself method to organize these criteria for the analysis of public policy issues,[348] for finding violations of antitrust laws, or for formulating remedies. There are no systematical patterns of indicators that can be related to automatic conclusions regarding competitiveness.[349]

The indicators demonstrate the importance of careful field analysis in dealing with competitive problems. At the same time, they indicate that the function of sophisticated economic analysis is to improve the basis for judgment, not to serve as a substitute for it.

To bemoan the indefiniteness of the indicators is fruitless. Scientific certainty is an illusion:[350] in this, as in other fields of analysis, such certainty has been disproven time after time. The need for assumptions and postulates together with the confines of observational methods set limits for certitude in almost every type of analysis—and those dealing with man's behavior have suffered more than any. Even in the biological sciences, diagnosis and prognosis are not set in judgmental absolutes. Consider, for example, the problems of the medical doctors and the opportunities for differences of opinion in their practice.

On the surface, it would appear that greater certainty can be achieved by using a more limited group of indicators. There has been some debate regarding which of the three types of criteria are more significant.[351] However, there has not been enough empirical progress to concentrate on a limited group of indicators. Perhaps, beyond present horizons there will be enough knowledge to determine that certain indicators are highly correlated. At that time, a more limited group might suffice. Today, however, the analytical tasks call for proper selections from the full kit of tools[352] and for alertness to the formulation of new ones.[353]

Indeed, there is room for arguing that more, rather than fewer, criteria should be employed in some antitrust fields. Robinson-Patman cases apply limited indicators of behavior. As a result, they tend to rule out consideration of the effects of price discrimination in many instances. Small companies, which have to contend with many market rivals, are treated in the same fashion as those that enjoy a dominating position in their markets.[354] Because of the difficult analytical problems they impose, indicators of performance are used infrequently. Yet, the ultimate questions concern the effect, present or future, on competition.

On the other hand, some indicators can be singled out as practical guides for the administration of policy, indicators that are so clearly tied up with anticompetitive forces that they provide a satisfactory basis for administration. These indicators have been classified under the clear per se category: agreements to fix prices, to allocate markets, to administer boycotts, and to limit production or capacity.

Even though a substantial number of indicators[355] are available, they can be applied in a practical fashion.[356] With appropriate clarification of the issues of a case, it is possible to select those criteria that are germane to the problem at bar. Hence, it is possible to consider all the pertinent indicators without burdening the proceedings with aimless meandering through a sea of inapplicable economic evidence.

There is a certain usefulness in the three classes of indicators. However, as has been demonstrated, there are no distinct lines of demarcation between them. Some indicators can fit two or even three classifications. Conceptually, the major advantage in the classification is that they provide a broad-brush distinction between those indicators that are valuable for diagnosis only and those that are useful for both diagnosis and remedy.[357]

Considerable progress has been made in developing and applying the indicators. However, much more is needed. More effective application of existing economic inquiry must be developed. At the same time, further refinement of the tools of analysis is required.

There is a pressing need to supply practical aids in such analysis for the guidance of judges in the trial of antitrust issues. This need affects all of the stages in litigation, from the definition of the issues to the final decision and the formulation of decrees.

Further experience with such analysis in antitrust administration should help to make the indicators more specific and better suited to the administration of antitrust. Practical application depends on a firmer understanding between the legal and economic disciplines.

# 8 / *Defining the Market**

A CENTRAL FEATURE in competitive analysis is the problem of defining the relevant market. This is essential for any final evaluation of a competitive situation or for the formulation of realistic programs for improvement. In such analyses the relevant market encompasses those goods or services that are considered to be competitive with each other, the sellers of these goods, and those buyers[1] who are regarded as rivals. [2]

The application of most indicators of competition requires the ascertainment of the market in which competition does or might take place. The attributes of structure and behavior are tested within a market context. Conditions of entry, concentration, and geographical distribution are analyzed within a specific market. The effects of exclusive contracts and price discrimination must be judged within the confines of a defined market.

As the discussion of the indicators demonstrates, however, analysis of competition within a market calls for inquiry into the economic power of the individual market rivals.[3] Alcoa competed with other fabricators of aluminum products. However, it had a striking advantage because it was integrated and could squeeze the margins of its competitors by maintaining high prices for the raw material and low prices for the finished product. A & P, as a national chain, could cut prices in some cities below those of local stores because it made good profits elsewhere. If a company enjoys a dominant position in one market, it can use its resources for militant competition in a second[4] and drive companies that operate exclusively in the latter market out of business.[5]

Therefore, while the definition of the market locates the site of the

* Footnotes for Chapter 8 begin on page 443.

competitive rivalry, it does not confine the analysis of competition. To understand the nature of the rivalry and the forces which affect its future course in any one market, inquiry must be made into the positions of the pertinent sellers and buyers in other markets.[6]

The task of market definition affects all manner of policy formulation and administration affecting competition. The evaluation of the general state of competition, prospective statutory developments, industry studies, public-utility regulation, tariffs, and price control are all affected by relevant market definitions. Issues of market rivalry arise under many guises—"monopolization," "like goods," "relative rates," "unfair methods of competition," "line of products," "restraint of trade," and "lessening competition." But, regardless of how the issue may develop, it involves a common problem: defining the area of competition.

Market definition requires a combination of the legal and economic disciplines.[7] While economic theory defines markets in general terms,[8] the legal concept of the market is specialized, varying with differences in statutory language, with the seriousness of the pertinent violation, and with its consequences. Law does not allow for a universal definition.[9] Statutes affecting competition, such as antitrust and tariff laws, are based on a number of concepts of the market. Some laws contemplate a wide variety of markets: national, international, local, and regional—markets with many buyers and sellers, operating at many locations, dealing with similar goods bearing different brands. A few laws are concerned only with the competition between two or more distributors who purchase the same goods from the same manufacturer and who sell to the same types of customers.

Given these legal differences, the economist engaged in administration must tailor his inquiry to the specific purpose at hand instead of relying on general-purpose definitions. He could not, for example, satisfy the requirements of every legal proceeding by defining a market to include all nonferrous metals in virgin and scrap form. For certain purposes, for example, under some sections of the Clayton Act, he would have to analyze the aluminum ingot market; while under another section, the relevant market might cover primary and secondary aluminum and copper.[10]

By the same token, the lawyer must cope with market definitions that are tailored to the requirements of the specific proceeding. In this task, economic analysis can be of considerable aid in clarifying the issues and developing theories and supporting evidence. In addition, economic analysis of the statutes and cases can aid in the interpretation of precedents precisely because the market is an economic concept.

The importance of the concept of the pertinent market is clearest in the trial of antitrust issues when the determination of what competition is relevant can be the key issue.[11] If a market covers many types of products, an individual company's position appears weaker than if it encompasses only one. On the other hand, if one corporation is attacked for acquiring another, it may prefer to argue that they operate in separate narrow markets.

The *Alcoa* case[12] presents an interesting illustration of the significance of the definition of the market. In that case, Judge Learned Hand said that if a company occupies 90 per cent[13] of the relevant market, that situation "is enough to constitute a monopoly; it is doubtful whether 60 or 64 per cent would be enough; and certainly 33 per cent is not."[14]

This oft-quoted formula highlights the import of the market definition. As a matter of happenstance, Judge Hand could have defined the market to match each of the three percentages he used as bench marks. Alcoa's production of virgin aluminum ingots represented 90 per cent of the ingots used by all fabricators of aluminum products in the United States. On the other hand, Alcoa's production accounted for two thirds of all aluminum available—including secondary and scrap aluminum as well as virgin ingots. Further, if the market definition covered ingots which are available for purchase, plus secondary and scrap, and if Alcoa's percentage was based solely on its sale of ingots to others (excluding its own use of the ingots it produced), Alcoa's share would be approximately one third of the market.[15]

This lack of mathematical certainty[16] disturbs many people. Some would like to see the formulation of a master classification which would catalog and define all the markets in the country. This quest for certainty is related to a desire for a practical, equitable antitrust administration as well as a clarification of its application to specific market situations.

However, no method has yet been contrived for setting up such uniform classifications.[17] Any definition depends on the purposes of, and the setting for, the analysis.[18] There appear to be no fixed boundaries for industries or markets.[19] The recent pace of technological changes maintains competition in an almost constant state of flux. For example, the developments in plastics, wood, nonferrous metals, and ceramics have provided new applications of these materials in place of steel. Meanwhile, steel has been used in place of existing products made of wood, cement, and clay. These developments in the uses of materials are paralleled by differences in the methods of fabricating final products. For example, steel trays are made by companies who purchase sheet steel which they stamp and enamel; plastic trays are produced by molders who follow totally different processes; wood trays are manufactured in still other ways.

## *Dimensions of a Market*

A market cannot be described by reference to a single factor such as similarity in the physical characteristics of the commodities, or of their end uses. Definition requires a balanced consideration of a number of characteristics or dimensions to meet the analytical needs of the specific problem under consideration. At one extreme a vague description of competition is that every item which competes for the consumer's dollar is in rivalry with every other item: shoes in competition with bread; furniture in competition with seashore vacations. As the court said in *Times-Picayune Publishing Co.*:[20] "For every product substitutes exist, but a relevant market cannot meaningly encompass that infinite range." At the other extreme, is the narrow-compass definition, which confines a market to items that have uniform quality and service. Such a test would show that there is a separate market for every trade-marked item and for almost every selling location. Ford Motor Company, a supermarket which is located two blocks from other food retailers, or the publisher of any textbook would be monopolists in their markets.

The analytical task calls for avoiding these extremes and for weighing the various factors that determine degrees of competition and the dimensions of a competitive situation. In this process, the market definition cannot be produced by a simple analytical exercise. It must be constructed with an eye to the purpose for which it is intended.

Two products may be in the same market in one inquiry and not in another. For example, coal, natural gas, and residual fuel oil may be regarded as competitive for some purposes[21] and not for others. A high excise tax, say $10 per ton on heating coal, would give fuel oil and natural gas great advantages. A sharp reduction in freight rates for coal would give it an advantage in its rivalry with oil.[22] On the other hand, if several major oil companies were to merge, it would seem unreasonable to belittle the effect of the merger by relating the sales of the companies with a broad market for energy, which includes fuel oil, coal, natural gas, firewood, charcoal, electrical power, and solar-heat systems.

Many attributes or dimensions can be considered in defining a market. Some are broad analytical factors, such as cross-elasticity of demand and relative costs of the sellers. Others are narrower characteristics, such as physical composition of the product and attractiveness to the buyer. In addition there are issues of another order: Should only present competition be considered or potential as well?[23] Should production or productive capacity be used to measure the size of the market?

No definition of a single market will call for the utilization of all of these attributes. In some instances, the definition may turn on only one dimension or two. However, in order to make a sharp delineation of the pertinent characteristics, it may be necessary to review all types before selecting the most relevant.

The more important market dimensions are discussed below. This outline is intended to be illustrative rather than exhaustive. The classifications used can be arranged in various ways. The organization here is influenced by convenience in analyzing available material, particularly the antitrust cases.

Among the important dimensions to be considered in the definition of a market are: physical characteristics, attractiveness to buyers, cross-elasticity of demand, sellers' costs, relative prices, end uses, stages of marketing, integration and stages of manufacture, methods of production or origin, regionalism, and actual and potential competition. Subsidiary to these factors is the question of how a market should be measured in order to determine a company's relative position, whether in units, dollar sales, or by other means.

*Physical Characteristics of Products*

The simplest basis for defining a market is to select products that have the same physical characteristics. Yet, subsidiary questions often can be quite important. How much variety in these characteristics will be encompassed in the definition? Does the origin of the product affect the classification? Should differences in the engineering and other services provided by the producer be considered? Should the criteria depend on laboratory tests or should they consider differences in origin and consumer preference?

Judicial decisions vary considerably. In some cases it has been held that products with fairly dissimilar physical characteristics are in the same market; in others, that products with the same physical characteristics but differing in origins or use, are not in the same market; while in some, apparently small differences in physical characteristics have been enough to persuade the courts that two products were not in the same market.

In the first *Alcoa* case,[24] Judge Hand held that only virgin aluminum ingots were in the relevant market. He excluded secondary and scrap aluminum, reasoning that the policies of Alcoa, the sole domestic producer of virgin aluminum, had an important bearing on the supply of secondary and scrap aluminum. However, several years later, in a proceeding to determine remedies, the court ruled that secondary and scrap aluminum should be included.[25] It justified the change in definition because the production of two new producers of virgin aluminum affected the supply of the secondary and scrap products.[26]

In other cases, materials with substantial differences in physical characteristics were included in the relevant market. In the *Cellophane* case,[27] the court held that the market included many types of flexible wrapping even though none of them had all of the qualities of cellophane.

On the other hand, physical characteristics were treated differently in *du Pont-General Motors.*[28] The court limited the market to finishes for automobiles and excluded paints used for other purposes. In fact, the defined market excluded 75 to 85 per cent of du Pont's production of the paint because it was used by other industries.[29] This conclusion was based on the defendants' evidence that the production of automobile finishes required special services and quality controls, and that not all paint manufacturers could satisfy the automotive requirements. In another proceeding, nationally advertised jeweled watches were considered as a market, excluding watches that were not nationally advertised as well as nonjeweled timepieces.[30] In the *Klearflax Linen Looms* proceeding[31] the court held that there was a separate market for linen rugs, despite the argument that they were in constant competition with other rugs.

The treatment of physical characteristics poses many problems in defining a market. How much attention should be paid to physical performance and how much to chemical composition or physical construction? For example, containers, made of tin-plate, aluminum, glass, or plastic may be used for the same purposes in the preservation and sale of identical foods. Yet their constructions are very different.

Should laboratory tests of physical construction prevail? Bayer's and all other aspirin tablets meet the requirements of the United States Pharmacopoeia and produce the same effects. Nevertheless, on many occasions the retail prices for the Bayer product have been as much as six times the retail prices for some other aspirin brands.[32] Are these tablets in the same market? This situation might be compared with the market for aluminum frying pans which might be considered separate from that for enameled-steel and other frying pans. However, if aluminum frying pans were sold at six times the price of the enameled steel, stainless steel, or glass products, would they enjoy a substantial sale?

While physical characteristics are among the primary factors to consider, they do not always produce the final answer by themselves. They must, on occasion, be considered along with other factors.

### *End Uses of Products*

In defining a market, the factor of end uses is closely related to physical characteristics. If the same product is destined for different uses in the hands of the buyers, the definition of the market may not be based solely on the physical specifications. Further, the same end use may place several items in the same market despite physical differences.

Consideration of differences in uses is particularly important in studying markets for services, such as transportation, news entertainment, and advertising. Thus, the problem arose in determining whether the following pairs were in single markets: morning and evening newspapers;[33] farm publications and general magazines;[34] taxi service and other transportation between railroad stations in Chicago.[35]

End use was of substantial importance in the Federal Trade Commission's definition of the market in the *Brillo* proceeding.[36] A sharp line of demarcation was made between industrial and household steel wool. Although both products are made by the same processes, they are packaged differently and sold to different users. Similarly, in *Reading Co.*[37] the court held that anthracite is not interchangeable with other fuels because of differences in some of the industrial uses of the fuels. A strategic element in this decision was the fact that the fuel which was used would depend on the equipment in the buyer's plant.

In several cases products that are interchangeable for certain purposes, but not for all, were held to be in different markets. Though hydraulic and sucker pumps can be used interchangeably in shallow and straight wells, they were held to be in different markets because hydraulic pumps are required for wells that are not straight or go beyond certain depths.[38] Similar results obtained in cases involving oil bits.[39]

End use criteria for defining a market affect many types of policy decisions. There may be a considerable number of products, differing in physical characteristics but with the same end use. Further products of the same or similar specifications may be used for a number of unrelated purposes. Thus, in discussing concentration of industry studies, Kaplan points to the "loosely-defined industry," floor and wall coverings:

> This industry in its current dimensions cannot be separated marketwise from competition with the related products in the building trades, with household equipment, carpets, rugs, paints,

boards, tiles, and sheet goods. More specifically, the resilient, smooth-surface coverings—of cork, wood-flour, felt, asphalt, asbestos, gypsum, rubber, etc., with linseed oil and various other binders—are found to compete more or less directly with the following types of products: Soft-surface floor coverings—rugs and carpets made from various types of natural and synthetic fibers; painted floors and walls of all types; wall covering materials such as pre-decorated panel board, plastic tile, fiberboard, paper, burlap, and plaster; wood flooring products including plywood and hardboard; ceramic material such as tile, brick, and architectural glass; and other inorganic materials such as terrazzo, stone, and cement.[40] . . . Erstwhile floor-covering materials have also found new uses in furniture, kitchen equipment, and transportation equipment.[41]

*Attractiveness to Buyers*

The factor of attractiveness to buyers blends in with physical characteristics. While this feature is most important for consumer goods, it may also influence producer goods markets.

The TNEC report on prices showed substantial differences in the prices paid by consumers for the same drug items sold under well-advertised brands and under their generic names. A tabulation of eleven drug items sold under proprietary and nonproprietary names showed total prices of $28.95 for an ounce of each trade-marked item, compared with $4.59 for the nonbranded goods.[42] Similar points have been made in the recent hearings of the Senate Antimonopoly Subcommittee.

In contrast the court was not impressed by the defense's argument in *American Crystal Sugar*[43] that cane sugar and beet sugar are not in the same market because the former product is more attractive to American consumers. It found that industrial buyers purchase the items entirely on the basis of price and that housewives do purchase the beet as well as the cane product whenever it is available.

Other factors influencing attractiveness to buyers are differences in service, guarantees, assurances of supply when there are shortages, prestige, and style elements. For example, it was held that women's dresses of original design constituted a market separate from other dresses because of their exclusiveness.[44]

## *Cross-Elasticity of Demand*

The term "cross-elasticity of demand"[45] is employed in economic studies of product substitutability.[46] The demands for two products have a high cross-elasticity if a change in the price of one has a strong effect on the purchases or prices of the other. For example, if consumers believe that two brands of equally priced coffee have the same quality and if one manufacturer raises his price, say five cents per pound, most consumers will shift to the other. At the other extreme, if changes in the prices of product A have no effect on the prices and sales of product B, there is no cross-elasticity of demand.[47]

While economists frequently use the concept cross-elasticity of demand, no method has been developed for gauging it.[48] Many observers, economists and others, have maintained that cross-elasticity of demand does or does not exist in specific situations. But the issue may be more complex than the mere existence of cross-elasticity. The problem is how to measure the degree of cross-elasticity.[49] As stated in the *Times-Picayune* case,[50] the problem is to draw the circle around the market. Many, possibly most, products are in some market rivalry with broad ranges of goods and services. The problem is to determine how strong the demand relationship is. It is possible that some day a method of measuring cross-elasticity of demand will be formulated. At present the term merely sums up a general impression.

Considerable doubt has been raised about the application of cross-elasticities.[51] Professor Machlup feels that they are "particularly hopeless unknowns." Regardless of the terminology, however, whether one prefers "substitutability" or "cross-elasticity," the basic problem of determining what should be encompassed in a market will continue as long as we are concerned with problems of competition.

## *Influences of Sellers' Costs*

Differences in the costs[52] of individual sellers may indicate that one enjoys a strong monopolistic position despite a high cross-elasticity of demand.[53] In the *Corn Products* case,[54] Judge Hand held that substitute items can be excluded from the market if their manufacturing costs are substantially greater than those of the product in question. Suppose that products A and B sell for approximately the same prices and have a high cross-elasticity of demand. Product A may be manufactured by several producers with costs that are just below their selling prices, while product B may be manufactured by a single producer whose costs are very low, say as an extreme, only one half of the market price. In that event, the manufacturer of product B could, if he chose, cut the price so low that he would drive product A out of the market. But he may decide that it would be more profitable to continue with the higher price and lesser volume. He would then enjoy the capacity to operate within a wide range of discretion without being hurt—a manifestation of monopoly power. Hence, while products A and B may have a high degree of cross-elasticity, the shape of the market would have been determined by one producer who could change it at will.[55]

### *Relative Prices of Goods*

The prices of goods may delimit the market. The six-dollar housedress and the sixty-dollar silk print both satisfy some of the same physical end uses. However, because of relative prices they would not be considered competitive. Similarly, differences in the prices of branded and nonbranded drugs may place them in different markets even though physical characteristics and end uses are the same.

In the 1946 *American Tobacco* case[56] the court held that the fifteen-cent and ten-cent cigarettes were not in the same market. Therefore, in reviewing the position of the leading manufacturers, the court considered their power in the narrow fifteen-cent market. It is interesting to note that the court later found[57] that the defendants had injured the producers of the ten-cent brands by collectively buying up cheaper grades of tobacco so that they would not be available for the lower-priced cigarettes.

In contrast, as Professor Stocking pointed out, the courts held in the *Cellophane* case[58] that several flexible wrapping materials were in the same market despite substantial differences in their prices. "Apparently du Pont could ignore the prices of rival papers in setting its own prices. From 1924 to 1950 the price of the principal type of moistureproof cellophane was at all times, for which figures are available, from two to seven times that of 25# bleached glassine and from two to four and one-half times that of 30# waxed paper, despite a reduction in the average price of cellophane from $2.51 to 49 cents a pound."[59]

Analysis of the influence of prices can cover relative movements of prices and their influences on volume. Such inquiry can cast some light on cross-elasticity. Thus, if the prices of product A were reduced while the prices of product B were constant, without influencing the relative sales volumes of the two, cross-elasticity would be low.

Such analysis is reflected in the debates regarding the *Cellophane* case.[60] Stocking and Mueller[61] argued that cellophane should not have been classed in the market with other flexible wrapping materials because of substantial differences in their price movements for several years. They pointed to large reductions in cellophane prices over a period of about fourteen years while the prices of the other products remained relatively stable. They interpreted the independence of the price movements as an indication of a low degree of substitution. Lishan differed with this analysis. He argued that the study was restricted to differences in the direction of price movements, down or up, and that it should have encompassed relative percentage changes of prices and sales.[62]

Relative movements of prices and sales volumes may reflect changes in cross-elasticities. They might, for example, indicate that two products, which had not been competitive, moved into the same market. For example, it is possible that the reductions in cellophane prices, relative to other flexible wrapping materials, indicate that the products had not been competitive several years ago, but that they are in the same market today.

### *Stages of Marketing*

Many distinctions in markets depend on marketing stages. Sales to consumers are not in the same market as sales to resellers. Parts sold to an assembler of a larger product are not in direct competition with the same parts going into the repair and replacement channels.

The administration of the Robinson-Patman Act has been strongly influenced by these dimensions of the market.[63] Differences in prices charged to wholesalers and to retailers have not been considered price discriminations because the two sets of buyers do not compete with each other. In line with this construction, it has been held that the act was violated when a wholesale discount was allowed on all purchases by a firm which sold at both wholesale and retail.[64]

Similarly, it was held that spark plugs sold to automobile manufacturers for car assembly are not in competition with replacement plugs.[65] On the other hand, the equipment sold to the same automobile manufacturers for resale as replacements was considered to be in the same market as the products sold to automobile accessory distributors.

### *Integration and Stages of Manufacture*

Differences in the degree of integration of members of an industry can raise some interesting questions regarding the market. If the market definition is based on one stage of manufacture, the analysis of competition may be cast in one mold. At another stage of manufacture, or distribution, another mold may be used.

Problems of integration arise because of differences between the activities of competitors. If every fabricator of aluminum products engaged in all the activities of Alcoa—mining, smelting, rolling, casting, and fabricating—there would be no problem of integration or market definition in the consideration of the charge that Alcoa had monopolized the industry. Nor would there be if all fabricators purchased their requirements of aluminum ingots and sheets.

If the *Alcoa* decision[66] had turned solely on competition in the sale of fabricated products, the market definition would have been quite different. Centering the issues on the sale of the metal, as the case did, it gave rise to substantial definitional problems: the exclusion or inclusion of imported virgin aluminum ingots, of secondary and scrap aluminum, of the metal sold on the market, of the metal used by the Aluminum Company, itself, and of such competing materials as copper.

The other side of the coin showed up in the *American Can Company* case[67] of 1916. American Can was prosecuted for monopolization, under the Sherman Act, because of its acquisition of competing plants. While the company sold its entire output to canners, some canners produced all or some of the cans they used. The court found that if the proportions of the market were based on the number of cans sold by can manufacturers, American Can had a 50 per cent share. On the other hand, if total cans produced (including those manufactured by canners for their own use) were taken as the market supply, American Can would account for only one third. It chose the latter definition and refused to dissolve the combination.

Both sides of the equation, buying and selling, were raised in the *Columbia Steel* case[68] since the acquisition promoted integration. The government argued that the acquisition of Consolidated by Columbia meant that rival producers of primary steel products would be foreclosed from the opportunity to sell to Consolidated, which was a steel fabricator. On the other hand, the acquisition interfered with the sources of raw material enjoyed by competitors of Consolidated since Columbia and its associated companies would confine their sales of primary steel to Consolidated whenever there were shortages. However, the court was not impressed and held that the Sherman Act had not been violated.

### *Methods of Production or Origin*

Methods of production or of origin have affected the definition of the market in a number of cases. A problem in *Alcoa*[69] was whether to include imported material in the market. The problem in another case was whether extruded steel pipes are in the same market as welded steel pipes.[70] The significance of differences in methods of production have, in some instances, been related to the consideration of relative costs.

In several cases market definitions have turned on the origin of materials without consideration of substitutability. Starch made from corn was held to constitute a market, excluding other starches.[71] Parchment paper was considered a market unto itself, excluding other papers which served the same purposes.[72]

In contrast, in the 1931 *Standard Oil of Indiana* case,[73] the relevant market was defined to include gasoline produced by the cracking process as well as gasoline produced in other ways. Similarly, in

*American Crystal Sugar*[74] the market was construed to cover both the cane and the beet products.

### *Actual and Potential Competition*

On occasion, a major element in competitive analysis is whether to confine the "market" to existing competition or to consider potential competition as well. Should the market cover the present suppliers alone or should account be taken of potential suppliers who can transfer some productive capacity to the manufacture of the pertinent item? If this potential is to be included in the productive capacity of the market, how far afield should the circle go? Should machinery that will require substantial modification be included? Should any allowance be made for companies which employ similar productive techniques and could easily tool up and enter the market if it became attractive?

Another issue of potential competition involves the inclusion of producers who do not customarily sell in a regional market. If transportation costs are high, relative to price, a product will not be moved over wide areas, as in the case of cement, and the relevant market falls within a circumscribed area. However, if prices in one area should rise substantially above the level of others, shipments might come from the "outside." Hence, the geographical dimensions of the market may be changed by price increases. Such situations are illustrated by the concern about "pricing American goods out of the market" if domestic costs rise too far above foreign costs.

An important issue in the *Columbia Steel* case[75] was whether steel plates and shapes constituted "a market distinct from other rolled steel products." The court held that "if rolled steel producers can make other products as easily as plates and shapes, then the effect of the removal of Consolidated's demand for plates and shapes must be measured not against the market for plates and shapes alone, but for all comparable rolled products." Further, "potential competition from producers of presently non-competitive articles . . . may be taken into consideration in weighing the effect of any acquisition of assets on restraint of trade."[76] Accordingly, the court was not concerned about U. S. Steel's purchase of the West Coast company.

On the other hand, Judge Weinfeld was not impressed with a comparable argument in the *Bethlehem-Youngstown* merger case.[77] "In practice steel producers have not been equipped to shift from product to product. . . . Moreover, the evidence establishes that the continuing relationships between buyers and sellers in the steel industry make such shifts unlikely." Nor was the Federal Trade Commission or the court swayed by *Crown-Zellerbach's*[78] contention that all paper machines could produce the coarse papers that were involved in the commission's attack on the acquisition of St. Helens, a competitor of Crown.

### *Regionalism of the Market*

The geographical dimensions of a market are frequently a key factor. Should the market be analyzed on a national basis, a regional, or a local community? Compare, for example, machine tools and milk. The market for most machine tools appears to be national: there are relatively few producers of each type of tool; transportation cost is not large in relation to the price of the machine; manufacturers may be found in various places throughout the country. In contrast, there is no national market for fluid milk; requirements of freshness and local regulations force milk markets into a local pattern.

A series of geographical problems have been considered in antitrust cases. Questions have been largely: Should the market be taken as national or regional? Should individual communities constitute the relevant market? How should the pertinent region be defined—using customary industry classification, comparative transportation,[79] and other costs? Which is more important, the distributive patterns of the bulk of the industry's sales or of the companies involved in the proceeding?

As the court stated in the *Indiana Farmers' Guide* case,[80] the provisions of the Sherman Act "have both a geographical and distributive significance and apply to any part of the United States as distinguished from the whole and to any part of the classes of things forming a part of interstate commerce." However, this does not necessarily mean that the market will be taken on a local or regional basis in every instance. Thus, in *Alcoa*[81] the relevant market considered for aluminum was national. Conversely, in *Columbia Steel*[82] the focus was on sales in the eleven West Coast states where the acquired company sold its products. In *Bethlehem-Youngstown Steel*[83] the court considered both national and regional markets for various classes of steel products and much of the proceeding turned on what were the appropriate regional markets.[84]

Regional markets were significant in *Standard Stations*,[85] which covered the sale of gasoline in several Western states, in the *Pillsbury*[86] proceeding, which dealt with the sale of cake mixes in the Southeast, and in *Crown-Zellerbach*,[87] which dealt with the sale of paper in West Coast states.

In some cases the regional market has been defined to cover a narrow area. Thus, in *Johnson Cement Block Co.* v. *Waylight Co.*[88] the issue was whether an exclusive dealing contract tended toward a monopoly. The contract covered the sale of lightweight aggregates for concrete building blocks in a region in northeastern Minnesota and northwest Wisconsin. This aggregate was the only lightweight material available within a distance of 150 miles. The court held that the high transportation costs of the material made it impracticable to manufacture the lightweight blocks with materials from the alternative source at a competitive price. Therefore, the market was confined to the narrow region.

There has been some tendency to classify markets for service on a city basis.[89] In the *Paramount Pictures* case,[90] the market considered was the exhibition of films in the first-run theaters in major cities. In the *Yellow Cab* proceeding,[91] the pertinent market was confined to taxi service in four large cities.

The geographical pattern of markets cannot be organized into a set formula. Account must be taken of the nature of the industry, the shape of competition, the buying and selling activities of the companies in question and of their competitors.

### *Unit of Measurement*

The unit of measurement is an important factor in certain market definitions because of its influence on calculations of market shares.

For example, *Besser Manufacturing Co.*[92] was the setting for a debate concerning the proportion of the total market for cement block-making machinery which was enjoyed by the defendant. Defense counsel argued that the market and its share should be measured by the number of machines manufactured and sold. The government's counsel persuaded the court that the more realistic unit of measurement would be dollar sales rather than the number of machines. This contention was based on the superiority of Besser machines, which had substantially greater capacity than competing products. Apparently, no attention was paid to the possibility of using the productive capacity of the machines—number of blocks produced per hour—as the unit of measurement.

Many types of units have been used in the cases: dollar sales, physical output, dollar production, capacity, circulation of newspapers. Miss Bock in analyzing the decisions under the Antimerger Act found that:

> Although it is more than apparent that shifts in units of measurement can cause substantial shifts in the apparent structure of an industry and in the apparent market shares or rank of the acquiring or acquired unit, the courts' and the commission's reasons for using one unit rather than another are seldom explicit. Indeed, it is frequently unclear as to whether a unit of measurement has been selected for its relevance or for its relative availability.[93]

## *Market Definition in Policy Analysis*

Market definitions affect competitive problems in three fields: the formulation of public policy; various types of government regulation, such as rate, price, and tariff controls; and the administration of antitrust laws. The applications of market definitions vary within as well as among these fields.

The determination of appropriate market definitions is of substantial import for a number of policy issues. It can have a central influence on industry studies. It has a profound effect on the measurement of industrial concentration as a clue to the state of competition. It bears on many aspects of legislative consideration in setting government regulatory policy.

The orientation of industry studies is necessarily influenced by the definition of the market. In his study of the rayon industry, Professor Markham concluded that rayon is part of a larger market for fibers.[94] This conclusion obviously had an influence on his findings of the workability of competition in the industry. On the other hand, in his study of the metal container industry Professor McKie concluded, "Cross-elasticities of demand between metal cans and substitute containers are very small."[95] It is interesting to speculate on what the nature of these two studies might have been had they covered the "fiber" industry and the "container" or the "food container" industry.

The concept of the market is a key element in the measurement of industrial concentration. In the general evaluation of the state of competition, one of the outstanding factors is the analysis of market shares. In such measurement, the definition of the market and the unit of measurement is a keystone.

Analyses of concentration are potentially useful in evaluating the over-all state of competition, the areas in the economy that require attention, and the general effects of antitrust campaigns.[96] However, without the firm footing of market definition such estimates cannot develop an accurate picture of market shares. Over-all figures of gigantism in the economy do portray some of the aspects of broad economic power. However, they do not, in themselves, provide practical clues regarding what might be done to change the situation.

Studies of concentration are based on data which often shed little light on competitive conditions within any market.[97] Financial data reflect the size of companies, not their position in any competitive market because of the great diversity of operations of large companies. The *Census of Manufactures* does not indicate substitute products, differences in end uses, the import-export balances of specific products, product alternatives for existing capacity, significant geographical dimensions, or appropriate units of measurement. These deficiencies are not the fault of the census which, after all, was designed for less specific purposes.

Census data, whether by industry or by product, are often either too broad or too narrow to portray concentration within a market.[98] Industry classifications necessarily follow the major products of each company. For example, if 70 per cent of a plant's output consisted of nails and 30 per cent of wire fence, the entire output would be included in the nails and spikes industry. As a result, the total production of the nail industry and the company's position in that industry would be overstated. Meanwhile, the total for the wire-drawing industry, which includes wire fence, would be understated, and the market positions of other companies in that industry would be set too high.

Census Bureau statisticians have reported that "the larger producers of particular products are frequently classified as firms in some other industry."[99] Professor Wilcox in his analysis of a TNEC study[100] pointed out the difficulties of product classification. "All pills, tablets, powders, and salts are lumped together, as are all tinctures, extracts, sirups, elixirs and solutions, and all flags, vestments, robes, badges and emblems."[101]

On the other hand, as Wilcox pointed out, many categories are too narrow. "Rubber combs are separated from other combs and furniture is treated as one product when made of wood, another when made of metal, and a third when made of fiber, rattan, reed or willow. . . . Beet sugar is again listed in one category and cane sugar in another."[102]

The data ignore exports and imports even when they are significant elements in the market. Hence, they may overstate a company's sales position or understate it. They may omit significant competition from abroad and overlook markets that are partly international in scope. For example, the international market for tin is hardly described by the picture of domestic production, which accounts for only a small fraction of total consumption.

The geographical aspects of many markets add further complexity to concentration ratios. Markets which are regional in nature do not respect state boundaries. Hence, neither national nor state data will adequately measure either the market or concentration within it.

The increasing complexity of markets has important implications for policy analysis. As technology blurs industry lines and brings more types of materials, fabrication, and distribution into competition with each other, the nature of many markets changes. Substitution and cross-elasticity of demand become more significant factors. Yet, limits of substitutability remain. Technological advances do not solve the problems of competition. Rather, they plague the analyst by weakening his most comfortable premise, *ceteris paribus*, for all other things do not remain equal.

On the other hand, the technological advances and the trend toward greater diversification of many companies have injected substantial competitive influences in many sectors. New producers, new products that compete with old ones, and new distributors have increased market rivalry in a number of areas. Man-made fibers compete with products of cotton and wool. Aluminum is substituted for steel and copper. Plastics are competing with wood, metals, glass, leather, and cotton in various products. Hence, the analytical problems multiply, while new competition develops.

## *Market Definition in Regulation Other Than Antitrust*

Problems of market definition are important in many phases of government regulation that bear on competition. Outside the antitrust field, among these regulatory functions are or have been: price control, transportation, tariffs, and communications.

In some regulation, the market must be defined specifically as in tariff procedures. In others, there is no occasion to define the market, as in the controls over transportation. However, the effect of the regulation, as well as the policy issues that pertain to it, call for a consideration of competitive forces.

### *Price Control*

In formulating price ceilings and other regulations, the Office of Price Administration found that market or industry definitions had a profound influence. If the price ceiling on one product was 10 per cent above 1940 prices, while the ceiling on a competing item was 20 per cent above, bothersome issues of equity and enforcement arose. Obviously, many manufacturers tried to come under industry definitions which would give them higher ceilings. Therefore, a considerable proportion of the agency's efforts were devoted to problems of industry definition.

After some experience, the Office of Price Administration attempted to formulate the factors that should be considered in defining a product. Its list of factors included: "(1) the general understanding of the industry regarding what constitutes a product or line of products; (2) the end-uses; (3) the similarity of specifications and manufacturing processes; (4) the similarity of reactions to common cost increases; (5) the stability of the price relationships between the items; and (6) the similarity of types of purchasers and marketing conditions."[103]

As the discussion of the dimensions of the market indicates, the list of factors did not allow any mechanical classification. While they served as general guides, they could not produce uniform results. Many decisions required substantial study. The problems of classification continued throughout the duration of price control during World War II only to be renewed and reconfirmed by the Office of Price Stabilization during the Korean episode.

### *Tariff Regulation*

The Tariff Commission has had to wrestle with definitions of the market throughout its existence. The specific problems it faces currently stem out of its conduct of investigations under the "escape clause," Section 7, of the Trade Agreements Extension Act of 1951, as amended.[104]

Under that act, tariff concessions were made on a product-by-product basis with a provision that each concession could be reduced if a domestic industry were injured seriously or threatened with such injury. Section 7 of the act defined the domestic industry as one which produced products that are "like or directly competitive with the foreign goods which were subject to the concession."

In response to a Senate inquiry, the commission said that it had "not found it practicable to formulate a standard interpretation" of like or directly competitive goods.[105] Accordingly, each commissioner formed his own interpretation in each investigation.

> In consequence, the Commission does not always reach a unanimous opinion on what domestic articles are "like or directly competitive" with the complained-of imports. Even when there is agreement on that matter, there is sometimes disagreement over the

precise scope of the domestic industry in question. When the domestic "like or directly competitive" article is either a joint product, a co-product, or a by-product, determination of the scope of the domestic industry is particularly troublesome.[106]

In the commission's report on zinc sheet it held that: "The statutory terms 'like' and 'directly competitive' are mutually exclusive."[107] (It is, of course, difficult to see how a "directly competitive" article *must* be different from a "like" article.) In its release about petroleum and its liquid derivatives, the commission defined "directly competitive" items as those which "do not have the same name, characteristics, and use, but which nevertheless come into direct competition . . . because, among other things, one is substantially substitutable for the other in principal use or uses." (It did not explain why a "like" article is not "directly competitive.")[108]

In the zinc sheet report the commission held that "the term 'like' . . . means the 'same' or 'identical' product and that a permissible method of determining whether products are 'like' is the method of tariff classification."[109]

In the report on lamb, mutton, sheep and lambs the majority of the commission voted that there was no reason to recommend a tariff change. They held that lambs and sheep are "different products . . . than the meat of these animals," and referred to differences in tariff classifications.[110] Further, they are not "directly competitive"; the law prevents the commission from considering injury to packers because of the import of live animals. "Each is a separate 'industry' under the law." Hence, even if this definition of industry "offends the economists' concept," the commission was bound by the law.[111]

In their dissent, Commissioners Schrieber and Sutton argued that while live domestic animals are not "like or directly competitive" with the imported meat, "domestic producers of lambs and sheep are part of the industry that produces lamb and mutton."[112]

## *Public Utility Regulation*

Many regulatory policies that have indirect bearing on the state of competition call for consideration of markets and the nature of competition. Thus, when the Interstate Commerce Commission considered whether to allow continuation of freight-rate reductions on Appalachian coal shipped to East Coast utilities, the Empire State Petroleum Association protested, arguing that the reductions forced down the price of residual oil unfairly.[113]

The competitive relationships in transportation involved market concepts even before modern regulation was started. After the Civil War, strong recommendations were made for federal water transport development in order to control the railroads. Instead of direct railroad regulation, the report of the Senate's Windom Committee of 1874, referred to in Chapter 3 above, advocated a program to control the railroads by a substantial improvement of the nation's inland water transportation.

In 1935 the Interstate Commerce Commission undertook the regulation of trucking as well as railroads.[114] Following the theory that the two means of transportation are in the same market, the I.C.C. has set trucking rates high enough to support the railroad charges. More recently, the situation was reversed when trucking interests protested against a possible reduction of railroad rates because it would hurt the truckers.

In substance, most regulatory functions of government are influenced by market concepts. Under some regulation, as in tariff and price control, specific findings must be made of market areas. Under others, as in transportation, public policy considerations are strongly influenced by broad competitive relations, though there is no procedure that requires a specific definition of the market.

## *Market Definition in Antitrust*

The concept of the market is central to most types of antitrust enforcement—central and complex. At first glance, there would be a neat orderliness in such proceedings if each one started with a clear-cut definition of the market, as a matter of law, before considering evidence of violations. However, the determination of what is covered by a "relevant market" is not a question of conventional precedent but a matter of judgment based on an inquiry into each specific situation.

The definition of a market is a continuing problem of economic analysis. No legal definition can describe the actual shape of competition. A decision "for all time" fixing the definitions of all markets for any purpose would have a quicksand base. New products may come into direct competition next year. Changes in service requirements may rearrange the geographical nature of the market. Evidence may be presented in a new case which would persuade another court—possibly, even the same judge—to consider a new market definition in another case.

Further, a market definition that would be appropriate for one statute would not necessarily fit another. As Irston Barnes has said:

> The very phrase "relevant market" implies that the definition must be relevant to something. . . . Given the pattern of behavior and intent of, let us say, Alcoa, one might well wish to exclude from the relevant market those products which the court did, in fact, exclude in finding that Alcoa had violated the Sherman Act in achieving dominance of ninety per cent of the primary ingot market. And yet, it would seem equally reasonable, in a Section 7 case, to prohibit Alcoa from acquiring, for example, a major manufacturer of copper on the grounds that, given the purposes of the Clayton Act—to reach in their incipiency acts which may adversely affect competition—copper is a sufficiently close substitute for aluminum to bring it into the market relevant in the *Clayton Act* case.[115]

Market definitions have been influenced in the cases by several conditions. To begin with, the phraseology of the statutes have implied differences. Some statutes seem to require narrow and some broad interpretations of the market. Second, the weight of the violation and the harshness of remedies seem to have had some effect. Lastly, judicial determinations of markets are influenced, of course, by the competence of the counsel for both sides and by the judges' own predilections.

### *Differences of Language of Antitrust Statutes*

The development of principles for delimiting the relevant market is complicated by the statutory language of the antitrust laws. There is no way to tell whether Congress consciously intended to apply different concepts of the market when it chose the phraseology of the various statutes, whether in an endeavor to write interesting prose it varied the language, whether it intended the same consequences to flow from the same language, or whether it simply overlooked problems of statutory interpretation.

The main antitrust laws present an interesting pattern of variation in their references to the relevant market. Differences are to be found in separate sections of the same enactment, as well as in different statutes.

Section 1 of the Sherman Act[116] relates to conspiracies "*in restraint of trade* among the several states, or with foreign nations." Section 2 relates to monopolizing, attempts to monopolize, or conspiracy to monopolize, "*any part of the trade or commerce* among the several states or with foreign nations."

The Miller-Tydings amendment[117] to Section 1, and the McGuire Act,[118] both of which permit resale price maintenance, refer to commodities which are "in *free and open competition* with commodities of the same general class produced or distributed by others."

Section 5 of the Federal Trade Commission Act[119] covers "unfair methods of competition *in commerce*."

Section 2 of the Clayton Act,[120] amended by the Robinson-Patman Act, covers discrimination in prices of "*commodities of like grade and quality* . . . where the effect of such discrimination may be substantially to lessen competition or tend to create a monopoly in *any line of commerce*." Section 2(d) relates to payment for services furnished by a *customer* unless it is available on proportionately equal terms to all other customers competing in the distribution of such products. Section 2(e) relates to furnishing *purchasers* services on terms not accorded to all purchasers "on proportionally equal terms."

Section 3 of the Clayton Act covers exclusive purchase agreements which may "substantially lessen competition or tend to create a monopoly in *any line of commerce*."

Section 7 of the Clayton Act, as amended, applies to acquisitions of stock or assets of another corporation where "the effect of such acquisition may be substantially to lessen competition or to tend to create a monopoly . . . *in any line of commerce in any section of the country*."

The old Section 7 referred to substantial lessening of competition between the acquired and the acquiring corporation and to restraint on "*such commerce in any section or community*" as well as to a tendency "to create a monopoly in *any line of commerce.*"

Section 3 of the Robinson-Patman Act[121] relates to discrimination "for the purpose of destroying competition, or eliminating a competitor . . . *in any part of the United States.*"

There is, then, a great variety in the nature of the violation and in the nature of the market visualized in these main provisions. Market references are to "trade . . . among the several states, or with foreign nations"; "*any part* of the trade or commerce among the several states, or with foreign nations"; "free and open *competition with commodities of the same general class*"; "in commerce"; "*any line* of commerce"; "competing in the distribution of such *products*"; "all *customers*"; "all *purchasers*"; "in *any line* of commerce in *any section* of the country"; "commerce in *any section or community*"; "competition . . . in *any part of the United States.*"

This variety in statutory language has been reflected in a confusing array of decisions regarding the relevant market. Some of the decisional differences appear to be founded on statutory distinctions. But there is no clear pattern.[122] Some differences have developed despite similar phraseology in the pertinent statutes. Some decisional similarities occur despite differences in statutory language.

### *Sherman Act Section 1*

Conspiracies to restrain trade involve such practices as the fixing of prices, the allocation of markets, the limitation of production, and boycotts. These violations do not require any consideration of competitive effects. Therefore, the consideration of market boundaries affects only the treatment of circumstantial evidence to prove a conspiracy.[123]

No substantial questions arose with regard to definitions of the market in such cases as: *Addyston Pipe and Steel Co.*[124] and *Socony-Vacuum*[125] involving price fixing; in *General Dyestuff Corp.*[126] concerning allocation of territories; in the 1905 *Swift & Co.*[127] case involving the elimination of competition in the purchase of livestock and in setting prices for prepared meats; and in the decision of the Supreme Court in *Klor's*[128] regarding a boycott.

*Sherman Act Section 2*

Most cases involving *attempts* to monopolize and conspiracy to monopolize do involve a substantial amount of commerce. While they do not call for any complex analysis of markets,[129] they are not always consistent. The *Lorain Journal* case[130] utilized a market concept of competing media since it turned on a newspaper's attempt to monopolize by refusing advertisements from any local advertiser who used an independent radio station; the *Times-Picayune* proceeding[131] turned on newspaper advertising without considering other forms of sales promotion; *Associated Press*[132] was confined to the news services of one agency; *Paramount Pictures*[133] considered only first-run exhibits of motion pictures; *National City Lines*[134] dealt with the sale of buses, tires, and supplies to bus lines in forty-five cities; *Affiliated Music Enterprises* was a private suit in which the relevant market was held to be performance rights in gospel music.[135]

Monopolization cases, under Section 2 of the Sherman Act, must be based on a finding that a monopoly does exist.[136] In the absence of a monopoly, there may be an *attempt* to monopolize but not a monopolization. Therefore, such cases call for a fairly clear-cut conclusion about what is the relevant market, a point that can be slurred over in trying many other types of violation.

The important recent monopolization cases produced no clearly consistent definitions of the market, as in two leading cases, *Alcoa*[137] and *Cellophane*.[138] Further, as stated above, there was an interesting shift in the two *Alcoa*[139] proceedings. In 1945 the Circuit Court excluded scrap and secondary aluminum; while in 1950 the District Court included them. In the *Cellophane* case, both the District and Supreme Courts were impressed by the "cross-elasticity of demand," which Judge Hand shunted aside in the first *Alcoa* proceeding, and held that the relevant market covered a wide range of flexible wrapping material.[140]

Interestingly, some economic studies arrived at conclusions in direct opposition to those of the courts. Stocking and Mueller[141] found little cross-elasticity between cellophane and other flexible wrapping materials. Robertson pointed to a high degree of substitutability between aluminum and copper.[142]

In another outstanding monopolization case, against *United Shoe Machinery Corp.*[143] Judge Wyzanski defined the shoe machinery market by the criterion of competitiveness of machinery for similar purposes. However, without spelling out his reasons, he excluded sewing machinery using dry thread, used in making uppers.[144]

*The Antimerger Statutes*

Recently, interest in the problem of market definition was given a new impetus by cases under the 1950 Celler-Kefauver amendment[145] to the Antimerger Act, Section 7 of the Clayton Act. This interest has developed in part, as a consequence of the increased attention devoted to mergers by the antitrust agencies; in part, because by their nature, the antimerger cases focus more attention on market definition than most other antitrust statutes; and, in part, because of the prominence of the recent well-publicized cases against du Pont and General Motors[146] under the old Section 7 and against Bethlehem Steel[147] under the new Section 7.

Two dimensions of the market have figured prominently in these cases: substitutability and the geographical territory covered. Substitutability has been construed both broadly and narrowly in these proceedings. By and large, there seems to be a general tendency to accept whatever geographical theory will support a finding of a violation, whether on national or regional grounds. This element may be due to the phraseology of Section 7 which refers to "any line of commerce in any section of the country."

The most prominent court proceeding under the new Section 7 to date has been the *Bethlehem-Youngstown Steel*[148] case. Judge Weinfeld's decision in the District Court was not appealed by the company. Therefore, we do not have the advantage of a Supreme Court decision. The question before the court was whether the second largest steel manufacturer in the United States should be permitted to acquire the sixth largest. In defining the line of commerce the court agreed that it should follow the standard of "peculiar characteristics and uses." It rejected the defendant's argument that the company's capacity should be compared with total industry capacity because of the flexibilities in the use of steel-making equipment. Therefore, it held that comparisons should be made by products. The defendants argued that in *Columbia Steel*[149] the Supreme Court held, in effect, that steel mill equipment can be shifted from one type of product to another, and that this flexibility shapes the contours of the product market. The court rejected this contention on the premise that, "the standard for determining product market differs according to the different sections of the antitrust laws. . . . It does not follow that the production flexibility recognized in a vertical integration case under Section 1 of the Sherman Act, like *Columbia Steel*, is controlling in a horizontal case under Section 7 of the Clayton Act."[150]

Nor was the judge impressed by the argument that substitute products should be considered. He found that there are no effective substitutes for the products under consideration, and held that the reasonable interchangeability test of the *Cellophane* case[151] was not applicable.

The case also involved an interesting point about the regional dimension. The defense urged that the relevant market was composed solely of the geographic areas in which each of the companies had made the bulk of their sales. Judge Weinfeld held that there is a national market for such products as well as lesser market areas which are based largely on important consuming centers. Therefore, the market included areas where trade would be affected by conditions in the sections where the companies sold. Hence, "if the change in price in one area has an effect on price in another area, both areas may be included in one geographic market." Further, he was concerned not only with the existing geographic distribution of products but also with the potential changes in the distribution after the merger had taken place.

The production flexibility theory of the *Columbia Steel* case[152] was rejected also by the Federal Trade Commission in *Crown-Zellerbach*,[153] another Section 7 proceeding. The respondents argued that many paper-making machines can produce a wide variety of papers; therefore, the market dimensions should cover productive capacity for all papers instead of being confined to the coarse product. The commission felt that there was no evidence of substantial merit that mills which manufactured other types of papers were likely to shift to coarse papers. It disposed of the geographical dimension with a holding that the eleven Western states comprised the relevant market and that the three coastal states could constitute such a market. On appeal, the court held that the relevant market was located in the three coastal states.[154]

On the other hand, the Federal Trade Commission seemed to follow the *Cellophane* case[155] in an opinion in another Section 7 proceeding. *Brillo Manufacturing Co.* involved the acquisition of a producer of steel wool by another. The hearing examiner declined to consider evidence that industrial steel wool was sold in a market which includes various abrasives that are used for the same purposes as the steel product in paint removal, furniture finishing, and floor finishing. He concluded that: "The relevant market in Section 7 proceedings is the line of commerce engaged in by the companies involved. . . . To broaden such line of commerce to include all acceptable substitutes would in nearly every case so enlarge the area of competition as to render not only Section 7 but Sections 2 and 3 of the Clayton Act impotent and for all practical purposes meaningless."[156] On appeal, the Commission felt that:

> The hearing examiner in concluding as a matter of law that industrial steel wool was a relevant market erred in basing his determination solely on the fact that those were the wares being produced by the acquired and the acquiring companies. The test instead is whether these products are shown by the facts to have such peculiar characteristics and uses as to constitute them sufficiently distinct from others to make them a "line of commerce" within the meaning of the Act.[157]

Therefore, the Commission felt that additional factors which should be taken into account related to:

> . . . the manner in which the products are marketed, their physical characteristics, prices, and possibly other things bearing on the question of whether or not they may be distinguished competitively from other wares. On the other hand, as the examiner in essence held, the mere fact that articles other than steel wool are marketed for industrial use as abrasives is not adequate legal warrant for including all abrasive products in the relevant line of commerce.[158]

The market has been construed in fairly narrow terms in a number of other Section 7 cases. *In the Matter of Reynolds Metals Co.*,[159] the Federal Trade Commission held that the Reynolds company violated Section 7 when it purchased a company that manufactured florist foil. The commission considered florist foil a distinguishable product market because it was a specific type of decorated aluminum foil which was used by the florist to wrap around potted plants and cut flowers. Therefore, it held that the vertical acquisition foreclosed a substantial proportion of the florist foil market from competing aluminum producers and affected competition in the sale of foil.

Similarly, in *Erie Sand and Gravel Co.*,[160] a proceeding about the merger of two companies engaged in dredging sand and gravel from lake bottoms, the F.T.C. held that the relevant market was composed exclusively of lake sand and excluded sand from other sources.[161] It held: "The evidence reveals, however, that most bank and pit sands mentioned in respondent's analysis are sold outside of the relevant market area. The quantities sold within the market are so small that consideration could not affect the final determination in this matter."[162] The relevant market area was confined to a twelve-mile strip along the south shore of Lake Erie. The Circuit Court of Appeals decided that the evidence showed that the two types of sand are "interchangeable" and that the F.T.C.'s findings about the quantities of pit sand sold within the twelve-mile strip were not supported by the evidence. Accordingly, it remanded the case to the commission for reconsideration.[163]

Similar narrow definitions were employed in *Hamilton Watch* v. *Benrus*,[164] a Section 7 case. It was held that nationally advertised jewelled watches represented the proper dimension of the market, excluding other types of timekeepers.[165] A narrow geographical region, the Washington, D.C. metropolitan area was regarded as the relevant market in *Maryland and Virginia Milk Producers*.[166] It has been held that a merger can have an adverse effect on competition even when two companies operate primarily in separate areas. In *American Crystal Sugar*[167] the court decided that competition may be substantially lessened because the enhanced strength of the merged company might give it an undue advantage in each trading area.

### *Resale Price Maintenance*

The market definition problem figured importantly in one case under the Miller-Tydings exemption from Section 1 of the Sherman Act. The act permitted resale price agreements for products that are "in free and open competition with commodities of the same general class" in those states which allowed such agreements. The Eastman Kodak Company entered into "fair trade" agreements covering "Kodachrome" color films.[168] The Federal Trade Commission issued a cease and desist order under Section 5 of the Federal Trade Commission Act, holding that this practice constituted an unfair method of competition because the agreements were not protected by the Miller-Tydings amendment. It found that color films are in a class by themselves, one which did not include black and white films. Therefore, Kodachrome was not "in free and open competition with commodities of the same general class." The Circuit Court of Appeals upheld the Commission.[169]

It should be noted that there is no issue of market definition in a prosecution for resale price control when the "fair trade" exemption from the Sherman Act is not applicable.[170] Market "control is not a material factor in cases involving resale restrictions. . . . The Sherman Act does not sanction the suppression by a manufacturer of competition among its purchasers or subpurchasers."[171]

### *Robinson-Patman Act*

The application of the Robinson-Patman Act has not involved substantial consideration of market definition. Probably because of this, no clear-cut principles of the relevant market have emerged. In his excellent review, *The Price Discrimination Law,* Corwin D. Edwards dealt at length with the concept of injury to competition in the primary line—that is, competition between the seller and his competitors—in cases concerning quantity and volume discounts.[172] He found that in the majority of such cases:

> The Commission's complaints and findings supply no information, other than a description of the discounts and a statement that seller was in competition with others, to show how it was determined that volume discounts were damaging to competition in the primary line. In one case the only further information given was that the price differences were substantial. In another, the conclusion is baldly based upon the probability that the discriminations will divert trade from competitors. In two others the Commission explained that many retailers had ceased, wholly or partly, to buy

> from the seller's competitors. In a fifth the nature of the diversion is briefly explained as the result of a tendency of buyers to concentrate their purchases in order to take advantage of higher rates of discount. . . . Though by piecing these brief statements together one can obtain a general idea of the nature of the injury the Commission believes volume discounts produce in the primary line, none of the cases contains any statement as to the number, size, and power of the seller's competitors nor as to the amount of trade that may be diverted.[173]

The absence of discussion regarding the relevant market in the orders of the Federal Trade Commission and in judicial decisions under the Robinson-Patman Act may stem from the assumptions about injury to competition that seem to be inherent in them. By and large, the concept of injury to competition under the act has been less complicated—perhaps less meaningful—than the concepts applied in other antitrust fields. There has been little economic inquiry into effects on competition, either past or potential. For the most part, it was presumed that any price discrimination would injure competition. Usually, the proceedings have involved competition among the customers of the respondent rather than his competition with his own rivals, or his purchasers' competition with customers of his rivals. This attitude is reflected in the Supreme Court opinion in the *Morton Salt Co.* case.[174]

> The Commission found what would appear to be obvious, that the competitive opportunities of certain merchants were injured when they had to pay respondents substantially more for their goods than their competitors had to pay. . . . That respondents' quantity discounts did result in price differentials between competing purchasers sufficient to influence their resale price of salt was shown by evidence. This showing in itself is adequate to support the Commission's appropriate findings.

The absence of clear concepts of the market in Robinson-Patman cases reflects the mechanical workings of the regulation and the absence of substantial consideration of competitive effects. Given this orientation, there has been no need to struggle with market concepts. Occasional attention has been paid to the geographical limits which separate markets. But no other feature has been considered pertinent. In effect, the act has been applied to problems of competition on what is probably the narrowest basis under the antitrust laws.

### *Clayton Act Section 3*

Section 3 of the Clayton Act[175] makes it unlawful to lease or sell commodities, or to fix a price or rebate for commodities, on the condition that the lessee or purchaser will not use or deal in the goods of a competitor of the lessor or seller when the effect "may be to substantially lessen competition or tend to create a monopoly in any line of commerce."

From this language, the section would appear to require consideration of the dimensions of the market.[176] However, the trend of the decisions under this section is not clear. For some time the cases seemed to follow the principle that a violation can be found without considering the effect on competition within a well-defined market. Then, in May 1961, in deciding the *Tampa Electric* case,[177] the Supreme Court felt that competitive effects and relevant markets are important.

In a leading case, *International Salt Co.* v. *U.S.*[178] the Supreme Court based its ruling of a violation on the ground that the volume of business restrained is not insignificant or insubstantial. Hence, it did not have to consider effect on competition or the relevant market. In the *Standard Stations* case,[179] the court based its decision that the act had been violated solely on the finding that the exclusive contracts, providing that the retail gasoline stations would purchase supplies exclusively from Standard, affected a substantial volume of business. The court concluded, "that the qualifying clause of Section 3 is satisfied by proof that competition has been foreclosed and a substantial share of the line of commerce affected. . . ."

The Federal Trade Commission took the position in its *Maico*[180] decision that it did have to inquire into competitive effects. However, more recently it seemed to adopt the Supreme Court's position in the *Mytinger* case[181] and avoided the need for market inquiry.

The Supreme Court seems to have modified its position by its decision in the recent *Tampa Electric* case.[182] That suit concerned a twenty-year agreement providing that the electric utility company would purchase all of its requirements of boiler fuel for one of its generating stations from a producer of bituminous coal. The court decided that competitive effect is important. It criticized the lower courts because they had not considered the relevant market area and shifted to the principle that the issue is "whether the contract forecloses competition in a substantial *share* of the line of commerce involved. . . ." It concluded that in the light of that principle the contract was not illegal. Of interest, is the court's dictum that it reached this conclusion on the assumption that bituminous coal constitutes the "line of commerce" and did not have to consider whether the market should include oil and gas as competing fuels.

Today, the future pattern of Section 3 decisions is not clear. Conceivably, the court may follow the *Standard Stations* rule when a manufacturer imposes exclusive contracts on a large number of small customers, and the *Tampa Electric* principle for a single contract between two substantial companies. Conceivably, it might follow the latter rule only when the contract brings new competition into a market.

### *Principles in Antitrust Law*

The development of a standard set of principles for setting the dimensions of a market under the antitrust law seems to be well-nigh impossible today. Several efforts have been made to distinguish the application of the statutes in this respect. Differences have been suggested in the definitions that apply to the merger law and the monopolization provisions, to attempts to monopolize, to combinations, and to monopolizing. Some have argued that constructions of the various laws should be the same when statutory language is similar. For example, it has been urged that because of similarity in the language of Sections 3 and 7 of the Clayton Act, the rule of the *International Salt* case[183] should be applied in merger cases.[184] If such a principle were adopted, a violation of the antimerger statute would require no more than a finding that a substantial amount of commerce is involved. However, this suggestion has not been followed in such proceedings as *Bethlehem Steel*[185] and *Pillsbury*.[186] Further, the *Tampa Electric* decision[187] raises new questions about the *International Salt* rule.

Many discussions reflect the assumption that the market definition should be based on one set of principles applying to all the statutes.[188] This assumption underlies some of the discussions concerning the apparent inconsistencies between the two du Pont cases—*Cellophane*[189] and *General Motors*[190]—and the *Bethlehem Steel* case.

The concern about the two du Pont cases boils down to the question whether markets will be defined broadly or narrowly. As will be recalled, in the *Cellophane* case the Supreme Court approved a broad construction of the market to cover many flexible wrapping materials which might be construed as substitutes for cellophane.[191] In the *General Motors* case, the court applied a particularly narrow concept,[192] confining the market to paints and fabrics used by automobile manufacturers.

In much of the discussion, several factors that might serve to explain the two decisions have been slighted or overlooked. One factor can explain the accident of the decisions without providing satisfactory clues for the future. Others can point to possible distinctions on legal and economic grounds. The first factor is the shift in the line-up of the justices: those who represented the minority position in the *Cellophane* case wrote the majority opinion in the *du Pont-General Motors* case. Second, is the possibility of reconciliation on analytical grounds, namely, that in each case the definition of the market was based on the use of the product by the purchaser. Third, the difference in the statutes—Section 2 of the Sherman Act and Section 3 of the Clayton Act—may explain the decisions. Last is the possibility that the court was influenced profoundly by the differences in the harshness of the possible remedies which were envisaged in the two cases.

The make-up of the justices participating in the consideration of each of these cases may have had a substantial influence on their outcomes.[193] In 1956, Justice Reed wrote the majority opinion in the *Cellophane* case, joined by Justices Burton, Frankfurter, and Minton; Justices Clark and Harlan did not participate. The three dissenters in the case (Justices Black, Douglas, and Warren) were in the majority in the *General Motors* case in 1957, along with Justice Brennan who wrote the majority opinion; Justices Clark, Harlan, and Whittaker did not participate while Justices Burton and Frankfurter dissented. Hence, the change in the composition of the court, when Reed and Minton retired and Brennan and Whittaker took their places, revised its general orientation in the field. Yet, some believe that future decisions might follow the *Cellophane* theory if the three nonparticipating justices should take part.[194] Accordingly, it is possible that efforts to reconcile the two decisions may be mere rationalization and that the only logical explanation can be the shift in the composition of the court.

One possible reconciliation[195] of the two cases might be that the market was consistently defined in terms of the requirements of the users.[196] The *Cellophane* case rested on the opinion that the "market is composed of products which have a reasonable interchangeability for the purposes for which they are produced—price, use and qualities considered."[197] On the other hand, as noted earlier, the majority in the *General Motors* case held that:

> The record shows that automobile finishes and fabrics have sufficient peculiar characteristics and uses to constitute them products sufficiently distinct from all other finishes and fabrics to make them "line of commerce" within the meaning of the Clayton Act. . . . Thus, the bounds of the relevant market for the purposes of this case are not coextensive with the total market for finishes and fabrics, but are coextensive with the automobile industry, the relevant market for automotive finishes and fabrics.[198]

The market basis for the *Cellophane* proceeding included materials used by the packagers who substituted cellophane and the other flexible wrapping materials for each other. On the other hand, in the *du Pont-General Motors* case, the market definition turned on the needs of the users of automobile fabrics and finishes. The court felt that the automobile industry required certain types of service and experimentation; therefore, its requirements could not be satisfied by manufacturers who did not possess the appropriate skills. Accordingly, both market definitions were based on the requirements of the pertinent industrial users.[199]

A third influence might be the objectives of the legislation[200] and the nature of the differences in the burden of proof associated with the two acts.[201] The Sherman Act is aimed at accomplished conditions: the *Cellophane* charge[202] was that monopolization had taken place. The Clayton Act is aimed at curtailing incipient monopolistic forces: the *du Pont-General Motors* charge[203] was that the relationship would probably tend to lessen competition or create a monopoly. Accordingly, a Clayton Act charge that is aimed at incipiency may make it appropriate to follow a narrower concept of the market than a Sherman Act case.[204]

The fourth influence that might have some bearing on the comparison of the two decisions—related, in good measure, to the third—might be the judges' reactions to the differences in the possible remedies.[205] In the *Cellophane* case a likely remedy would have been to order the break-up of the Cellophane Division of du Pont into two or more separate companies—one might have remained as the division of du Pont—or to compel the development of new companies. Such a decision would have involved serious consideration of the effect of a dissolution on costs, on the capacity to meet industry's requirements, and on future developmental work. The courts have demonstrated a vigorous reluctance to apply harsh remedies that might have wide economic repercussions.[206]

In contrast, the basic issue in *du Pont-General Motors* was how much control du Pont should have over a separate company that obviously has no need for outside assistance.[207] The economic repercussions of a change of this type could not be serious, although the specific procedure to be followed to effectuate the divorce was troublesome because of tax and stock-market consequences. Therefore, the *du Pont-General Motors* interpretation is apt to be confined to cases in which the remedies are not as radical as the break-up of operating units.[208]

## *Future Development of Market Definition*

Where does all of this take us? How can practical principles for defining markets be established? What are the requirements for any principles? How can precedents be established for market definition, which is primarily a problem in economic analysis?

Several types of bench marks are needed for market definition. In the administration of the laws, guiding principles are needed which take into account the nature of the violation[209] and the remedies which are involved in the proceeding. Such definitional principles are required not only for the prosecution, but for any subsequent review of the effects of the proceeding and any consideration of possible revisions in the decree.

Another set of bench marks is desirable for other areas of government administration that affect competition. For example, regulation in the transportation industries calls for clearer understanding of the nature of the competition among the various methods of transportation. This is a key element in the development of a transportation policy. Similarly, the examination of the effect of trade barriers—whether they take the form of tariffs, quotas, or other restrictions—require another set of principles for gauging markets.

There are a number of features of policy formulation and review which involve the concept of the market: evaluation of the over-all state of competition; analyses of measurements of industrial concentration and power; assessments of the effectiveness of the existing laws; and considerations of new laws. The most immediate need for improvements in setting market dimensions is in the analysis of industrial concentration. Without substantial improvement these measurements will continue to be too limited for effective policy consideration.

In the development of a methodology for defining markets, we must guard against undue rigidity[210] and the counsel of perfection. Competitive forces are too varied and too dynamic to permit fixed mathematical formulas that avoid the need for judgment. Possibly, some day the "social science" quantifiers will show the way. At the moment, their triumphs in gauging consumer reaction, in dealing with a multitude of cost influences, and in competitive game theories indicate *prospective* methods for applying mathematical formulas successfully. Until and unless these are demonstrated and attain general acceptance, we shall have to struggle with the tools we have, improving methods of analysis which depend on judgment and not on conceptual models.

We do have several worthwhile clues for affirmative development. First, market definitions require economic analysis and cannot be settled by conventional "rules of law."[211] Second, such definitions must be integrated with the other analytical elements of the specific proceeding.[212] A mechanical two-step operation—first defining the market and then examining competition in it—is not appropriate. The dimensions of a market must be set in the light of the nature of the alleged violation and the potential remedies. Third, more rigorous analysis of the range of past decisions is needed to begin to evolve a body of principles for future proceedings. Fourth, methods should be developed for providing improved assistance in these considerations to judges, hearing examiners, and commissions. And lastly, further understanding of this range of analytical problems should be developed through more specific work in measuring industrial concentration and industry studies.

In many respects, the task of market definition reflects two broader issues: the rationalization of the antitrust laws and competitive policies; and the improvement in the use of economic analysis in administering the laws. This calls for continuing efforts to develop a firm body of principles in the statutes and their interpretation. A phase of this program would deal with the remedies in the light of differences between monopolistic situations, restraints of trade, unfair competition, and practices that reflect incipient monopolistic forces.

These problems serve to highlight again the need for improving the relationships between economists and lawyers, with greater understanding of the differences between the disciplines. Experience indicates that the definition of the market is a problem in economic analysis that cannot be treated exclusively by conventional rules of law. We cannot, merely as a matter of technicality, decide which products are in a market and which products are out, what geographical area should be included, what level of distributors, what potential entrants exist, and what capacity can be shifted.[213]

Obviously, rules of law must be applied in defining the market in court proceedings. However, these rules require the exercise of the economic discipline. Any meaningful application of precedent in this area calls for the comparison of market definitions, clearly an economic problem.[214] Thus, a possible reconciliation of the *Cellophane* and *du Pont-General Motors* cases calls for the development of principles regarding the bases of the market definitions, for example, the application of a principle of consumer use, as suggested above.

Such a reconciliation is important not only to avoid inconsistency, but also to provide a reasonable public explanation for the decisions.

Without such understanding public impressions can develop that the law is capricious—a feeling that would weaken respect for the judicial system. At the same time, a lack of comprehension of the principles would reduce the effectiveness of the law because businessmen and their lawyers would not know what the law permits.

The definition of a market in a vacuum is neither helpful nor significant. The definition must be related to broader concepts relating to market control. As Lucile Keyes has pointed out, "there is no accepted (or even any suggested) common denominator by means of which such factors as market share, the competition of imperfect substitutes, or the ability of competitors to expand can be considered together in any given instance and their combined effects in terms of market control ascertained."[215] Further, "this lack of clarity regarding market definition is only part of the broader ambiguity that affects the whole legal concept of market control."[216]

Some lawyers have approached the problem mechanically. For example, Victor Hansen, then the Assistant Attorney General in charge of the Antitrust Division, said: "Definition of the market as such may be said to be the initial step that must be undertaken in a monopolization case. At the outset we must determine the product or products which are to be included as being within the relevant market."[217]

However, as Professor Turner has pointed out, "if economic criticism is to be made, it should be directed at the potentially misleading aspects of the traditional 2-step legal approach of first defining the market and then deciding whether monopoly power exists. Percentage share of a market based on a particular definition of the market does not in itself indicate the extent of monopoly power."[218]

Some economists have doubted the possibility of developing a satisfactory market definition. For example, Professor Chamberlin has argued that " 'industry' or 'commodity' boundaries are a snare and a delusion—in the highest degree arbitrarily drawn and, wherever drawn, establishing at once wholly false implications both as to competition of substitutes within their limits . . . and as to the possibility of ruling on the presence or absence of oligopolistic forces by the simple device of counting the number of producers included."[219]

But this position is surely an argument against literal nominalists. It does not imply that market definition is impossible, for setting the general boundaries of markets is essential in any evaluation of competitive conditions, whether the classification is spelled out or assumed. Rather, the statement is a protest against rigid definitions on the basis of which simple counts of producers and simple measures of concentration would be sufficient.

Moreover, as suggested above, analysis of competitive forces cannot be confined within the circumference of a defined market. The nature of competition is influenced by many outside factors. A market rival who earns substantial profits in other markets may use them to reinforce his power in the market in question. Alcoa could afford to take small margins between the prices of virgin aluminum and fabricated products because of its gains in producing ingots. A & P could sell groceries with small mark-ups in one town because of its broad base in the rest of the country.

Above all, the tools of economic inquiry that can be employed in the analysis of markets must be improved. Such concepts as cross-elasticity of demand must be made more specific to be useful in the administration of the law. Professor Stocking has expressed doubts about judges' ability to utilize the concept of cross-elasticity properly. If one grants this contention, the next questions may be: How can we inject more precise meaning into the concept? What can be done to help judges to understand its meaning and use? Should we suspend the use of such a concept in antitrust until the economic analysis is on a firmer base and can be made clear enough to be employed productively by judges and lawyers?

In substance, there are few areas of competition, in antitrust and in other governmental functions, which do not involve intricate problems of market definition. The policy requirements are varied and complex. They do not lend themselves to simple classifications.[220] They will not be satisfied by theoretical exercises in taxonomy. They call for specific empirical analysis which is tailored to the individual problems at issue. At the same time, they require comparisons of the definitions utilized in the trials of similar cases. Such comparisons will make it possible to avoid capricious differences. This feature makes it all the more important to employ economic analysis which is based on an understanding of the differences in the objectives and requirements of the regulation in point.

# 9 / *Statistical Evidence**

CONSIDERATION OF COMPETITIVE ISSUES frequently requires the employment of statistical evidence.[1] The utility of statistics in the analysis of broad policy problems has been well established. While there has been considerable progress in the practical utilization of statistical material in litigation and administrative procedures,[2] there is considerable room for improvement.[3]

Judges, lawyers, and administrative agencies have had great difficulty in employing statistical material satisfactorily. Established litigation procedures, especially technical rules of evidence, do not readily accommodate statistical evidence.[4] The rules of evidence, which can be changed only through a slow evolutionary process, were formulated originally for jury trials. The judicial procedures were developed to meet the requirements of simple trials which turned on oral testimony about uncomplicated fact situations. While administrative agencies were developed, in part, as a means of avoiding the limitations of judicial procedures, they have been strongly influenced by such processes.

Despite obstacles, the legal profession has made substantial headway in the use of statistical material. Archaic rules of evidence[5] have been revised gradually to permit the practical employment of quantitative data in litigation. Statistical tabulations and charts, the results of surveys,[6] and the products of statistical samplings,[7] which would not have been considered by courts at the turn of the century, have been admitted in evidence in recent years.

Yet, the needs for further development are great. With few exceptions, our legal procedures still do not permit adequate use of modern statistical methodology.[8] The techniques for handling quantitative data are not as advanced in legal administration as they are in such other fields as economics, engineering, and industrial management.

* Footnotes for Chapter 9 begin on page 454.

While statistical material is currently applied in many legal proceedings, there is a substantial need to improve its utilization and interpretation. Technical rules of evidence frequently make it difficult to introduce such data. Practical, low-cost methods of providing data, through such means as statistical sampling, are not used as effectively as they might be. Judges find difficulty in interpreting conflicting data in testing quantitative evidence for pitfalls,[9] and in cutting through the obfuscating maneuvers of litigants' lawyers.[10] Such well-established technical methods of statistical inference as correlation, extrapolation, interpolation, and analysis of variance, are rarely employed.

The problem is broader than the mathematics of statistical method. For example, testing the quality and reliability of a field survey requires evaluation of the questions asked as well as of the sampling methods followed.[11] Surveys of costs, profits, price, and new entrants into the market call for accounting, statistical, and economic skills. Surveys of consumer reaction call for an understanding of sociological and psychological analysis.[12]

Methods need to be developed for assisting the courts and administrative agencies in their application of statistical evidence. Progress in this direction depends importantly on the mutual understanding of several professional groups: lawyers, economists, statisticians, and psychologists.[13] We must learn how to relate litigation methods, economic analysis, statistical and accounting techniques, and sociological and psychological analysis. Consideration of such factors as price and cost movements, misleading advertising, definitions of markets, indicators of competition, and competitive influences call for the cooperative application of these disciplines. In the definition of pertinent issues, construction of surveys, formulation of questions, development of tabulations, statistical inference, and interpretation, each of these professions has a substantial contribution to make.

## *Uses of Statistical Method*

Statistical method is a basic tool of inquiry. Few competitive issues can be understood without the application of some quantitative data.[14] Indeed, quantitative analysis is a feature of most economic studies, whether they cover business conditions, international trade, fiscal and monetary problems, labor conditions, or industry-market studies.

The application of statistical method in economic inquiry calls for considerable analytical judgment. Few, if any, economic problems can be solved by the mechanical application of statistics. The definition of the problem, the relation of the data to the problem, the determination of the limits of the quantitative data all call for analysis.

As we have seen in the discussions of the indicators of competition and of circumstantial evidence, there are many analytical problems which cannot be solved by statistical methods alone.[15] For example, judging the influence of a business practice on competition[16] calls for a review of methods of production, procurement, and distribution; in turn, such inquiry requires conclusions about the relevant market.[17] In these studies, various uses are made of statistics to confirm or support analytical hypotheses. However, in the final analysis qualitative judgments must be made of the cumulative effects of the quantitative and qualitative evidence.

On many occasions, judgment depends on factors that have not been quantified. Frequently, no applicable data are readily available.[18] For example, in the absence of a survey of consumer reaction, a decision may be required about the misleading influences of certain representations or about the cross-elasticity in the demand for certain products. On other occasions, no quantitative methods may be available. How can the intent to monopolize be measured?

The application of statistical methods depends on several factors: understanding of the uses of quantitative data in the solution of the specific problem under consideration; knowledge of the data which are readily available through census and other compilations made by government agencies and trade groups; construction of special field surveys either to supplement the existing data or to study phenomena which have not been covered; and utilization of the data within the limitations which are set by judicial and administrative procedures.

### *Statistics in Policy Analysis*

Policy analysis calls for a wide range of statistical treatment. Among the most frequently used statistical evidence in such policy review are: business population and concentration;[19] costs and productivity;[20] price movements and flexibilities;[21] and the statistics of antitrust enforcement.[22] These materials provide clues to competitive trends, the effects of present policies, and the desirability of alternative policies.

Industrial concentration is a widely used indicator of competitive conditions.[23] In broad economy-wide terms, it can shed some light on concentration of economic power—a factor of importance in the consideration of social and political as well as economic objectives. Such a measure can be useful in the analysis of trends in competitive conditions in individual markets. As can be seen in Chapter 8, however, the current measurements of industrial concentration do not offer satisfactory signposts of either concentration of power or competitive conditions.

Business population data are employed in general studies of the health of small business. Figures on the number of business enterprises, new businesses, sales of businesses, and discontinuances through bankruptcy or liquidation are helpful to studies of the conditions of small business.[24] However, these series do not, by themselves, offer final evaluations. A high mortality rate may be taken to indicate that small business is suffering. On the other hand, it may have come about because business conditions enabled many unskilled people to start new ventures, or because a recession "boiled out" enterprises that will be replaced in number during a subsequent recovery.

Industry statistics showing new entrants and exits[25] provide clues to the state of competition within a defined market. Such analysis can throw light on one of the principal indicators of competition—ease of entry into the market.[26] But currently available data do not always provide direct answers. Industry figures do not necessarily reflect what is taking place in a market.[27] For example, since products of steel may enter into new rivalry with wood, plastics, rubber, copper, aluminum, and glass, conventional industry categories frequently fail to portray market competition. Nor do series on new entrants into an industry always reflect the entry, through diversification, of established businesses.

Data on price movements have been employed in policy formulation in many fields including inflation, wage rates, and competition.[28] During the great depression, a new pricing issue was created: the influence of relatively rigid prices on fluctuations of production and employment.[29] As indicated in Chapter 7, this issue has been prominent in recent studies of competitive policy. These analyses have raised several interesting statistical-interpretive problems. Differences have developed regarding such questions as: What should be examined—selling prices or the margins between what firms pay for labor and materials and what they receive for the final product?[30] Are the available statistics regarding price changes an accurate reflection of relative stability or do they fail to take account of quality changes[31] and are the statistical results unduly influenced by the mechanisms for gathering data?[32] Do price statistics portray actual prices paid or list prices which are subject to substantial unpublicized discounts?[33] Finally, what is the basis for the presumption that more flexible prices would help to maintain stable production?

The statistics of antitrust activity have been used to gauge the effectiveness of enforcement. The Antitrust Division of the Department of Justice and the Federal Trade Commission are encouraged to institute more proceedings and to win more cases in order to demonstrate their effectiveness and to win increased budgets. However, as we have seen, reliance on the accomplishment-gauge of case statistics can actually reduce the effectiveness of the antitrust program. Such counts have probably encouraged government lawyers and administrators to institute many proceedings against small companies in unimportant industries and to win many minor skirmishes through the consent procedures, without affecting the state of competition appreciably.

Industry studies call for considerable statistical treatment.[34] They deal with such factors as the size and growth of an industry, trends in concentration, interindustry and foreign competition, trends in labor conditions, costs, productivity, volume, prices, profits, and investment, the nature of geographic markets, and transportation costs. Much of this material is applied in the litigation of specific antitrust attacks.[35]

As this brief sampling of the use of statistics in policy consideration implies, no data provide mathematically inevitable conclusions. Such consideration must take account of a number of factors—some statistical and some qualitative—to formulate tolerably significant policy conclusions. In the process, economic analysis is required to formulate the issues to be considered in testing the various policy alternatives;

to determine which quantitative data may be germane to the issues; and to provide a sophisticated interpretation of the data. For example, economic analysis must be brought to bear on the consideration of measurements of industrial concentration as a clue to the state of competition in the economy.[36]

### *Application of Statistical Analysis in Litigation*

Potential uses of statistical evidence in antitrust litigation are many and varied. A complete catalog would be impossible. Because of the current trend toward increased use of statistical evidence, especially in the merger cases, many new applications of statistical methods are developing. Following are a few illustrations.

Statistical compilations of prices and price movements can be used to test hypotheses about price conspiracy and anticompetitive influences as in the *Tag Manufacturers* case.[37]

Measurements of dominance in a market have been compiled by studying sales of individual companies and of their competitors as in the *Pillsbury*[38] and *Crown-Zellerbach*[39] proceedings. *Pillsbury* involved an interesting sampling problem. Respondents' evidence about the size of the market, based on data about two metropolitan areas, was rejected on the ground that it was not representative of the entire market covered.

Statistical proof of the geographical limits of various regional markets was offered in the *Bethlehem Steel* case.[40]

Price movements were used to test contentions about the definition of a market in the *Cellophane* proceedings.[41]

Complaints regarding misleading representation were tested by surveys of doctors and dentists in the *Rolaid*[42] and *Ipana*[43] proceedings.

Cost data[44] have been employed to test power to raise prices and exclude competitors in the *Alcoa*[45] and *Cellophane*[46] cases; to test intent to monopolize in *American Tobacco;*[47] to test predatory intent in *A & P;*[48] to test the existence of a price conspiracy in *Pevely Dairy*[49] and *Eli Lilly;*[50] and to justify price discrimination in Robinson-Patman cases.[51]

Proof of the exposure of many products to customers and the absence of exclusive dealing agreements was presented through statistical studies in the proceeding against *J. I. Case*.[52]

## *Problems in the Application of Statistics*

The uses of quantitative data in litigation and administrative proceedings involve a number of problems. When should original data be used? When and how should statistical tabulations, charts, and other visual aids be employed? How should field surveys be made, checked, and interpreted? What are proper statistical samples, and how can their reliability be checked? Finally, what uses can be made of statistical inference to interpret the meaning of the data?

A quick review of these problems will help to interpret the issues that surround the use of statistics in litigation. By relating the features of statistical methods of the technical rules of evidence one can understand and evaluate the lawyer's resistance to the use of quantitative data and the problems of the courts in utilizing statistical material.

It should be noted, parenthetically, that the employment of statistical evidence in litigation is not confined to antitrust. Similar problems can be encountered in such other legal fields as public utility rates, fraud, contract interpretation, taxes, medical malpractice, paternity suits, and trade-marks. Each such field has its own unique problems in statistical application.

### *Tabulations*

Tabulations must be employed whenever a substantial number of transactions or observations are made.[53] It would hardly be practical to examine each invoice[54] prepared by a company over a ten-year period in order to picture its sales trends. Nor would anyone want to look at each employee of the company during those years to see how many were employed.

Yet, the use of tabulations is not devoid of technical problems.[55] Categories must be defined and related to each other. Many tabulations lend themselves to manipulation through chart presentation. The years selected for starting a tabulation can have a profound influence on interpretation. Sources of data must be found; for example, government studies, trade association statistics, company figures, and surveys or special tabulations based on one or more of such sources.

Categories and bases for statistical interpretation can be strategic. Suppose a company maintains a stable work force but changes the number of hours of work from week to week to reflect changes in sales volume. A tabulation of the *number of workers* employed will show stable employment, while *hours worked* might reflect great instability.[56] Suppose that Bethlehem sells one product to General Motors and Youngstown sells another;[57] then a tabulation of total dollar sales to the same customer would develop an illusion of competition between the two suppliers.

Consider a company which had sold a given product at retail for years and later manufactured the product, integrating raw material production, parts manufacturing, and assembly. If only its dollar sales volume is considered, its retail sales might show no increase, and the tabulation would not reflect the expansion in its employment, investment, and volume of activity. On the other hand, a table of value added (dollar sales less purchases) would show up the expansion.

Geographical categories can be of great moment. A comparison of a steel mill's sales with industry volume for the entire country would be quite different from a comparison which was made for each market region. For example, the *Affidavit in Support of the Plaintiff's Motion for Summary Judgment*[58] in *Bethlehem Steel*[59] showed that Bethlehem's shipments of steel sheets and strip in 1953 accounted for 13.5 per cent of the national totals, 100 per cent of shipments to the District of Columbia, and 73.5 per cent of shipments to Maryland.[60]

The starting date for a time series can have a profound effect on the interpretation of trends. Some computations based on the *Background Statistics Bearing on the Steel Dispute*[61] illustrate the point. If the series starts with 1940, steel prices rose by 174 per cent between 1940 and 1958 while the wholesale prices of all commodities rose by 133 per cent; in contrast, if the series starts in 1944, steel prices would show an increase of 172 per cent between 1944 and 1958 while general prices rose only 76 per cent; hence, steel prices in 1958 look more reasonable in a tabulation starting in 1940 than one which starts in 1944.

Wage and price comparisons offer similar results. Starting in 1940,[62] one wage series presented in the same report indicates a wage increase of 146 per cent between 1940 and 1958, compared with the price increase of 174 per cent. On the other hand, wages and prices seemed to move together between 1950 and 1958 with a 58 per cent increase for labor and a 60 per cent increase for price. Between 1956 and 1958 employment costs showed a greater increase (19 per cent) than price (13 per cent).

Methods of presentation of tabulations can influence impressions.[63] Should a bar court, a series of pie charts or a line chart be used? Should one chart be drawn to prove one point or a substantial number of points? How large a scale should be used? A chart that shows ten workers to the inch will rise by three inches when thirty workers are added, while a scale of one hundred workers to the inch will show a rise of only 3/10 of an inch for the same increase.

Presentations can be made in original data or in relative figures. A table of annual dollar sales may be less impressive than a table of indexes, showing the first year as one hundred and the following years as percentages of the first. Conversely, a chart showing percentage change from the previous year may accentuate fluctuations from year to year and underplay an expansion over a period of years.

### *Sampling*

Probably the most difficult quantitative concept to apply in litigation is the statistical sample. Briefly stated, a sample is intended to reflect what would be found if everything in a "universe" were examined.[64] After reading a chapter in a new textbook, a lawyer may decide to buy it; after tasting a martini, he may decide not to drink it; after interviewing ten dealers, he may feel that no dealer was forced into an exclusive arrangement with his client. In each instance, he has used a sample. Each sample represented a universe—a book, a cocktail, a retailer's experience with his client.

Common experience tells the lawyer that there are differences in the reliability of samples.[65] He has read books which contain only one good chapter. On the other hand, he knows that one unsatisfactory sip means that the entire martini is not to his taste. He also knows that, if his client selected the ten dealers he interviewed, they probably do not represent the attitudes of all; whereas, if he saw dealers "at random" around the country, he would obtain more reliable reactions.

Stripped of its jargon and of its technicalities, sampling technique is frequently employed by every lawyer. These everyday samples are based on common sense rather than on mathematical findings.[66] They call for evaluation of the reliability of the samples and an unstated acceptance of the mathematical laws of probability.

Indeed, as the discussion of circumstantial evidence shows, judicial findings of fact are frequently based on probability theory.[67] The circumstantial evidence is not proof conclusive.[68] It merely demonstrates the probability, or likelihood, that an event occurred.[69] For example, circumstantial evidence might show an overwhelming probability that the defendant in a criminal case did steal a TV set. The probabilities are that certain ascertainable events would not have taken place unless he stole. Yet, there always remains the remote possibility that he did not commit the crime.

In practice, methods of sampling depend also on the frequency of the procedure. A cigarette factory which buys many hogsheads of tobacco can rely on a small sample extracted from an inner section of each.[70] However, a cigar-maker who works alone would have to exercise much more care in inspecting a hogshead. The cigarette plant could rely on the average quality of the samples as an accurate gauge of the average of all of the hogsheads. The lone cigar-maker cannot average out the quality of a number of hogsheads; hence, his sampling method must be more precise than that of the factory.

When many who employ sensible sampling procedures in daily activities are confronted with a planned sample, suspicion arises.[71] A judge who is willing to base a decision on the testimony of a handful of dealer or consumer witnesses, can have serious doubts about the fairness and adequacy of a carefully constructed opinion survey of four thousand consumers.[72] Similarly, a lawyer who has permitted opponents to use the testimony of a handful of consumer witnesses can rise to the attack when the other side presents the results of an organized survey. Of course, the legal profession has no monopoly on this suspicion. Nor is the attitude entirely without foundation in every case. However, there has been some progress in the use of practical sampling methods in litigation.

The essential task of sampling is to secure the same information which would be obtained by a complete census. The goal of sampling procedures is to select the smallest number of observations that will describe the universe adequately.[73] A sample has several practical advantages over a census: it is less costly; it can provide more detailed information[74] and employ better-trained observers;[75] in some instances it is the only way to make practical observations.[76] For example, testing every drop of a drug mixture would leave no product to sell. In many situations it can provide more reliable information than a complete census.

An accepted classification of samples divides them into two classes: "judgmental" and "probability."[77] In its pure form, a judgmental sample is based on the surveyor's judgment about what sample will best represent the universe. In contrast, a probability sample is based on a mathematical design which substitutes standard, objective methods of selection for personal judgment.[78] Obviously, this simple classification does not reflect two watertight compartments. Some types of mathematical aids are employed in competent judgmental samples. Skilled judgment is required in the bulk of probability samples.

The probability sample has two advantages. Because many of its elements are standardized,[79] they provide a rational basis for expert agreement about the quality of the sample. Secondly, it provides a basis for estimating its own accuracy. Probability methods help to plan a survey by indicating: how large a sample should be taken; how to make random selections so that the sample will be representative; and what is the probable margin of error that may be reflected in the results.

The margin of error sets the limits within which a complete count would fall. A small margin of error indicates very reliable results. But even a substantial margin may provide an accuracy which is satisfactory for the purpose at hand. Suppose, for example, that a sample study shows that 30 per cent of the sales of a given product takes place in syndicate stores, and that the probable error of the sample is 4 per cent. This would mean that syndicate stores account for between

26 and 34 per cent of total sales. If a court's decision would be the same whether the per cent was 26 or 34, there would be no need for further study. On the other hand, if the decision would depend on which of these figures was right, the survey would have to be designed to produce a narrower range of probable error. Hence, this method enables the planner to set up a survey which would be sufficiently accurate for the purposes at hand.

Such estimates of probable error cannot be made for judgmental samples. Therefore, the reliability of such samples must be gauged by examining the reasonableness of the methods followed and by considering corroborating evidence of its results.[80] On the other hand, in many instances, a judgmental sample provides survey results more quickly, at lower cost.[81] In addition, its common-sense approach is more appealing to many who distrust the probability sample because they do not understand its mathematical foundations.

The design of a sample starts with a review of the universe to be covered.[82] Do we want to know what proportion of all stores selling drugs—including supermarkets, department stores, variety stores, and drugs stores—display Brand X lipstick? Or are we interested in drug stores only, or in drug stores in large towns? Until the universe is defined, it is not possible to tell what a sample will do. For example, a sample of pertinent retailers in Washington, D.C. would probably not be representative of large cities, small towns, suburbs, and rural areas. Nor would it reflect the average for the country because of regional differences.

The next step, for many surveys, is to divide the total population into groups or "frames." A frame might cover a type of retailer, a type of community, or a geographical region. The classification and distribution of the frames may indicate that certain groups should be studied more carefully than others. The jargon classes this as a "stratified" sample.[83] For example, if it were known that 60 per cent of all Brand X lipsticks were sold through 25 chain organizations of drug, variety, and supermarket stores, an effort might be made to secure all the pertinent information from each of those organizations. For, if the sampling procedure should overlook most of the chains, it would have obvious shortcomings.[84]

Another step would be the determination of how many individual outlets to survey. This number would be based on mathematical probability formulas, which indicate what margin of error can be expected for any given number of stores. After deciding what margin of error would be satisfactory, the number of observations would be set.

The relationship between margin of error and the number of observations is not easy for the non-mathematician to understand.[85] Sampling error depends much more on the total number of observations than on the proportion of the universe to be covered.[86] A one per cent sample of all families in the United States would cover about 500,000. A one per cent sample of male teachers in elementary and high schools, age 55 or over, would cover only about 500 observations, while a 5 per cent sample would cover only 2,500. Hence, a sample of one per cent of all families might give a margin of error of plus or minus 1 against a figure of 60 per cent, or a range of 59 to 61. A sample of 5 per cent of the teachers might produce a margin of error of 15 against an average of 60 per cent, or a range of 45 to 75.

The heavier dependence on the absolute size of the sample, rather than on its proportion of the population, has a mathematical basis.[87] The average income of the five men in a car pool cannot be determined by interviewing one man. On the other hand, the mathematicians tell us that the incomes of 100,000 messenger boys in one city could be sampled with a 98 per cent accuracy by interviewing 217 boys selected at random. If there were only 1,000 messengers in the city, a sample of 179 would be sufficient; for 200 messengers a sample of 105 would be needed for 98 per cent accuracy.[88]

Information from other surveys or census material might show that certain cities are representative of groups of cities. Or, it might be found that the bulk of the products which are covered by a survey are sold in the largest thirty-two metropolitan areas; in which event, more attention would be given to those locations.

After selecting the types of stores and areas to be surveyed, the specific stores to cover might be chosen by a system of "random numbers." All stores which operate in each town and county would be assigned numbers. With this numerical list, numbers would be chosen from standard tables of "random numbers" which is a sequence of numbers that was developed by mathematicians to reflect chance only without being influenced by the immediate survey in any way.

The judgmental sample requires decisions about what frames or groups to use and what samples to take for each. Using previous information about the universe to set up the sample, the judgment process can produce satisfactory results. For example, in making a survey of average prices charged for a special size of Brand X canned peaches in chain stores in Manhattan, one might start with the following information: the number and location of stores in each chain; past surveys showed that there tended to be price differences among stores in twenty distinct neighborhoods; and the volume of shipments of Brand X to stores in each of these neighborhoods. With this knowledge it would be possible to select specific stores in each of the twenty neighborhoods, choosing one store for each chain in each neighborhood. Prices in the selected stores would be averaged for each neighborhood. These neighborhood averages would then be combined into a weighted average based on the shipments that were made. Such a sample might be a fair representation of the various classes which are involved, reflecting regional differences as well as differences in the price policies of all of the chains.

In this, as in every area of analysis, no single tool is best suited for all occasions. Nor are the differences between the two types of samples sharply marked in each case. The probability sample calls for judgment[89] while the judgmental sample frequently calls for understanding of mathematical probability. Many surveys call for a combination of the two types. For example, a stratified sample may cover five types of plants, classified by number of employees and production methods; full counts may be taken of some classes; a 40 per cent sample taken of another; a 1 per cent sample of a third.[90] These can be presented as a combination of judgment and probability, or a probable error may be computed for the total sample as well as for individual frames.

Sampling methods are employed more widely than generally has been recognized. Most surveys do not provide complete coverage even if they do not bear a "sample" label. For a census survey cannot ensure the complete coverage of every person in the population or every company in the industry. Many census reports are based on samples. For example, in the recent census certain questions were asked of every fifth family interviewed.[91] Nevertheless, the census reports are accepted as "factual" without reservation—a reasonable conclusion.

Sampling must be used in many phases of antitrust.[92] Even a company's regular operating data may not provide the evidence required. Consider the determination of cost differences to justify a price differential under the Robinson-Patman Act.[93] No company has been able to devise books of account which will produce figures on such cost difference regularly.[94] Therefore, any proof of cost differences requires special studies. Such a survey would be prohibitively expensive if it covered a full year's operation and would probably take a year to finish. The study might have to cover the length of time it takes to make a sales call on specific types of customers, the time it takes for a shipping clerk to make up orders of specified sizes, and the number of minutes required to write and post an invoice. Maintaining special records of the time taken for these steps, together with wage and other costs over a full year, would be very costly, and the record-keeping itself would reduce the efficiency of the operation. Therefore, the F.T.C. recognizes the need to accept sample studies that are made over a limited period of time, say a week or a month.[95] It may be noted that these studies have been based on judgmental rather than probability samples. Judgmental considerations include analysis of the period covered to see if it is representative of operations during the year, or if the company branch or branches that were reviewed are typical of the operations of all of its branches.

It has been suggested that some samples may produce more accurate results than a complete census.[96] Joel Dean advanced this conclusion in comparing the Bureau of the Census monthly samples of unemployment with the results of its Decennial Census in April 1950. The bureau has regularly constructed estimates of unemployment through sample surveys covering 25,000 families. After the 1950 Census was taken, a significant discrepancy was noted between the estimates based on the sample and the census. Subsequent investigation indicated that the sample was more accurate than the full census. Professor Dean felt that the sample survey was superior since it employed fewer interviewers who were better trained to follow directions than the large number of enumerators required for the Decennial Census.[97]

One of the analytical problems that affects both judgment and probability samples is how to define the universe which is described by a sample.[98] A mathematical measurement of accuracy relates to a specified universe. The definition of such a universe must be based on judgment rather than a wholly mathematical formula. Mathematical evaluation cannot tell the appropriateness of the survey, or its application to the problem at hand.[99]

The relationship between the sample and the universe it represents can be illustrated simply. Suppose that two separate investigators were asked to survey the distribution of family incomes in New York City. Investigator A might visit all the boroughs, spending a substantial time in travel and collecting three thousand replies. On the other hand, Investigator B, for laziness or lack of time, might concentrate on apartment houses in the Park Avenue area and complete his three thousand interviews in short order. If they were applied mechanically, many gauges of sampling would show the two surveys to have the same accuracy. One type of test would show that the Park Avenue sample is superior. In fact, it probably would be the more accurate sample—but it would reflect the distribution of incomes in the Park Avenue area, not in New York City.[100]

The relationship between the sample and the universe is not an academic exercise. In antitrust, it affects practical problems of prosecution and defense. It can determine the final outcome of a proceeding.

Consider the case of *Tag Manufacturers Institute, et al.* v. *F.T.C.*[101] The court was critical of the Federal Trade Commission's study of prices which it made to substantiate a charge of price fixing. On the basis of a sample study of invoices of competing manufacturers the commission argued that the survey indicated that prices were fixed. The defendants contended that the commission's survey gave too much weight to stock tags and too little to special tags; that stock tags, which accounted for only 13 per cent of total sales, were given a weight of 71.69 per cent; that it was only reasonable to suppose that there would be greater uniformity in the prices of the stock items because of competition; that the study excluded sales to wholesalers and to government agencies; that the sample was confined to sales on two days during periods of stable market conditions; and that a sample taken during unstable market conditions would produce greater price diversity. This argument persuaded the court that the F.T.C.'s study was deficient.

The complaint in this case covered the pricing of all the industry products. The sample did appear to be deficient as a sample of that universe. However, the sample might have been used to describe another universe more accurately, and the prosecution might have been successful.

If the complaint had covered an agreement to fix prices for the stock tags which were sold to private users, part of the F.T.C.'s sample could have been employed as an adequate picture of that universe. There would have been no debate about weighting the prices for non-stock items or about sales to wholesalers and government. The Commission might have proved its price-fixing charge by relating the complaint to the showing of a smaller, more adequate sample. To establish an antitrust violation, there is no need to prove that all prices were fixed. Indeed, Justice Douglas' opinion in *Socony-Vacuum Oil Co.*[102] indicates no requirement to show a rigid fixing of prices to sustain an antitrust charge. Here, then, is another instance of the need for relating the issues of the case to the economic analysis employed.

## *Survey Methods*

There is a vital distinction between the problems of sampling and those of the survey methods.[103] Survey methods refer to the design of the questions, the methods of collecting the information, and the circumstances surrounding the collection.[104] W. E. Deming, one of the outstanding mathematical specialists in sampling has stressed this difference. "The issues involved in the survey should be considered separately from the issues involved in the sample. For in many cases criticisms of sampling have really not related to the sampling, but have related to the way in which the survey was put up, the way in which the problems were defined, and the way in which the survey was conducted."[105]

Professor Deming used the controversy about the 1950 Census estimates of unemployment, discussed above, as an illustration of this point. He argued that while most critics of the census referred to possible errors of sampling, the problem was really one of defining unemployment.[106] He suggested, for example, that if a man fears that he may lose his job, his wife may feel that she should find employment to supplement their income; as soon as she plans to look for a position, she considers herself unemployed; therefore, she would report herself as being unemployed. Hence, responses to unemployment questions merely reflect a frame of mind. This feature would have the same influence on any survey—a full census or a sample. Therefore, the problem relates to survey techniques rather than sampling methods.

The way in which questions are asked during a survey can exert a strategic influence on its results.[107] A case in point is *Sears Roebuck & Company* v. *Johnson,*[108] a suit for a trade-mark infringement. The defendant used the name "All-State Driving School." The plaintiff had employed the trade name "Allstate" for some time. During the survey, interviewers asked a number of consumers oral questions about the names and found that many thought that there was a connection between the two. The district judge held that the survey was not reliable because while the two words sound alike, they do not look alike. However, the Circuit Court of Appeals reversed this decision, and accepted the survey results.[109]

*Oneida Ltd.* v. *National Silver Co.*[110] involved the question whether the defendant's design of silver flatware led consumers to believe that the product was made by the plaintiff. Each side polled consumers. The plaintiff took a poll of one thousand women who were asked to designate which company they believed to be the manufacturer of the silverware. The court held that the housewife's off-the-cuff answer was not a reliable gauge of her reactions as a buyer; if she contemplated the purchase of silverware, she would be much more careful. Therefore, a survey of potential buyers would be more significant.[111] Further, the court was critical of the evidence presented because the plaintiff conducted its survey in a community near its plant, while the defendants conducted another survey in the area where the plaintiff's competitors were located. Though the plaintiff's survey was admitted into evidence, the court held the results to be inconclusive.

In *Coca-Cola Co.* v. *Nehi Corp.*[112] the plaintiff attempted to prove that the word "Cola" was associated with its product.[113] Word association tests were used in college psychology classrooms. The court held that: "It is manifest that the mental reaction of the student in the classroom to the word Cola is bound to differ from the buyer in the market place when confronted with the name of the beverage in the size and dress of the bottle and package."[114]

*Lerner Stores Corp.* v. *Lerner*[115] involved another opinion survey with built-in bias. Interviewers asked passers-by in front of the plaintiff's San Francisco store what they understood by the term "Lerner Shops." The responses were used in a suit to enjoin the defendant from opening a store using the name "Lerner" in San Jose, California. The trial court ignored the results of the survey. The appellate court held that the survey was of little value because its location predetermined the conclusion.

## *Statistical Interpretation*

The task of statistical interpretation calls for an understanding of the pertinent mathematical procedures. It requires a sophisticated appreciation of the meanings and shortcomings of such procedures as "extrapolation," "interpolation," and "correlation." While these methods help to analyze various relationships, they have not been widely employed in litigation because of their technical complexities. Yet, they are of great value not only in the social but also in the biological and physical sciences.

In their simplest forms interpolation and extrapolation are used in everyday business analysis. They provide a method for estimating what would be the probable results of given conditions on certain happenings. Thus, a company which knows its overhead and variable costs can estimate its total costs at various volumes by setting up a trend line and estimating costs for each level of production. Such a method is employed on every break-even chart.

Forecasts of many types are made by extending trend lines—a method of extrapolating. With a set of charts of population trends, it is possible to predict the country's population in 1965 or 1968. Such population forecasts require the use of a number of subsidiary trends showing such factors as: age composition of the population, birth rates of various groups, death rates, and immigration. The resulting trends can be understood by most judges if they are given logical explanations with a minimum of technical jargon.

Statistical methods can be used also to determine, within a reasonable degree of probability, what happened during past periods when no observations were made. Unfortunately, these techniques require somewhat involved calculations for many purposes. The trajectory of a bullet cannot be described by a layman merely because he knows where the gun and target are located. Nor can intervening price movements be described merely by looking at prices on two days that are three years apart. Seasonal, cyclical, and other movements which influence the economy and the specific industry make such estimates somewhat involved. Nevertheless, in the hands of a competent economist, reasonably accurate reconstruction may frequently be achieved and explained.

The use of such methods is not successful if the basic data are not persuasive. In the recent *Pillsbury* proceeding,[116] the F.T.C. rejected estimates submitted by the respondent based on such interpolation and extrapolation. A witness for the company used his own estimates on flour consumption during 1945-46 and 1951-52 and estimates for the intervening and subsequent years. The F.T.C. held that these estimates were unreliable because they were based on the unsupported judgment of the witness who "corrected" the data of several field surveys.[117]

Correlation methods can be of substantial help in economic interpretation. Such methods can shed light on the relationships between two or more series or conditions. For example, such a measurement would indicate whether there is a closer relationship between the market supply of cotton and its price or between national income and the price of cotton. This index might indicate that the same market factors influenced the prices of an item before and after a merger. Such a result might be used to prove that the mergers had no effect on prices.

Interpretations of mathematical relationships cannot be mechanical. The fact that two series vary together does not prove a causal connection. A number of statistical curios show the danger of accepting all measures of high correlation. For example, over a period of years, the salaries of Presbyterian ministers in Massachusetts was highly correlated with the prices of rum in Jamaica.[118] Obviously, other evidence which corroborates the causal relation is needed for sensible conclusions.

While the more involved types of statistical inference have not been widely used in litigation, some of the simpler methods are employed frequently. Any tabulation of quantitative data over a period of time requires inference for interpretation. Is it likely that a company's sales or profits will increase over a period of years, judging from its past sales and profits? Did wage rates in the steel industry advance as quickly as prices? Did steel prices merely keep pace with general price levels? Will a company's position in a market continue to decline? Do the data on prices charged by various competitors indicate a price conspiracy? Is the similarity in price movements due to the same cost and demand conditions? Are the price similarities due to competition and absence of price-shading because of the Robinson-Patman Act?

All of these inferences call for the skills of the economist and the statistician. They require, also, that the technical interpretation should be translated into language and concepts that the lawyer can employ. In their application, they accentuate the need for providing the judges with satisfactory help in carrying their heavy burdens.

## *Trial Procedures*

The application of statistical methods within the framework of litigation, outlined in Chapter 5, above, poses a number of significant problems. What data should be admitted into evidence and considered? How can the courts gauge the reliability of the evidence? How can a judge decide what statistical analysis is more reliable in the face of conflicting material and conflicting testimony from opposing experts? How can a court interpret the statistical evidence and relate it to other types of testimony, some of which may appear to be in conflict with the data?

The established techniques of trial are not patterned for the effective use of quantitative evidence.[119] Most courtroom procedures were designed for oral testimony in cases in contract, torts, and real estate which required findings by a jury composed of inexperienced peers. These conventional procedures have been adequate for treating simple fact situations. However, they have required laborious modification to accommodate the complexities of economic analysis. For example, the price movements of an industry's products cannot be described by oral testimony alone. To study such price movements in an industry of fifty companies, which manufacture several hundred products and sell to thousands of customers, through oral testimony without tabulation would be impossible.

Given the historical influences on litigation procedures and the slow pace of their revision, much of the treatment of statistical information has been influenced by technical maneuvers regarding the admission of such evidence,[120] rather than by consideration of its analytical value. In many instances, judges have ruled that such evidence cannot be presented to the court. In some cases, the legal infighting has taken so much time it has interfered with effective court administration and has substantially reduced the possibilities of applying such economic analysis effectively. In fact, the extended discussions might well have riveted the judge's attention on the technical problems of evidence rather than the merits of the case.[121]

As Professor Dession has pointed out, because of these methods of trying cases, "many realities of the situations in question tend to recede from the focus of attention as litigation progresses, and the situations themselves tend to be replaced by verbal patterns more manageable because artificially simplified."[122]

While substantial progress[123] has been made in handling quantitative data in litigation, there is a great need for the development of effective methods of presenting such material and for giving it adequate consideration. Many jurists have accepted statistical evidence and would like to see improvements in methods of presentation. Some feel, like Judge Noonan, "that a visual presentation of summaries and statistics and graphic illustrations of economic material are not only a great saving of trial time but of immeasurable aid to a proper understanding of the material."[124] However, many other judges are loath to consider such evidence, while others are willing to accept the evidence but have great difficulty in applying it in their factual analysis.

The application of statistical material in antitrust cases raises many practical problems.[125] Procedures must be developed to utilize quantitative tabulations in evidence. Such procedures must afford adversaries adequate opportunity to review the underlying data so that the tabulations and their interpretations may be tested adequately.[126] It has been suggested that the courts undertake to test such data independently.[127] However, as discussed above in Chapter 6, such a step would call for a radical revision in the judicial function—one which should not be taken lightly.

Part of the problem concerns the judge's inability to analyze conflicting reports and interpretations.[128] The underlying uncertainty created by this incapacity may account, in large measure, for the resistance to tabulations and surveys. Old beliefs linger on regarding the "trickiness" of statistics. "Figures don't lie, but liars figure" is a long-remembered adage. It will probably take years of productive experience to erode this underlying attitude.

The specific requirements of the judicial procedure play an important role in any improvements in handling quantitative evidence. The effective utilization of data regarding economic forces depends on clear-cut definitions of the issues before the trial is started.[129] The level of craftsmanship in defining complex economic issues has not been as high as in many areas of litigation. Similarly, technical rules regarding the admissibility and utilization of evidence have an important bearing on the tasks of defining the issues, deciding what quantitative evidence may be introduced in the trial, presenting the evidence, and interpreting it. For a proper perspective of these problems one must consider the rules of evidence and the reasons for their development.

## *Rules of Evidence*

The introduction of statistical data in antitrust litigation is controlled by the general rules covering the admissibility of evidence.[130] These rules have evolved over the centuries starting with the early development of the common law in England. During the course of this evolution, they have taken on the inherited superstitions of many generations of lawyers.[131]

Rules of evidence were designed originally to keep unreliable evidence from the inexperienced people who serve on juries. It was felt that inexperienced jurors would not be competent to differentiate between unsubstantiated rumor and specific testimony based on direct observation.

As equity jurisprudence developed, other types of evidentiary rules developed. Since the equity trials were held without a jury, the need for "protecting" the triers of fact became less important. The judges felt that their experience enabled them to gauge the reliability of evidence more effectively than lay juries. However, they were not willing to accept radical changes in the rules.

An important influence on the application of the rules of evidence is the nature of the possible consequences of a trial. Thus, the rules covering criminal cases differ from those of civil proceedings. Further, the seriousness of the crime and the ensuing penalties affect the court's judgment. For example, the defendant in a murder trial is allowed more freedom in introducing evidence than a man accused of speeding. Similarly, if the ultimate issue in a case is whether to issue an order regarding future behavior, the plaintiff would have greater leeway in introducing evidence than in a case which might call for a fine or imprisonment. In antitrust, the courts require a higher "standard of proof" in a criminal price-fixing case than in a civil case, which could at worst result in an injunction to discontinue the arrangement. At the same time, if the prospective cure in the civil case were the break-up of a company, the courts would probably tend to permit the defendants greater latitude in introducing evidence.

The application of rules of evidence has a substantial bearing on the trial of issues relating to competition. As we have seen, such trials turn on circumstantial evidence and the tests of hypotheses.[132] Further, such evidence and hypotheses cannot be described in simple factual terms. As a result, competitive issues provide some of the most complex evidentiary problems facing the courts.

The rules regarding admissibility and application of evidence encompass three major issues: relevancy, materiality, and competence.[133] Problems of relevancy deal with whether the information relates to the issues in the case. Without such a rule, individual litigants could filibuster freely by producing all manner of evidence. Further, in the absence of such rules litigants might well produce information that would cater to bias rather than to the issues.

This rule is of substantial import in antitrust cases. It limits the quantity of evidence, and it serves to compel the parties to define the issues clearly. Unless an issue is defined, the judge may not permit the presentation of evidence dealing with it. Because of this feature, there are occasions, no doubt, when counsel will attempt to obfuscate issues in order to provide a peg on which to hang some evidence.

The effects of the rules regarding materiality are hard to pin down firmly. "Materiality" relates to the question of how reliable and convincing is the evidence which is presented. A thorough understanding of materiality might require psychological analyses of the mental paths followed by the judge in arriving at his conclusions. On occasion, it is possible to tell whether or not a judge was impressed by some evidence. However, it seems impossible to define any rules that would provide substantial control over the intellectual mastication of evidence during a judge's private deliberation.

### *Hearsay Rule*

Finally, the rules of competence govern the determination of whether the evidence offered is reliable enough to be admitted. The most prominent feature among these rules applies to hearsay evidence,[134] a subject of particular importance to the introduction of statistical evidence.

The hearsay rule was formulated to eliminate statements of fact made by a person who is not present at the trial.[135] At one time, almost all hearsay evidence was excluded because it did not give either the jury or the judge an opportunity to gauge the reliability of the personal source of the information. The party who was hurt by the hearsay rule was not afforded an opportunity to test the reliability of the personal source of the evidence by cross-examination.[136] The judge and the jury had no opportunity to evaluate the sincerity, perception, memory, or narrative ability of the original teller-of-the-tale.

Frequently, witnesses testify through the depositions that are taken outside of the courtroom. Under this procedure, a witness under oath is asked questions before an impartial reporter, and the opposition has an opportunity to cross-examine him at the time. The full deposition is then submitted in evidence. This procedure gives neither a judge nor a jury an opportunity to form its own impressions of the personality of the witness. But the opposition can employ its cross-examination to test the witness and his statements while the deposition is being taken.

Over the years, many exceptions[137] to the hearsay rule developed.[138] Some exceptions covered stategic information which could be obtained only through testimony about what a witness heard from others. For example, in considering whether a will should be admitted to probate, the court must have no question about the soundness of a testator's mind when he signed the document. By definition, the testator is not available to testify in this proceeding. Therefore, the only way to obtain the necessary evidence on this point is through the testimony of witnesses who had observed the testator at or about the time when he signed the will. Such testimony frequently requires the repetition of statements made by the testator.

A related development has been the acceptance of testimony regarding somebody's opinion,[139] rather than as a statement of fact.[140] An extreme illustration will demonstrate the difference. Testimony that Mr. Jones said that he is Napoleon would be admitted as evidence of the state of his mind. However, the statement could not be introduced to prove that Mr. Jones is Napoleon. Mr. Jones himself would have to testify to that.

With these developments, the hearsay rule calls for two sets of questions. One: Is the testimony offered hearsay? Two: If it is hearsay, should it be admitted under one of the exceptions?

The exceptions[141] to the hearsay rule have gained increased importance with modern industrial development. The proprietor of a one-man shop could be expected to give direct testimony about his transactions. The customers of a handicraft shop were known and could offer direct testimony about their transactions, the quality of the goods, and their satisfaction with the products. However, the sheer numbers of suppliers, customers, and sales-clerks in a modern department store require a division of labor; entries are made on books showing customers' and suppliers' accounts by clerks who never see the individuals and companies; credits are allowed and collections are made by others; complaints are handled in separate departments, as are receipts and deliveries of merchandise.

Therefore, the only practical evidence regarding the experience of a substantial institution—rather than an individual—must come from people whose testimony is based on books of account. Similarly, it is no longer possible to hear the direct testimony of a large number of customers, actual and potential, when the court is trying a case about misleading use of a trade-mark. To keep testimony within manageable limits, in many cases the opinions of customers must be polled and summed up for the court.

Economic evidence may be admitted[142] if the information is produced through direct testimony of a witness, based on his own knowledge, if the testimony is about someone's state of mind,[143] or if it is hearsay evidence, which may be tested for reliability, and there is no other way of providing the information.[144] For example, a survey of consumers' impressions about which company manufactured a specific item could be admitted under the rule that covers opinion evidence.[145] Similarly, evidence from books of account, which are kept in the regular course of business, with no reference to the problems involved in the litigation, could be admitted on the ground that the evidence is reliable, was not rigged to prove a point, and is the sole source of needed information. Again, reports of the Bureau of Census and other governmental agencies could be admitted even though the information is not presented directly by the companies covered in the tabulation. Thus, census data on industry shipments could be admitted without testimony from each of the companies in the industry. However, such admission is not automatic.

The basic questions, then, regarding quantitative evidence boil down to such issues as: Should the information be admitted into evidence so that it can be considered by the courts?[146] How can the information be tested for its reliability? When conflicting statistical evidence is produced by each side, how can the courts determine which is more reliable?[147] How much weight should be given to the statistical evidence when it runs counter to other types of information? Finally, what aid can be given to the courts to provide data that would be helpful, to determine the reliability and significance of statistical evidence, and to utilize the data properly within the purview of a broader economic analysis?

*Evidence in Administrative Agencies*

The rules of admissibility of evidence—especially the hearsay rule—have been less significant in the proceedings of the Federal Trade Commission and other agencies[148] than they have been in the courts.[149] Evidentiary rules of regulatory agencies have not been influenced by the problems of trial by jury for several reasons. To begin with, since the administrative agencies came into being long after the development of the common law, they could make a fresh start. Second, since administrative agencies do not use lay juries, their traditions were more influenced by the rules of equity courts which were more flexible. Third, the agencies were set up, in part, to avoid this dependence on narrow rules of evidence. In theory, the agencies have more technical capacity to analyze data than individual judges because of the special *expertise* of their staffs.[150] Further, since they have investigatory powers, they do not have to rely on witnesses to the same extent as the courts.[151]

A fourth reason for the greater liberality of the agencies' rules has been the nature of their activity. Administrative agencies focus on prospective activity rather than on penalties for past actions. As the court said in the *Cement Institute* case, "rules which bar certain types of evidence in criminal or quasi-criminal cases are not controlling in proceedings . . . where the effect of the Commission's order is not to punish or fasten liability on respondents for past conduct, but to ban specific practices for the future in accordance with the general mandate of Congress."[152]

These differences have made it easier for the administrative agencies to handle economic problems than for the courts. It is interesting to note that because of these differences some judges feel that: "To preserve their own jurisdiction against the inroads of the agencies, the courts must in this type of antitrust controversy relax the rigidity of the hearsay rule."[153] Further, "So far as this court is aware, the Supreme Court has never reversed or criticized a trial court for admitting hearsay evidence in a civil antitrust case tried without a jury."[154]

The differences between the evidentiary rules of agencies and the courts pose a substantial issue of public policy. Since the Federal Trade Commission and the courts exercise many of the same functions but follow different evidentiary rules, the application of statistical data will depend in good part on the way in which a case arises. If the proceeding takes place before the F.T.C., quantitative evidence may be admitted freely. But the same evidence might be excluded from consideration were the same case tried in a court. Yet, there is no difference between the substantive antitrust law applied by the Commission and that applied by the court.

The distinction between the evidentiary rules of the courts and the F.T.C. is one of degree. It is true that the administrative agencies are not bound by the same technical evidentiary rules as the courts.[155] Nevertheless, the agencies frequently have great difficulty in determining how to utilize quantitative evidence. Many of the pleas for improving methods for handling such data have emanated from the F.T.C. as well as from the judiciary.[156]

## *Lawyers' Resistance to Statistical Analysis*

Despite the heritage of the rules of evidence, there has been substantial progress in the use of tabulations, surveys, and statistical samples.[157] In food and drug cases, for example, the practice of sampling "has generally been sanctioned by the courts, so that it is not necessary for the inspector to check every can or package or even every case."[158] In antitrust, progress is made in practice and in the attitudes of the bar, as reflected in the reports of the Judicial Conference and committees of the American Bar Association,[159] which favored the use of tabulations, surveys, and statistical samples.

Yet, there remains a core of resistance to the use of surveys and of statistical samples. Because of their customary reliance on direct personal testimony, many lawyers and judges turn the proverbial jaundiced eye on impersonal survey material. Many "common-law" lawyers are uneasy because of their difficulties in controlling the use and interpretation of the unfamiliar statistical forms. Judges have been uncomfortable in dealing with conflicting statistical reports since they have no solid basis for evaluation.[160] Frequently, the use of such data has been bothersome because of the legal maneuvering about the issues of admissibility. Some uncertainty has been engendered by the difficulties that lawyers encounter in examining and understanding the data supporting tabulations that are presented by their opponents. Such a shortcoming presents a serious problem because it eliminates the intelligent criticism of the opposition—a factor that weighs heavily in the judicial process. Finally, there is an inherent suspicion of sample surveys because of possible subtle biases that are not fully grasped by either the opposition or the judge.

The legal traditions that underlie the hearsay rule play an important role in judicial attitudes toward statistical samples. Judges seem confident of their own *expertise* in evaluating personal testimony.[161] It is true that when statistical material is presented, impressions can be formed of the reliability of the economist or statistician who presents the data. However, there is no chance to judge the reliability of the people who have been covered by the survey or of the field interviewers. Further, the witness's testimony may be unconvincing because of difficulty in following his technical discussion.

Some students of the problem feel that surveys can produce more reliable information than personal testimony in court, despite the attitudes of many lawyers.[162] They are impressed with the difficulty of obtaining a fair picture of consumer reaction in a court room.[163] They argue that when consumer witnesses are subjected to the strain of a trial, they are ill at ease and will try to give testimony that will satisfy the questioner. In contrast, the same consumers can give more truthful information to a poll-taker because they are not under tension and do not know that the poll will be used in litigation.[164]

Judicial difficulties in using tabulations are compounded by trial debates concerning technical problems of tabulation and sampling. The niceties of the differences of opinion among the experts have confounded some courts in their evaluations of survey results.[165] There are indications that the economists and statisticians who testify are persuaded by the heat of the trial, and the drives of the rival lawyers, to bend their testimony to support the positions of their clients instead of furnishing the courts with objective, informed testimony. Thus, Professor Kennedy has been impressed by differences between the attitudes of these experts when they are in and out of court.

"Disagreement among experts in court over acceptable methodologies, however, may be expected to induce judicial caution in accepting the results of polls conducted according to any sampling plan. Contrary to the impression that one may get from such conflict of opinion as that described, engendered by the necessities of litigation, it appears, nevertheless, that authorities in their out-of-court discussions of sampling problems are not seriously at odds over methodology."[166]

The use of statistical evidence in legal proceedings entails another procedural problem—how to subject the data to fair tests through cross-examination and countervailing evidence.[167] As has been suggested, a key factor in adversary proceedings is the opportunity afforded to the opposition to test, challenge, and counter any evidence considered by the court. To carry out these gambits, the adversary must have ample opportunity to examine the raw data from which a tabulation is compiled. If the underlying information was obtained in confidence, however, the exposure of such material to the opposition raises many troublesome problems.

The problem of how to treat confidential information usually arises when a government agency presents tabulations that are based on confidential surveys which were made for the specific case.[168] For example, if the Federal Trade Commission uses its investigatory power to obtain market information from a number of competitors, the replies are confidential, and they may not be disclosed in a public hearing. Hence, the use of such tabulations presents a dilemma either to the hearing examiner or to the judge.

The dilemma is not easy to resolve. On the one hand, the defendant company might use the confidential information for its competitive advantage, or it might harm a small competitor or a customer for giving an unfavorable reply. On the other hand, it cannot challenge the government's survey and tabulation without examining the returns. Nor can it bring in contradictory evidence or interpretation.

One solution that has been applied is to permit the defendant's counsel to examine the returns in confidence. He may use his observations to test the tabulation—a method which has been applied successfully. But he may not divulge individual returns to his client.[169]

This problem involves issues of equity and fairness. The government has investigatory powers for obtaining information from anyone connected with a market—sellers, customers, and suppliers. The private defendant or respondent does not have such extensive powers. In a judicial proceeding he can exercise subpoena powers. However, this is not a practicable method for obtaining information at reasonable cost,[170] and it is not freely available in a proceeding before an administrative agency.[171] Hence, the government agency does have a stronger position than the private defendant or the private plaintiff.[172]

Recently, an effort was made to limit the government's powers. One circuit court of appeals held that the F.T.C. cannot require a company to produce a duplicate of its report to the Bureau of the Census because such reports are confidential.[173] However, another court upheld a similar Commission subpoena.[174] This difference was resolved by the Supreme Court on December 11, 1961 when it decided that the Commission does have the power to require a copy of a company's census report.[175]

Many courts have exhibited notable suspicion of statistical polls. Apparently, this suspicion is not without foundation. Support for it may be found among some of the students of the problem. For example, Fred M. Kecker, after reviewing the leading cases in which courts have discussed samples, concludes that, "There has been a tendency of professional poll-takers to devise polls so as to ensure the attainment of desired results."[176] Probably because of the lack of recognized standards for such polls, no effort has been made to censure either the poll-takers or the lawyers who arrange for misleading surveys. Indeed, the organized bar has paid little attention to this problem.

Because of this uncertainty many judges tend to accept surveys if their results conform with their own preconceptions.[177] From his study of the use of survey research findings as legal evidence, Hiram C. Barksdale concluded that "Generally, in deciding such cases [trademark, false and misleading advertising, unfair competition, adulterated and misbranded foods, drugs, and cosmetics, and design infringement], the courts attempt to place themselves in the position of the ordinary purchaser and to weight the probability of deception and the likelihood of confusion. Under this procedure, personal notions of how ordinary buyers will react become the basis for judgment."[178]

In some cases, judges have reflected considerable confusion about what to do with survey data. For example, Judge Nordbye in *U.S.* v. *J. I. Case*[179] seemed at a loss in deciding what to do with an Iowa State College survey of the accessibility of farm machinery in Iowa. Possibly to justify his position, he went so far as to say, "It may be stated that the [government's] chief objection to the exhibit was that courts usually do not indulge in, or entertain, economic investigations in determining the pertinent issues in antitrust litigation. That is true."

The picture is not clear even when statistical samples have been admitted into evidence. "The review of cases also indicates," said Barksdale, "that survey evidence has played a relatively insignificant role in most cases where it has been admitted."[180]

It is interesting to note that judicial concern about sampling developed after statistical methods were introduced. Even today a judge who has reservations about statistical samples will accept samples without question if the "survey" procedure takes place in the courtroom and if it is not so labeled.

Courts and administrative agencies have always employed samples without awareness of their pitfalls and limitations. In *Gorham Co.* v. *White*,[181] testimony from several men in the trade was accepted as satisfactory evidence regarding the infringement of a design patent. *Jacob Siegel Co.* v. *F.T.C.*[182] involved a Federal Trade Commission order to discontinue use of the word "alpacuna" on a label for garments, based on a finding that it led consumers to believe that the cloth contained vicuna and wool. Testimony about consumer belief had been accepted from a small number of housewives and store personnel. The court felt that the F.T.C. had substantial evidence for the order.[183]

*Lifesavers Corp.* v. *Curtiss Candy Co.*[184] involved the confusion of products. After hearing seventy witnesses, the judge refused to listen to any more. No consideration was given to the fairness and adequacy of the sample. Similarly, in a Coca-Cola case,[185] which turned on misleading similarities in names, the court accepted the limited work of two investigators who testified.[186]

A few judges have relied on their own samples with confidence in the competence of their survey. Judge Jerome Frank relied on his own sample in two significant cases giving neither adversary any opportunity to test his survey and, possibly, stretching the limits of a judge's function. In his opinion in *La Touraine Coffee Co., Inc.* v. *Lorraine Coffee Co., Inc.*,[187] he said, "I have asked a dozen American men and women, selected at random, what Touraine means; their invariable reply was 'a part of France'."[188] Professor Kennedy reported, "I have tried the same question on members of several of my classes in Trade Regulation, and have not yet obtained the reply Judge Frank invariably received."[189]

Again, Judge Frank made his own survey when considering the issues in *Triangle Publications, Inc.* v. *Rohrlich et al.*,[190] a trade-mark infringement case in which the court held for "Seventeen" magazine in a suit regarding the use of "Seventeen" as a brand for girdles. In his dissenting opinion he wrote, "I have questioned some adolescent girls and their mothers and sisters, persons I have chosen. I have been told uniformly by my questionees that no one could reasonably believe that any relation existed between the plaintiff's magazine and the defendant's girdles."[191]

## *Judicial Needs*

The use of statistical evidence in court is a key factor affecting the effective judicial consideration of economic issues.[192] Since they are not experienced in evaluating such evidence and lack technical advice in the field, judges have been at a loss in dealing with such quantitative material. Administrative agencies have a similar problem.[193]

To employ statistical evidence effectively, practicable methods should be developed for aiding judges,[194] hearing examiners, and commissioners in evaluation and interpretation. This need is of special import when conflicting reports and interpretations[195] are offered by the litigants. Even when one survey is presented, there are many opportunities for employing technical arguments about the accuracy and significance of the statistical data.[196]

The task of improving the application of statistical material in the trial of economic issues starts with the pleadings and the pre-trial conferences. It calls for clear definitions of the issues of the case and of the specific application of the evidence to these issues. The best statistical study has no place in a trial unless it can be tied to the issues in understandable terms.

Effective use of statistical evidence will require more efficient treatment of the technical problems of evidence in judicial and administrative proceedings.[197] Long drawn out maneuvers surrounding the introduction of evidence can assume such importance that the point of the data may be blurred. This condition affects not only special surveys but published material as well.

Much progress has been made to develop satisfactory procedures[198] —but not enough. Many judges make effective use of pre-trial conferences, especially in "Big Cases," in order to define the issues and to settle as many evidentiary problems as possible before the trial proper begins. Through such informal discussions a judge may force both parties into agreement regarding: the nature and order of evidence; what opportunities will be given before the trial to examine the material supporting statistical tabulations so that criticism and counterevidence may be prepared; and, on occasion, sample tests or field surveys which will be undertaken for the trial.[199] These procedures require affirmative participation by the judge in defining the issues and the application of statistical material.[200] Indeed, technical advice could be most useful to the judge and the parties during the course of these pre-trial proceedings.

Another factor influencing the application of statistical evidence is the development of methods of presentation that will affirmatively assist the court. Such progress seems to require considerable attention to the improved use of visual aids, charts, and tabulations.[201] Improvement requires cooperation among the lawyers and the economists and statisticians.

Above all, future progress will depend in large part on the imaginative application of statistics by the lawyers. For example, the combination of survey results and live witnesses may help many judges to overcome their hesitation in using statistical data.[202] The results of a tabulation of consumer attitudes can be made more meaningful, as well as more persuasive, when several "typical" consumers testify before the judge and the litigating lawyers.[203] The story told by the data can "come alive."

Similarly, lawyers can utilize a survey to excellent advantage even without presenting it in evidence. Such a survey may serve to upset the force of the opposition because it can arm a lawyer with a clear picture of an underlying situation. Consider a highly simplified example: careful analysis of a dealer survey may indicate that inexperienced retailers usually sell only one brand of a specific product while better established dealers carry several brands; further, that about four fifths of the dealers fit into the latter category, having been in business for five years or more. Then, if the opposition witnesses testify that they sell only one brand, cross-examination may well establish the fact that they are not typical of the great bulk of the retailers. It may not be necessary to introduce the survey into evidence at all.

It has been suggested, on several occasions, that the judges' burdens in handling statistical evidence could be eased by setting up an impartial body to review surveys and other data and to report directly to the courts.[204] This suggestion parallels the proposal for the employment of special masters-in-chancery composed of experts or panels of experts to advise the courts. A related proposal has been that the judge select an expert who will review the data and testify on it in open court.[205] Such a procedure would parallel some experiments in the treatment of medical problems and suggestions regarding the use of experts in patent litigation.

It has also been proposed that standards[206] be set up for adequate samples so that the courts can apply recognized yardsticks to test the reliability of surveys presented to them. However, little progress has been made in formulating standards that can be employed by the courts without technical advice.[207]

Indeed, it is difficult to see how it would be possible to establish basic standards for sampling that would take into consideration the relationships between the issues of the case, the standards of accuracy required in the sample, the types of other information which may be available, and the practical problems faced in the specific field survey. Further, as has been pointed out, many issues which are couched as sampling problems relate to the survey method rather than the sample. Hence, it would seem that the problems of sampling and surveys are far too complex to be encompassed by any simple, nontechnical set of standards. Yet, with technical advice a judge could gauge the accuracy and meaning of a survey, especially if he hammers the problem out in pre-trial proceedings, which permit him to be more active in informal give-and-take discussion.

Some judges have felt that courts should be equipped to conduct field surveys on their own. For example, in *Repouille*,[208] Judge Learned Hand was sorry that the courts have no Gallup Poll to aid them in discovering the general public feeling regarding the meaning of "good moral character" which is required of applicants for naturalization. Similarly, in *RCA* v. *Decca Record, Inc.*[209] Judge Woolsey "suggested the possibility of deputizing a peripatetic commissioner or examiner who would conduct surveys as an agent of the court."

Judge Frank in *Triangle Publications, Inc.*[210] felt that: "We should have a staff of investigators like those supplied to administrative agencies."

The report of the Judicial Conference on "Procedure in Antitrust and Other Protracted Cases," suggested the submission of technical facts of unusual complexity to experts and special masters. This expert or panel would hold hearings, receive evidence and permit cross-examination. Then the written report would be submitted to the court.[211]

Judge Prettyman, then Chief Judge of the Circuit Court of Appeals for the District of Columbia, referred to an interesting suggestion[212] during a discussion of the judge's problem when experts and other witnesses present conflicting views. He urged that a judge should be enabled to summon disinterested authorities for advice whenever a scientific fact is a major factor in a proceeding, and he is dissatisfied with the testimony. The advice of these authorities would be presented on the witness stand, subject to cross-examination.

The successful application of statistical methods is a major factor affecting the practical application of economic analysis in the trial of competitive issues. Until the treatment of statistical evidence is improved, there will continue to exist sharp limitations on the effective use of economic analysis.

Further improvements will depend on several groups.[213] Lawyers and prosecuting agencies must find practical means for handling the data. Economists, statisticians, and mathematicians have to increase their efforts to develop statistical tools of analysis which fit the requirements of the judicial system. Judges will require substantial aids in the trial of such issues. All will have to cooperate in devising practical means for judicial assistance.

One feature of such development stands out clearly. Ultimate progress will not be made by bringing statistical technicians, whether as masters, witnesses or advisers, into the proceeding only during the trial proper. The task starts with the basic inception of the case. The complaint, the answers, the subsequent pleadings and conferences must define the issues—the legal, the economic, and the statistical issues. If the economist and the statistician are to make satisfactory contributions, they must participate in all phases of pre-trial planning as well as the trial itself.

# 10 / *Summary and Recommendations*[*]

CONSIDERATION OF POLICIES regarding competition reflects many of the dilemmas of society today. Policies are influenced by a variety of ultimate public goals, some consistent and some contradictory. Regulatory activity is directed at all the points of the compass—favoring militant competition; raising the plane of competition; blunting some edges of competition; driving toward monopoly; and regulating monopolies. The state of competition is affected also by such other government activities as purchasing, research, subsidies, and other forms of industry promotion, and taxes. Some tend to enliven competition; some have anticompetitive effects.

## *Public Goals and Policies*

The situation is complicated by the maze of uncoordinated policies which are followed by the several levels of government. Market competition is influenced by the countless regulations of the federal government, those of the fifty states, and of thousands of local governments. There is little semblance of order or agreement in the myriad rules and regulations that affect market competition.

This potpourri of regulations reflects our general ambivalence regarding the functions of government. In theory, Americans prefer as little government as possible. Tradition favors an economy which is regulated by market competition, with government hovering overhead to protect health and safety and to umpire disputes. Yet, in recent years the nation has looked to government to solve a multitude of economic and social problems, including full employment, growth, and monetary stability.

[*] Footnotes for Chapter 10 begin on page 467.

This ambivalence might well be an intellectual heritage. The Founding Fathers felt it desirable to minimize the role of public authority. They visualized the functions of government as those of a neutral policeman. However, this philosophy reflected attitudes toward the new federal government and did not encompass all public activity. State and local governments apparently continued to carry out many types of industry regulation and even of participation in industrial ventures.

The dilemmas of competition may be only a reflection of a basic problem of mid-century society: the conflict between the desire for personal security and the incentive system. Modern man wants both. Personal security means comfort and freedom from strain. On the other hand, the incentive system applies the stick to the lazy and ineffective ones as well as awarding the carrot to the energetic and the efficient. Unfettered competition can be ruthless in its treatment of employer and employee. Where then is the proper balance—to temper competition without destroying it?

The broad range of political, social, and economic goals complicates all efforts to draw up simple, consistent policies regarding competition. There is deep respect for efficiency, which is induced by the spur of competition. Yet, there is also profound concern about the political power giant successful enterprises can wield. There exists a strong tradition for public reliance on free competition instead of government regulation or private controls. Yet, there is substantial public support for barriers to foreign competition, such private controls as resale price maintenance, which might protect some small retailers, and limitations on the entry of new entrepreneurs in many industries and trades.

The policy confusion is reflected in a variety of government activities. Most antitrust laws are dedicated to competition; some are not. Despite a strong policy favoring competition within the United States, substantial import barriers have been maintained, and domestic manufacturers have been permitted to organize associations in order to avoid competition in their foreign activities. The substantial program of government purchases and research contracts favors large, well-entrenched companies despite some insubstantial small business programs. Little progress has been made in determining how the public interest should be reflected in national policies regarding the unions and agricultural programs. Some tax laws favor corporate mergers and disfavor corporate split-ups. Many controls over the regulated industries seem dedicated to the exclusion of market rivalry.

State governments undertake sporadic antitrust efforts. Nevertheless, the bulk of state and local regulation seems to favor limits to intrastate competition and barriers to interstate commerce. The total national influences of these activities have largely been ignored.

In substance, we combine a general tradition in favor of a free market economy with an amazing array of exceptions. We tend to satisfy our beliefs in competition by concentrating on a traditional antitrust policy. However, little attention is devoted to the wide range of government activities—federal, state, and local—which insulate many groups from the rigors of market rivalry. It is abundantly clear that public policy is not dedicated to *laissez faire* in its extreme form. However, society seems to be drifting into a confused river of conflicting cross currents without broad understanding or purpose. There is a clear need today for developing a balance of the nation's ultimate goals in order to set a clearer course for public policy regarding the workings of the market economy.

## *Antitrust Administration*

Antitrust administration reflects the disorganized state of public policies. Functions are divided among so many agencies that no one bears the ultimate responsibility for their over-all coordination. The functions of the two principal agencies—the Federal Trade Commission and the Antitrust Division of the Department of Justice—overlap. Some antitrust rules are enforced by both agencies. There is no clear division of responsibilities. On occasion, both agencies have prosecuted the same companies for the same practices. Despite public claims to the contrary, the activities of the two are not affirmatively coordinated. The Antitrust Division has not employed the investigative powers of the F.T.C. until recently. The Commission has not asked the Antitrust Division to use its authority to sue for injunctions when they seem necessary.

Neither agency is charged with the continuing review of competitive conditions. Neither has the authority to operate outside the frame of reference of the antitrust laws. Nor have they customarily been called on for policy recommendations regarding other government activities.[1]

There never has been a concerted effort to review the administrative framework. Even when an attempted improvement was made through the passage of the Federal Trade Commission Act in 1914, the words about the functions of the F.T.C. were not accompanied by commensurate action. The Commission was established in 1914 in order to bring *expertise* to bear on the treatment of competitive problems because many felt that the courts were not sufficiently skilled. Yet, the powers of the Commission were limited to issuing orders to cease and desist from engaging in specific practices. It has not been accorded authority to change a market structure. Nor does it have affirmative power to compel companies to follow specified practices, except for divestiture orders under the antimerger statute. Such positive authority was still confined to equity decrees, which were formulated by the "unskilled" judges. Hence, the new administrative *expertise* was hobbled before it started.

As a matter of fact, the Antitrust Division exercises more affirmative regulatory powers than the F.T.C. Since most antitrust decrees are negotiated before the Antitrust Division files a complaint with a court, it actively operates as a regulatory agency. Its consent decrees can be as broad as any equity court can write, with much more latitude than a cease and desist order. A number of these decrees provide for direct regulation of prices and royalties.

Much of the work of the F.T.C. lies outside the antimonopoly area. It prosecutes more companies for misleading advertising than for other anticompetitive activities. Its original assignment has been broadened to cover the policing of consumer information in textiles and furs, as well as foods, drugs, and cosmetics.

About twenty other federal agencies participate in antitrust administration. Some are entrusted with the enforcement of antitrust laws in specific markets. Some have authority to grant antitrust exemptions. Most of these agencies exhibit no zeal for antitrust policies. Many suffer from the conflicting duality of their tasks—to promote their industries and to protect the public interest. On occasion, they have granted exemptions to practices that had been under antitrust attack by the Department of Justice. Some have construed their primary functions to call for checkreining competition and for maintaining high prices, rather than encouraging market rivalry when it is feasible.

## *Attention to the Remedies*

Remarkably little attention has been devoted to the development of effective methods for injecting competition into markets. By and large, the agencies and the courts have been preoccupied with the question whether the laws were violated. Despite seventy years of experience, there are no practical guides for formulating effective decrees. We experiment with various kinds of orders, but do not observe their effects. We have no policy-administrative mechanism for coordinating antitrust decrees with other means of stimulating competition, such as reducing tariffs or using government purchases to induce substantial companies to enter a market.[2]

There has been almost no attention devoted to the differences between a finding that a market is dominated by monopolistic forces and the formulation of an order which will make it competitive. Decrees are directed mainly to eliminating the manifestations of anticompetitive forces rather than to curing the underlying market situations that permit them. If a price discrimination really reflects monopolistic power, merely prohibiting the discrimination hardly touches the competitive problem. If a requirements contract implements market domination, the cancellation of the contract may have no practical effect on competition; in fact, the exclusion of competitors may continue without benefit of contract. When patents are controlled by an antitrust violator, compulsory licensing may have little or no significance: witness the large proportion of instances when such licensing was required by a decree, but no licenses were given, and there were no inquiries from potential licensees.

No one is charged with maintaining a continuing examination of competitive conditions in strategic industries. There is no organization to study the efficacy of antitrust in revitalizing competition in markets that require attention, or to analyze the effects of competition on the social performance of any markets. Practically no consideration is given to the possible advantages of legislative programs which are tailored for specific markets, programs which would coordinate antitrust with such other activities as government purchasing and research, tariffs, and even patents and taxes. Nor is there any mechanism for reporting to Congress, when antitrust remedies cannot effectively inject competition into a market, with suggestions regarding legislative action to reorganize the structure of the pertinent industry. (It will be recalled that such a step was taken in the Public Utility Act of 1935, which was drafted after a study of the public utility companies, in order to revise the industry according to a carefully developed plan.)

In effect, there exists no mechanism for a continuing policy review of the effects of antitrust programs and related government activities. Judicial review does not provide such a function. A judge can consider only the case at hand, a proceeding which usually concerns one company. Further, even judicial review is not available for much antitrust activity, most of which is carried on through the negotiation of consent decrees.

Because of the lack of substantive review, the agencies are encouraged to strive for many proceedings and a large proportion of victories. There is little concern about the broad influences of their efforts on the economy—or the lack thereof. A proceeding against a food broker who gave part of his commission to a customer is given the same attention as a case against a corporate merger which may have long-run influences on a market structure. Prosecutions of small companies in unimportant markets, combined with a substantial flow of consent orders and decrees, build up records of great activity. The incentive to play a "numbers game" is stimulated by Congress, which considers numbers but which has, with few exceptions, paid little attention to effects in its considerations of agency budgets. The devoted public servants in the agencies cannot be expected to resist these spurious yardsticks because the numbers provide important supports for budget requests.

## *Improvements in the Litigation Process*

Much of the enforcement and policy development of the laws of competition depend on litigation. Many prosecutions and private suits are carried on in the courts. The administrative agencies tend to follow the litigation procedures. Negotiated decrees and orders are influenced by what the parties would expect from a contested proceeding.

Yet, the process of litigation was not designed to cope with the types of problems that are encompassed by antitrust enforcement. Judicial procedures were developed when courts were concerned with fairly simple problems that could be investigated through the direct evidence of witnesses who could be seen and heard. They were clearly not constructed for the trial of complex economic issues.

There are, nevertheless, many aspects of litigation which comport with our sense of justice, and which can be adapted to the improved treatment of economic problems. The judicial impartiality, the open proceeding, and the rights of appeal are so strongly entrenched in our framework of government that any effort to change them would be unsuccessful. Many litigation procedures can be adapted to effective trial of antitrust problems: clarifying the issues; making information available to both sides; and offering reasonable opportunities to present evidence and argument in support of one's position and in opposition to the other side. Further, the technique of testing hypotheses, which is employed in the treatment of circumstantial evidence, is common to both legal and economic analysis.

In order to increase the effectiveness of litigation in the trial of antitrust issues, a number of procedures would have to be modified. New methods would have to be devised to handle economic issues of substantial complexity. Means would have to be developed to alleviate the heavy tasks that are assigned to the judges in the prosecution of a Big Case.

The weight of the essential judicial burden has not been appreciated. A single judge has more power, and related responsibility, in antitrust than in any other field. He can formulate orders which guide the basic structures and practices of important firms. He can split a company up into several parts. He can divest it of important patent rights and profoundly alter its ways of doing business.

This judicial authority is severely tempered by uncertainty. Without practical assistance, it is hard to see how a single judge can develop strong enough convictions to exercise this power except in highly unusual situations. Obviously, we do not want to swing to the other extreme—to encourage exercise of power lightly. If we are seriously resolved to nurture competition, however, means must be found to strengthen the use of judicial discretion. For without such support judges will continue their preoccupation with the finding of a violation rather than devoting attention to the formulation of effective remedies. Lacking a background in economic analysis—especially in such technical areas as statistics and sampling—many jurists have demonstrated remarkable skill in handling economic issues. However, they require substantial aids for these tremendously difficult analytical tasks.

Because of a deficiency in economic analysis, the use of judicial precedent in antitrust has not been as competent as in other fields. For example, the judicial criteria for defining the relevant market within which competition operates has been quite unclear. Understandable precedents for the determination of the relevant market and the interpretation of indicators of competition require economic analysis. Basically, the use of precedent calls for comparing the factual situations under review with those covered by previous decisions in order to determine which are analogous. Hence, the application of precedent in determining what is a relevant market requires comparisons with previous cases to decide what principles apply. This analysis by analogy is an exercise in economics. Lacking technical understanding, judges cannot be expected to develop a high degree of consistency. Further, their opinions cannot produce adequate guides for either the government or industry. Even if economic analysis could demonstrate that the courts are consistent, clear judicial explanations of the decisions are necessary to promote business certainty and voluntary compliance with antitrust regulation.

## *Economic Analysis in Policy Formulation*

The contributions of economic analysis to the formulation and administration of national policies bearing on competition are affected by the inconsistent variety of public goals. Because of the conflicts among our goals we cannot adopt a policy favoring untrammeled competition. At the same time, economic inquiry must be employed as one of the analytical aids, probably the most important one, for the development of policies that maintain appropriate balances among these public aims.

Effective policy development requires clear definitions of the available alternatives as well as reasonable predictions of the consequences of such alternatives. In this consideration economic inquiry has great potential value. It can help to formulate issues, to determine what data are pertinent, to collect and interpret the evidence, and to develop and test hypotheses regarding the policy alternatives and their consequences.

Against these needs, how effective is the contribution of economics in this area of policy development? Has the economics profession paid sufficient attention to these problems? Has it reached out for cooperation with other professions, or has it been content to converse within its own ranks? Has it depended so much on a closed-system theory and its peculiar jargon that it has failed to communicate with the policy makers? Has it produced enough hard-headed empirical work to make an impression?

Or, does the difficulty lie in the other direction: Have others, especially the legal profession, managed to keep the economists at arms-length? Have policy makers and administrators given sufficient attention to economic inquiry to encourage able economists to labor in the field of competitive issues? Have they expected too many unconditional analyses and forecasts from the economists?

Relatively few economists seem to be concerned about issues of industrial regulation today. Many, who are interested, have been occupied with extending theoretical treatments that have not been related to observation. Much of the discussion has been enveloped in a technical jargon, which sounds strange in the ears of the policy makers.

On the other hand, much of the public consideration of these problems has been on a basis that is too narrow for profitable economic analysis of policy. Lawyers have been occupied with procedural problems of antitrust, such as investigative powers and preliminary injunctions. With some exceptions, legislators have been concerned with the same procedural aspects. Economists have not been called on extensively for advice concerning the effects of antitrust and of other governmental activities, or regarding the broader questions about the state of competition and the uses of the various government capacities to curb monopoly powers.

In general, there has not been an affirmative interest in investigating the workings and effects of competition. Although market rivalry takes many forms—such as price, quality, packaging, service, and warranties—economists have been preoccupied with price competition. Little attention has been given to the importance of field studies of the effects of price and other forms of competition on costs, efficiency, price stability, or production and employment. Assumptions, which appear logical, have been made about the effects of competition. However, there have been few investigations of these influences.

Because of the absence of affirmative proof of the favorable consequences of competition, policy makers have not developed strong convictions about the issues and remain satisfied with general statements favoring a free market. Such lack of conviction makes it easier to adopt policies that appear to improve the condition of such groups as automobile and tire dealers, textile and garment manufacturers, food brokers, wheat farmers, textile workers, and petroleum producers, to mention a few, without considering the effects of such steps on the general state of competition.

## *Economic Analysis in Administration*

Economic analysis has not been widely used either by the administrative agencies or by the courts. To begin with, market studies have not been generally employed to decide which sectors of the economy need antitrust attention. Decisions to prosecute have been based largely on complaints received from the general public and from competitors.

Economic inquiry has not been employed effectively by prosecutors or defendants during antitrust proceedings. Economists have rarely participated in defining the issues of the case, in setting the strategy of presentation, or in developing the arguments. Nor have they participated regularly in the negotiation of consent decrees and orders.

The principal use of economic analysis in prosecution and negotiation has concerned the proof of a violation. It has been largely neglected in formulating decrees and orders. Therefore, what is probably the most productive use of economic study—the capacity to forecast the effects of alternative orders—has been missing.

Neither the agencies nor the courts have been given sufficient help in economic analysis. Judges have been required to consider long, involved records without satisfactory assistance in reviewing statistical and other economic evidence. By and large, neither the plaintiffs nor the defendants have excelled in supplying the judges with the evidence and arguments which are prerequisite to an understanding of the economic issues. A number of judges have expressed the need for clearer presentations of economic issues and evidence. While sporadic advances have been made, there is little evidence that satisfactory progress will develop in the future.

## *Cooperation Between Lawyers and Economists*

Part of the difficulty of applying economic analysis in antitrust enforcement is the lack of understanding between lawyers and economists.[3] Because antitrust is a regulatory activity, effective tools of economic analysis must fit the frame of reference of legal procedures. On the other hand, the full advantages of economic inquiry cannot be obtained through expert witnesses and data processors; it requires the participation of economists in the selection of cases, definitions of issues, and preparation of evidence and arguments, as well as in the consent procedures.

Considerable progress toward the mutual understanding of the two professions has been made in recent decades. However, further advance will depend on a clear appreciation of the differences between the disciplines.

Each profession looks for a higher degree of certainty than the other can offer. Economists would like legal decisions to be more consistent and would like the legal rules spelled out in black-letter terms. Lawyers would like economists to furnish them with precise rules about such problems as how to define a market, what is a satisfactory statistical survey, and how to measure degree of competitiveness. But neither desire can be satisfied completely.

There are basic differences in the nature of the two disciplines. Lawyers operate within a well-organized framework. Their problems are limited by definable issues within the structure of law. Terms are defined by statute and by judicial decisions. There is a recognized means for settling differences of opinion. The decision of the highest court is the correct one. Since legal predictions refer to what the court will do, their worth is subject to specific test.

In contrast, economists have no orderly framework for terminology or decision. There is no recognized group to set definitions, to determine correctness of positions, or to test predictions. Even when other economists agree with a prediction, there is no final test. The ultimate proof might be what happens in the market. However, even this is not reliable. There is always the possibility that some unconsidered factors had such influence that the accuracy of a prediction could result from coincidence.

Economists and lawyers have difficulty in understanding each other's language and values. Lawyers have no problem in using words in specific, technical senses. They can deal with a word or phrase as it is defined in a statute or prior case. Economists, in contrast, attempt to use terms on a consistent basis throughout their analysis. For example, in economic theory "price discrimination" has a universal meaning; in law it could have one meaning under the Robinson-Patman Act and another under a public utility regulation.

Lawyers, as advocates, feel that their function is to present their cases as forcefully as possible. "Everyone is entitled to his day in court." Economists, in the main, have difficulty in understanding or accepting special pleaders. Since most economic analysis is policy-oriented or academic, it seems fair to say that many economists—especially in the universities—retain an innate suspicion of practicing lawyers.

Lawyers, in general, have difficulty in understanding the work of many economists. Some economists are engaged in model-building. Their analysis follows long, indirect chains of reasoning. Some economic theorizing resembles intellectual gymnastics; there are few observational counterparts for their findings; they tend to minimize the number of factors that must be taken into account. As a result, their tools of analysis are not operational—they do not fit the specific needs of the lawyer who has a practical problem to solve either through litigation or negotiation.

The need for improvement in the working relations of lawyers and economists is great. Many of society's vital problems—economic, social, and political—depend on improvements in the regulatory process. These improvements will be sharply limited unless the two professions learn to work together effectively in the formulation and administration of public policy.

## *Conclusions*

There is a pressing need to clarify public policies regarding competition and to improve their administration. A key factor in satisfying this need is the effective application of economic analysis. To achieve such clarification and improvement, several steps should be taken:

Develop more affirmative conclusions about the influences of the various forms of competition on efficiency, costs, innovation, consumer sovereignty, economic growth, and stability.

Produce a better coordinated structure of government regulation—federal, state, and local—bearing on competition.

Coordinate the operations of the pertinent federal agencies.[4]

Eliminate those elements of tax policy that seem to hinder competition, such as present regulations that impose a tax penalty on dividing a large company into several smaller ones.

Develop the means for conducting a continuing review of policies, the state of competition in the economy, and for spotting those markets that require special legislative or executive attention.

Undertake a series of studies of the effects of antitrust enforcement on market competition, and the accomplishments of various types of decrees in order to develop a better understanding of the remedies which may be required to alleviate monopolistic situations.

Improve the capacity of the judicial system and the administrative agencies to try economic issues, and to formulate effective remedies.

## *Recommendations*

The key element in achieving these objectives is to improve the use of economic analysis. Progress in this direction calls for two phases: first, to better employ economic inquiry as it stands today; and second, to find ways to improve its methods of analysis. Clearly, the two go hand-in-hand. Productive developments in economic analysis will depend, in large part, on its use. The spur of practical problems of policy and administration would induce progress.

The mutual understanding of the legal and economic professions will not be achieved through general discussion. It can be developed by working together on specific cases and policies. It requires that economists work directly with lawyers, supplying ideas, information, and analysis to both the prosecution and the defense.

In theory, the government agencies should take the lead in this development. They have more experience than any private law office or defendant. They have a sufficient volume of activity to employ a staff of first-rate economists. In addition, since they are the attackers, they have a greater influence in setting the "field of battle."

The government has not taken the lead heretofore.[5] It has not upgraded the positions of economists in the antitrust agencies. It has not generally used the economists on the staffs of the agencies very effectively.

It is important to recognize that practical improvement in the application of economic analysis will be evolutionary rather than revolutionary. Substantial progress has been made by economists, lawyers, judges, and policy makers. However, it seems possible that further development will require more attention to fundamental problems of methodology. The improvement to date has been to overcome some of the more obvious hurdles. Future development may provide a more difficult task.

Recommendations for effectuating such a program must be set in general terms at this stage. The form of each project would depend on which institution undertakes it—whether one of the antitrust agencies, another government agency, a university or research institution, the Judicial Conference, or an independent research worker. Similarly, the range of educational programs is so great that any suggestions in that area must be general. A few specific studies can be used as illustrations of a general need.

### *Basic Studies Needed*

A number of basic studies are needed. These can be prosecuted in part by government agencies and in part by research and academic institutions. The following is only a general indication of the more important areas.

*Competitive Operations.* What are the forms of price and "non-price" competition? How are they affected by market structure, buying habits, and distributive practices? How does cost affect competition? How responsive is cost to competitive pressures? How responsive are total costs to fluctuations in business activity? What is the competitive relationship between prices, design, service, distribution methods, the costs of these functions, long-run costs decisions, and other forms of investment decisions?

Such studies call for a better understanding of how competition works, especially its effect on costs. Since ever-increasing proportions of cost are incurred through long-term decisions and do not respond quickly to changes in volume, their behavior may have a profound effect on the future nature of competition and what we can expect from it. Additionally, the degree of competitiveness may have a strategic influence on the pressures to reduce or control costs.

*Definitions of Competition.* What criteria can be employed as practicable indicators of competition? How can these criteria be developed in litigation, negotiation, and in the formulation of decrees? A series of market studies, covering some which have been involved in antitrust litigation and some which have not, can help to organize this material and set it in proper perspective.

The major purpose of such a study would be to forge tools of economic analysis which could be applied effectively in litigation. How have the criteria been employed in litigation and industry studies? Can a general framework be devised to select the pertinent indicators for purposes of comparisons of previous cases and of markets; for example, what criteria can be employed to identify markets in which price discrimination tends to promote competition and those in which it serves to impair competition?

One of the needs in this area is a clearer treatment of the relationships between indicators of structure, behavior, and performance. It is only through a better understanding of such relationships that headway can be made in differentiating diagnosis and prognosis in the competitive area. Clearer understanding is needed of the differences between finding antitrust violations and formulating remedies.

*Effects of Competition.* What pressures does competition exert on prices, efficiency, innovation, product variety and quality, costs, volume of production, consumer guidance, and investment? What has happened in industries which were subjected to new competitive forces, for example: the optical goods manufacturers when foreign quality products started to flow into the United States; the automobile industry under the same conditions; Alcoa when new companies started to produce aluminum? What are the effects of competition in expanding and contracting industries? Are there substantial differences in the influence of competition during various phases of business fluctuation?

Such analyses would take into account a number of previous industry and other surveys as well as a series of new ones. Some projects would best be undertaken after important antitrust proceedings, for example, after the break-up of a price conspiracy or a patent pool. Valuable insights might be obtained from studies in other countries, such as British experience after the decision against the cotton spinners agreement, or the Common Market experience under its program for breaking down international barriers.

*The Regulatory Process.* Such studies call for a consideration of the relationships between the ultimate aims of the regulation, the industry pressures for and against those aims, and the relationship between those pressures and the specific regulations. How much competitive latitude is permitted in the regulatory process? What methods have been used to foster competition? What is their relationship to the agencies' responsibilities for promoting the development of the industry? Studies of the "regulated" industries are needed. Additionally, empirical work would be desirable in a number of other areas. What is the nature of the regulatory process which starts with an antitrust decree? How do the administrative agencies operate? How is policy formulated, administered, reviewed by the agencies, the Congress, and the Executive? What is the relationship between the regulatory agencies and the courts in the development and the application of policy?

*Application of Economic Analysis in Litigation.* Such studies would call for detailed review of how various problems of economic analysis are handled in litigation. They would require detailed inquiry into how such analysis is used in the definition of the issues, in the collection of material, in the presentation of evidence and arguments, and in judicial determination. They would cover separate consideration of the tasks of determining violations and formulating remedies. The studies would, of course, be oriented to practical programs for supplying technical aid to judges within the framework of the judicial system. They would require careful observations of litigation procedures in process.

### *Continuing Reviews*

There is a substantial need for continuing analysis of the operations and influences of the antitrust laws. Basic field work should be carried on by government agencies since they possess investigatory powers and ready access to government files. These studies differ from the first group in two respects: first, they should be carried on as a continuing review whereas the first group includes spot studies; and second, they require basic work by government agencies.

Ideally such studies would be carried on by a central agency. One might well be organized on a basis similar to that of the Council of Economic Advisers, free of the administrative responsibility of prosecution and enforcement. The following is a tentative list of the types of studies which would be useful.

*Range and Effects of Government Regulation.* This would call for continuing studies of the structure of regulation at federal, state, and local levels. Additionally, it would provide studies of and reports on new proposals analyzing their relations to the existing structure of regulation. Ideally, such reports would be available to the Executive, the Congress, and the agencies while the proposals are under consideration.

*Administrative Agencies.* Such an inquiry would include a review of the relationships between the Federal Trade Commission and the Antitrust Division and other agencies involved in the regulation of competition. It would be directed to recommendations regarding overlapping functions and cooperative programs. What functions are best carried out by a commission and what by the Department of Justice? Can the investigatory powers of the Federal Trade Commission be better utilized? Can the work of the antitrust agencies and the regulatory agencies be coordinated more effectively?

*Competitive Trends.* Such a continuing study would call first for the development of a methodology for reviewing total competitive trends. The inquiry would require the forging of new methods of analysis. In part, this analysis would call for new statistical exploration. For example, it would require the evolution of meaningful measurements of trends in industrial concentration.[6] It could not rely on current census reports that are not geared for such inquiry. Rather, it would have to strike out for new statistical concepts and surveys that would produce concentration measurements for well-defined markets. Such concentration measurements would be related to the broader analysis of competitive forces and trends.

This inquiry would be difficult. Currently, there are few clues regarding such analysis. The broad generalizations which have been made about the state of competition are not persuasive. There is no clear conceptual framework today for such analyses.

These studies would necessarily be experimental. Although there would be many false starts, any progress would be useful. So many policy decisions must be made in the dark that any light would improve them.

This does not imply that any decisions—policy or administrative—

should be postponed until progress can be made along these lines. We have to make do with what we have.

*Effects of Decrees.* A meaningful review of the effects of decrees and orders should be undertaken on a continuing basis. Investigations should start within a reasonable time after a decree is issued. The surveys could develop significant empirical material that would help to tailor decrees for specific market situations. To start with, the project could cover decrees which have been formulated in the recent past, say the last five years. Several existing industry studies, as well as congressional investigations, would help to shed some light on what has taken place.

*Market Studies.* Such investigations would be devoted to spotting problem areas and analyzing means of injecting competition. These analyses would help to direct the antitrust agencies to concentrate their efforts on more important market situations. At the same time, they would indicate what use could be made of such programs as lowering tariffs, guiding government purchasing and research, and revising tax laws regarding corporate "spin offs" of divisions. These studies could support recommendations to Congress for specific programs when conventional antitrust means are not sufficient to make markets more competitive.

## *Education and Development*

There is a manifest need for cultivating a closer relationship between the legal and the economic disciplines. This effort would require programs on a number of fronts. It would be dedicated to helping lawyers to acquire a substantial understanding of the economic discipline and of its usefulness.[7] At the same time, it would aim at the development of economists who could supply the needs.

*Education.* Many problems of our society indicate the need for law and economics professors with broader capacities than their current disciplines. To that end, it would be desirable to make it possible for those faculties to develop greater breadth. For example, it would be desirable to inaugurate a program of fellowships for younger men who are preparing for professional careers; conferences could be organized for existing faculties; and cooperative projects for the preparation of educational materials could be financed. There are many opportunities for joint studies of specific problems that would develop men who can work effectively with other professions. At the same time, these studies could make a substantial contribution to the consideration of a wide range of policy problems.

*Litigation.* The most important forward moves for coordinating the two professions would be through litigation itself. The strengthening of the economic sections of the antitrust agencies would be a keystone in such a program. Such improvement would require specific agency programs to bring in top-flight economists. If the government were to take the lead, it would have a profound effect on the antitrust bar. Educational programs, of the type referred to in the preceding paragraph, could be of substantial aid. They could help to uncover both economists and lawyers who could contribute to such a program. At the beginning, the agencies might find it necessary to employ a number of economists as consultants rather than full-time employees. Since the few economists who might be available for such work are engaged in private practice or in the universities, the agencies might not be able to attract many on a fixed-tenure basis. However, it would be possible to attract outstanding economists if they were given high enough rank.

Comparatively few economists seem to find many attractions in competition and government regulation. Able economists are more interested in government activities relating to fiscal, monetary, and labor problems, rather than in the regulatory functions where they rank only as "handmaidens" to the lawyers. Until this situation is changed, outstanding economists will not undertake assignments in the regulatory agencies. Furthermore, unless the change takes place, promising graduate students will not be interested in working in this area.

More effective applications of economic analysis in the litigation of competitive issues require several cooperative efforts. Among them are:

1. The development of methods whereby lawyers can translate economic data into terms that will be meaningful to judges. Such a task is similar to that faced by the patent bar in litigating complex patent issues.

2. The formulation of specific procedures to aid judges in: clarifying the issues of the case; sorting and organizing the evidence which is presented and relating it to the issues; winnowing out irrelevant and redundant economic evidence; testing the reliability of conflicting evidence and expert opinion; coordinating hypotheses with evidence; defining the pertinent markets; analyzing the economic precedents; and analyzing the effects of the alternative remedies under consideration. Such a development would require close cooperation of bench, bar, and economists. It would call for careful experimentation with various methods.

3. A concerted effort to develop substantive rules which will provide appropriate balances for the evidentiary burden in various classes of cases. There is a need to develop an appropriate balance between the need for expedition and certainty in administration and the competitive importance of more careful economic inquiry. This effort may call for a larger group of clear per se rules; for a set of presumptions which places the burden of justification on the defendant; for a set which places the burden on the prosecution—with possible differences between the treatment of small and large defendants.

4. Joint discussions between lawyers and economists to review and analyze the specific procedures followed in various cases to determine what methods helped to implement public policies in this area. Such discussions might be organized by the Judicial Conference and by various professional organizations such as the Practicing Law Institute, antitrust sections of bar associations, and law schools.

## *The Basic Problem*

Substantial progress in formulating and administering national policies regarding competition will, in the final analysis, depend on the extent of public interest in these important policy issues. Attitudes about competition have a profound effect on the type of society in which we live. Competitive issues are inextricably tied up with the complex of society's objectives. The political consequences of concentrated economic power, the functions of government regulation, the economic consequences of centralized and decentralized decision-making, all are intimately related to how much competition we want and what we expect it to accomplish.

Because of the differences in ultimate political, social, and economic goals, as well as changing domestic and international conditions, we cannot hope to achieve an uncomplicated, fixed set of policies regarding competition. These policies must continue to be flexible. They cannot be rigid in the face of the dynamics of technology, business conditions, and international economic and political developments.

However, greater consistency can be achieved. Clearer definitions of our policies are necessary. A policy-making process can be developed that permits us to update our regulatory framework instead of letting inertia dictate that we continue a mass of inherited public attitudes which stem from a host of historical conditions.

To these ends, our methods of policy formulation and review must be improved. In fast-moving times, such improvement requires constant questioning, some of it uncomfortable. Does Sherman Act policy fit current needs after seventy years of drastic economic and social change? Does the philosophy of the Clayton and Federal Trade Commission Acts meet today's problems? Should our historical belief in forbidding cartels be continued or should a more flexible policy be adopted and regulation applied where it seems to be the preferable alternative? Do current international conditions, particularly the development of such international economic integration as the European Common Market, indicate that we should attempt to develop closer coordination with other large economies in our attitudes toward competition? Do we need a wholesale revision of antitrust and related laws in order to provide a clearer basis for an effective program for injecting stronger competitive influences into the economy?

Public attention has been accorded to narrow problems in this area. There has been general interest in such issues as the electric equipment conspiracy, drug prices, agricultural programs, barriers to international trade, to mention a few. Business, legal, and academic groups have been concerned with antitrust, union power, corporate power, Robinson-Patman, fair trade, and similar problems.

However, we have not, as a nation, recognized the need to devote some attention to the broader policy issues and to their far-reaching implications. We have not developed wide understanding of the nature of this range of problems affecting the body politic. Nor have we realized that mere repetition of theological cant about free enterprise and competition does not meet our needs and that the problems require serious analytical consideration.

The significance of these issues cannot be overstated. They have far-reaching influences on basic national goals—political, social, and ethical. They bear importantly on many aspects of international relations. They influence the picture that the peoples of other countries see when they look toward the United States.

The needs for progress are great. The achievement of an affirmative structure of policies in the competitive-regulatory complex would serve to improve many elements in modern industrial economies, here and abroad.

We have the resources, economic and intellectual, for substantial progress. Will we recognize the need?

# Footnotes

## Chapter 1

[1] 15 U.S.C. 1-7.

[2] Egon Sohmen states that, "It is often held that enforcement of competition through prohibition of cartel agreements and the breakup of large combines can never be effective." However, he points out that, "If that were true, it would be hard to understand why German industrialists have fought so bitterly, and unfortunately with some measure of success, for the repeal of the Allied ordinances." "Competition and Growth: The Lesson of West Germany," *American Economic Review,* Vol. 49 (December 1959), pp. 986, 994.

[3] See, for example, comments of Ben W. Lewis in "The Sherman Act and Enforcement-Discussion," *American Economic Review,* Vol. 38 (1948), p. 212. He feels that "the free enterprise system, as a system, is on its way out, and the most that we can expect from antitrust laws is that they will make the transition process less painful." Judge Frank took an extreme position in *Standard Brands* v. *Smidler.* "Monopoly-phobia, like most phobias, is both a symptom and a cause of a neurotic tendency which, in refusing bravely to face facts, cannot yield intelligent guidance." 151 F. 2d 34, 42. See also Dudley F. Pegrum, *Regulation of Industry* (1949), p. 473; William J. Fellner, *Competition Among the Few* (1949), pp. 309-10.

[4] Adam Smith, *The Wealth of Nations* (Cannan ed., 1904), p. 130.

[5] Prominent jurists were not sanguine about the operations of the act. Justice Holmes regarded it as "a foolish law." *Holmes-Laski Letters,* Vol. 1 (Howe ed., 1953), p. 248. Justice Brandeis felt that the act was merely part of our folklore. *Ibid.*, p. 719.

[6] John Bates Clark, "The Limits of Competition," *Political Science Quarterly,* Vol. 2 (1887), pp. 55, 61; Edwin R. A. Seligman, "Railway Tariffs and the Interstate Commerce Law," *ibid.*, p. 373; and Richard T. Ely, *Monopolies and Trusts* (1912), p. 243.

[7] J. M. Clark, "Competition and the Objectives of Government Policy," in Edward H. Chamberlin ed., *Monopoly and Competition and Their Regulation* (1954), pp. 324-25.

[8] Gosta Mickwitz, "The Means of Competition at Various Stages of Production and Distribution," *Kyklos,* Vol. 11 (1958), p. 509. This article presents the results of investigations of the forms of market rivalry in Denmark, Sweden, and Finland. It indicates variations in these forms as one progresses through the stages of production and distribution from raw materials to the consumer.

[9] See discussion of "non-price competition" in Edward S. Mason, *Economic Concentration and the Monopoly Problem* (1957), pp. 155-59. See also Corwin D. Edwards, "Issues in the Monopoly Problem," in Edward H. Chamberlin, ed., *Monopoly and Competition and Their Regulation* (1954), p. 188.

[10] Some believe that competition is essentially self-destructive. See Joan Robinson, "The Impossibility of Competition," in *ibid.*, p. 245.

[11] Almarin Phillips, "A Critique of United States Experience with Price-Fixing Agreements and the Per Se Rule," *Journal of Industrial Economics,* Vol. 8 (October 1959), pp. 14, 30.

[12] For a stimulating discussion of the relationships between "wealth" and the "power process" see Harold D. Lasswell, "The Interplay of Economic, Political and Social Criteria in Legal Policy," *Vanderbilt Law Review,* Vol. 14 (March 1961), p. 451.

[13] See "Message from the President of the United States," *Final Report and Recommendations of the Temporary National Economic Committee,* S. Doc. 35, 77 Cong. 1 sess. (1941), pp. 11, 14-15. See also *Financing Small Business,* Report to the Committees on Banking and Currency and the Select Committees on Small Business by the Federal Reserve System, 85 Cong. 2 sess. (April 11, 1958), Pts. 1 and 2.

[14] Though he stated his thesis more in political terms and took a somewhat extreme position, this conflict seemed to be one of the basic sources of concern in Friedrich A. Hayek's, *The Road to Serfdom* (1944). Yet Hayek was not a devotee of *laissez faire.*

[15] See J. M. Clark, *Alternative to Serfdom* (1948), pp. 61 *et seq.*

[16] J. K. Galbraith, *The Affluent Society* (1958).

[17] For an interesting piece about majority attitudes in favor of security over income found in the United States, Britain, Sweden, Canada, and Australia, see "More or Less Competition?", *The Economist* (July 2, 1949), p. 7.

[18] See R. S. Edwards and H. Townsend, *Business Enterprise* (1958), p. 562.

[19] "Competition, if it be allowed to operate fully, is merciless. . . ." *Ibid.*, p. 398. Jacob Weissman feels that "if we accept—perhaps have already accepted—the primacy of norms stressing security and minimum standards of living, oligopoly may demand major modification, even abandonment of the antitrust program." "Is Oligopoly Illegal? A Jurisprudential Approach," *Quarterly Journal of Economics,* Vol. 74 (August 1960), pp. 437, 463.

[20] J. M. Clark, *Competition as a Dynamic Process* (1961), pp. 81-82.

[21] See Donald H. Wallace, ed., *Economic Standards of Government Price Control,* Technical National Economic Committee Monograph No. 32 (1941), pp. 404-05.

[22] See *Staff Report on Employment, Growth, and Price Levels,* Prepared for consideration by the Joint Economic Committee, 86 Cong. 1 sess. (1959), Chap. 6.

[23] Benjamin N. Selekman, *A Moral Philosophy for Management* (1959).

[24] Carl Kaysen, perhaps in an ironic mood, refers to "the soulful corporation." "The Social Significance of the Modern Corporation," *American Economic Review,* Supplement, Vol. 47 (1957), p. 311. See also C. Wright Mills, *The Power Elite* (1956) and Earl Latham, "Anthropomorphic Corporations, Elites, and Monopoly Power," *American Economic Review,* Supplement, Vol. 47 (1957), p. 303.

[25] The most prominent supporter of this creed is Adolph A. Berle, Jr. See his *The 20th Century Capitalist Revolution* (1954).

[26] Ernest Dale makes the point rather forcefully. "Thus social responsibility may merely serve as a thinly disguised ideological weapon to retain power for 'daddy who knows best.'" *American Economic Review,* Vol. 51 (May 1961), pp. 540, 542.

[27] See Louis B. Schwartz, "Institutional Size and Individual Liberty: Authoritarian Aspects of Bigness," *Northwestern University Law Review,* Vol. 55 (March-April 1960), pp. 4, 13-14.

[28] Adam Smith, *The Wealth of Nations* (Modern Library ed., 1937).

[29] These teachings of the neoclassical economists, it should be noted, did not call

for a literal *laissez-faire* policy. See Harvey J. Levin, "Standards of Welfare in Economic Thought," *Quarterly Journal of Economics,* Vol. 70 (February 1956), p. 117.

[30] The position has been stated in Berle, *op. cit.,* and David Lilienthal, *Big Business: A New Era* (1953). See critical discussion of this point of view in John C. Stedman, "A New Look at Antitrust: The Report of the Attorney General's Committee," *Journal of Public Law,* Vol. 4 (1956), p. 223.

[31] See W. H. Ferry, *The Corporation and the Economy* (1959), p. 8.

[32] "If their directors begin to act as if they really were general trustees for the public at large, they may well imperil their present freedom." Eugene V. Rostow, "To Whom and For What Ends is Corporate Management Responsible?", in Edward S. Mason, ed., *The Corporation in Modern Society* (1960), pp. 46, 68; see also Eugene V. Rostow, "The New Sherman Act: A Positive Instrument of Progress," *University of Chicago Law Review,* Vol. 14 (1947), pp. 567, 573.

[33] Ben Lewis states the position strongly. "Our giant firms are sitting like fat, delectable ducks, virtually inviting the Government to open fire with something more effective than antitrust." *Administered Prices,* Hearings before the Senate Judiciary Committee, 86 Cong. 1 sess. (1959), Pt. 9, p. 4719.

[34] *U.S.* v. *United Shoe Machinery Corp.,* 110 F. Supp. 295 (D.C. Mass. 1953).

[35] See Robert M. Hutchins, *Two Faces of Federalism* (1961).

[36] For a general review of these criticisms see M. S. Massel, "The Regulatory Process," *Law and Contemporary Problems,* Vol. 26 (Spring 1961), p. 181.

[37] Charles J. Hitch referred to a tendency "to recommend government action on the quite insufficient grounds that a function is performed less than perfectly in the private sector." "The Uses of Economics," *Research for Public Policy: Brookings Dedication Lectures* (1961), pp. 91, 107.

[38] For example, Edward S. Mason points out that our antitrust policies would be much simpler if we were not concerned about efficiency and desired only to limit market power. "Market Power and Business Conduct: Some Comments," *American Economic Review,* Supplement, Vol. 46 (1956), pp. 471, 476.

[39] *U.S.* v. *Southern Pacific Co.,* 259 U.S. 214 (1922). See discussion in *Report of the Attorney General's National Committee to Study the Antitrust Laws* (1955), p. 264. Similar conflicts are discussed in Jerome K. Kuykendall, "Remarks," *New Theories of Federal Trade Commission Enforcement,* Trade Regulation Reports, No. 153 (Extra ed., June 8, 1960), p. 49.

[40] *Business Week,* Aug. 12, 1961, p. 31.

[41] A report in the *New York Times* of Oct. 23, 1961, indicates that the policy of permitting a private communications satellite system is being reviewed in the White House.

[42] See, for example, Edward R. Johnston, "The Defense of an Antitrust Case," *Proceedings,* Section of Antitrust Law, American Bar Association (April 1957), pp. 9, 12.

[43] See Frank H. Knight, "Methodology in Economics—Part II," *Southern Economic Journal,* Vol. 27 (April 1961), pp. 273, 282; Jacob Viner, "International Trade Theory and Its Present Day Relevance," *Economics and Public Policy: Brookings Lectures 1954* (1955), p. 122.

## *Chapter 2*

[1] The combination of these goals is reflected in the Supreme Court's opinion in *Northern Pacific Railway Co.* v. *U.S.*, 356 U.S. 1, 5 (1958). "The Sherman Act was designed to be a comprehensive charter of economic liberty aimed at preserving free and unfettered competition as the rule of trade. It rests on the premise that the unrestrained interaction of competitive forces will yield the best allocation of our economic resources, the lowest prices, the highest quality and the greatest material progress, while at the same time providing an environment conducive to the preservation of our democratic political and social institutions."

[2] *Goals for Americans,* Report of the President's Commission on National Goals (1960), p. 9.

[3] See Edward H. Mason, "Workable Competition Versus Workable Monopoly," *Business Practices Under Federal Antitrust Laws,* Proceedings of the Third Annual Meeting of the New York State Bar Association, Section on Antitrust Law (Jan. 24, 1951), pp. 67, 71.

[4] See discussion of these two goals in Edward S. Mason, *Economic Concentration and the Monopoly Problem* (1957), p. 375.

[5] John Heath of the University of Manchester observes that, "In Britain the desire to promote competition is derived to a lesser extent from the area of political philosophy than in the United States, on the theory perhaps that power is in general exercised responsibility." *Not Enough Competition?,* Institute of Economic Affairs, Hobart Paper II (London, 1961), p. 7.

[6] Carl Kaysen argues that, "The chief virtue of a competitive market in practice is not necessarily that it leads to economic efficiency but that it constrains private economic power." "The Social Significance of the Modern Corporation," *American Economic Review,* Supplement, Vol. 47 (1957), pp. 311, 316. See also A. D. Neale, *The Antitrust Laws of the United States of America* (1960), p. 422.

[7] Cartels and monopolies have been associated with the rise of the Nazi party in Germany. J. M. Wood, *The Challenge of Monopoly* (1960), p. 19. W. H. Ferry is pessimistic about the community's interest in freedom. *The Corporation and the Economy* (1959).

[8] Frank H. Knight feels that "An ideally competitive market is practically the only setting of complete mutual freedom. . . ." "Methodology in Economics—Part II," *Southern Economic Journal,* Vol. 27 (April 1961), pp. 273, 282. See also J. M. Clark, *Competition as a Dynamic Process* (1961), pp. 85-87.

[9] For an illuminating account of many conflicts about competition, private power, state regulation, and state ownership from the Revolution to the Civil War see Louis Hartz, *Economic Policy and Democratic Thought: Pennsylvania, 1776-1860* (1948). As Hartz points out, many misinterpretations of *laissez-faire* policies have been based on examinations of federal activities and overlook state functions that were more important in the economic life of the day.

[10] Eugene V. Rostow, "The New Sherman Act: A Positive Instrument of Progress," *University of Chicago Law Review,* Vol. 14 (1947), pp. 569, 570. An effective argument for focusing antitrust policy on power is contained in Carl Kaysen and Donald Turner, *Antitrust Policy: An Economic and Legal Analysis* (1959).

[11] Thomas Jefferson defined a "wise and frugal Government" as one "which shall restrain men from injuring one another, shall leave them otherwise free to regulate their own pursuits of industry and improvement. . . ." "First Inaugural Address" in James D. Richardson, *A Compilation of the Messages and Papers of the Presi-*

*dents* (1897), pp. 309, 311. See also Emmette S. Redford, *Potential Public Policies to Deal with Inflation Caused by Market Power,* Study Paper No. 10, Study of Employment, Growth, and Price Levels, Joint Economic Committee, 86 Cong. 1 sess. (Dec. 11, 1959), pp. 3, 4.

[12] Eugene V. Rostow, "British and American Experience with Legislation Against Restraints of Competition," *Modern Law Review,* Vol. 23 (September 1960), pp. 477, 480-81.

[13] Hans B. Thorelli, *The Federal Antitrust Policy* (1954), pp. 570-71.

[14] *U.S.* v. *Columbia Steel Co. et al.,* 334 U.S. 495, 536 (1948).

[15] See Ralph J. Cordiner, "Competitive Private Enterprise in Space," *Peacetime Uses of Space Series,* Lecture V, University of California, Los Angeles (May 4, 1960), p. 6.

[16] George W. Stocking, *Workable Competition and Antitrust Policy* (1961), p. 2.

[17] For an interesting discussion of this attitude see Sumner H. Slichter, "A Defense of Bigness," in American Management Association, *Legal, Financial, and Tax Aspects of Mergers and Acquisitions* (1957).

[18] Adolph A. Berle, Jr., *The 20th Century Capitalist Revolution* (1954) and David Lilienthal, *Big Business: A New Era* (1953).

[19] Eugene V. Rostow, "To Whom and For What Ends is Corporate Management Responsible?", in Edward S. Mason, ed., *The Corporation in Modern Society* (1960), pp. 46, 68; Ben W. Lewis, "Power Blocs and the Operation of Economic Forces: Economics by Admonition," *American Economic Review,* Vol. 49 (May 1959), p. 384.

[20] For example, Clark, *op. cit.,* p. 11.

[21] See Derek C. Bok, "Section 7 of the Clayton Act and the Merging of Law and Economics," *Harvard Law Review,* Vol. 74 (December 1960), pp. 226, 235-36, about fears that bigness will lead to political collectivism. See also pp. 306-07.

[22] For example, Lucile S. Keyes, "The Shoe Machinery Case and the Problem of the Good Trust," *Quarterly Journal of Economics,* Vol. 68 (1954), p. 287; Fred I. Raymond, *The Limitist* (1947); Henry C. Simons, *A Positive Program for Laissez-Faire* (1934), p. 20; A. Papandreou and J. Wheeler, *Competition and Its Regulation* (1954), pp. 487-88. See Justice Brandeis' comment in *Liggett Co.* v. *Lee,* 288 U.S. 517, 541 (1933) and Louis B. Brandeis, *The Curse of Bigness* (Fraenkel ed., 1934). See also Milton Handler, "Introductory—The Brandeis Conception of the Relationship of Small Business to Antitrust," *Proceedings,* Section of Antitrust Law, American Bar Association (April 1960), p. 13.

[23] Michael L. Hoffman makes an interesting point, in this connection, about a semantic difficulty. In a dispatch from Geneva he said, "American businessmen customarily fail to realize that when European businessmen talk about getting rid of controls they mean only getting rid of government controls." "Business Statesmen Held Greatest Need of Europe," *New York Times,* Nov. 22, 1949.

[24] Walter S. Owen, "A New Emphasis: The Law in a Changing World," *American Bar Association Journal,* Vol. 45 (November 1959), p. 1172.

[25] Louis B. Schwartz, "Institutional Size and Individual Liberty: Authoritarian Aspects of Bigness," *Northwestern University Law Review,* Vol. 55 (March-April 1960), p. 4. M. Rotondi has pointed out that freedom of competition requires "equal opportunities in all aspects of competition and complete freedom to benefit from its results." However, this must take place within the limits imposed by the state. Therefore, he suggests that "it would be better to speak of *equality* in competition rather than *freedom* of competition." "Unfair Competition in Europe," *American Journal of Comparative Law,* Vol. 7 (Summer 1958), p. 329.

[26] Thorelli argues that antitrust "helps us to distinguish liberty from license." *Op. cit.,* p. 608. For a contrary view see Donald Dewey, "Mergers and Cartels:

Some Reservations about Policy," *American Economic Review,* Vol. 51 (May 1961), pp. 255, 261-62.

[27] See Thorelli, *op. cit.,* pp. 276-77; see also Edward H. Levi, "The Antitrust Laws and Monopoly," *University of Chicago Law Review,* Vol. 14 (1947), pp. 153, 154-55.

[28] The National Association of Manufacturers says, "Businessmen believe in competition because they recognize that the alternative to it is comprehensive government direction, which would be far worse in its consequences." *Foreign Competition* (1960), p. 7. See also Clair Wilcox, *Public Policies Toward Business* (1955), p. 853; and *Goals for Americans,* Report of the President's Commission on National Goals (1960), p. 9.

[29] On the other hand, Edward H. Levi points out the tendency to regulate in the enforcement of antitrust. "The Monopoly Problem as Viewed by a Lawyer," *American Economic Review,* Supplement, Vol. 47 (1957), p. 293.

[30] Gunnar Myrdal makes the point that "The whole discussion of a 'free' versus a 'planned' economy has thus become strangely unrelated to reality. . . ." *Beyond the Welfare State* (1960), p. 11.

[31] See, for example, W. H. Ferry, *The Economy Under Law* (1960), pp. 9, 22.

[32] Howard H. Hines is concerned about the influence of "big business" on public opinion regarding political and social issues. "Effectiveness of 'Entry' by Already Established Firms," *Employment, Growth, and Price Levels,* Hearings before the Joint Economic Committee, 86 Cong. 1 sess. (1959), Pt. 7, pp. 1981, 1996-97. See also Earl Latham, "The Commonwealth of the Corporation," *Northwestern University Law Review,* Vol. 55 (1960), p. 25; and Lee Loevinger, "Antitrust, Economics and Politics," *Antitrust Bulletin,* Vol. 1 (1955), pp. 225, 256-57. A stimulating discussion of the relationship between political theory and economic theory, centering on the choice-making of the market, may be found in C. B. Macpherson, "Market Concepts in Political Theory," *Canadian Journal of Economics and Political Science,* Vol. 27 (1961), p. 490.

[33] For an account of the political influences of cartels see Heinrich Kronstein and Gertrude Leighton, "Cartel Control: A Record of Failure," *Yale Law Journal,* Vol. 25 (1946), p. 297. See also Theodore J. Kreps, *An Evaluation of Antitrust Policy: Its Relation to Economic Growth, Full Employment and Prices,* Study Paper No. 22, Study of Employment, Growth, and Price Levels, Joint Economic Committee, 86 Cong. 2 sess. (1960), p. 9.

[34] Eugene V. Rostow, *Planning for Freedom* (1959), p. 32.

[35] See Hines, *op cit.,* p. 1981; Eugene V. Rostow, "Market Organization and Stabilization Policy," in M. F. Millikan, ed., *Income Stabilization for a Developing Democracy* (1953), p. 439; Clare E. Griffin, *An Economic Approach to Antitrust Problems* (1951), p. 57.

[36] Thorelli, *op cit.,* pp. 570-71.

[37] Robert C. Brooks, Jr., "Businessmen's Concepts of 'Injury to Competition,'" *California Management Review,* Vol. 3 (1961), pp. 89, 92-93. See also Lee Loevinger, *The Law of Free Enterprise* (1949), pp. 137-38.

[38] See Lee Loevinger, "Recent Developments in Antitrust Enforcement," *Proceedings,* Section of Antitrust Law, American Bar Association (April 1961), pp. 102, 103.

[39] Such practices were involved in *Puerto Rican American Tobacco Co.* v. *American Tobacco Co.,* 30 F. 2d 234 (C.C.A.-2d 1929). The court found that the defendant reduced its prices below cost in Puerto Rico, where it had only one competitor, in order to punish the competitor for stimulating tax legislation which hurt the American Tobacco Co. More recently a price cut of some 25 per cent in a limited area was found to violate the Clayton Act. The court held that the reduction "was initiated for the purpose of driving the competitor out of business."

*Maryland Baking Co.* v. *F.T.C.*, 243 F. 2d 716, 718 (C.C.A.-4th 1957). See also *Pittsburgh Coal Co. of Wisconsin* v. *F.T.C.*, 8 F.T.C. 480 (1925), and *In the Matter of Fleischman Co.*, 1 F.T.C. 119 (1918).

[40] Wilcox, *op. cit.*, p. 862.

[41] See Marketing Laws Survey, *State Price Control Legislation* (1940).

[42] See Edward S. Mason's discussion of the writings of Schumpeter, Berle, Lilienthal, and Galbraith in "The Apologetics of 'Managerialism,'" *Journal of Business*, Vol. 31 (1958).

[43] See John C. Stedman, "A New Look at Antitrust: The Report of the Attorney General's Committee," *Journal of Public Law*, Vol. 4 (1956), p. 223.

[44] W. W. Rostow, *The Stages of Economic Growth* (1960).

[45] C. Dupont and F. A. G. Keesing, "The Yugoslav Economic System and Instruments of Yugoslav Economic Policy: A Note," in International Monetary Fund, *Staff Papers*, Vol. 8 (November 1960), p. 77. See *The Economist*, Jan. 7, 1961, p. 20. This article indicates a further loosening of administrative controls and additional reliance on profits and productivity.

[46] For a discussion of progress and problems see Paul Landy, "Reforms in Yugoslavia," *Problems of Communism*, Vol. 10 (November-December 1961), p. 24.

[47] Personal discussions with a Yugoslavian economist.

[48] J. M. Clark, *Competition as a Dynamic Process* (1961), esp. p. 65. See also J. M. Clark, *Social Control of Business* (2d ed., 1939). Professor Clark has presented the clearest exposition of the relationship between a competitive policy and the efforts to raise the plane or level of competition.

[49] An interesting tie-up between state and local regulation and union activity is suggested by James W. McKie: "In some areas unions have been able to control (or at least influence) state and local licensing and inspection of certain kinds of business, which enables them to control entry and competition in these lines." "Collective Bargaining and the Maintenance of the Market Competition," in Philip D. Bradley, ed., *The Public Stake in Union Power* (1959), p. 86.

[50] See G. E. Hale and Rosemary D. Hale, *Market Power: Size and Shape Under the Sherman Act* (1958), p. 4.

[51] Peter A. Stone and Harold Denton, *Toward More Housing*, Temporary National Economic Committee Monograph No. 8 (1940).

[52] After a broad study the authors concluded that, "Promotion of public health is definitely a secondary objective of state milk control laws." University of Arizona, Agricultural Experiment Station, *Barriers to the Interstate Movement of Milk and Dairy Products in the Eleven Western States*, Bulletin 255 (April 1945).

[53] An elementary illustration of the need for standards is provided by the differences in the sizes of the "standard" barrel. The standard in Maine contains 5,914 cubic inches compared with 7,056 cubic inches in the Federal Standard. George R. Taylor, Edgar L. Burtis, and Frederick V. Waugh, *Barriers to Internal Trade in Farm Products* (March 1939), p. 76.

[54] Corwin D. Edwards refers to the use of standardization programs to exclude new competitors from a market and misleading grades which support price differentials but do not reflect quality differences. *Maintaining Competition* (1949), p. 29.

[55] Colston E. Warne, "The Influence of Ethical and Social Responsibilities on Advertising and Selling Practices," *American Economic Review*, Vol. 51 (May 1961), p. 527.

[56] See Tibor Scitovsky, *Welfare and Competition* (1951), p. 446; and James Edward Meade, *Planning and the Price Mechanism* (1949), pp. 59-60.

[57] See discussion of the influence of brands on drug prices in Senate Judiciary Committee, Subcommittee on Antitrust and Monopoly, *Antitrust and Monopoly*

*Activities, 1960,* 87 Cong. 1 sess. (1961), pp. 10-18. See also Corwin D. Edwards, "Standards and Product Differentiation," in Dickson Reck, ed., *National Standards in a Modern Economy* (1956), p. 327.

[58] Testimony of L. R. Walker, *Investigation of Concentration of Economic Power,* Hearings before the Temporary National Economic Committee, 75 Cong. (1939), Pt. 8, Problems of the Consumer, p. 3413.

[59] The problem of finding a satisfactory balance is illustrated in Joel B. Dirlam and Irwin M. Stelzer, "The Insurance Industry: A Case Study in the Workability of Regulated Competition," *University of Pennsylvania Law Review,* Vol. 107 (December 1958), p. 199.

[60] For a valuable discussion of the relationship between efficiency and competition see Scitovsky, *loc. cit.* See also *1960 Joint Economic Report,* Report of the Joint Economic Committee on the January 1960 Economic Report of the President, 86 Cong. 2 sess. (1960), pp. 3, 18.

[61] Some see conflicts in these objectives. "As is often the case, the goals of public policy conflict: efficiency requires fewer units of larger size, and competition requires many units." Stephan Stykolt and Harry C. Eastman, "A Model for the Study of Protected Oligopolies," *Economic Journal,* Vol. 70 (June 1960), pp. 336, 347.

[62] Edward S. Mason, "Price Policies and Full Employment," in Carl J. Friedrich and Edward S. Mason, eds., *Public Policy* (1940), pp. 25, 38. The relationship between competition and efficiency has influenced lawmakers as well. See Emanuel Celler, "The Study of Monopoly Power," *Business Practices under Federal Antitrust Laws,* Proceedings of the Third Annual Meeting of the New York State Bar Association, Section on Antitrust Laws (Jan. 24, 1951), pp. 58, 64; and *1961 Joint Economic Report,* Joint Economic Committee, 87 Cong. 1 sess. (1961), pp. 41-42. See also Clark, *Competition as a Dynamic Process,* pp. 72-74.

[63] The term "invisible hand" was originated, of course, in Adam Smith, *The Wealth of Nations* (Modern Library ed., 1937).

[64] An interesting observation is made by *Business Week,* June 10, 1961, p. 46. In an article on the difficulties faced by airlines and plane builders, "When Supersonic Travel Comes," it said, "if the world's airlines were all controlled by bankers, equipment purchasing might well have stopped with the DC-6B, one of the most profitable airplanes ever built. By now the 6B would have paid for itself and profits would be pouring in. Instead, airlines are controlled by men and by governments that are constantly trying to steal someone else's business without losing any themselves. The best way to do this is to fly the fastest plane."

[65] "The price of monopoly is upon every occasion the highest which can be got. The natural price, or the price of free competition, on the contrary, is the lowest which can be taken, not upon every occasion indeed, but for any considerable time together. The one is upon every occasion the highest which can be squeezed out of the buyers, or which, it is supposed, they will consent to give: The other is the lowest which the sellers can commonly afford to take, and at the same time continue their business." Adam Smith, *op. cit.,* p. 61.

[66] See testimony of Richard V. Gilbert in *The Relationship of Prices to Economic Stability and Growth,* Commentaries submitted by economists from labor and industry appearing before the Joint Economic Committee, 85 Cong. 2 sess. (Oct. 31, 1958), p. 228.

[67] See, for example, Merrill J. Roberts, "The Regulation of Transport Price Competition," *Law and Contemporary Problems,* Vol. 24 (Autumn 1959), p. 557; and Henry Clay, "The Campaign Against Monopoly and Restrictive Practices," *Lloyd's Bank Review,* Vol. 24 (1952), p. 14.

[68] The outstanding proponent of this point of view is J. A. Schumpeter. See his

*Capitalism, Socialism and Democracy* (1942). See also W. Rupert Maclaurin, "Technological Progress in Some American Industries," *American Economic Review,* Vol. 44 (1954), p. 178, and *Innovation and Invention in the Radio Industry* (1949).

[69] C. F. Carter and B. R. Williams, *Industry and Technical Progress* (1957), p. 169.

[70] See Calvin B. Hoover, "The Relevance of the Competitive, *Laissez-Faire* Economic Model to Modern Capitalistic National Economies," *Kyklos,* Vol. 8 (1955), p. 40, esp. p. 51. The evidence about the effect of size on cost is reviewed in Caleb A. Smith, "Survey of the Empirical Evidence on Economies of Scale," in National Bureau of Economic Research, *Business Concentration and Price Policy* (1955), p. 213.

[71] For a discussion of the relationship between efficiency and size see James A. Duesenberry, "Small Business in the American Economy," *Financing Small Business,* Report to the Committees on Banking and Currency and the Select Committees on Small Business by the Federal Reserve System, 85 Cong. 2 sess. (1958), Pts. 1 and 2, p. 172.

[72] D. Hamberg, "Size of Firm, Monopoly and Economic Growth," *Employment, Growth, and Price Levels,* Hearings before the Joint Economic Committee, 86 Cong. 1 sess. (1959), Pt. 7, p. 2337. Hamberg cites several studies which conclude that "new firms are very often needed if radically new innovations are to take place. . . ." (P. 2350.) Duesenberry argues that "Small and medium sized firms make a much more important indirect contribution to progress than their size or direct contribution to the development of new techniques would indicate." Testimony of James S. Duesenberry, *ibid.,* p. 2325. For a criticism of this position see Joel B. Dirlam and H. John Thorkelson, "Implications of the Individualist Theory of Invention," *Antitrust Bulletin,* Vol. 6 (1961), p. 173.

[73] One study of 61 important inventions developed since 1900 shows that independent inventors were responsible for more than half of them. I. Jewkes, D. Sawers, and R. Stillerman, *The Sources of Invention* (1958). See *Staff Report on Employment, Growth, and Price Levels,* Prepared for consideration by the Joint Economic Committee, 86 Cong. 1 sess. (1959), p. 431.

[74] For a discussion of "a number of important disadvantages associated with being large" see Pauline Lesley Cook, *Effects of Mergers* (1958), esp. p. 435.

[75] See, for example, "Address of Alfred Marshall" in *Memorials of Alfred Marshall* (1925), pp. 279-80.

[76] See testimony of Fritz Machlup, *Administered Prices,* Hearings before the Senate Judiciary Committee, 86 Cong. 1 sess. (1959), Pt. 10, pp. 4954-55.

[77] Laurence I. Wood, *Patents and Antitrust Law* (1941), Chap. 1.

[78] See Fritz Machlup, *An Economic Review of the Patent System,* Study No. 15, Senate Judiciary Committee, Subcommittee on Patents, Trademarks, and Copyrights, 85 Cong. 2 sess. (1958); and Seymour Melman, *The Impact of the Patent System on Research,* Study No. 11, *ibid.*

[79] "Almost invariably within the last twenty-five years—certainly more often than not—when a patent had been sufficiently exploited to get to the courts, it was declared invalid because the subject matter was *not deemed to be an invention.*" Emanuel R. Posnack, "Inventions, Patents and Society: An Evaluation and Re-evaluation," *Federal Bar Journal,* Vol. 20 (Summer 1960), p. 263. "In 80 per cent of all the Circuit Court of Appeals and United States Supreme Court cases involving patent validity and infringement decided during 1941 to 1945, the patents were declared invalid or not infringed." Sigmund Timberg, "Equitable Relief Under the Sherman Act," *University of Illinois Law Forum,* Vol. 1950 (Winter Number), pp. 629, 645.

[80] See *Report of the Attorney General's National Committee to Study the Antitrust Laws* (1955), pp. 229-59.

[81] See, for example, Henry H. Villard, "Competition, Oligopoly and Research," *Journal of Political Economy,* Vol. 66 (December 1958), p. 483.

[82] Discussion with an official of the Netherlands government.

[83] See Sumner H. Slichter, "A Defense of Bigness in Business," in American Management Association, *Legal, Financial, and Tax Aspects of Mergers and Acquisitions* (1957), p. 157.

[84] J. K. Galbraith, *American Capitalism: The Concept of Countervailing Power* (1952); J. K. Galbraith, "Countervailing Power," *American Economic Review,* Supplement, Vol. 44 (1954), p. 1; and Earl Latham, "Anthropomorphic Corporations, Elites and Monopoly Power," *American Economic Review,* Supplement, Vol. 47 (1957), p. 303.

[85] Consumer cooperatives have been urged as a countervailing power in dealing with monopoly. J. M. Wood, *The Challenge of Monopoly* (1960), p. 11. The use of a producers' agreement to counteract the power of a preponderant buyer was involved in the *Water-Tube Boilermakers'* case before the Restrictive Practices Court in the United Kingdom. This is the only case up to 1961 "in which the restrictions as a whole have been found by the Court not to be contrary to the public interest." R. L. Sich, "Developments Under the Restrictive Trade Practices Act, 1956, of the United Kingdom," *Proceedings,* Section of Antitrust Law, American Bar Association (August 1960), pp. 285, 290.

[86] See, for example, George J. Stigler, "The Economist Plays with Blocs," *American Economic Review,* Supplement, Vol. 44 (1954), p. 7; John Perry Miller, "Competition and Countervailing Power: Their Roles in the American Economy," *ibid.,* p. 15; William J. Fellner, *Competition Among the Few* (1949), pp. 252-53.

[87] W. H. Ferry, *The Corporation and the Economy* (1959), p. 14; Louis B. Schwartz, "Institutional Size and Individual Liberty: Authoritarian Aspects of Bigness," *Northwestern University Law Review,* Vol. 55 (March-April 1960), pp. 14-15; Bernard Nossiter, "The Hidden Affair Between Big Business and Labor," *Harper's Magazine,* July 1959, p. 32; Bayless Manning, "Corporate Power and Individual Freedom: Some General Analysis and Particular Reservations," *Northwestern University Law Review,* Vol. 55 (March-April 1960), pp. 38, 45.

[88] See James W. McKie, "Collective Bargaining and the Maintenance of Market Competition," in Philip D. Bradley, ed., *The Public Stake in Union Power* (1959), p. 86, esp. pp. 87-89.

[89] See, for example, R. S. Edwards and H. Townsend, *Business Enterprise* (1958), p. 205.

[90] Abe Fortas, "The Grievances of the Small Business Man—A Bill of Particulars," *Proceedings,* Section of Antitrust Law, American Bar Association (April 1960), pp. 33, 35.

[91] Consider, for example, such statements as, "As growth is the enemy of monopoly, there is good reason to believe that monopoly is equally the enemy of growth." Testimony of William H. Martin, *Employment, Growth, and Price Levels,* Hearings before the Joint Economic Committee (1959), pp. 2000-01.

[92] Jesse Markham says that "most analysts of antitrust policy would undoubtedly agree that in the broad sweep of its history since 1890 antitrust policy has stimulated growth of the economy as a whole. . . ." "Growth Incentives and Antitrust Policy," in Klaus Knorr and William J. Baumol, eds., *What Price Economic Growth?,* (1961), p. 93. Later he refers to the theory "that strict application of the Robinson-Patman Act stifles some competitive growth." (P. 102.) See also testimony of John Perry Miller in *Employment, Growth, and Price Levels,* Hearings, pp. 2123-24.

[93] Theodore J. Kreps concluded that "the impact of antitrust policy" on economic growth, employment, and private levels "seems to be incapable of quantitative measurement; it is presumably small and indirect." *An Evaluation of Antitrust Policy: Its Relation to Economic Growth, Full Employment, and Prices,* Study Paper No. 22, Study of Employment, Growth, and Price Levels, Joint Economic Committee (1960), p. 43. See also Donald Dewey, *Monopoly in Economics and Law* (1959), pp. 302-08; and Simon N. Whitney, *Antitrust Policies,* Vol. 2 (1958), p. 392.

[94] Professors Sohmen and Roskamp present an interesting difference of opinion about the influence of competition on the growth of West Germany. Egon Sohmen, "Competition and Growth: The Lesson of West Germany," *American Economic Review,* Vol. 49 (December 1959), p. 986; and Karl W. Roskamp, "Competition and Growth–The Lesson of West Germany: Comment," *ibid.,* Vol. 50 (December 1960), p. 1018.

[95] See also Edwards and Townsend, *op. cit.,* p. 563.

[96] Anglo-American Council on Productivity, *Industrial Engineering* (1954), p. 2.

[97] Anglo-American Council on Productivity, *Management Accounting* (1950), p. 7. See also Anglo-American Council on Productivity, *Steel Founding* (1949).

[98] Gosta Mickwitz, "The Means of Competition at Various Stages of Production and Distribution," *Kyklos,* Vol. 11 (1958), p. 509.

[99] See (British) Monopolies and Restrictive Practices Commission, *Report on the Supply and Export of Certain Semi-Manufactures of Copper and Copper-based Alloys* (1955), par. 287.

[100] Edward S. Mason, "Price Policies and Full Employment," in Carl J. Friedrich and Edward S. Mason, eds., *Public Policy* (1940), pp. 25, 48-49.

[101] See J. M. Clark, *Competition as a Dynamic Process* (1961).

[102] See, for example, Charles L. Schultze, *Recent Inflation in the United States,* Study Paper No. 1, Study of Employment, Growth, and Price Levels, Joint Economic Committee (September 1959); and Ruth P. Mack, "Inflation and Quasi-Elective Changes in Costs," *Review of Economics and Statistics* (1959), p. 225.

[103] This relationship was an important influence on a team that was sent to the U.S. to study industrial accounting methods. Anglo-American Council on Productivity, *Management Accounting* (1950).

[104] See Edwards and Townsend, *op. cit.,* p. 181.

[105] See, for example, R. L. Hall and C. J. Hitch, "Price Theory and Business Behavior," *Oxford Economic Papers,* No. 2 (1939), and Fritz Machlup's criticism of this paper in "Marginal Analysis and Empirical Research," *American Economic Review,* Vol. 36 (1946), p. 519. See also Joe S. Bain, "Price and Production Policies," in Howard S. Ellis, ed., *A Survey of Contemporary Economics* (1948), p. 129.

[106] Friedrich A. Hayek, *Individualism and Economic Order* (1948), p. 105.

[107] See J. M. Clark, *Competition as a Dynamic Process,* pp. 134-40, and his *The Economics of Overhead Costs* (1923), a pioneering analysis.

[108] See Charles L. Schultze, *Prices, Costs, and Output for the Postwar Period: 1947-1957* (1960) and *Recent Inflation in the United States, op. cit.;* and Ruth P. Mack, "Inflation and Quasi-Elective Changes in Costs," *Review of Economics and Statistics* (August 1959), p. 225.

[109] See Wilson Senay, "The Changing Cost-Volume-Profit Relationship," *N.A.A. Bulletin,* Vol. 40 (September 1958), p. 3.

[110] Some of the intricacies of costs and cost-price relations are reviewed in Richard B. Heflebower, "Full Costs, Cost Changes and Prices," in National Bureau of Economic Research, *Business Concentration and Price Policy* (1955), p. 361.

[111] An interesting discussion of these relationships is contained in Paul W. Mc-

Cracken, "Price-Level Stability for or vs. Growth?", *Michigan Business Review,* Vol. 13 (May 1961), p. 11. See Emmette S. Redford, *Potential Public Policies to Deal with Inflation Caused by Market Power,* Study Paper No. 10, Study of Employment, Growth, and Price Levels, Joint Economic Committee (Dec. 11, 1959), pp. 3, 4; and J. K. Galbraith, "Monopoly and the Concentration of Economic Power," in Howard S. Ellis, ed., *A Survey of Contemporary Economics* (1948), pp. 99, 109-15.

[112] Jesse Markham suggests that there is a welfare need for a "stable general price level and flexible individual commodity and service prices." "The Methodology and Policy Implications of Price Flexibility," Address delivered at the meeting of the Group of Experts on Restrictive Business Practices, May 27-29, 1959 (mimeo.), p. 12.

[113] See, for example, William Fellner and Others, *The Problem of Rising Prices* (1961), Chap. 6, "The Role of Monopolistic Pricing," pp. 69-72. See also *Staff Report on Employment, Growth, and Price Levels,* Prepared for consideration by the Joint Economic Committee, 86 Cong. 1 sess. (1959), Chap. 10. Edward S. Mason feels that it would be impossible to bring about a competitive adjustment of prices to changes in cyclical conditions through antitrust. Indeed, he feels that such a result would be "dubiously desirable." "Competition, Price and Policy and High-Level Stability," in U.S. Chamber of Commerce, *Economic Institute on Pricing Problems and the Stabilization of Prosperity* (1947), p. 29. Fritz Machlup made an interesting point in his testimony before the Joint Economic Committee. He reported that Minister Erhardt of Germany had told him that a substantial reduction in German tariffs helped to take the drive out of a "big wage push." *Employment, Growth, and Price Levels,* Hearings, (1959), Pt. 9A, p. 2857. See also testimony of Walter W. Heller in *January 1961 Economic Report of the President and the Economic Situation and Outlook,* Hearings before the Joint Economic Committee, 87 Cong. 1 sess. (1961), p. 305; and J. M. Clark, *The Wage-Price Problem* (1960), p. 53.

[114] See testimony of J. K. Galbraith, *Administered Prices,* Hearings before the Senate Judiciary Committee, 86 Cong. 1 sess. (1959), Pt. 10, pp. 4929, 4930.

[115] For an interesting debate regarding the influence of price flexibility on full employment see Don Patinkin, "Price Flexibility and Full Employment," *American Economic Review,* Vol. 38 (September 1948), p. 543; and Thomas C. Schelling, "The Dynamics of Price Flexibility," *American Economic Review,* Vol. 39 (September 1949), p. 911. Patinkin is impressed with the possibility that when prices fall, expectations of future decline will lead consumers to postpone purchases while producers liquidate inventories and postpone investment.

[116] Markham feels that "rigid prices and rigid margins which persist over long periods of time are *prima facie* evidence that competition is being restrained." "The Methodology and Policy Implications of Price Flexibility," *op. cit.*

[117] Gardiner C. Means, *Industrial Prices and Their Relative Inflexibility,* S. Doc. 13, 74 Cong. 1 sess. (1935).

[118] For a review of the literature about price flexibility, see Richard Ruggles, "The Nature of Price Flexibility and the Determinants of Relative Price Changes in the Economy," in National Bureau of Economic Research, *Business Concentration and Price Policy* (1955), p. 441.

[119] For his latest analysis see Gardiner C. Means, *Administrative Inflation and Public Policy* (1959).

[120] On the other hand, Alfred C. Neal suggests that "if prices were perfectly flexible, large changes would result from small causes. A small increase in the effective supply of money (MV) could start a one-way movement of prices which sweeps like wildfire through the economy." "Pricing Aspects of Business Cycle

History," in U.S. Chamber of Commerce, *Economic Institute on Pricing Problems and the Stabilization of Prosperity* (1947), pp. 32, 36-37. Edward S. Mason seems to agree with Neal. However, he points out that economic thought is divided on this point. "Competition, Price Policy and High-Level Stability," *ibid.*, pp. 19, 27.

[121] However, see testimony of Gardiner C. Means in *Administered Prices*, Hearings before Senate Judiciary Committee, 85 Cong. 1 sess. (1957), Pt. 1, p. 85.

[122] For example, Alfred C. Neal, *Industrial Concentration and Price Inflexibility* (1942), and his article "Pricing Aspects of Business Cycle History," *op. cit.*, p. 32.

[123] M. A. Adelman, "What is 'Administered Pricing' "?, *The Conference Recorder* (1958), p. 19.

[124] Eugene V. Rostow, "To Whom and For What Ends is Corporate Management Responsible?", in Edward S. Mason, ed., *The Corporation in Modern Society* (1960), pp. 46, 66. See also Eugene V. Rostow, "British and American Experience with Legislation Against Restraints of Competition," *Modern Law Review*, Vol. 23 (September 1960), p. 447.

[125] For example, Paul W. McCracken, "Price-Level Stability for or vs. Growth?" *Michigan Business Review*, Vol. 13 (May 1961), p. 11.

[126] Milton Friedman argues that union power is not a significant factor in inflationary developments. His article appears in David McCord Wright, ed., *The Impact of the Union* (1951). See also Philip Bradley, ed., *The Public Stake in Union Power* (1959). In a recent study, Harold M. Levinson concluded that "there was no generally applicable relationship between union strength and wage increases in various industries." *Postwar Movement of Prices and Wages in Manufacturing Industries*, Study Paper No. 21, Joint Economic Committee, 86 Cong. 2 sess. (1960), p. 21. For a strong argument supporting the "cost-push" see H. G. Moulton, *Can Inflation Be Controlled?* (1958).

[127] See Committee for Economic Development, *The Public Interest in National Labor Policy* (1961). The general tenor of this report is that the problem "deserves careful consideration." However, it is only one of a number of possible causes. Among those considered are changes in the money supply and business monopoly. (Pp. 113-15.)

[128] It might be noted, parenthetically, that this line of reasoning negates or ignores theories about the beneficent effects of countervailing power between big unions and big industry. In fact it implies that while concentrated power on one side begets similar power on the other, it is most likely that the two will join forces and collect whatever the traffic will bear. See J. K. Galbraith, *American Capitalism and the Concept of Countervailing Power* (1952) and Emmette S. Redford, *Potential Public Policies to Deal With Inflation Caused by Market Power*, Study Paper No. 10, Study of Employment, Growth, and Price Levels, Joint Economic Committee (Dec. 11, 1959), p. 5.

[129] Some doubts are cast on this assumption in William G. Bowen, *Wage Behavior in the Postwar Period: An Empirical Analysis* (1960), pp. 95-96.

[130] For an endorsement of voluntary programs see testimony of Walter W. Heller, *January 1961 Economic Report of the President and the Economic Situation and Outlook*, Hearings before the Joint Economic Committee, 87 Cong. 1 sess. (1961), p. 306. Richard B. Heflebower sees the "jawbone" method of regulation as the first stage of "a gradual drift toward more direct regulation. . . ." "Book Commentary, Antitrust Policy," *Northwestern University Law Review*, Vol. 56 (1961), pp. 315, 331.

[131] A related proposal has been to require large corporations in concentrated industries to file advance public notice of price increases. See Louis B. Schwartz, "Institutional Size and Individual Liberty: Authoritarian Aspects of Bigness," *Northwestern University Law Review*, Vol. 55 (March-April 1960), pp. 4, 22-23,

and Arthur J. Goldberg, "The Role of the Labor Union in an Age of Bigness," *ibid.*, pp. 54, 58.

[132] A useful account of the controversy may be found in *Business Week*, Sept. 30, 1961, p. 84. The article contains a review of attitudes of a number of economists on each side.

[133] As Edward S. Mason has pointed out, "many proposals for public action designed to promote economic stability and re-employment are apt to assume price behavior as given. In part this minimizing of price problems is probably the result of the very great difficulty of distinguishing between price behavior which promotes and that which retards recovery and full employment. . . ." "Price Policies and Full Employment," in Carl J. Friedrich and Edward S. Mason, eds., *Public Policy* (1940), pp. 25, 27.

[134] See Alfred C. Neal's contention that perfect price flexibility would accentuate the inflationary influences of an increase in the money supply. "Pricing Aspects of Business Cycle History," in *Economic Institute on Pricing Problems and the Stabilization of Prosperity* (1947), pp. 32, 36-37.

[135] Indeed, there is a need to clarify what we mean by inflation, itself. See Fritz Machlup, "Another View of Cost-Push and Demand-Pull Inflation," *Review of Economics and Statistics*, Vol. 42 (May 1960), p. 125.

[136] See "Competition and Prices," *The Statist*, Aug. 15, 1959, p. 76; and Clark, *The Wage-Price Problem*, p. 48.

[137] "It may be observed that excessive wage increases are more likely to spread in oligopolistic industries than in industries where price competition is intense. . . ." William Fellner and Others, *The Problem of Rising Prices* (1961), p. 51.

[138] See Fellner, *ibid.*, p. 70, for argument that there "cannot be a profit-price spiral" which is comparable to a "wage-price spiral." The thesis presented is that higher profits will have a dampening effect on sales because of the higher prices; on the other hand, higher wages will increase consumer incomes.

[139] Eugene V. Rostow feels that a "competitive economy" would be more responsive to governmental measures than a "monopolistic one." "The New Sherman Act: A Positive Instrument of Progress," *University of Chicago Law Review*, Vol. 14 (1947), pp. 567, 569. Henry Simons held that "no amount of monetary stabilization or stimulation can make an economy function better or tolerably as it becomes increasingly monopolized and syndicalized." "Economic Stability and Antitrust Policy," *University of Chicago Law Review*, Vol. 2 (1944), pp. 338, 345.

[140] Mason, "Price Policies and Full Employment," in *Public Policy*, pp. 25, 27. See also Gardiner C. Means, *Administrative Inflation and Public Policy* (1959), esp. pp. 37-42; and Bowen, *op. cit.*, pp. 338, 345.

[141] See testimony of William J. Fellner, *Employment, Growth, and Price Levels*, Hearings before the Joint Economic Committee, 86 Cong. 1 sess. (1959), Pt. 7, pp. 2333, 2334.

[142] See Sir Robert Hall, "Britain's Economic Problem," Pt. 2, *The Economist*, Vol. 200 (Sept. 23, 1961), p. 1132.

[143] See George W. Stocking, *Workable Competition and Antitrust Policy* (1961), p. 5.

[144] See *The Definition of "Small Business" Within the Meaning of the Small Business Act of 1953 as Amended*, Interim Report of Subcommittee No. 2 on Government Procurement, Disposal and Loan Activities to the House Select Committee on Small Business, 85 Cong. 2 sess. (Jan. 3, 1959).

[145] See *Antitrust and Monopoly*, Report of the Senate Judiciary Committee, Antitrust Subcommittee, 86 Cong. 1 sess. (1960), p. 18.

[146] Edward S. Mason, *Economic Concentration and the Monopoly Problem* (1957), p. 196.

[147] See Arthur Goldberg, "Labor and Antitrust," *Industrial Union Department Digest,* Vol. 3 (1958), p. 61.

[148] Fellner and Others, *The Problem of Rising Prices,* p. 57.

[149] Milton C. Denbo, a lawyer, argues that the antitrust exemption of labor unions is "unconscionable." "Labor Exemption—An Anti View," *Federal Bar Journal,* Vol. 20 (Winter 1960), p. 30.

[150] Edward H. Chamberlin, "Labor Union Power and the Public Interest," in Philip D. Bradley, ed., *The Public Stake in Union Power* (1959), pp. 3, 10. See also Edward H. Chamberlin, "Can Union Power be Curbed?", *Atlantic Monthly* (June 1959), pp. 46, 48.

[151] Chamberlin, "Labor Union Power and the Public Interest," *op. cit.,* p. 18.

[152] For example, the by-laws of the Bakery and Confectionery Workers' Union provide that workers will be withdrawn from companies which engage in "unfair or unwarranted competition." See Corwin D. Edwards, *Maintaining Competition* (1949), p. 91. Other practices along these lines were involved in *U.S.* v. *Brims,* 272 U.S. 549 (1926); *U.S.* v. *United Brotherhood of Carpenters,* 313 U.S. 539 (1941); *U.S.* v. *Employing Plasterers',* 347 U.S. 186 (1954).

[153] James W. McKie, "Collective Bargaining and the Maintenance of Market Competition," in Philip D. Bradley, ed., *The Public Stake in Union Power* (1959), p. 88.

[154] See, for example, *Allen Bradley Co.* v. *Local No. 3,* 325 U.S. 727 (1945). See also Theodore J. Kreps, *An Evaluation of Antitrust Policy: Its Relation to Economic Growth, Full Employment, and Prices,* Study Paper No. 22, Study of Employment, Growth, and Price Levels, Joint Economic Committee, 86 Cong. 2 sess. (1960), pp. 33-34; Committee for Economic Development, *The Public Interest in National Labor Policy* (1961), p. 143; *U.S.* v. *Milk Drivers & Dairy Employees Union, Local No. 471,* 153 F. Supp. 803 (D.C. Minn. 1957); and *U.S.* v. *Hamilton Glass Co.,* 155 F. Supp. 878 (N.D. Ill. 1957).

[155] See *Staff Report on Employment, Growth, and Price Levels,* Prepared for consideration by the Joint Economic Committee, 86 Cong. 1 sess. (1959), p. 437; and Clark, *The Wage Price Problem,* p. 55.

[156] See discussion of national wage policies in Fellner and Others, *The Problem of Rising Prices.* A statement in favor is contained on pp. 56-57. An argument against such policies is presented on pp. 63-64. See *1960 Joint Economic Report,* Report of the Joint Economic Committee. "The Federal Government could . . . bring together in an annual labor-management conference the leaders of both of these groups so that they could be given the general economic outlook and informed of the relation of their actions to the national economic welfare." (P. 19). See also Mark W. Leiserson, *A Brief Interpretive Survey of Wage-Price Problems in Europe,* Study Paper No. 11, Study of Employment, Growth and Price Levels, Joint Economic Committee, 86 Cong. 1 sess. (1959). See also testimony of J. K. Galbraith in *Administered Prices,* Hearings before the Senate Judiciary Committee, 86 Cong. 1 sess. (1959), p. 4932; and Joseph W. Garbarino, "Wage Escalation and Wage Inflation," in American Statistical Association, *1959 Proceedings of the Business and Economic Statistics Section.* An independent study group financed by the Committee for Economic Development opposes the proposal of the Fellner committee report in a section which reviews this and several other suggestions. Committee for Economic Development, *op. cit.,* pp. 112-22. See esp. p. 117.

[157] See "Competition and Prices," *The Statist,* Aug. 15, 1959, p. 76.

[158] The Council on Prices, Productivity and Incomes appointed by the Government of the United Kingdom warned that national announcements of suggested standards for wage increases would become minimum increases. *First Report* (1958). See *Staff Report on Employment, Growth, and Price Levels,* Prepared for

consideration by the Joint Economic Committee, 86 Cong. 1 sess. (1959). It is suggested that an annual conference be held; however, the report does not exhibit any faith in moral suasion, pp. xxxvii, 434-37.

[159] An excellent review of experience in various countries is contained in William Fellner and Others, *The Problem of Rising Prices* (1961), pp. 60-62, together with a useful summary of "Wage Determination in Selected Countries," pp. 281-488.

[160] It has been suggested that such policies be tied up with recommendations from a fact-finding board of inquiry appointed by the President. See, for example, discussion in *Employment Growth, and Price Levels,* Hearings before the Joint Economic Committee, 86 Cong. 1 sess. (1959), Pt. 7, pp. 2852-53.

[161] Emmette S. Redford discusses the problems of administration and standards in *Potential Public Policies to Deal with Inflation Caused by Market Power,* Study Paper No. 10, Study of Employment, Growth, and Price Levels, Joint Economic Committee, 86 Cong. 1 sess. (Dec. 11, 1959). See also Committee for Economic Development, *loc. cit.*

[162] Edward S. Mason, *Economic Concentration and the Monopoly Problem* (1957), Chap. 10, p. 196. See also Arthur J. Goldberg, "The Role of the Labor Union in an Age of Bigness," *Northwestern University Law Review,* Vol. 55 (March-April 1960), pp. 54, 58. Mr. Goldberg advocates the development of "a better way quickly of asserting the public interest" in union-management conflicts in "big" industries. (P. 58.) However, he makes no affirmative suggestions. He does object to suggestions that corporations file advance notice of price increases.

[163] See T. W. Schultz, *Agriculture in an Unstable Economy* (1945), and W. H. Nicholls, *Imperfect Competition Within Agricultural Industries* (1941).

[164] For a fairly comprehensive review of one aspect of this problem see Joseph J. Saunders, "The Status of Agricultural Cooperatives Under the Antitrust Laws," *Federal Bar Journal,* Vol. 20 (Winter 1960), p. 35.

[165] Theodore J. Kreps feels that "in the businesses which buy, process, and distribute agricultural products there has been undiminished concentration of economic control." Kreps, *op. cit,* p. 39.

[166] See Frank Robotka "Capper-Volstead and the Cooperatives," *Journal of Farm Economics,* Vol. 41 (1959), p. 1213; and Edwin G. Nourse, *The Legal Status of Agricultural Cooperation* (1928).

[167] A leading agricultural economist feels that "in most lines the competitiveness of agriculture has not been reduced, except for short periods and then only to a moderate extent." M. R. Benedict, "Attempts to Restrict Competition in Agriculture: The Government Programs," *American Economic Review,* Supplement, Vol. 44 (1954), pp. 93, 106. The article contains an excellent summary of developments starting with the 1920's. To somewhat the same effect, see D. Gale Johnson, "Competition in Agriculture: Fact or Fiction," *ibid.,* p. 107.

[168] See Ramsay Wood, "Public Policies Affecting Small Business," *Financing Small Business,* Report to the Committees on Banking and Currency and the Select Committees on Small Business by the Federal Reserve System, 85 Cong. 2 sess. (1958), Pts. 1 and 2, p. 306.

[169] Judge Hand said that the motivation behind the Sherman Act was broader than the economic objectives. "It is possible, because of its indirect social or moral effect, to prefer a system of small producers, each dependent for his success upon his own skill and character, to one in which the great mass of those engaged must accept the direction of a few." *U.S.* v. *Aluminum Co. of America,* 148 F. 2d 416, 427 (C.C.A.-2d 1945).

[170] See statement by Senator Sherman in the 1890 debates. *Congressional Record,* Vol. 21 (51 Cong. 1 sess.), pp. 2457, 2460, and 2598.

[171] For a discussion of state efforts in this direction see Reinhold P. Wolff, "Monopolistic Competition in Distribution," *Law and Contemporary Problems,* Vol. 8 (Spring 1941), p. 303.

[172] Eugene D. Bennett argues that we can maintain our "mythological preference for the small, independent person" because of the high level of our economy. He contrasts this with the European point of view. "Comparison of United States and Foreign Antitrust Laws," *Section of International and Comparative Law Bulletin,* Vol. 3 (1958), pp. 14, 21.

[173] *U.S.* v. *Aluminum Co. of America,* 148 F. 2d 416, 430 (1945). See also *U.S.* v. *Morgan,* 118 F. Supp. 621, 737 (S.D.N.Y. 1953); and Herbert Pope, "The Legal Aspect of Monopoly," *Harvard Law Review,* Vol. 20 (1907), p. 167.

[174] B. Fog cites several large companies that refrain from aggressive policies which might drive small competitors out of the market because of a fear of monopoly attacks and government control. *Industrial Pricing Policies* (1960), pp. 149, 151. See Sumner H. Slichter, "A Defense of Bigness in Business," in American Management Association, *Legal, Financial, and Tax Aspects of Mergers and Acquisitions* (1957); and Calvin B. Hoover, "The Relevance of the Competitive, Laissez-Faire Economic Model to Modern Capitalistic National Economies," *Kyklos,* Vol. 8 (1955), p. 40.

[175] Blackwell Smith, "Effective Competition: Hypothesis for Modernizing the Antitrust Laws," *New York University Law Review,* Vol. 26 (July 1951), p. 405.

[176] See Federal Trade Commission, *The Merger Movement, A Summary Report* (1948). The report refers to increased concentration after prosecution for price-fixing in the cement, salt, white lead, and book paper industries. (Pp. 8-14.)

[177] *U.S.* v. *Addyston Pipe and Steel Co.,* 85 F. 271 (C.C.A.-6th 1898), aff'd 175 U.S. 211 (1899). Wendell Berge, "Problems of Enforcement and Interpretation of the Sherman Act," *American Economic Review,* Vol. 38 (1948), pp. 172, 174. The same point has been made about the railroads in Almarin Phillips, "A Critique of United States Price-Fixing Agreements and the Per Se Rule," *Journal of Industrial Economics,* Vol. 8 (October 1959), pp. 13, 15.

[178] John Heath, *Not Enough Competition?,* Institute of Economic Affairs, Hobart Paper II (London, 1961), p. 32.

[179] See Friedrich Kessler and Richard H. Stern, "Competition, Contract, and Vertical Integration," *Yale Law Journal,* Vol. 69 (November 1959), p. 1; and Justice Douglas' dissent in *Standard Oil Co.* v. *U.S.,* 337 U.S. 293, 318 (1949).

[180] For a discussion of vertical integration to avoid the effects of a monopolistic situation see R. S. Edwards and H. Townsend, *Business Enterprise* (1958), p. 205.

[181] See Edward H. Chamberlin, "Labor Union Power and the Public Interest," in Philip D. Bradley, ed., *The Public Stake in Union Power* (1959), pp. 3, 18.

[182] See, for example, the discussion of U.S. sugar policy in *Staff Papers Presented to the Commission on Foreign Economic Policy* (1954), p. 207. See also *Subsidy and Subsidylike Programs of the U.S. Government,* Materials prepared for the Joint Economic Committee, 86 Cong. 2 sess. (1960), pp. 35-36.

[183] See, for example, Senate Judiciary Committee, Subcommittee on Antitrust and Monopoly, *Petroleum, the Antitrust Laws and Government Policies,* 85 Cong. 1 sess. (1957). See also *United States* v. *Economic Concentration and Monopoly,* Staff Report to the Monopoly Subcommittee of the House Committee on Small Business, 79 Cong. 2 sess. (1946), pp. 93-95. The report lists fourteen cartels which magnified the effects of industrial concentration.

[184] See Kingman Brewster, Jr., "Extraterritorial Effects of the U.S. Antitrust Laws: 'An Appraisal,'" *Proceedings,* Section of Antitrust Law, American Bar Association, New York and London, July 13 and 25, 1957, p. 65, and his *Antitrust and American Business Abroad* (1958); Victor R. Hansen, "Extraterritorial Effects of the

U.S. Antitrust Laws: 'The Enforcement of the United States Antitrust Laws by the Department of Justice to Protect Freedom of United States Foreign Trade,'" *Proceedings,* Section of Antitrust Law, American Bar Association, New York and London, July 13 and 25, 1957, p. 75.

[185] For discussions of international cooperation in antitrust see Sigmund Timberg, "The Case for an International Agreement," *Cartel* (January 1956), p. 2; Eugene D. Bennett, "Comparison of United States and Foreign Antitrust Laws," *Section of International and Comparative Law Bulletin,* Vol. 3 (1958), pp. 14, 21, 22.

[186] See Edward H. Chamberlin, ed., *Monopoly and Competition and Their Regulation* (1954); European Productivity Agency, *Guide to Legislation on Restrictive Business Practices* (1960); and Kingman Brewster, Jr., *Antitrust and American Business Abroad* (1958), Chap. 3. See also a provocative series of discussions in *Proceedings, International Conference on Control of Restrictive Business Practices,* University of Chicago (1960).

[187] See, for example, J. M. Jeanneney, "Nationalization in France," in Edward H. Chamberlin, ed., *Monopoly and Competition and Their Regulation* (1954), p. 471.

[188] See, for example, F. Vito, "Monopoly and Competition in Italy," in *ibid.,* p. 43.

[189] See C. D. Edwards, T. J. Kreps, B. W. Lewis, F. Machlup, and R. P. Terrill, *A Cartel Policy for the United Nations* (1945).

[190] "Buy American" Act of 1933, 410 S.C. 10. See Sec. (13) of Appendix VI of *Staff Papers Presented to the Commission on Foreign Economic Policy* (1954), pp. 315-20; and *Subsidy and Subsidylike Programs of the U.S. Government, op. cit.,* p. 47.

[191] Edwards, Kreps, Lewis, Machlup, and Terrill, *op. cit.,* p. 100.

[192] Søren Gammelgaard, *Resale Price Maintenance,* European Productivity Agency (1958).

[193] A plea for further efforts to control cartels and a review of past efforts may be found in J. J. Lador Lederer, "Prospect and Retrospect," *Cartel,* Vol. 11 (1961), p. 42. For a discussion of treaty provisions designed to curtail the effect of restrictive business practices see James T. Haight, "The Restrictive Business Practices Clause in United States Treaties: An Antitrust Tranquilizer for International Trade," *Yale Law Journal,* Vol. 70 (December 1960), p. 240.

[194] See Allen C. Phelps, "Export and the Webb-Pomerene Act," *Business Practices Under Federal Antitrust Laws,* Proceedings of the Third Annual Meeting of the New York State Bar Association, Section on Antitrust Law (Jan. 24, 1951), p. 178.

[195] See O. D. K. Norbye, *Mission Report on Restrictive Business Practices in the United States,* European Productivity Agency (1959), pp. 21, 22.

[196] See discussion of international commodity agreements in Edward S. Mason, *Economic Concentration and the Monopoly Problem* (1957), pp. 85-89.

[197] Our experience with the wheat, sugar, wool, and cotton agreements are covered in Committee for Economic Development, *The Public Interest in National Labor Policy* (1961), pp. 201-12. See also Edward S. Mason, *Controlling World Trade* (1946), pp. 252-65.

[198] See Senate Judiciary Committee, Antitrust Subcommittee, *Foreign Trade Conferences,* Staff Memorandum, 84 Cong. 1 sess. (1955), esp. p. 10; William Dwight Whitney, "International Trade," *Business Practices Under Federal Antitrust Laws,* Proceedings of the Third Annual Meeting of the New York State Bar Association, Section on Antitrust Law (Jan. 24, 1951), p. 171. James T. Haight discusses cooperation between antitrust and foreign commerce agencies regarding antitrust prosecution. *Loc. cit.*

[199] *U.S.* v. *Imperial Chemical Industries, Ltd.,* 105 F. Supp. 215 (S.D.N.Y. 1952).

[200] *Timken Roller Bearing Co.* v. *U.S.*, 83 F. Supp. 284 (N.D. Ohio 1949), modified 341 U.S. 593 (1951).

[201] See Kingman Brewster, Jr., *Law and United States Business in Canada* (1960), pp. 16-22. A Canadian point of view may be found in Davie E. Fulton, *CCH Antitrust Law Symposium* (1959), p. 39.

[202] Notes and Comments, "Extraterritorial Application of the Antitrust Laws: A Conflict of Laws Approach," *Yale Law Journal*, Vol. 70 (December 1960), p. 259. This article presents a fairly comprehensive review of foreign reactions against the consequences of some U.S. proceedings, and of the decrees which order performance of acts abroad.

[203] See H. Thomas Austern, "Aberrant Antitrust," *Proceedings*, Section of Antitrust Law, American Bar Association (August 1958), and "Report of the Special Committee on the Antitrust Aspects of the Atomic Energy Program," *ibid.*, p. 158.

[204] The relationship between national defense and competition is a key factor in *Petroleum, the Antitrust Laws and Government Policies*, Report of the Subcommittee on Antitrust and Monopoly to the Senate Judiciary Committee, 85 Cong. 1 sess. (1957).

[205] This problem entered into judicial consideration in *U.S.* v. *Aluminum Co. of America*, 91 F. Supp. 333, 347 (S.D.N.Y. 1950).

[206] W. H. Ferry denies that we ever had such a policy in the United States. *The Corporation and the Economy* (1959), p. 12.

[207] For example, Emmette S. Redford points out, in his discussion of inflation, that "Public policy encompasses many objectives which may conflict with that of preventing inflation, including such objectives as national security, conservation of resources, and support of the purchasing power of various groups." *Potential Public Policies to Deal With Inflation Caused by Market Power*, Study Paper No. 10, Study of Employment, Growth, and Price Levels, Joint Economic Committee 86 Cong. 1 sess. (Dec. 11, 1959), p. 8.

[208] "The economist can tell the policy maker how best to get wherever he wants to go." Clair Wilcox, "From Economic Theory to Public Policy," *American Economic Review*, Supplement, Vol. 50 (May 1960), p. 27.

## *Chapter 3*

[1] See testimony of Fritz Machlup, *Administered Prices*, Hearings before the Senate Judiciary Committee, 86 Cong. 1 sess. (1959), Pt. 10, pp. 4955, 4956.

[2] 15 U.S.C. 68.

[3] Walter Adams and Leonard Gray conclude that the federal government "has by a process of functional perversion become one of the principal bulwarks of concentration and monopoly." *Monopoly in America* (1955), p. 145.

[4] "I regard the law of regulated industries as one of the most urgent fields of research and reform in the whole of our law dealing with economic affairs. The present role of the state and federal regulatory agencies controlling railroads, utilities, and the transportation and communications industries raises fundamental questions both of substance and of procedure. The statutes which they seek to enforce are usually out of date, often confused, ill-drawn, and needlessly complex. Many of their rules echo forgotten battles, and guard against dangers which no longer exist. They comprise vast codes, understood only by a jealous priesthood which protects these swamps and thickets from all prying eyes. In the main, the

agencies follow routines established for the control of local gas companies and street railways. The relevance of the model is not immediately apparent, in dealing with progressive and expanding industries like air transport or trucking." Eugene V. Rostow, *Planning for Freedom* (1959), pp. 311-12.

[5] "Students . . . have expressed the belief that a specialized independent agency, insulated from national political climate, whose function is the day-to-day supervision of a particular segment of the Nation's industry, inevitably tends to become imbued with and to express the special viewpoint of the regulated industry, to the possible exclusion or undue subordination of the overriding public interest." *Judicial Doctrine of Primary Jurisdiction as Applied in Antitrust Suits,* Staff Report to the House Judiciary Committee, 84 Cong. 2 sess. (1956), p. 2. See also Lucile Sheppard Keyes, "The Protective Functions of Commission Regulation," *American Economic Review,* Supplement, Vol. 48 (1958), p. 544; Carl Fulda, "Antitrust Considerations in Motor Carrier Mergers," *Michigan Law Review,* Vol. 56 (1938), p. 1237; and Louis B. Schwartz, "Legal Restriction of Competition in the Regulated Industries: An Abdication of Judicial Responsibility," *Harvard Law Review,* Vol. 67 (1954), p. 436.

[6] See testimony of Walter Adams, *Administered Prices,* Hearings (1959), Pt. 9, pp. 4785, 4786, 4791; *Report of the Attorney General's National Committee to Study the Antitrust Laws* (1955), pp. 265, 269.

[7] Walter Adams, "The Regulatory Commissions and Small Business," *Law and Contemporary Problems,* Vol. 24 (Winter 1959), pp. 147, 151. In *American Export Airlines, Inc.—Certificate of Public Convenience and Necessity* (1940), the Civil Aeronautics Board said that "competition in air transportation is not mandatory, especially when considered in relation to any particular route or service." Cited in *The Airlines Industry,* Report of the House Judiciary Committee, 85 Cong. 2 sess. (1958), p. 68. A contrary view about the importance of competition is set forth in the board's report, *The Role of Competition in Commercial Air Transportation,* Report submitted to the Senate Small Business Committee, Subcommittee on Monopoly, 82 Cong. 2 sess. (1952).

[8] See *The Airlines Industry,* esp. pp. 110-13.

[9] See discussion of these arguments in Everette MacIntyre, "The Role of the Robinson-Patman Act in the Antitrust Scheme of Things—The Perspective of Congress," *Proceedings,* Section of Antitrust Law, American Bar Association (August 1960), p. 325, esp. footnote 28, p. 336.

[10] See Frederick M. Rowe, "Expectation Versus Accomplishment Under the Robinson-Patman Act, 1936-1960: A Statement of the Issues," *ibid.,* p. 298, esp. p. 304; and Corwin D. Edwards, *The Price Discrimination Law* (1959), p. 151.

[11] See Marcus A. Hollabaugh, "What is New on Capitol Hill," *Proceedings,* Section of Antitrust Law, American Bar Association (August 1960), p. 260, for discussion of several proposed amendments. See also H.R. 10922, 86 Cong. 2 sess. (providing for one-price policy to all competitors); H.R. 2868 and H.R. 4530, 86 Cong. 1 sess. (providing limits on the right to meet a competitor's price). See discussion of S. 11, 84 Cong., in Edwards, *op. cit.,* pp. 571-80.

[12] H.R. 1253 (Harris Bill). Pressures for resale price controls are described in Notes and Comments, "The Enforcement of Resale Price Maintenance," *Yale Law Journal,* Vol. 69 (November 1959), p. 168.

[13] See *Functional Discounts,* Hearings before the House Judiciary Committee, Antitrust Subcommittee, on H.R. 848, H.R. 927, H.R. 2788, H.R. 2868, and H.R. 4530 (June 1959). See also "Recommendation Against a Mandatory Functional Discount Amendment to the Robinson-Patman Act," *Proceedings,* Section of Antitrust Law, American Bar Association (April 1959), p. 90.

[14] 15 U.S.C. 1-7.

[15] 15 U.S.C. 8-11.

[16] Public Law 85-909 (1958). The McGuire Act was passed as an amendment to the Federal Trade Commission Act, but it amends all antitrust law.

[17] Public Law 75-314 (1937).

[18] It should be noted the resale price control still involves dangers. J. Lee Rankin, "The *Parke, Davis* Case," *Sales and Pricing Policies Under the Antitrust Laws,* Trade Regulation Reports (1961), p. 63. See Joro Hertwig, "Price Discrimination Deceives Consumers," *Cartel,* Vol. 10 (October 1960), p. 127, for discussion of German experience.

[19] 29 U.S.C. 105.

[20] 15 U.S.C. 12.

[21] Public Law 74-692 (1936).

[22] This provision, Sec. 7, was amended in 1950 by the Celler-Kefauver Act. For a history of the prior provision see David D. Martin, *Mergers and the Clayton Act* (1960).

[23] 15 U.S.C. 41. Technically, the F.T.C. Act is not described as an antitrust law in the statutes. The major significance of this distinction relates to the right of injured parties to sue for treble damages under the Clayton Act.

[24] Public Law 75-447 (1938).

[25] For a general description of the application of Sec. 5 see Edward F. Howrey, "Utilization by the F.T.C. of Section 5 of the Federal Trade Commission Act as an Antitrust Law," *Antitrust Bulletin,* Vol. 5 (March-April 1960), p. 161.

[26] The Packers and Stockyards Act of 1921 makes it unlawful for packers to: engage in unjust discrimination or deceptive practices; apportion supplies between packers if it tends to restrain commerce or create a monopoly; manipulate or control prices; create a monopoly; and conspire to apportion territories, purchases, or sales, or to control prices. Additionally, discriminatory rates for stockyard services are unlawful. (7 U.S.C. 181.) The Department of Agriculture recently issued orders against arrangements not to compete. Swift & Co., P. & S. Docket 2358, Nov. 21, 1961, *CCH Trade Regulation Reports,* Par. 50,111; Heath and Holley, P. & S. Docket 2612, Dec. 8, 1961, *CCH Trade Regulation Reports,* Par. 50,112.

[27] The Federal Alcohol Administration Act of 1935 makes it unlawful for a producer, importer, or wholesaler of alcoholic beverages to enter into exclusive dealing contracts in interstate or foreign commerce, or to accomplish the same result through other enumerated practices. It forbids interlocking directors among such companies unless they have been approved by the Secretary of the Treasury through the Bureau of Internal Revenue. (27 U.S.C. 205 and 208.)

[28] The Bank Holding Company Act of 1956 requires prior approval of the Federal Reserve Bank for bank holding companies to merge, to acquire more than 5 per cent of the voting shares of any bank, or to acquire substantially all the assets of any bank. (12 U.S.C. 1841.)

[29] The Federal Deposit Insurance Act was amended in 1960 to provide that no insured bank could merge with or acquire the assets of any other bank without the approval of the Comptroller of the Currency, the Board of Governors of the Federal Reserve System, or the Federal Deposit Insurance Corporation. The selection of the agency depends on the status of the bank. In considering requests for such approval, the agency having jurisdiction must request a report on the competitive factors involved from the Attorney General and from the other two agencies. (12 U.S.C. 1828.) In a recent decision the Comptroller of the Currency said that the issue of the competitive effect of a bank merger is "charged with emotionalism and characterized at the present time by an almost complete lack of clarity and objectivity. . . ." He disapproved of the proposed merger on grounds related to the local community's banking needs. *CCH Trade Regulation Reports,* Par. 50,114.

[30] The Federal Power Act of 1920 provides that all licenses issued by the Federal Power Commission shall be on condition that agreements to limit the output of electrical energy are prohibited. Further, it prohibits all arrangements to limit the output of electrical energy, to restrain trade or to fix prices. (16 U.S.C. 803.)

[31] The Atomic Energy Act of 1954 permits the Atomic Energy Commission to revoke or suspend any license which becomes involved in an antitrust violation. The commission must report to the Attorney General when it has information regarding the use of special nuclear materials or atomic energy which appears to violate the antitrust laws or to restrict free competition. The Attorney General is to notify the commission whether a proposed license would tend to support an antitrust violation. (42 U.S.C. 2011.)

[32] The Tariff Act of 1930 has provisions against "unfair methods of competition and unfair acts in the importation of articles . . . the tendency of which is to destroy or substantially injure an industry, efficiently and economically operated . . . or to restrain or monopolize trade and commerce in the United States." The Revenue Act of 1916 authorizes the President to declare a retaliatory embargo against goods from countries which unfairly prohibit the importation of U.S. products. (15 U.S.C. 71.) The Trade Agreements Extension Act of 1955 has a similar provision. (19 U.S.C. 1351.) The Revenue Act of 1916 also provides against the "dumping" of foreign products in the U.S. The act makes it unlawful to import articles at prices which are substantially less than the prices in the principal markets in the producing country, plus the costs of importing, if there is an intent to injure a domestic industry or to restrain domestic trade. The Unfair Practices in Imports Act of 1930 (19 U.S.C. 1337) has similar provisions.

[33] *Report of the Attorney General's National Committee to Study the Antitrust Laws* (1955), Chap. 6, pp. 261-314.

[34] Norris-La Guardia Act of 1932 (29 U.S.C. 105).

[35] The Webb-Pomerene Act of 1918 permits the organization and operation of export associations which do not restrain domestic commerce or the export trade of a competitor. (15 U.S.C. 61-65.) See *Study of Monopoly Power,* Hearings before the Subcommittee on Study of Monopoly Power, House Judiciary Committee, 81 Cong. 2 sess. (1950), Pt. 3, p. 79 *et seq.*

[36] The Defense Production Act of 1950 exempts voluntary agreements and programs which contribute to national defense from the antitrust laws, when they are approved by the President. (50 U.S.C. App. 2158.)

[37] The Small Business Act of 1958, in effect, authorizes the Small Business Administrator to exempt corporations from the antitrust laws when they are organized by small businesses to obtain materials and equipment and to engage in research. Such exemptions require the approval of the Attorney General. (15 U.S.C. 636.)

[38] The Capper-Volstead Act of 1922 exempts farm marketing cooperatives from the antitrust laws. However, if the Secretary of Agriculture finds that prices are "unduly enhanced," he can order an association to cease monopolizing or restraining trade. (7 U.S.C. 291, 292.) For a review of these exemptions see Joseph J. Saunders, "The Status of Agricultural Cooperatives Under the Antitrust Laws," *Federal Bar Journal,* Vol. 20 (Winter 1960), p. 35.

[39] The Agricultural Marketing Agreement Act of 1938 and the Agricultural Adjustment Act of 1933 permit the Secretary of Agriculture to enter into marketing agreements with producers, processors, and handlers of agricultural products. Such arrangements are exempt from the antitrust laws. (7 U.S.C. 671.)

[40] The Fisherman's Collective Marketing Act of 1934 exempts associations of fishermen from the antitrust laws. However, if the Secretary of the Interior feels

that the actions of any association has "unduly enhanced" prices, he can issue appropriate cease and desist orders. (15 U.S.C. 521, 522.)

[41] The Ship Mortgage Act of 1920 exempts associations of marine insurance companies from the antitrust laws. (46 U.S.C. 885.)

[42] The Mineral Leasing Act of 1920 limits leases on federal mineral lands. However, the Secretary of the Interior can permit lessees of oil and coal lands to combine in order to construct and run refineries and common carriers. (30 U.S.C. 184.)

[43] The McCarran Act of 1945 exempts insurance companies from antitrust laws to the extent that state laws control. (15 U.S.C. 1011-15.) See Joel B. Dirlam and Irwin M. Stelzer, "The Insurance Industry: A Case Study in the Workability of Regulated Competition," *University of Pennsylvania Law Review*, Vol. 107 (1958), p. 199, for a review of the results of state regulation. See also Melvin G. de Chazeau and Alfred E. Kahn, *Integration and Competition in the Petroleum Industry* (1959), esp. p. 559; James B. Donovan, "Insurance—The Case in Favor of Existing Exemptions from the Antitrust Laws," *Federal Bar Journal*, Vol. 20 (Winter 1960), p. 56; Franklin P. Michels, "Insurance—The Case Against Broad Exemptions from the Antitrust Laws," *ibid.*, p. 66. Baddia J. Rashid, "A New Look at the McCarran Act and Its Aftermath," address before the National Association of Independent Insurers, Nov. 15, 1961. Reported in *CCH Trade Regulation Reports*, Par. 50,109.

[44] The State Tobacco Compact Act of 1936 permits interstate compacts controlling the production of tobacco. (7 U.S.C. 515.)

[45] The Interstate Oil Compact Act of 1959 approves interstate oil compacts which limit production. (Public Law 84-185.)

[46] The Connally Act of 1935 prohibits interstate shipments of petroleum and of products which do not comply with state regulations. The President can suspend the operation of the act when he finds that there is an undue burden on interstate commerce. (15 U.S.C. 715.) See testimony of Walter Adams regarding federal cooperation, *Administered Prices*, Hearings before the Senate Judiciary Committee, 86 Cong. 1 sess. (1959), Pt. 9, p. 4791.

[47] *Ibid.*

[48] For a discussion of "primary jurisdiction" and the exemptions see William L. McGovern, "Antitrust Exemptions for Regulated Industries," *Federal Bar Journal*, Vol. 20 (Winter 1960), p. 10. See also House Judiciary Committee, Antitrust Subcommittee, *Judicial Doctrine of Primary Jurisdiction as Applied in Antitrust* (Staff Report 1956), 84 Cong. 2 sess.; and *Proceedings*, Section of Antitrust Law, American Bar Association (August 1958), esp. Carl H. Fulda, "A Critique of the Doctrine of Primary Jurisdiction," p. 68.

[49] *Report of the Attorney General's National Committee to Study the Antitrust Laws* (1955), p. 264.

[50] House Judiciary Committee, Antitrust Subcommittee, *Report on Consent Decree Program of the Department of Justice*, 86 Cong. 1 sess. (1959), p. 300.

[51] The Interstate Commerce Act of 1887 provides antitrust exemptions for transactions relating to pooling and acquisitions of rail carriers when they are approved by the Interstate Commerce Commission. (49 U.S.C. 1 *et seq.*) See Carl Fulda, "Antitrust Considerations in Motor Carrier Mergers," *Michigan Law Review*, Vol. 56 (1938), p. 1237. It also contains provisions against discriminatory rates. See *Great Northern Ry. Co.* v. *Merchants Elevator Co.*, 259 U.S. 285 (1922).

[52] The Reed-Bulwinkle Act of 1948 allows rate agreements between carriers if they are approved by the Interstate Commerce Commission. (49 U.S.C. 5b).

[53] The Shipping Act of 1916 permits agreements which set rates and control competition between water carriers when they are approved by the Federal Mari-

time Board. In the absence of proper approval, the act outlaws certain deferred rebates and discriminatory rates of water carriers. (46 U.S.C. 822). The recent Shipping Bill exempts international shipping conferences from the antitrust laws. It authorizes the Federal Maritime Commission to disapprove any conference rate which is detrimental to U.S. commerce and to permit lower rates to a shipper who agrees to give all or a set proportion of his business to a carrier or a conference of carriers. (Public Law 87-346.)

[54] The Communications Act of 1934 provides antitrust exemptions for mergers and consolidations of domestic telephone and telegraph carriers which are approved by the Federal Communications Commission. (47 U.S.C. 221(a), 222(c)(1).) It also permits interlocking directorates of such carriers if they are approved by the Federal Communications Commission. It reaffirms the application of the antitrust laws to the manufacture and sale of radio apparatus. No one in the radio transmitting and receiving business can acquire an interest in a cable, wire, telegraph, or telephone system if the purpose or effect of the acquisition is to lessen competition substantially or to restrain interstate or foreign commerce. The same rule applies to a carrier of wire communications which acquires an interest in radio. The statute is not clear regarding antitrust violations in the broadcast industry. The Federal Communications Commission cannot exempt or prosecute practices which are forbidden by antitrust laws. It can deny or revoke broadcast licenses. The Attorney General's power to prosecute for such violations is unclear. See *Black River* v. *McNinch*, 101 F. 2d 235 (D.C.Cir. 1938) cert. denied 307 U.S. 623 (1939); "Antitrust Immunity in the Communications Industries," *Virginia Law Review*, Vol. 44 (November 1958), p. 1131; and *Antitrust Consent Decrees and the Television Broadcasting Industry*, Hearings before the House Judiciary Committee, 87 Cong. 1 sess. (1961), Serial No. 6, esp. pp. 15-21. The Federal Communications Commission asked the General Electric Company and the Westinghouse Corporation for information regarding their antitrust violations. This information will be considered in acting on the companies' applications for renewal of broadcasting licenses. The letters were sent on Nov. 1, 1961. *CCH Trade Regulation Reports*, Par. 50,107.

[55] The Federal Aviation Act of 1958 gives the Civil Aeronautics Board the power to grant antitrust exemptions to consolidations and mergers of air carriers, interlocking directorates, and inter-carrier agreements apportioning income, traffic, equipment, or settling rates. (Public Law 85-726.)

[56] See Richard B. Heflebower, "Mergers Between Competing Railroads: A Preliminary View," Address delivered at Conference on Transportation Mergers and Acquisitions, Aug. 29, 1961 (mimeo.), for an argument in favor of further limitations on entry. Interstate Commerce Act, 49 U.S.C. 1 (18) regarding railroads and 49 U.S.C. 306 regarding trucklines.

[57] 16 U.S.C. 803 creating Federal Power Commission.

[58] Communications Act, 47 U.S.C. 151 *et seq.*

[59] *Ibid.* For a discussion of the commission's "pro-competitive" functions see Harvey J. Levin, "Broadcast Regulation and Inter-Medium Competition," *Virginia Law Review*, Vol. 45 (1959), p. 1104.

[60] The Perishable Agricultural Commodities Act of 1930 provides for licenses by the Agricultural Marketing Service for dealers, brokers, and commission merchants who handle fresh and frozen fruits and vegetables. (7 U.S.C. 499.)

[61] The Atomic Energy Act of 1954 provides for licenses by the Atomic Energy Commission. See H. Thomas Austern, "Aberrant Antitrust," *Proceedings*, Section of Antitrust Law, American Bar Association (August 1958), p. 99. See also "Report of the Special Committee on Antitrust Aspects of Atomic Energy Program," *ibid.*, p. 158.

[62] Public Law 60-151 (1908); Public Law 63-216 (1914) (48 U.S.C. 443).

[63] Federal Aviation Act of 1958, Sec. 401.

[64] Sec. 3 of the Federal Alcohol Administration Act (27 U.S.C. 203).

[65] For example, importers of milk or cream must have a permit from the Secretary of Health, Education, and Welfare under the Import Milk Act; under the Federal Seed Act of 1939, samples of seed offered for importation must be approved by the Agricultural Marketing Service (7 U.S.C. 1551 *et seq.*); licenses from the Secretary of Agriculture are required for the importation of veterinary biologics under the Virus-Serum-Toxin Act of 1913 (21 U.S.C. 151-58); the Imported Meat Act requires pre-inspection of all meat and meat products offered for importation (19 U.S.C. 1306).

[66] Federal Aviation Act of 1958; Interstate Commerce Act (49 U.S.C. 1); Intercoastal Shipping Act of 1933; Shipping Act of 1916.

[67] Communications Act of 1934.

[68] Federal Power Act of 1920 (16 U.S.C. 792-825).

[69] Natural Gas Act of 1938 (15 U.S.C. 717).

[70] For a severe criticism of the law of regulated industries see Eugene V. Rostow, *Planning for Freedom* (1959), esp. pp. 311-12. Other immunities are granted by the Attorney General for programs related to defense operations. For a critique see Senate Judiciary Committee, Subcommittee on Antitrust and Monopoly, *Petroleum, The Antitrust Laws and Government Policies,* 85 Cong. 1 sess. (1957). See also *Judicial Doctrine of Primary Jurisdiction as Applied in Antitrust Suits,* Staff Report to the House Committee on the Judiciary, 84 Cong. 2 sess. (1956). This report is somewhat critical of the judicial tendency to reduce the power of the Department of Justice. (See pp. 30 and 31.) See also Louis Schwartz, "Legal Restriction of Competition in the Regulated Industries," *Harvard Law Review,* Vol. 67 (1954), p. 67; and Walter Adams, "The Regulatory Commissions and Small Business," *Law and Contemporary Problems,* Vol. 29 (Winter 1959), p. 147.

[71] Federal Aviation Act of 1958; Interstate Commerce Act (49 U.S.C. 1(5) and 2 regarding railroads and 49 U.S.C. 316 and 317 regarding trucklines); Intercoastal Shipping Act of 1933; Shipping Act of 1916.

[72] Communications Act of 1934. The rate-making power applies to interstate telephone and telegraph services.

[73] Federal Power Act of 1920 (16 U.S.C. 792-825); Natural Gas Act of 1938 (15 U.S.C. 717).

[74] See testimony of Walter Adams, *Administered Prices,* Hearings before the Senate Judiciary Committee, 86 Cong. 1 sess. (1959), Pt. 9, p. 4791.

[75] The control of marketing of hog-cholera serum and virus is in the hands of a committee of producers and wholesalers selected by the secretary who has authority to veto its actions. Their orders are enforced by the Department of Agriculture. (7 U.S.C. 851 *et seq.*).

[76] Agricultural Marketing Agreement Act of 1937. See Warren C. Waite, "Federal Price Fixing in Milk Markets," *Economic Standards of Government Price Control,* Temporary National Economic Committee Monograph No. 32 (1941), p. 65.

[77] Henry P. Caulfield, Jr., "Federal Electric Power Policy," Resources for the Future, 1958 (mimeo.).

[78] *Ibid.,* p. 1.

[79] See, for example, Harvey J. Levin, *Broadcast Regulation and Joint Ownership of Media* (1960). Professor Levin discusses the relationship between such competing media as newspapers and television stations and its influence on broadcasting licenses. See also Walter Adams, "The Regulatory Commissions and

Small Business," *Law and Contemporary Problems*, Vol. 24 (Winter 1959), p. 147.

[80] See, for example, testimony of Walter Adams in *Administered Prices*, Hearings, Pt. 9, p. 4785. He suggests discontinuing regulation of trucking to make transportation more competitive. For another point of view see Richard B. Heflebower, "Mergers Between Competing Railroads: A Preliminary View," Address delivered at Conference on Transportation Mergers and Acquisitions, August 29, 1961 (mimeo.).

[81] Caulfield, *op. cit.*

[82] S. Rept. 307, 43d Cong. 1 sess. (1874).

[83] S. Rept. 46, 49th Cong. 1 sess. (1886).

[84] An informative review of these federal activities is contained in *Consumer Protection Activities of Federal Departments and Agencies*, Eighth Report by the House Committee on Government Operations, 87 Cong. 1 sess. (1961).

[85] See Joe S. Bain, *Barriers to New Competition* (1956). Professor Bain makes an interesting point that adequate consumer information will make it easier for new companies to enter many markets. See discussion of Entry in Chap. 7, below.

[86] See Abraham Ribicoff, Statement before the Subcommittee on Antitrust and Monopoly of the Senate Judiciary Committee, Sept. 13, 1961 (mimeo.), p. 3, re proposed regulation of consumer information to stimulate price competition. See also p. 23 re need for simple common names for drugs for doctors' guidance.

[87] Food and Drug Act of 1906 (21 U.S.C. 1-15); Food, Drug and Cosmetic Act (21 U.S.C. 321 *et seq.*). For a description of the acts and their enforcement, see *Consumer Protection Activities of Federal Departments and Agencies*, pp. 208-28. See also Tea Importation Act (21 U.S.C. 41 *et seq.*).

[88] Public Health Service Act of 1944 (58 Stat. 682) and Food, Drug and Cosmetic Act (21 U.S.C. 321).

[89] U.S. Food and Drug Administration, *Requirements of the United States Food, Drug, and Cosmetic Act* (1958).

[90] *Ibid.*

[91] 21 U.S.C. 451-69.

[92] 21 U.S.C. 71-91, 96.

[93] 19 U.S.C. 1306.

[94] 26 U.S.C. 4811-19.

[95] 21 U.S.C. 151-58. This act forbids ineffective biologicals for the treatment of animals. Secretary Ribicoff, in testimony for further drug regulation, said, "For the plain fact is that until we are allowed to require that a drug be proven effective before it is marketed, we must say to the American people: a hog is protected against worthless drugs, but you are not." *Op. cit.*, p. 5.

[96] 15 U.S.C. 1191-1200.

[97] 15 U.S.C. 68.

[98] 15 U.S.C. 69.

[99] 15 U.S.C. 70.

[100] Public Law 86-613. See S. Rept. 1158 (March 10, 1960) and H. Rept. 1861 (June 14, 1960).

[101] 7 U.S.C. 135.

[102] 7 U.S.C. 91-99.

[103] 27 U.S.C. 201 *et seq.*

[104] Organic Act of the National Bureau of Standards (15 U.S.C. 272(d)). See also 5 U.S.C. 133, 272.

[105] 7 U.S.C. 71-87.

[106] 7 U.S.C. 1551-1609.

[107] 7 U.S.C. 511.

[108] 7 U.S.C. 51-65, 471-76; 26 U.S.C. 1920-35.

[109] 7 U.S.C. 499.

[110] Standard Container Act of 1916 (15 U.S.C. 251-56) and Standard Hamper Act of 1928 (15 U.S.C. 257).

[111] 7 U.S.C. 2.

[112] Securities Act of 1933, Securities Exchange Act of 1934, Trust Indenture Act of 1939, Investment Company Act of 1940, Investment Advisers Act of 1940, and Public Utility Holding Company Act of 1935.

[113] 15 U.S.C. 1231-33.

[114] The commission's activity during the fiscal years 1957-60 can be gauged through the number of complaints it issued. The record shows the following:

| | Complaints in Antimonopoly Cases | Complaints in Deceptive Practice Cases |
|---|---|---|
| 1957 | 57 | 187 |
| 1958 | 86 | 268 |
| 1959 | 79 | 271 |
| 1960 | 157 | 346 |

Source: Federal Trade Commission, *Annual Report,* 1960, p. 40.

[115] The commission's lack of selectivity is criticized in Glen E. Weston, "Improving the Antitrust Laws and Their Enforcement," *Antitrust Bulletin,* Vol. 5 (January-February 1960), pp. 33, 40-41.

[116] Corwin D. Edwards pointed to the lack of "high-level centralized responsibility" concerning antitrust policy in the federal government. *Administered Prices,* Hearings before the Senate Judiciary Committee, 86 Cong. 1 sess. (1959), Pt. 9, p. 4806. See also *U.S.* v. *Economic Concentration and Monopoly,* Staff Report to the Monopoly Subcommittee of the House Committee on Small Business, 79 Cong. 2 sess. (1946), p. 34.

[117] Corwin D. Edwards wrote, "There is a clear and sustained record of interaction" on the part of the regulatory agencies in enforcing antitrust. *Maintaining Competition* (1949), p. 308. See also statement by Jerome K. Kuykendall, then chairman of the Federal Power Commission. "Remarks," *New Theories of Federal Trade Commission Enforcement,* CCH Trade Regulation Reports, No. 153 (Extra ed., June 8, 1960), p. 49.

[118] Federal Trade Commission, *Annual Report,* 1960, pp. 90-93.

[119] Edward F. Howrey, "Analysis of Present Problems and Suggestions for Administrative Change," *Proceedings,* Section of Antitrust Law, American Bar Association (April 1957), p. 40.

[120] 26 Federal Register 6015.

[121] F.T.C., *Annual Report,* 1960, pp. 84-90.

[122] *American Life and Accident Insurance Co.* v. *F.T.C.* (C.C.A.–8th 1958), *CCH Trade Cases,* Par. 69,040; *Automobile Owners Safety Insurance Co.* v. *F.T.C.* (C.C.A.–8th 1958), *CCH Trade Cases,* Par. 69,041.

[123] See Earl W. Kintner, "A Challenge to the Food Industry," Address delivered at the 51st Annual Meeting of the Grocery Manufacturers of America, Inc., Nov. 9, 1959 (mimeo.). The F.T.C. has issued the following Guides: "Cigarette Advertising," in 1955; "Tire Advertising," and "Deceptive Pricing," in 1958; "Bait Advertising," in 1959; "Deceptive Advertising of Guarantees," and "Advertising Allowances and Other Merchandising Payments and Services," in 1960. It should be noted that these Guides are not regarded as binding rulings. See *In the Matter of Arnold Constable Corporation,* Docket 7657, Opinion of the Commission, Jan. 12, 1961 (mimeo.), p. 3.

[124] F.T.C. *Annual Report,* 1960, p. 33.

[125] The proceedings are detailed in Robert M. Parrish, "Voluntary Procedures," *An Antitrust Handbook,* Section of Antitrust Law, American Bar Association (1958), pp. 395, 402-03.

[126] F.T.C., *Annual Report,* 1960, p. 36. See also Henry D. Stringer, "The Piece Goods Buyer and the New Textile Labeling Act," Remarks made at a meeting of the Piece Goods Buyers Association, Inc. (mimeo.) and "The New Textile Labeling Act and the Wholesaler," Remarks made at the 33rd Annual Convention of the National Wholesale Dry Goods Association, Jan. 19, 1960 (mimeo.).

[127] F.T.C., *Annual Report,* 1960, p. 78.

[128] These remedies are reviewed in William D. Kilgore, Jr., "Antitrust Judgments and Their Enforcement," in *An Antitrust Handbook,* Section of Antitrust Law, American Bar Association (1958), p. 331.

[129] The consent procedure is outlined in Stanley N. Barnes, "Settlement by Consent Judgment," *ibid.,* p. 235.

[130] Release of the Department of Justice, June 29, 1961; Order No. 246-61 of the Attorney General, June 29, 1961.

[131] The F.T.C. has used Sec. 5 to carry out some rules which are related to the Clayton Act, notably Sec. 2, the Robinson-Patman amendment. This development is discussed in Milton Handler, "Recent Antitrust Developments," *Yale Law Journal,* Vol. 71 (November 1961), pp. 75, 90-98.

[132] The F.T.C. has also used Sec. 5 to stop practices which are within the area covered by the Clayton Act, but which could not be prosecuted successfully as Clayton Act cases. *In the Matter of Foremost Dairies,* it attacked the acquisition of partnerships and intrastate corporate enterprises, a practice which is not subject to the Antimerger Act, Sec. 7, which covers the acquisition of interstate corporate business. (Docket 6495.) *In the Matter of Food Fair,* the commission used Sec. 5 to attack the practice of obtaining discriminatory advertising allowances, an advantage which is not covered specifically by Sec. 2 of the Clayton Act (Robinson-Patman Act). Docket 6458.

[133] See Joseph W. Burns, "A Summary of a Study of the Antitrust Laws," *Antitrust Bulletin,* Vol. 1 (1956), pp. 695, 720-27; Joseph W. Burns, *A Study of the Antitrust Laws* (1958), p. 72.

[134] Victor R. Hansen, "Functioning of the Antitrust Division—Its Relationship to the Federal Trade Commission and Current Policies of the Division," *Proceedings,* Section of Antitrust Law, American Bar Association (August 1958), pp. 20, 21.

[135] In 1948, one week after an F.T.C. order was issued, the Department of Justice filed suit against the same companies for the same offense. Burns, *A Study of the Antitrust Laws,* p. 73.

[136] 5 U.S.C. 1003.

[137] 15 U.S.C. 41.

[138] F.T.C., *Annual Report,* 1960, p. 163.

[139] See Burns, *A Study of the Antitrust Laws.*

[140] House Judiciary Committee, Antitrust Subcommittee, *Report on Consent Decree Program of the Department of Justice,* 86 Cong. 1 sess. (1959), p. 303, for further criticism.

[141] *Antitrust Consent Decrees and the Television Broadcasting Industry,* Hearings before the House Judiciary Committee, 87 Cong. 1 sess. (1961), Serial No. 6.

[142] For example, "For many years there has been an effective liaison arrangement between the Antitrust Division of the Department of Justice and the Federal Trade Commission." *Law-Enforcement Activities Affecting Small Business,* Report to the House Select Committee on Small Business, 85 Cong. 2 sess. (1959), p. 4. See also p. 5.

[143] "Remarks of William C. Kern, Commissioner, Federal Trade Commission,

Before the Mechanical Contractors Associations of Texas, Inc.," Jan. 14, 1961 (mimeo.), p. 9.

[144] *Ibid.*

[145] See Kern, *op. cit.*, pp. 9, 10, and Burns, *A Study of the Antitrust Laws*, p. 80. In a statement made shortly after taking office as Assistant Attorney General, Antitrust Division, Lee Loevinger held that Robinson-Patman is compatible with antitrust. "Recent Developments in Antitrust Enforcement," *Proceedings*, Section of Antitrust Law, American Bar Association (April 1961), pp. 102, 104-05.

[146] During the period 1936 to 1957, 47.6 per cent of the Commission's Robinson-Patman orders involved the payment or receipt of brokerage. Corwin D. Edwards, *The Price Discrimination Law*, p. 70.

[147] The F.T.C. studies are listed in its *Annual Report*, 1960, pp. 141-65.

[148] Some students have questioned some of its premises. See, for example, Joseph Palamountain, *The Politics of Distribution* (1955), pp. 62-68.

[149] See Attorney General's order, "Organization of the Department of Justice," 24 Federal Register 2452.

[150] 42 U.S.C. 2135.

[151] 15 U.S.C. 631 *et seq.*

[152] 50 U.S.C. App. 1941.

[153] 12 U.S.C. 1828, as amended by Public Law 86-463 (approved May 13, 1960).

[154] Armed Services Procurement Act of 1947 and Federal Property and Administrative Services Act of 1949.

[155] It will be recalled that the Connally Act of 1935 prohibits interstate shipments of petroleum and products which do not comply with state regulations. The operation of the act can be suspended by the President when he finds that there is an undue burden on interstate commerce. (15 U.S.C. 715.)

[156] Unfair Practices in Imports Act of 1930 (19 U.S.C. 1337). Under the Revenue Act of 1916 the President can declare a retaliatory embargo against goods from countries which unfairly embargo goods from the U.S. (15 U.S.C. 71). A similar provision is contained in the Trade Agreements Extension Act of 1955 (19 U.S.C. 1351).

[157] The Atomic Energy Commission is required to report to the Attorney General regarding the use of special nuclear material or atomic energy that appears to violate the antitrust laws or to restrict free competition. Additionally, it may revoke or suspend any license which is involved in an antitrust violation. Atomic Energy Act of 1954 (42 U.S.C. 2135).

[158] The Federal Reserve Board enforces Sec. 7 of the Clayton Act concurrently with the Attorney General in its application to banks and trust companies and may grant exemptions from Sec. 8 for interlocking directors of banks. Additionally, the board administers provisions of the Bank Holding Company Act relating to the merger of holding companies and the acquisition of more than 5 per cent of the voting shares of any bank. (12 U.S.C. 1841.)

[159] The Federal Deposit Insurance Act was amended in 1960 to provide that each of these agencies will give an advisory report on the competitive factors involved in any contemplated bank merger. (12 U.S.C. 1828.)

[160] The Interstate Commerce Commission can exempt transactions approved by it from the antitrust laws, under the Interstate Commerce Act. It enforces the Clayton Act in its application to carriers under its jurisdiction. It is empowered to exempt mergers of such carriers from the application of Sec. 7 of the Clayton Act. It enforces a provision against discriminatory rates under the Interstate Commerce Act. The Reed-Bulwinkle Act authorizes the commission to approve rate agreements exempting them from antitrust. (49 U.S.C. 5.)

[161] The Federal Communications Commission enforces the Clayton Act as it applies to its regulated carriers. It may exempt mergers from the operation of Sec. 7, and may approve interlocking directorates.

[162] The Civil Aeronautics Board enforces the Clayton Act in its application to its regulated constituents and can exempt transactions from the antimerger statute.

[163] The Federal Power Commission's approval of an acquisition or merger provides an automatic exemption from the operation of Sec. 7. All licenses which it grants under the Federal Power Act must include agreements that there shall be no limits on the output of electrical energy. (16 U.S.C. 803.) The Natural Gas Act requires that the commission transmit evidence regarding violations of the antitrust laws to the Attorney General under the Natural Gas Act. (15 U.S.C. 717.)

[164] The Federal Maritime Board may grant exemptions under Sec. 7 of the Clayton Act. It enforces Sec. 14 of the Shipping Act of 1916 against granting rebates, driving other carriers out of business through "fighting ships," discriminating against a shipper who uses another carrier, and making unfair or unjust discriminatory contracts. (46 U.S.C. 801 *et seq.*) Sec. 15 of the act authorizes the board to exempt price-fixing agreements and pooling arrangements. The recent Shipping Bill exempts international shipping from the antitrust laws and authorizes the board to disapprove any conference rate which is detrimental to U.S. commerce. (Public Law 87-346.)

[165] Under the Capper-Volstead Act, the Secretary of Agriculture is empowered to issue cease and desist orders against farm cooperatives if their actions enhance prices "unduly." (7 U.S.C. 291, 292.) The Agricultural Adjustment Act of 1933 authorizes him to exempt agricultural marketing agreements from the antitrust laws. (7 U.S.C. 608.) He is charged with the enforcement of the antitrust provisions of the Packers and Stockyards Act (7 U.S.C. 181 *et seq.*), and he is empowered to approve exemptions from the antimerger statute for all transactions under his jurisdiction.

[166] Packers and Stockyards Act (7 U.S.C. 181 *et seq.*)

[167] The Secretary of the Interior is authorized to issue cease and desist orders against cooperatives of fishermen if he feels that their actions have enhanced prices "unduly." Fisherman's Collective Marketing Act (15 U.S.C. 521, 522).

[168] The Secretary of the Interior has the authority to approve combinations of lessees under the Mineral Leasing Act of 1920, for constructing or running refineries and common carriers. (43 U.S.C. 970.)

[169] The Securities and Exchange Commission can approve transactions under the Public Utility Holding Company Act of 1935, which is a deconcentration statute. Such approval provides an exemption from the antimerger statute. (15 U.S.C. 79.)

[170] The Secretary of the Treasury, operating through the Internal Revenue Service, has the power to approve interlocking directorates of producers, importers, and wholesalers of alcoholic beverages. The I.R.S. regulates the packaging, labeling and size and fill of such beverages. Federal Alcohol Administration Act (27 U.S.C. 20 *et seq.*).

[171] Unfair Practices in Imports Act of 1930 (19 U.S.C. 1337).

[172] Revenue Act of 1916, Secs. 802, 803 (15 U.S.C. 71-77).

[173] The Tariff Commission is directed to investigate alleged violations of Sec. 337(a) of the Tariff Act of 1930 which makes unlawful "unfair methods of competition and unfair acts in the importation of articles . . . the tendency of which is to destroy or substantially injure an industry, efficiently and economically operated . . . or to restrain or monopolize trade and commerce in the United States."

[174] 15 U.S.C. 172 charges the Secretary of Commerce to investigate "what articles are controlled by trusts" and the effect of such trusts on production and prices "when required to do so by the President or either House of Congress." See

comment in *U.S. vs. Economic Concentration and Monopoly,* Staff Report to the Monopoly Subcommittee of the House Committee on Small Business, 79 Cong. 2 sess. (1946), p. 8.

[175] The Small Business Administration has the power, with the approval of the Attorney General, to exempt certain corporations formed by small businesses from the antitrust laws. (15 U.S.C. 631 *et seq.*)

[176] Federal Property and Administrative Services Act of 1949 (40 U.S.C. 488). Similar provisions regarding bids are in the Armed Services Procurement Act of 1956 (10 U.S.C. 2301 *et seq.*).

[177] One is the merger of the Philadelphia National Bank and the Girard Trust Corn Exchange Bank. Suit was filed the day after the merger was approved by the Comptroller of the Currency. Another is the merger of the First National Bank and Trust Co. and the Security Trust Co. in Lexington, Kentucky. See *Business Week,* March 4, 1961, p. 28, and Notes and Comments, "Bank Charter, Branching, Holding Company and Merger Laws: Competition Frustrated," *Yale Law Journal,* Vol. 71 (January 1962), p. 502. On January 15, 1962 a district court judge in Pennsylvania dismissed the government's suit in *U.S.* v. *Philadelphia National Bank et al., CCH Trade Regulation Reports,* Jan. 22, 1962.

[178] The board approved the merger of State Street Bank and Trust Co. and Rockland-Atlas National Bank of Boston. See *Business Week,* April 22, 1961.

[179] *U.S.* v. *Southern Pacific Co.,* 259 U.S. 214 (1922).

[180] *Control of Central Pacific Railway by Southern Pacific,* 76 I.C.C. 508 (1923). See also *Report of the Attorney General's National Committee to Study the Antitrust Laws* (1955), p. 264.

[181] *Ibid.,* pp. 272-73.

[182] The Antitrust Division of the Department of Justice agreed with the plan in principle. See testimony of Lee Loevinger, Assistant Attorney General, in *Antitrust Consent Decrees and the Television Broadcasting Industry,* Hearings before the House Judiciary Committee, Antitrust Subcommittee, 87 Cong. 1 sess., June 14 and 15, 1961, pp. 22-35.

[183] See *Business Week,* Aug. 12, 1961, p. 31.

[184] Sherman Act, Sec. 4.

[185] Clayton Act, Sec. 15.

[186] Sec. 22 of the Clayton Act provides for a fine of no more than $1,000 and imprisonment of no more than six months.

[187] Federal Trade Commission Act, Sec. 5(6)(b).

[188] *Ibid.,* Sec. 5(6)(l).

[189] *Ibid.,* Sec. 10. Fines may be levied up to $5,000 and imprisonment for not more than one year may be ordered if the subpoena is not obeyed. A fine of $100 can be levied for each day of refusal to file a report.

[190] *Ibid.* Fines up to $5,000 and imprisonment up to three years are provided.

[191] For a list of fines and improvements under the antitrust laws up to July 1946, see *U.S. vs. Economic Concentration and Monopoly,* Staff Report to the Monopoly Subcommittee of the House Committee on Small Business, 79 Cong. 2 sess. (1946), pp. 257-65.

[192] Sherman Act, Sec. 3.

[193] Clayton Act, Sec. 14(a).

[194] Packers and Stockyards Act, Sec. 205.

[195] 46 U.S.C. 801 *et seq.*

[196] 15 U.S.C. 1064, 1115. See *Bart Schwartz International Textiles, Ltd.* v. *F.T.C.,* U. S. Court of Customs and Patents Appeals, April 14, 1961. *CCH Trade Cases,* Par. 70,040.

[197] Atomic Energy Act, Sec. 105(a) (42 U.S.C. 2135).

[198] Communications Act of 1934, Sec. 313 (47 U.S.C. 314). This power was not mentioned in the recent Philadelphia electric case though some defendants are licensees.

[199] Panama Canal Act, Sec. 11 (15 U.S.C. 31).

[200] Shipping Act, Sec. 14(a) (46 U.S.C. 812).

[201] Similar provisions are contained in Unfair Practices in Imports Act of 1930 (19 U.S.C. 1337), Revenue Act of 1916 (15 U.S.C. 71), and Trade Agreements Extension Act of 1955 (19 U.S.C. 1351).

[202] Sherman Act, Sec. 6. An effort to enforce this provision was unsuccessful. *U.S.* v. *Addyston Pipe and Steel Co.*, 85 F. 271 (C.C.A.-6th 1898) mod. 175 U.S. 211 (1899). The Circuit Court of Appeals held that a trial by jury would be required if the forfeiture provision was to be enforced.

[203] Public Law 60-151 (1908) and Public Law 63-216 (1914) (48 U.S.C. 443).

[204] 15 U.S.C. 8-11 (1894).

[205] These provisions were passed in order to provide an "ancillary force of private investigators" who would help to enforce the antitrust laws. *Quemos Theatre Co., Inc.* v. *Warner Bros.*, 35 F. Supp. 949, 950 (D.C.N.J. 1940). An amendment of the income tax law in 1958 provided for favorable tax treatment of the damages recovered in such suits (26 U.S.C. 1306).

[206] The number of treble damage suits has been increasing. Only 175 such cases were reported up to 1940. In 1952 alone there were 261 private suits filed. The history of numbers of suits may be found in Robert A. Bicks, "The Department of Justice and Private Treble Damage Actions," *Antitrust Bulletin*, Vol. 4 (1959), pp. 5, 6. See also Lee Loevinger, "Enforcement of Robinson-Patman Act by Private Parties," *How to Comply with Robinson-Patman Act*, 1957 Antitrust Law Symposium (1957), p. 145.

[207] 15 U.S.C. 1221 *et seq.*

[208] A very useful series of studies, regarding patents, trademarks, and copyrights, has been prepared under the direction of Professor John C. Stedman for the Senate Judiciary Committee, Subcommittee on Patents, Trademarks, and Copyrights. A list of these studies may be found in the Subcommittee's *Report*, S. Rept. 1202, 86 Cong. 2 sess. (1960), hereinafter referred to as the Senate Patent Studies.

[209] A history of the patent acts is contained in Victor L. Edwards, *Efforts to Establish a Statutory Standard of Invention*, Study No. 7, Senate Patent Studies (1958).

[210] See, for example, Laurence I. Wood, "Restrictions Normally and Reasonably within the Patentee's Pecuniary Reward," *Proceedings*, American Bar Association (August 1959), p. 318.

[211] For example, *U.S.* v. *Columbia Steel Co. et al.*, 334 U.S. 495 (1948); *International Salt Co.* v. *U.S.*, 332 U.S. 392 (1947); *Times-Picayune Publishing Co.* v. *U.S.*, 345 U.S. 594 (1953).

[212] Jerrold G. Van Cise, "Antitrust Consent Decrees: The Trend and Defendants' Viewpoint," *Antitrust Bulletin*, Vol. 5 (1960), p. 319.

[213] See Fritz Machlup, *An Economic Review of the Patent System*, Study No. 15, Senate Patent Studies (1958), p. 12.

[214] See, for example, Arthur R. Burns, *The Decline of Competition* (1936), p. 11; F. A. Hayek, *The Road to Serfdom* (1944), p. 28; Lionel Robbins, *The Economic Basis of Class Conflict* (1939), p. 73.

[215] *International Salt Co.* v. *U.S.*, 332 U.S. 392 (1947).

[216] A rather complete review of patent-antitrust problems is set forth in *Report of the Attorney General's National Committee to Study the Antitrust Laws* (1955), Chap. V.

[217] Walton Hamilton and Irene Till, *Antitrust in Action,* T.N.E.C. Monograph No. 16 (1940).

[218] See Catherine S. Corry, *Compulsory Licensing of Patents—A Legislative History,* Study No. 12, Senate Patent Studies (1958).

[219] "Ironically, in some respects, the patent laws of foreign countries may be more 'antitrust' minded than the Sherman Act itself, supposedly the zenith of zealous antitrust policy." Sigmund Timberg, "International Patent Licensing and National Antitrust Laws," Paper delivered at the Twelfth Conference of Inter-American Bar Association, Bogota, Colombia (mimeo.), p. 7.

[220] William H. Davis, "Our National Patent Policy," *American Economic Review,* Vol. 38 (May 1948), pp. 235, 237-38.

[221] See, for example, *National Patent Policy,* Hearings before the Senate Judiciary Committee, Subcommittee on Patents, Trademarks, and Copyrights, 87 Cong. 1 sess. (June 2, 1961). For a general review see "Symposium on Government Contract Patent Policy," *Federal Bar Journal,* Vol. 21 (1961), pp. 3-163.

[222] Davis, *loc. cit.*

[223] See testimony of D. Hamberg, "Government Patent Policies and Government-Financed R & D," Statement presented to the Senate Small Business Committee on Dec. 8, 1959 in connection with the committee's hearings on the patent policies of the departments and agencies of the federal government (mimeo.). On the other hand, many argue that innovation will be stimulated by vesting the monopoly right in the inventors or contractors. See *Patent Policies of Departments and Agencies of the Federal Government—1959,* Hearings before the Senate Select Committee on Small Business, 86 Cong. 1 sess. (1960), esp. statement of William H. Davis, p. 439.

[224] Hamberg, *op. cit.,* p. 10.

[225] For a review of the present status of copyright law see *Copyright Law Revision,* Report of the Register of Copyrights, House Judiciary Committee, Committee Print, 87 Cong. 1 sess. (1961).

[226] 17 U.S.C. 1(b) (1952). See Harry G. Henn, *The Compulsory License Provisions of the U.S. Copyright Law,* Copyright Law Revision Study No. 5, Senate Judiciary Committee, Subcommittee on Patents, Trademarks and Copyrights, 86 Cong. 1 sess. (1960).

[227] W. M. Blaisdell, *The Economic Aspects of the Compulsory License,* Copyright Law Revision Study No. 6 (1960), p. 110.

[228] *Ibid.,* p. 111.

[229] *Ibid.,* p. 113.

[230] 15 U.S.C. 1051 *et seq.*

[231] See *U.S.* v. *Timken Roller Bearing Co.,* 83 F. Supp. 284 (N.D. Ohio 1949).

[232] See testimony of R. A. Gordon in *Employment, Growth, and Prices Levels,* Hearings before the Joint Economic Committee, 86 Cong. 1 sess. (1959), Pt. 9A, pp. 2963, 2968, and of Fritz Machlup, pp. 2827, 2857.

[233] A curious type of protection is found in Sec. 16 of the U. S. Copyright Law (Title 17, U.S.C.) The section provides that English language publications must be produced in the U.S. in order to obtain copyright protection. It does not prohibit the importation of the publications. A limited five-year copyright may be secured for a five-year period if a limited number of copies are imported under Sec. 22. During the five-year period a normal twenty-eight year copyright may be obtained if the publication is produced in the U.S. The application of this regulation to the works of foreign authors was modified substantially by the Universal Copyright Convention, adopted in 1952. *Copyright Bulletin,* Vol. 5, No. 3/4 (1952). See also *Copyright Law Revision,* Report of the Register of Copyrights (1961), Chap. 10. Under Sec. 337 of the Tariff Act of 1930 goods can be embargoed if unfair

methods of competition are employed in the importation. This provision can be used to protect a domestic patent. See release of U.S. Tariff Commission of Jan. 12, 1960 regarding its sewing machine investigation.

[234] Sec. 22 of the Agricultural Adjustment Act authorizes the President to restrict the importation of commodities, by imposing fees or quotas, when the importation tends to materially interfere with programs of the Department of Agriculture relating to agricultural commodities. The section authorizes the President to direct the Tariff Commission to survey and report to the President. (49 Stat. 750, 62 Stat. 1247, 64 Stat. 261, 7 U.S.C. 624.) Sec. 8 of the Trade Agreements Extension Act of 1951 provides that no trade agreement may be applied in a manner which is inconsistent with the requirements of Sec. 22. (65 Stat. 72.) The Sugar Act provides for import quotas. See also Sec. 104 of the Trade Agreements Extension Act of 1953 (67 Stat. 472). For a review of the status of Tariff Commission investigations see U. S. Tariff Commission, *Investigations Under Section 22 of the Agricultural Adjustment Act* (1960). Quota restrictions have been set on a number of agricultural commodities. Under Sec. 8 of the Trade Agreements Extension Act of 1958, the Office of Civil and Defense Mobilization determined that imports of crude oil and its principal derivatives threatened to impair the national security. In early 1959 the President announced a program of mandatory restrictions on imports of oil from overseas to be administered by the Department of the Interior. "The combination of state production controls and federal import restrictions has been a factor in maintaining United States oil prices at a level about 50 per cent higher than those abroad." [F. Gerard Adams and Leslie E. Grayson, "The Question of a National Fuels Policy," *Quarterly Review of Economics and Business*, Vol. 1 (August 1961), p. 7.] Import quotas were imposed on lead and zinc under Section 7 of the Trade Agreements Extension Act of 1951, the so-called escape-clause provision. See Release of the Press Secretary to the President, Sept. 2, 1958. For interesting general accounts of these developments see Constant Southworth and W. W. Buchanan, *Changes in Trade Restrictions Between Canada and the United States* (1960) and Willard L. Thorp, "Trade Barriers and National Security," *American Economic Review*, Vol. 50 (May 1960), p. 433.

[235] Sec. 201, Anti-Dumping Act (1921); Sec. 303, Tariff Act of 1930. See Commission on Foreign Economic Policy, *Staff Papers* (1954), pp. 160, 229-93.

[236] Edward S. Mason, *Controlling World Trade* (1946), pp. 249-52.

[237] See Commission on Foreign Economic Policy, *op. cit.*, pp. 443-52.

[238] An interesting effect may be found in the history of Canadian antitrust legislation. The "Anti-Combines" law was passed in 1899. During the legislative debate the principal purpose suggested for the legislation was to prevent Canadian businessmen from making price agreements to take advantage of the protective tariffs which were instituted at the time. Hazen Hansard, Q.C., "The 'Antitrust' Laws of Canada," *Proceedings*, Section of Antitrust Law, American Bar Association (August 1960) pp. 447, 450.

[239] See Adams and Grayson, *op. cit.*, p. 7. Crude oil prices are $1.00 a barrel more than foreign oil delivered in the U.S.

[240] Stephan Stykolt and Harry C. Eastman, "A Model for the Study of Protected Oligopolies," *Economic Journal*, Vol. 70 (June 1960), p. 336.

[241] *Ibid.*

[242] The "danger that these sanitary controls can be utilized as a form of economic protection" was pointed out after a review of the regulation in Commission on Foreign Economic Policy, *op. cit.*, p. 323. In a related field, interstate commerce, "Quarantines are sometimes enforced against areas that never were infested or diseased or which have become free of the pest or disease since the quarantine

was promulgated." George R. Taylor, Edgar L. Burtis, and Frederick V. Waugh, *Barriers to Internal Trade in Farm Products* (March 1939), p. 91. See also University of California, Agricultural Experiment Station, *The Efficacy and Economic Effects of Plant Quarantine in California* (1933).

[243] Commission on Foreign Economic Policy, *op. cit.*, p. 322.

[244] *Ibid.*, p. 207.

[245] See *Consumer Protection Activities of Federal Departments and Agencies*, Eighth Report by the House Committee on Government Operations, 87 Cong. 1 sess. (1961), pp. 93, 94.

[246] For a discussion of international commodity agreements see Commission on Foreign Economic Policy, *op. cit.*, pp. 188-212.

[247] Joint Economic Committee, Subcommittee on Foreign Economic Policy, *Trade Restraints in the Western Community*, 87 Cong. 1 sess. (1961), p. 17.

[248] These programs are reviewed in Commission on Foreign Economic Policy, *op. cit.*, pp. 315-20.

[249] *Ibid.* 41 U.S.C. 10.

[250] See, for example, Defense Appropriation Act of 1960, Par. 623, 73 Stat. 382 (1959), and Cargo Preference Act, 46 U.S.C. 1241.

[251] For a review of these provisions and their application see Harry R. Van Cleve, Jr., "The Use of Federal Procurement to Achieve National Goals," *Wisconsin Law Review*, Vol. 1961 (1961), p. 566.

[252] Notably Texas, Wisconsin, New York, and Missouri. See James A. Rahl, "Toward a Worthwhile State Antitrust Policy," *Texas Law Review*, Vol. 39 (June 1961), p. 753. A notable recent victory for the Texas Attorney General was to force the Sinclair Oil Corporation to discontinue its effort to acquire control of Texas Pacific Coal & Oil Co. *Business Week*, Oct. 28, 1961, p. 38. For information about current developments, especially in New York, see Louis J. Lefkowitz, "Protecting the New York Consumer," *Sales and Pricing Policies Under the Antitrust Laws*, Trade Regulation Reports (1961), p. 55 and "Remarks," *New Theories of Federal Trade Commission Enforcement*, Trade Regulation Reports, No. 153 (Extra ed., June 8, 1960), p. 63.

[253] An argument for active state enforcement, together with a discussion of state activity, is contained in Will Wilson, "The State Antitrust Laws," *American Bar Association Journal*, Vol. 47 (February 1961), p. 161. Mr. Wilson is the Attorney General of the State of Texas, one of the states which has been active in antitrust enforcement. Richard H. Stern says, "Probably more state antitrust suits are pending in the courts now [1961] than at any other time since the enactment of the bulk of such state legislation around the turn of the century." "A Proposed Uniform State Antitrust Law: Text and Commentary on a Draft Statute," *Texas Law Review*, Vol. 39 (June 1961), p. 717, footnote 1. Rahl points to "some recent signs of a revival." However, he feels that, "There is no basis for thinking that there is more than a mild stir, if that, in the majority of state capitals." Rahl, *op. cit.*, p. 754. Before he became Assistant Attorney General in charge of the Antitrust Division, Lee Loevinger had this to say about state antitrust activity: "It is a notorious fact that state antitrust laws, with one or two notable exceptions, are virtually a dead letter. This is not because these laws are substantively inferior to the federal statute, as many of them are similar and some are more specific. Nor does the increasing importance of interstate commerce wholly account for inactivity at the state level. Rather the explanation seems to be that the states have not established staffs for public enforcement of their antitrust laws and have not encouraged private enforcement by providing treble damage actions for injured parties." "Treble Damage Litigation and the Small Business Man," *Proceedings*, Section of Antitrust Law, American Bar Association (April 1960), pp. 106, 113.

[254] Paul T. Truitt, "Interstate Trade Barriers in the United States," *Law and Contemporary Problems,* Vol. 8 (Spring 1941), p. 209.

[255] Marketing Laws Survey, *State Price Control Legislation* (1940), p. xxxv, footnote 25.

[256] *Ibid.*

[257] See Clifton H. McCall, "The Present Status of State Fair Trade Laws," *Texas Law Review,* Vol. 39 (June 1961), p. 851.

[258] Marketing Laws Survey, *State Occupational Legislation* (1942).

[259] John A. McIntire and Charles S. Rhyne, "Municipal Legislative Barriers to a Free Market," *Law and Contemporary Problems,* Vol. 8 (Spring 1941), p. 359.

[260] Frank Bane, "Administrative Marketing Barriers," *ibid.,* p. 376.

[261] An interesting feature is the requirement that milk containers must be dated to ensure fresh milk. There seems to be substantial evidence that this practice is costly and unnecessary in view of other milk regulations. The Dairy Employees Union objected to the elimination of this requirement in Chicago, because it might eliminate 50 jobs. *Chicago Daily News,* June 20, 1961, p. 14, editorial and letter to editor from Professor L. D. Witter, University of Illinois microbiologist.

[262] University of Arizona, Agricultural Experiment Station, *Barriers to the Interstate Movement of Milk and Dairy Products in the Eleven Western States,* Bulletin 255 (April 1954). The authors of this report concluded that, "Promotion of public health is definitely a secondary objective of state milk control laws," p. 12.

[263] Marketing Laws Survey, *Interstate Trade Barriers and Outlines of Studies* (1942), p. 44.

[264] Efforts in the same direction may be found on the federal level. See H.R. 10922, 86 Cong. 2 sess. (1960).

[265] New Mexico set a markup of 17.5 per cent for wholesalers and 38.8 per cent for retailers of alcoholic beverages; Rhode Island set similar markups of 17 per cent and 45 per cent for cordials and cocktails. Distilled Spirits Institute, *State Laws and Regulations Relating to Distilled Spirits* (October 1959).

[266] For a history of Minnesota's "8 per cent law," see Brief of Respondent, *Minnesota* v. *Applebaum,* Supreme Court of Minnesota (1960).

[267] Marketing Laws Survey, *State Price Control Legislation* (1940), p. LV. These loss-leader provisions bear an interesting relation to premium stamp plans. In Oklahoma, Safeway Stores, a national chain which does not use stamps, was prosecuted for selling below minimum markup prices when it reduced prices to meet the competition of local grocers who did use stamps. Safeway lost the case although its price reductions were no more than the cost of the stamps to the competing retailers. *Safeway Stores, Inc.* v. *Oklahoma Retail Grocers Assn., Inc.,* 322 P. 2d 179 (1957), aff'd 360 U.S. 334 (1959). The laws have been used by retailers' associations to "police price-cutters" in action which is contrary to antitrust policy. See *Food and Grocery Bureau of Southern California, Inc.* v. *Harold B. Garfield,* 125 P. 2d 3 (Cal. Sup. Ct. 1942); and *Food and Grocery Bureau of Southern California, Inc.,* v. *U.S.* 139 F. 2d 973 (C.C.A.-9th 1943).

[268] For example, Minnesota Act of March 20, 1932, C.61, Sec. 5.

[269] Montana Rev. Codes Ann. (Anderson and McFarland, 1935), Sec. 2620.68.

[270] Oregon, Sec. 15., L. 1st Ex. 1935, Chap. 65; and Washington Rev. Stat. Ann., Sec. 6284-9.

[271] Oregon, *ibid.*

[272] Iowa, Sec. 5093.04, L.1937, C.136; New Jersey, Sec. 56:6-2, Rev. Stat. (Supp. 1938).

[273] A fairly comprehensive description of these controls is contained in Joint Committee of the States to Study Alcoholic Beverage Laws, *Alcoholic Beverage Control* (1960).

[274] Distilled Spirits Institute, *op. cit.*, pp. 2-23.

[275] *Ibid.*, pp. 81-85.

[276] Irwin W. Silverman, L. T. Bennett, Jr., and Irvin Lechliter, "Control by Licensing over Entry into the Market," *Law and Contemporary Problems*, Vol. 8 (Spring 1941), p. 234.

[277] Marketing Laws Survey, *State Occupational Legislation* (1942).

[278] See Peter A. Stone and R. Harold Denton, *Toward More Housing*, T.N.E.C. Monograph No. 8 (1940), p. 39.

[279] See Corwin D. Edwards, "Legal Requirements that Building Contractors be Licensed," *Law and Contemporary Problems*, Vol. 12 (1947), p. 76.

[280] Stone and Denton, *loc. cit.*

[281] See Joel B. Dirlam and Irwin M. Stelzer, "The Insurance Industry: A Case Study in the Workability of Regulated Competition," *University of Pennsylvania Law Review*, Vol. 107 (December 1958), p. 199.

[282] Marketing Laws Survey, *State Milk and Dairy Legislation* (1941), pp. 36-40.

[283] It is suggested by Melvin G. de Chazeau and Alfred E. Kahn that state prorationing of crude production and restrictions on imports are primarily responsible for any failure to serve the public interest. Further, the industry could be workably competitive and "there would be little room for price leadership. . . ." They present an argument for unitizing productive fields in order to "restore a goodly element of competition." *Integration and Competition in the Petroleum Industry* (1959), pp. 559, 567. See also Eugene V. Rostow, *A National Policy for the Oil Industry* (1948), p. 45; and Alfred E. Kahn, "Economic Issues in Regulating the Field Price of Natural Gas," *American Economic Review*, Supplement, Vol. 50 (1960), p. 506, for a discussion of the relationships between oil and gas regulation.

[284] Edith N. Cook, "Legislative Restrictions on Marketing Integration," *Law and Contemporary Problems*, Vol. 8 (Spring 1941), p. 273.

[285] In Idaho, for example, a company operating one store would pay an annual tax of $5.00; another with twenty stores would pay a tax of $500 each. See American Retail Federation, *Chain Store Taxes* (Jan. 1, 1937), p. 10; F. Eugene Melder, "Interstate Tax Barriers," in Walter J. Kress, ed., *National Tax Association Proceedings of the Fifty-first Annual Conference on Taxation, October 27-31, 1958* (1959), pp. 280, 290; George J. Feldman, "Legislative Opposition to Chain Stores and its Minimization," *Law and Contemporary Problems*, Vol. 8 (Spring 1941), p. 334. Feldman discusses several types of programs against chains.

[286] Melder, *op. cit.*, p. 291. See also F. Eugene Melder, *State Trade Walls* (1939).

[287] For a discussion of some efforts to cope with the problem see Corwin D. Edwards, *Maintaining Competition* (1949), pp. 312-13.

[288] F. Eugene Melder, *State and Local Barriers to Interstate Commerce in the United States* (1937); Charles E. Noyes, "Barriers Against Interstate Commerce," *Editorial Research Reports*, Vol. 1 (1939), p. 191; Robert Wallace McMillan, *Federal Centralization and Certain Interstate Trade Barriers* (1941); Council of State Governments, *Trade Barriers Among the States* (April 1939).

[289] U.S. Bureau of Agricultural Economics, *Barriers to Internal Trade in Farm Products* (1939), p. III.

[290] For rather extensive listings see Julia E. Johnsen, *Interstate Trade Barriers* (1940) and Marketing Laws Survey, *Interstate Trade Barriers* (1942).

[291] *Ibid.*, p. 44; Robert Wallace McMillan, *Federal Centralization and Certain Interstate Trade Barriers* (1941).

[292] Sec. 31, Chap. 1, Title 29, *Code of Alabama* (1940). For a fairly comprehensive catalog of the alcoholic beverage laws which constitute interstate trade bar-

riers, see Joint Committee of the States to Study Alcoholic Beverage Laws, *Trade Barriers Affecting Interstate Commerce in Alcoholic Beverages* (1952), pp. 35-39.

[293] Marketing Laws Survey, *Interstate Trade Barriers,* p. 45.

[294] *Ibid.,* p. 44. A nontremulous air cell is the air pocket found in newly laid eggs between the egg-white and the shell at one end. This air is dispersed as the egg ages or when it is moved about in substantial degree.

[295] See University of Arizona, Agricultural Experiment Station, *Barriers to the Interstate Movement of Milk and Dairy Products in the Eleven Western States,* Bulletin 255 (April 1954), regarding dairy products.

[296] See University of Arizona, Agricultural Experiment Station, *Restrictions on the Production and Interstate Distribution of Margarine in the Eleven Western States,* Report 112 (July 1953). Many other restrictions have been developed on the production, sale, and use of margarine. See National Association of Margarine Producers, "Progress in the Repeal of Restrictions on Margarine," June 30, 1958 (mimeo.), and Public Law 81-459 regarding federal limitations on serving yellow margarine.

[297] Marketing Laws Survey, *Interstate Trade Barriers,* p. 23; Julia E. Johnsen, *Interstate Trade Barriers* (1940).

[298] The U.S. Department of Agriculture publishes a regular series, *Summary of State Nursery-Stock Shipping Requirements and Plant Quarantines and Regulations Affecting Interstate Shipments,* by states.

[299] Marketing Laws Survey, *Interstate Trade Barriers,* p. 21.

[300] *Ibid.;* Johnsen, *loc. cit.*

[301] See Donald V. Harper, "Economic Regulation of the Motor Trucking Industry by States," *Illinois Studies in the Social Sciences,* Vol. 43 (1959), for an extensive treatment of state regulation of the trucking industry; see also McMillan, *loc. cit.*

[302] Truck-Trailer Manufacturers Association, *Watch Your Weight* (1959). "Of the 20 States . . . considered in this study . . . from the southern borders of Virginia, Kentucky, and Illinois . . . to the Canadian border—no 2 contiguous States had size and weight laws which were uniform in every respect." U.S. Department of Agriculture, *Highway Transportation Barriers in 20 States,* Marketing Research Report 157 (1957).

[303] The Marketing Committee of the National Association of Commissioners, Secretaries, and Directors of Agriculture felt that the problem was serious as long ago as 1939. See statement of the committee in U.S. Bureau of Agricultural Economics, *Barriers to Internal Trade in Farm Products* (1930), p. IV. See also James Harvey Rogers, "From State Rights to State Autarchy," *Harper's Magazine* (November 1938), p. 646 and Charles A. Beard, "Forty-eight Sovereigns," *Today* (June 11, 1936), p. 21.

[304] Reynold E. Carlson, "Interstate Barrier Effects of the Use Tax," *Law and Contemporary Problems,* Vol. 8 (Spring 1941), p. 223.

[305] See *Miller Bros. Co.* v. *Maryland,* 347 U.S. 340 (1954) and *General Trading Co.* v. *State Tax Commission,* 322 U.S. 335 (1944).

[306] For example, a Connecticut resident may not bring a full gallon of liquor into the state without a license; California permits one gallon from outside the United States; the District of Columbia, Florida, and Hawaii permit one gallon; Maryland permits one quart at a time and not over two quarts per month. Distilled Spirits Institute, *State Laws and Regulations Relating to Distilled Spirits* (October 1959). See also Joint Committee of the States to Study Alcoholic Beverage Laws, *Trade Barriers Affecting Interstate Commerce in Alcoholic Beverages* (1952).

[307] F. Eugene Melder, "Interstate Tax Barriers," in Walter J. Kress, ed., *Na-*

*tional Tax Association Proceedings of the Fifty-first Annual Conference on Taxation, October 27-31, 1958* (1959), pp. 280, 290. On Jan. 18, 1961, the *Washington Post* reported such a seizure and arrest. On Nov. 22, 1961, the *Washington Evening Star* reported that Maryland officials are "marshalling their border patrol for a crackdown" on consumers who bring alcoholic liquors into the state. The chief of the state's alcohol tax unit said that "100 arrests were made during the last year for illegal importation of liquors and for bootlegging."

[308] F. Eugene Melder, "Interstate Tax Barriers," *op. cit.*, pp. 280, 291.

[309] See Paul Studenski, "State Taxes Threaten U.S. Common Market," *Harvard Business Review*, Vol. 38 (July-August 1960), p. 57.

[310] *Northwestern States Portland Cement Co.* v. *Minnesota*, 358 U.S. 450 (1959).

[311] Public Law 86-272 (1959). See Senate Small Business Committee, *Eleventh Annual Report*, Report 51, 87 Cong. 1 sess. (1961), p. 33.

[312] See Floyd E. Britton, "Taxation Without Representation Modernized," *American Bar Association Journal*, Vol. 46 (April 1960), p. 369, and (May 1960), p. 526.

[313] See Senate Small Business Committee, *State Taxation on Interstate Commerce—1959*, Hearings, Pts. 1, 2, and 3, and Report, 86 Cong. 1 sess. (1959); and John Sparkman, "The Problems of Multi-State Taxation of Interstate Commerce Income," *American Bar Association Journal*, Vol. 46 (April 1960), p. 375.

[314] See also Senate Small Business Committee, *State Taxation on Interstate Commerce*, Report, pp. 3-6.

[315] *Northwestern States* v. *Minnesota*, 358 U.S. 450 (1959). See also Sparkman, *loc. cit.*; and Joe C. Barrett, "State of the States in Taxing Multi-State Income," *American Bar Association Journal*, Vol. 48 (1962), p. 35.

[316] One program of the Public Health Service calls for state cooperation on milk and shellfish. Various states accept inspections of sister states whose requirements satisfy the standards set by P.H.S. The F.T.C. cooperates with state agencies in avoiding deceptive practices. See *Consumer Protection Activities of Federal Departments and Agencies*, Eighth Report by the House Committee on Government Operations, 87 Cong. 1 sess. (1961), pp. 43-45.

[317] For example, the Connally Act of 1935 (regarding controls of the production of oil), the McCarran Act of 1945 (regarding insurance companies), and the McGuire Act (regarding resale price control).

[318] Robert A. Bicks, "Antitrust Today," *Sales and Pricing Policies Under the Antitrust Laws*, Trade Regulation Reports (1961), p. 15.

[319] For a review of experience under the act, see Joel B. Dirlam and Irwin M. Stelzer, "The Insurance Industry: A Case Study in the Workability of Regulated Competition," *University of Pennsylvania Law Review*, Vol. 107 (December 1958), p. 199.

[320] See, for example, *F.T.C.* v. *National Casualty Co.* and *F.T.C.* v. *American Hospital and Life Ins. Co.*, 357 U.S. 560 (1958) (decided jointly).

[321] See Richard A. Wiley, "Pups, Plants and Package Policies—or the Insurance Antitrust Exemptions Re-examined," *Villanova Law Review*, Vol. 6 (Spring 1961), p. 281.

[322] George R. Taylor, Edgar L. Burtis, and Frederick V. Waugh, *Barriers to Internal Trade in Farm Products* (March 1939), p. IV.

[323] F. Eugene Melder, *State Trade Walls* (1939).

[324] The law is explained, in detail, in Commerce Clearing House, Inc., *Hazardous Substances Labeling Act* (1960).

[325] M. A. Copeland, C. C. Linnenberg, and D. M. Barbour, *Government Purchasing—An Economic Commentary*, T.N.E.C. Monograph No. 19 (1940) contains an interesting review of identical bidding in sales to the federal government in 1938. See pp. 32, 312.

[326] Robert A. Bicks, "The Federal Government's Program on Identical Bids," September 1960 (mimeo.).

[327] Act of May 26, 1938; 15 U.S.C. 13(c).

[328] For example, *General Shale Products Corp.* v. *Struck Construction Co.*, 37 F. Supp. 598 (D.C.Ky. 1941); *Sperry Rand Corp.* v. *Nassau Research and Development Associates, Inc.* (D.C.N.Y. 1957), *CCH Trade Cases,* Par. 68,786. See also *Opinion of the Attorney General of the United States* (Dec. 28, 1936), *CCH Trade Cases,* Par. 55,145.

[329] See G. E. Hale and Rosemary D. Hale, *Market Power: Size and Shape Under the Sherman Act* (1958), p. 4.

[330] "For example, tax laws enacted after 1940 are alleged to have increased significantly the volume of mergers." Jesse Markham, "Growth Incentives and Antitrust Policy," in Klaus Knorr and William J. Baumol, eds., *What Price Economic Growth?* (1961), pp. 92, 111. See also Philip D. Bradley, "The Direct Effects of a Corporate Income Tax," *Quarterly Journal of Economics,* Vol. 56 (August 1942), p. 638.

[331] See Corwin D. Edwards' suggestion that means be found to encourage corporations to split up. Testimony in *Administered Prices,* Hearings before the Senate Judiciary Committee, 86 Cong. 1 sess. (1959), Pt. 9, p. 4814.

[332] See J. Keith Butters, John Lintner, and William L. Cary, *Effects of Taxation, Corporate Mergers* (1951), p. 16.

[333] See John Lintner and J. Keith Butters, "Effects of Taxes on Concentration," in National Bureau of Economic Research, *Business Concentration and Price Policy* (1955), pp. 239, 252-64.

[334] Sumner H. Slichter, "A Defense of Bigness in Business," in American Management Association, *Legal, Financial, and Tax Aspects of Mergers and Acquisitions* (1957), p. 156.

[335] The Department of Justice did have some difficulty in deciding what position to take on this tax issue. See Press Release of Jan. 15, 1960 (letter from Attorney General Rogers); Release of July 19, 1961 (letter from Attorney General Kennedy); and Release of Aug. 24, 1961 (covering testimony on several bills for tax relief by L. F. Oberdorfer, Assistant Attorney General, Tax Division).

[336] *U.S.* v. *Hilton Hotels Corporation* (D.C.N.D. Ill. 1956), *CCH Trade Cases,* Par. 68,253.

[337] *Taxation of Exchanges and Distributions Pursuant to Antitrust Decrees,* Hearings before the House Committee on Ways and Means on H.R. 8126, 86 Cong. 1 sess. (1959).

[338] 15 U.S.C. 79.

[339] Public Law 87-403 approved Feb. 2, 1962.

[340] See discussion of the problem in J. Keith Butters, "Taxation, Incentives and Financial Capacity," *American Economic Review,* Vol. 44 (May 1954), pp. 504, 517. For a description of efforts to alleviate the tax burden on small business see Robert M. Schmidt, "The Correlation of Federal Taxation of Small Business and Antitrust Policy," *University of Detroit Law Journal,* Vol. 39 (December 1961), p. 181.

[341] Butters, Lintner, and Cary, *op. cit.,* p. 9.

[342] *Ibid.* See especially discussion about the feeling that the tax authorities tend to over-value the stock of closely held corporations. (Pp. 11-12.)

[343] See James O. Wynn, "Relation of Carry-Forward and Carry-Back Provisions to Business Concentration," in Tax Institute, *Taxation and Business Concentration* (1950), p. 69; and Gustave Simons, "Comment on Tax Provisions which Promote Concentration," in *ibid.,* p. 78.

[344] *Ibid.*

[345] See J. Keith Butters, "Recent Trends in Industrial Concentration and Taxa-

tion," in *ibid.*, pp. 3, 6; and Maurice Austin, "Effect of Present Corporate Tax Rates on Business Concentration," in *ibid.*, p. 218.

[346] See *Financing Small Business,* Report to the Committees on Banking and Currency and the Select Committees on Small Business by the Federal Reserve System, 85 Cong. 2 sess. (1958), Pts. 1 and 2, pp. 541-45.

[347] Sec. 124 of the Internal Revenue Code, enacted in October 1940, Second Revenue Act of 1940, 54 Stat. 998.

[348] For an illuminating study of the relationships between competition and direct government regulation see Leland L. Johnson, *Communications Satellites and Telephone Rates: Problems of Government Regulation,* RAND Corporation (1961).

[349] About half of the research engineers and scientists employed by industry in January 1952 were on contract research with either the Department of Defense or the Atomic Energy Commission. W. Rupert Maclaurin, "Technological Progress in Some American Industries," *American Economic Review,* Vol. 44 (1954), pp. 178, 188.

[350] *Economic Report of the President* (January 1962).

[351] Standard Oil Company (New Jersey) reports that more than 3,200 "space related" products or processes had been developed by mid-1961. *The Lamp* (Summer 1961), p. 9.

[352] See D. Hamberg, "Size of Firm, Monopoly, and Economic Growth," *Employment, Growth, and Price Levels,* Hearings before the Joint Economic Committee, 86 Cong. 1 sess. (1959), Pt. 7, p. 2337. He points to heavy government expenditures for research and development in aircraft, electronics, electrical equipment, atomic energy, and guided missile industries. (P. 2355.)

[353] See Robert A. Bicks, "An Appropriate Role Under Our Federal System for a State Antitrust Enforcement Program," *Antitrust Bulletin,* Vol. 5 (1960), pp. 503, 509-10. An interesting illustration of such government efforts is related in Dickson Reck, *Government Purchasing and Competition* (1954). In response to requests for bids for automobile tires for 1937-38, bids were submitted which were identical and high. The procurement agency negotiated a contract with Sears, Roebuck at lower prices. After that experience the tire manufacturers changed their policies. (Pp. 160-61.)

[354] See M. A. Copeland, C. C. Linnenberg, and D. M. Barbour, *Government Purchasing—An Economic Commentary,* T.N.E.C. Monograph No. 19 (1940) for a study of 1938 bids.

[355] 10 U.S.C. 2305.

[356] 41 U.S.C. 151.

[357] The significance of this provision in the act of 1949 is difficult to evaluate. Dickson Reck found, "In the three years following the establishment of the General Services Administration, however, the Administrator found no occasion to refer any bid to the Attorney General." *Government Purchasing and Competition,* p. 185. Some agencies, such as the Tennessee Valley Authority, regularly conduct investigations of bids. T.V.A. purchases between $120 million and $500 million of supplies each year; electrical generating and transmission equipment; construction equipment and materials; and thousands of other items. It has worked with the antitrust authorities in developing information about price rigging. *Business Week,* April 1, 1961, pp. 62-70.

[358] U.S. Department of Justice, "The Federal Government's Program on Identical Bids," Sept. 7, 1960 (mimeo.), p. 8.

[359] For an account of this experience and of the entry of three additional members of the aluminum industry in the 1950's see William T. Hogan and Frank Koelble, "Technology and Competition," *University of Detroit Law Journal,* Vol. 38 (1960), pp. 113, 122-27.

[360] "Defense contracts go largely to the very largest companies. . . . These con-

tracts are most important in those fields where technology is advancing most rapidly." Testimony of W. H. Martin, *Employment Growth, and Price Levels,* Hearings, Pt. 7, p. 2003.

[361] *U.S. vs. Economic Concentration and Monopoly,* Staff Report to the Monopoly Subcommittee of the House Committee on Small Business, 79 Cong. 2 sess. (1946), p. 9. See also Smaller War Plants Corporation, *Economic Concentration and World War II,* S. Doc. 206, 79 Cong. 2 sess. (1946).

[362] A balanced discussion of the small business problem in World War II procurement is presented in R. Elberton Smith, *The Army and Economic Mobilization,* United States Army in World War II: War Department (1959).

[363] See testimony of James S. Duesenberry, for an interesting short discussion of research and development and the favored position of large firms, especially in the case of government financed research. *Employment, Growth, and Price Levels,* Hearings, Pt. 7, pp. 2326-28.

[364] Hamberg found that during 1953, 1954, and 1955 only 1 per cent of the R and D contracts of the Atomic Energy Commission went to "small firms." "Government Patent Policies and Government-Financed R & D," Statement presented to the Senate Small Business Committee on Dec. 8, 1959 in connection with the committee's hearings on the patent policies of the departments and agencies of the federal government (mimeo.), p. 9.

[365] Hamberg found that during 1957 only 6 per cent of the Defense Department's R & D contracts were awarded to companies employing less than 500 people. Hamberg, *loc. cit.*

[366] See discussion of "Restrictions on Competition," *Federal Bar News,* Vol. 9 (January 1962), pp. 16-20.

[367] See Senate Small Business Committee, *Eleventh Annual Report,* Report 51, 87 Cong. 1 sess. (1961), pp. 5, 17-22; and *Small Business Administration—1961,* Report 1117, 87 Cong. 2 sess. (1962), p. 8.

[368] *Ibid.,* p. 7.

[369] Based on discussion with procurement personnel.

[370] Observations of the writer during war-time services as chief of the price policy section, Purchases Divisions, Headquarters, Army Service Forces.

[371] Many illustrations of civilian applications of the products of military R & D are contained in Herbert E. Striner, Richard V. Sherman, Jr., and Leon Karadbil, *Defense Spending and the U.S. Economy* (2 vols., Operations Research Office, Johns Hopkins University, 1958).

[372] This argument does not touch on other important policy issues: What are the effects of the practice on the advances of technology? How does it affect the government's contract costs? Some of these issues are dealt with in a study at George Washington University, published in *The Patent, Trademark and Copyright Journal of Research and Education,* Vol. 4 (Winter 1960).

[373] A good discussion of the patent policies of the departments may be found in the "Symposium on Government Contract Patent Policy," *Federal Bar Journal,* Vol. 21 (Winter 1961), p. 1.

[374] For a contrary view see William M. Allen, "Lawyers and the National Purpose," *American Bar Association Journal,* Vol. 47 (October 1961), p. 981.

[375] For a competent review see Harry R. Van Clever, Jr., "The Use of Federal Procurement to Achieve National Goals," *Wisconsin Law Review,* Vol. 1961 (1961), p. 566.

[376] 41 U.S.C. 35-45.

[377] 40 U.S.C. 276.

[378] Related statutes are the Eight-Hour Law (40 U.S.C. 324-26) and the Copeland and Anti-Kickback acts (40 U.S.C. 376 and 18 U.S.C. 874).

[379] In the course of setting "prevailing wages" union rates are taken into account but not followed. However, in the coal industry union rates set the "prevailing wages."

[380] 7 U.S.C. 1903.

[381] See K. F. Johnson, "Humane Slaughter Program," *Journal of the American Veterinary Association,* Vol. 136 (1960), p. 388. A release of the U.S. Department of Agriculture, dated July 18, 1960, states that over two thirds of the establishments under Federal Meat Inspection were using the methods approved under the act.

[382] See *The Washington Post,* Oct. 22, 1961, p. 2.

[383] 40 U.S.C. 488.

[384] Rubber Producing Facilities Disposal Act of 1953 (50 U.S.C. App. 1941).

[385] On May 2, 1961, President Kennedy established a White House Committee on Small Business, chaired by the administrator of the Small Business Administration, to develop "new constructive policies and programs in behalf of small business." Release, White House Press Secretary, May 2, 1961.

[386] See A. D. H. Kaplan, *Small Business: Its Place and Problems* (1948), Chap. 6.

[387] Agricultural education has had a long history. A short description is contained in *Consumer Protection Activities of Federal Departments and Agencies,* Eighth Report by the House Committee on Government Operations, 87 Cong. 1 sess. (1961), pp. 101-02.

[388] See Senate Small Business Committee, *Small Business Administration—1961,* S. Rept. 1117, 87 Cong. 2 sess. (1962), p. 10.

[389] 15 U.S.C. 1221 *et seq.* See discussion in Friedrich Kessler and Richard H. Stern, "Competition, Contract, and Vertical Integration," *Yale Law Journal,* Vol. 69 (November 1959), pp. 1, 103-14.

[390] See Earl W. Kintner, "Governmental Measures Apart from Antitrust Litigation for the Furtherance of Small Business," *Proceedings,* Section of Antitrust Law, American Bar Association (April 1960), pp. 38, 41-43. See also "Symposium on the Small Business Investment Act of 1958," *Federal Bar Journal,* Vol. 20 (1960), pp. 292, 388; Everette MacIntyre, "Small Business and the Antitrust Laws," *University of Detroit Law Journal,* Vol. 39 (December 1961), p. 169; and *Small Business Investment Act—1960,* Report of the Senate Select Committee on Small Business, 86 Cong. 2 sess. (April 27, 1960). The act may be found in 15 U.S.C. 661-96.

[391] Small Business Investment Act of 1958 (15 U.S.C. 661, 695, 696); Small Business Tax Revision Act (15 U.S.C. 631-61); Technical Amendments Act of 1958 (15 U.S.C. 57). This program is reviewed in Robert M. Schmidt, "The Correlation of Federal Taxation of Small Business and Antitrust Policy," *University of Detroit Law Journal,* Vol. 39 (December 1961), p. 181.

[392] An appeal for coordination is presented in Andreas Papandreou and John Wheeler, *Competition and Its Regulation* (1954), pp. 488-89.

[393] The problem of reconciling regulation and competition is brought out in the discussion of the communication satellites. Since "only one commercial system seems feasible within the near future," the Antitrust Division and the Federal Communications Commission have had to struggle with this reconciliation. The Antitrust Division has argued for a joint venture open to all interested businesses. *Antitrust Consent Decrees and the Television Broadcasting Industry,* Hearings before the House Judiciary Committee, 87 Cong. 1 sess. (1961), p. 22. See also pp. 23-35 and 56-59.

[394] For example, the Antitrust Subcommittee of the House Judiciary Committee found that "the oil pipeline industry has been able to use the I.C.C. as an instrument for protection against the requirements of the *oil pipeline* consent decree." House Judiciary Committee, Antitrust Subcommittee, *Report on Consent*

*Decree Program of the Department of Justice,* 86 Cong. 1 sess. (1959), p. 300.

[395] A recent conflict between the Department of Justice and the Federal Power Commission is in point. After the F.P.C. approved the acquisition of one pipeline company by another, the Department of Justice joined in an attack on the acquisition. The commission's approval was upheld on the grounds that such approval provided an antitrust exemption. *California* v. *F.P.C. respondent, and El Paso Natural Gas Co., intervenor, CCH Trade Cases,* Par. 69,967 (C.C.D.C. 1961). See also *U.S.* v. *Bank Stock Corp. of Milwaukee* (D.C. Wisc. filed 1961).

[396] See, for example, Jerome K. Kuykendall, "Remarks," *New Theories of Federal Trade Commission Enforcement,* CCH Trade Regulation Reports, No. 153 (Extra ed., June 8, 1960), p. 49; and John C. Doerfer, "Federal Communications Commission and the Antitrust Law," *ibid.*, p. 57.

## *Chapter 4*

[1] As Robert A. Dahl points out, we have attempted to analyze these problems in terms of "grand alternatives," using mutually exclusive categories, for example, "planning *vs.* no planning, price system *vs.* centralized allocations." "Hierarchy, Democracy, and Bargaining in Politics and Economics," *Research Frontiers in Politics and Government: Brookings Lectures 1955* (1955), pp. 45, 46.

[2] See Derek C. Bok, "Section 7 of the Clayton Act and the Merging of Law and Economics," *Harvard Law Review,* Vol. 74 (December 1960), pp. 226, 306-07.

[3] Charles Lindblom presents another reason for the lack of clarity in "The Science of Muddling Through," *Public Administration Review,* Vol. 19 (1959), p. 79.

[4] An interesting opportunity for such a review is contained in Public Law 87-305 (75 Stat. 666), passed Sept. 26, 1961. Sec. 5(a) provides that the Attorney General shall survey government activities which may affect small business "for the purpose of determining any factors which may tend to eliminate competition, create or strengthen monopolies. . . ." He may direct the F.T.C. to make such studies for him and must report to Congress and the President at least once a year on these surveys. Corwin D. Edwards has suggested the development of a new agency for competitive policy. *Maintaining Competition* (1949), p. 288.

[5] See Clair Wilcox, "From Economic Theory to Public Policy," *American Economic Review,* Supplement, Vol. 50 (May 1960), p. 27.

[6] For an incisive discussion of the difficulties of making such evaluation see Theodore J. Kreps, *An Evaluation of Antitrust Policy: Its Relation to Economic Growth, Full Employment, and Prices,* Study Paper No. 22, Study of Employment, Growth, and Price Levels, Joint Economic Committee (1960), pp. 24-27. See also Theodore J. Kreps, *Measurement of the Social Performance of Business,* Temporary National Economic Committee Monograph No. 7 (1940).

[7] See Jesse W. Markham, "Economic Analysis," *Proceedings,* Section of Antitrust Law, American Bar Association (April 1954), pp. 145, 152.

[8] See discussion of the place of competition in the regulation of civil air transportation in House Committee on the Judiciary, Antitrust Subcommittee, *The Airlines Industry,* 85 Cong. 1 sess. (1957), Chap. 3, and Civil Aeronautics Board, *The Role of Competition in Commercial Air Transportation,* Report submitted to the Senate Small Business Committee, Subcommittee on Monopoly, 82 Cong. 2 sess. (1952).

[9] See Richard B. Heflebower, "Mergers Between Competing Railroads: A Preliminary View," Address delivered at Conference on Transportation Mergers and Acquisitions, Aug. 29, 1961.

[10] See Harvey Levin, "Regulatory Efficiency, Reform and the FCC," *Georgetown Law Journal*, Vol. 50 (1961), pp. 1, 42.

[11] See *U.S.* v. *Economic Concentration and Monopoly*, Staff Report to the Monopoly Subcommittee of the House Committee on Small Business, 79 Cong. 2 sess. (1946), p. 12. "At the present time there is no test of the effectiveness of the Government's efforts to prevent concentration."

[12] For a review of studies up to 1948 see Harrison F. Houghton, "The Growth of Big Business," *American Economic Review*, Vol. 38 (May 1948), p. 72. See also Richard B. Heflebower, "United States of America," in Edward H. Chamberlin, ed., *Monopoly and Competition and Their Regulation* (1954), p. 110. Professor Heflebower concludes that competition outweighs monopoly in the United States.

[13] G. Warren Nutter made a rough estimate "that 45 per cent of national income is produced under continuously competitive conditions and an additional 25 per cent under irregularly competitive conditions." "Competition: Direct and Devious," *American Economic Review*, Supplement, Vol. 44 (1954), pp. 69, 76. Heflebower seems to be optimistic, placing considerable reliance on "seller's reaction to uncertainty. . . ." "Toward a Theory of Industrial Markets and Prices," *American Economic Review*, Vol. 44 (1954), pp. 121, 139.

[14] See, for example, Rufus S. Tucker, "Concentration and Competition," *Journal of Marketing* (April 1940), p. 358; Clair Wilcox, *Public Policies Toward Business* (1955), pp. 837, 838; A. D. H. Kaplan, *Big Enterprise in a Competitive System* (1954), p. 71; George L. Mehren, "Bigness—Goodness or Badness?", Address before the Commonwealth Club of California, Nov. 7, 1958, Giannini Foundation (mimeo.).

[15] See evaluation of the Antitrust Division, reprinted in *U.S.* v. *Economic Concentration and Monopoly*, *op cit.*, p. 209. See also Joe S. Bain, *Industrial Organization* (1959), pp. 529-30; G. W. Stocking and M. W. Watkins, *Monopoly and Free Enterprise* (1951).

[16] See, for example, W. H. Ferry, *The Economy Under Law* (1960), p. 6; Heflebower, "Toward a Theory of Industrial Markets and Prices," *op. cit.*, pp. 138-39. Stigler feels that at least three fourths of our commodity markets closely approximate pure competition. George Stigler, *Five Lectures on Economic Problems* (1950), Chap. 5.

[17] Two outstanding studies which did not profess to be complete were made some years ago. Arthur R. Burns, *The Decline of Competition* (1936), and Clair Wilcox, *Competition and Monopoly in American Industry*, Temporary National Economic Committee Monograph No. 21 (1940).

[18] See W. H. S. Stevens, "Has Competition Declined?" *Journal of Marketing* (April 1939), p. 346.

[19] Adam Smith, *The Wealth of Nations* (Modern Library ed., 1937).

[20] *Principals of Political Economy*, Ashley ed. (1928), p. 242. As Professor J. M. Clark sees it, "We need to be on our guard against this form of homesickness for an historical past that is mythical." *Competition as a Dynamic Process* (1961), p. 31.

[21] "Competition is a composite of actions in four different fields. These include methods of production, selection and design of products, selling activities, and pricing." J. M. Clark, "The Uses of Diversity: Competitive Bearings of Diversities in Cost and Demand Functions," *American Economic Review*, Supplement, Vol. 48 (1958), pp. 474, 476. See also Gösta Mickwitz, "The Means of Competition at Various Stages of Production and Distribution," *Kyklos*, Vol. 11 (1958), p. 509.

[22] Discussion with a top executive in one of the Big Three of the automobile industry.

[23] Clair Wilcox, *Public Policies Toward Business* (1955), p. 838.

[24] A. D. H. Kaplan, *Big Enterprise in a Competitive System* (1954), esp. pp. 192-94.

[25] See *U.S.* v. *Columbia Steel Co. et al.*, 334 U.S. 495 (1948).

[26] Clark, *Competition as a Dynamic Process*, p. 113.

[27] See William T. Hogan and Frank Koelble, "Technology and Competition," *University of Detroit Law Journal*, Vol. 38 (1960), p. 113.

[28] A general statement against rigidity in rules and policies is given in C. J. Friedrich, "The Dilemma of Administrative Responsibility," *Responsibility* (Nomos III, 1960), pp. 189, 197-98. "Politics, like laws, cannot be made sufficiently detailed to fit all situations, and therefore must leave much to the discretion of those who operate and execute policies. The extent of such discretion varies and is extended or contracted to some extent at least as a result of technical considerations, but as we said at the outset, it always involves three notions, namely (1) that a choice between several existing alternatives can be and indeed must be made, or that (2) a novel solution is found, an innovation or invention made, and (3) that such a choice or innovation is not made arbitrarily, wantonly, or carelessly, but in accordance with the requirements of the situation."

[29] See *Northern Pacific Railway Co.* v. *U.S.*, 356 U.S. 1, 5 (1958), for a statement of the need for definitive rules of the *per se* category in order to avoid "incredibly complicated and prolonged economic investigation."

[30] See John C. Stedman, "A New Look at Antitrust: The Report of the Attorney General's Committee," *Journal of Public Law*, Vol. 4 (1956), pp. 223, 260-62. Professor Stedman takes a strong stand in favor of the certainty of *per se* rules. (Pp. 256, 259.)

[31] See William B. Lockhart and Howard R. Sacks, "The Relevance of Economic Factors in Determining Whether Exclusive Arrangements Violate Section 3 of the Clayton Act," *Harvard Law Review*, Vol. 65 (April 1952), p. 919. The authors plea for more economics analysis in such cases.

[32] A typical business attitude is expressed by John E. Swearingen, President of Standard Oil Company (Indiana). He criticizes "the present confusion of antitrust policies, which vary from day to day as to what the law means." *Span*, Vol. 1 (1961), Standard Oil Company (Indiana) p. 25. A more analytical position may be found in H. Thomas Austern, "Inconsistencies in the Law," *Business Practices Under Federal Antitrust Laws*, Proceedings of the Third Annual Meeting of the New York State Bar Association, Section on Antitrust Law (Jan. 24, 1951), esp. p. 169. See also Clare E. Griffin, *An Economic Approach to Antitrust Problems* (1951).

[33] "To seek both flexibility and certainty in the same laws is a logical contradiction." Lee Loevinger, "Recent Developments in Antitrust Enforcement," *Proceedings*, Section of Antitrust Law, American Bar Association (April 1961), p. 104. See also Louis B. Schwartz, "The Schwartz Dissent," *Antitrust Bulletin*, Vol. 1 (1955), p. 37; Joel B. Dirlam and Alfred E. Kahn, *Fair Competition* (1954), pp. 261-68.

[34] It is interesting to note that the Clayton Act was proposed in order to develop greater certainty in antitrust. See President Wilson's message recommending additional antitrust legislation in *Congressional Record*, Vol. 51 (1914), p. 1963. See also Gerard Henderson, *The Federal Trade Commission* (1924).

[35] See Clair Wilcox's criticism of the "rule of reason," which he feels is unclear. *Public Policies Toward Business* (1955), p. 868. However, he feels that "Complete predictability, in the area of combination and monopolization, is not to be obtained." (P. 871.)

[36] A listing of the *per se* rules may be found in Blackwell Smith, "Effective Competition: Hypothesis for Modernizing the Antitrust Laws," *New York University Law Review*, Vol. 26 (July 1951), Footnote, p. 422.

[37] The "rule of reason" stems from *Standard Oil Co. (N.J.)* v. *U.S.*, 221 U.S. 1 (1911). For a history of the development of the rule of reason see Milton Handler, "The Judicial Architects of the Rule of Reason," *American Bar Association, Antitrust Section, Report 21* (1957), p. 21.

[38] Richard A. Givens argues that the *per se* rules are not exceptions to the rule of reason since the courts held that price-fixing agreements are "in themselves unreasonable." "Parallel Business Conduct Under the Sherman Act," *Antitrust Bulletin*, Vol. 5 (May-June 1960), pp. 273, 276.

[39] See *U.S.* v. *Bausch and Lomb Co.*, 321 U.S. 707 (1944), and *U.S.* v. *Addyston Pipe and Steel Co.*, 85 F. 271 (C.C.A.-6th, 1898), aff'd 175 U.S. 211 (1899). In *U.S.* v. *White Motor Co.*, a district court judge held that a manufacturer who set up exclusive selling territories for distributors had committed a *per se* violation. *CCH Trade Cases-1961*, Par. 70,025 (D.C.N.D. Ohio, April 21, 1961).

[40] For a strong criticism of this principle see Almarin Phillips, "A Critique of United States Experience With Price-Fixing Agreements and the Per Se Rule," *Journal of Industrial Economics*, Vol. 8 (October 1959), p. 13, esp. p. 14; and E. D. Bennett, "Comparison of United States and Foreign Antitrust Laws," *Section of International and Comparative Law Bulletin*, Vol. 3 (1958), pp. 14, 19.

[41] *U.S.* v. *Trenton Potteries Co.*, 273 U.S. 392, 397-98 (1927).

[42] *U.S.* v. *Socony-Vacuum Oil Co., Inc. et al.*, 310 U.S. 150 (1940), footnote 59. "But it is well established that a person 'may be guilty of conspiring although incapable of committing the objective offense.' . . . And it is likewise well settled that conspiracies under the Sherman Act are not dependent on any overt act other than the act of conspiring. . . . It is the 'contract, combination . . . or conspiracy in restraint of trade or commerce' which § 1 of the Act strikes down, whether the concerted activity be wholly nascent or abortive on the one hand, or successful on the other. . . . And the amount of interstate or foreign trade involved is not material. . . . Whatever economic justification particular price-fixing agreements may be thought to have, the law does not permit an inquiry into their reasonableness."

[43] Edward S. Mason, *Economic Concentration and the Monopoly Problem* (1957), p. 394.

[44] *Standard Oil Co. of California* v. *U.S.*, 337 U.S. 293 (1949).

[45] *International Salt Co.* v. *U.S.*, 332 U.S. 392 (1947).

[46] A contrary decision was made in *Tampa Electric Co.* v. *Nashville Coal Co.* (Feb. 27, 1961), *CCH Trade Cases*, Par. 69,940. In that case, which involved an electric utility company's requirements contract for coal, the Supreme Court held that it was "necessary to weigh the probable effect of the contract on the relevant area of effective competition. . . ."

[47] For a critique of this principle, see Alfred E. Kahn, "A Legal and Economic Appraisal of the 'New' Sherman and Clayton Acts," *Yale Law Journal*, Vol. 63 (January 1954), pp. 293, 325. Efforts to apply the same rule in Sec. 7 cases, against mergers, have not been successful despite similarity in language. See *U.S.* v. *Brown Shoe Co., Inc.* (E. D. Mo. 1956), *CCH Trade Cases*, Par. 68,244.

[48] See discussion in *Report of the Attorney General's National Committee to Study the Antitrust Laws* (1955) and Note, "Competitive Injury Under the Robinson-Patman Act," *Harvard Law Review*, Vol. 74 (June 1961), p. 1597. Alfred Kahn feels that the Commission has gone to absurd lengths in this direction. *Op. cit.*, p. 335.

[49] See *Anheuser-Busch* v. *F.T.C.*, 363 U.S. 536 (1960). For an argument against

a *per se* approach see Jules Backman, "An Economist Looks at the Robinson-Patman Act," *Proceedings,* Section of Antitrust Law, American Bar Association (August 1960), p. 343. See also Milton Handler, "Recent Antitrust Developments," *Yale Law Journal,* Vol. 71 (November 1961), pp. 75, 99-102. It has been held that economic effects do not need to be considered in enforcing another antidiscrimination provision under the Packers and Stockyards Act. *Wilson & Co.* v. *Ezra Taft Benson, Secretary of Agriculture, CCH Trade Cases* (1961), Par. 69,931.

[50] *In the Matter of Yale & Towne Mfg. Co.,* 52 F.T.C. 1580 (1956). See discussion of this proceeding in Julian O. von Kalinowski, "Price Discrimination and Competitive Effects," *Proceedings,* Section of Antitrust Law, American Bar Association (August 1960), pp. 360, 369-71. See also *Whitaker Cable Corp.* v. *F.T.C.,* 293 F. 2d 253 (C.C.A.-7th 1957) cert. denied 353 U.S. 938 (1957), and *In the Matter of Fred Bonner Corporation,* Docket 7068, Opinion of the Commission (Sept. 29, 1960) (mimeo.), pp. 2-6. An effective statement against a *per se* approach may be found in the initial decision of the hearing examiner *In the Matter of United Biscuit Co. of America,* Docket 7817 (July 26, 1961). For a discussion of changes in the commission's attitudes see Frederick M. Rowe, "Borderline Issues in Court and Commission Cases Under Section 2 and 3 Cases," *Proceedings,* Section of Antitrust Law, American Bar Association (April 1956), pp. 60-72, 80-82.

[51] An outstanding *per se* case was *U.S.* v. *Socony-Vacuum Oil Co., Inc. et al.,* 310 U.S. 150, 60 S.Ct. 811 (1940). It clearly established the rule that price-fixing is illegal regardless of economic effects. Yet, the record of the case covered 12,000 pages plus more than 1,000 exhibits. Almarin Phillips, "Policy Implications of the Theory of Interfirm Organization," *American Economic Review,* Vol. 51 (1961), pp. 245, 254.

[52] *Eastern States Lumber Ass'n* v. *U.S.,* 234 U.S. 600, 612 (1914); see also *Interstate Circuit* v. *U.S.,* 306 U.S. 208, 227 (1939).

[53] Richard B. O'Donnell, "Civil Antitrust Trials," *Proceedings,* Section of Antitrust Law, American Bar Association (April 1954), p. 73.

[54] Almarin Phillips concludes that a "rule of reason approach" would be more appropriate than *per se* even in price fixing cases. "A Critique of United States Experience with Price-Fixing Agreements and the Per Se Rule," *Journal of Industrial Economics,* Vol. 8 (October 1959), pp. 13, 14.

[55] Corwin D. Edwards suggests the use of rebuttable presumptions in merger cases. *Administered Prices,* Hearings before the Senate Judiciary Committee, 86 Cong. 1 sess. (1959), Pt. 9, p. 4811.

[56] George Stigler suggests the following rule in merger cases: (1) a presumption in favor of a firm with "less than 5 to 10 per cent of an industry's output (after merger)"; (2) a presumption against a firm with one fifth or more of the industry's output; (3) an investigation of all firms in between if their annual sales are $5 million or more. "Mergers and Preventative Antitrust Policy," *University of Pennsylvania Law Review,* Vol. 104 (1955), pp. 176, 182.

[57] According to *Business Week* Lee Loevinger, Assistant Attorney General, Antitrust Division, "raises the question whether the antitrust laws should be applied to small business in a different way from large companies." (March 25, 1961, p. 66.) See John C. Stedman, "A New Look at Antitrust: The Report of the Attorney General's Committee," *Journal of Public Law,* Vol. 4 (1956), pp. 223, 273.

[58] See Seymour D. Lewis, "Orderly Marketing and the Small Business Man," *Proceedings,* Section of Antitrust Law, American Bar Association (April 1960), p. 73; and Abe Fortas, "The Grievances of the Small Business Man—A Bill of Particulars," *ibid.,* pp. 33, 34.

[59] For example, Edward S. Mason suggests that there may be occasions when

a price-fixing agreement may lead to a more competitive market structure. However, "this outcome is sufficiently infrequent not to be worth bothering about." "Market Power and Business Conduct: Some Comments," *American Economic Review,* Supplement, Vol. 46 (1956), pp. 471, 477.

[60] See Mason's discussion of the argument concerning *per se* and rule of reason in *ibid.,* pp. 471, 478-79.

[61] *U.S.* v. *E. I. du Pont de Nemours & Co.,* Supreme Court (May 22, 1961). See also Edward Levi, "The Antitrust Laws and Monopoly," *University of Chicago Law Review,* Vol. 14 (1947), pp. 153, 182.

[62] Hans B. Thorelli, *The Federal Antitrust Policy* (1945), p. 571.

[63] See Jesse W. Markham, "An Alternative Approach to the Concept of Workable Competition," *American Economic Review,* Vol. 40 (June 1950), pp. 349, 361; Carl Kaysen, *United States* v. *United Shoe Machinery Corporation, An Economic Analysis of an Anti-Trust Case* (1956), pp. 271, 340; Edward H. Mason, "Workable Competition Versus Workable Monopoly," *Business Practices Under Federal Antitrust Laws,* Proceedings of the Third Annual Meeting of the New York State Bar Association, Section on Antitrust Law (Jan. 24, 1951), pp. 67, 68.

[64] The Supreme Court said that the courts "may not impose penalties in the guise of preventing future violation." *Hartford-Empire Co.* v. *U.S.,* 323 U.S. 386 (1945).

[65] Walton H. Hamilton states a strong case for developing specific, rather than general, remedies in *Price and Price Policies* (1938), p. 4. See Justice Douglas' opinion in *U.S.* v. *Crescent Amusement Co.,* 323 U.S. 173, 186 (1944).

[66] Baddia J. Rashid is impressed with the "infinite varieties of injunctive relief." At the same time, he points to the similarities in decrees. "What is Right with Antitrust?" *Antitrust Bulletin,* Vol. 5 (January-February 1960), pp. 5, 18.

[67] An interesting suggestion regarding the use of an additional import duty to remedy a "monopolistic" situation is contained in Senate Judiciary Committee, Antitrust and Monopoly Subcommittee, *Petroleum, the Antitrust Laws and Government Policies* (1957), p. 7.

[68] Several countries provide for such remedies. The Brazil Law on Customs Tariff of 1940 provides that import duties may be reduced or eliminated if competing domestic goods are produced or dealt with by cartels. United Nations Economic and Social Council, *Restrictive Business Practices, Annex C, Supplement No. 11B* (1953), p. 39. Canada has a similar provision in the Combines Investigation Act. *Ibid.,* p. 49. The Union of South Africa authorizes the Minister of Economic Development to reduce duties to the minimum applicable rate if an industry protected by a maximum rate acts "in a manner which tends to such a restraint of trade . . . as is detrimental to the public interest." *Ibid.,* p. 201. An interesting point of view is suggested in an article in *The Economist* of June 3, 1961. "Britain, for its part, had at least begun to realize last year that even unilateral tariff cuts would be good for the British economy, because they would foster more competition. . . ." (P. 983.) See testimony of R. A. Gordon, *Employment, Growth, and Price Levels,* Hearings before the Joint Economic Committee, 86 Cong. 1 sess. (1959), Pt. 9A, p. 2968. He suggests that foreign competition will help to dampen inflationary wage increases. See also testimony of Walter Adams, *Administered Prices,* Hearings before the Senate Judiciary Committee, 86 Cong. 1 sess. (1959), Pt. 9, p. 4786; and Nathan Probst, Jr., "The Failure of the Sherman Antitrust Law," *University of Pennsylvania Law Review,* Vol. 75 (1926), p. 122.

[69] George W. Stocking remarked, after reviewing several prominent antitrust cases, "The decisions banned the monopolistic practices but left unmodified the structure of the industry which may have shaped practices." "Economic Change

and the Sherman Act: Some Reflections on 'Workable Competition,'" *Virginia Law Review,* Vol. 44 (1958), pp. 537, 545. See also Robert C. Brooks, Jr., "Price Cutting and Monopoly Power," *Journal of Marketing,* Vol. 25 (1961), pp. 44, 49; and Corwin D. Edwards, *Maintaining Competition* (1949), p. 288.

[70] Joe S. Bain, *Industrial Organization* (1959), pp. 535, 536.

[71] S. Rept. 597, 63 Cong. 2 sess. (1914), pp. 9, 11. See also Gerard Henderson, *The Federal Trade Commission* (1924), p. 92.

[72] Sec. 5(b), Federal Trade Commission Act, 15 U.S.C. 41; and Sec. 11, Clayton Act, 15 U.S.C. 12. While it might be argued that the commission has the power to require specific practices as a means of implementing its cease and desist orders, it has not interpreted its authority in that way. A change may be in the offing. A January 1962 order requires specific practices. The consent order, *In the Matter of the Rubber Manufacturers Assn., Inc.,* Docket 7505 (Order dated Jan. 6, 1962), provides that the respondents cease a price conspiracy. Each company is ordered to review its prices "on the basis of its own costs, the margin of profit individually desired, and other lawful considerations." It must then establish new prices based on this review.

[73] *In the Matter of Pillsbury Mills, Inc.,* Docket 6000, Opinion of the Commission (mimeo.), pp. 10, 11. *U.S.* v. *Standard Oil of California,* 78 F. Supp. 850, 866-67 (D.C.S.D.Cal., 1948).

[74] Barbara Burt, "Antitrust Laws—Judicial Relief for Violations of Section Seven of the Clayton Act—Disenfranchisement in *United States* v. *E. I. du Pont de Nemours & Co.,*" *Michigan Law Review,* Vol. 58 (May 1960), pp. 1024, 1041.

[75] See *Standard Fashion Co.* v. *Magrane-Houston Co.,* 258 U.S. 346, 356 (1922); *F.T.C.* v. *Raladann Co.,* 283 U.S. 643 (1931), p. 647; *Dictograph Products* v. *F.T.C.,* 217 F. 2d 821 (C.C.A.-2d 1954), pp. 821, 826-27; *Transamerica Corp.* v. *Federal Reserve Board,* 206 F. 2d 163 (1953). A former chairman of the F.T.C. went one step further, maintaining that "the Federal Trade Commission Act was designed . . . to stop in their incipiency acts and practices which, when full blown, would violate" the Clayton Act as well as the Sherman Act. Edward F. Howrey, "Utilization of the F.T.C. of Section 5 of the Federal Trade Commission Act as an Antitrust Law," *Antitrust Bulletin,* Vol. 5 (March-April 1960), pp. 161, 172. Thus, incipiency precedes incipiency. See also *F.T.C.* v. *Motion Picture Advertising Service Co.,* 344 U.S. 392, 394 (1953).

[76] Probably because of this difference, antitrust authorities seem to prefer trying Clayton Act cases to Sherman Act proceedings. See Victor H. Kramer, "The Trial of a Protracted Antitrust Case—A Proposal," *American Bar Association Section of Antitrust Law,* Vol. 18 (1961), pp. 41, 42; and Robert A. Bicks, "Current Enforcement Policies," *New Theories of Federal Trade Commission Enforcement,* CCH Trade Regulation Reports, No. 153 (Extra ed., June 8, 1960), pp. 25, 28.

[77] *U.S.* v. *E. I. du Pont de Nemours & Co.,* 353 U.S. 586 (1957).

[78] "Relative severity of the sanction or remedy which may be imposed has often been considered a sufficient reason to require a higher degree of probability in proof than would otherwise be required in a civil action." George H. Dession, "The Trial of Economic and Technological Issues of Fact: I," *Yale Law Journal,* Vol. 58 (June 1949), pp. 1019, 1045.

[79] Walton H. Hamilton, *The Politics of Industry* (1957), p. 143.

[80] John A. Duncan makes a considerable point of the latitude permitted the department in drafting consent decrees. "Post-Litigation Resulting from Alleged Non-Compliance with Government Antitrust Consent Decrees," *Western Reserve Law Review,* Vol. 8 (1957), p. 45.

[81] This issue is not that of enforcement; yet it is tied in with active enforcement procedures. There has been sharp criticism of the agencies because they have

negotiated orders and have not checked compliance with them. See, for example, *Patent Policies of Departments and Agencies of the Federal Government—1959,* Hearings before the Senate Select Committee on Small Business, 86 Cong. 1 sess. (1960), pp. 16, 23, and *U.S. vs. Economic Concentration and Monopoly,* Staff Report to the Monopoly Subcommittee of the House Committee on Small Business, 79 Cong. 2 sess. (1946), pp. 26, 46.

[82] There are bits and pieces of interesting information. See, for example, letter from Robert A. Bicks, Acting Assistant Attorney General, *Patent Policies of Departments and Agencies of the Federal Government—1959,* Hearings, p. 422. He points out several instances when new competition was developed through decrees requiring patent licenses. R. L. Sich, the Registrar of Restrictive Trading Agreements in Great Britain, has said, "In some cases the ending of common price agreements has been marked by immediate and quite considerable price reductions; in others there has been no immediate change, but that, of course, does not mean that there never will be." "Developments Under the Restrictive Trade Practices Act, 1956, of the United Kingdom," *Proceedings,* Section of Antitrust Law, American Bar Association (August 1960), pp. 285, 293. Later he pointed out that, "The ending of restrictive agreements has also in a number of cases been accompanied or shortly followed by mergers." *Ibid.* See John Heath, *Not Enough Competition?*, Institute of Economic Affairs, Hobart Paper II (London, 1961), for a quick analysis of the effects of various decisions under the British Restrictive Trade Practices Act of 1956. A purchasing agent for the State of Florida reported that there was a 20 per cent reduction in the prices paid on state bakery contracts after successful criminal proceedings for price-fixing. *Consumer Protection Activities of Federal Departments and Agencies,* Eighth Report by the House Committee on Government Operations, 87 Cong. 1 sess. (1961), p. 295. See Hans B. Thorelli, *The Federal Antitrust Policy* (1954), p. 606, and "Antitrust: Consent Decree: The History and Effect of Western Electric Co. *v.* United States," *Cornell Law Quarterly,* Vol. 45 (Fall 1959), p. 88.

[83] A Federal Trade Commission report indicates that a number of corporate mergers took place shortly after participating firms were cited for price collusion. *The Merger Movement* (1948). Simon Whitney reports the merger of defendants after a price-fixing case [*U.S.* v. *Addyston Pipe and Steel Co.,* 85 F. 271 (C.C.A.-6th 1898), aff'd 175 U.S. 211 (1899)]. Simon N. Whitney, *Antitrust Policies,* Vol. 2 (1958), p. 13. See also Thorelli, *loc cit.;* and Almarin Phillips, "A Critique of United States Experience with Price-Fixing Agreements and the Per Se Rule," *Journal of Industrial Economics,* Vol. 8 (October 1959), p. 15.

[84] In the *International Salt* case it was held that district courts enjoy "large discretion to model their judgments to fit the exigencies of the particular case." *International Salt Co.* v. *U.S.,* 332 U.S. 392, 400-01 (1947).

[85] *U.S.* v. *E. I. du Pont de Nemours & Co.,* U.S. Supreme Court (May 22, 1961).

[86] See, for example, Judge Wyzanski's opinion in *U.S.* v. *United Shoe Machinery,* 110 F. Supp. 295 (D.C. Mass., 1953), aff'd *per curiam* 347 U.S. 521 (1954).

[87] For a discussion of some of the problems regarding the scope of decrees or orders see Harry L. Shniderman, "Federal Trade Commission Orders Under the Robinson-Patman Act: An Argument for Limiting Their Impact on Subsequent Pricing Conduct," *Harvard Law Review,* Vol. 65 (March 1952), p. 750.

[88] *F.T.C.* v. *National Lead Co.,* 352 U.S. 419, 429 (1957).

[89] George W. Stocking, "Economic Change and the Sherman Act: Some Reflections on 'Workable Competition,' " *Virginia Law Review,* Vol. 44 (1958), p. 537.

[90] Earl A. Jinkinson, "Observations on the Trial of An Antitrust Case," *Antitrust Bulletin,* Vol. 5 (1960), pp. 551, 555.

[91] Estimated from table in House Small Business Committee, *Congress and the Monopoly Problem,* H. Doc. 240, 85 Cong. 1 sess. (1957), p. 660, and "Workload Statement" of Antitrust Division (mimeo.).

[92] Earl W. Kintner, "The Role of Robinson-Patman in the Antitrust Scheme of Things—The Perspective of Enforcement Officials," *Proceedings,* Section of Antitrust Law, American Bar Association (August 1960), p. 315.

[93] Information furnished by the Federal Trade Commission. For a breakdown of the orders issued before Sept. 30, 1956, by statutory provisions, see H. Doc. 240, 85 Cong. 1 sess., p. 661.

[94] The wide variety in decree provisions is demonstrated in Philip Marcus, "Impact on Business of Antitrust Decrees," *Vanderbilt Law Review,* Vol. 11 (1958), p. 309. See also Vernon A. Mund, "Refusal to Sell," *ibid.,* p. 354, for list of decrees with compulsory selling provisions.

[95] John Heath proposes that such analysis be undertaken in the United Kingdom. *Not Enough Competition?,* Institute of Economic Affairs, Hobart Paper II (London, 1961), p. 39.

[96] For example, Michael Conant, *Antitrust in the Motion Picture Industry: Economic and Legal Analysis* (1960).

[97] Several pieces of evidence are contained in the testimony of Robert A. Bicks, Acting Assistant Attorney General, Antitrust Division, Department of Justice in *Employment, Growth, and Price Levels,* Hearings before the Joint Economic Committee, Pt. 7, 86 Cong. 1 sess. (1959). See also House Judiciary Committee, Antitrust Subcommittee, *Report on Consent Decree Program of the Department of Justice,* 86 Cong. 1 sess. (1959); Senate Judiciary Committee, Subcommittee on Antitrust and Monopoly, *Antitrust and Monopoly Activities, 1960,* 87 Cong. 1 sess. (1961), p. 30.

[98] For example, James W. McKie found that the decree in *U.S.* v. *American Can Co.* [87 F. Supp. 18 (N.D. Cal., 1949)] led to "The Decline of Monopoly in the Metal Container Industry," *American Economic Review,* Vol. 45 (May 1955), p. 499. He felt that there was an extensive breakdown of exclusive supply arrangements, that price leadership had weakened, that smaller firms were establishing firmer bases, and that food packers were beginning to manufacture their own cans. "A forecast of workable competition appears to be justified." (P. 508.) See also statement by J. H. Stauss, who is not as sanguine as McKie but who agrees that the case "has improved the economic health" of the industry. *Ibid.,* p. 528.

[99] *U.S.* v. *Gold Filled Mfrs. Assn., Inc.,* (D.C. Mass. 1957), *CCH Trade Cases,* Par. 68,760. See also *U.S.* v. *L. A. Young Spring and Wire Corp.* (D.C.E.D. Mich. 1951), *CCH Trade Cases,* Par. 62,905; *U.S.* v. *Foster Wheeler* (D.C.E.D. Penn., Consent Decree Filed May 22, 1961); *In the Matter of the Rubber Manufacturers Assn., Inc.,* F.T.C. Docket 7505, Order dated Jan. 6, 1962.

[100] *U.S.* v. *Standard Oil of California,* 337 U.S. 293 (1949).

[101] "Outlawing of requirements contracts between producers and distributors has on occasion been an inducement to the large company to integrate for reasons of law rather than economics." A. D. H. Kaplan, *Big Enterprise in a Competitive System* (1954), p. 247. See also Friedrich Kessler and Richard H. Stern, "Competition, Contract, and Vertical Integration," *Yale Law Journal,* Vol. 69 (November 1959), p. 1, esp. pp. 122-27. The article discusses various uses of vertical integration to avoid the incidence of antitrust laws.

[102] John Heath raises a similar question. "A price agreement and an oligopoly may be real alternatives, the removal of one resulting in the other." *Op. cit.,* p. 20.

[103] Senate Judiciary Committee, Subcommittee on Patents, Trademarks and

Copyrights, *Compulsory Patent Licensing Under Antitrust Judgments,* Staff Report, 86 Cong. 2 sess. (1960).

[104] *Ibid,* p. 13

[105] *Ibid.,* p. 14.

[106] *Ibid.,* pp. 14, 18.

[107] *Ibid.,* p. 21.

[108] *Ibid.,* p. 22.

[109] *Report on Consent Decree Program of the Department of Justice,* 86 Cong. 1 sess. (1959), p. 119.

[110] Fritz Machlup regards price discrimination as a symptom, not a cause, of monopoly. Fritz Machlup, *The Political Economy of Monopoly* (1952), pp. 136-37. Following this theory, a Robinson-Patman order would not get at the root of the problem.

[111] Provisions against discrimination are contained in decrees under other acts as well as Robinson-Patman. Philip Marcus, "Impact on Business of Antitrust Decrees," *Vanderbilt Law Review,* Vol. 11 (March 1958), p. 310.

[112] See Harry L. Shniderman, "Federal Trade Commission Orders Under the Robinson-Patman Act: An Argument for Limiting Their Impact on Subsequent Pricing Conduct," *Harvard Law Review,* Vol. 65 (1952), p. 772.

[113] For a similar suggestion see J. B. Heath, "Restrictive Practices and After," *The Manchester School of Economic and Social Studies,* Vol. 29 (May 1961), pp. 173, 202.

[114] Corwin D. Edwards, *The Price Discrimination Law* (1959).

[115] Kaysen argues that this procedure is undesirable. Carl Kaysen, *U.S.* v. *United Shoe Machinery Corporation, An Economic Analysis of an Anti-Trust Case* (1956), p. 271.

[116] Hartford-Empire *Co. et al.* v. *U.S.,* 323 U.S. 386 (1945); 324 U.S. 570 (1945).

[117] See *Compulsory Patent Licensing Under Antitrust Judgments,* Staff Report of the Senate Judiciary Committee, Subcommittee on Patents, Trademarks and Copyrights, 86 Cong. 2 sess. (1960), pp. 24, 25.

[118] *U.S.* v. *American Society of Composers, Authors and Publishers* (D.C.S.D.N.Y. 1941), *CCH Trade Cases,* Par. 56,104. Under the provisions of ASCAP, consent decree royalty rates charged for the use of copyright material are fixed, together with the rules for the administration of the society and the distribution of its income. Further proceedings for modification of the decree were held in 1950 and 1959. See *Sam Fox Publishing Co., Inc.* v. *U.S.* (S. Ct. May 1961) *CCH Trade Cases,* Par. 70,030, for a discussion of the history of the modifications and for an illustration of the types of problems which may arise under such a decree; that case turned on the effort of some members of the society who wanted to intervene in order to object to certain phases of the decree modification; it was decided that they could not intervene. See also "Comment, ASCAP and the Antitrust Laws: The Story of a Reasonable Compromise," *Duke Law Journal,* Vol. 1959 (1959), p. 259; and Sigmund Timberg, "The Antitrust Aspects of Merchandising Modern Music: The ASCAP Consent Judgment of 1950," *Law and Contemporary Problems,* Vol. 19 (1954), p. 294.

[119] Such provisions raise a new and difficult problem: how to determine what are "reasonable" royalties. Neither theory nor the administration of these decrees have provided any substantial basis for gauging such license fees. Systematic analysis, which might provide significant criteria and yardsticks, has not been undertaken.

[120] *Compulsory Patent Licensing Under Antitrust Judgments* (1960).

[121] See Justice Brennan's opinion in *U.S.* v. *E. I. du Pont de Nemours & Co.* (U.S. Supreme Court, May 22, 1961). He rejected the company's argument that an

injunction which would eliminate its voting rights in General Motors should be issued instead of requiring it to divest itself of GM stock. He felt that "the policing of an injunction would probably involve the courts and the Government in regulation of private affairs more deeply than the administration of a simple order of divestiture."

[122] See *Compulsory Patent Licensing Under Antitrust Judgments* (1960). It is suggested that the Antitrust Division should supervise compulsory patents, since "applicants may be reluctant to institute royalty proceedings." (P. 53.)

[123] Yale Brozen discusses the problem of foreign competition and its stimulation of new efficiency in U.S. business in "The New Competition—International Markets: How Should We Adapt?", *Journal of Business,* Vol. 33 (October 1960), esp. p. 325. Administrative decisions to reduce or remove a protective tariff in order to increase market competition may be feasible if recent recommendations regarding an amendment to the Trade Agreements Act are accepted. It was suggested that the President be granted "authority to negotiate tariff reductions across the board in place of his present authority to negotiate item by item." Joint Economic Committee, *A New Look at Foreign Economic Policy,* 87 Cong. 1 sess. (1961), p. 6. See Sir Robert Hall, "Britain's Economic Problem," *The Economist,* Pt. 2, Vol. 200 (Sept. 23, 1961), pp. 1132, 1133. He refers to the possible desirability of compensating declining industries instead of protecting them against foreign competition.

[124] Such a program was probably envisaged in the formation of the Monopolies and Restrictive Practices Commission in the United Kingdom. Parliament has passed only one order covering an industry, Dental Goods. The order merely required that certain practices be discontinued. See John Heath, *Not Enough Competition?,* Institute of Economic Affairs, Hobart Paper II (London, 1961), p. 23.

[125] 15 U.S.C. 79.

[126] 17 U.S.C. 1.

[127] 15 U.S.C. 1221 *et seq.*

[128] Such a procedure is inherent in the controls of some other countries. For example, the functions of the Monopolies Commission of the United Kingdom include the reporting of recommendations to Parliament. Legislation may follow. C. Hilary Scott, "The 'Antitrust' Laws of the United Kingdom," *Proceedings,* Section of Antitrust Law, American Bar Association (August 1960), pp. 436, 438-39.

[129] See, for example, *Report of the Attorney General's National Committee to Study the Antitrust Laws* (1955), Chap. 8.

[130] Donald Dewey, *Monopoly in Economics and Law* (1959), pp. 156, 246-49, 308.

[131] See Marver H. Bernstein, *Regulating Business by Independent Commissions* (1955).

[132] Corwin D. Edwards, *Maintaining Competition* (1949), p. 293.

[133] See Emmette S. Redford, *Administration of National Economic Control* (1952), esp. pp. 277-83; James M. Landis, *Report on Regulatory Agencies to the President-Elect* (1960), p. 30.

[134] General statements of congressional committees have not had much influence. See, for example, *1960 Joint Economic Report,* Report of the Joint Economic Committee on the January 1960 Economic Report of the President, 86 Cong. 2 sess. (1960). The committee states that the Antitrust Division's budget of less than $4.5 million is "much too meager an amount for the functions it is expected to perform." (P. 18.) The division's budget was increased to $5 million for 1961. *Consumer Protection Activities of Federal Departments and Agencies,* Eighth

Report by the House Committee on Government Operations, 87 Cong. 1 sess. (1961), p. 296. See also Corwin D. Edwards, *Maintaining Competition* (1949).

[135] "The regulatory process necessitates the development of more detailed lines of policy from rather general legislative declarations and also the application of these more detailed policies to specific cases." *Investigation of Executive Agencies of the Government,* Preliminary Report of the Select Committee to Investigate the Executive Agencies of the Government, S. Rept. 1275, 75 Cong. 1 sess. (1937), p. 770.

[136] Hugh M. Hall, Jr., "Responsibility of President and Congress for Regulatory Policy Development," *Law and Contemporary Problems,* Vol. 26 (Spring 1961), p. 261.

[137] See Robert Ginnane, "The Control of Federal Administration by Congressional Resolution and Committees," *Harvard Law Review,* Vol. 66 (1952), p. 569.

[138] Ferrel Heady and Eleanor Tabor Linenthal, "Congress and Administrative Regulation," *Law and Contemporary Problems,* Vol. 26 (Spring 1961), p. 238.

[139] "As a charter of freedom, the [Sherman] Act has a generality and adaptability comparable to that found to be desirable in constitutional provisions." Chief Justice Hughes in *Appalachian Coals, Inc.,* v. *U.S.,* 288 U.S. 344, 359-60 (1933).

[140] Hugh M. Hall, Jr., describes equally vague provisions in other acts. *Op. cit.,* pp. 276-77.

[141] See *ibid.,* pp. 278-80.

[142] President's Committee on Administrative Management, *Administrative Management in the Government of the United States* (1937); Robert E. Cushman, *The Independent Regulatory Commissions* (1941).

[143] See James M. Landis, *The Administrative Process* (1938).

[144] For a discussion of congressional influences on the independent commissions, especially regarding procedures, see Heady and Linenthal, *loc. cit.* See also Winston M. Fick, "Issues and Accomplishments in Administrative Regulation: Some Political Aspects," *Law and Contemporary Problems,* Vol. 26 (Spring 1961), pp. 283, 294.

[145] Hall, *op. cit.,* p. 269.

[146] See Emmette S. Redford, *Administration of National Economic Control* (1952). Professor Redford deals with the independence of the agencies and argues that they are not free of presidential control.

[147] An extension of the discussion of the relative positions of departments and commissions may be found in Mark S. Massel, "The Regulatory Process," *Law and Contemporary Problems,* Vol. 26 (Spring 1961), p. 181.

[148] Herbert A. Simon points out the deficiencies of an outmoded theory that administration is only "the neutral instrument of policy." "Recent Advances in Organization Theory," *Research Frontiers in Politics and Government: Brookings Lectures 1955* (1955), pp. 23, 24.

[149] *U.S.* v. *Standard Oil of California,* 337 U.S. 293 (1949).

[150] *In the Matter of The Maico Co., Inc.,* F.T.C. Docket 5822, *CCH Trade Regulation Reports* (Dec. 15, 1953), Par. 11,577.

[151] For example, *In the Matter of Mytinger & Casselberry,* F.T.C. Docket 6962. Order to cease and desist, Sept. 28, 1960. Opinion of the Commission, p. 3, same date.

[152] Kahn is critical of the commission's tendency to follow mechanical judicial rules. He feels that the commission "has failed to realize the anticipated advantages of flexible and expert regulation of business practices by administrative commissions, rather than by judicial combat, and has come perilously close to undermining its very reason for existence." Alfred E. Kahn, "A Legal and Economic Appraisal of the 'New' Sherman and Clayton Acts," *Yale Law Journal,* Vol. 63 (1954), footnote p. 335.

[153] *U.S.* v. *National Lead Co. et al.,* 332 U.S. 319 (1947), *CCH Trade Cases,* Par. 57,575.

[154] Earl W. Kintner, "The Current Ordeal of the Administrative Process," Address delivered to Antitrust Section of the Illinois State Bar Association, Nov. 5, 1959 (mimeo.), p. 14. See also Henry D. Stringer, "The Piece Goods Buyer and the New Textile Labeling Act," Jan. 12, 1960 (F.T.C. mimeo.).

[155] See, for example, the following Guides: *Deceptive Advertising* (October 1958); *Tire Advertising* (May 1958); *Bait Advertising* (November 1959); *Deceptive Advertising of Guarantees* (April 1960); and *Advertising Allowances* (May 1960).

[156] See Harry L. Shniderman, "Collateral Discriminations Under the Robinson-Patman Act—Section 2(c), (d) and (e)," *Proceedings,* Section of Antitrust Law, American Bar Association, Vol. 17 (1960), p. 410, esp. the discussion of *Exquisite Form* on p. 417.

[157] Discussed in Mark S. Massel, "What the Delivered Pricing Problem is All About," in U.S. Chamber of Commerce, *Delivered Pricing and the Future of American Business* (1948), pp. 10, 11.

[158] See Kintner, "The Current Ordeal of the Administrative Process," *op. cit.,* p. 11.

[159] *U.S.* v. *E. I. du Pont de Nemours & Co.,* 351 U.S. 377 (1956).

[160] *U.S.* v. *E. I. du Pont de Nemours & Co.,* 353 U.S. 586 (1957).

[161] *U.S.* v. *Aluminum Co. of America,* 148 F. 2d 416 (C.C.A.-2d 1945).

[162] See discussion of rule-making in Marver H. Bernstein, *Regulating Business by Independent Commissions* (1955), esp. pp. 179-82. For a review of the mechanics of promulgating rules see Council of State Governments, "Administrative Rule-Making Procedure in the States" (mimeo., 1961).

[163] For example, Louis Hector, "Problems of the CAB and the Independent Regulatory Commissions," *Yale Law Journal,* Vol. 69 (1960), p. 931.

[164] This distinction is made in the Administrative Procedure Act (5 U.S.C. 1001-11), which sets different procedural rules for each phase.

[165] It is interesting to note President Wilson's assurance in 1913, that uncertainty can be eliminated by explicit statutes—probably such as the Clayton Act. His statement is reprinted in *Law-Enforcement Activities Affecting Small Business,* Report to the House Select Committee on Small Business, 85 Cong. 2 sess. (1959), p. 21.

[166] Everette MacIntyre, on being sworn in as a member of the Federal Trade Commission, expressed the hope that the commission would undertake the promulgation of rules "which would condemn harmful trade practices industry by industry rather than case by case." Release of F.T.C., Sept. 26, 1961, p. 2. Commissioner MacIntyre expanded on this suggestion in an address before the American Marketing Association on Dec. 28, 1961. *CCH Trade Regulation Reports,* Par. 50,110. See also *Law-Enforcement Activities Affecting Small Business,* p. 20; and Corwin D. Edwards, *Maintaining Competition* (1959), pp. 304-06.

[167] Marver H. Bernstein, "The Regulatory Process: A Framework for Analysis," *Law and Contemporary Problems,* Vol. 26 (Spring 1961), pp. 329, 331-33.

[168] For a more extended discussion see Mark S. Massel, "The Regulatory Process," *ibid.,* p. 181.

[169] The report of the Senate Judiciary Committee on the act stated that the cost provision "leaves trade and industry free from any restriction or impediment to the adoption and use of more economic processes. . . ." S. Rept. 1502, 74 Cong. 2 sess. (1936), p. 5. See also John E. Murray, Jr., "Cost Justification and the Robinson-Patman Act: Suggestions for a More Workable Defense," *Saint Louis University Law Journal,* Vol. 6 (Spring 1960), pp. 20, 21.

[170] Corwin D. Edwards referred to an O.P.A. report that 85 per cent of the

companies with which O.P.A. dealt during World War II could not supply costs for individual products. *Administered Prices,* Hearings before the Senate Judiciary Committee, 86 Cong. 1 sess. (1959), Pt. 9, pp. 4804, 4805.

[171] Jules Backman, "An Economist Looks at the Robinson-Patman Act," *Proceedings,* Section of Antitrust Law, American Bar Association (August 1960), pp. 343, 349; Arthur Andersen, *An N.R.A. Enigma: What Constitutes "Selling Below Cost"?* (1933). Mr. Andersen, head of a leading accounting firm, asked, "What sound basis then can possibly be set for the allocation of selling and advertising expense to all products, when the only common factor is their dollar cost or dollar sales value?" (P. 4.)

[172] See "Advisory Committee on Cost Justification Report to the Federal Trade Commission," reproduced in Herbert F. Taggart, *Cost Justification* (1959).

[173] B. Fog, *Industrial Pricing Policies* (1960), pp. 222, 223.

[174] See "Advisory Committee on Cost Justification Report to the Federal Trade Commission," Taggart, *op cit.,* p. 555.

[175] For a general argument in support of the theory see Note, "Competitive Injury under the Robinson-Patman Act," *Harvard Law Review,* Vol. 75 (June 1961), p. 1597.

[176] "The recorded cases suggest that the Commission has permitted respondents to show any reasonable cost differences which are based upon some showing of factual cost analysis." Murray, *op. cit.,* p. 20. See also Mark S. Massel, "The Robinson-Patman Act: Cost Justification," *Conference on the Antitrust Laws and the Attorney General's Committee Report* (1955), p. 197.

[177] See Justice Benjamin N. Cardozo's discussion of the need for such coordination in the field of private law. "A Ministry of Justice," in Margaret E. Hall, ed., *Selected Writings of Benjamin Nathan Cardozo* (1947), p. 357.

[178] Corwin D. Edwards, *Maintaining Competition* (1949), p. 288.

[179] Corwin D. Edwards' testimony in *Administered Prices,* Hearings before the Senate Judiciary Committee, 86 Cong. 1 sess. (1959), Pt. 9, p. 4806.

[180] John C. Stedman argues that the strength of the position of the Antitrust Division is "that it *does* play the role of prosecutor. . . ." "The Committee's Report: More Antitrust Enforcement—Or Less?", *Northwestern University Law Review,* Vol. 50 (July-August 1955), pp. 316, 321.

[181] For a discussion of the problem of bringing the policy maker and the social scientist together see Max F. Millikan, "Inquiry and Policy: The Relation of Knowledge to Action," in Daniel Lerner, ed., *The Human Meaning of the Social Sciences* (1959), p. 158.

[182] Political is used not "to convey any undertone of disparagement (as 'politician,' say, often does), but rather merely to refer to the contentious and more dynamic aspects of government." Winston M. Fick, "Issues and Accomplishments in Administrative Regulation: Some Political Aspects," *Law and Contemporary Problems,* Vol. 26 (Spring 1961), p. 283.

[183] Charles E. Lindblom presents an intriguing discussion of the differences in the types of analysis used in policy-making and in theory in "The Science of 'Muddling Through,'" *Public Administration Review,* Vol. 19 (1959), p. 79.

[184] See G. A. Lundberg, *Can Science Save Us* (1947).

[185] "It of course goes without saying that man does not live by real income alone, and that noneconomic considerations must and will play a part in the policy-making process. But the responsibility of the economist, *qua* economist, ends when he has brought into the decision-making process the economic facts and the economic objectives relevant to the problem under consideration." Jacob Viner, "International Trade Theory and Its Present Day Relevance," *Economics and Public Policy: Brookings Lectures 1954* (1955), p. 122.

[186] Donald C. Blaisdell has described the pressure groups and their influences on government regulation in the 1930's in *Economic Power and Political Pressures,* T.N.E.C. Monograph No. 26 (1941).

[187] See E. Benoit-Smullyan, "Value Judgments and the Social Sciences," *Journal of Philosophy,* Vol. 42 (1945), p. 197.

[188] Julius Cohen, "Towards Realism in Legisprudence," *Yale Law Journal,* Vol. 59 (April 1950), esp. p. 897. See also Herbert A. Simon, "Recent Advances in Organization Theory," *Research Frontiers in Politics and Government: Brookings Lectures 1955* (1955), pp. 23, 33, 38.

[189] See Robert A. Dahl's discussion of the relationship between the "policy scientist" and the "policy-maker." "Hierarchy, Democracy, and Bargaining in Politics and Economics," *ibid.,* pp. 45, 67-69.

[190] See Fritz Morstein Marx, "The Mind of the Career Man," *Public Administration Review,* Vol. 20 (1960), p. 133.

[191] A thoughtful discussion of the role of the technician in the policy-making process is developed in Henry A. Kissinger, "The Policymaker and the Intellectual," *The Reporter,* March 5, 1959, p. 30.

[192] For a suggestion that various groups must work together in the "modernization of the law" see Arthur T. Vanderbilt, *The Challenge of Law Reform* (1955), pp. 156-57.

[193] See M. A. Adelman, "Economic Analysis and Critique of the Factors Considered in Judging the Legality of Mergers," *Mergers and Competition: Recent Developments,* Current Business Studies, No. 21 (December 1954), p. 21.

[194] Marver H. Bernstein, *Regulating Business by Independent Commission* (1955); Emmette S. Redford, *Administration of National Economic Control* (1952).

[195] For a brief commentary on the differences between the economist's functions in administration and policy-making see J. B. Heath, "The Restrictive Practices Court on Competition and Price Restriction," *The Manchester School of Economic and Social Studies,* Vol. 28 (January 1960), p. 18.

[196] Clair Wilcox points to the effects on choices of "careful analysis of alternatives." "From Economic Theory to Public Policy," *American Economic Review,* Supplement, Vol. 50 (May 1960), pp. 27, 34. See also Jesse W. Markham, "Economic Analysis," *Proceedings,* Section of Antitrust Law, American Bar Association (April 1954), pp. 145, 152.

[197] Hans B. Thorelli's findings regarding the passage of the Sherman Act are interesting in this connection. He points out that, "Congress and the social scientists were out of touch with one another. . . ." *The Federal Antitrust Policy* (1954), p. 567.

[198] Charles E. Lindblom raises some basic questions about the application of theory in policy formulation. "Policy Analysis," *American Economic Review,* Vol. 48 (1958), p. 298.

[199] See Jacob Viner, "International Trade Theory and its Present Day Relevance," *Economics and Public Policy: Brookings Lectures 1954* (1955), pp. 121-22.

[200] Clair Wilcox raises some provocative questions about the influence of economic theory on policy in "From Economic Theory to Public Policy," *American Economic Review,* Supplement, Vol. 50 (May 1960), p. 27.

[201] See J. Wiseman, "Economic Analysis and Public Policy," *Economic Journal,* Vol. 70 (September 1960), p. 455.

[202] See Charles E. Lindblom, *op. cit.,* p. 299.

# *Chapter 5*

[1] The setting for these problems is discussed in George D. Reycraft, "Practical Problems Presented in the Trials of Recent Merger Cases," *Antitrust Bulletin,* Vol. 4 (September-October 1959), p. 635.

[2] Dudley F. Pegrum feels that "enforcement, which depends upon presentation of evidence under regular rules of court procedure, has proved to be a severe handicap to the development of a readily adaptable policy of industrial control. The issues involved in establishing the patterns of modern industry are too complex for court battles. Broad judgment on what constitutes sound business policy must be exercised, and the courts are not fitted for this." *The Regulation of Industry* (1949), p. 308.

[3] Corwin D. Edwards, "Preserving Competition v. Regulating Monopoly," *American Economic Review,* Supplement, Vol. 30 (1940), Pt. 2, p. 164; E. Barrett Prettyman, "Needed: New Trial Technique: Suggestions for the Trial of Complicated Cases," *ABA Journal,* Vol. 34 (September 1948), p. 766; Henry M. Hart, Jr. and John T. McNaughton, "Evidence and Inference in the Law," in Daniel Lerner, ed., *Evidence and Inference* (1958), pp. 48, 52-53. "A resort to judicial process is an essential of a system of justice. But an attempt to amend or revise the structure and practices of an industry by resort to judicial process is a task fraught with uncertainty. The legal process was intended to do justice in the instant case, to end conflict between two belligerent individuals. It was never shaped for so stupendous and alien a task as causing the channels of commerce to run straight, or fitting an industry out with a new and different set of practices. It is in its nature a bothersome and interminable technique beset with ceremonial and irrelevance. It is possessed of all the frailties which attach to the use of a procedure ill-fitted for the work at hand." Walton H. Hamilton, *The Politics of Industry* (1957), pp. 143-44.

[4] Milton Handler, *A Study of the Construction and Enforcement of the Federal Antitrust Laws,* Temporary National Economic Committee Monograph No. 38 (1941), pp. 90-92.

[5] Stanley N. Barnes, "Settlement by Consent Judgment," *Proceedings,* Section of Antitrust Law, American Bar Association (Spring 1954), pp. 8, 10. See also *U.S.* v. *Economic Concentration and Monopoly,* Staff Report to the Monopoly Subcommittee of the House Committee on Small Business, 79 Cong. 2 sess. (1946), p. 42.

[6] Testimony of George Romney in *Administered Prices,* Hearings before the Senate Judiciary Committee, 85 Cong. 2 sess. (1958), Pt. 6, p. 2887. "In the first place, Sherman Act procedures are too slow. It took exactly 20 years in the courts to terminate the proceedings against the Aluminum Company of America.

"It took 14 years between the filing and conclusion of the cases against General Motors Acceptance Corp.

"It took more than 10 years in the courts to try and settle the problems of monopoly in the motion-picture industry. In the meantime the advent of television had completely changed industry patterns."

[7] Edward F. Howrey, "Analysis of Present Problems and Suggestions for Administrative Change," *Proceedings,* Section of Antitrust Law, American Bar Association (April 1957), pp. 40, 43.

[8] For a discussion of the role of the hearing examiner see Fletcher G. Cohn, "Some Practical Aspects of Conducting An Antitrust Hearing before the Federal Trade Commission," *Antitrust Bulletin,* Vol. 4 (September-October 1959), p. 665,

and William R. Tincher, "Practical Aspects of Conducting Antitrust Proceedings: Post Hearing," *ibid.*, p. 683.

[9] See Earl W. Kintner, "Post-Hearing Procedures and Compliance," in Section of Antitrust Law, American Bar Association, *An Antitrust Handbook* (1958), p. 425.

[10] Edward F. Howrey, "Revaluation of Commission's Responsibilities," *Federal Antitrust Laws* (1953), pp. 202, 206.

[11] J. H. Wigmore, *Anglo-American System of Evidence in Trials at Common Law*, Vol. 9 (3d ed., 1940), p. 266; C. T. McCormick, "Some Observations Upon the Opinion Rule and Expert Testimony," *Texas Law Review*, Vol. 23 (1945), p. 132; E. M. Morgan, "Hearsay Dangers and the Application of the Hearsay Concept," *Harvard Law Review*, Vol. 62 (1948), p. 185.

[12] See Judge Gregory F. Noonan's discussion of two opposite decisions on the same problem in two courts and the influence of the evidence presented by two different defendants who were sued by the same plaintiff. "The Need for Acceptable Standards of Proof," *The Growing Role of Economic Data in Judicial and Administrative Proceedings*, Current Business Studies No. 18 (March 1954), pp. 11, 14, 15.

[13] Dissent in *Harmar Drive-In Theatre* v. *Warner Bros.*, 239 F. 2d 555, 559 (C.C.A.-2d 1956).

[14] "The simple fact is that the Anglo-Saxon system of law is essentially the product of adversary proceedings." Simon H. Rifkind, "Reflections of a Former Judge," *Federal Bar Journal*, Vol. 19 (1959), pp. 268, 273.

[15] Charles E. Wyzanski, Jr., "A Trial Judge's Freedom and Responsibility," *Harvard Law Review*, Vol. 65 (June 1952), pp. 1295, 1296.

[16] Lon Fuller, *The Problems of Jurisprudence* (1949), p. 707.

[17] C. T. McCormick, *Evidence* (1954), p. 708.

[18] "A judge does not merely sit in judgment in a big case; he administers it." Victor H. Kramer, "The Trial of a Protracted Antitrust Case—A Proposal," *American Bar Association Section of Antitrust Law*, Vol. 18 (1961), p. 41. See also "Report of Sherman Act Subcommittee on Cost Data Problems in Sherman Act Cases," *Proceedings*, Section of Antitrust Law, American Bar Association (August 1960), p. 521.

[19] See James R. Withrow, Jr., "A Defense Counsel's View of a Government Civil Antitrust Suit," *Antitrust Bulletin*, Vol. 3 (1958) p. 49; E. Barrett Prettyman, "Six Suggestions for Improvement," *Business Practices Under Federal Antitrust Laws*, Proceedings of the Third Annual Meeting of the New York State Bar Association, Section on Antitrust Law (Jan. 25, 1951), pp. 34, 35.

[20] For a rather complete, though short, treatment of the technical problems of defining issues see Fred A. Freund, "The Pleading and Pre-Trial of an Antitrust Claim," *American Bar Association Section of Antitrust Law*, Vol. 18 (1961), p. 15.

[21] The importance of clarifying the issues is ably stressed in "Report of Sherman Act Subcommittee on Cost Data Problems in Sherman Act Cases," *Proceedings*, Section of Antitrust Law, American Bar Association (August 1960), p. 521.

[22] A forceful statement may be found in Moses Lasky, "Proof of Complicated Economic and Technical Facts and Handling of Documents," 23 F.R.D. 606 (1959).

[23] However, in its *Handbook of Recommended Procedures for the Trial of Protracted Cases* (1960), the Judicial Conference of the United States does not seem to be impressed with pleadings as the means for framing the issues in a protracted case. It recommends that counsel should be directed to submit separate statements elaborating and clarifying the issues and it places much of the burden of compelling clarification on the judge. See especially Sec. IV on "Pre-Trial Procedure: Civil Cases."

[24] Some aspects of "pretrial" are covered in Joseph E. McDowell, "Pretrial Procedure: Pretrial v. Procedure," *Antitrust Bulletin,* Vol. 4 (September-October 1959), p. 675.

[25] *Handbook of Recommended Procedures for the Trial of Protracted Cases,* p. 35.

[26] See "'The Big Case,' Developments in the Law—Discovery," *Harvard Law Review,* Vol. 71 (March 1961), p. 1000.

[27] *U.S.* v. *General Motors,* 121 F. 2d 376 (C.C.A.-7th 1941), cert. denied 314 U.S. 618 (1941).

[28] The theory that a corporate parent may conspire with its subsidiary or that two subsidiaries of the same parent may conspire is rather recent in development. Several cases involved the theory: *U.S.* v. *Yellow Cab,* 338 U.S. 338 (1949); *Kiefer-Stewart* v. *Seagram,* 340 U.S. 211 (1951); *Timken Roller Bearing Company* v. *U.S.,* 341 U.S. 593 (1951). Strong criticism of the theory was expressed in *Report of the Attorney General's National Committee to Study the Antitrust Laws* (1955), pp. 30-36. A contrary view may be found in Robert A. Solo, "Intra-Enterprise Conspiracy and the Theory of the Firm," *Journal of Business,* Vol. 34 (April 1961), p. 153.

[29] 15 U.S.C. 12 *et seq.*

[30] *U.S.* v. *Standard Oil of California,* 337 U.S. 293 (1949).

[31] *International Salt Co.* v. *U.S.,* 332 U.S. 392 (1947).

[32] *Tampa Electric Co.* v. *Nashville Coal Co.,* 81 S. Ct. 623 (1961).

[33] *Automatic Canteen Co. of America* v. *F.T.C.,* 194 F. 2d 433 (C.C.A.-7th 1952), reversed 346 U.S. 61 (1953).

[34] See Mark S. Massel and R. James Gormley, "Business Methods and Antitrust Policy: The Automatic Canteen Case," *Antitrust Bulletin,* Vol. 1 (1955), pp. 361-95, 467-91.

[35] *U.S.* v. *Morgan,* 118 F. Supp. 621, 737 (S.D.N.Y. 1953).

[36] Breck P. McAllister, "The Big Case: Procedural Problems in Antitrust Litigation," *Harvard Law Review,* Vol. 64 (November 1950), pp. 27, 50, footnote 92.

[37] *U.S.* v. *United Shoe Machinery Corp.,* 110 F. Supp. 295 (D.C. Mass. 1953), aff'd *per curiam* 347 U.S. 521 (1954).

[38] See discussion of expert witnesses in "Report of Sherman Act Subcommittee on Cost Data Problems in Sherman Act Cases," *Proceedings,* Section of Antitrust Law, American Bar Association (August 1960), Sec. VII. *The Handbook of Recommended Procedures for the Trial of Protracted Cases* (1960), Judicial Conference of the United States, recommends that the expert testimony be confined "to those issues which are properly the subject of such testimony. . . ." It notes a "tendency, particularly in antitrust litigation, for the parties to proffer expert opinions on issues which in essence are legal rather than factual. . . ." (P. 63.)

[39] See discussion of the hearsay rule in Henry M. Hart, Jr. and John T. McNaughton, "Evidence and Inference in the Law," in Daniel Lerner, ed., *Evidence and Inference* (1958), p. 48. The authors regard it as "largely archaic." (P. 56.)

[40] A number of pretrial orders which reflect this liberalization are reproduced in *Report of the Committee on Practice and Procedure in the Trial of Antitrust Cases,* Section of Antitrust Law, American Bar Association (1954), pp. 85, 110, 114.

[41] Corwin D. Edwards, "Can the Antitrust Laws Preserve Competition?", *American Economic Review,* Supplement, Vol. 30 (March 1940), pp. 164, 173.

[42] Reprinted in *Report of the Committee on Practice and Procedure in the Trial of Antitrust Cases,* pp. 89, 90.

[43] *Ibid.,* pp. 107-11.

[44] *Ibid.,* p. 114.

[45] Edwards, "Can the Antitrust Laws Preserve Competition?", *op. cit.*, p. 173.

[46] Eugene Kozik, "Oligopoly and the Concept of Workable or Effective Competition: An Economic Analysis of Recent Antitrust Cases," *University of Pittsburgh Law Review*, Vol. 21 (June 1960), pp. 621, 645.

[47] *Automatic Canteen Co. of America* v. *F.T.C.*, 346 U.S. 61 (1953).

[48] A. L. Levin and R. J. Levy, "Persuading the Jury with Facts Not in Evidence: The Fiction-Science Spectrum," *University of Pennsylvania Law Review*, Vol. 105 (December 1956), p. 139.

[49] Joel B. Dirlam and Irwin M. Stelzer, "The Cellophane Labyrinth," *Antitrust Bulletin*, Vol. 1 (1956), pp. 633, 638.

[50] Edward F. Howrey, "Economic Evidence in Antitrust Cases," *Journal of Marketing*, Vol. 19 (1954).

[51] *Eastern States Lumber Association* v. *U.S.*, 234 U.S. 600 (1914).

[52] For an adequate nut-shell description of criminal proceedings see Allen A. Dobey, "Criminal Antitrust Trials," in Section of Antitrust Law, American Bar Association, *An Antitrust Handbook* (1958), p. 277.

[53] See Morris R. Cohen and Ernest Nagel, "An Introduction to Logic and Scientific Method," *War Department Education Manual*, EM621, U.S. Armed Forces Institute, Madison, Wisconsin (1934), esp. pp. 207, 392-96, for an excellent discussion of the uses of hypotheses.

[54] For a discussion of the functions of experts see David W. Louisell, "The Psychologist in Today's Legal World," *Minnesota Law Review*, Vol. 39 (February 1955), p. 235 and George D. Reycraft, "Practical Problems Presented in the Trials of Recent Merger Cases," *Antitrust Bulletin*, Vol. 4 (September-October 1959), p. 635.

[55] When one defendant argued that various points of evidence should be considered separately, the court held that the "character and effect of a conspiracy are not to be judged by dismembering it and viewing the separate parts, but only by looking at it as a whole." *U.S.* v. *General Electric*, 82 F. Supp. 753 (D.C. N.J. 1959), pp. 903-04, citing *U.S.* v. *Patten*, 226 U.S. 525, 544 (1913).

[56] Consider, for example, the Supreme Court's point that the Big Three cigarette producers raised prices in 1931 when tobacco prices were at the lowest level since 1905 and manufacturing costs had been declining. *American Tobacco Co.* v. *U.S.*, 328 U.S. 781 (1946), p. 208.

[57] See M. A. Adelman's argument that industry background must be taken into account. *A & P: Study in Price-Cost Behavior and Public Policy* (1959), p. 414.

[58] A similar issue was developed in *U.S.* v. *Eli Lilly & Co.* (D.C. N.J. 1959), *CCH Trade Cases*, Par. 69,536. The court in that case was impressed with the influence of an agreement between the vaccine manufacturers and the federal government providing that the government would pay the lowest prices charged to anyone.

[59] An interesting use of circumstantial evidence to prove that uniform prices did not indicate a price conspiracy may be found in *Pevely Dairy Co.* v. *U.S.*, 178 F. 2d 363 (C.C.A.-8th 1949), cert. denied 339 U.S. 942 (1950). One factor which supported the finding that there was no price conspiracy was evidence of the uniformity of defendants' costs. See also *Continental Baking Co. et al.* v. *U.S.*, 218 F. 2d 137 (C.C.A.-6th 1960).

[60] Almarin Phillips is critical of the "fictional dichotomy of hypotheses" which are employed in price conspiracy cases. "Policy Implications of the Theory of Interfirm Organization," *American Economic Review*, Vol. 51 (May 1961), pp. 245, 251-52.

[61] Cohen and Nagel, *op. cit.*, p. 393.

[62] It has been urged by some that the government should indicate the type of decree it has in mind at the time the issues are defined; such a procedure, it is be-

lieved, will serve to clarify the objectives of the proceeding. See William L. McGovern, "Toward the Integrated Trial of an Antitrust Case," *Antitrust Bulletin,* Vol. 4 (November 1950), p. 27.

[63] See Richard B. O'Donnell, "Civil Antitrust Trials," in Section of Antitrust Law, American Bar Association, *An Antitrust Handbook* (1958), pp. 301, 326-29.

[64] A committee of the American Bar Association recommends that "The court should make separate and specific findings of fact." Also, that the parties should be permitted to propose such findings. *Report of the Committee on Practice and Procedure in the Trial of Antitrust Cases,* Section of Antitrust Law, American Bar Association (1954), p. 55. See also Holmes Baldridge, "Simplifying and Expediting Cases," *Business Practices Under Federal Antitrust Laws,* Proceedings of the Third Annual Meeting of the New York State Bar Association, Section on Antitrust Law (Jan. 24, 1951), pp. 23, 30.

[65] This practice is criticized in Breck P. McAllister, "The Big Case: Procedural Problems in Antitrust Litigation," *Harvard Law Review,* Vol. 64 (November 1950), pp. 27, 60.

[66] *U.S.* v. *Forness,* 125 F. 2d 928, 942 (C.C.A.-2d 1942).

[67] *Report of the Committee on Practice and Procedure in the Trial of Antitrust Cases,* p. 21.

[68] Carl Kaysen, *United States* v. *United Shoe Machinery Corporation, An Economic Analysis of an Anti-trust Case* (1956), p. 271.

[69] Even in a handbook, which advises judges on how to organize and manage an antitrust trial, there is a strange silence about the problem of formulating a decree. *Report of the Committee on Practice and Procedure in the Trial of Antitrust Cases.*

[70] In *U.S.* v. *Oregon State Medical Society,* 343 U.S. 326, 333 (1952), the Supreme Court held that the function of a decree "is to forestall future violation" and that it is not meant to punish.

[71] *Hartford-Empire Co.,* v. *U.S.,* 323 U.S. 386, 409-10 (1945).

[72] *International Salt Company, Inc.* v. *U.S.,* 332 U.S. 392 (1947).

[73] See Joe S. Bain, *Industrial Organization* (1959), pp. 530, 535.

[74] *Hartford-Empire Co. et al.* v. *U.S.,* 323 U.S. 386 (1945); 324 U.S. 570 (1945).

[75] *U.S.* v. *E. I. du Pont de Nemours & Co.,* 353 U.S. 586 (1957).

[76] Public Law 87-403, approved Feb. 2, 1962.

[77] Sigmund Timberg suggests the desirability of separate hearings on relief because the formulation of a decree required "mental processes" and facts which are not the same as the hearings regarding a violation. "Equitable Relief Under the Sherman Act," *University of Illinois Law Forum,* Vol. 1950 (Winter Number), pp. 629, 634.

[78] 15 U.S.C. 41 *et seq.*

[79] Separate hearings have been recommended only with regard to divorce, dissolution, or divestiture in *Report of the Committee on Practice and Procedure in the Trial of Antitrust Cases,* p. 57. The *Report* gives several illustrations (pp. 109, 114, 126).

[80] The work of the Judgments and Judgment Enforcement Section is described by William D. Kilgore, Jr., chief of the section, in "Antitrust Judgments and Their Enforcement," Section of Antitrust Law, American Bar Association, *An Antitrust Handbook* (1958), p. 331.

[81] F.T.C. Consent Order Procedure, Sec. 3.2. *CCH Trade Regulation Reports,* Par. 9815.02.

[82] See *U.S.* v. *Swift & Co.,* 286 U.S. 106, 114 (1932); *Tobin* v. *Alma Mills,* 192 F. 2d 133 (1951); *U.S. Gypsum* v. *National Gypsum,* 352 U.S. 457, 463 (1957).

[83] Consent decrees usually contain a provision along the following lines: Jurisdic-

tion is retained for the purpose of enabling any of the parties to this Final Judgment to apply to this Court at any time for such further orders and directions as may be necessary or appropriate for the construction or carrying out of this Final Judgment, for the modification or termination of any of the provisions herein and for the enforcement of compliance therewith and punishment of violations thereof. Victor H. Kramer, "Modification of Consent Decrees: A Proposal to the Antitrust Division," *Michigan Law Review,* Vol. 56 (May 1958), pp. 1051, 1053.

[84] See *ibid.*, p. 1060.

[85] *U.S.* v. *Aluminum Co. of America,* 148 F. 2d 416 (C.C.A.-2d 1945).

[86] *U.S.* v. *United Shoe Machinery,* 110 F. Supp. 295 (D.C.Mass. 1953), aff'd *per curiam* 347 U.S. 521 (1954).

[87] *U.S.* v. *United Fruit Co.* (D.C.E.D. La. 1958), *CCH Trade Cases,* Par. 68,941.

[88] *U.S.* v. *International Business Machines Corp.* (D.C.S.D. N.Y. 1956), *CCH Trade Cases,* Par. 68,245.

[89] There are peculiar problems in modifying a consent decree because the court cannot turn to a record or a judicial opinion in a proceeding covering the existing decree. Victor H. Kramer, "Modification of Consent Decrees: A Proposal to the Antitrust Division," *Michigan Law Review,* Vol. 56 (1958), p. 1055.

[90] Seth M. Dabney, "Antitrust Consent Decrees: How Protective an Umbrella?", *Yale Law Journal,* Vol. 68 (June 1959), p. 1391. See *U.S.* v. *Swift & Co.,* 286 U.S. 106, 119 (1932).

[91] Dabney, *op. cit.*, pp. 1399-1400.

[92] *U.S.* v. *Swift & Co., CCH Trade Regulation Reports,* Par. 6267; 276 U.S. 311 (1928); 286 U.S. 106 (1932).

[93] Kramer, *op. cit.*, pp. 1051, 1064.

[94] *The Hartford-Empire Co.* v. *U.S.*, 46 F. Supp. 541 (N.D. Ohio 1942), 323 U.S. 386 (1945).

[95] *U.S.* v. *American Society of Composers, Authors and Publishers* (D.C.S.D. N.Y. 1941), *CCH Trade Cases,* Par. 56,104.

[96] See "ASCAP and the Antitrust Laws: The Story of a Reasonable Compromise," *Duke Law Journal* (Spring 1959), p. 258.

[97] Sigmund Timberg, "Equitable Relief Under the Sherman Act," *University of Illinois Law Forum,* Vol. 1950 (Winter Number), pp. 629, 638-39.

[98] *U.S.* v. *United Shoe Machinery Corp.,* 110 F. Supp. 295 (D.C. Mass. 1953), aff'd *per curiam* 347 U.S. 521 (1954).

[99] A trend in the direction of regulation in antitrust decrees is emphasized in Myron W. Watkins and Joel B. Dirlam, "Government Policy Toward Competition and Private Pricing," *The Relationship of Prices to Economic Stability and Growth,* Compendium of Papers Submitted by Panelists Appearing before the Joint Economic Committee (March 31, 1958), p. 513.

[100] Derek C. Bok, "Section 7 of the Clayton Act and the Merging of Law and Economics," *Harvard Law Review,* Vol. 74 (December 1960), pp. 226, 291, 295.

[101] George H. Dession, "The Trial of Economic and Technological Issues of Fact: II," *Yale Law Journal,* Vol. 58 (July 1949), p. 1242.

[102] E. Barrett Prettyman, "Six Suggestions for Improvement," *Business Practices Under Federal Antitrust Laws,* Proceedings of the Third Annual Meeting of the New York State Bar Association, Section on Antitrust Law (Jan. 24, 1951), p. 34.

[103] E. Barrett Prettyman, "Needed: New Trial Technique: Suggestions for the Trial of Complicated Cases," *ABA Journal,* Vol. 34 (September 1948), p. 766.

[104] *Ibid.*, p. 770.

[105] Judge Gregory F. Noonan, "The Need for Acceptable Standards of Proof," *The Growing Role of Economic Data in Judicial and Administrative Proceedings,* Current Business Studies No. 18 (March 1954), p. 11.

[106] *Ibid.*

[107] This term was used first, within the writers' knowledge, by Breck P. McAllister. His article on the subject has aroused considerable attention. "The Big Case: Procedural Problems in Antitrust Litigation," *Harvard Law Review*, Vol. 64 (November 1950), p. 27.

[108] *Sugar Institute* v. *U.S.*, 297 U.S. 553 (1936).

[109] McAllister, *op. cit.*, p. 58.

[110] 92 F. Supp. 868 (S.D. N.Y. 1950).

[111] "Report of Sherman Act Subcommittee on Cost Data Problems in Sherman Act Cases," *Proceedings*, Section of Antitrust Law, American Bar Association (August 1960), p. 521.

[112] *U.S.* v. *National Lead Co.*, 332 U.S. 319 (1947).

[113] McAllister, *op. cit.*, p. 32.

[114] *U.S.* v. *United Shoe Machinery Corp.*, 110 F. Supp. 295 (D.C. Mass. 1953), aff'd *per curiam* 347 U.S. 521 (1954).

[115] McAllister, *op. cit.*, p. 44.

[116] *U.S.* v. *Henry S. Morgan et al.*, 118 F. Supp. 621, 737 (S.D. N.Y. 1953).

[117] Pretrial Order No. 2 and Memorandum of Judge Medina, May 25, 1950, pp. 13, 14. Reprinted in McAllister, *op. cit.*, p. 52. The McAllister article contains an illuminating description of the problems of evidence in this case.

[118] M. A. Adelman refers to courts which are "buried in undigested gobs of fact which they do not understand." "Economic and Legal Concepts of Competition," *Journal of Farm Economics*, Vol. 41 (December 1959), pp. 1197, 1202. See also his article on "The du Pont-General Motors Decision," *Virginia Law Review*, Vol. 43 (1957), p. 873.

[119] *Hartford-Empire Co. et al.* v. *U.S.*, 323 U.S. 386 (1945); 324 U.S. 570 (1945).

[120] However, a committee of the American Bar Association has appealed for an effort to limit "the period of inquiry." *Report of the Committee on Practice and Procedure in the Trial of Antitrust Cases*, Section of Antitrust Law, American Bar Association (1954).

[121] The "hostility" of trial courts against "big" antitrust cases was referred to by Chief Judge Clark of the Court of Appeals for the 2d Circuit in *Eagle Lion Studios* v. *Loew's, Inc.*, 248 F. 2d 438, 451 (1957).

[122] The desire to simplify affects the opinions of some judges regarding the substantive law. For example: Justice Black favored a *per se* approach in *Northern Pacific* because it "avoids the necessity for an incredibly complicated and prolonged investigation . . . [which is] so often wholly fruitless. . . ." *Northern Pacific Ry. Co.* v. *U.S.*, 356 U.S. 1, 5 (1958). See comment on the case in S. Chesterfield Oppenheim, "Selected Developments in the courts and the Federal Trade Commission," *Proceedings*, Section of Antitrust Law, American Bar Association (August 1959), pp. 33, 39-41.

[123] *Tampa Electric Co.* v. *Nashville Coal Co.*, 276 F. 2d 766 (C.C.A.-6th 1960), reversed 81 S. Ct. 623 (1961).

[124] In 1959 almost 700 antitrust cases were pending in the U.S. courts. The Southern District of New York had "at least 300 long and complicated cases." Warren Olney, III, "Meeting the Impact of Antitrust Litigation in the United States District Courts," *New Theories of Federal Trade Commission Enforcement*, CCH Trade Regulation Reports, No. 153 (Extra ed., June 8, 1960), pp. 3, 4, 6.

[125] The same problem has attracted the attention of observers in other countries. See, for example, William Arthur Lewis, *Overhead Costs* (1949), p. 161. Mr. Lewis feels that the judge's lack of understanding was the reason for the British judicial development in favor of monopoly.

[126] See Justice Frankfurter's opinion in *U.S.* v. *Standard Oil of California*, 337

U.S. 293 (1949), about the problems of adjudication of complex economic issues by "Judges unequipped for it, either by experience or by the availability of skilled assistance." A somewhat different view may be found in Justice Jackson's minority opinion. He felt that judges should hear "all the relevant evidence" for "without it a judicial decree is but a guess in the dark."

[127] An incisive description of some of the problems of dissolution is presented by Corwin D. Edwards in a book review, *American Economic Review*, Vol. 50 (December 1960), pp. 1102, 1106, 1107. See also Joe S. Bain, *Industrial Organization* (1959), p. 530; Walton H. Hamilton, *The Politics of Industry* (1957), pp. 145-46; Donald Dewey, *Monopoly in Economics and Law* (1959), pp. 246-54.

[128] *U.S.* v. *United Shoe Machinery Corp.*, 110 F. Supp. 295 (D.C. Mass. 1953). Justice Douglas seems to take another point of view. See his dissent in *U.S.* v. *Columbia Steel*, 334 U.S. 495, 527 (1948).

[129] Irston Barnes, "Competitive Mores and Legal Tests in Merger Cases: The du Pont-General Motors Decision," *Georgetown Law Journal*, Vol. 46 (1958), pp. 564, 579. Barbara Burt feels that this condition is undergoing change. "The trend is clear—the courts are more ready to find divestiture necessary than in past years." "Antitrust Laws—Judicial Relief for Violations of Section Seven of the Clayton Act—Disenfranchisement in United States *v.* E. I. du Pont de Nemours & Co.," *Michigan Law Review*, Vol. 58 (May 1960), pp. 1024, 1040.

[130] See Carl Kaysen, *United States* v. *United Shoe Machinery Corporation, An Economic Analysis of an Anti-trust Case* (1956), p. 340.

[131] Eugene V. Rostow, "The New Sherman Act: A Positive Instrument of Progress," *University of Chicago Law Review*, Vol. 14 (1947), p. 567.

[132] See M. S. Isenbergh and S. J. Rubin, "Antitrust Enforcement through Consent Decrees," *Harvard Law Review*, Vol. 53 (1940), p. 386.

[133] This method was followed in the enforcement of Sec. 8 of the Clayton Act which forbids interlocking directorates of large competitors. Victor H. Kramer "Interlocking Directorships and the Clayton Act after 35 Years," *Yale Law Journal*, Vol. 59 (1950), pp. 1266, 1271.

[134] Sigurd Anderson, "Settlement and Compliance Procedures," *Proceedings*, Section of Antitrust Law, American Bar Association, (April 1959), pp. 60, 62-63.

[135] *CCH Trade Regulation Reports*, Par. 50,104.

[136] See House Judiciary Committee, Antitrust Subcommittee, *Report on Consent Decree Program of the Department of Justice*, 86 Cong. 1 sess. (1959), p. 301, and table on p. 8. Between 1890 and 1940 over half of the 270 civil proceedings instituted under the Sherman Act resulted in consent decrees. Walton Hamilton and Irene Till, *Antitrust in Action*, Temporary National Economic Committee Monograph 16 (1940), p. 68. Between 1935 and 1954 about 72 per cent of civil actions brought were terminated by consent decrees. *Report of the Attorney General's National Committee to Study the Antitrust Laws* (1955). See also House Select Committee on Small Business, *Law-Enforcement Activities Affecting Small Business*, 85 Cong. 2 sess. (1959), p. 15.

[137] Calculated from tables supplied by the Antitrust Division. A table in the *Report on Consent Decree Program of the Department of Justice*, p. 8, indicates that 77 per cent of equity actions terminated were consent decrees between 1955 and 1958. The 1958 figure was 87 per cent.

[138] Calculated from tables supplied by the F.T.C. During the fiscal year ending June 30, 1958, the commission entered 217 consent orders and 47 contested orders, or 82 per cent and 18 per cent. Anderson, *op. cit.*, p. 61.

[139] Stanley N. Barnes, "The Department of Justice and the Antitrust Laws," in Practising Law Institute, *Understanding the Antitrust Laws* (1955), pp. 125, 134-36.

[140] John C. Stedman, "The Committee's Report: More Antitrust Enforcement—or Less?", *Northwestern University Law Review,* Vol. 50 (July-August 1955), pp. 316, 323. See also "The Modification of Antitrust Consent Decrees," *Harvard Law Review,* Vol. 63 (1949), pp. 320, 322. Barnes, *op. cit.*, pp. 125, 133.

[141] Stanley N. Barnes, former Assistant Attorney General, said, "In the ten year period from 1935 to 1945, approximately 106 antitrust actions ended in consent decrees. Of these, 80 were entered within three days after the complaint was filed. . . . Indeed, in many proceedings decrees were entered at the same time complaints were filed." "Settlement by Consent Judgment," *Proceedings,* Section of Antitrust Law, American Bar Association (Spring 1954), pp. 8, 9.

[142] Stedman is critical of this feature. *Op. cit.*, pp. 316, 324.

[143] Edward T. Tait, "Equitable Treatment of Competitors," *New Theories of Federal Trade Commission Enforcement,* CCH Trade Regulation Reports, No. 153 (Extra ed., June 8, 1960), pp. 75, 79. Commissioner Tait described negotiations with members of an industry before complaints were issued and commented on the unusual treatment.

[144] The Judicial Conference has approved proposals in congressional bills which would require that all consent decrees and orders should be published in the *Federal Register* at least thirty days before their entry. *Report of the Proceedings of the Annual Meeting of the Judicial Conference of the United States,* H. Doc. 321, 86 Cong. 2 sess. (1960), p. 35.

[145] Release of the Department of Justice, June 29, 1961; Order No. 246-61 of the Attorney General, June 29, 1961. See also statement of Lee Loevinger, Assistant Attorney General, Antitrust Division, before the House Judiciary Committee, Antitrust Subcommittee, June 14, 1961 (mimeo.).

[146] *Revised Rules of Practice,* issued by the F.T.C., June 29, 1961, Pt. 3—Consent Order Procedure.

[147] Stedman, *op. cit.*, pp. 316, 324.

[148] John T. Loughlin, "Investigation and Trial of Robinson-Patman Act Cases before the Federal Trade Commission," *Antitrust Bulletin,* Vol. 5 (January-February 1960), pp. 45, 50.

[149] Victor R. Hansen, "What Antitrust Means to the American Business Man," in American Management Association, *Legal, Financial and Tax Aspects of Mergers and Acquisitions* (1957), p. 142.

[150] Judge Yankwich feels that "a consent decree may be more effective in stopping a monopolistic practice in an industry than the more-heralded contested case which reached the higher courts. . . ." "Observations on Antitrust Procedures," 10 F.R.D. 165, 180 (1950).

[151] This point is implied in Hansen, *op. cit.*, p. 143. It is made directly by William D. Kilgore, Jr., "Antitrust Judgments and Their Enforcement," *Proceedings,* Section of Antitrust Law, American Bar Association (April 1954), pp. 102, 104.

[152] The advantages of third-party comments seem to underlie several proposals that antitrust consent decrees and orders should be published in the *Federal Register* at least 30 days prior to their entry. See S. 1337, H.R. 6253, H.R. 5942 of the 86th Congress. These bills were approved by the Judicial Conferences. *Report of the Proceedings of the Annual Meeting of the Judicial Conference of the United States, op. cit.*, p. 35. See House Judiciary Committee, Antitrust Subcommittee, *Report on Consent Decree Program of the Department of Justice,* 86 Cong. 1 sess. (1959).

[153] See *ibid.*, esp. p. 302.

[154] For a strong critique of the consent decree see *ibid.*

[155] A subcommittee of the House Small Business Committee pointed out that "numbers, whether large or small, do not provide an accurate index of the sig-

nificance of antitrust actions." *Law-Enforcement Activities Affecting Small Business,* Report to the House Select Committee on Small Business, 85 Cong. 2 sess. (1959), p. 3. See also p. 12.

[156] See, for example, Earl W. Kintner, "The Federal Trade Commission in 1960—Apologia Pro Vita Nostra," Address delivered at the 1961 Annual Meeting of the New York State Bar Association, Section on Antitrust Law, Jan. 26, 1961 (mimeo.). Kintner, then chairman of the F.T.C., boasted of the number of complaints and orders issued in 1960, compared with previous years, after pointing out that "statistics can be inaccurate measurements of an agency's effectiveness. . . ." (P. 14.) Robert A. Bicks, then Acting Assistant Attorney General, Antitrust Division, made a similar boast saying that "this year's record of 63 cases spells more than 50 per cent increase in new proceedings." Department of Justice Release, Jan. 4, 1960, p. 1. On the other hand, some congressional committees have raised doubts about such a yardstick. See, for example, *Law-Enforcement Activities Affecting Small Business.*

[157] Walter Adams complained because antitrust agencies ignore giant mergers while prosecuting "strawberry growers with a net income of $900 a year, and the lobster fishermen of Maine. . . ." *Administered Prices,* Hearings before the Senate Judiciary Committee, 86 Cong. 1 sess. (1959), Pt. 9, p. 4784.

[158] A few congressional investigations have been made. The *Report on Consent Decree Program of the Department of Justice,* House Judiciary Committee, Antitrust Subcommittee, 86 Cong. 1 sess. (1959), covers two consent decrees: A.T.&T. and the Oil Pipeline orders. The Antitrust Subcommittee of the House Judiciary Committee contended that there is a "complete absence of procedures to bring to the attention of the Antitrust Division instances where defendants have failed to comply with their [antitrust decrees] requirement." (P. 302.) See also *U.S. vs. Economic Concentration and Monopoly,* Staff Report to the Monopoly Subcommittee of the House Committee on Small Business, 79 Cong. 2 sess. (1946).

[159] Myron W. Watkins and Joel B. Dirlam, "Government Policy Toward Competition and Private Pricing," *The Relationship of Prices to Economic Stability and Growth,* Compendium of Papers Submitted by Panelists appearing before the Joint Economic Committee, (March 31, 1958), pp. 513, 521 *et seq.*

[160] See, for example, "Antitrust: Consent Decree: The History and Effect of *Western Electric Co.* v. *U.S.*," *Cornell Law Quarterly,* Vol. 45 (1959), p. 88.

[161] See Seth M. Dabney, "Antitrust Consent Decrees: How Protective an Umbrella?" *Yale Law Journal,* Vol. 68 (1959), p. 1391.

[162] John A. Duncan, "Post-Litigation Resulting from Alleged Non-Compliance with Government Antitrust Consent Decrees," *Western Reserve Law Review,* Vol. 8 (1957), pp. 45, 50.

[163] See Charles A. Horsky "Settlement," in Section of Antitrust Law, American Bar Association, *An Antitrust Handbook* (1958), pp. 507, 509.

[164] Sec. 4 of the Clayton Act, 15 U.S.C. 12 *et seq.*

[165] This advantage may be reduced by a recent decision, *Radiant Burners, Inc.* v. *Peoples Gas Light and Coke Co.,* decided by the U.S. Supreme Court in January 1961. *CCH Trade Cases,* Par. 69,896. In that case the court held that a treble-damage plaintiff did not always have to prove "public injury" to win his case; injury to himself stemming from an antitrust conspiracy would be enough. The significance of the case is discussed in Charles E. Mueller, "Antitrust Conspiracies—Doctrine of Public Injury," *Federal Bar News,* Vol. 8 (June 1961), p. 145.

[166] Lee Loevinger, "Handling a Plaintiff's Antitrust Damage Suit," *Antitrust Bulletin,* Vol. 4 (1959), pp. 29, 38, 43.

[167] See criticism of enforcement in *Law-Enforcement Activities Affecting Small Business,* Report to the House Select Committee on Small Business, 85 Cong. 2

sess. (1959), pp. 11-18, and testimony of Walter Adams, *Administered Prices,* Hearings before the Senate Judiciary Committee, 86 Cong. 1 sess. (1959), pp. 4784, 4786.

[168] Sigmund Timberg compares consent procedures with other administrative procedures in "Recent Developments in Antitrust Consent Judgments," *Federal Bar Journal,* Vol. 10 (1949), p. 351.

[169] See Corwin D. Edwards, *Maintaining Competition* (1949), pp. 298-304.

[170] For a discussion of the problem and of commission efforts to overcome it, see Edward T. Tait, "Equitable Treatment of Competitors," *New Theories of Federal Trade Commission Enforcement,* CCH Trade Regulation Reports, No. 153, (Extra ed., June 8, 1960), p. 75.

[171] See Jerome Frank, *Courts on Trial* (1949).

[172] See Erwin Griswold, "The Need for a Court of Tax Appeals," *Harvard Law Review,* Vol. 57 (1944), p. 1153; Simon Rifkind, "A Special Court for Patent Litigation? The Danger of a Specialized Judiciary," *American Bar Association Journal,* Vol. 37 (1951), p. 425; Henry J. Friendly, "Reactions of a Lawyer—Newly Become Judge," *Yale Law Journal,* Vol. 71 (1961), pp. 218, 220-22; Earl W. Kintner, "Developments in Congress of Special Interest to the Federal Trade Commission," *Proceedings,* Section of Antitrust Law, American Bar Association (August 1959), pp. 198, 203-05; Earl W. Kintner, "The Trade Court, the ABA, the lawyer and the Public Interest," *ibid.* (April 1957), p. 72; and Herbert W. Clark, "The Judicial Functions of the Federal Trade Commission should be Transferred to the District Courts," *ibid.,* p. 51.

## *Chapter 6*

[1] For a contrary view see Samuel M. Fahr, "Why Lawyers are Dissatisfied with the Social Sciences," *Washburn Law Journal,* Vol. 1 (1961), p. 161. He feels that "there is now some question as to whether the use of economic studies may not be overblown in areas such as antitrust administration. . . ." (P. 167.)

[2] See discussion and illustrations in Edward F. Howrey, "Merger Problems Confronting F.T.C.," Address delivered before the Section on Antitrust Law of the New York State Bar Association, Jan. 26, 1955 (mimeo.). See also Richard B. O'Donnell, "Civil Antitrust Trials," *Proceedings,* Section of Antitrust Law, American Bar Association (April 1954), pp. 73, 89.

[3] See, for example, the use of psychologists in antitrust as developed in David W. Louisell, "The Psychologist in Today's Legal World," *Minnesota Law Review,* Vol. 39 (February 1955), p. 235.

[4] Lee Loevinger stated that "the preliminary investigation is probably far more important in antitrust cases than in many other classes of litigation." "Handling a Plaintiff's Antitrust Damage Suit," *Antitrust Bulletin,* Vol. 4 (1959), pp. 29, 38.

[5] See Earl W. Kintner, "The Federal Trade Commission in 1960—Apologia Pro Vita Nostra," Address delivered at the 1961 Annual Meeting of the New York State Bar Association, Section of Antitrust Law, Jan. 26, 1961 (mimeo.), pp. 52, 53. Recently, the F.T.C. announced the appointment of a "Program Review Officer" who "will study the various areas of our economy, locate the primary trouble spots, and make recommendations as to how and where the Commission's efforts should be directed." Release, Oct. 13, 1951.

[6] *U.S. v. Economic Concentration and Monopoly,* Staff Report to the Monopoly

Subcommittee of the House Committee on Small Business, 79 Cong. 2 sess. (1946), p. 49. See recommendation of Herbert Brownell, then attorney general, "The Department of Justice in Antitrust," *New Theories of Federal Trade Commission Enforcement,* CCH Trade Regulation Reports, No. 153 (Extra ed., June 8, 1960), pp. 12, 20; see also Victor R. Hansen, "Current Antitrust Policy," in 1957 Antitrust Law Symposium, *How to Comply with Robinson-Patman Act* (1957), pp. 25, 30.

[7] A former assistant attorney general stated that "on the whole, the course of antitrust enforcement tends to be plotted by the flow of intelligence in the form of complaints from the public generally and from injured parties in particular." Robert A. Bicks, "The Federal Government's Program on Identical Bids," Address delivered before the Annual Meeting of the Association of State Purchasing Officials, Sept. 6, 1960 (mimeo.), p. 8. A similar statement is contained in Federal Trade Commission, *Annual Report,* 1960, p. 30. See also W. Hamilton and I. Till, *Antitrust in Action,* Temporary National Economic Committee Monograph No. 16 (1940), p. 36.

[8] See Commission on Organization of the Executive Branch of the Government, *Task Force Report on Regulatory Commissions* (1949).

[9] Edward F. Howrey, "Revaluation of Commission's Responsibilities," *Federal Antitrust Laws,* Summer Institute on International and Comparative Law, University of Michigan Law School (1953), p. 202.

[10] See testimony of E. T. Grether, *Employment, Growth, and Price Levels,* Hearings before the Joint Economic Committee, 86 Cong. 1 sess. (1959), Pt. 7, p. 2117.

[11] "It might thus be suggested that the enforcement policy would be improved if the selection of cases were derived in much larger degree from a general economic analysis of industry structure and behavior within the economy, with attention to the actual incidence of poor market performance and suspect market structure, and in lesser degree from the volume of complaints by private parties. This would imply the strengthening of the function of general economic analysis within the Antitrust Division, as a guide to the policy strategy and tactics of the Division. A more reasoned regulatory policy might then emerge." Joe S. Bain, *Industrial Organization* (1959), p. 613.

[12] A subcommittee of the House Small Business Committee points out that many antitrust proceedings appear to have been insignificant and that many cases were brought against firms which are not nationally known. *Law-Enforcement Activities Affecting Small Business,* Report to the House Select Committee on Small Business, 85 Cong. 2 sess. (1959), pp. 11-18.

[13] *U.S.* v. *Economic Concentration and Monopoly,* p. 5.

[14] John T. Loughlin, "Investigation and Trial of Robinson-Patman Act Cases before the Federal Trade Commission," *Antitrust Bulletin,* Vol. 5 (January-February 1960), pp. 45, 71-72.

[15] For a description of an F.T.C. proceeding which covered several competitors at one time see Edward T. Tait, "Equitable Treatment of Competitors," *New Theories of Federal Trade Commission Enforcement,* CCH Trade Regulation Reports, No. 153 (Extra ed., June 8, 1960), pp. 75, 79.

[16] See discussion of price discrimination and its relation to competition in Chap. 7, Indicators of Competition, below.

[17] Glen E. Weston, "Improving the Antitrust Laws and Their Enforcement," *Antitrust Bulletin,* Vol. 5 (January-February 1960), pp. 33, 40.

[18] Jesse W. Markham, "Economic Analysis," *Proceedings,* Section of Antitrust Law, American Bar Association (April 1954), pp. 145, 154.

[19] *U.S.* v. *Imperial Chemical Industries, Ltd.,* 100 F. Supp. 504 (D.C.S.D. N.Y. 1951).

[20] Breck P. McAllister, "The Big Case: Procedural Problems in Antitrust Litigation," *Harvard Law Review,* Vol. 64 (November 1950), pp. 27, 34.

[21] *Ibid,* p. 35.

[22] *U.S. v. United Shoe Machinery,* 110 F. Supp. 205 (D.C. Mass. 1953), aff'd *per curiam* 347 U.S. 251 (1954).

[23] McAllister, *op. cit.,* p. 40.

[24] The construction of the original Sec. 7 of the Clayton Act is in point. For many years both F.T.C. and the Department of Justice had interpreted the statute to cover only the purchase of the capital stock of a competitor. Then in the *du Pont-General Motors* complaint, the Antitrust Division inserted a charge under the old Sec. 7 as an afterthought. (See Irston R. Barnes, "Competitive Mores and Legal Tests in Merger Cases: The du Pont-General Motors Decision," *Georgetown Law Journal,* Vol. 46 (1958), pp. 564, 571.) The Supreme Court seized the opportunity to say that the section could be applied to purchases of stock in customer companies.

[25] John C. Stedman feels that it would be advisable to set some limits on such judicial attitudes. "The Committee's Report: More Antitrust Enforcement—Or Less?", *Northwestern University Law Review,* Vol. 50 (July-August 1955), p. 316.

[26] Edward F. Howrey, "Revaluation of Commission's Responsibilities," *Federal Antitrust Laws* (1953), p. 202.

[27] E. T. Grether, "Economic Analysis in Antitrust Enforcement," *Antitrust Bulletin,* Vol. 4 (1959), pp. 55, 70. "Economic 'evidence,' strictly speaking, is not enough. Economic argument is also required. The 'facts' must be placed in a conceptual framework provided by economic conceptions—theory, if you will."

[28] Howrey, former chairman of the F.T.C., feels that the commission, itself, needs the services of an economic adviser. *Op. cit.,* pp. 202, 206.

[29] Grether, "Economic Analysis in Antitrust Enforcement," *op. cit.,* p. 74.

[30] See Victor H. Kramer, "The Trial of a Protracted Antitrust Case—A Proposal," *American Bar Association Section of Antitrust Law,* Vol. 18 (1961), pp. 41, 45. Mr. Kramer feels that failure "to formulate the issues not only may waste weeks of trial time; it is particularly unfair to the defendant." (P. 45.)

[31] Barnes, *op. cit.,* pp. 564, 588-89.

[32] See M. A. Adelman, *A & P: A Study in Price-Cost Behavior and Public Policy* (1959), pp. 414, 415.

[33] Jesse W. Markham, "Economic Analysis," *Proceedings,* Section of Antitrust Law, American Bar Association (April 1954), p. 154. See also Corwin D. Edwards, *Maintaining Competition* (1949), p. 301.

[34] This lack is clearly demonstrated in *Report of the Committee on Practice and Procedure in the Trial of Antitrust Cases,* Section of Antitrust Law, American Bar Association (May 1, 1954), p. 521. Despite a serious effort to review and improve procedures in the trial of antitrust cases no attention was paid to the difficult problem of formulating decrees. At one point reference is made to a discussion of the relief contemplated by the plaintiff (p. 21). However, this discussion serves only to help clarify the issues of the trial, taking place at the pretrial conference. No point is made about the evidence needed to decide what type of decree is needed if a violation is found.

[35] "Whether he wills it or not, the antitrust advocate, if he desires to make an adequate approach to problems of antitrust relief, becomes a practicing economist. . . ." Sigmund Timberg, "Equitable Relief under the Sherman Act," *University of Illinois Law Forum,* Vol. 1950 (Winter Number), pp. 629, 658. See also Howrey, *op. cit.,* p. 202.

[36] "There is no merit in the ceremony of finding a violation unless something like adequate relief is to be granted. The courts have consistently underestimated

the requirements for adequate relief." Edward H. Levi, "The Antitrust Laws and Monopoly," *University of Chicago Law Review*, Vol. 14 (1947), pp. 153, 182.

[37] See Eugene Kozik, "Oligopoly and the Concept of Workable or Effective Competition: An Economic Analysis of Recent Antitrust Cases," *University of Pittsburgh Law Review*, Vol. 21 (June 1960), pp. 621, 623.

[38] See House Judiciary Committee, Antitrust Subcommittee, *Report of Consent Decree Program of the Department of Justice*, 86 Cong. 1 sess. (1959).

[39] *Hartford-Empire Co. et al.* v. *U.S.*, 323 U.S. 386 (1945); 324 U.S. 570 (1945).

[40] *U.S.* v. *American Society of Composers, Authors and Publishers* (D.C.S.D.N.Y. 1941), *CCH Trade Cases*, Par. 56, 104.

[41] See William I. Greenwald, "The Measurement of Damages in Private Antitrust Suits," *Antitrust Bulletin*, Vol. 5 (1960), p. 293. Herbert A. Bergson, "Proof of Damage," *Antitrust Law Symposium, 1952*, Proceedings of the Fourth Annual Meeting, Section on Antitrust Law, New York State Bar Association, Jan. 23-24, 1952, p. 78.

[42] See Lee Loevinger, "Enforcement of Robinson-Patman Act by Private Parties," 1957 Antitrust Law Symposium, *How to Comply with Robinson-Patman Act* (1957), p. 147.

[43] Of course, if there is no antitrust decree, the plaintiff must undertake the task of proving the violation. In such cases plaintiffs are required to prove that the violation caused "public injury." In a recent case the Supreme Court held that public injury need not be proven if the claim rested on a charge of conspiracy. *Radiant Burners, Inc.* v. *Peoples Gas Light and Coke Co.*, Supreme Court (1961), *CCH Trade Cases*, Par. 69,896. See Charles E. Mueller, "Antitrust Conspiracies—Doctrine of Public Injury," *Federal Bar News*, Vol. 8 (June 1961), p. 145.

[44] On occasion, damages may be measured by the gain of the violator from his illegal conduct. See H. D. Nims, "Damages and Accounting Procedure in Unfair Competition Cases," *Cornell Law Quarterly*, Vol. 31 (1946), p. 36; Thomas C. McConnell, "The Treble Damage Action," *University of Illinois Law Forum*, Vol. 1950 (1950), p. 659.

[45] For several specific illustrations see Herbert F. Taggart, *Cost Justification* (1959), Chap. 17.

[46] *Twentieth Century-Fox Film Corp.* v. *Brookside Theatre*, 194 F. 2d 846, 855 (C.C.A.-8th 1952), cert. denied 343 U.S. 942; *Bigelow* v. *RKO Radio Pictures*, 327 U.S. 251, 264-65 (1946).

[47] See Lee Loevinger, "Handling a Plaintiff's Antitrust Damage Suit," *Antitrust Bulletin*, Vol. 4 (1959), pp. 29, 31.

[48] For a listing of the types of reconstructions which have been used successfully see *ibid.*, pp. 33-34.

[49] *Hanover Shoe, Inc.* v. *United Shoe Machinery Corp.*, 185 F. Supp. 826 (D.C.Pa. 1960).

[50] See Note, "The Defense of 'Passing On' in Treble Damage Suits Under the Antitrust Laws," *Yale Law Journal*, Vol. 70 (1961), p. 469.

[51] From 1890 to 1940 only 175 private suits were filed. Between 1947 and 1952, inclusive, 423 private suits were entered and the plaintiffs won 130. Senate Small Business Committee, *The Role of Private Antitrust Enforcement in Protecting Small Business*, S. Rept. 1855, 85 Cong. 2 sess. (1958). In 1960 about 600 private antitrust actions were pending in the federal courts, compared to 93 government cases. Warren Olney, III, "Meeting the Impact of Antitrust Litigation in the United States District Courts," *New Theories of Federal Trade Commission Enforcement*, CCH Trade Regulation Reports, No. 153 (Extra ed., June 8, 1960), pp. 3, 4.

[52] As Kaysen pointed out in the *United Shoe Machinery* case, the record was so long—12,000 pages of oral testimony and 5,000 documents—that "one person can-

not read all of this detail, even in two years. . . ." Carl Kaysen, *United States* v. *United Shoe Machinery Corporation, An Economic Analysis of an Anti-Trust Case* (1956), p. 20.

[53] See Olney, *loc. cit.*

[54] The British Restrictive Practices Court is an interesting variation. The Court has a majority of lay members "qualified by virtue of their knowledge of or experience in industry, commerce or public affairs." See 4 (1) of the Restrictive Trade Practices Act of 1956. The Canadian Restrictive Practices Commission has an economic adviser. *Report of the Director of Investigation and Research, Combines Investigation Act,* 1961.

[55] See discussion of such suggestions in Henry M. Hart, Jr. and John T. McNaughton, "Evidence and Inference in the Law," in Daniel Lerner, ed., *Evidence and Inference* (1958), pp. 48, 64-65.

[56] For approval of this procedure see Kintner, "The Federal Trade Commission in 1960—Apologia Pro Vita Nostra," Address delivered at the 1961 Annual Meeting of the New York State Bar Association Section of Antitrust Law, Jan. 26, 1961 (mimeo), p. 12.

[57] The role of an "adviser to the court" is discussed in Judicial Conference of the United States, *Handbook of Recommended Procedures for the Trial of Protracted Cases* (1960), p. 67. It suggests that the advantage of such a practice is "simplicity." The only disadvantage it covers is the "antagonism of the bar and of litigants."

[58] "A Trial Judge's Freedom and Responsibility," *Harvard Law Review,* Vol. 65 (June 1952), pp. 1281-1304.

[59] Judicial Conference of the United States, *Handbook of Recommended Procedures* (1960). See also *Report of the Judicial Conference of the United States on Procedures in Antitrust and Other Protracted Cases,* Sept. 26, 1951, 13 F.R.D. 62; *Report of the Committee on Practice and Procedure in the Trial of Antitrust Cases,* Section of Antitrust Law, American Bar Association (1954); and "Report of Sherman Act Subcommittee on Cost Data Problems in Sherman Act Cases," *Proceedings,* Section of Antitrust Law, American Bar Association (August 1960) p. 52.

[60] The limitations on such witnesses have not been defined. As experts they would probably be subject to the types of limits discussed in Anthony Lloyd, "The Lawyer's Point of View," *Economic Journal,* Vol. 70 (September 1960), pp. 467, 470.

[61] The case for such neutral experts is ably treated in Senate Judiciary Committee, Subcommittee on Patents, Trademarks and Copyrights, *The Role of the Court Expert in Patent Litigation,* 85 Cong. 1 sess. (1958). See also "Report of the Sherman Act Subcommittee on Cost Data Problems in Sherman Act Cases," *Proceedings,* Section of Antitrust Law, American Bar Association (August 1960), p. 521; Roscoe Pound, "Legislation as a Social Function," *Publications American Sociological Society,* Vol. 7 (1913), pp. 148, 161.

[62] For a discussion of the present limitations of the use of a master-in-chancery see *La Buy* v. *Howes Leather Co., Inc. et al.,* 352 U.S. 249 (1957).

[63] Judicial Conference of the United States, *Handbook of Recommended Procedures* (1960), pp. 32, 65. See also Note, *Harvard Law Review,* Vol. 61 (1948), pp. 657, 701.

[64] See discussion of masters and court-appointed experts against the background of a review of the problems of using cost evidence in "Report of Sherman Act Subcommittee on Cost Data Problems in Sherman Act Cases," *Proceedings,* Section of Antitrust Law, American Bar Association (August 1960), esp. pp. 553-55.

[65] See E. Barrett Prettyman, "Six Suggestions for Improvement," *Business Practices Under Federal Antitrust Laws,* Proceedings of the Third Annual Meeting of

the New York State Bar Association, Section on Antitrust Law, Jan. 24, 1951, pp. 34, 40.

[66] There have been a number of objections to the use of masters. See, for example, discussion in "'The Big Case' Developments in the Law—Discovery," *Harvard Law Review*, Vol. 74 (March 1961), p. 1000.

[67] 15 U.S.C. 41 *et seq.*

[68] The courts have not been unaware of the provision. The Supreme Court cited the section as evidence of Congress' intention that decrees "deal with the future economic condition of the enterprise as well as past violations." *International Salt Co.* v. *U.S.*, 332 U.S. 392 (1947), footnote 10. Edward Levi feels that such recommendations should probably come from an agency which does not have regulatory functions. "The Antitrust Laws and Monopoly," *University of Chicago Law Review*, Vol. 14 (1947), pp. 153, 183.

[69] Phillip C. Newman reproduced an extract of a letter from an unnamed Supreme Court Justice who felt that if economic advisers were available no solutions would be developed by the Court. "The Place of Economic and Market Analysis in Antitrust Administration," *Antitrust Bulletin*, Vol. 1 (May-July 1956), pp. 743, 752.

[70] *Report of the Attorney General's National Committee to Study the Antitrust Laws* (1955), p. 366. Compare this position with a recommendation made in 1950 by Professor S. Chesterfield Oppenheim, co-chairman of the Attorney General's Committee, *A New Look at Antitrust Enforcement Trends*, Antitrust Law Symposium (1950), pp. 69, 80. See also Holmes Baldridge, "Simplifying and Expediting Cases," *Business Practices Under Federal Anti-Trust Laws*, Proceedings of the Third Annual Meeting of the New York State Bar Association, Section on Antitrust Law, Jan. 24, 1951, pp. 23, 29.

[71] Leon R. Yankwich, "'Short Cuts' in Long Cases," 13 F.R.D. 41 (1953).

[72] In 1908 W. H. Humble suggested that perhaps lawyers should be trained as economists and economists trained as lawyers. *American Law Review*, Vol. 42 (1908), p. 379.

[73] See testimony of E. T. Grether, *Employment, Growth, and Price Levels*, Hearings before the Joint Economic Committee, 86 Cong. 1 sess (1959), Pt. 7, p. 2115.

[74] Eugene V. Rostow, "The New Sherman Act: A Positive Instrument of Progress," *University of Chicago Law Review*, Vol. 14 (1947), p. 567, esp. pp. 574-75.

[75] Consider, for example, Paul Samuelson's leading economic's textbook *Economics*. He feels that lawyers and judges "have concentrated on the wrong things" and "have adopted a drily literal approach toward the antitrust laws." (3rd ed., 1955, p. 470.) On the other side, consider statements by Judge Yankwich cited earlier in this chapter. *Op. cit.*, p. 41.

[76] J. Wiseman, "Economic Analysis and Public Policy," *Economic Journal*, Vol. 70 (September 1960), pp. 455, 463, 464. See Henry M. Hart, Jr. and John T. McNaughton, "Evidence and Inference in the Law," in Daniel Lerner, ed., *Evidence and Inference* (1958), p. 61. For a discussion of the influence of lawyers in government regulation see Marver H. Bernstein, *Regulating Business by Independent Commission* (1955), esp. pp. 15-16.

[77] David Riesman, "Law and Sociology," *Stanford Law Review*, Vol. 9 (1957), p. 651.

[78] See S. M. Fahr, "Why Lawyers Are Dissatisfied With the Social Sciences," *Washburn Law Journal*, Vol. 1 (1961), p. 161. Professor Fahr is more concerned with psychologists and sociologists than with economists. However, he does not overlook the economic profession.

[79] "It is utterly impossible to analyze the role of antitrust . . . in legal terms. The issues are basically economic." Testimony of E. T. Grether, *Employment, Growth, and Price Levels,* Hearings, p. 2116. "It will hardly do to discuss the matter by insisting that economists complicate and confuse the issues and that judgment and common sense will suffice." Derek C. Bok, "Section 7 of the Clayton Act and the Merging of Law and Economics," *Harvard Law Review,* Vol. 74 (December 1960), pp. 226, 227. See also Jesse W. Markham, "Economic Analysis," *Proceedings,* Section of Antitrust Law, American Bar Association (April 1954), pp. 145, 152.

[80] Economists have been used in antitrust work more widely in Europe than in the U.S. E. D. Bennett, "Comparison of United States and Foreign Antitrust Laws," *Section of International and Comparative Law Bulletin,* Vol. 3 (1958), pp. 14, 19.

[81] Hart and McNaughton, *op. cit.,* pp. 48, 61-62.

[82] For a discussion of limitations on expert witnesses see Anthony Lloyd, "The Lawyer's Point of View," *Economic Journal,* Vol. 70 (September 1960), pp. 467, 470.

[83] "Handmaiden" is E. T. Grether's term. See "Economic Analysis in Antitrust Enforcement," *Antitrust Bulletin,* Vol. 4 (1959), pp. 55, 56. "But to date economists and economic analysis have not been equal partners in antitrust enforcement. At the very best, economics has been a poor junior partner in both public and private actions." Testimony of E. T. Grether, Hearings, pp. 2115, 2116. "Within enforcing agencies the status of staff economist is generally subordinate to the status of attorneys, and perhaps largely because of this fact, economists, as interpreters of the facts, are held in rather low regard by many examiners in administrative tribunals." Joel Dean and John Duffy, "How the Business Economist Can Help in Management's Antitrust Problems," *Antitrust Bulletin,* Vol. 4 (November-December 1959), pp. 801, 813. The authors are "skeptical about the value of expert testimony by professional economists, especially in F.T.C. cases."

[84] *Harvard Law Review,* Vol. 10 (1897), pp. 457, 469.

[85] See, for example, James H. McGlothlin, "Some Practical Problems in Proof of Economic, Scientific and Technical Facts," 23 F.R.D. 467, 480 (1959). McGlothlin seems to be concerned about differences of opinion among the economists. (Footnote 13.) He regards the existence of monopoly power as an issue of fact for the court to decide. (Pp. 480-81.) See also Yankwich, *op. cit.,* p. 58. Judge Yankwich argues against "economic theories" in antitrust.

[86] There are many indications of this "blind spot." The most recent one is contained in "Report of Sherman Act Subcommittee on Cost Data Problems in Sherman Act Cases," *Proceedings,* Section of Antitrust Law, American Bar Association (August 1960), p. 521. In urging that neutral experts are not useful, the report divides the field of the experts into two distinct parts: "calculation or other conclusion from known data" and "theory." It finds that the competence of such calculation or conclusion is easily discerned "so that the adversary expert usually makes plain what is correct." Contrariwise, if the dispute is a theory, "every acceptable expert is likely to be an adherent to some school of theory, every acceptable expert is likely to be an adherent to some school of thought and so his mere selection is tantamount to a selection of an answer to the problem." This analysis falls short of the mark: evidence about cost and cost differences must depend on theory; evidence about "cross-elasticity" of demand rests on theory about cross-elasticity and about the concept of the market, as we shall see in the chapter on defining the market; testimony about the number of competitors rests on some theory of the market and the nature of competition. Indeed, in many cases the implication that certain "facts" are pertinent to the issues of the case depends upon theories about what competition is and what influences it.

[87] As Professor Clare E. Griffin points out, Judge Hand's findings about monopoly in the *Alcoa* case "implies an economic judgment." *An Economic Approach to Antitrust Problems* (1951), p. 48.

[88] Philip C. Newman points to a lack of financial incentives in the field for economists. "The Place of Economic and Market Analysis in Antitrust Administration," *Antitrust Bulletin,* Vol. 1 (May-July 1956), pp. 743, 748.

[89] E. T. Grether, "Economic Analysis in Antitrust Enforcement," *Antitrust Bulletin,* Vol. 4 (1959), pp. 55, 57. For an interesting discussion of experts in psychology see David W. Louisell, "The Psychologist in Today's Legal World," *Minnesota Law Review,* Vol. 39 (February 1955), p. 235. The use of economists as experts in several proceedings is discussed in George D. Reycraft, "Practical Problems Presented in the Trials of Recent Merger Cases," *Antitrust Bulletin,* Vol. 4 (September-October 1959), p. 635.

"The professional expert is only too often the thick and thin advocate of the party employing him, whose chief aim is to win the case for his client, and in doing so oftentimes to befog it for his adversaries by resorting to technicalities and hairspun distinctions. Of course there are many professional experts not justly subject to this criticism, but as a general rule greater dependence should be placed upon intelligent witnesses, not professionally employed, who from practical knowledge and experience are competent to testify as to the nature and practice of patented inventions and who are free from suspicion as to the fairness of their opinion." *Union Sulphur Co.* v. *Freeport Texas Co.,* 251 F. 634 (D.C. Del. 1918).

[90] See Eugene Kozik, "Oligopoly and the Concept of Workable or Effective Competition," *Pittsburgh Law Review,* Vol. 21 (1960), pp. 621, 645.

[91] This attitude toward economists is reflected in Edward R. Johnston, "Defense of an Antitrust Case," *Proceedings,* Section of Antitrust Law, American Bar Association (April 1957), p. 9.

[92] Eugene V. Rostow, *Planning for Freedom* (1959), pp. 362-63.

[93] Marshall Harris, "Legal-Economic Interdisciplinary Research," *Journal of Legal Education,* Vol. 10 (1958), pp. 452, 462. See Samuel M. Fahr's complaint about "the state of uncertainty, doubt, and disagreement among social scientists themselves. . . ." "Why Lawyers Are Dissatisfied with the Social Sciences," *Washburn Law Journal,* Vol. 1 (1961), pp. 161, 175.

[94] Jesse W. Markham, "Economic Analysis," *Proceedings,* Section of Antitrust Law, American Bar Association (April 1954), pp. 145, 146.

[95] See Henry M. Hart, Jr. and John T. McNaughton, "Evidence and Inference in the Law," in Daniel Lerner, ed., *Evidence and Inference* (1958), pp. 48, 52-53.

[96] Dean Rostow throws new light on this problem. He recounts the discussions about the treatment of dissents in the *Report of the Attorney General's National Committee to Study the Antitrust Laws* (1955). Academic members of the committee, in both law and economics, believed that each member would assume responsibility for each part of the report and would submit signed dissents. In contrast, many lawyers in practice "felt that a rule of anonymity would give them more professional and intellectual freedom. . . ." Otherwise, they were concerned about being embarrassed in their relationships with clients and in their future pleadings. Eugene V. Rostow, "The Lawyer and His Client," *American Bar Association Journal,* Vol. 48 (1962), pp. 25, 26.

[97] See discussion in *Report of the Attorney General's National Committee to Study the Antitrust Laws* (1955), p. 340.

[98] An interesting side-light on this difference may be found in the following statement by Lee Loevinger, who subsequently became the Assistant Attorney General, Antitrust Division. "Today's symposium is concerned with the effect of

antitrust law upon the small businessman. However, the essential topic of consideration, as I understand it, is not the substantive or procedural rules of law as such, but an attempt to evaluate the economic and social effects of antitrust law. A discussion of this character is more difficult for a lawyer than one concerned with more conventional legal questions. There are established techniques and sources for answering the ordinary legal questions—although they do not always yield completely lucid answers—but there are not established techniques or sources for seeking the answers to these questions." "Treble Damage Litigation and the Small Business Man," *Proceedings,* Section of Antitrust Law, American Bar Association (Spring 1960), p. 106.

[99] Donald F. Turner, "Antitrust Policy and the Cellophane Case," *Harvard Law Review,* Vol. 70 (December 1956), pp. 281, 313-14.

[100] See discussion in *Report of the Attorney General's National Committee to Study the Antitrust Laws* (1955), pp. 339, 340.

[101] Walton H. Hamilton has expressed an economist's point of view in *Politics of Industry* (1957). "It is little short of a fiction to state an antitrust case in terms of the innocence or guilt of a corporation and of its executives. The real question is whether its activities are moving toward objectives of which the law approves. To cloak the inquiry as a research for personal and corporate guilt is to blur the issue of holding a going concern within channels which serve the public interest." (Pp. 146-47.) See also testimony of George Romney in *Administered Prices,* Hearings before the Senate Judiciary Committee, Subcommittee on Antitrust and Monopoly, 85 Cong. 2 sess. (1958), Pt. 6, p. 2887.

[102] Edward H. Levi, "The Antitrust Laws and Monopoly," *University of Chicago Law Review,* Vol. 14 (1957), pp. 153, 158-60; Lee Loevinger, "Recent Developments in Antitrust Enforcement," *Proceedings,* Section of Antitrust Law, American Bar Association (April 1961), pp. 102, 103. For a contrary view see Eugene V. Rostow, "The New Sherman Act: A Positive Instrument of Progress," *University of Chicago Law Review,* Vol. 14 (1947), p. 567.

[103] See discussion of "abuse theory" in G. E. Hale and Rosemary D. Hale, *Market Power: Size and Shape Under the Sherman Act* (1958), esp. p. 86.

[104] Jesse W. Markham, "Economic Analysis," *Proceedings,* Section of Antitrust Law, American Bar Association (April 1954), pp. 145, 146.

[105] See Philip C. Newman, "The Place of Economic and Market Analysis in Antitrust Administration," *Antitrust Bulletin,* Vol. 1 (May-July 1956), pp. 743, 749.

[106] See, for example, Myron W. Watkins, "Book Review of E. S. Mason, *Economic Concentration and the Monopoly Problem,*" *American Economic Review,* Vol. 47 (1957), pp. 747, 751-52; Alfred E. Kahn, "Standards for Antitrust Policy," in American Economic Association, *Readings in Industrial Organization and Public Policy* (1958), p. 352; Joel B. Dirlam and Alfred E. Kahn, *Fair Competition: The Law and Economics of Antitrust Policy* (1945), Chap. 2, p. 41.

[107] Dean Levi states, "The truth is, of course, that in most monopoly cases, if the court has a mind to do so, it can find abuses." *Op. cit.,* pp. 153, 158.

[108] 15 U.S.C. 79.

[109] It should be noted that the courts have held that it is not necessary to find "specific intent" in monopolization cases. Judge Hand said, "In order to fall within Sec. 2, the monopolist must have both the power to monopolize and the intent to monopolize. To read the passage as demanding any 'specific' intent, makes nonsense of it, for no monopolist monopolizes unconscious of what he is doing." *U.S.* v. *Aluminum Co. of America,* 148 F. 2d 416, 432 (C.C.A.-2d 1945). See also *U.S.* v. *Paramount Pictures, Inc.,* 334 U.S. 131 (1948); and *U.S.* v. *Griffith,* 334 U.S. 100 (1948).

[110] See Edward Johnston, "Monopolize or Attempt to Monopolize," *Proceedings,*

Section on Antitrust Law, American Bar Association (Summer 1953), p. 72. A contrary position may be found in Rostow, "The New Sherman Act: A Positive Instrument of Progress," *op. cit.*, p. 567. *Contra* Edward Johnston and John P. Stevens, "Monopoly or Monopolization—A Reply to Professor Rostow," *Illinois Law Review*, Vol. 44 (1949), p. 269.

[111] Turner, *op cit.*, pp. 281, 313-14.

[112] Dean Rostow makes the point that law must "transcend the limits of economics, and draw [its] strength from a wider range of aspirations." These include "social and human goals." *Planning for Freedom* (1959), pp. 362-63.

[113] For a somewhat different view, see Lee Loevinger, "Antitrust, Economics and Politics," *Antitrust Bulletin*, Vol. 1 (1955), p. 225.

[114] Edward S. Mason, "Monopoly in Law and Economics," *Yale Law Journal*, Vol. 47 (1937), p. 34. Mason felt that monopoly in law means restraint of individual behavior, rather than market control; freedom of contract not of competition. In economics, he believed, monopoly is coming to have an analytical meaning rather than a classification. Malcolm T. Dungan feels that "if lawyers and economists are ever going to communicate (and particularly concerning antitrust, their most frequent and important meeting ground) they had better start trying to talk each other's language." Book Review in *Journal of Public Law*, Vol. 8 (1959), pp. 295, 298.

[115] Edward F. Howrey refers to several differences. "Lawyers frequently complain that they must exercise great care because the economist's use of a particular word may be misleading from a legal standpoint. Words like 'monopoly,' 'competition,' 'discrimination,' etc., are given a meaning in economics which may sometimes differ considerably from the meaning in law, and vice versa." "Coalescence of Legal and Economic Concepts of Competition," Address delivered before the Section on Antitrust Law of the New York State Bar Association, Jan. 26, 1955 (mimeo.), pp. 3-4.

[116] Robert C. Brooks, Jr., "Injury to Competition Under the Robinson-Patman Act," *University of Pennsylvania Law Review*, Vol. 109 (April 1961), pp. 777, 785; John S. McGee, "Price Discrimination and Competitive Effects: The Standard Oil of Indiana Case," *University of Chicago Law Review*, Vol. 23 (1956), p. 398.

[117] Jules Backman, "An Economist Looks at the Robinson-Patman Act," *Proceedings*, Section of Antitrust Law, American Bar Association (August 1960), pp. 343, 344.

[118] Chief Justice Warren has said that "a price discrimination within the meaning of that provision [Sec. 2(a) of the Clayton Act] is merely a price difference." *F.T.C.* v. *Anheuser-Busch, Inc.*, 363 U.S. 536 (1960).

[119] See Harold D. Lasswell, "The Interplay of Economic, Political and Social Criteria in Legal Policy," *Vanderbilt Law Review*, Vol. 14 (March 1961), pp. 451, 458.

[120] For an interesting discussion of interrelationships between economics and jurisprudence see *ibid.*

[121] The *Annual Report, 1958-1959,* of the Russell Sage Foundation has an interesting description of the substantial problems of developing effective working relations between the social sciences and the older professions of medicine, theology, and law. In its endeavors, the foundation points out, it found that the law "which is the most difficult profession for social scientists to work with, has no model for working with scientists except that of treating them as expert witnesses. The legal profession does not approach its problems within a scientific orientation and neither the lawyer nor the social scientist has yet developed an appropriate perception of each other's role." (Pp. 13-14.)

[122] Henry M. Hart, Jr. and John T. McNaughton, "Evidence and Inference in the Law," in Daniel Lerner, ed., *Evidence and Inference* (1958), pp. 48, 52-53. See also Lee Loevinger, "Treble Damage Litigation and the Small Business Man," *Proceedings,* Section of Antitrust Law, American Bar Association (Spring 1960), p. 106.

[123] "For so far as the particular dispute and the litigants then before the Court are concerned, there is no law governing the case until the justices have spoken." Arthur S. Miller, "A Note on the Criticism of Supreme Court Decisions," *Journal of Public Law,* Vol. 10 (1961), pp. 139, 146.

[124] See Oswald W. Knauth, "Economic Theory and Postulates Pertaining to Today's Business Practices," *Mergers and Competition: Recent Developments,* Current Business Studies, No. 21 (December 1954), p. 5.

[125] Lack of agreement among social scientists is a source of irritation for many lawyers. Samuel M. Fahr discusses the problem in "Why Lawyers Are Dissatisfied with the Social Sciences," *Washburn Law Journal,* Vol. 1 (1961), p. 161.

[126] "The prophecies of what the courts will do in fact, and nothing more pretentious, are what I mean by the law." Oliver Wendell Holmes, "The Path of the Law," *Harvard Law Review,* Vol. 10 (1897), pp. 457, 461. Marshall Harris feels that economists look for too much predictability in the law and "are inclined to believe that all court decisions are determined with mechanical precision by the logical application of known rules of law." "Legal-Economic Interdisciplinary Research," *Journal of Legal Education,* Vol. 10 (1958), pp. 452, 466.

[127] Hart and McNaughton point out that practical settlement of cases is more important than "perfect correctness of particular decisions." *Op. cit.,* pp. 48, 53.

[128] Friedrich A. Hayek, *Individualism and Economic Order* (1948), p. 73.

[129] *Ibid.,* p. 74.

[130] Alfred North Whitehead, *Science and the Modern World* (1926), p. 288.

[131] The science of political economy "fixes attention on a definite group of abstractions, neglects everything else. . . ." *Ibid.* In Charles Hitch's words, "like the practitioners of nearly every science, we [economists] have a marked tendency to go it alone." "The Uses of Economics," *Research for Public Policy: Brookings Dedication Lectures* (1961), pp. 91, 107.

[132] David Riesman, *Individualism Reconsidered* (1955), p. 435.

[133] Julius Cohen, "Towards Realism in Legisprudence," *Yale Law Journal,* Vol. 59 (April 1950), pp. 886, 887.

[134] An extreme illustration of this self confidence may be found in Morris L. Ernst, "The Need for Reappraisal of Leadership of the Bar," *American Bar Association Journal,* Vol. 47 (October 1961), p. 959. "I believe that history will prove that the legal profession, in our culture, is the only skill or discipline equipped, fit and qualified to lead the people."

[135] See J. W. Markham's objection to basing precedents regarding monopoly on legal points. "Economic Analysis," *Proceedings,* Section of Antitrust Law, American Bar Association (April 1954), pp. 145, 150.

[136] Benjamin Nathan Cardozo, *The Nature of the Judicial Process* (1921), pp. 20, 21.

[137] Judicial Conference of the United States, *Handbook of Recommended Procedures for the Trial of Protracted Cases* (1960), p. 63.

[138] See Robert M. Hutchins, *Two Faces of Federalism* (1961), p. 21. He argues that "the development of the law has been in the hands of craftsmen who did not ask themselves questions of principle, but only how do I do what needs to be done, in court or in office, on behalf of the interests I represent?" Further, "the law schools have seldom been much affected by the universities of which they are nominally a part." See also M. McDougal, "Law as a Process of De-

cision," *Natural Law Forum,* Vol. 1 (1956), p. 53; and Harold Lasswell, *The Decision Process* (1956).

[139] For a review of the applications of economic analysis in a number of problem areas see *Economics and the Policy Maker: Brookings Lectures 1958-1959* (1959).

[140] J. Wiseman, "Economic Analysis and Public Policy," *Economic Journal,* Vol. 70 (September 1960), p. 455, esp. p. 456.

[141] See, however, Carl Kaysen's discussion of the use of a model in *United States v. United Shoe Machinery Corporation, An Economic Analysis of an Anti-Trust Case* (1956), pp. 17, 18.

[142] See Richard Ruggles, "The Value of Value Theory," *American Economic Review,* Vol. 44 (May 1954), pp. 140, 145.

[143] *Ibid.,* p. 145.

[144] See Alfred Marshall, *Principles of Economics* (8th ed., 1927); Edward H. Chamberlin, *The Theory of Monopolistic Competition* (1933); J. M. Clark, *Competition as a Dynamic Process* (1961), pp. 118-27. Richard B. Heflebower discusses the more recent theories of cost-price relationships in "Full Costs, Cost Changes, and Prices," in National Bureau of Economic Research, *Business Concentration and Price Policy* (1955), p. 361.

[145] "Some theorists, pursuing their analysis on a high plane, refer to their work as 'tool making' rather than 'tool using.' A 'toolmaker,' however, who constructs tools which no 'tool user' can use is making a contribution of little significance. Some knowledge of the use of tools is probably indispensable to their effective fabrication." Edward S. Mason, *Economic Concentration and the Monopoly Problem* (1957), footnote 5, p. 57. Carl Kaysen raises an interesting question about the usefulness of models in empirical analysis. "The student of actual markets must continue for some time to use his present miscellaneous kit of theoretical tools, inadequate as it is, rather than plan to trade it in for a neatly graded set of game-theoretic models, guaranteed to fit all problems." Book Review, *American Economic Review,* Vol. 50 (December 1960), pp. 1036, 1040.

[146] Consider, for example, the impossibility of persuading a court to employ a mathematical model. An interesting example of the lack of practicability can be found in Martin Shubik, *Strategy and Market Structure* (1959). It presents an application of mathematical theory of games to the analysis of antitrust problems.

[147] See Joe S. Bain, *Industrial Organization* (1959), pp. 321-24.

[148] See discussion of "non-price" competition in Edward S. Mason, "Price Policies and Full Employment," in Carl J. Friedrich and Edward S. Mason, eds., *Public Policy* (1940), p. 25.

[149] See National Bureau of Economic Research, *Cost Behavior and Price Policy* (1943), Chap. 3.

[150] *Ibid.,* Chap. 9.

[151] J. Fred Weston, *The Role of Mergers in the Growth of Large Firms* (1953), p. 94. For a review of many of these models see John Perry Miller, "Measures of Monopoly Power and Concentration: Their Economic Significance," in National Bureau of Economic Research, Business Concentration and Price Policy (1955), p. 119.

[152] Perfect monopoly is equated with the absence of cross-elasticity, while perfect competition is equated with maximum cross-elasticity of the demand for the products of several suppliers. This indicator states extremes. Yet, there may be infinite cross-elasticity in the demand for the products of only two sellers in a market—which does not, of itself, assure active competition. See Nicholas Kaldor, "Market Imperfection and Excess Capacity," *Economica* (February 1935), p. 33. See also K. W. Rothschild, "The Degree of Monopoly," *Economica* (February

1942), p. 214, for an index based on relative demand curves, which is similar to the index based on cross-elasticity. Another index which combines cross-elasticity of demand and availability of capacity was suggested in A. G. Papandreou, "Market Structure and Monopoly Power," *American Economic Review*, Vol. 39 (September 1949), p. 883.

[153] See, for example, Joe S. Bain, "The Profit Rate as a Measure of Monopoly Power," *Quarterly Journal of Economics*, Vol. 55 (1941), p. 271, and "Relation of Profit Rate to Industry Concentration: American Manufacturing, 1936-1940," *ibid.*, Vol. 65 (1951), p. 293.

[154] A. P. Lerner, "The Concept of Monopoly and the Measurement of Monopoly Power," *Review of Economic Studies*, Vol. 1 (1934), p. 157. Professor Papandreou says, "Measures focusing on different aspects of monopoly power have been suggested by economists, but none has been as popular with the profession as the Lerner index." *Op. cit.*, p. 884.

[155] For a perceptive discussion of the relationship between marginal and average, or total, costs see B. Fog, *Industrial Pricing Policies* (1960).

[156] J. M. Clark, "Competition and the Objectives of Government Policy," in Edward H. Chamberlin, ed., *Monopoly and Competition and Their Regulation* (1954) pp. 317, 330.

[157] Tibor Scitovsky, "Economic Theory and the Measurement of Concentration," in National Bureau of Economic Research, *Business Concentration and Price Policy* (1955), pp. 101, 105. Scitovsky suggests adding the difference between average variable costs and marginal costs to the equation on the ground that this difference reflects imperfections "in the market where the firm sells and in the markets where it buys." This modification would, as he recognizes, simply measure the margin between price and average variable costs. That margin, taken as a percentage of price, becomes a type of profit measurement. It is hard to see much difference between this suggestion and the Lerner formula.

[158] See, for example, Leon R. Yankwich, " 'Short Cuts' in Long Cases," 13 F.R.D. 41 (1953).

[159] Albert Kocourek, *Jural Relations* (1927); Wesley Newcomb Hohfeld, *Fundamental Legal Conceptions as Applied in Judicial Reasoning and Other Legal Essays* (1923).

[160] "An economist can be helpful to bench and bar in two ways. First, he is a specialist in the collection and analysis of economic facts, and in using them to test hypotheses; he has learned a set of techniques which permit him to be wrong somewhat less frequently in these areas than the rest of humankind. Second, he is a specialist simply in economic logic, and can, while waiving any comment on facts, help discern the economic content or economic meaning of a court decision, or a statute, or a report. Of course any given document may have noneconomic aspects which are far more important; but while they may justly overbear the economics, they do not contradict or remove them." M. A. Adelman, "The du Pont-General Motors Decision," *Virginia Law Review*, Vol. 43 (1957), p. 873.

[161] See Sigmund Timberg, "The Right of Customer-Seller Selection," *CCH Symposium* (1951), pp. 150, 154.

[162] Eugene V. Rostow, *Planning for Freedom* (1959), p. 362.

[163] For a criticism of this lack see James H. McGlothlin, "Some Practical Problems in Proof of Economic, Scientific and Technical Facts," 23 F.R.D. 467, 478 (1959). He feels that it is useful to bring opposing experts together before the trial on such matters as chemistry and physics; however, there is no point in a conference between an economist who believes in structural tests and one who believes in the "behaviorist" tests. For an explanation of the differences in these tests see Chap. 7 below.

[164] See Carl Kaysen, *United States* v. *United Shoe Machinery Corporation, An Economic Analysis of an Anti-Trust Case* (1956), regarding insufficient bases for the government's requested relief (pp. 340-43); Eugene Kozik, "Oligopoly and the Concept of Workable or Effective Competition: An Economic Analysis of Recent Antitrust Cases," *University of Pittsburgh Law Review*, Vol. 21 (June 1960), pp. 621, 645.

[165] *U.S.* v. *Columbia Pictures Corp. et al.* (D.C.S.D.N.Y.), *CCH Trade Cases* (July 1960), Par. 69,766.

[166] *U.S.* v. *Besser Mfg. Co.*, 96 F. Supp. 304 (D.C.E.D.Mich. 1951); 343 U.S. 444 (1952).

[167] E. T. Grether, "Economic Analysis in Antitrust Enforcement," *Antitrust Bulletin*, Vol. 55 (1959), p. 55.

[168] *Ibid.*, p. 74.

[169] *U.S.* v. *Columbia Steel Co. et al.*, 334 U.S. 495 (1948).

[170] Grether, *op. cit.*, pp. 61-64.

[171] *U.S.* v. *Paramount Pictures, Inc.*, 66 F. Supp. 323 (1946); 334 U.S. 131 (1948).

[172] Grether, *op. cit.*, pp. 66-68.

[173] *U.S.* v. *E. I. du Pont de Nemours & Co.*, 351 U.S. 377 (1956).

[174] *U.S.* v. E. I. *du Pont de Nemours & Co.*, 353 U.S. 586 (1957).

[175] Jesse W. Markham feels that the "most obvious use to which analytical economics can be put" is to develop the framework for policy. "Economic Analysis," *Proceedings*, Section of Antitrust Law, American Bar Association (April 1954), pp. 145, 151.

[176] This point is illustrated by Commissioner Philip Elman's concurring opinion *In the Matter of Union Carbide Corporation*, Docket 6826 (Sept. 25, 1961) (mimeo.). He contrasted the analysis of an economist with the more limited inquiry required by the Antimerger Act (Sec. 7 of the Clayton Act) (pp. 1-4). See also the dissenting opinion of Commissioner William C. Kern (pp. 1-8). He objected to the use of "rigid yardsticks" (p. 6).

[177] See M. T. Dungan, "Book Review," *Journal of Public Law*, Vol. 8 (1959), pp. 295, 298.

[178] Lee Loevinger, "Treble Damage Litigation and the Small Business Man," *Proceedings*, Section of Antitrust Law, American Bar Association (April 1960), p. 106.

[179] "The economist has been too little aware of the legal requirements and the lawyer too little versed in the fundamentals of economics and business for either to get an adequate grasp of the issues involved in the organization and operation of cooperatives." Harold G. Moulton in preface to Edwin G. Nourse, *The Legal Status of Agricultural Co-operation* (1927).

## *Chapter 7*

[1] J. M. Clark, *Competition as a Dynamic Process* (1961).

[2] Eugene V. Rostow, "Problems of Size and Integration," *Business Practices Under Federal Antitrust Laws*, Proceedings of the Third Annual Meeting of the New York State Bar Association, Section on Antitrust Law (Jan. 24, 1951), pp. 117, 133.

[3] Several courts have attempted definitions. In *F.T.C.* v. *Sinclair Refining Co.*, competition was described as "conflict for advantage." [261 U.S. 463, 476 (1923).] In *U.S.* v. *Standard Oil Co.* the expression used was "a contest for trade." [47

F. 2d 288, 297 (E.D. Mo. 1931).] In *U.S.* v. *Aluminum Co. of America,* Judge Knox referred to "independent endeavor of two or more persons . . . within the . . . market place, to obtain the business patronage of others. . . ." [91 F. Supp. 333 (S.D.N.Y. 1950).] In *U.S.* v. *Griffith* monopoly was assumed to be power to exclude competition. [334 U.S. 100, 107 (1948).] Monopolization required, in addition to a monopoly, a desire to exclude competition and the intent to exercise the power.

[4] E. H. Chamberlin, *The Theory of Monopolistic Competition* (7th ed., 1956), esp. pp. 6, 7.

[5] An interesting commentary on this point is made in a statement by Professors G. W. Stocking and W. F. Mueller. "Business rivalry is itself a symptom of the absence of pure competition." "The Cellophane Case and the New Competition," *American Economic Review,* Vol. 45 (March 1955), pp. 29, 31.

[6] See *Report of the Attorney General's National Committee to Study the Antitrust Laws* (1955), pp. 337, 338.

[7] See Adam Smith, *The Wealth of Nations* (Modern Library ed., 1937), p. 61.

[8] See Lionel Robbins, *The Theory of Economic Policy* (1953), p. 57.

[9] Some legal dicta are somewhat similar to this concept of monopoly and equally vague. Consider the classic statement that monopoly is power over price or power to exclude competition. *American Tobacco Co.* v. *U.S.,* 328 U.S. 781 (1946).

[10] "The price of monopoly is upon every occasion the highest which can be got." Adam Smith, *op. cit.,* p. 61.

[11] Paul Samuelson, *Economics—An Introductory Analysis* (1948), p. 493; see also Note, "Definition of the Market in Tying Arrangements," *Yale Law Journal,* Vol. 63 (1954), pp. 389, 396.

[12] "We have not and probably never had perfect market competition of the kind described by the classical economists. . . ." Corwin D. Edwards, "Preserving Competition vs. Regulating Monopoly," *American Economic Review,* Vol. 30 (1940), pp. 164, 170.

[13] Adam Smith, *op. cit.*

[14] *Ibid.,* Book IV.

[15] John Stuart Mill, *Principles of Political Economy* (Ashley ed., 1928), p. 42.

[16] Alfred Marshall, *Principles of Economics* (1920).

[17] See, for example, Arthur R. Burns, *Decline of Competition* (1936) and *Final Report and Recommendations of the Temporary National Economic Committee,* S. Doc. 35, 77 Cong. 1 sess. (1941).

[18] Joan Robinson, *The Economics of Imperfect Competition* (1934).

[19] See, however, Joan Robinson, "Imperfect Competition Revisited," *Economic Journal,* Vol. 63 (1953), p. 579.

[20] Chamberlin, *op. cit.*

[21] Colston E. Warne feels that these developments have not eliminated the "sterile exercises in logic and mathematics" of classical economic theory. "Advertising and Consumer Behavior," *Cartel,* Vol. 10 (1960), pp. 82, 87.

[22] See Richard Ruggles, "The Value of Value Theory," *American Economic Review* Vol. 44 (May 1954), p. 140.

[23] "Toward a Concept of Workable Competition," *American Economic Review,* Vol. 30 (1940), p. 243. He defined the concept to mean "rivalry in selling goods in which each selling unit normally seeks maximum net revenue, under conditions such that the price or prices each seller can charge are effectively limited by the free option of the buyer to buy from a rival seller or sellers of what we think of as 'the same' product. . . ." Recently, Professor Clark has indicated that he prefers the term "effective competition." *Competition as a Dynamic Process* (1961), p. ix.

[24] Almarin Phillips believes that workable competition is the "foundation" of the argument against *per se* rules. "A Critique of United States Experience With

Price-Fixing Agreements and the Per Se Rule," *Journal of Industrial Economics,* Vol. 8 (October 1959), pp. 13, 29-30.

[25] See, for example, Jesse W. Markham, *Competition in the Rayon Industry* (1952); R. B. Tennant, *The American Cigarette Industry* (1950); Melvin G. de Chazeau and Alfred E. Kahn, *Integration and Competition in the Petroleum Industry* (1959); William H. Nicholls, *Price Policies in the Cigarette Industry* (1951).

[26] See Eugene V. Rostow, "Problems of Size and Integration," *Business Practices Under Federal Antitrust Laws,* Proceedings of the Third Annual Meeting of the New York State Bar Association, Section on Antitrust Law (Jan. 24, 1951), pp. 117, 133.

[27] See Stephen H. Sosnick, "A Critique of Concepts of Workable Competition," *Quarterly Journal of Economics,* Vol. 72 (August 1958), p. 380.

[28] Professor Friedrich A. Hayek is critical of this point of view. "What our theoretical models of separate industries conceal is that in practice a much bigger gulf divides competition from no competition than perfect from imperfect competition." *Individualism and Economic Order* (1948), p. 105.

[29] See Edward S. Mason, *Economic Concentration and the Monopoly Problem* (1957), pp. 352-57. In discussing workable competition Mason compares the writings of J. M. Clark with C. D. Edwards, C. Wilcox, and G. Stigler. He feels that the latter three writers "clearly think of workable competition in terms of market conditions imposing a set of limitations on the scope of action of the individual buyer or seller. These limitations prevent the exploitation of buyers by sellers too few in number or in collusion with each other and prevent the exploitation of sellers by buyers. . . . Clark's conception of workable competition also emphasizes these limitations, but it appears from his discussion that limitations are not enough." See also George W. Stocking, "Economic Change and the Sherman Act: Some Reflections on 'Workable Competition,'" *Virginia Law Review,* Vol. 44 (May 1958), p. 537. Professor Stocking feels that the concept of workable competition is "vague." (p. 553.)

[30] See Charles F. Phillips, Jr., "Workable Competition in the Synthetic Rubber Industry," *Southern Economic Journal,* Vol. 28 (October 1961), p. 154. The paper applies theories of workable competition to the government's program of selling synthetic rubber plants and the industrial effects of the disposal program.

[31] For strong criticisms of the concept and an argument that it is meaningless see George A. Stigler, "Report of the Attorney General's Committee on Antitrust Policy, Discussion," *American Economic Review,* Supplement, Vol. 46 (1956), pp. 504-07, and Ben Lewis, *Administered Prices,* Hearings before the Senate Judiciary Committee, 86 Cong. 1 sess. (1959), Pt. 9, p. 4716. George W. Stocking does not believe "that the standard of workability is an appropriate one by which to determine the legality of business arrangements under the antitrust statutes." "Economic Tests of Monopoly and the Concept of the Relevant Market," *Antitrust Bulletin,* Vol. 2 (1957), pp. 479, 481.

[32] "An industry may be judged to be workably competitive when, after the structural characteristics of its market and the dynamic forces that shaped them have been thoroughly examined, there is no clearly indicated change that can be effected through public policy measures that would result in greater gains than social losses." Jesse W. Markham, "An Alternative Approach to the Concept of Workable Competition," *American Economic Review,* Vol. 40 (June 1950), pp. 349, 361; Carl Kaysen, *United States* v. *United Shoe Machinery Corporation, An Economic Analysis of an Anti-Trust Case* (1956); George W. Stocking, "The Rule of Reason, Workable Competition and Monopoly," *Yale Law Journal,* Vol. 64 (1955), p. 1107.

[33] This aspect of the theory is probably the basis for its use in an attack on the

*per se* rules. Phillips argues, "The foundation of the argument that the *per se* rule is an improper policy instrument is the notion of 'workable competition.'" *Op. cit.*, p. 29.

[34] See Richard B. Heflebower, "Toward a Theory of Industrial Markets and Prices," *American Economic Review*, Vol. 44 (May 1954), p. 121.

[35] An interesting critique of price theory which is not based on an "empirical framework" is presented in Richard Ruggles, "The Value of Value Theory," *ibid.*, p. 140. He argues that value theory is tautological, that many of its concepts have no factual counterparts, that it relies too much on *certeris paribus*, that it omits many important factors, and that it considers only the simple situation of single-product plants.

[36] For a persuasive statement of this point of view see Clark, *op. cit.*, esp. Chap. 1.

[37] Irston R. Barnes, "Competitive Mores and Legal Tests in Merger Cases: The du Pont-General Motors Decision," *Georgetown Law Journal*, Vol. 46 (1958), pp. 564, 593.

[38] "If science is not to degenerate into a medley of *ad hoc* hypotheses, it must become philosophical and must enter upon a thorough criticism of its own foundation." A. N. Whitehead, *Science and the Modern World* (1926), p. 24.

[39] See Clark, *op. cit.*, pp. 419-25. The first classification was structure and performance. Some referred to "behavior" as a combination of the two. Later "market conduct" was added. In this book, behavior and conduct are taken as synonymous.

[40] "Thus it is not useful to attempt to maintain too rigid a distinction between structure and conduct; structure in a broad sense can be taken to include both structure proper and conduct." Carl Kaysen and Donald F. Turner, *Antitrust Policy, An Economic and Legal Analysis* (1959), pp. 59-60.

[41] However, William H. Martin argues that, "In recent years, economists seem to have become increasingly disenchanted with attempts to measure 'degrees of monopoly.'" Testimony in *Employment, Growth, and Price Levels*, Hearings before the Joint Economic Committee, 86 Cong. 1 sess. (1959), Pt. 7, p. 2000.

[42] For example, Fritz Machlup argues that price discrimination is made possible by the existence of some degree of monopoly. On this theory, the remedy for a finding of price discrimination would call for means of weakening the monopoly forces rather than merely forbidding the discrimination. *The Political Economy of Monopoly* (1952), pp. 136-37.

[43] See Edward S. Mason, "Workable Competition Versus Workable Monopoly," *Business Practices Under Federal Antitrust Laws*, Proceedings of the Third Annual Meeting of the New York State Bar Association, Section on Antitrust Law (Jan. 24, 1951), pp. 67, 68-69.

[44] Howard H. Hines relates concentration and monopoly and concludes that if there is a trend in either it is probably downward. Testimony in *Employment, Growth, and Price Levels*, Hearings before the Joint Economic Committee, 86 Cong. 1 sess. (1959), Pt. 7, pp. 1977, 1978.

[45] Donald Wallace refers to following issues: size of firms relative to efficiency, progress and locational factors; allocation of resources between industries, utilization of resources, and returns to owners; level of use of resources; severity of business cycle; and progressiveness. "Individual Markets and Public Policy: Some Major Problems," *Public Policy*, Vol. 59 (1940), pp. 99-100.

[46] See Blackwell Smith, "Effective Competition: Hypothesis for Modernizing the Antitrust Laws," *New York University Law Review*, Vol. 26 (July 1951), p. 405. One of his chief complaints seems to be that no rules have been laid down prescribing "given percentages" of an industry "as necessary to violation." (P. 421.)

[47] Such a desire seems to underlie much of the material in a recent study of

market power. G. E. Hale and Rosemary D. Hale, *Market Power: Size and Shape Under the Sherman Act* (1958). (See esp. pp. 120-22.) See also testimony of William H. Martin in *Employment, Growth, and Price Levels,* Hearings (1959), Pt. 7, p. 2000.

[48] Kenneth S. Carlston, "Tests and Evidence of Monopoly Under the Sherman Act: A Restatement," *Federal Antitrust Laws,* University of Michigan Law School (1953), pp. 16, 19-20.

[49] See formulas proposed for judging mergers in George Stigler, "Mergers and Preventive Antitrust Policy," *University of Pennsylvania Law Review,* Vol. 104 (1955), p. 176.

[50] For a discussion of these measurements see E. H. Chamberlin, "Measuring the Degree of Monopoly and Competition," in Edward H. Chamberlin, ed., *Monopoly and Competition and Their Regulation* (1954), p. 255. Professor Chamberlin argues against any single measure.

[51] "Detecting monopoly is simpler than measuring it." G. W. Stocking and W. F. Mueller, "The Cellophane Case and the New Competition," *American Economic Review,* Vol. 45 (March 1955), pp. 29, 30.

[52] Dean Edward S. Mason feels that "it is not possible, nor will it ever be possible to present an unambiguous measure of the degree of monopoly." "Market Power and Business Conduct: Some Comments," *American Economic Review,* Supplement, Vol. 56 (1956), pp. 471, 480. Professor Fritz Machlup concludes that "so many different elements enter into what is called a monopolistic position and so complex are their combined effects that a measurement of 'the' degree of monopoly is even conceptually impossible." *The Political Economy of Monopoly* (1952), p. 527. See also Donald F. Turner, "Antitrust Policy and the Cellophane Case," *Harvard Law Review,* Vol. 70 (December 1956), pp. 281, 313.

[53] See Albert R. Connelly's protest against the indiscriminate use of concentration percentages. "Emerging Theories of Mergers," *New Theories of Federal Trade Commission Enforcement,* CCH Trade Regulation Reports, No. 153 (Extra Ed., June 8, 1960), p. 111.

[54] Clair Wilcox, *Public Policies Toward Business* (1955), p. 836.

[55] Professor Joe S. Bain has suggested the use of profit rates as a measure of "deviations from competitive equilibrium." He defined profit rates as "the ratio of the net earnings . . . to the replacement cost of service value of those assets of the firm which it could economically hold at a minimum and produce its present output." This ratio would be compared with the current rate of interest to provide the indicator. "The Profit Rate as a Measure of Monopoly Power," *Quarterly Journal of Economics* (February 1941), pp. 271, 287-88.

[56] Carl Kaysen and Donald F. Turner, *Antitrust Policy, An Economic and Legal Analysis* (1959), p. 63. They suggest also a rule of thumb for measuring market power: if one company accounts for 50 per cent or more of an industry's sales for five years or more, or if four or fewer companies account for 80 per cent. (P. 98.)

[57] *Ibid.,* p. 64.

[58] Friedrich A. Hayek, *Individualism and Economic Order* (1948), p. 101.

[59] Office of Temporary Controls, *Economic Data Series,* No. 26, reports average chain store food gross margins in 1941 were 16.7 per cent of net sales. In contrast, Heflebower points out that an O.P.A. survey showed an average margin of 16-17 per cent of sales for independent retailers and 5-7 per cent for wholesalers in the industry. Richard B. Heflebower, "Mass Distribution: A Phase of Bilateral Oligopoly or of Competition?", *American Economic Review,* Supplement, Vol. 47 (1957), pp. 274, 275.

[60] Based on observations and discussions with supermarket chain owners.

[61] Professor Derek C. Bok makes a strong plea for this position with regard to the administration of the antimerger statute. He suggests using as a guide "the extent to which that merger has increased the superiority in the leader's size beyond the margin of superiority enjoyed five years prior to the merger." However, he quickly proceeds to a consideration of "exceptional cases." "Section 7 of the Clayton Act and the Merging of Law and Economics," *Harvard Law Review*, Vol. 74 (December 1960), pp. 226, 283. See also pp. 293, 315, 316.

[62] Betty Bock, "Mergers and Market Size—1. Product Dimensions," *The Conference Board Business Record*, Vol. 16 (April 1959), pp. 192, 193. William H. Martin points to the need for further development "to provide discernible insight into the probable effect of corporate mergers and acquisitions." *Mergers and the Clayton Act* (1959), p. 326.

[63] On the other hand, G. Warren Nutter feels that we are developing too many criteria. "Competition: Direct and Devious," *American Economic Review*, Supplement, Vol. 44 (1954), p. 69.

[64] "It is not possible nor will it ever be possible, by calculating market shares, dividing price minus marginal cost by price, or other hocus pocus, to present an unambiguous measure of the degree of monopoly. Market power has many dimensions." Edward S. Mason, *Economic Concentration and the Monopoly Problem* (1957), p. 400.

[65] For example, see discussion of "exceptional cases" in Derek C. Bok, *op. cit.*, pp. 226, 283.

[66] *U.S.* v. *Bethlehem Steel*, 168 F. Supp. 576 (1958).

[67] *U.S.* v. *E. I. du Pont de Nemours & Co.*, 353 U.S. 586 (1957), cert. denied 314 U.S. 618 (1941).

[68] *In the Matter of Brillo Manufacturing Co., Inc.*, F.T.C. Docket 6557 (Nov. 26, 1958).

[69] *U.S.* v. *E. I. du Pont de Nemours & Co.*, 351 U.S. 377 (1956).

[70] Clair Wilcox, *Public Policies Toward Business* (1955), p. 871.

[71] Joe S. Bain, "Price Leaders, Barometers, and Kinks," *Journal of Business*, Vol. 33 (1960), pp. 193, 194.

[72] Almarin Phillips, "A Critique of United States Experience with Price-Fixing Agreements and the Per Se Rule," *Journal of Industrial Economics*, Vol. 8 (October 1959), p. 13.

[73] *Schine Chain Theatres, Inc.* v. *U.S.*, 334 U.S. 110, 130 (1948).

[74] Some writers equate tests of market structure with the defendant's share of the market. G. E. Hale and Rosemary D. Hale, *Market Power: Size and Shape under the Sherman Act* (1958), p. 89; see *Report of the Attorney General's National Committee to Study the Antitrust Laws* (1955), pp. 325, 326.

[75] Bain, "Price Leaders, Barometers, and Kinks," *op. cit.*, pp. 193, 194.

[76] A comprehensive treatment of concentration measures is contained in Betty Bock, *Concentration Patterns in Manufacturing*, National Industrial Conference Board Studies in Business Economics, No. 65 (1959). On the application of percentage share as a test of market control see Edward Levi, "A Two Level Anti-Monopoly Law," *Northwestern Law Review* (December 1952), p. 567.

[77] "The fact that large numbers of buyers and sellers *will* insure workable competition does not mean, however, that such numbers are necessary." Edward S. Mason, "Competition, Price Policy, and High-Level Stability," in U.S. Chamber of Commerce, *Economic Institute on Pricing Problems and the Stabilization of Prosperity* (1947), pp. 19, 31. *In the Matter of Brillo Manufacturing Co., Inc.*, (Docket 6557), the F.T.C. Hearing Examiner held that concentration was not an

important factor since there were seven companies in an industry with annual sales of $5 million. Initial Decision, Nov. 25, 1958 (mimeo.), p. 6.

[78] Professor Kingman Brewster points to "the realization that competition may be workable and effective even though there are not many firms in an industry." This observation, he feels, serves "to make the law's job hard." "Enforceable Competition: Unruly Reason or Reasonable Rules?", *American Economic Review*, Supplement, Vol. 46 (1956), p. 482. See also Corwin D. Edwards, *Maintaining Competition* (1949), p. 10; Jesse W. Markham, *Competition in the Rayon Industry* (1952), p. 204; Vernon A. Mund, *Government and Business* (2d ed., 1955), p. 71.

[79] *U.S.* v. *Aluminum Co. of America*, 148 F. 2d 416 (C.C.A.-2d 1945).

[80] *In the Matter of Brillo Manufacturing Co., Inc.*, F.T.C. Docket 6557 (Nov. 26, 1958).

[81] *In the Matter of Crown Zellerbach Corp.*, F.T.C. Docket 6180 (Decided Dec. 26, 1957). A tabulation of percentages of the market "held to be illegal" is contained in G. E. Hale and Rosemary D. Hale, *op. cit.*, footnote pp. 120-21, *American Tobacco Co.* v. *U.S.*, 328 U.S. 781 (1946).

[82] H. T. Brown defines market power as "control over a certain percentage of the market." "Monopoly—The 1953 Model," *Federal Antitrust Laws* (1953), pp. 3, 14.

[83] R. L. Andreano and S. L. Warner, "Professor Bain and Barriers to New Competition," *Journal of Industrial Economics*, Vol. 7 (October 1958), pp. 66, 67.

[84] See Lucile Sheppard Keyes, "The Bethlehem-Youngstown Case and the Market-Share Criterion," *American Economic Review*, Vol. 51 (September 1961), pp. 643, 650, 651. *U.S.* v. *Columbia Steel Co. et al.*, 334 U.S. 495 (1948), p. 528.

[85] Eugene V. Rostow points to the uncritical use of percentage of markets. "The New Sherman Act: A Positive Instrument of Progress," *University of Chicago Law Review*, Vol. 14 (1947), p. 567. See also Betty Bock, "Mergers and Market Size—3. Other Factors," *Conference Board Business Record*, Vol. 16 (July 1959), p. 347.

[86] *U.S.* v. *Brown Shoe Co., Inc.*, *CCH Trade Cases* (1956), Par. 68,244. See also *U.S.* v. *National Lead Co. et al.*, 334 U.S. 319 (1947); *CCH Trade Cases* (1946-47), Par. 57,575. In that case the court held that there was no showing that four competitors would be better than two, or six better than four.

[87] Fred J. Weston, *The Role of Mergers in the Growth of Large Firms* (1953), pp. 89-90; Myron W. Watkins, "Book Review of E. S. Mason, *Economic Concentration and the Monopoly Problem*," *American Economic Review*, Vol. 36 (1946), pp. 747, 750.

[88] An interesting tie-up of behavior and structure is presented in Arthur H. Kahn, "Discriminatory Pricing As a Barrier to Entry: The Spark Plug Litigation," *Journal of Industrial Economics*, Vol. 8 (1959), p. 1. Professor J. M. Clark points to the need to consider freedom of exit as an important feature. *Competition as a Dynamic Process* (1961), p. 112. See also Joe S. Bain, "Conditions of Entry and the Emergence of Monopoly," in Edward H. Chamberlin, ed., *Monopoly and Competition and Their Regulation* (1954), p. 215.

[89] The most complete discussion of this factor may be found in Joe S. Bain, *Barriers to New Competition* (1956). He does not deal extensively with entry by existing firms in other markets. See criticism in Andreano and Warner, *op. cit.*, p. 75. See also Alfred R. Oxenfeldt, *New Firms and Free Enterprise* (1943); Preben Munthe, *Freedom of Entry into Industry and Trade*, European Productivity Agency (1958); and Howard H. Hines, "Effectiveness of 'Entry' by Already Established Firms," *Quarterly Journal of Economics*, Vol. 70 (1957), p. 132 (reprinted in *Employment, Growth, and Price Levels*, Hearings before the Joint Economic Committee, 86 Cong. 1 sess., Pt. 7 (1959), p. 1981). Hines' article contains an interesting bibliography in footnote 1.

[90] *Ibid.* See also William T. Hogan and Frank Koelble, "Technology and Competition," *University of Detroit Law Journal,* Vol. 38 (1960), p. 113, esp. p. 122. For a view of recent developments see George D. McCarthy, "Premeditated Merger," *Harvard Business Review,* Vol. 39 (January-February 1961), p. 74.

[91] *American Crystal Sugar Co.* v. *Cuban American Sugar Co.,* 259 F. 2d 524 (1958).

[92] *In the Matter of A. G. Spalding & Bros., Inc.,* Docket 6478. Order to cease and desist, March 30, 1960.

[93] Richard B. Heflebower raises a profound question: "whether economic effects of entry stem from the fear of entry or from the force of actual entry." "Toward a Theory of Industrial Markets and Prices," *American Economic Review,* Vol. 44 (May 1954), pp. 121, 131.

[94] See *U.S.* v. *United Shoe Machinery Corp.,* 110 F. Supp. 295 (D.C. Mass. 1953), aff'd *per curiam,* 347 U.S. 521 (1954).

[95] "A patent . . is at least *prima facie* evidence of [market] control." *U.S.* v. *Standard Oil of California,* 337 U.S. 293, 307 (1949). See also Munthe, *op. cit.,* p. 20.

[96] Sigmund Timberg points to the "almost monotonous regularity with which the Supreme Court finds patents lacking in inventiveness." From 1941 to 1945 patents were not upheld in 80 per cent of cases in the Circuit Court of Appeals and the Supreme Court. "Equitable Relief under the Sherman Act," *University of Illinois Law Forum,* Vol. 1950 (Winter Number), pp. 629, 645.

[97] *Hartford-Empire Co. et al.* v. *U.S.,* 323 U.S. 386 (1945); 324 U.S. 570 (1945).

[98] *U.S.* v. *General Electric et al.,* 82 F. Supp. 753 (D.C.N.J. 1949).

[99] Jesse W. Markham, "Economic Analysis," *Proceedings,* Section of Antitrust Law, American Bar Association (April 1954), pp. 145, 149. Markham regards this factor as the "most important single determinant of the degree of competition in a given industry." See Joe S. Bain, *Industrial Organization* (1959); *Report of the Attorney General's National Committee to Study the Antitrust Laws* (1955), pp. 326, 327.

[100] Joe S. Bain, *Barriers to New Competition* (1956).

[101] See affidavits in support of defendant submitted in *U.S.* v. *Bethlehem Steel Corp.,* 168 F. Supp. 576 (1958).

[102] Joe S. Bain, *Industrial Organization* (1959).

[103] *American Tobacco Co.* v. *U.S.,* 328 U.S. 781 (1946). The court was impressed with the large advertising expenditures of the Big Three in the cigarette industry. It felt that these expenditures, together with large investments required for inventories and federal taxes, tended to forestall potential competition. (P. 797.)

[104] Robert C. Brooks, Jr., "Volume Discounts as Barriers to Entry and Access," *Journal of Political Economy,* Vol. 69 (February 1961), p. 63.

[105] *In the Matter of American Optical Co.,* 28 F.T.C. 169 (1939).

[106] *In the Matter of A. G. Spalding & Bros., Inc.,* Docket 6478. Order to cease and desist, March 30, 1960.

[107] Corwin D. Edwards gives this indicator substantial prominence. "Preserving Competition vs. Regulating Monopoly," *American Economic Review,* Supplement, Pt. 2, Vol. 30 (1940), pp. 164, 170.

[108] *Erie Sand and Gravel Co.* v. *F.T.C.* (C.C.A.-3d May 1961), *CCH Trade Cases,* Par. 70,028.

[109] See discussion of this problem in J. M. Clark, *Competition as a Dynamic Process* (1961), Chaps. 12, 13, 14.

[110] *U.S.* v. *Bethlehem Steel,* 168 F. Supp. 576 (1958).

[111] *F.T.C.* v. *Cement Institute,* 333 U.S. 683 (1948).

[112] See Clark, *op. cit.,* Chap. 14.

[113] *U.S.* v. *New York Great A & P Tea Co.*, 67 F. Supp. 626 (E.D. Ill. 1946), aff'd 173 F. 2d 79 (C.C.A.-7th 1949).

[114] *Anheuser-Busch* v. *F.T.C.*, 265 F. 2d 677 (C.C.A.-7th 1959). Reviewed and remanded 363 U.S. 536 (1960). See also Edgar R. Barton, "The *Anheuser-Busch* Case," *Sales and Pricing Policies Under the Antitrust Laws*, CCH Trade Regulation Reports (1961), p. 72.

[115] *Report of the Attorney General's National Committee to Study the Antitrust Laws* (1955), p. 327.

[116] *Hamilton Watch Co.* v. *Benrus Watch Co.*, 114 F. Supp. 397 (D.C. Conn. 1953), aff'd 206 F. 2d 738 (C.C.A.-2d 1953).

[117] *Kiefer-Stewart Co.* v. *Joseph E. Seagram & Sons, Inc.*, 340 U.S. 211 (1951).

[118] See Joseph A. Sheehy, "Implications of Intra-Enterprise Conspiracy Doctrine in Clayton Act Sections 2 and 3 Cases," *Proceedings*, Section of Antitrust Law, American Bar Association (April 1956), p. 83.

[119] 15 U.S.C. 16, 18.

[120] See 49 Stat. 717.

[121] For a rather full discussion of vertical integration see Friedrich Kessler and Richard H. Stern, "Competition, Contract, and Vertical Integration," *Yale Law Journal*, Vol. 69 (November 1959), p. 1. Preben Munthe deals with the relationship between vertical integration and freedom of entry in *Freedom of Entry into Industry and Trade*, European Productivity Agency (1958), pp. 39-40.

[122] See A. D. H. Kaplan's treatment of integration as a stimulator of competition and of the limits of integration as a means of market control. *Big Enterprise in a Competitive System* (1954), pp. 208-18.

[123] *U.S.* v. *Aluminum Co. of America*, 148 F. 2d 416 (C.C.A.-2d 1945).

[124] *In the Matter of Reynolds Metals Co.*, Docket 7009. Order to cease and desist, Jan. 21, 1960.

[125] See Corwin D. Edwards, "Economic Implications of Business Boundary Laws," *Law and Contemporary Problems*, Vol. 8 (Spring 1941), p. 292, and *U.S.* v. *Bethlehem Steel Co.*, 168 F. Supp. 576, 612 (1958).

[126] Vernon Mund is impressed with the effects of the refusal of integrated producers to sell basic products to non-integrated competitors. *The Right to Buy—1959*, Staff Report prepared for the Senate Select Committee on Small Business, 86 Cong. 1 sess. (1959), esp. p. 16.

[127] *Report of the Attorney General's National Committee to Study the Antitrust Laws* (1955), pp. 330, 331.

[128] Joe S. Bain, "Price Leaders, Barometers, and Kinks," *Journal of Business*, Vol. 33 (1960), pp. 193, 194.

[129] J. M. Clark, *Competition as a Dynamic Process* (1961), Chap. 9.

[130] Corwin D. Edwards, *The Price Discrimination Law* (1959), p. 31.

[131] Docket 3264, 26 F.T.C. 303. See also U.S. Rubber, Docket 3685, 28 F.T.C. 1489 (Order 4/25/39); Whitaker Cable, Docket 5722, 51 F.T.C. 938.

[132] Corwin D. Edwards pointed out the significance of private brands in "Standards and Product Differentiation," in Dickson Reck, ed., *National Standards in a Modern Economy* (1956), p. 327. He stated that the aggregate price of ten private brands listed in an advertisement was about 53 per cent of the aggregate for equivalent nationally advertised brands. (Pp. 329-30.)

[133] Joe S. Bain, *Barriers to New Competition* (1956).

[134] *U.S.* v. *Sugar Institute*, 15 F. Supp. 817 (S.D.N.Y. 1934).

[135] Carpet Manufacturers—*CCH Trade Cases*, Par. 56,079 (1941); Battery Separator—*CCH Trade Cases*, Par. 56,154 (1941).

[136] *U.S.* v. *American Linseed Oil*, 262 U.S. 371 (1932).

[137] J. K. Galbraith, *American Capitalism: The Concept of Countervailing Power*

(1952), and his "Countervailing Power," *American Economic Review,* Supplement, Vol. 44 (1954) p. 1; George J. Stigler, "The Economist Plays with Blocs," *ibid.,* p. 7; John Perry Miller, "Competition and Countervailing Power: Their Roles in the American Economy," *ibid.,* p. 15.

[138] See *In the Matter of Champion Spark Plug Co.,* Docket 3977. Order to cease and desist, July 10, 1953.

[139] See *U.S.* v. *New York Great A & P Tea Co.,* 67 F. Supp. 626 (D.C.E.D. Ill. 1946), aff'd 173 F. 2d 79 (C.C.A.-7th 1949).

[140] See, for example, Almarin Phillips' discussion of the railroad-shipper relationships towards the end of the last century. "A Critique of United States Experience with Price-Fixing Agreements and the Per Se Rule," *Journal of Industrial Economics,* Vol. 7 (October 1959), p. 13.

[141] *Bradley Co.* v. *Local Union No. 3,* 325 U.S. 797 (1945).

[142] See Richard B. Heflebower, "Toward a Theory of Industrial Markets and Prices," *American Economic Review,* Vol. 44 (May 1954), pp. 121, 131.

[143] A. D. H. Kaplan, *Big Enterprise in a Competitive System* (1954), pp. 192-94.

[144] See Arthur H. Kahn, "Discriminatory Pricing as a Barrier to Entry: The Spark Plug Litigation," *Journal of Industrial Economics,* Vol. 8 (October 1959), p. 1. He points to the potential competition from customers who may start to manufacture the product they purchase.

[145] Some economists prefer to use the term "conduct" and define "behavior" as a combination of conduct and performance. Stephen H. Sosnick, "A Critique of Concepts of Workable Competition," *Quarterly Journal of Economics,* Vol. 72 (August 1958), pp. 380, 387.

[146] For example, Richard B. Heflebower traces the relationship between oligopoly (few sellers) and "the somewhat elastic glue of collusion" in "Stability in Oligopoly," *The Manchester School of Economic and Social Studies,* Vol. 29 (January 1961), pp. 79, 93.

[147] *U.S.* v. *Aluminum Co. of America,* 148 F. 2d 416 (1945).

[148] This indicator is employed by most economists who have considered criteria of competition. See, for example, Alfred R. Oxenfeldt, *Industrial Pricing and Market Practices* (1951); George W. Stocking and Myron W. Watkins, *Monopoly and Free Enterprise* (1951).

[149] *U.S.* v. *Socony-Vacuum Oil Co., Inc. et al.,* 310 U.S. 150 (1940).

[150] *Johnson* v. *Schlitz,* 33 F. Supp. 176 (D.C. Tenn. 1940).

[151] *Hartford-Empire Co. et al.* v. *U.S.,* 323 U.S. 386 (1945); 324 U.S. 572 (1945).

[152] *Kiefer-Stewart Co.* v. *Seagram & Sons,* 340 U.S. 211 (1951).

[153] Judge Hand raised a substantial question about the relationship between prices fixed by agreement and monopoly prices. He argued that monopolies have "an equal, or even greater, power to fix prices. . . ." Hence, "it would be absurd to condemn (price-fixing) contracts unconditionally, and not to extend the condemnation to monopolies; for the contracts are only steps toward that entire control which monopolies confer; they are really partial monopolies." *U.S.* v. *Aluminum Co. of America,* 148 F. 2d 416, 427-28 (C.C.A.-2d 1945).

[154] *Klor's, Inc.* v. *Broadway-Hale Stores, Inc. et al.,* 359 U.S. 207 (1959).

[155] *Report of the Attorney General's National Committee to Study the Antitrust Laws* (1955), pp. 329, 330.

[156] For a discussion of the relationship between parallelism and agreement see Almarin Phillips, "Policy Implications of the Theory of Interfirm Organization," *American Economic Review,* Vol. 51 (May 1961), pp. 245, 251-52.

[157] See Richard A. Givens, "Parallel Business Conduct Under the Sherman Act," *Antitrust Bulletin,* Vol. 5 (May-June 1960), p. 273; Almarin Phillips and George R. Hall, "The Salk Vaccine Case: Parallelism, Conspiracy and Other Hypotheses,"

*Virginia Law Review*, Vol. 46 (1960), p. 717; Bernard R. Sorkin "Conscious Parallelism," *Antitrust Bulletin*, Vol. 2 (1957), p. 281.

[158] See criticism of the concept in J. M. Clark, *Competition as a Dynamic Process* (1961), pp. 19, 20. See also *Report of the Attorney General's National Committee to Study the Antitrust Laws*, pp. 36-42.

[159] "[T]his court has never held that proof of parallel business behavior conclusively establishes agreement or, phrased differently, that such behavior itself constitutes a Sherman Act offense." *Theater Enterprise, Inc.* v. *Paramount Film Distributing Corp.*, 346 U.S. 537 (1954). In this connection, see Edward Levi's discussion of "concert of action." "The Antitrust Laws and Monopoly," *University of Chicago Law Review*, Vol. 14 (1947), pp. 153, 177-78. See also Jerome G. Shapiro, "The Salk Vaccine," *Sales and Pricing Policies Under the Antitrust Laws*, CCH Trade Regulation Reports (1961), p. 91; *Standard Oil Co. of California* v. *Moore*, 251 F. 2d 188 (C.C.A.-9th 1957); and *Orbo Theatre Corp.* v. *Loew's Inc.*, 156 Supp. 771 (D.C.D.C. 1957).

[160] Joe S. Bain feels that this indicator is likely to be a "relatively fruitless" device in antitrust. "Price Leaders, Barometers, and Kinks," *Journal of Business*, Vol. 33 (1960), pp. 193, 203.

[161] *Interstate Circuit, Inc. et al.* v. *U.S.*, 306 U.S. 208 (1939). See also *Milgrim* v. *Loew's Inc.*, 192 F. 2d 579 (C.C.A.-3d 1951); cert. denied 343 U.S. 929 (1952).

[162] For a comprehensive discussion of price leadership see Arthur R. Burns, *Decline of Competition* (1936), Chap. 3.

[163] Bain, *op. cit.*, p. 197.

[164] *U.S.* v. *U.S. Steel Corp.*, 223 F. 55, 89 (1915).

[165] *U.S.* v. *International Harvester*, 274 U.S. 693 (1927). Justice Sanford held that "the fact that competitors may see proper, in the exercise of their judgment, to follow the prices of another manufacturer, does not establish any suppression of competition or show any sinister domination." (P. 708.)

[166] *In the Matter of Crown Zellerbach Corp.*, F.T.C. Docket 6180 (Decided Dec. 26, 1957).

[167] See George J. Stigler's discussion of "barometric" price leadership. "The Kinky Oligopoly Demand Curve and Rigid Prices," *Journal of Political Economy*, Vol. 55 (1947), p. 432. See also Jesse W. Markham, "The Nature and Significance of Price Leadership," in American Economic Association, *Readings in Industrial Organization and Public Policy* (1958), p. 176, for a refinement of the "barometric" concept.

[168] See Edwin G. Nourse and Horace B. Drury, *Industrial Price Policies and Economic Progress* (1938), p. 124.

[169] See Fritz Machlup, *The Basing-Point System* (1949); Carl Kaysen, "Basing Point Pricing and Public Policy," *Quarterly Journal of Economics*, Vol. 63 (1949), p. 289; and Corwin D. Edwards, *The Price Discrimination Law* (1959), Chaps. 11-13.

[170] *F.T.C.* v. *Staley Manufacturing Co.*, 324 U.S. 746 (1945).

[171] See Corwin D. Edwards, "The Effect of Recent Basing Point Decisions Upon Business Practices," *American Economic Review*, Vol. 38 (1948), p. 828.

[172] The strongest opponent of any departure from f.o.b. prices was Professor Frank Fetter. See his *Masquerade of Monopoly* (1931) and "Exit Basing Point Pricing," *American Economic Review*, Vol. 38 (1948), p. 816.

[173] See J. M. Clark, "Law and Economics of Basing Points: Appraisals and Proposals," *American Economic Review*, Vol. 39 (1949), p. 430 and his *Competition as a Dynamic Process* (1961).

[174] *F.T.C.* v. *Cement Institute*, 333 U.S. 683 (1948).

[175] Melvin G. de Chazeau and Alfred E. Kahn feel that the policy emphasis of

large firms with few competitors is to meet, not beat, competitive prices. *Integration and Competition in the Petroleum Industry* (1959), p. 380. See also *Report of the Attorney General's National Committee to Study the Antitrust Laws,* pp. 331, 332. The committee felt that "effective competition also involves freedom to undercut rivals' prices."

[176] *Standard Oil Co. (Indiana)* v. *F.T.C.,* 173 F. 2d 210 (C.C.A.-7th 1949); 340 U.S. 231 (1951).

[177] A new issue was developed *In the Matter of Sunshine Biscuits, Inc.,* Docket 7708. In writing the Opinion of the Commission (Sept. 25, 1961, mimeo.), Commissioner Sigurd Anderson held that the defense of meeting competition was valid only when a price was reduced "to hold customers rather than to gain new ones." (P. 4.) In a strong dissent Commissioner Philip Elman argued that the majority's rule would curtail competition and that it is "practically unworkable." (P. 3.)

[178] *Anheuser-Busch* v. *F.T.C.,* 265 F. 2d 677 (C.C.A.-7th 1959). Reversed and remanded 363 U.S. 536 (1960).

[179] See National Resources Committee, *Structure of the American Economy,* Pt. I (1939), p. 132. An excellent summary of the literature regarding price flexibility is presented in Richard Ruggles, "The Nature of Price Flexibility and the Determinants of Relative Price Changes in the Economy," in National Bureau of Economic Research, *Business Concentration and Price Policy* (1955), p. 441.

[180] See, for example, Jesse W. Markham, "The Methodology and Policy Implications of Price Flexibility," address delivered at the Meeting of the Group of Experts on Restrictive Business Practices, May 27-29, 1959 (mimeo.); Gardiner C. Means, *Administrative Inflation and Public Policy* (1959). Corwin D. Edwards refers to "flexibility of business policies toward prices and other important terms of the market bargain." "Preserving Competition vs. Regulating Monopoly," *American Economic Review,* Supplement, Pt. 2, Vol. 30 (1940), pp. 164, 171. Fritz Machlup refers to the use of price flexibility as a means of detecting "the presence and degree of monopoly." However, he is not enthusiastic about such use. *The Political Economy of Monopoly* (1952), p. 475. J. K. Galbraith raises doubts about price flexibility as a guide to monopoly in "Monopoly Power and Price Rigidities," *Quarterly Journal of Economics,* Vol. 50 (May 1936), p. 456. See also Richard Ruggles, *op. cit.,* p. 441.

[181] Gardiner C. Means, *Industrial Prices and Their Relative Inflexibility,* S. Doc. 13, 74 Cong. 1 sess. (1935). However Means said, "Administered prices should not be confused with monopoly." (P. 1.)

[182] Alfred C. Neal, *Industrial Concentration and Price Inflexibility* (1942).

[183] See National Resources Committee, *loc. cit.*

[184] See discussion of this relationship in *Frequency of Change in Wholesale Prices, A Study of Price Flexibility,* A Study Prepared for the Joint Economic Committee by the United States Department of Labor, Bureau of Labor Statistics, 85 Cong. 2 sess. (1959), p. 9.

[185] See Edward S. Mason, *Economic Concentration and the Monopoly Problem* (1957), p. 53, and Gardiner C. Means "Notes on Inflexible Prices," *American Economic Review,* Supplement, Vol. 26 (March 1936), p. 23.

[186] Robert F. Lanzillotti was impressed by the differences between published and transaction prices in his study of *The Hard-Surface Floor-Covering Industry* (1955), pp. 87, 145.

[187] *Frequency of Change in Wholesale Prices, A Study of Price Flexibility,* p. 6.

[188] Richard B. Heflebower discusses the pricing practices for tailor-made products in "Full Costs, Cost Changes, and Prices," in National Bureau of Economic Research, *Business Concentration and Price Policy* (1955), pp. 361, 378-85.

[189] *U.S.* v. *Engineering Survey and Audit Co.* (D.C. La. 1940), *CCH Trade Cases,* Par. 56,019; *U.S.* v. *Brooker Engineering Co.* (D.C. Mich. 1942), *CCH Trade Cases,* Par. 56,183; *Zion's Service Corp.* v. *H. A. Danielson* (Supreme Court of Utah, 1961), *CCH Trade Cases,* Par. 70,165.

[190] Under some systems the bids are not shown to competitors until the award is made. Corwin D. Edwards reported the manager of such a system had assured him that "the use of the system had raised the average level of bids at least 30 per cent." *Maintaining Competition* (1949), footnote 26, p. 28.

[191] See, for example, *Tag Manufacturers Institute,* 174 F. 2d 452 (C.C.A.-1st 1949); *U.S.* v. *Reno Merchant Plumbing and Heating Contractors, Inc.* (D.C. Nev. 1952), *CCH Trade Cases,* Par. 67,361.

[192] *Report of the Attorney General's National Committee to Study the Antitrust Laws* (1955), pp. 333, 336. The Committee felt that some price discrimination stimulates competition and some may evidence an "effective monopoly." See Fritz Machlup, "Characteristics and Types of Price Discrimination," *Business Concentration and Price Policy* (1955), p. 397.

[193] Carl Kaysen refers to price discrimination as an aspect of performance. *United States* v. *United Shoe Machinery Corporation, An Economic Analysis of an Antitrust Case* (1956), p. 20. Arthur H. Kahn feels that price discrimination may produce better performance "if the existing monopoly power cannot be removed." "Discriminatory Pricing as a Barrier to Entry: The Spark Plug Litigation," *Journal of Industrial Economics,* Vol. 8 (1959), p. 1.

[194] An interesting presentation of the use of cumulative or volume discounts as a device for blocking entry is contained in Robert C. Brooks, Jr., "Volume Discounts as Barriers to Entry and Access," *Journal of Political Economy,* Vol. 69 (February 1961), p. 63. Fritz Machlup sees price discrimination as a symptom, not a cause, of monopoly power. *The Political Economy of Monopoly* (1952), pp. 136-37.

[195] See J. M. Clark, *Studies in the Economics of Overhead Cost* (1923), p. 416; M. A. Adelman, "Price Discrimination as Treated in the Attorney General's Report," *University of Pennsylvania Law Review,* Vol. 104 (1955), p. 224; John F. Savage, "Not All Price Discriminations are Unlawful under the Robinson-Patman Act," *Marquette Law Review,* Vol. 42 (Fall 1958), p. 201. Savage lists a number of market factors which he feels would be useful in analyzing the competitive effects of price discrimination. See also Arthur H. Kahn, "Discriminatory Pricing as a Barrier to Entry," *op. cit.,* p. 1; John McGee, "Price Discrimination and Competitive Effects: The Standard Oil of Indiana Case," *University of Chicago Law Review,* Vol. 23 (1956), p. 398; and Robert C. Brooks, Jr., "Injury to Competition Under the Robinson-Patman Act," *University of Pennsylvania Law Review,* Vol. 109 (April 1961), pp. 777, 786.

[196] Pauline Lesley Cook, *Effects of Mergers* (1958), pp. 432-33.

[197] Almarin Phillips discusses instances of price discrimination due to powerful positions of some buyers in "A Critique of United States Experience with Price-Fixing Agreements and the Per Se Rule," *Journal of Industrial Economics,* Vol. 8 (1959), p. 13.

[198] For a full description of the types of price discrimination see Fritz Machlup, "Characteristics and Types of Price Discrimination," in National Bureau of Economic Research, *Business Concentration and Price Policy* (1955), p. 397.

[199] H. Thomas Austern, "Inconsistencies in the Law," *Business Practices Under Federal Antitrust Laws,* Proceedings of the Third Annual Meeting of the New York State Bar Association, Section on Antitrust Law (Jan. 24, 1951), pp. 158, 164-65.

[200] Corwin D. Edwards discusses the influence of the power of big buyers on

discriminatory advantages in "Conglomerate Bigness as a Source of Power," in National Bureau of Economic Research, *Business Concentration and Price Policy* (1955), pp. 331, 337-40.

[201] See *Automatic Canteen Co. of America* v. *F.T.C.*, 346 U.S. 61 (1953).

[202] *American Motor Specialties Co., Inc.* v. F.T.C., 298 F. 2d 225 (C.C.A.-2d 1960), cert. denied 364 U.S. 884 (1960).

[203] *U.S.* v. *New York Great A & P Tea Co.*, 67 F. Supp. 626 (E.D. Ill. 1946), aff'd 173 F. 2d 79 (C.C.A.-7th 1940).

[204] *In the Matter of Luxor, Ltd.*, Docket 3736. Order to cease and desist, July 31, 1940.

[205] *In the Matter of Food Fair Stores, Inc.* Docket 6458.

[206] *U.S.* v. *New York Great A & P Tea Co., loc. cit.*

[207] See M. A. Adelman's thesis that predatory behavior will not occur in retailing, *A & P: A Study in Price-Cost Behavior and Public Policy* (1959), pp. 409-19. See also *Report of the Attorney General's National Committee to Study the Antitrust Laws* (1955), pp. 327, 328; Robert C. Brooks, Jr., "Price Cutting and Monopoly Power," *Journal of Marketing*, Vol. 25 (1961), p. 44.

[208] The predatory practices of the Standard Oil Company figured prominently in early antitrust days. See Commissioner of Corporations, *Transportation of Petroleum*, Garfield's Report (1906). *Standard Oil Co.* v. *U.S.*, 221 U.S. 1 (1911). John S. McGee concluded, in a recent study, that Standard Oil did not follow predatory practices but gained through the merger process. "Predatory Price Cutting: The Standard Oil (N.J.) Case," *Journal of Law and Economics*, Vol. 1 (1958), p. 137.

[209] See Professor Clair Wilcox's point about the difficulty of defining a predatory practice because of the problem of gauging intent. *Competition and Monopoly in American Industry*, Temporary National Economic Committee Monograph No. 21 (1940).

[210] *Mead's Fine Bread Co.* v. *Moore*, 348 U.S. 115 (1954); *U.S.* v. *New York Great A & P Tea Co.*, 67 F. Supp. 626 (E.D. Ill. 1946), aff'd 173 F. 2d 79 (C.C.A.-7th 1949). See Robert C. Brooks, Jr., "Injury to Competition Under the Robinson-Patman Act," *University of Pennsylvania Law Review*, Vol. 109 (April 1961), pp. 777, 785, 790.

[211] See, for example, *Holland Furnace Co.* v. *F.T.C.* (C.C.A.-7th 1961), F.T.C. Docket 6203. Practices involved were: representing its employees as representatives of government agencies or utility companies, or as engineers; misrepresenting the condition of competitors' furnaces and the lack of parts; dismantling furnaces without permission and refusing to reassemble them. Details are given in *Initial Decision* (Oct. 23, 1957).

[212] See discussion of need for broader analysis of exclusive arrangements in Alfred E. Kahn, "A Legal and Economic Appraisal of the 'New' Sherman and Clayton Acts," *Yale Law Journal*, Vol. 63 (January 1954), pp. 293, 335.

[213] *U.S.* v. *Standard Oil of California*, 337 U.S. 293 (1949).

[214] *In the Matter of Mytinger & Casselberry*, Docket 6062, Order to cease and desist Sept. 28, 1960.

[215] Richard B. Heflebower pointed to the case of integration backwards, when a distributive organization sets up brands and specifications and enters the market as a producer though it does not actually manufacture. "Toward a Theory of Industrial Markets and Prices," *American Economic Review*, Vol. 44 (May 1954), pp. 121, 131.

[216] See *U.S.* v. *General Electric Co.*, 272 U.S. 476 (1926), and *U.S.* v. *General Electric Co. et al.*, 82 F. Supp. 753 (D.C. N.J. 1949).

[217] See *U.S.* v. *Bendix Home Appliances, Inc.* (S.D.N.Y. 1948), *CCH Trade Cases,* Par. 63,346, and *U.S.* v. *Seeburg Corp.* (N.D. Ill. 1947), *CCH Trade Cases,* Par. 68,613. See also H. Thomas Austern, "Inconsistencies in the Law," *Business Practices Under Federal Antitrust Laws,* Proceedings of the Third Annual Meeting of the New York State Bar Association, Section on Antitrust Law (Jan. 24, 1951), pp. 158, 162, 163; and Stanley D. Robinson, "Providing for Orderly Marketing of Goods," *Proceedings,* Section of Antitrust Law, American Bar Association (August 1959), p. 282.

[218] Vernon A. Mund argues that antitrust should make it more difficult for a seller to refuse to sell to others. See "Refusal to Sell," *Vanderbilt Law Review,* Vol. 11 (March 1958), and *The Right to Buy—1959,* Staff Report prepared for the Senate Select Committee on Small Business, 86 Cong. 1 sess. (1959). J. M. Wood argues for strengthening the right to buy in England, referring to refusals to sell to consumer cooperatives. *The Challenge of Monopoly* (1960), pp. 22-23.

[219] *In the Matter of Container Stapling Corp.,* Docket 8082.

[220] *In the Matter of International Staple and Machine Co.,* Docket 8083.

[221] An argument for allowing small manufacturers to use territory restrictions may be found in Seymour D. Lewis, "Orderly Marketing and the Small Business Man," *Proceedings,* Section of Antitrust Law, American Bar Association (April 1960), pp. 73, 77-80.

[222] Friedrich Kessler and Richard H. Stern, "Competition, Contract, and Vertical Integration," *Yale Law Journal,* Vol. 69 (November 1959), p. 1.

[223] *U.S.* v. *Standard Oil of California,* 337 U.S. 293 (1949).

[224] *U.S.* v. *American Can Co.,* 87 F. Supp. 18 (N.D. Cal. 1949).

[225] *Tampa Electric Co.* v. *Nashville Coal Co.,* 276 F. 2d 766 (C.C.A.-6th 1960).

[226] J. E. Vaizey, "The Brewing Industry," in Pauline Lesley Cook, *Effects of Mergers* (1958), p. 421.

[227] See Notes, "Definition of the Market in Tying Arrangements: Another Aspect of Times-Picayune," *Yale Law Journal,* Vol. 63 (1954), p. 389; Alfred E. Kahn, "A Legal and Economic Appraisal of the 'New' Sherman and Clayton Acts," *ibid.,* pp. 293, 322.

[228] William B. Lockhart and Howard R. Sacks, "The Relevance of Economic Factors in Determining Whether Exlusive Arrangements Violate Section 3 of the Clayton Act," *Harvard Law Review,* Vol. 65 (April 1952), pp. 919, 942.

[229] *International Salt Co.* v. *U.S.,* 332 U.S. 392 (1947); *International Business Machines Corp.* v. *U.S.,* 293 U.S. 131 (1936); *Times-Picayune Publishing Co.* v. *U.S.,* 345 U.S. 594 (1953).

[230] See, for example, *U.S.* v. *Paramount Pictures, Inc.,* 334 U.S. 131 (1948).

[231] See *Report of the Attorney General's National Committee to Study the Antitrust Laws* (1955), pp. 250-54.

[232] *National Harrow Co.* v. *Hench,* 83 F. 36 (C.C.A.-3d 1897).

[233] *Hartford-Empire Co. et al.* v. *U.S.,* 323 U.S. 386 (1945); 324 U.S. 570 (1945).

[234] *Cutter Laboratories* v. *Lyophile-Cryochem Corp.,* 170 F. 2d 80 (C.C.A.-9th 1949).

[235] *U.S.* v. *Rail Joint Co. et al.* (D.C. Ill. 1944; D.C. Ill. 1945), *CCH Trade Cases,* Par. 57,287, Par. 57,469.

[236] See *Report of the Attorney General's National Committee to Study the Antitrust Laws,* Chap. V.

[237] Myron W. Watkins, "Book Review of E. S. Mason, *Economic Concentration and the Monopoly Problem,*" *American Economic Review,* Vol. 47 (1957), p. 747.

[238] It is contrasted with action which "springs from business requirements." *U.S.* v. *Columbia Steel Co. et al.,* 334 U.S. 495, 527 (1948).

[239] See Betty Bock, *Mergers and Markets,* N.I.C.B. Studies in Business Economics, No. 69 (1960), p. 82.

[240] *U.S.* v. *Aluminum Co. of America,* 148 F. 2d 416 (C.C.A.-2d 1945).

[241] Corwin D. Edwards, "Doing Business Under the Law as it Now Stands," in U.S. Chamber of Commerce, *Economic Institute on Delivered Pricing and the Future of American Business,* December 9-10, 1948, pp. 90, 94.

[242] Edward S. Mason argues "that 'satisfactory performance' is a concept far too slippery for any practical use to an antimonopoly policy." *Economic Concentration and the Monopoly Problem* (1957), p. 330.

[243] Carl Kaysen and Donald Turner discuss the difficulty of applying performance standards. *Antitrust Policy, An Economic and Legal Analysis* (1959), pp. 54-55. However, they propose to use them. (Pp. 52-53.) Theodore J. Kreps is pessimistic about the possibilities of using performance tests because they are not "measurable." *An Evaluation of Antitrust Policy: Its Relation to Economic Growth, Full Employment, and Prices,* Study Paper No. 22, Study of Employment, Growth, and Price Levels, Joint Economic Committee, 86 Cong. 2 sess. (1960), pp. 24-25. Edward S. Mason feels that it would be "extremely difficult to devise (performance) tests that can be administered by a court of law." *Op. cit.,* p. 367.

[244] See, for example, Charles Phillips' interesting treatment of "Workable Competition in the Synthetic Rubber Industry," *Southern Economic Journal,* Vol. 28 (October 1961), p. 154. While Phillips finds satisfactory performance in the industry, he presents no yardsticks for such evaluation. In the *Standard Stations* case the Supreme Court sustained a ruling against evidence of the beneficial effects of a practice on the ground that such an inquiry "would be a standard of proof if not virtually impossible to meet, at least most ill-suited for ascertainment by courts." *Standard Oil Co.* v. *U.S.,* 337 U.S. 293, 310 (1949). For a criticism of this aspect of performance tests see Eugene V. Rostow, "Problems of Size and Integration," *Business Practices Under Federal Antitrust Laws,* Proceedings of the Third Annual Meeting of the New York State Bar Association, Section on Antitrust Law (Jan. 24, 1951), p. 117; John C. Stedman, "A New Look at Antitrust: The Report of the Attorney General's Committee," *Journal of Public Law,* Vol. 4 (1956), pp. 223, 271.

[245] Stephen H. Sosnick, "A Critique of Concepts of Workable Competition," *Quarterly Journal of Economics,* Vol. 72 (August 1958), pp. 380, 392, 393, 396. Sosnick argues that no "set of structure or conduct requirements" will guarantee that "performance will be satisfactory." (P. 397.) However, he would not rely on performance alone.

[246] See statement of Committee on Cartels and Monopoly of the Twentieth Century Fund in George Stocking and Myron W. Watkins, *Monopoly and Price Enterprise* (1951), pp. 552-53.

[247] Myron W. Watkins suggests a novel theory about the use of performance tests: that they serve as a clue to intent. "Book Review of E. S. Mason, *Economic Concentration and the Monopoly Problem,*" *American Economic Review,* Vol. 47 (1957), pp. 747, 752.

[248] Sosnick, *op. cit.,* p. 398.

[249] Myron W. Watkins argues that "courts are not fitted" for such a task and that Congress never intended it. *Op. cit.,* p. 750. The Supreme Court held that differences between legal and illegal conduct cannot depend on so uncertain a test as the reasonableness of prices. *U.S.* v. *Trenton Potteries Co.,* 273 U.S. 392, 396-98 (1927). See also Clare E. Griffin, *An Economic Approach to Antitrust Problems* (1951), pp. 63-68.

[250] Victor R. Hansen suggests that an underlying assumption of antitrust is that good market performance without strong competition might be even better if

competition were active. Further, that "antitrust policies strive to promote competition as such and not only desirable economic performance." "The Current Federal Policy on Antitrust Matters," *Antitrust Bulletin,* Vol. 4 (July-August 1959), pp. 541, 546-47.

[251] See Eugene Kozik, "Oligopoly and the Concept of Workable or Effective Competition: An Economic Analysis of Recent Antitrust Cases," *University of Pittsburgh Law Review,* Vol. 21 (June 1960), p. 621.

[252] For a criticism of this aspect of the performance indicators see Clair Wilcox, *Public Policies Toward Business* (1955), pp. 870-71.

[253] Joseph W. Garbarino, "A Theory of Interindustry Wage Variation," *Quarterly Journal of Economics,* Vol. 64 (1950), p. 285.

[254] Carl Kaysen, "Market Definition in Anti-Trust Law Proceedings," *The Growing Role of Economic Data in Judicial and Administrative Proceedings,* Current Business Studies, No. 18 (March 1954), pp. 18, 22. Fritz Machlup refers to profits as having been regarded as "the monopoly index *par excellence.*" *The Political Economy of Monopoly* (1952), p. 474. He is not convinced of its use. See also Joe S. Bain, "The Profit Rate as a Measure of Monopoly Power," *Quarterly Journal of Economics,* Vol. 55 (1941), p. 271; and K. W. Rothschild, "A Further Note on the Degree of Monopoly," *Economica,* New Series, Vol. 10 (1943), p. 69.

[255] The court held that high profits were required by the cost structure of the industry and did not constitute substantial evidence in *U.S.* v. *E. I. du Pont de Nemours & Co.,* 351 U.S. 377 (1956).

[256] *American Tobacco Co. et al.* v. *U.S.,* 328 U.S. 781 (1946).

[257] *U.S.* v. *Sugar Institute,* 15 F. Supp. 816 (S.D.N.Y. 1934).

[258] *U.S.* v. *Eli Lilly & Co.,* 24 F.R.D. 285 (D.C.N.J. 1959).

[259] Wilcox, *op. cit.,* pp. 842-43, 867.

[260] "Much more serious than the fact that prices may not correspond to marginal cost is the fact that, with intrenched monopoly, costs are likely to be much higher than is necessary." Friedrich A. Hayek, *Individualism and Economic Order* (1948), p. 105.

[261] Clare E. Griffin looks to competition as a means of producing a "socially useful profit pattern." This entails high profits for more efficient firms and no profits for the inefficient. "Economic Objections and Antitrust Policy," *Federal Antitrust Laws,* University of Michigan Law School (1953), p. 30.

[262] Machlup, *op. cit.,* p. 490.

[263] See Joe S. Bain, "Relation of Profit Rate to Industry Concentration: American Manufacturing, 1936-1940," *Quarterly Journal of Economics,* Vol. 65 (1951), p. 293. Bain found low correlation between profit rates and degree of concentration. See also David Schwartzman, "The Effects of Monopoly on Prices," *Journal of Political Economy,* Vol. 67 (1959), p. 352. Both writers feel that there may be differences in profit rates of highly concentrated and relatively unconcentrated industries, but that there is no continuous relationship between the two. In his *Barriers to New Competition* (1956), Bain found a positive correlation between higher barriers to entry and high profits. However, no such correlation existed in his examination of industries with "substantial" or with "moderate to low" entry barriers. Again, the marked differences in profit rates were found at the extremes.

[264] Machlup, *op. cit.,* pp. 493-96.

[265] Divisional profits were used by the government in *U.S.* v. *E. I. du Pont de Nemours & Co.,* 351 U.S. 377 (1956). The court was not impressed with using profits as an indicator. See also *Times-Picayune Publishing Co.* v. *U.S.,* 345 U.S. 594 (1953).

[266] *Contra,* Carl Kaysen and Donald Turner. "In most industrial multiproduct

firms . . . price-cost margins for the separate products can be defined." *Antitrust Policy, An Economic and Legal Analysis* (1959), p. 64.

[267] Judge Hand felt that "it is no excuse for 'monopolizing' a market that the monopoly has not been used to extract from the consumer more than a 'fair' profit." *U.S.* v. *Aluminum Co. of America,* 148 F. 2d 416, 427 (C.C.A.-2nd 1945).

[268] Clair Wilcox, *Public Policies Toward Business* (1955), p. 869; Edward S. Mason, *Economic Concentration and the Monopoly Problem* (1957).

[269] Also called "responsiveness of prices to changes in costs." Edward F. Howrey, "Coalescence of Legal and Economic Concepts of Competition," Address delivered before the Section on Antitrust Law, New York State Bar Association, Jan. 26, 1955 (mimeo.), p. 6.

[270] Joseph W. Garbarino, "A Theory of Interindustry Wage Variation," *Quarterly Journal of Economics* Vol. 64 (1950), p. 285.

[271] Carl Kaysen suggests this criterion and points out the difficulty of judging it. *United States* v. *United Shoe Machinery Corporation, An Economic Analysis of an Anti-Trust Case* (1956), p. 18.

[272] The court felt that good performance in research should not be attacked in antitrust on the ground that it is a legitimate competitive activity. *U.S.* v. *E. I. du Pont de Nemours & Co.,* 351 U.S. 377 (1956). See also Mason, *op. cit.,* p. 367; Jesse W. Markham, *Competition in the Rayon Industry* (1952).

[273] Joseph A. Schumpeter, *Capitalism, Socialism, and Democracy* (1947), p. 106.

[274] C. F. Carter and B. R. Williams, *Industry and Technical Progress* (1957), p. 169.

[275] Schumpeter, *op. cit.,* pp. 84, 85.

[276] Clare E. Griffin feels that "it is more feasible to judge the progressiveness of an industry than it is to evaluate its absolute level of efficiency." *An Economic Approach to Antitrust Problems* (1951), p. 73.

[277] *Report of the Attorney General's National Committee to Study the Antitrust Laws* (1955), pp. 328, 329. The committee felt that rate of growth is not a "direct economic indicator of the state of competition"; however, it may be important in evaluating other factors.

[278] *U.S.* v. *Aluminum Co. of America,* 148 F. 2d 416 (1945).

[279] Wilcox, *op. cit.,* p. 869; Mason, *op. cit.,* p. 368.

[280] See *Report of the Attorney General's National Committee to Study the Antitrust Laws* (1955), pp. 332, 333.

[281] Wilcox, *op. cit.,* p. 870.

[282] Stephen H. Sosnick regards this as a "specious test" since he feels that competition "is just the process of providing options or alternatives." "A Critique of Concepts of Workable Competition," *Quarterly Journal of Economics,* Vol. 72 (August 1958), p. 380. He does not explain why such a test could not be developed into a final evaluation if his definition of competition were correct.

[283] Edward F. Howrey refers to "effective" consumer choice. "Coalescence of Legal and Economic Concepts of Competition," Address delivered before Section on Antitrust Law, New York State Bar Association, Jan. 26, 1955 (mimeo.); see Notes, "Definition of the Market in Tying Arrangements: Another Aspect of Times-Picayune," *Yale Law Journal,* Vol. 63 (1954), pp. 389, 396.

[284] Corwin D. Edwards, "Preserving Competition vs. Regulating Monopoly," *American Economic Review,* Supplement, Pt. 2, Vol. 30 (1940), pp. 164, 170; Melvin G. de Chazeau and Alfred E. Kahn, *Integration and Competition in the Petroleum Industry* (1959), p. 384; M. A. Adelman, "Business Size and Public Policy," *Journal of Business,* Vol. 24 (1951), p. 272.

[285] Corwin D. Edwards, *Maintaining Competition* (1949), p. 9.

[286] Clair Wilcox, *Public Policies Toward Business* (1955), p. 869; Edward S. Mason, *Economic Concentration and the Monopoly Problem* (1957), p. 354.

[287] For an interesting discussion of distribution costs and their relationship to oligopoly and countervailing power, see Richard B. Heflebower, "Mass Distribution: A Phase of Bilateral Oligopoly or of Competition?", *American Economic Review,* Supplement, Vol. 47 (1957), p. 274.

[288] Morris A. Adelman reviews some difficulties in distinguishing between selling and production costs in his paper, "The 'Product' and 'Price' in Distribution," *American Economic Review,* Supplement, Vol. 47 (1957), p. 266. He states, "It would be difficult to consider the annual model change in automobiles as a production cost, for example." (p. 271.)

[289] Wilcox, *op. cit.,* p. 870; Howrey, *op. cit.,* p. 6; Blackwell Smith, "Effective Competition: Hypothesis for Modernizing the Antitrust Laws," *New York University Law Review,* Vol. 26 (July 1951), pp. 405, 441.

[290] Eugene Kozik, "Oligopoly and the Concept of Workable or Effective Competition: An Economic Analysis of Recent Antitrust Cases," *University of Pittsburgh Law Review,* Vol. 21 (June 1960), p. 621. This goal was an element in Judge Hand's opinion in *U.S.* v. *Aluminum Co. of America,* 148 F. 2d 416 (C.C.A.-2d 1945). See also C. E. Griffin, *Economic Approach to Antitrust Problems* (1951), pp. 82-85.

[291] Wilcox, *op. cit.,* p. 870.

[292] See Alfred R. Oxenfeldt, *Industrial Pricing and Market Practices* (1951); Stephen H. Sosnick, "A Critique of Concepts of Workable Competition," *Quarterly Journal of Economics,* Vol. 72 (August 1958), pp. 380, 417; Smith, *op. cit.,* p. 441.

[293] Joseph W. Garbarino, "A Theory of Interindustry Wage Variation," *Quarterly Journal of Economics,* Vol. 64 (1950), p. 285; J. K. Galbraith, *American Capitalism: The Concept of Countervailing Power* (1952); David Schwartzman, "Monopoly and Wages," *Canadian Journal of Economics and Political Science,* Vol. 26 (August 1960), p. 428. George J. Stigler, "The Statistics of Monopoly and Merger," *Journal of Political Economy* Vol. 64 (1956), pp. 33, 35.

[294] 15 U.S.C. 1-7.

[295] 15 U.S.C. 12 *et seq.*

[296] 15 U.S.C. 21(a).

[297] 15 U.S.C. 41 *et seq.*

[298] Ephraim Jacobs discusses the relationship between Secs. 3 and 7 in "Reasoning Behind and Explanation of the Factors Considered in Deciding the Legality of Mergers," *Mergers and Competition: Recent Developments,* Current Business Studies No. 21 (December 1954), pp. 11, 18-19.

[299] An interesting application of the section is reflected in *U.S.* v. *Jerrold Electronics Corp.,* 187 F. Supp. 545 (E. D. Pa. 1960), aff'd *per curiam* March 20, 1961.

[300] See Robert C. Brooks, Jr., "Injury to Competition under the Robinson-Patman Act," *University of Pennsylvania Law Review,* Vol. 109 (April 1961), p. 777; Note, "The Use of Tie-ins in New Industries," *Yale Law Journal,* Vol. 70 (1961), p. 804, discusses the problem of tie-in sales for new products and the problems of applying a *per se* rule.

[301] *International Salt Co.* v. U.S., 332 U.S. 392 (1947).

[302] *U.S.* v. *Standard Oil of California,* 337 U.S. 293 (1949).

[303] *Tampa Electric Co.* v. *Nashville Coal Co.,* 276 F. 2d 766 (C.C.A.-6th 1960), reversed 81 S. Ct. 623 (1961).

[304] *U.S.* v. *Bethlehem Steel,* 168 F. Supp. 576 (1958).

[305] *In the Matter of Crown Zellerbach Corp.*, Docket 6180 (Decided Dec. 26, 1957).

[306] *In the Matter of Pillsbury Mills, Inc.*, Docket 6000, 50 F.T.C. 555 (1953).

[307] Irston R. Barnes, "Markets, Competition, and Monopolistic Tendencies in Merger Cases," *Marquette Law Review*, Vol. 40 (1956), p. 141.

[308] *U.S.* v. *Sugar Institute*, 15 F. Supp. 817 (S.D.N.Y. 1934).

[309] *U.S.* v. *Aluminum Co. of America*, 148 F. 2nd 416 (C.C.A.-2d 1945).

[310] *U.S.* v. *E. I. du Pont de Nemours & Co.*, 351 U.S. 377 (1956).

[311] *U.S.* v. *General Electric*, 82 F. Supp. 753 (D.C.N.J. 1949).

[312] *Banana Distributors, Inc.* v. *United Fruit Co.* (D.C.S.D.N.Y. 1958), *CCH Trade Cases*, Par. 69,057.

[313] *U.S.* v. *Socony-Vacuum Oil Co., Inc. et al.*, 310 U.S. 150, 60 S. Ct. 811 (1940).

[314] *U.S.* v. *Sugar Institute*, *loc. cit.*

[315] *Hartford-Empire Co. et al.* v. *U.S.*, 323 U.S. 386 (1945); 324 U.S. 570 (1945).

[316] *Klor's, Inc.* v. *Broadway-Hale Stores, Inc. et al.*, 359 U.S. 207 (1959). See James A. Rahl, "Per Se Rules and Boycotts Under the Sherman Act," *Virginia Law Review* (November 1959), p. 1173.

[317] *U.S.* v. *U.S. Steel Corp.*, 223 Fed. 55 (1915).

[318] *American Tobacco Co. et al.* v. *U.S.* 328 U.S. 781 (1946).

[319] *U.S.* v. *E. I. du Pont de Nemours & Co.*, *loc. cit.*

[320] *U.S.* v. *Aluminum Co. of America*, 148 F. 2d 416 (C.C.A.-2d 1945).

[321] *U.S.* v. *United Shoe Machinery Corp.*, 110 F. Supp. 295 (D.C. Mass. 1953), aff'd *per curiam* 347 U.S. 521 (1954).

[322] *U.S.* v. *General Motors*, 121 F. 2d 276 (C.C.A.-7th 1941), cert. denied 314 U.S. 618 (1941).

[323] *Lorain Journal* v. *U.S.*, 343 U.S. 143 (1951).

[324] *In the Matter of Food Fair Stores, Inc.*, Docket 6458.

[325] *National Silver Co.* v. *F.T.C.*, 88 F. 2d 425 (C.C.A.-2d 1937).

[326] *F.T.C.* v. *Cement Institute*, 333 U.S. 683 (1948).

[327] *Fashion Originators' Guild of America, Inc. et al.* v. *F.T.C.*, 312 U.S. 457 (1941).

[328] *Standard Oil Co. (Indiana)* v. *U.S.*, 340 U.S. 231 (1951).

[329] *In the Matter of Hansen Inoculator Co., Inc.*, Docket 3264. Order to cease and desist, Jan. 12, 1938.

[330] *Anheuser-Busch* v. *F.T.C.*, 265 F. 2d 677 (C.C.A.-7th 1959), reversed and remanded 363 U.S. 536 (1960).

[331] *U.S.* v. *Standard Oil of California*, 337 U.S. 293 (1949).

[332] *International Salt Co.* v. *U.S.*, 332 U.S. 392 (1947).

[333] *In the Matter of The Maico Co., Inc.*, F.T.C. Docket 5822 (Dec. 15, 1953), *CCH Trade Regulations*, Par. 11,577.

[334] *In the Matter of Mytinger and Casselberry Inc.*, Docket 6962. Opinion of the Commission, Sept. 28, 1960 (mimeo.), p. 3.

[335] *Tampa Electric Co.* v. *Nashville Coal Co.*, 365 U.S. 320 (1961).

[336] See discussion in Milton Handler, "Recent Antitrust Developments," *Yale Law Journal*, Vol. 71 (November 1961), pp. 75, 81-88.

[337] *U.S.* v. *Bethlehem Steel*, 168 F. Supp. 576 (1958).

[338] *In the Matter of Brillo Manufacturing Co., Inc.*, F.T.C. Docket 6557 (Nov. 26, 1958).

[339] *American Crystal Sugar Co.* v. *The Cuban American Sugar Co.*, 259 F. 2d 524 (1958).

[340] *In the Matter of A. G. Spalding & Bros., Inc.*, Docket 6478. Order to cease and desist, March 30, 1960.

[341] *U.S. v. Bethlehem Steel, loc. cit.*

[342] *In the Matter of A. G. Spalding & Bros., Inc., loc. cit.*

[343] *U.S. v. Brown Shoe Co., Inc., CCH Trade Cases* (1956), Par. 68,244.

[344] *In the Matter of Erie Sand and Gravel Co.,* F.T.C. Docket 6670 (Oct. 26, 1959).

[345] *U.S. v. Bethlehem Steel, loc. cit.*

[346] *Hamilton Watch Co. v. Benrus Watch Co.,* 114 F. Supp. 307 (D.C. Conn. 1953), aff'd 206 F. 2d 738 (C.C.A.-2d 1953).

[347] *American Crystal Sugar Co. v. The Cuban American Sugar Co., loc. cit.*

[348] See Richard B. Heflebower, "Recent American Anti-trust Experience," *Three Banks Review,* Vol. 46 (1960), pp. 3, 6, 9.

[349] " 'Workable' or 'effective' competition supplies no formula which can substitute for judgment. It suggests leads to data of significance, and a means of organizing the data bearing on the question whether a given market of itself is sufficiently competitive in its structure and behavior to be classified as workably competitive. And it provides some bench-marks or criteria, representing somewhat different points of vantage, for the process of making that judgment." *Report of the Attorney General's National Committee to Study the Antitrust Laws* (1955), p. 337.

[350] Thorstein Veblen, *The Place of Science in Modern Civilization* (1919). "Science creates nothing but theories." (P. 19.)

[351] For example, Carl Kaysen argues that ideally indicators of structure would be used. *United States v. United Shoe Machinery Corporation, An Economic Analysis of an Anti-Trust Case* (1956), p. 17. Blackwell Smith argues for performance. "Effective Competition: Hypothesis for Modernizing the Antitrust Laws," *New York University Law Review,* Vol. 26 (July 1951), pp. 405, 412. Alfred E. Kahn favors the use of indicators of conduct, particularly collusion, unfairness, coercion, predatory practices, and exclusion, on grounds of practicability. "Standards for Antitrust Policy," *Harvard Law Review,* Vol. 67 (1953), p. 39.

[352] See Edward S. Mason, *Economic Concentration and the Monopoly Problem* (1957), p. 366.

[353] See Jesse Markham, "The Per Se Doctrine and the New Rule of Reason," *Southern Economic Journal,* Vol. 22 (1955), p. 22.

[354] Yet, "small firms will be better able to pursue a flexible pricing policy." B. Fog, *Industrial Pricing Policies* (1960), p. 143.

[355] Edward F. Howrey, then chairman of the Federal Trade Commission, was not concerned about the number of indicators. He cited sixteen. "Economic Evidence in Antitrust Cases," *Journal of Marketing,* Vol. 19 (1954). Reprinted in *The Role of Sampling Data as Evidence in Judicial and Administrative Proceedings,* Current Business Studies No. 19 (October 1954), pp. 69, 74.

[356] See Irston R. Barnes, "Quantitative Data and Sample Surveys as Evidence in Judicial and Administrative Procedures," in *ibid.,* pp. 33, 37.

[357] E. T. Grether points out the need for deciding "whether action can be successful if directed only at business conduct, or whether structural adjustments are necessary in order to enhance the effectiveness of competition." Testimony in *Employment, Growth, and Price Levels,* Hearing before the Joint Economic Committee, 86 Cong. 1 sess. (1959), Pt. 7, pp. 2115, 2117. Joe S. Bain, does not have much confidence in conduct remedies in Sherman Act cases. *Industrial Organization* (1959), p. 520.

## *Chapter 8*

[1] As Professor Clark states it, "The point is that competition is a two-sided activity . . ." J. M. Clark, *Competition as a Dynamic Process* (1961), p. 394.

[2] Joe S. Bain, *Industrial Organization* (1959), p. 7.

[3] See Corwin D. Edwards, "Conglomerate Bigness as a Source of Power," *Business Concentration and Price Policy* (1955), p. 331, and "Issues in the Monopoly Problem," in Edward D. Chamberlin, ed., *Monopoly and Competition and Their Regulation* (1954), p. 188. See also Robert C. Brooks, Jr., "Injury to Competition Under the Robinson-Patman Act," *University of Pennsylvania Law Review,* Vol. 109 (April 1961), pp. 777, 785, 790.

[4] See Robert F. Lanzillotti, *The Hard-Surface Floor-Covering Industry* (1955), Chap. 6. For a contrary view see M. A. Adelman, "The Antimerger Act, 1950-1960," *American Economic Review,* Vol. 51 (May 1961), pp. 236, 242-43.

[5] The problem is discussed in Philip Marcus, "Monopoly Profits, Economic Impossibility, and Unfairness as Anti-Trust Tests," *Vanderbilt Law Review,* Vol. 14 (March 1961), p. 581.

[6] Robert C. Brooks, Jr. develops this point in a discussion of predatory price cutting in his article on "Price Cutting and Monopoly Power," *Journal of Marketing,* Vol. 25 (1961), p. 44. (See esp. p. 47.) See also John S. McGee, "Predatory Price Cutting: The Standard Oil (N.J.) Case," *Journal of Law and Economics,* Vol. I (1958), p. 137.

[7] See Federal Trade Commission, *Report on Corporate Mergers and Acquisitions,* (May 1955), p. 148.

[8] See Bain, *Industrial Organization,* p. 7; Carl Kaysen, "Market Definition in Anti-Trust Law Proceedings," *The Growing Role of Economic Data in Judicial and Administrative Proceedings,* Current Business Studies No. 18 (March 1954), p. 18. Kaysen feels that "in practice, the economist's definition and the businessman's definition boil down to the same thing . . . when an economist defines a market area, he uses those facts and that kind of information which a businessman in the course of business uses to do business. . . ." (Pp. 18-19.) On the other hand, N. Kaldor seems to feel that the industry "group" can be defined only from the point of view of the individual seller. Hence, there would be a specific group for each seller, composed of himself and the firms which compete with him. "Mrs. Robinson's 'Economics of Imperfect Competition,' " *Economics,* Vol. 1 of new series (1934), p. 335.

[9] "The boundaries of an 'industry' or 'market' will often be uncertain and controversial, and a definition appropriate in one case may be inappropriate in another." *Report of the Attorney General's National Committee to Study the Antitrust Laws* (1955), p. 322.

[10] For a discussion of the competition between aluminum and other metals see Ross M. Robertson, "On the Changing Apparatus of Competition," *American Economic Review,* Supplement, Vol. 44 (May 1954), pp. 41, 54-55.

[11] Philip Marcus presents a strong attack on the use of the concept in his article, "Antitrust Bugbears: Substitute Products—Oligopoly," *University of Pennsylvania Law Review,* Vol. 105 (December 1956), p. 185.

[12] *U.S.* v. *Aluminum Co. of America,* 44 F. Supp. 97 (S.D. N.Y. 1941); 148 F. 2d 416 (C.C.A.—2d 1945); 91 F. Supp 333 (S.D. N.Y. 1950).

[13] Professor Donald F. Turner points out the shortcomings of the use of percentage of a market as an indicator. "Antitrust Policy and the Cellophane Case," *Harvard Law Review,* Vol. 70 (December 1956), pp. 281, 309. See also Carl

Kaysen, "Market Definition in Anti-Trust Law Proceedings," *op. cit.*, pp. 18, 21-22.

[14] 148 F. 2d 416 (C.C.A.-2d 1945).

[15] 148 F. 2d 416, 424-25. See Edward S. Mason, *Economic Concentration and the Monopoly Problem* (1957), p. 360, for a criticism of Judge Hand's inference of degree of market control directly from the 90 per cent figure; and Clair Wilcox, *Public Policies Toward Business* (1955). Alfred E. Kahn disagrees with Mason. He feels that "no better economic measure . . . is available." "A Legal and Economic Appraisal of the 'New' Sherman and Clayton Acts," *Yale Law Journal*, Vol. 63 (January 1954), pp. 293, 298.

[16] "The relative effect of percentage command of a market varies with the setting in which that factor is placed." *U.S.* v. *Columbia Steel*, 334 U.S. 495, 528 (1948).

[17] See discussion of "How Much Market Power is Needed to Constitute Monopoly?", in *Report of the Attorney General's National Committee to Study the Antitrust Laws* (1955), pp. 48-55.

[18] M. A. Adelman, "Economic and Legal Concepts of Competition," *Journal of Farm Economics*, Vol. 41 (December 1959), pp. 1197, 1198-99.

[19] Baddia J. Rashid points to changes in the interpretation of markets, under Sec. 2, over a period of time due to technological changes in products, processes, and competition. "What is Right with Antitrust?", *Antitrust Bulletin* Vol. 5 (January-February 1960), pp. 5, 10.

[20] *Times-Picayune Publishing Co.* v. *U.S.*, 345 U.S. 594 (1953).

[21] For example, Professor Heinrich Kronstein reports, "Now we find the American coal corporations attempting to persuade Europe to keep out Venezuelan oil by fixing import quotas." *Government and Business in International Trade* (1961). Similarly, during a coal crises in Europe, the German authorities approved "a cartel agreement between coal and oil producers which restricted competition from oil." "The High Authority," *Cartel*, Vol. 9 (1959), p. 106.

[22] When the coal-hauling railroads filed lower rates on coal transported from the Appalachian fields to the East Coast, the Empire State Petroleum Association, representing 275 marketers of oil, protested before the Interstate Commerce Commission. *Business Week*, Oct. 31, 1959, p. 82.

[23] See *U.S.* v. *Columbia Steel Co.*, 334 U.S. 495, 528 (1948).

[24] *U.S.* v. *Aluminum Co. of America*, 148 F. 2d 416, 424-25 (C.C.A.-2d 1945).

[25] *U.S.* v. *Aluminum Co. of America*, 91 F. Supp. 333, 355-59 (S.D. N.Y. 1950).

[26] Competing materials were not considered in defining the market. Yet, A. D. H. Kaplan cites a long list of materials which compete with aluminum. *Big Enterprise in a Competitive System* (1954), pp. 97-99.

[27] *U.S.* v. *E. I. du Pont de Nemours & Co.*, 351 U.S. 377 (1956).

[28] *U.S.* v. *E. I. du Pont de Nemours & Co.*, 353 U.S. 586 (1957).

[29] Alfred Nicols, "Economic Issues in the du Pont-General Motors Case," *Journal of Business*, Vol. 33 (July 1960), pp. 227, 235.

[30] *Hamilton Watch Co.* v. *Benrus*, 114 F. Supp. 307, 315 (D.C. Conn. 1953), aff'd 206 F. 2d 738 (C.C.A-2d 1953).

[31] *U.S.* v. *Klearflax Linen Looms, Inc.*, 63 F. Supp. 92 (D.C. Minn. 1945).

[32] Saul Nelson and Walter Keim, *Price Behavior and Business Policy*, Temporary National Economic Committee Monograph No. 1 (1940), p. 81.

[33] *Times-Picayune Publishing Co.* v. *U.S.*, 345 U.S. 594 (1953).

[34] *Indiana Farmer's Guide Publishing Co.* v. *Prairie Farmer Publishing Co.*, 293 U.S. 268 (1934); and *In the Matter of Farm Journal, Inc.*, Docket 6388, Initial Decision June 6, 1956, Order July 17, 1956.

[35] *U.S.* v. *Yellow Cab Co.*, 80 F. Supp. 936 (D.C. N.D. Ill. 1948), aff'd 338 U.S. 338 (1949).

[36] *In the Matter of Brillo Manufacturing Co., Inc.*, Docket 6557 (Nov. 26, 1958).

[37] *U.S.* v. *Reading Co.*, 253 U.S. 26 (1920).

[38] *Kobé, Inc.* v. *Dempsey Pump Co.*, 198 F. 2d 416 (C.C.A.-10th 1952), cert. denied 344 U.S. 837 (1952).

[39] *Hughes Tool Co.* v. *Ford*, 114 F. Supp. 525 (E.D. Okla. 1953), rev'd 215 F. 2d 924 (C.C.A.-10th 1954), cert. denied 348 U.S. 927 (1955).

[40] A. D. H. Kaplan, *Big Enterprise in a Competitive System* (1954), p. 105. See also Robert F. Lanzillotti, *The Hard-Surface Floor-Covering Industry* (1955), pp. 4-8.

[41] Kaplan, *op. cit.*, p. 105.

[42] Nelson and Keim, *op. cit.*, p. 81.

[43] *American Crystal Sugar Co.* v. *The Cuban American Sugar Co.*, 259 F. 2d 524 (1958).

[44] *Fashion Originators' Guild, Inc.* v. *F.T.C.*, 114 F. 2d 80 (C.C.A.-2d 1940), aff'd 312 U.S. 457 (1941).

[45] See R. L. Bishop, "Elasticities, Cross-Elasticities, and Market Relationships," *American Economic Review*, Vol. 42 (December 1952), p. 779.

[46] Carl Kaysen refers to "near substitutes." *United States v. United Shoe Machinery Corporation, An Economic Analysis of an Anti-Trust Case* (1956), p. 17. For discussions of the concept of cross-elasticity in economic theory and its relationship to monopoly see Joe S. Bain, *Price Theory* (1952), esp. p. 52; and George J. Stigler, *The Theory of Price* (1952). For an attack on the use of the concept in antitrust see Philip Marcus, "Antitrust Bugbears: Substitute Products—Oligopoly," *University of Pennsylvania Law Review*, Vol. 105 (December 1956), p. 185.

[47] Robert Triffin suggests that cross-elasticity of demand is zero for a pure monopolist and infinite for a pure competitor. *Monopolistic Competition and General Equilibrium Theory* (1940).

[48] "It must be admitted, however, that the concept of cross-elasticity is not crystal clear and that disputes exist among economists as to how it should be formulated." G. E. Hale and Rosemary D. Hale, *Market Power: Size and Shape Under the Sherman Act* (1958), footnote, p. 109, which contains a number of references.

[49] See Triffin, *op. cit.*, pp. 88-89.

[50] *Times-Picayune Publishing Co.* v. *U.S.*, 345 U.S. 594 (1953).

[51] George W. Stocking has said, "In the hands of judges in antitrust the concept [of cross-elasticity] is probably not of much use." "Economic Change and the Sherman Act: Some Reflections on 'Workable Competition,'" *Virginia Law Review*, Vol. 44 (May 1958), pp. 537, 570.

[52] See "Report of Sherman Act Subcommittee on Cost Data Problems in Sherman Act Cases," *Proceedings*, Section of Antitrust Law, American Bar Association (August 1960), esp. pp. 532-33, for a discussion of the uses of cost data.

[53] Stocking, *op. cit.*, p. 571.

[54] *U.S.* v. *Corn Products Refining Co.*, 234 F. 964, 975-76 (S.D. N.Y. 1916).

[55] "The monopolists of a product with some near substitutes at prices considerably higher than his production costs has a choice of having a high-price cost margin and a low "market share" in the combined market, defined by his outputs and that of the substitutes at the high price, or a much higher market share and a low-price cost margin, since at the lower price, many of the higher price products would cease to be substitutes. Failure to deal with this point was the major error in the reasoning of Judge Leahy in the Du Pont case (Cellophane)." Carl Kaysen and Donald Turner, *Antitrust Policy, An Economic and Legal Analysis* (1959), footnote 2, p. 102.

[56] *American Tobacco Co. et al.* v. *U.S.*, 328 U.S. 781 (1946).

[57] *Ibid.*, p. 803.

[58] *U.S.* v. *E. I. du Pont de Nemours & Co.*, 351 U.S. 377 (1956).

[59] A tabulation of comparative prices in 1949 for cellophane and other flexible wrapping materials shows a substantial range in the prices. The price per square inch of saran was 265 per cent of that of moistureproof cellophane, while plain waxed sulphite 25# coated opaque paper was priced at 30.4 per cent of the cellophane product. George W. Stocking and Willard F. Mueller, "The Cellophane Case and the New Competition," *American Economic Review*, Vol. 45 (March 1955), pp. 29, 50.

[60] *U.S.* v. *E. I. du Pont de Nemours & Co.*, 351 U.S. 377 (1956).

[61] Stocking and Mueller, *op. cit.*, p. 29.

[62] John M. Lishan, "The Cellophane Case and Cross-Elasticity of Demand," *Antitrust Bulletin*, Vol. 4 (1959), pp. 593, 594.

[63] The clearest discussion of this feature may be found in Corwin D. Edwards, *The Price Discrimination Law* (1959), Chap. 10.

[64] *Ruberoid Co.* v. *F.T.C.*, 70 S.CT. 800 (1952).

[65] For example, *In the Matter of Champion Spark Plug Co.*, Docket 3977. See discussion in Edwards, *op. cit.*, pp. 294-99.

[66] *U.S.* v. *Aluminum Co. of America*, 148 F. 2d 416 (C.C.A.-2d 1945).

[67] *U.S.* v. *American Can Co.*, 234 F. 1019 (1916).

[68] *U.S.* v. *Columbia Steel Co. et al.*, 334 U.S. 495 (1948).

[69] *U.S.* v. *Aluminum Co. of America, loc. cit.*

[70] *U.S.* v. *Bethlehem Steel Corp.*, 168 F. Supp. 576 (1958).

[71] *U.S.* v. *Corn Products Refining Co.*, 234 F. 964 (D.C.S.D.N.Y. 1916), 249 U.S. 621 (1919).

[72] *Story Parchment Co.* v. *Paterson Parchment Paper Co.*, 228 U.S. 555 (1931).

[73] *Standard Oil of Indiana* v. *U.S.*, 283 U.S. 163 (1931).

[74] *American Crystal Sugar Co.* v. *The Cuban American Sugar Co.*, 259 F. 2d 524 (1958).

[75] *U.S.* v. *Columbia Steel Co.*, 334 U.S. 495 (1948).

[76] *Ibid.*, p. 528.

[77] *U.S.* v. *Bethlehem Steel Corp.*, 168 F. Supp. 576 (1958).

[78] *In the Matter of Crown Zellerbach Corp.*, Docket 6180. Final Decision Dec. 26, 1957.

[79] See, for example, Initial Decision, *In the Matter of Crown Zellerbach Corp.*, Docket 6180 (Feb. 25, 1957), p. 24.

[80] *Indiana Farmers' Guide* v. *Prairie Farmer*, 293 U.S. 268 (1934); 299 U.S. 156 (1936).

[81] *U.S.* v. *Aluminum Co. of America*, 148 F. 2d 416 (C.C.A.-2d 1945).

[82] *U.S.* v. *Columbia Steel Co. et al.*, 334 U.S. 495; *CCH Trade Cases* (1948), Pars. 62,260, 62,560.

[83] *U.S.* v. *Bethlehem Steel Corp.*, 168 F. Supp. 576 (1958).

[84] This position is attacked bitterly in M. A. Adelman, "The Antimerger Act, 1950-1960," *American Economic Review*, Vol. 51 (May 1961), pp. 236, 237.

[85] *U.S.* v. *Standard Oil of California*, 337 U.S. 293 (1949).

[86] *In the Matter of Pillsbury Mills, Inc.*, Docket 6000, 50 F.T.C. 555 (1953).

[87] *In the Matter of Crown Zellerbach Corp.*, Docket 6180 (Decided Dec. 26, 1957).

[88] D.C. Minn. April 20, 1960, *CCH Trade Cases*, Par. 69,689.

[89] In *U.S.* v. *Brown Shoe Co.*, 179 F. Supp. 721 (E. D. Mo. 1959), each of a number of cities with a population of 10,000 or more with the surrounding area was treated as a market. Probable jurisdiction to consider an appeal was noted by the Supreme Court. 363 U.S. 825.

[90] *U.S.* v. *Paramount Pictures, Inc.*, 334 U.S. 131 (1948).

[91] *U.S.* v. *Yellow Cab*, 80 F. Supp. 936 (N.D. Ill. 1948), aff'd 338 U.S. 338 (1949).

[92] *U.S.* v. *Besser Manufacturing Co.*, 96 F. Supp. 304 (D.C.E.D. Mich. 1951), aff'd 343 U.S. 444 (1952).

[93] Betty Bock, "Mergers and Market Size–2. Geographic Dimensions," *The Conference Board Business Record*, Vol. 16, No. 6 (June 1959), p. 285.

[94] Jesse W. Markham, *Competition in the Rayon Industry* (1952), p. 2.

[95] J. W. McKie, "The Decline of Monopoly in the Metal Container Industry," *American Economic Review*, Vol. 45 (1955), pp. 499, 500.

[96] For a summary review of the analysis of concentration see Jesse W. Markham, "Trends in the Relative Importance of Small Business," *Financing Small Business*, Report to the Committees on Banking and Currency and the Select Committees on Small Business by the Federal Reserve System, 85 Cong. 2 sess. (1958), p. 197.

[97] "The most serious defect of a concentration index as an index of degree of monopoly is its failure to reflect competition from 'other industries.'" Fritz Machlup, *The Political Economy of Monopoly* (1952), p. 486. See also Jesse J. Friedman, "The Senate Antitrust Subcommittee Report on Concentration–What It Is and What It Is Not," in *Economic Concentration Measures: Uses and Abuses*, 41st Annual Meeting of the National Industrial Conference Board, May 17, 1957, pp. 6, 12-13.

[98] "It is often assumed that universe data for market and industry studies are available in census reports. However, census information on a product basis is available only for a limited number of relatively broad product classes and only for selected years. Also, figures . . . may include only those corporations which are primarily engaged in that line of manufacture . . . and may exclude other important producers whose primary activity classifies them elsewhere. Moreover, it may include all of the products or shipments of companies a substantial part of whose activity may relate to products or markets which are not in issue.

". . . attorneys and economists rarely find census categories which satisfactorily fit the markets under consideration." Irston R. Barnes, "Quantitative Data and Sample Surveys as Evidence in Judicial and Administrative Procedures," *The Role of Sampling Data as Evidence in Judicial and Administrative Proceedings*, Current Business Studies No. 19 (October 1954), pp. 33, 39.

[99] Maxwell R. Conklin and Harold T. Goldstein, "Census Principles of Industry and Product Classification, Manufacturing Industries," in National Bureau of Economic Research, *Business Concentration and Price Policy* (1955), p. 15.

[100] Willard L. Thorp and Walter F. Crowder, *The Structure of Industry*, T.N.E.C. Monograph No. 27 (1941).

[101] Clair Wilcox, "On the Alleged Ubiquity of Monopoly," *American Economic Review*, Vol. 40 (May 1950), pp. 67, 69.

[102] *Ibid.*

[103] H. Levinson, "The Minimum Product Standard," *Problems in Price Control: Pricing Standards* (1947). Cited in *OPA Manual*, Vol. 5, Sec. 5-5303-02.

[104] 19 U.S.C. 1364.

[105] U.S. Tariff Commission, *Lamb, Mutton, Sheep and Lambs, Report on Escape-Clause Investigation No. 7-83* (1960), p. 77.

[106] *Ibid.*

[107] U.S. Tariff Commission, *Zinc Sheet, Report on Escape-Clause Investigation No. 81* (1960), p. 54.

[108] U.S. Tariff Commission, Press Release of Nov. 3, 1958.

[109] U.S. Tariff Commission, *Zinc Sheet, Report on Escape-Clause Investigation No. 81* (1960), p. 58.

[110] U.S. Tariff Commission, *Lamb, Mutton, Sheep and Lambs, Report on Escape-Clause Investigation No. 7-83* (1960).

[111] *Ibid.*, pp. 60, 61.

[112] *Ibid.*, p. 85.

[113] *Business Week*, Oct. 31, 1959, p. 82. In another proceeding, barge operators challenged rate cuts by the railroads, *Business Week*, July 23, 1960, p. 40. Commenting on the 1959 coal crisis in Europe, *Cartel* reported that a cartel agreement was approved between coal and oil producers which restricted competition from oil. "The High Authority," *Cartel*, Vol. 9 (July 1959), p. 106.

[114] 40 U.S.C. 314.

[115] Irston R. Barnes, "Competitive Mores and Legal Tests in Merger Cases: The du Pont-General Motors Decision," *Georgetown Law Journal*, Vol. 46 (1958), footnote 119, p. 603.

[116] 15 U.S.C. 1.

[117] Public Law 75-314 (1937).

[118] Public Law 85-909, Sept. 2, 1958.

[119] 15 U.S.C. 41 *et seq.*

[120] 15 U.S.C. 13.

[121] 15 U.S.C. 13, 21a.

[122] Professor Donald F. Turner suggests a possible classification which, he points out, may be oversimplified.

(1) *Attempts and Conspiracies*—Monopoly is control over *any appreciable amount of commerce,* even though that amount is not a market in any meaningful economic sense.

(2) *Combinations*—Monopoly is control over a *market from which qualitatively distinct substitutes are prima facie (and possibly conclusively) excluded.*

(3) *Individual Monopolizing*—Monopoly is control over a *market in which qualitatively distinct substitutes are included* (either prima facie or conclusively) *once it is shown that they are reasonably interchangeable.* "Antitrust Policy and the Cellophane Case," *Harvard Law Review*, Vol. 70 (December 1959), pp. 281, 304.

[123] Notes, "Definition of the Market in Tying Arrangements: Another Aspect of Times-Picayune," *Yale Law Journal*, Vol. 63 (January 1954), pp. 389, 396.

[124] *U.S.* v. *Addyston Pipe and Steel Co.*, 85 F. 271 (C.C.A.-6th 1898), aff'd 175, U.S. 211 (1899).

[125] *U.S.* v. *Socony-Vacuum Oil Co., Inc. et al.*, 310 U.S. 150 (1940).

[126] *U.S.* v. *General Dyestuff Corp.*, 57 F. Supp. 642 (S.D. N.Y. 1944).

[127] *U.S.* v. *Swift & Co.*, 286 U.S. 106, 116 (1932).

[128] *Klor's Inc.* v. *Broadway-Hale Stores, Inc. et al.*, 359 U.S. 207 (1959).

[129] Turner feels that, "It is reasonable to discard any refined concept of market in attempt and conspiracy cases because the conduct involved is so egregious that it may be appropriately condemned *per se.*" Turner, *loc. cit.*, p. 307. To the same effect see *U.S.* v. *Standard Oil of California*, 337 U.S. 293, 299 (1949). Judge Swan made a significant distinction between monopolization and conspiracy-to-monopolize tests of relevant markets in *U.S.* v. *Consolidated Laundries Corp. et al.* (C.C.A.-2d, May 1961), *CCH Trade Cases*, Par. 70,039. He held that the conspiracy case did not require a market definition.

[130] *Lorain Journal* v. *U.S.*, 342 U.S. 143 (1951).

[131] *Times-Picayune Publishing Co.* v. *U.S.*, 345 U.S. 594 (1953).

[132] *Associated Press* v. *U.S.*, 326 U.S. 17 (1946).

[133] *U.S.* v. *Paramount Pictures, Inc.*, 334 U.S. 121 (1948).

[134] *U.S.* v. *National City Lines, Inc.*, 186 F. 2d 562 (C.C.A.-7th 1951), cert. denied 341 U.S. 916 (1951).

[135] *Affiliated Music Enterprises, Inc.,* v. *Sesac, Inc.,* 268 F. 2d 13 (C.C.A.-2d 1959), cert. denied 361 U.S. 831.

[136] *Report of the Attorney General's National Committee to Study the Antitrust Laws* (1955), p. 44.

[137] *U.S.* v. *Aluminum Co. of America,* 148 F. 2d 416 (C.C.A.-2d 1945).

[138] *U.S.* v. *E. I. du Pont de Nemours & Co.,* 351 U.S. 377 (1956).

[139] *U.S.* v. *Aluminum Co. of America,* 148 F. 2d 416 (C.C.A.-2d 1945) and 91 F. Supp. 333 (S.D. N.Y. 1950)

[140] The Supreme Court felt that "in considering what is the relevant market . . . no more definite rule can be declared than that commodities reasonably interchangeable . . . make up that 'part of the trade or commerce,' monopolization of which may be illegal." (*U.S.* v. *E. I. du Pont de Nemours & Co., op. cit.,* p. 395.) Further, "An element for consideration as to cross-elasticity of demand between products is the responsiveness of the sales of one product to price changes of the other." (P. 400.) Finally, the Supreme Court accepted the lower court's findings that "sensitivity of customers in the flexible packaging markets to price or quality changes prevented du Pont from possessing monopoly control. . . ."

[141] George W. Stocking and Willard F. Mueller, "The Cellophane Case and the New Competition," *American Economic Review,* Vol. 45 (March 1955), pp. 29, 50.

[142] "Given aluminum and copper prices prevalent in the last few years," according to R. M. Robertson, "copper has almost entirely lost the high-voltage transmission line business and is rapidly losing in the so-called secondary distribution field." "On the Changing Apparatus of Competition," *American Economic Review,* Vol. 44 (May 1954), pp. 51, 54.

[143] *U.S.* v. *United Shoe Machinery Corp.,* 110 F. Supp. 295 (D.C. Mass. 1953), aff'd *per curiam,* 347 U.S. 521 (1954).

[144] See criticism of this feature in L. S. Keyes, "The Shoe Machinery Case and the Problem of the Good Trust," *Quarterly Journal of Economics,* Vol. 68 (1954), footnote p. 295. Carl Kaysen points out that the defense did not present "a positive definition of the market, but criticized the definition implied by the government." "Market Definition in Anti-Trust Law Proceedings," *The Growing Role of Economic Data in Judicial and Administrative Proceedings,* Current Business Studies No. 18 (March 1954), pp. 18, 20.

[145] Public Law 81-899, Dec. 29, 1950; 15 U.S.C. 18.

[146] *U.S.* v. *E. I. du Pont de Nemours & Co.,* 353 U.S. 586 (1957).

[147] *U.S.* v. *Bethlehem Steel,* 168 F. Supp. 576 (1958).

[148] *Ibid.*

[149] *U.S.* v. *Columbia Steel Co. et al.,* 334 U.S. 495 (1948).

[150] *U.S.* v. *Bethlehem Steel,* 168 F. Supp. 576 (1958), footnote 34.

[151] *U.S.* v. *E. I. du Pont de Nemours & Co.,* 351 U.S. 377 (1956).

[152] *U.S.* v. *Columbia Steel Co. et al.,* 335 U.S. 495 (1948).

[153] *In the Matter of Crown Zellerbach Corp.,* Docket 6180 (Decided Dec. 26, 1957).

[154] *Crown Zellerbach Corp.* v. *F.T.C.* (C.C.A.-9th 1961), *CCH Trade Cases,* Par. 70,038.

[155] *U.S.* v. *E. I. du Pont de Nemours & Co.,* 351 U.S. 377 (1956).

[156] *In the Matter of Brillo Manufacturing Co., Inc.,* Docket 6557. Order Granting in Part and Denying in Part Respondent's Motion to Discuss the Complaint (Oct. 15, 1957, mimeo.), p. 6.

[157] Order Remanding Case to Hearing Examiner (May 23, 1958), Opinion of the Commission, p. 2.

[158] *Ibid.,* pp. 2-3.

[159] *In the Matter of Reynolds Metals Co.*, Docket 7009, Order to Cease and Desist (Jan. 21, 1960).

[160] *In the Matter of Erie Sand and Gravel Co.*, Docket 6670, Opinion of the Commission (Oct. 26, 1959). On appeal, the case was remanded to the commission to reconsider the definition of the market, taking account only of geographic issues. The Circuit Court of Appeals held that the evidence showed no quality differences. *Erie Sand and Gravel Co.* v. *F.T.C.* (C.C.A.-3d May 29, 1961), *CCH Trade Cases,* Par. 70,028.

[161] *Ibid.* Opinion of the Commission (Oct. 26, 1959), p. 6. The Hearing Examiner had decided that lake sand "is generally of higher quality" than pit sand. Initial Decision (filed Dec. 2, 1958), p. 5.

[162] *Ibid.* Opinion of the Commission, pp. 5-6.

[163] *Erie Sand and Gravel Co.* v. *F.T.C.* (C.C.A.-3d 1961), *CCH Trade Cases,* Par. 70,028.

[164] 114 F. Supp. 307, 315 (D.C. Conn. 1953), aff'd 206 F. 2d 738 (C.C.A.-2d 1953).

[165] Competition between jeweled-lever and the cheaper pin-lever watches is growing in intensity. See "Watch Producers Battle for Markets," *Business Week,* Jan. 7, 1961, p. 82.

[166] *U.S.* v. *Maryland and Virginia Milk Producers Assn., Inc.*, 167 F. Supp. 799 (D.C. D.C. 1958); 362 U.S. 458 (1960).

[167] *American Crystal Sugar Co.* v. *The Cuban American Sugar Co.*, 259 F. 2d 524 (1958).

[168] *In the Matter of Eastman Kodak Co.*, Docket 4322.

[169] The court said that "the argument is that all photographic film, whether Kodachrome or black and white, is in the 'same general class' being film for taking pictures, and that color film is in free and open competition with black and white film because each competes for 'the consumer dollar' inasmuch as a person about to take a picture must choose between buying a color film or a black and white film. By analogous reasoning it may be argued that champagne and Poland Spring water are competing commodities of the same general class because both are beverages and a person desiring to quench his thirst must choose which to buy; or similarly, that the various types of fuel—coal, wood, oil, gas, etc.—are all competing commodities of the same general class." *Eastman Kodak Co.* v. *F.T.C.*, 158 F. 2d 592 (C.C.A.-2d 1946), cert. denied 330 U.S. 828 (1947).

[170] *U.S.* v. *The White Motor Co.* (D.C. N.D. Ohio, April 21, 1961), *CCH Trade Cases,* Par. 70,025. See also *U.S.* v. *Bausch & Lomb Optical Co. et al.*, 45 F. Supp. 387 (1942); *Dr. Miles Co.* v. *Parks,* 220 U.S. 373 (1911).

[171] *U.S.* v. *The White Motor Co., loc. cit.* See also *Ethyl Gasoline Corp.* v. *U.S.*, 309 U.S. 436 (1940), and *U.S.* v. *Parke, Davis & Co.*, 362 U.S. 29 (1960).

[172] Corwin D. Edwards, *The Price Discrimination Law* (1959).

[173] *Ibid.*, pp. 219-20.

[174] *F.T.C.* v. *Morton Salt Co.*, 334 U.S. 37 (1948).

[175] 15 U.S.C. 14.

[176] See Notes, "Definition of the Market in Tying Arrangments: Another Aspect of Times-Picayune," *Yale Law Journal,* Vol. 63 (January 1954), p. 389; and William B. Lockhart and Howard R. Sacks, "The Relevance of Economic Factors in Determining Whether Exclusive Arrangements Violate Section 3 of the Clayton Act," *Harvard Law Review,* Vol. 65 (April 1952), p. 919.

[177] *Tampa Electric Co.* v. *Nashville Coal Co.*, 276 F. 2d 766 (C.C.A.-6th 1960), reversed 81 S.Ct. 623 (1961).

[178] 332 U.S. 392 (1947).

[179] *U.S.* v. *Standard Oil of California,* 337 U.S. 293 (1949).

[180] *In the Matter of the Maico Co., Inc.,* Docket 5822. Initial Order to cease and desist, Nov. 25, 1952; Consent Order, June 3, 1955.

[181] *In the Matter of Mytinger & Casselberry,* Docket 6962, Order to cease and desist, Sept. 28, 1960.

[182] *Tampa Electric Co.* v. *Nashville Coal Co.,* 276 F. 2d 766 (C.C.A.-6th 1960), reversed 81 S.Ct. 623 (1961).

[183] *International Salt Co.* v. *U.S.,* 332 U.S. 392 (1947).

[184] A similar suggestion is made regarding the geographical dimensions of the market in Notes and Comments, " 'Substantially to Lessen Competition . . .': Current Problems of Horizontal Mergers," *Yale Law Journal,* Vol. 68 (July 1959), pp. 1627, 1631.

[185] *U.S.* v. *Bethlehem Steel,* 168 F. Supp. 567 (1958).

[186] *In the Matter of Pillsbury Mills, Inc.,* Docket 6000, 50 F.T.C. 555. See Opinion of the Commission (Dec. 28, 1953), and Order (Dec. 16, 1960).

[187] *Tampa Electric Co.* v. *Nashville Coal Co.,* 276 F. 2d 766 (C.C.A.-6th 1960), reversed 81 S.Ct. 623 (1961).

[188] See, for example, Philip Marcus, "Antitrust Bugbears: Substitute Products—Oligopoly," *University of Pennsylvania Law Review,* Vol. 105 (December 1956), p. 185.

[189] *U.S.* v. *E. I. du Pont de Nemours & Co.,* 351 U.S. 377 (1956).

[190] *U.S.* v. *E. I. du Pont de Nemours & Co.,* 353 U.S. 586 (1957).

[191] See debate on the definition in *Antitrust Bulletin,* Vol. 2 (1957). Gerhard A. Gesell favors the *Cellophane* decision in "Legal Problems Involved in Proving Relevant Markets." (P. 463.) George W. Stocking presents a contrary view in "Economic Tests of Monopoly and the Concept of the Relevant Market." (P. 479.)

[192] Jesse W. Markham feels that it was "an exceedingly narrow definition." He suggests that this market definition might hurt the government in later cases, *e.g.,* in an attack on a merger of a large auto-paint manufacturer with a large producer of refrigerator-paint. "The *du Pont-General Motors* Decision," *Virginia Law Review,* Vol. 43 (October 1957), pp. 881, 887-88.

[193] See George W. Stocking, "Economic Change and the Sherman Act: Some Reflections on 'Workable Competition,' " *Virginia Law Review,* Vol. 44 (May 1958), pp. 537, 581-82.

[194] William F. Rogers, "*U.S. v. du Pont*—A Judicial Revision of Section 7," *Antitrust Bulletin,* Vol. 2 (1957), pp. 577, 581.

[195] Another reconciliation was suggested by Judge Herlands in *U.S.* v. *Columbia Pictures Corp. et al.* (D.C. S.D. N.Y.), *CCH Trade Cases* (1960), Par. 69,766 (July 1, 1960). "The tests enunciated by the authorities are consistent. Effectively, the test 'reasonable interchangeability for the purposes for which (the products) are produced—price, use and qualities considered' [citing *Cellophane*] and the test 'sufficient peculiar characteristics and uses to constitute them products sufficiently distinct . . . to make them a line of commerce within the meaning of the Clayton Act' [citing *du Pont-General Motors*] are but different verbalizations of the same criterion."

[196] See Betty Bock, *Mergers and Markets,* National Industrial Conference Board, Studies in Business Economics No. 69 (1960), pp. 27-29. Alfred Nicols feels that the "critical element" in the definition of the market in *General Motors* turned on the buyer's requirements. Alfred Nicols, "Economic Issues in the *du Pont-General Motors Case,*" *Journal of Business,* Vol. 33 (July 1960), pp. 227, 234. However, he argues that this analysis was in error. "No rational basis was provided for restricting the market finding to the buyer." *Ibid.,* p. 237.

[197] *U.S.* v. *E. I. du Pont de Nemours & Co.,* 351 U.S. 377, 378 (1956).

[198] *U.S.* v. *E. I. du Pont de Nemours & Co.*, 353 U.S. 586, 595 (1957).

[199] See Robert A. Bicks, "Mergers and Acquisitions: 'A Government Lawyer's Views,'" *Proceedings*, Section of Antitrust Law, Annual Meeting of the American Bar Association, New York and London, July 13 and 25, 1957, pp. 20, 29.

[200] See Betty Bock, *op. cit.*, p. 92.

[201] For a contrary view see Edward F. Howrey, "Advising Clients in the Light of the du Pont (General Motors) Decision," *Antitrust Bulletin*, Vol. 3 (1958), p. 13. "The fact that they [*General Motors* and *Cellophane*] were decided under different sections of the antitrust laws . . . does not, insofar as the relevant product market is concerned, assist either the lawyer or the businessman in rationalizing the two decisions." (P. 16.)

[202] *U.S.* v. *E. I. du Pont de Nemours & Co.*, 351 U.S. 377 (1956).

[203] *U.S.* v. *E. I. du Pont de Nemours & Co.*, 353 U.S. 586 (1957).

[204] In *Cellophane* the court distinguished between Sherman Act charges of conspiring to monopolize and monopolization. It felt that in a conspiracy case such as *Story Parchment*, "the scope of the market was not in issue." *U.S.* v. *E. I. du Pont de Nemours & Co.*, 351 U.S. 377 (1956), footnote p. 395.

[205] See George H. Dession, "The Trial of Economic and Technological Issues of Fact: I," *Yale Law Journal*, Vol. 58 (June 1949), pp. 1019, 1045.

[206] As A. D. Neale points out, this feature "is not an unfamiliar idea in other branches of law. It became very difficult to get juries to convict in England at a time when quite minor thefts were visited with capital punishment." *The Antitrust Laws of the United States of America* (1960), p. 460.

[207] Holmes Baldridge offers a different interpretation. He feels that the remedies of divorce, divestiture and dissolution "are more likely to be applied under Section 7 of the Clayton Act than under Section 2 of the Sherman Act, because Section 7 deals specifically with mergers, because the quantum of proof is much less exacting, and because such remedies are much more effective in dissipating the monopolistic effects of merger than is an injunction." "The Present Status of Large Corporations Under Section 7 of the Clayton Act," *Antitrust Bulletin*, Vol. 3 (1958), pp. 25, 30.

[208] Judge Weinfeld attempted to relate the varying definitions of the market under different statutes in his opinion on *Bethlehem-Youngstown*, 168 F. Supp. 576 (1958). In footnote 36 he said, "It should be noted that the basic issue in the *Cellophane* case was that of monopoly power and the Supreme Court expressly limited the market definition there to the monopolization clause of Section 2 of the Sherman Act. There is a basic distinction between Section 2 of the Sherman Act and Section 7 of the Clayton Act. Further, monopoly power was defined by the Supreme Court in the *Cellophane* case as 'the power to control prices or exclude competition.' Obviously, when the question is power over price, substitute products may be relevant because they can limit that power. The issue under Section 7 of the Clayton Act is not whether a merger may result in a company having power over price or the power to exclude competition. The issue under Section 7 is whether there is a reasonable probability of substantial lessening of competition. There can be a substantial lessening of competition with respect to a product whether or not there are reasonably interchangeable substitutes. The merger of two producers of a product may substantially lessen competition or tend to create a monopoly in the market for that product even though it does not substantially lessen competition or tend to create a monopoly in the broader market embracing all the products which are reasonably interchangeable with their product. . . . This does not, however, mean that interchangeability can be ignored—a high degree of interchangeability may under certain circumstances make it more or less the same product."

Judge Weinfeld's interpretation of Section 7 calls for a market definition which would be quite different from the one that would be used under Section 2 of the Sherman Act. However, the basis for his distinction is not clear. He gave no clue regarding what "degree of interchangeability" would satisfy a Section 7 market definition. Nor did he explain the difference between the definition of monopoly power in *Cellophane,* "the power to control prices and exclude competition," and the standard of lessening of competition which he would apply under Section 7.

[209] Chairman Kintner of the F.T.C. pointed out that one must start with the market as defined in the statute. "A market so defined does not necessarily comport with an economist's definition of a market." *In the Matter of Pillsbury Mills, Inc.,* Docket 6000, Opinion of the Commission (Dec. 16, 1961, mimeo.), p. 4.

[210] Some seem to want to seize on any clue in order to formulate a mechanical rule. For example, it has been suggested that because of *Columbia Steel* "the law today appears to be that a consolidation involving no more than 24 per cent of the business in the relevant geographic market does not constitute an infringement of Section 2 of the Sherman Act." G. E. Hale and Rosemary D. Hale, *Market Power: Size and Shape Under the Sherman Act* (1958), p. 72. This percentage is obtained by adding U.S. Steel's percentage of sales of the "market" to the sales of consolidated, 13 plus 11. No account is taken of differences, under Section 2, in charges of monopolization, attempt to monopolize, and conspiracy to monopolize. Nor is allowance made for analyses covering sizes of competitors, trends, pricing, difficulties of entry, etc.

[211] "The market, then, does not perform the function of a rule of law. It operates, rather, to orient, systematize and classify factual situations so that antitrust policies can be properly applied. As a tool of factual analysis, the market concept should not be a draw-string, which is tightened for illegality and slackened for lawfulness. To attain the clarity of thought necessary for intelligent policy formulation and the rudiments of predictability essential to the administration of this body of law, the concept of the market should remain a constant." Note, "The Market: A Concept in Anti-trust," *Columbia Law Review,* Vol. 54 (1954), pp. 580, 603.

[212] Betty Bock, "Mergers and Market Size—1. Product Dimensions," *Conference Board Business Record,* Vol. 16 (April 1959), pp. 192, 194-95.

[213] The Attorney General's Committee stated, "Identification of markets required for solution of an antitrust problem is primarily one of fact." *Report of the Attorney General's National Committee to Study the Antitrust Laws* (1955), p. 44. The committee then went on to discuss principles followed in the cases in the same manner it applied in discussing legal principles. As long as the dichotomy of "law" and "fact" are not involved in jury cases of this type, we shall have no test of this question. However, the quest for principles is a matter of jurisprudence in this area.

[214] For a critique of the court's inconsistent treatment of market definition see Joe S. Bain, *Industrial Organization* (1959), pp. 512-13.

[215] "The Shoe Machinery Case and the Problem of the Good Trust," *Quarterly Journal of Economics,* Vol. 68 (1954), pp. 287, 296.

[216] *Ibid.,* p. 295.

[217] Victor R. Hansen, "The Current Federal Policy on Antitrust Laws," *Antitrust Bulletin,* Vol. 4 (1959), pp. 541, 548. A similar point of view is implied in Justice Reed's opinion in *U.S.* v. *Columbia Steel Co. et al.,* 334 U.S. 495 (1948), pp. 527-28.

[218] Donald F. Turner, "Antitrust Policy and the *Cellophane* Case," *Harvard Law Review,* Vol. 60 (December 1956), pp. 281, 309. See also Irston R. Barnes, "Competitive Mores and Legal Tests in Merger Cases: The *du Pont-General Motors* Decision," *Georgetown Law Journal,* Vol. 46 (1958), pp. 564, 603.

[219] Edward H. Chamberlin, "Product Heterogeneity and Public Policy," *American Economic Review,* Vol. 40 (May 1950), pp. 85, 86-87.

[220] See Judge Herlands' objections to the use of a "pat formula" in *U.S.* v. *Columbia Pictures et al.* (D.C.S.D.N.Y.), *CCH Trade Cases* (1960), Par. 69,766, July 1, 1960. He pointed out, also, that, "Statistical evidence can rarely, if ever, supply all the facts needed for a definitive judgment."

## *Chapter 9*

[1] Irston R. Barnes, "Quantitative Data and Sample Surveys as Evidence in Judicial and Administrative Procedures," *The Role of Sampling Data as Evidence in Judicial and Administrative Proceedings,* Current Business Studies No. 19 (October 1954), pp. 33, 34.

[2] Thomas Kiernan, "Observations on the Problem of Cross-Examination in Antitrust Cases," *American Bar Association Section of Antitrust Law,* Vol. 18 (1961), p. 71.

[3] William N. Early, "The Use of Survey Evidence in Antitrust Proceedings," *Washington Law Review and State Bar Journal,* Vol. 33 (Winter 1958), p. 380.

[4] "Even in the presentation of evidence relevant to a single conspiracy, the rules of evidence which were developed for personal crimes and torts are misfits as means to bring out the facts of an industrial market. Judicial evidence is that which individuals have done, seen, heard, felt, smelt, and tasted. There are few techniques for bringing before the court broad situations of which no single person has direct firsthand experience." Corwin D. Edwards, "Can the Antitrust Laws Preserve Competition?", *American Economic Review,* Supplement, Vol. 30 (March 1940), pp. 164, 173.

[5] Albert E. Sawyer, "Standards of Proof of Sampling Data," *The Role of Sampling Data as Evidence in Judicial and Administrative Proceedings,* Current Business Studies No. 19 (October 1954), pp. 46, 62.

[6] For an imposing list of cases in which opinion surveys were employed see Fred M. Kecker, "Admissibility in Courts of Law of Economic Data Based on Samples," *Journal of Business* (April 1955), pp. 114, 118.

[7] For another imposing list of cases in which samples were used see *ibid.,* p. 117.

[8] W. Edwards Deming, "On the Presentation of the Results of Sample Surveys as Legal Evidence," *Journal of American Statistical Association,* Vol. 49 (December 1954), p. 814.

[9] Hiram C. Barksdale concluded that "defective research has, in some cases, received more attention than it probably deserved." *The Use of Survey Research Findings as Legal Evidence* (1957), p. 106. See also p. 141.

[10] See Corwin D. Edwards, "Preserving Competition vs. Regulating Monopoly," *American Economic Review,* Supplement, Pt. 2, Vol. 30 (1940), p. 164, for illustration.

[11] See Hans Zeisel, "The Uniqueness of Survey Evidence," *Cornell Law Quarterly,* Vol. 45 (Winter 1960), p. 322.

[12] See David W. Louisell, "The Psychologist in Today's Legal World," *Minnesota Law Review,* Vol. 39 (February 1955), esp. pp. 249, 250.

[13] A number of efforts are being made in this direction. See, for example, the series of Current Business Studies of the Society of Business Advisory Professions,

Inc., especially No. 19, *The Role of Sampling Data as Evidence in Judicial and Administrative Proceedings,* and No. 26, *Standards of Probability Sampling for Legal Evidence.*

[14] Consider, for example, the issue of a price conspiracy which must be established through circumstantial evidence. The *Socony-Vacuum* case required a long, detailed analysis of thousands of transactions to tell how prices behaved. Tabulations were made by the government and by the defendants covering several months and sales in 28 cities. Without such tabulations it would have been impossible for the courts to review price movements. *U.S.* v. *Socony-Vacuum Oil Co. et al.,* 310 U.S. 150 (1940). See also *Tag Manufacturers Institute* v. *F.T.C.,* 174 F. 2d 452 (C.C.A.-1st 1949); and *Bristol-Myers Co.* v. *F.T.C.,* 185 F. 2d 58 (C.C.A.-4th 1950).

[15] See Barnes, in Current Business Studies No. 19, pp. 33, 44. Homer I. Mitchell, "Preparing and Trying an Antitrust Claim—The Defendant's Case," in American Bar Association, *Section of Antitrust Law,* Vol. 18 (1961), pp. 50, 58.

[16] This topic is dealt with in Chap. 7 above.

[17] See Chap. 8 above.

[18] "In the antitrust field, problems press for solution, and the absence of complete evidence does not justify inaction. Thus, in default of other evidence, administrative commissions have relied on outdated studies . . . or, they have at times resorted to inferring economic consequences where the relations of cause and effect have seemed to justify resting a decision on inferences." Barnes, in Current Business Studies No. 19, pp. 33, 34.

[19] See, for example, National Bureau of Economic Research, *Cost Behavior and Price Policy* (1943).

[20] See, for example, *ibid.*

[21] See, for example, Alfred C. Neal, *Industrial Concentration and Price Inflexibility* (1942).

[22] See, for example, tabulation of "Antitrust Cases Commenced" in *Annual Report of the Director of the Administrative Office of the United States Courts 1960,* p. 118.

[23] See, for example, M. A. Adelman, "A Current Appraisal of Concentration Statistics," *Proceedings of the Business and Economic Statistics Section of the American Statistical Association,* Annual Meeting 1957, p. 227; Federal Trade Commission, *Industrial Concentration and Product Diversification in the 1,000 Largest Manufacturing Companies: 1950* (1957), *Concentration in Industries Defined on an Establishment Basis* (1957), *The Concentration of Productive Facilities, 1947* (1949), *The Divergence Between Plant and Company Concentration, 1947* (1950), and *Report on Corporate Mergers and Acquisitions* (1955); Gideon Rosenbluth, *Concentration in Canadian Manufacturing Industries* (1957); *Mergers and Possible Growth of Concentration in the Trucking Industry,* Hearings before the Senate Small Business Committee, 85 Cong. 1 sess. (1957); *Banking Concentration and Small Business,* Staff Report to the House Select Committee on Small Business, 86 Cong. 2 sess. (1960); U.S. Department of Commerce, *Concentration of Industries Report* (December 1949); U.S. Bureau of the Census, *The Proportion of the Shipments (or Employees) of Each Industry, or the Shipments of Each Group of Products Accounted for by the Largest Companies as Reported in the 1954 Census of Manufacturers* (July 1957).

[24] See Eleanor J. Stockwell, "What is a 'Small' Business?", *Financing Small Business,* Report to the Committees on Banking and Currency and the Select Committees on Small Business by the Federal Reserve System, 85 Cong. 2 sess. (1958).

[25] See, for example, Jesse W. Markham, "Trends in the Relative Importance of Small Business," *ibid.*, esp. pp. 211-14.

[26] For an extended discussion see Joe S. Bain, "Economies of Scale, Concentration, and the Condition of Entry in Twenty Manufacturing Industries," in American Economic Association, *Readings in Industrial Organization and Public Policy* (1958), p. 46.

[27] For a discussion of the census data which are usually used see Maxwell R. Conklin and Harold T. Goldstein, "Census Principles of Industry and Product Classification, Manufacturing Industries," in National Bureau of Economic Research, *Business Concentration and Price Policy* (1955), p. 15.

[28] See, for example, *Economic Report of the President* for any year.

[29] Gardiner C. Means, *Industrial Prices and Their Relative Inflexibility,* S. Doc. 13, 74 Cong. 1 sess. (1935); Alfred C. Neal, *Industrial Concentration and Price Inflexibility* (1942); Richard Ruggles, "The Nature of Price Flexibility and the Determinants of Relative Price Changes in the Economy," in National Bureau of Economic Research, *Business Concentration and Price Policy* (1955), p. 441.

[30] See Means, *loc. cit.*, and Neal, *loc. cit.*

[31] See *Government Price Statistics,* Hearings before the Subcommittee on Economic Statistics of the Joint Economic Committee, 87 Cong. 1 sess. (1961) Pt. 1, p. 35; Deere & Company, *Facts About John Deere Tractor Wholesale Prices* (1961), presents an interesting demonstration of changes in quality. It shows that while list prices for a standard tractor rose from $733 to $2,122 between 1935 and 1961, the cost per drawbar horsepower decreased from $59.26 to $54.41; and price per pound rose from 30 to 46 cents. Further, if prices are adjusted to take account of changes in the Bureau of Labor Statistics' Wholesale Price Index for Agricultural Machinery, the list prices were increased by 29 per cent, while the price per horsepower fell 59 per cent and the price per pound fell 31 per cent.

[32] *Frequency of Change in Wholesale Prices, A Study of Price Flexibility,* Study prepared for the Joint Economic Committee by the U.S. Department of Labor, Bureau of Labor Statistics, 85 Cong. 2 sess. (1959).

[33] *Ibid.*

[34] See Barnes, in Current Business Studies No. 19, pp. 33, 34.

[35] For illustrations see cases reviewed in Chaps. 7, 8, and 9.

[36] Tibor Scitovsky, "Economic Theory and the Measurement of Concentration," in National Bureau of Economic Research, *Business Concentration and Price Policy* (1955), p. 101.

[37] *Tag Manufacturers Institute et al.* v. *F.T.C.*, 174 F. 2d 452 (C.C.A.-1st 1949), *CCH Trade Cases,* Par. 62,421 (C.C.A.-1st, May 12, 1949). In discussing this case, Albert E. Sawyer referred to "tens of thousands of invoices of nearly 40 corporations involved. There we selected a two-week period. The complaint covered six or seven years of time. We suggested to the Commission that it select any other two-week period . . . and then we made a very thoughtful comparison." "Standards of Proof of Sampling Data," *The Role of Sampling Data as Evidence in Judicial and Administrative Proceedings,* Current Business Studies No. 19 (October 1954), pp. 46, 63.

[38] *In the Matter of Pillsbury Mills, Inc.*, 50 F.T.C. 555 (1953), Docket 6000.

[39] *In the Matter of Crown Zellerbach Corp.*, Docket 6180. See criticism of the survey because changes were made in the figures of reporting companies, without consulting the companies, when the commission's economist tabulated the data. Initial Decision of the Hearing Examiner (Feb. 25, 1957), p. 27.

[40] *U.S.* v. *Bethlehem Steel,* 168 F. Supp. 576 (1958).

[41] *U.S.* v. *E. I. du Pont de Nemours & Co.*, 351 U.S. 377 (1956).

[42] *In the Matter of American Chicle Co.,* Docket 6791. Consent Order 1958.

[43] *Bristol-Myers Co.* v. *F.T.C.,* 185 F. 2d 58 (C.C.A.-4th 1950).

[44] For an interesting discussion of the applications of cost data see "Report of Sherman Act Subcommittee on Cost Data Problems in Sherman Act Cases," *Proceedings,* Section of Antitrust Law, American Bar Association (August 1960), p. 521.

[45] *U.S.* v. *Aluminum Co. of America,* 148 F. 2d 416 (C.C.A.-2d 1945).

[46] *U.S.* v. *E. I. du Pont de Nemours &Co., loc. cit.*

[47] *American Tobacco Co. et al.,* v. *U.S.,* 328 U.S. 781 (1946).

[48] *U.S.* v. *New York Great A & P Tea Co.,* 67 F. Supp. 626 (E.D. Ill. 1946), aff'd. 173 F. 2d 79 (C.C.A.-7th 1949).

[49] *Pevely Dairy Co.* v. *U.S.,* 178 F. 2d 363 (C.C.A.-8th 1949).

[50] *U.S.* v. *Eli Lilly & Co.,* 24 F.R.D. 285 (D.C.N.J. 1959).

[51] See Herbert F. Taggart, *Cost Justification* (1959) and Mark S. Massel, "The Robinson-Patman Act: Cost Justification," *Conference on the Antitrust Laws and the Attorney General's Committee Report* (1955), p. 197.

[52] *U.S.* v. *J. I. Case Co.,* 101 F. Supp. 856 (D.C. Minn. 1951).

[53] Edward F. Howrey, "Coalescence of Legal and Economic Concepts of Competition," Address delivered before the Section on Antitrust Law of the New York State Bar Association, Jan. 26, 1955 (mimeo.).

[54] For an illustration of the difficulties encountered in developing evidence of sales in the early cases see *Northern Pacific Ry.* v. *Keyes,* 91 F. 47, 59 (C.C.D.N. D. 1898).

[55] See M. J. Moroney, *Facts from Figures* (1952); G. W. Snedecor, *Statistical Methods* (1956).

[56] For example, compare Table D-23 "Average Weekly Hours of Work" and Table D-22 "Number of Wage and Salary Workers" in *Economic Report of the President* (1961). While number of workers in manufacturing increased from 1933 to 1934, average weekly hours decreased.

[57] A question which was involved in *U.S.* v. *Bethlehem Steel,* 168 F. Supp. 576 (1958).

[58] Affidavit of Harrison F. Houghton (D.C. S.D. N.Y. June 12, 1957).

[59] *U.S.* v. *Bethlehem Steel, loc. cit.*

[60] Affidavit cited, p. 37.

[61] U.S. Department of Labor, *Bulletin No. S-1* (October 1959), Tables 12a and 14a.

[62] *Ibid.*

[63] Moroney, *op. cit.*

[64] For an excellent and amusing introduction to sampling see Morris James Slonim, *Sampling in a Nutshell* (1960).

[65] "Every schoolboy knows enough not to judge a basket of fruit by the specimens on top. Every reader of a newspaper must doubt whether the readers whose letters are chosen for print are really representative of opinion in general." M. G. Kendall, "Sampling as an Exact Science," *Lloyd's Bank Review,* No. 51 (January 1949), pp. 34, 36.

[66] *Ibid.*

[67] See H. Thomas Austern, "Use of Statistical Techniques in Antitrust and Trade Regulation Proceedings," *Antitrust in Action* (April 1960) (mimeo.), p. 2.

[68] See William N. Early, "The Use of Survey Evidence in Antitrust Proceedings," *Washington Law Review and State Bar Journal,* Vol. 33 (Winter 1958), p. 380.

[69] See discussion in Henry M. Hart, Jr. and John T. McNaughton, "Evidence and Inference in the Law," in Daniel Lerner, ed., *Evidence and Inference* (1958), pp. 48, 54.

[70] See Theodore H. Brown, "Quality Control," *Harvard Business Review*, Vol. 29 (1951), p. 69 for discussion of use of sampling to check quality of deliveries.

[71] See Kendall, *op. cit.*, p. 35.

[72] Hans Zeisel points to the use of mortality tables which are "admitted almost daily without much legal argument in our courts, and probably without awareness that it is a sample survey . . ." "The Uniqueness of Survey Evidence," *Cornell Law Quarterly*, Vol. 45 (Winter 1960), pp. 322, 325, footnote 13.

[73] *Standards of Probability Sampling for Legal Evidence*, Current Business Studies No. 26 (1957), p. 4.

[74] See *Illinois Bell Telephone Co.*, 7 P.U.R. 3d 41; 606 Illinois Commerce Commission 493,506 (1955).

[75] Joel Dean, "Sampling to Produce Evidence on Which Courts Will Rely," *The Role of Sampling Data as Evidence in Judicial and Administrative Proceedings*, Current Business Studies No. 19 (October 1954), pp. 5, 8.

[76] "A party endeavoring to establish the public state of mind on a subject, which state of mind cannot be proved except by calling as witnesses so many of the public as to render the task impracticable, should be allowed to offer evidence concerning a poll which the party maintains reveals that state of mind." *People v. Franklin National Bank*, 105 N.Y.S. 2d 81.

[77] Dean, in Current Business Studies No. 19, pp. 5, 8.

[78] A committee of the Society of Business Advisory Professions, Inc. formulated the following definition: "Probability sampling is a procedure by which one obtains a result from a selected portion of a total number of establishments, accounts or other items, that will be the same, within calculable limits of uncertainty, as the result which would have come from an equal complete coverage. . . ." *Standards of Probability Sampling for Legal Evidence*, Current Business Studies No. 26 (1957), p. 4.

[79] Standards for sampling are published in the following: *Military Standard Sampling Procedures and Tables for Inspection by Attributes, Mil-Std-105A*, Washington, 1950; American Society for Testing Materials, *Tentative Recommended Practice for Probability Sampling of Materials* (1954); U.S. Bureau of the Budget, *Standards for Statistical Surveys* (1952); Statistical Office of the United Nations, *The Preparation of Sampling Survey Reports* (1950).

[80] ". . . a judgment sample may be more representative and efficient than a probability sample. Usually it is more plausible. But the trouble is there is no way of knowing how reliable or unreliable, a subjective sample is." Dean, in Current Business Studies No. 19, pp. 5, 10.

[81] W. G. Cochran, F. Mosteller, and J. W. Turkey, "Principles of Sampling," *Journal of American Statistical Association*, Vol. 49 (March 1954), p. 13. The article has an interesting discussion of the relationships between the two types of samples. See also Barnes, in Current Business Studies No. 19, pp. 33, 38.

[82] W. Edwards Deming seems to imply that on occasion the expert in subject matter relies too much on the statistician without evaluating the entire problem himself. "Statistical theory does not relieve the expert in the subject matter—the economist, accountant, or lawyer, marketing expert, engineer—of stating the problem and knowing what he is doing. Statistical theory will help him to get the answer when he knows what frame he wishes to study, and what questions would be useful to him if he were to cover that frame one hundred per cent." *Standards of Probability Sampling for Legal Evidence*, Current Business Studies No. 26 (1957), p. 20.

[83] The application of a stratified sample may be demonstrated by the practice of the Internal Revenue Service in compiling statistics of income and taxes. It uses the following samples for the designated classes:

| Class—By Amount of Adjusted Gross Income | Per Cent of Returns Covered |
|---|---|
| $7,000 and under | 3/10 of 1% |
| $7,000 to $25,000 | 10% |
| $25,000 to $50,000 | 25% |
| $50,000 and over | 100% |

In all, the sample covers 680,000 out of 52,000,000 returns. Morris James Slonim, *Sampling in a Nutshell* (1960), p. 117.

[84] W. Edwards Deming, an outstanding mathematical statistician and a strong proponent of sampling methods, says that "important and rare transactions" must be given separate treatment. Further, these choices must be made by "the expert in subject-matter" rather than the statistician. "On the Contributions of Standards of Sampling to Legal Evidence and Accounting," *The Role of Sampling Data as Evidence in Judicial and Administrative Proceedings,* Current Business Studies No. 19 (October 1954), pp. 14, 21.

[85] M. G. Kendall, "Sampling as an Exact Science," *Lloyd's Bank Review,* No. 51 (January 1949), pp. 34, 42.

[86] "The size of sample is no criterion of its precision. The procedure of stratification, the choice of sampling unit, the formulas prescribed for the estimations are important. Once these features are fixed, then as we increase the size we gain precision (though the point of diminishing returns comes rapidly)." Deming, in Current Business Studies No. 19, p. 23. The lower limits for sample size are discussed in Kendall, *op. cit.,* p. 40.

[87] See W. Edwards Deming, "On the Presentation of the Results of Sample Surveys as Legal Evidence," *Journal of American Statistical Association,* Vol. 49 (December 1954), pp. 814, 819.

[88] Morris James Slonim, *Sampling in a Nutshell* (1960), p. 74.

[89] See Deming, in Current Business Studies No. 19, esp. p. 21.

[90] Slonim, *op. cit.,* p. 117.

[91] Hans Zeisel, "The Uniqueness of Survey Evidence," *Cornell Law Quarterly,* Vol. 45 (Winter 1960), pp. 324, 325.

[92] Commissioner Humphrey of the F.T.C. showed the need for sampling when he registered a vociferous dissent when testimony was taken from "about a thousand witnesses" regarding the meaning of "Castile" soap. He felt that the procedure "has caused the F.T.C. to waste hundreds of thousands of dollars." Further, "piling up of cumulative evidence is an inexcusable outrage on the public." *In the Matter of James S. Kirk & Co.,* 12 F.T.C. 272, 289 (1928).

[93] Herbert F. Taggart, *Cost Justification* (1959).

[94] Herbert F. Taggart, "Work of the Cost-Justification Committee," *Antitrust Bulletin,* Vol. 1 (1956), pp. 585, 586-87. A discussion of this possibility is contained in R. A. Kosloske, *N.A.C.A. Bulletin,* Vol. 34 (December 1952).

[95] See *Report of Advisory Committee on Cost Justification of the Federal Trade Commission* (1956). Reprinted in Taggart, *Cost Justification,* pp. 555, 562.

[96] Zeisel, *op. cit.,* pp. 322, 328; Kendall, *op. cit.,* pp. 34, 39.

[97] Joel Dean, "Sampling to Produce Evidence on Which Courts Will Rely," *The Role of Sampling Data as Evidence in Judicial and Administrative Proceedings,* Current Business Studies No. 19 (October 1954), pp. 5, 8.

[98] Kendall defines this problem in terms of "bias in choice" of the sample. Kendall, *op. cit.,* pp. 36, 37. See *In the Matter of Pillsbury Mills,* Docket 6000, Opinion of the Commission (Dec. 16, 1930), p. 11, for a criticism of a consumer survey which covered two trading areas and was offered as a sample of the Southeastern States.

[99] W. Edwards Deming, "On the Contributions of Standards of Sampling to

Legal Evidence and Accounting," *The Role of Sampling Data as Evidence in Judicial and Administrative Proceedings,* Current Business Studies No. 19 (October 1954), p. 14.

[100] See Kendall, *op. cit.,* pp. 36-37, for a similar illustration.

[101] C.C.A.-1st, May 12, 1949, *CCH Trade Cases,* Par. 62,421. See also Albert E. Sawyer, "Standards of Proof of Sampling Data," in Current Business Studies No. 19, p. 46.

[102] *U.S.* v. *Socony-Vacuum Oil Co., Inc. et al.,* 310 U.S. 218 (1940).

[103] See Judicial Conference of the United States, *Handbook of Recommended Procedures for the Trial of Protracted Cases* (1960), p. 75, esp. footnote 134 (reprinted in 25 F.R.D. 351). "Sampling cannot overcome fundamental defects in definitions and in methods for eliciting information. In fact, these defects afflict complete coverages and samples alike." See also *Standards of Probability Sampling for Legal Evidence,* Current Business Studies No. 26 (1957), p. 9; and *The Role of Sampling Data as Evidence in Judicial and Administrative Proceedings,* Current Business Studies No. 19 (October 1954), pp. 58-60.

[104] A realistic illustration of the problem is presented in a reprint of the transcript of part of the proceedings in a treble-damage action in David W. Louisell, "The Psychologist in Today's Legal World," *Minnesota Law Review,* Vol. 39 (February 1955), pp. 235, 258-72.

[105] Deming, in Current Business Studies No. 19, pp. 14, 27.

[106] Deming, *ibid.,* p. 22. The importance of the definition shows up on many occasions. Monthly statistics showed that both civilian employment and civilian unemployment were reduced between June and July 1961. This peculiar change was probably due to the "unemployment" in June of college students who stopped looking for work in July because they felt that no jobs would be available during their summer vacation. "Employment and Population" table in *Survey of Current Business* (August 1961), p. S-11.

[107] See *S. C. Johnson & Sons, Inc.* v. *Gold Seal Co.,* 90 U.S.P.Q. 373 (1951).

[108] 121 F. Supp. 955 (E.D.Pa. 1954) revised 219 F. 2d 590 (C.C.A.-3d 1955).

[109] Sears was not as successful in another suit to protect this trademark. *Sears Roebuck & Co.* v. *All States Life Insurance Co.,* 246 F. 2d 161 (C.C.A.-5th 1957). The court criticized Sears' survey because the sequence of questions affected the final results. The sequence was: What does "All State" mean to you?; If you wanted All State Insurance where would you go?; Have you ever heard of All States Life Insurance Company?; Who would you say owns All States Life Insurance Company?

[110] 25 N.Y.S. 2d 271 (S. Ct. 1940).

[111] To the same effect see *American Luggage Works* v. *U.S. Truck Co.,* 158 F. Supp. 50 (D.C. Mass. 1957).

[112] 27 Del. Ch. 318, 36A. 2d 156 (1944).

[113] See also *Cleo Syrup Corp.* v. *Coca-Cola,* 139 F. 2d 416 (C.C.A.-8th 1943) cert. denied 321 U.S. 781 (1944).

[114] *Coca-Cola* v. *Nehi Corp.,* 27 Del. Ch. 318, 36A. 2d 156, 160 (1944).

[115] 162 F. 2d 160 (C.C.A.-9th 1947).

[116] *In the Matter of Pillsbury Mills,* Docket 6000. Opinion of the Commission (Dec. 16, 1960).

[117] *Ibid.,* pp. 7-9.

[118] Darrell Huff, *How to Lie With Statistics* (1954), p. 90.

[119] See statement by Sawyer in Current Business Studies No. 19, p. 62.

[120] Deming feels strongly about the treatment of statistics in court. ". . . the ridiculous spectacle of waste and frustration that takes place every day in our own commissions and courts through failure of lawyers and accountants to recognize existing standards of statistical practice. Instead, they argue interminably about ex-

hibits of data that come from surveys or tests scrupulously conducted, while they admit, agree, and pass judgment on statistical evidence that any statistician would disown and repudiate. . . ." Current Business Studies No. 19, pp. 14, 15.

[121] See, for example, a discussion of the evidentiary problems entailed in introducing a table of aluminum imports in Corwin D. Edwards, "Can the Antitrust Laws Preserve Competition?", *American Economic Review,* Supplement, Vol. 30 (March 1940), pp. 164, 173.

[122] George H. Dession, "The Trial of Economic and Technological Issues of Fact: II," *Yale Law Journal,* Vol. 58 (July 1949), pp. 1242, 1271.

[123] Many judges seem to feel that technical rules to exclude evidence should be liberalized. For example, Chief Judge Clark stated in *U.S.* v. *Appuzzo,* 245 F. 2d. 416, 420-21 (C.C.A.-2d 1957), "And we have often admonished our trial judge to err, if at all, on the side of the admission, rather than the exclusion, of evidence. A trial judge must rule on admissibility quickly and almost by instinct; his instinct ought to be to bring out the truth rather than to permit a party to cover up a part of his case."

[124] Judge Gregory F. Noonan, "The Need for Acceptable Standards of Proof," *The Growing Role of Economic Data in Judicial and Administrative Proceedings,* Current Business Studies No. 18 (March 1954), p. 11.

[125] See "Public Opinion Polls as Evidence in Unfair Competition Cases," *The Practical Lawyer* (October 1956).

[126] See *Report of the Committee on Practice and Procedure in the Trial of Antitrust Cases,* Section of Antitrust Law, American Bar Association (1954), p. 43.

[127] For a rounded discussion of the problem of employing neutral experts and of state and federal efforts to develop adequate procedures see Senate Judiciary Committee, Subcommittee on Patents, Trademarks, and Copyrights. *The Role of the Court Expert in Patent Litigation,* 85 Cong. 1 sess. (1958).

[128] See, for example, Judge Herlands' opinion in *U.S.* v. *Columbia Pictures Corp.* (D.C.S.D.N.Y. 1960), *CCH Trade Cases,* Par. 69,857.

[129] James H. McGlothlin, "Some Practical Problems in Proof of Economic, Scientific and Technical Facts," 23 F.R.D. 467, 477 (1959). McGlothlin recommends that plans for sampling and public opinion polls be discussed with the judge in pretrial.

[130] The classic work on evidence is J. H. Wigmore, *Anglo-American System of Evidence in Trials at Common Law* (3d ed., 1940).

[131] As Albert E. Sawyer sees it, "the thinking in terms of admissible evidence is still rather archaic in the minds of most courts." "Standards of Proof of Sampling Data," *The Role of Sampling Data as Evidence in Judicial and Administrative Proceedings,* Current Business Studies No. 19 (October 1954), pp. 46, 62.

[132] " 'Competition' is a phenomenon that has never been defined precisely and which is constantly changing. Injury to it must be inferred from surrounding circumstances rather than by direct testimony." William N. Early, "The Use of Survey Evidence in Antitrust Proceedings," *Washington Law Review and State Bar Journal,* Vol. 33 (Winter 1958), p. 380.

[133] See John MacArthur Maguire, *Evidence: Common Sense and Common Law* (1947).

[134] See Wigmore, *op. cit.,* Vol. 5, Par. 1362.

[135] Thus in *Elgin National Watch Co.* v. *Elgin Clock Co.,* 26 F. 2d 376 (D.C. Del. 1928), an affidavit based on a mail survey of retail jewelers was rejected as hearsay because it was based on the opinions of people who were not witnesses.

[136] See E. M. Morgan, "Hearsay Dangers and the Application of the Hearsay Concept," *Harvard Law Review,* Vol. 62 (1948), p. 177.

[137] Wigmore, *op. cit.*, Par. 1420.

[138] It has been suggested that the courts avoid the hearsay rule by taking "judicial notice" of a survey. As will be recalled in Chapter 5, it was pointed out that a court may take notice of information which is generally known, for example, published general reference material or "general knowledge." This procedure would avoid the technicalities of the hearsay rule. However, any judge who would go this far to admit a survey would not have any great difficulty with the hearsay rule. The suggestion is discussed in Hiram C. Barksdale, *The Use of Survey Research Findings as Legal Evidence* (1957), p. 117; F. R. Kennedy, "Law and the Courts," in Norman C. Meier and Harold W. Saunders, eds., *The Polls and Public Opinion* (1949), pp. 92, 102; R. C. Sorensen and T. C. Sorensen, "The Admissibility and Use of Opinion Research Evidence," *New York University Law Quarterly*, Vol. 28 (November 1953), p. 1221; and L. E. Waterbury, "Opinion Surveys in Civil Litigation," *Public Opinion Quarterly*, Vol. 17 (Spring 1953), p. 73. The judge ruled that survey findings corroborated a fact of which he took judicial notice in *Metropolitan Opera Association, Inc.* v. *Pilot Radio Corp.*, 68 N.Y.S. 2d 789 (1947).

[139] See Edward W. Hinton, "State of Mind and the Hearsay Rule," *University of Chicago Law Review*, Vol. 1, (1934), p. 394.

[140] This rule should not be confused with the rule against "opinion" evidence which rules out the opinions of witnesses unless they qualify as experts. Henry M. Hart, Jr. and John T. McNaughton, "Evidence and Inference in the Law," in Daniel Lerner, ed., *Evidence and Inference* (1958), pp. 48, 56.

[141] "Each exception, to be sure, has come into existence and been maintained independently and amid considerations peculiar to itself alone." Wigmore, *op. cit.*, Par. 1420.

[142] For a plea to liberalize the hearsay rule see J. S. Strahorn, Jr., "A Reconsideration of the Hearsay Rule and Admissions," *University of Pennsylvania Law Review*, Vol. 85 (March 1937), pp. 484, 486. "To the extent to which the extra-judicial utterance is in writing, or is perceived by a trained observer, or is of a sort itself likely to be well perceived, briefly or accurately remembered and simply narrated, the secondary danger of untrustworthiness in its reproduction is avoided and more reason is present than otherwise for allowing the statement to be proven despite the hearsay rule."

[143] For an interesting discussion of the state-of-mind rule and the safeguards which it requires see *American Luggage Works* v. *U.S. Trunk Co.*, 158 F. Supp. 50, 53 (D.C. Mass. 1957).

[144] An interesting question arose in the F.T.C. proceeding against *Carnation Co. et al.*, Docket 6172. The Hearing Examiner was not impressed with testimony from ice-cream manufacturers regarding the reasons given to them by former customers for switching to other sources of supply. Initial Decision June 1959, pp. 21-26, remanded to examiner, March 24, 1961.

[145] See discussion and cases in Judicial Conference of the United States, *Handbook of Recommended Procedures for the Trial of Protracted Cases* (1960), p. 74 (reprinted in 25 F.R.D. 351)

[146] See F. R. Kennedy, "Law and the Courts," in Norman C. Meier and Harold W. Saunders, eds., *The Polls and Public Opinion* (1949), p. 92, for discussion of cases when surveys were not admitted into evidence.

[147] In *du Pont Cellophane Co.* v. *Waxed Products Co.* the District Court solved the problem of conflicting surveys by rejecting both, holding them to be incompetent, immaterial, and irrelevant. Later the Court of Appeals stated that "such proofs have no great weight." 6 F. Supp. 859 (E.D.N.Y. 1934); 85 F. 2d 75 (C.C.A.-2d 1936); cert. denied 299 U.S. 601 (1936).

[148] Edward F. Howrey, "Economic Evidence in Antitrust Cases," *The Role of Sampling Data as Evidence in Judicial and Administrative Proceedings,* Current Business Studies No. 19 (October 1954), pp. 71, 78.

[149] Yet, the agencies are not free of problems. Chairman Edward F. Howrey of the F.T.C. argued that "summaries, tabulations, charts, graphs, sampling and polls of opinion should be admitted into evidence if antitrust enforcement is to succeed as a practical matter." Speech of Jan. 26, 1955, "Coalescence of Legal and Economic Concepts of Competition" (mimeo.).

[150] See, for example, *Illinois Bell Telephone Co., CCH Utilities Law Reporter,* Sec. 16,714 (Ill. Com. Comn. 1955). The company submitted reproduction cost estimates based on probability samples of its physical property. A statistical expert reviewed the sample for the commission, which concluded that "the Company's sample should be accepted as a fair cross section of the plant as a whole." It reflected a distinct preference for "a scientifically drawn sample" as opposed to "random inspections."

[151] For example, the Food and Drug Administration conducted its own survey of consumer opinion about the ingredients contained in Bireley's Orange Beverage. The survey served as the basis of the agency's decision and was admitted into evidence by the trial judge. The Court of Appeals supported him. "The hearsay objection is unfounded. The survey was not taken to prove that the Beverage is not orange juice but to show what consumers thought when shown a bottle of the Beverage." *U.S.* v. *88 Cases,* 187 F. 2d 967 (C.C.A.-3d 1951), cert. denied 342 U.S. 861 (1951).

[152] *F.T.C.* v. *Cement Institute,* 333 U.S. 683 (1948).

[153] *U.S.* v. *United Shoe Machinery Corp.,* 89 F. Supp. 349, 356 (D.C. Mass. 1950).

[154] *Ibid.*

[155] William N. Early, "The Use of Survey Evidence in Antitrust Proceedings," *Washington Law Review and State Bar Journal,* Vol. 33 (Winter 1958), pp. 380, 389.

[156] Chairman Howrey of the F.T.C. enunciated this point *In the Matter of Crown Zellerbach,* 51 F.T.C. 1105 (1955). During an argument on appeal from an examiner's ruling regarding a mail survey, he said, "We have to find some way to try these cases under this merger statute. . . . One of our great problems is how we are going to prove the probability of (injury) to competition . . . and if counsel in support of the complaint has to bring in 500 corporations we will just have to report to Congress that the law enforcement agencies have broken down and we cannot do anything about mergers or Section 7." Transcript April 26, 1955, p. 24.

[157] For an interesting application of survey results see *Initial Decision in the Matter of Carnation Co. et al.,* Docket 6178 (June 1959). The results of a survey of ice cream dealers seemed to be the most influential evidence in the proceeding. A sample of dealers was selected at random and each selected dealer was interviewed. See also the *Rolaids* proceeding which involved a mail questionnaire that had been mailed to a random sample of 500 doctors. State courts are making use of surveys. For example, in *Alexander's Department Stores* v. *Rapoport* a telephone survey of 7,000 people was accepted and the defendant was enjoined from using the name "Alexander." 113 N.Y.S.2d 718 (1952), aff'd 120 N.Y.S.2d 239 (1953). See also *Household Finance Corp.* v. *Federal Finance Corp.,* 105 F. Supp. 164 (D.C. Ariz. 1952), a survey that showed public recognition of a trade symbol was accepted.

[158] F. R. Kennedy, "Some Legal Aspects of Sampling," *Industrial Quality Control,* Vol. 7 (January 1951), pp. 24, 27. The use of samples has been recognized

in the following: *U.S.* v. *2,205 Cases of Canned Salmon,* F & D Act Decision 1133 (W.D. Texas 1925); *A. O. Andersen & Co.* v. *U.S.,* 284 F. 542 (C.C.A.-9th 1922); *U.S.* v. *431/2 Gross Rubber Prophylactics,* 65 F. Supp. 534 (D.C. Minn. 1946), aff'd in *Gellman* v. *U.S.* 159 F. 2d 881 (C.C.A.-8th 1947).

[159] *Report of the Committee on Practice and Procedure in the Trial of Antitrust Cases of the Section of Antitrust Law of the American Bar Association* (1954).

[160] The frequent introduction of conflicting surveys "has a tendency to cause judges to discredit surveys generally." F. R. Kennedy, "Law and the Courts," in Norman C. Meier and Harold W. Saunders, eds., *The Polls and Public Opinion* (1949), pp. 92, 98.

[161] Consider, for example, the following statement: "It may well be that an accurate estimate of public opinion or practice can be obtained by a sampling process or survey, but the record is devoid of information on this subject and in the absence of the proof of the scientific principles, if any, which underlie the practice, we must rely upon the impression which the advertisements would be likely to make upon the mind of a man of ordinary intelligence. This is not to express the opinion that all advertisements based upon surveys must be barred, but merely that the information in the possession of the manufacturer in this case was insufficient to support its advertisements, and hence that the action taken by the Commission in this respect was within its authority." *Bristol-Myers Co.* v. *F.T.C.,* 185 F. 2d 58, 60-61 (C.C.A.-4th 1950).

[162] See F. R. Kennedy, "Law and the Courts," *op. cit.,* pp. 92, 96. "Those engaged in opinion research have not found the duplication of courtroom techniques conducive to accurate probing of the public mind."

[163] See Fred M. Kecker, "Admissibility in Courts of Law of Economic Data Based on Samples," *Journal of Business* (April 1955), pp. 114, 120. "The door-to-door poll simulates market conditions better than the witness stand."

[164] Hans Zeisel, "The Uniqueness of Survey Evidence," *Cornell Law Quarterly,* Vol. 45 (Winter 1960), pp. 322, 336.

[165] Differences in survey results were involved in a number of cases. See, for example, *Oneida, Ltd.* v. *National Silver Co.,* 25 N.Y.S.2d 271 (1940); *Quaker Oats Co.* v. *General Mills, Inc.,* 134 F. 2d 429 (C.C.A.-7th 1943); *du Pont Cellophane Co.* v. *Waxed Products Co.,* 6 F. Supp. 859 (E.D.N.Y. 1934), modified 85 F. 2d 75 (C.C.A.-2d 1936); *Alexander Young Distributing Co.* v. *National Dairy Products Corp.,* 40 F. Supp. 748 (E.D. Pa. 1941).

[166] F. R. Kennedy, "Some Legal Aspects of Sampling," *Industrial Quality Control,* Vol. 7 (March 1951), p. 12.

[167] Irston R. Barnes, "Quantitative Data and Sample Surveys as Evidence in Judicial and Administrative Procedures," *The Role of Sampling Data as Evidence in Judicial and Administrative Proceedings,* Current Business Studies No. 19 (October 1954), pp. 40, 41.

[168] *Ibid.*

[169] This problem arose *In the Matter of the Crown Zellerbach Corp.,* 51 F.T.C. 1105, 1111 (1955). In the course of a survey of the sources of supply of coarse paper products in the Western states, the F.T.C. mailed a questionnaire to 500 jobbers and converters. About 490 replies were received. There were objections to the introduction of the evidence on the grounds that the information consisted of hearsay, unsworn evidence, was not subject to cross-examination, and was biased because it was prepared for the purpose of the trial. The commission did admit the survey into evidence. However, it ruled that the returns could be examined by the respondent in order to prepare for a cross-examination of the economist who conducted the survey. Cross-examination did show up inaccuracies

in the construction of the survey and the hearing examiner refused to make a finding of fact based on it.

[170] Barnes, in Current Business Studies No. 19, p. 40.

[171] H. Thomas Austern, "Use of Statistical Techniques in Antitrust and Trade Regulation Proceedings," *Antitrust in Action* (April 1960) (mimeo.), p. 16.

[172] William N. Early, "The Use of Survey Evidence in Antitrust Proceedings," *Washington Law Review and State Bar Journal,* Vol. 33 (Winter 1958), pp. 380, 393.

[173] *F.T.C.* v. *Dilger,* 276 F. 2d 739 (C.C.A.-7th 1960).

[174] *U.S.* v. *St. Regis Paper Co.* (C.C.A.-2d 1960); *CCH Trade Cases,* Par. 69,880.

[175] *St. Regis Paper Co.* v. *U.S.* (Sup. Ct. 1961), *CCH Trade Cases,* Par. 70,167.

[176] Fred M. Kecker, "Admissibility in Courts of Law of Economic Data Based on Samples," *Journal of Business* (April 1955), pp. 114, 127.

[177] *Ibid.,* p. 115; and Early, *op. cit.,* p. 387.

[178] Hiram C. Barksdale, *The Use of Survey Research Findings as Legal Evidence* (1957), p. 7. In *Standard Oil Co.* v. *Standard Oil Co. et al.,* 110 U.S. P.Q. 122 (D.C. Wyoming 1956), the court said (p. 132), "It seems to be the rule that in a case of this character a trial judge may reach his own conclusion as to a trade-mark being of an infringing character on account of appearance, sound and meaning independent of testimony supporting the claim." See also Judge Frank's dissent in *General Time* v. *U.S. Time,* 165 F. 2d 853 (1948). F. R. Kennedy is quite critical of such judicial notice, which he feels the courts seem to have engaged in for a long time. "Law and the Courts," in Norman C. Meier and Harold W. Saunders, eds., *The Polls and Public Opinion* (1949), p. 97. Morton J. Simon points to "the fact that courts have admitted survey evidence but have still decided the issue against the evidence of the survey." *The Law for Advertising and Marketing* (1956), p. 478, see also p. 472.

[179] 101 F. Supp. 856, 868 (D.C. Minn. 1951).

[180] Barksdale, *op. cit.,* p. 141. See also Simon, *loc. cit.*

[181] 10 Fed. Cas. 829, No. 5621 (C.C.S.D.N.Y.) 1870.

[182] 150 F. 2d 751 (C.C.A.-3d 1944).

[183] A contrary view was taken in *Coca-Cola Co.* v. *Nehi Corp.,* 27 Del. Ch. 318 (1944). The court gave little weight to the testimony of 13 witnesses about what "cola" meant to them. It held that the testimony of 13 out of millions of customers was of minor importance.

[184] 87 F. Supp. 16 (N.D. Ill. 1949).

[185] *Coca-Cola Co.* v. *National Nu Grape Co.,* 97 U.S.P.Q. 481 (1953).

[186] The same results obtained in *Coca-Cola Co.* v. *Victor Syrup Corp.,* 97 U.S.P.Q. 478 (1953), aff'd 218 F. 2d 596 (C.C. Pa. 1954).

[187] 157 F. 2d 115, 120 (C.C.A.-2d 1946).

[188] Judge Frank took the same tack in *Eastern Wine Corp.* v. *Winslow-Warren, Ltd., Inc.,* 137 F. 2d 955.

[189] Kennedy, "Law and the Courts," *op. cit.,* p. 106.

[190] 167 F. 2d 969 (C.C.A.-2d 1948).

[191] *Ibid.,* p. 976.

[192] Progress continues on various fronts. In a discussion of the operations of the Restrictive Practices Court of the United Kingdom, it was reported: "The aim of the Court and of the Registrar has been to keep down to an essential minimum the amount of evidence presented. Thus the Court has expressed the view that the evidence of one trade witness need not be duplicated unless the other witness can speak of matters from a different angle; and accountancy work has usually been limited, by agreement between the Registrar and Respondents, to a sample of the field. For example, in the Yarn Spinners' case costings were prepared for a

small sample of counts for a small sample of firms." "Presenting a Case," *Cartel,* Vol. 10 (April 1960), p. 74.

[193] See statement of Chairman Howrey of the F.T.C. *In the Matter of Crown Zellerbach,* Transcript of Hearing on Appeal, April 26, 1955, p. 24.

[194] Hans Zeisel, "The Uniqueness of Survey Evidence," *Cornell Law Quarterly,* Vol. 45 (Winter 1960), pp. 322, 344; Albert E. Sawyer, "Standards of Proof of Sampling Data," *The Role of Sampling Data as Evidence in Judicial and Administrative Proceedings,* Current Business Studies No. 19 (October 1954), p. 46, esp. p. 49.

[195] See, for example, Judge Herlands' comments, *U.S.* v. *Columbia Pictures Corp.* (D.C.S.D.N.Y. April 1960), *CCH Trade Cases,* Par. 69,857.

[196] Consider, for example, Judge Herlands' problem in *U.S.* v. *Columbia Pictures Corp.* in *ibid.* "Not only are the experts in diametrical disagreement as to their respective evaluation and critique of the particular exhibits and the methods by which they are prepared, but counsel disagree as to the extent to which Professor Arkin's testimony adversely affects defendant's contentions in respect to particular exhibits."

[197] See Judicial Conference of the United States, *Handbook of Recommended Procedures for the Trial of Protracted Cases* (1960), esp. pp. 71-76. (Reprinted in 25 F.R.D. 351.)

[198] A leading antitrust lawyer concludes that "over the last two decades, particularly in the field of antitrust and trade regulation, there has been a growing acceptance of statistical proof." H. Thomas Austern, "Use of Statistical Techniques in Antitrust and Trade Regulation Proceedings," *Antitrust in Action* (April 1960) (mimeo.), p. 4.

[199] Zeisel, *op. cit.,* pp. 322, 345.

[200] The appendix of the *Report of the Committee on Practice and Procedure in the Trial of Antitrust Cases,* Section of Antitrust Law, American Bar Association (1954) contains a number of pretrial orders which show considerable progress in this direction.

[201] A plea for summarizations when they are appropriate is made in Judicial Conference of the United States, *op. cit.,* p. 71.

[202] Austern, *op. cit.,* p. 15. Zeisel maintains that "Cross-examination of selected survey interviewers is likely to be misleading." *Op. cit.,* p. 337. William N. Early is doubtful about the desirability of this procedure because he feels that the "best method of testing the survey would be by examining the methods by which it was compiled." "The Use of Survey Evidenced in Antitrust Proceedings," *Washington Law Review and State Bar Journal,* Vol. 33 (Winter 1958), pp. 380, 396.

[203] See Note, "Public Opinion Surveys as Evidence," *Harvard Law Review,* Vol. 66 (1953), p. 498.

[204] For example, see Irston R. Barnes, "Quantitative Data and Sample Surveys as Evidence in Judicial and Administrative Procedures," *The Role of Sampling Data as Evidence in Judicial and Administrative Proceedings,* Current Business Studies No. 19 (October 1954), pp. 33, 41.

[205] Zeisel, *op. cit.,* pp. 344-45.

[206] Reference is made to "generally accepted standards of objective procedure and statistics in the field of such surveys" in Judicial Conference of the United States, *op. cit.* However, no standards are suggested.

[207] One attempt to set up standards is contained in *Standards of Probability Sampling for Legal Evidence,* Current Business Studies No. 26 (1957). However, a technician is needed to apply the suggested standards. Further, the "Disclaimer" is an excellent discussion of the limitations of such a standard. (Pp. 3, 4.)

[208] 165 F. 2nd 152, 153 (C.C.A.-2nd 1947).

[209] S.D.N.Y. 1943, cited in F. R. Kennedy, "Law and the Courts," in Norman C. Meier and Harold W. Saunders, eds., *The Polls and Public Opinion* (1949), pp. 92, 99.

[210] *Triangle Publications, Inc.* v. *Rohrlich et al.*, 167 F. 2d 969 (C.C.A.-2d 1948).

[211] Such recommendations have not been welcomed by all. A committee of the American Bar Association was not impressed by them. *Report of the Committee on Practice and Procedure in the Trial of Antitrust Cases,* Section of Antitrust Law, American Bar Association (1954), pp. 44, 45.

[212] E. Barrett Prettyman, "Six Suggestions for Improvement," *Business Practices Under Federal Antitrust Laws,* Proceedings of the Third Annual Meeting of the New York State Bar Association, Section on Antitrust Law (Jan. 24, 1951), pp. 34, 40.

[213] "More effective communication between lawyers and research practitioners is needed. Integrating of the knowledge of both fields is necessary to achieve maximum usefulness. Greater cooperation is also needed. The responsibilities of both parties must be recognized. The research practitioner must become sufficiently familiar with legal procedures so that he can formulate more precisely the research that is needed and plan the presentation of findings more effectively. At the same time the lawyer must seek to understand the concept of survey research and become familiar with the limitations of survey techniques, as well as the application of those techniques to problems encountered in litigation." Hiram C. Barksdale, *The Use of Survey Research Findings as Legal Evidence* (1957), p. 149.

## *Chapter 10*

[1] See Corwin D. Edwards' recommendation in *Maintaining Competition* (1949), p. 288.

[2] There have been a few efforts in this direction, for example, the use of government contracts during World War II to induce Reynolds and Kaiser to enter the aluminum industry.

[3] Derek C. Bok feels that the relation of law and economics has generally received "a more facile treatment than it deserves." "Section 7 of the Clayton Act and the Merging of Law and Economics," *Harvard Law Review,* Vol. 74 (December 1960), pp. 226, 227.

[4] See testimony of Corwin D. Edwards in *Administered Prices,* Hearings before the Senate Judiciary Committee, 86 Cong. 1 sess. (1959), Pt. 9, p. 4806, and his letter, p. 4853.

[5] Carl Kaysen has expressed the view, "based on information from private sources, that defendants are already ahead of the Government in utilizing economists in assisting in the preparation of anti-trust cases." *United States v. United Shoe Machinery Corporation, An Economic Analysis of an Anti-Trust Case* (1956), footnote 8, p. 338.

[6] See testimony of Corwin D. Edwards in *Administered Prices,* Hearings, Pt. 9, p. 4808.

[7] "The law schools have seldom been much affected by the universities of which they are nominally a part." Robert M. Hutchins, *Two Faces of Federalism* (1961), p. 21.

# *Subject Index*